SHIMMERING DETAILS

VOLUME 2

SHIMMERING DETAILS

A Memoir

VOLUME 2

PÉTER NÁDAS

TRANSLATED FROM THE HUNGARIAN BY
JUDITH SOLLOSY

FARRAR, STRAUS AND GIROUX
NEW YORK

Farrar, Straus and Giroux
120 Broadway, New York 10271

Printed in the United States of America
Originally published in Hungarian in 2017 by Jelenkor Kiadó,
Budapest, as *Világló részletek*
English translation published in the United States by
Farrar, Straus and Giroux
First American edition, 2023

Library of Congress Cataloging-in-Publication Data
Names: Nádas, Péter, 1942– author. | Sollosy, Judith, translator.
Title: Shimmering details : a memoir / Péter Nádas ; translated from the
    Hungarian by Judith Sollosy.
Other titles: Világló részletek. English
Description: First American edition. | New York : Farrar, Straus and
    Giroux, 2023.
Identifiers: LCCN 2023021275 | ISBN 9780374174590 (v. 1 ; hardcover) |
    ISBN 9780374611644 (v. 2 ; hardcover)
Subjects: LCSH: Nádas, Péter, 1942– | Authors, Hungarian—20th
    century—Biography. | LCGFT: Autobiographies.
Classification: LCC PH3291.N297 Z46 2023 | DDC 894/.511334 [B]—
    dc23/eng/20230811
LC record available at https://lccn.loc.gov/2023021275

www.fsgbooks.com
www.twitter.com/fsgbooks • www.facebook.com/fsgbooks

10 9 8 7 6 5 4 3 2 1

SACRIFICING MARCELLINA

THERE WAS NO HELPING IT, I set off from Paris accompanied by the silent clamor of the dead. To tell the truth, I wasn't sure where I was headed. I couldn't find the place, not even on the Net. I set off because, after all those years, it was something I felt I had to do. From what I'd read, I knew that I should head for Toulouse first, from where, by all odds, I could catch the local train to Latour-de-Carol. Even the name sounded intriguing. It must have been the tower of one Charles or another. I must have been around eight when I heard the name of the town for the first time. But before I set off, I headed for the nearby rue Geoffroy l'Asnier, where Serge Klarsfeld's museum is located, and where the walls are inscribed with the names of the victims. I also wanted to see Klarsfeld's collection of the portraits of murdered children, seventy-six thousand names in all. The names of those who do not exist.

As the years passed, the mass murders of the twentieth century turned into a professional problem for me, as well as for others. I could never deal with these thousands and millions by resorting to fiction. The first anonymous victim impedes my progress. No matter where I begin or with whom, I can't get to the end. Given that I am a single individual and given my imagination, I simply can't imagine this many anonymous individuals, I can't track their progress, nor can my fictional heroes do so. My hero cannot pretend that he never existed, or that he is not bound to find an explanation for his own survival, on this side of the narrative or beyond. Serge Klarsfeld hurled himself headlong into the thick of the story, and with decades of dogged labor he has retrieved amateur photographs from its depths that took everyone by surprise. But then, why should anyone remember the faces and dead bodies of the murdered children of people they don't even know.

I am professionally bound to confine myself to people with names. Which is ridiculous, of course, because not a moment passes without an infinite mass of humanity by my side, frozen into a state of anonymity, my familial and anthropological plurals; and yet I must leave out whoever does not have a first name and who does not rise from the tempestuous sea of conflicts or the infinite desert of boredom. Their murderers plunged these individuals into the profoundest impersonality, they deprived them of their human face, and Klarsfeld found this intolerable, he found it unacceptable, and so he brought them back, he writes. On the other hand, the shimmering glance of these dead children cracks open, if fleetingly, the marble slab of theological thinking, something that he could not have counted on, say I. It cracks it open even if for decades Christian theology has pretended to have no knowledge of the absence of these individuals, as if the story of their massacre and the story of their absence had not penetrated the daily lives of European society, whereas if it acknowledged this absence, it could retrieve and salvage their memory from the maw of time and rectify the damage done to the concept of divine mercy and preordination.

But though I bought a first-class ticket in order to be at a safe distance from everything and everyone with their small lunch boxes and their small cooler boxes, my awful petit bourgeois train companions got on my nerves just the same. As soon as the celebrated high-speed train, the *train à grande vitesse*, wrenched itself from the crowds at Gare de Lyon and took off in all its majesty, they, as if on cue, began eating. The French petit bourgeois must satisfy his hedonism on what you might call a tight budget. I couldn't abide the sight of them fussing about to no purpose, opening and closing, pulling out and jamming back in, putting things down and picking things up strictly for their own benefit, and to the accompaniment of the relentless rustle of their paper bags and the unremitting crackle of their plastic lunch boxes, as in line with some hedonistic rite they methodically guzzled up their prescribed four courses. But before they were done, they first ate three kinds of cheese and a bit of fruit, then drank a bit of coffee from their thermos bottles. Which went on till their stomachs were fit to burst. No one can be that hungry. No one has an appetite as voracious as that. They didn't eat because they were hungry, and they didn't eat because they couldn't resist the pleasure of eating, they ate because their style of living prescribes the duty to heap pleasure on top of pleasure. Whether it rains or shines, they must eat four courses. Their daily portion of baguette must be fresh and crispy, and it better be crispy enough to cover everything with crumbs within a ten-meter radius. Also, they must drink some wine from their two small travel flasks and some water from their plastic bottles with which they poison the environment. They first put all these things up on the racks, then they took them down, they took them out and put them back in, they bunched them up and discarded them, they uncapped them and recapped them, they unwrapped them and rewrapped them, they uncorked them and recorked them. I beat a quick retreat. I fled their first-class hedonistic sense of duty and their Cartesian rigidity. I fled the devastating spirit of Descartes and Sade. I couldn't bear watching them any longer, I couldn't listen to their champing, their indecent chewing, the noisy swallowing of their food, the smacking of their lips in public, their Adam's apples bobbing up and down from the loud, unrestrained gulping of their drinks, and so I went in search of an unoccupied seat someplace else, except I couldn't find one anywhere, I don't know why. There wasn't a single unoccupied seat on this accursed train, as if on this accursed day all of humanity were heading for Bordeaux and Toulouse, and not just me. In this madly speeding train, the corridors, too, were packed with passengers. Considering the speed, the passengers would have never been allowed to stand like this on a proper German or Swiss train.

Once again, I was at a loss to understand.

From time to time the train gave me a jolt, and had a man with strong arms not reached out after me, had he not grabbed me, I'd have plunged headlong into the abyss of the train's stairs. Even so, I managed to hit my head against an iron pole. On the other hand, the gash, the split-open skin, the blood oozing down my forehead made me regain my sanity somewhat.

I looked for the place by the names familiar to me from my reading, but at first I couldn't find it either under the name of Vernet or Le Vernet, the names by which the town was known to me. I couldn't find it on any of the maps, not even the most detailed; look as I might, I couldn't even find it on the Internet. On the other hand, I found an idyllic bathing resort in the Pyrenees by the name of Vernet-les-Bains, which was pleasant to explore. This Vernet-les-Bains is rich in thermal springs, it is profuse with flowers and even has a water park. It must have been a miserable little hole in the wall before the war, with a handful of inhabitants and a handful of goats high up in the mountains, but I needed to find my own place or, as Pierre Nora called it, my place of remembrance, somewhere in the foothills. Ariège. And then, when I looked under the entries for the region and the rushing mountain stream from which it received its name, I found the page I'd been looking for. Le Vernet d'Ariège. I could now identify it from my readings on history and from what I'd heard about my own uncle's life. But there was nothing else on the page. Also, I'd reached Toulouse by then, and thanks to my hosts, the following day I lost even this one clue.

They said that there's a place by that name just south of the city, it shouldn't take me more than twenty minutes by train. We found it on a map of the region in the vicinity of the commune of Venerque. No d'Ariège, they said twice, *pas d'Ariège, pas d'Ariège*, it's really simple, as if they were talking to an idiot or someone hard of hearing. *Et voilà.* It's Le Vernet, *simplement Le Vernet*. On the other hand, they had no knowledge of anything happening there sixty or a hundred years ago, or even earlier. In the evening, a couple they were friends with came over for dinner, both doctors like them. They were cheerful and talkative, like them, because they also hailed from the south. By all odds, their lack of knowledge is the fault of bourgeois historiography, which is to be blamed for other deficiencies as well. Again and again, their obvious ignorance appalled me. On the other hand, it suited these decent bourgeois and Spiessbürgers, who'd rather not be confronted with anything that might unsettle their much valued worldview, specifically, the course of their businesses and their expense accounts. In turn, bourgeois historiography is pleased to oblige them. They treat political history and political philosophy without considering the workers' movements as well, or only as little as possible, and the peasants' movements even less, as a result of which the continent's social history can't be properly understood, and the picture of its human condition remains irrevocably distorted. We can recognize neither our former selves nor our present selves in it. They concern themselves with colonialism, militant missionary work, and the slave trade, in short, the fire-and-brimstone history of a series of genocides only obliquely, in line with their national and religious biases, in line, one might say, with their domestic sense of aesthetics. Given half a chance, they balk at incorporating even the sheer fact of the series of genocides into their national consciousness. It would be far too awkward for them to have to come face-to-face with the history of their religious universalism and superstitious racism as reflected in their institutions, administrative systems, and human sciences.

My Parisian friends had not heard the story of the internment camp at Le Vernet either, whereas they were well-informed Frenchmen otherwise, men and women for whom Drancy and Les Milles say something. And yet Le Vernet is not simply a camp in the universe of French camps, it was the largest camp, and it was a penal camp or, according to the official terminology of the time, a *camp spécial*. On the basis of Anne Grynberg's investigative work, *Les Camps de la honte*, I counted eighty-eight camps. In his *La France des camps: L'internement 1938–1946*, Denis Peschanski identifies an even greater number and speaks of approximately 600,000 internees in two hundred camps. Of course, at this point I might ask where I might find a Hungarian compatriot of mine with knowledge of the internment camps at Ricse, Csörgő, and Garany in former Zemplény County, or whether he can show us where his fellow Hungarians had suffered in these towns.

But that day, I willingly accepted the version offered by my hosts and their loud southern guests, just as I had willingly accepted the ignorance of my Parisian friends. I was a guest. I couldn't very well start shouting at the dinner table while we were stuffing ourselves with foie gras, strewing the kilim rug with crumbs of their wretched baguettes, and drinking Henri Bourgeois's Sancerre from Chavignol. I accepted their proposition without a word, to wit, that this Le Vernet, this *simplement* that shares a station with Venerque, *il faut prêter attention, s'il vous plaît ne pas échanger les deux*, one must pay attention in order not to confuse the two; in short, I did not doubt them; after all, these two that I must not confuse also lie along the Toulouse-Barcelona line, and so even when I bought my ticket, I thought great, I'm on track, I'm going in the direction of Latour-de-Carol, and that happens to be the station on the French border where, after the collapse of the Catalonian front in February 1939, the defeated Republicans sneaked across, individually and in groups, about twelve thousand of them, practically the entire 26th Division, Spanish anarchists, Spanish Communists, members of the International Brigade, including Hungarians, my father's envied friends and comrades.

My father had wanted to fight on the side of the Republicans, he had wanted to show his solidarity. *No pasarán.* It may have been the greatest political ambition of his youthful years. Except, the illegal Communist doctors at the illegal recruitment center weeded him out, they did not consider him physically fit. He was thus prevented from going and killing people and dying a hero of his own free will whereas, had he fallen at the Battle of the Ebro, it would have been an entirely different story as far as I'm concerned because I would not have been conceived. When my father objected to something, it always turned out to be too loudly and far too unsympathetically, and when he next tried to reason with the recruitment board, he gave the impression of a hysterical child.

Not only did he want justice, not only did he want to right erroneous thinking, he wanted unequivocal truth, and he wanted it pronto.

He was a quiet man, gentle like his brothers, attentive and courteous to a fault, a person who, quite unexpectedly for the outside world, was nevertheless given to bursts of hysteria.

They explain to him that he has chronic scoliosis and whether he knows it or not, his condition is serious. Perhaps nobody told him, but he should be wearing a back brace. Yet I see from his surviving medical records that he must have known about his illness when he went for the secret recruitment. On October 4, 1934, about three years before he was turned away, he'd been X-rayed by Dr. Dezső Markó at the Charité X-ray Institute, and, on the basis of the lateral X-rays of the vertebrae of the lower back and the upper lumbar vertebrae, the doctor concluded that the spine showed a pronounced kyphosis, a discontinuity in the alignment of the spine. His condition may have been due to the wounds he'd suffered at the Hadik Barracks. The corpus vertebrae are flattened and widened in the area of the curvature. The spaces between the vertebrae are healthy, of medium width. The contours of the vertebrae are sharp. The doctor gave the summary professional opinion that he had kyphoscoliosis caused by rickets.

And so he couldn't show his solidarity, he couldn't go to his death voluntarily. He argued with the illegal Communist doctors that he was as perfectly fit for expeditions into the Tatra and the Alps, for climbing rocks, rowing on the Danube and the Tisza for weeks on end, skiing in the Tatra and the Alps, as anyone else, but his reasoning fell on deaf ears. Also, he was short of stature. According to his military records from the same period, he was just 165 centimeters, or five feet six inches. On the other hand, in the surviving summer pictures and as I remember him, he was sporty and well built, handsome, hardy, healthy; his bones may have been at risk, but you couldn't tell by just looking at him. Only before our mother's death, when he buckled under the strain and walked with hunched shoulders, did he give the impression that he was slightly hunchbacked. Later, he envied even the prisoners, the executed, and the fallen for their participation in the glorious struggle that ended in defeat. At most, his features became distorted, the scar he received as a child turned white, and he trembled under the weight of his lifelong self-restraint when, for the benefit of the family, my Uncle Pali and Aunt Magda gave an impassioned account of the cleansing actions of the anti-Trotskyite firing squads that were acting on orders from Moscow. There was something unfamiliar in their manner, a striving for superiority I had not detected before, as if each was trying to outdo the other, as if each could say something even graver, even more horrible. They were bursting with the amount of knowledge that, to be sure, they should have shared with the others at a much earlier date. Granted that in a dictatorship being in possession of confidential information confers special privileges, the members of my own family were never among the most privileged. It's not that they gradually found themselves at a remove from the mighty, dictatorial power of the Party; they were never part of it. They would have been ill-suited to the task to begin with, except they didn't have what it takes to admit it, and their ostentatious display of knowledge was meant to hide this fact, whereas what they were displaying was something they should have been ashamed of to begin with. In this instance, it meant that in spite of their personal views, they had to acknowledge that the attempt to do away with the anarchist and the Trotskyite movements can't be blamed on Franco's fascists, not even in retrospect. Even back then, they should have written it off to the account of the Muscovite faction of Communists, what's more, they should have done so publicly, when they were editing leftist newspapers for their party. And if they knew back then but did not publish what they knew, neither in *Femmes*, nor in the Paris-based *Hungarian Worker*, nor in *Regards*, because they felt that in the interest of the unity of the European antifascist movement they must keep quiet about this series of murders, then they, too, must share the blame. They pretended they'd heard about the postwar show trials and the series of Stalinist purges only from brief, confidentially whispered accounts of speeches delivered at secret meetings, whereas many of their closest friends had fallen victim to the purges of the thirties.

To a child's mind, the most interesting aspect of their silence was their denial. All the while they were speaking about things they'd never spoken about earlier, they even denied that they might have been keeping quiet about anything at all. For instance, they kept quiet about the cheating during the free elections of 1947, about the so-called blue slips, whereas they printed them and transported them on their trucks, and bragged about it to one another in my presence. Too many of them had been involved for it to be kept secret. On that summer afternoon, under the open sky, they cut one another short, vying to outdo one another to see who could come up with more lies or who knew about more secrets and murders of which for a long time, a very long time, not only was it not right for them to speak, it was expressly forbidden, and had anyone so much as whispered about them, they would have been bound to consider such confidentially relayed information scaremongering, the disruptive machinations of reactionaries, and would have had to report it.

It was summer and very hot, the conversation took place at our home, first inside, but they were restless, they said that there was not enough air, and besides, in those days they had every reason to suspect that the walls had ears. It was their job to make sure that the walls everywhere had ears. Thanks to his telecommunications experience, my father, whose code name had been Jupi in the illegal Communist movement, made sure of it, as did my uncle Endre Nádas, whose code name had been Vadas. And so they continued their conversation out on the big terrace, then moved out to the big lawn under the giant copper beech. Probably, this family gathering took place during the hot summer of 1954. But only the Communist members of the family had gathered for the occasion. Even my grandfather the inveterate Garamist, the social democrat, could not be present, and as for my Uncle Pista, he came alone, without his quick-tempered, outspoken wife, Teréz, a descendant of the composer Karl Goldmark, who was educated by Wallachian nuns and who, with her finely chiseled but extremely pushy manners, stood out from the rest of the family like a sore thumb and got on everyone's nerves.

It was the last summer that our mother was still with us, if barely. Ruffled by so many obviously criminal acts, the men and women were standing in groups under the shade of the greenish-purple branches of the tree, holding the pink-edged, flower-patterned pink teacups from Erzsébet Mezei's pink salon in their hands, and they were shouting and making sweeping gestures as they stood on the green lawn, each bent on outdoing the other with their murders, each bent on outdoing themselves. It had been a long afternoon and by then the sky was overcast, but they were bent on reviewing their lives in the movement as the summer storm was brewing, but then did not erupt. No wonder I wanted to make sense of it; no wonder I paid very close attention.

Up in the mountains, two thousand meters above sea level, the French police grabbed the fighters as they crossed the Spanish border. About five thousand were taken to Mazères, where there was an abandoned kiln once used to make bricks, the rest were taken to Le Vernet d'Ariège.

As for me, I already had my suspicions the previous day, because in the memoirs and in what I read about its history, there was no mention of the closeness of Toulouse, but there was plenty of mention of the closeness of the Spanish border and the mountains, in which case I was on the wrong track. The defeated troops had to cross the frontier up high, above the vegetation, over impassable, secret paths. My uncle, who was not conducted down to Le Vernet d'Ariège from the mountains but was arrested in 1939 in Paris one morning in early fall, also writes in detail about the nearby mountains. At the time of his arrest, he was no longer secretary of the editorial committee, or *secrétaire du comité de rédaction*, which for all intents and purposes meant editor-in-chief of *Regards*, the illustrated weekly of the anti-fascist People's Front which he had launched, and whose masthead declared that it was *Le grand hebdomadaire illustré du Front Populaire* but, because in the wake of the events produced by the war and on orders from the Party in Moscow or, to be precise, in answer to the courteous summons from the journalist and Communist politician Gyula Alpári, he had taken over the management of the *Rundschau*, the paper of the illegal International Information Bureau of the Party. In one of the two notebooks that have survived, he even mentions that according to a superstitious camp belief, all calamity comes from the nearby Pyrenees. Which is a pretty hair-raising statement. Probably, it's the furious take on *ex montibus salus*, salvation comes from the mountains.

When out of simple courtesy, my uncle took over editorship of the illegal *Rundschau* from Alpári, meaning that in line with Party discipline he gave up a professionally significant job for a professionally worthless one, they had just come back to Paris from the daisy-covered hills and deep green forests of Asnières, they'd just returned from vacation, my Aunt Magda writes in her memoirs, but by then she'd been haunted by some sort of vague fear for many months. Dread. This was one of my Aunt Magda's favorite words, but she didn't use it in her memoirs. On the other hand, she mentions that her husband had undergone a profound change. They should leave Paris immediately, this was what her instincts told her. Disappear, make themselves scarce, get away. In the twenty years following the Commune, this was the sixth place they'd lived, and with so much turmoil behind them, my Aunt Magda's instincts dictated that they must now leave their beloved Paris as well. At the time she was senior editor of the women's magazine *Femmes*, the illustrated journal of an international antiwar and antifascist women's group with a wide political base. She had no way of knowing that another world war had broken out, but she knew that the German Luftwaffe was dropping bombs on Polish cities, that the German army was on the march with intent to occupy Poland, and that it was only a matter of days, possibly hours, before Britain and France would declare war on Germany. The German occupation was nowhere yet when, as a political preamble, the left-wing liberal Daladier government had already caused a rift in the antifascist united front, and had begun its obsessive pursuit of Communists and foreigners in order to appease its own fascists, hoping to take the wind out of their sails, and also to send a message to the Nazis as well. At least, this is how my Aunt Magda characterized Daladier's politics in word and in writing. We are good negotiating partners because we love neither the Bolsheviks nor the Jews. Even thirty years on, Daladier would still get her fuming mad. Probably, he reminded her of her own hated and despised liberal-bourgeois scum, her own liberal-conservative ancestors. Clearly, Daladier would have liked to forestall the eventuality of the French having to go to war because of the Poles, and so he began persecuting those who could have been his allies in defending the nation, something that would soon be painfully evident, indeed.

I am not convinced that my Aunt Magda did not have a good reason for her rage. With their pragmatic political speculations, the conservative liberals and the leftist liberals generally end up kicking themselves in the ass. My own experience tells me the same.

On the other hand, the eventuality of policing aliens was part of French domestic tradition. They had gathered up aliens as soon as the First World War broke out, they locked them in internment camps, and for the four years that the war lasted, they kept them under tight surveillance, as if they'd been hardened criminals.

For safety considerations, my uncle had to relocate the editorial offices of the *Rundschau* from the most conspicuous part of the city, the Champs-Élysées, to the Place des Victoires, where they thought that the distinguished address would protect them. Which proved to be the naïve calculation of a man who had lived a long time in peace. But the truth is that my uncle was trusting to a fault, which was part of his appeal. My Aunt Magda wrote down the reasons she gave her husband for fleeing, and how her husband turned a deaf ear to her reasonable arguments. The manhunt for Communists won't stop at their doorstep, they won't get away, and also, in the days to come, their chances of being active in this town would be nil. They must decamp. But he's considered French, my Uncle Pali retorted. At which my aunt shouted angrily that the question is not what your friends consider you, the question is how long the police will put up with your activities. Don't count on their forbearance. Don't you think they know why Maurice Thorez's automobile is parked in front of your office every day for hours on end, she asked, beside herself with anger and frustration. Thorez chose my uncle's office as the scene of his confidential meetings and made his confidential phone calls from there.

Don't go thinking there's a single traffic cop in all of Paris who doesn't see, who doesn't know where the general secretary of the Communist Party goes, my aunt shouted. Do you really think that they don't recognize him in his automobile or that they don't recognize the car or the driver. Rest assured, she shouted, they even know that he gave his first interview yesterday sitting behind your desk because, in the interest of his own safety, the correspondent of *The Times* didn't want to meet him at Party headquarters. Which goes without saying.

They always lead you by the nose.

But he's relocated his office to a safer place.

The hell it is, when you make long-distance calls to Moscow every day, the hell it is, my aunt shouted. Do you really believe they don't know who you talk to and what you talk about. The French police may like their comforts, but they're no fools.

This is how we fought for two whole days and two whole nights, she writes in her memoirs, but my Uncle Pali wouldn't hear of leaving Paris, even though she kept at him, saying that she'd grow vegetables in the countryside, dig, replant the fresh growth, plant new ones and weed the garden, and they could live on that until the war ended. With her premonition and her intention to flee, she presents herself in her memoirs as if she were the only one who saw what was coming. But only in her memoirs, because she told me a different story. She portrays herself as if it had never occurred to her that if they fled, they'd be turning their backs on their voluntary legal as well as illegal activities. She makes it look like her husband was not in his right mind, as if he were, in fact, out of his mind, and so she had to think and act for the both of them. Whereas my Uncle Pali probably did not want to abandon his station, meaning the Party, like a coward. He simply couldn't do it. He couldn't do it because of himself, and he couldn't do it because of the others. My aunt was engaged with the life of her instincts and without a doubt she was right, her instinct to flee was justified, while my uncle was engaged with the ethical premises of his profession and activities in the movement, in which case his decision to remain was legitimate. This is the stuff of drama. In a crisis, a person will not desert his friends and colleagues in favor of a fabulous vegetable garden and his wife's seductive instinctual life. His decision is honorable. Still, he should not put his freedom or his life on the line unnecessarily. There can be no doubt about the sanity of this line of reasoning either.

Certainly, my aunt did not take the drama with which the era had confronted them into full consideration. They couldn't be sober-minded and honorable at the same time, and in order to hide the real drama, with her inclination for betrayal, which she called sober-mindedness, she later depicted her husband as slightly deranged. And to make sure that those who read her memoirs should accept the idea of her husband being deranged, she prepared the way for this insinuation with the idyllic description of their vacation in Asnières, in which she seasoned the clash of sober-mindedness and honor with a pinch of anachronism.

In fact, from the early fifties on, my Uncle Pali began to go soft in the head; the process could not be reversed medically, and by the early sixties, it had ended. His going soft in the head should not be understood metaphorically but as a reality, it was a physiological condition that made my uncle as well as the people around him suffer. The cerebral structures lose their shape, the cells responsible for the shape of the brain tissue are damaged. The individual suffering from dementia can no longer make the connection, for the benefit of the outside world, between sensual impressions, linguistic information, and the various layers of stored memory; in short, the preshaped content of consciousness is lost, or else survives only in part. What a person like this says or writes is as lacking in shape or form as the structures of his brain, which have lost their ability to provide structure. We don't know what he is thinking or feeling.

And yet the news of what's happening to them in the indistinct outside world reaches them all the same. When he couldn't manage to answer a question, my Uncle Pali would sometimes break into tears, much like my friend and mentor Miklós Mészöly years later when, having fallen prey to dementia, he couldn't connect the various layers of his consciousness, and would fly into a rage. I once wanted to ask him about his role in the illegal Hungarian Collective, which came into being in the early twentieth century, and which was both anti-German and anti-Semitic, and which, improbably, is still in existence today. I wanted to ask him everything he knows about the collective, and I wanted to hear once again what he'd told me earlier, to garner from him all the minute details he had not mentioned before, information I needed to help me understand. I could tell by his expression that he was searching for the place the question occupied in his conscious mind, but could not find it. We were at dinner, and he shouted, he was beside himself, wanting to know why I was asking such idiotic questions. I first noticed that something was not right with him at least ten years earlier. What's more, at the time, he himself had a premonition of his future. He made me promise that if I were to detect the first sign of dementia in him I would tell him, because he would then put an end to his life. I must promise. I must promise on my word of honor. It is my duty as a friend. I made no such promise, much less on my word of honor. I laughed. I may have been laughing at him, I may not have taken him seriously, the stance of a young man whose shoulders are not yet burdened with the question of whether life is worth living with a deficient mind. It is not. It is as clear as day. But at the time I considered pathetic the fact that he would even think of asking me anything of the sort.

He quoted Aristotle, who felt that if a friend is about to say or do something foolish, a man should beat him over the head. He is bound to do so by the ideal of friendship. I countered by asking, what if I'm wrong. If my judgment is at fault. Besides, anger, envy, and feelings of revenge can also lead to faulty judgment.

In which case I don't understand what antiquity meant by friendship.

Meaning that I'm not a good friend, meaning that he's been lavishing his friendship on someone undeserving of it.

Which, needless to say, I didn't like either, and I told him that it's as if he were bent on forcing me to make an unethical promise by appealing to my vanity and calling me his friend.

We argued over this until both of us forgot what we'd been arguing about.

Still, he kept at me, wanting me to promise.

I would not.

My aunt discovered the first signs of my uncle going soft in the head, as she put it, on the daisy-covered, or as she writes, the oxeye daisy–covered hills and dark green woods of Asnières. However, it seems to me that what she took for early signs of senility was probably my uncle's strange behavior, because he was regularly cheating on her by then, and he probably acted strangely as a result.

Possibly, it was as she writes, and she detected signs of change in her husband's manner, though it is more likely that for the first time in their marriage, she felt that her husband was cheating on her, and not for the first time either, and that she projected her later experiences with her husband onto the earlier ones, something that a professional historian like her, with several hefty historical monographs and biographies to her credit, should not have done. Normally, when a person notices that something is not right with the workings of another person's mind, that he is constantly confused, he or she does not look to dementia for an explanation. He or she might entertain the possibility that the other has gone crazy, and they say to themselves that the other is off his rocker, he's gaga, soft in the head, but then, he was an idiot to begin with. The law of rationality will not allow the observer to conclude that the other is suffering from an illness. He or she will look for all sorts of petty excuses, as if he or she were deceiving themselves on purpose. We prefer to think that the other is lying. That he's taking us for fools. Or that he has something up his sleeve. And so on.

The oxeye daisy bursts into bloom in early June, and if this is what my aunt remembered most vividly, then they didn't just go on vacation someplace, as they used to do, but moved out of Paris to Asnières-sur-Oise for the summer. She writes that her husband befriended the milkman who picked him up every morning on his truck, saving him from having to trek up the hillside to the railroad station of Viarmes. If she had to go to Paris herself to attend to the urgent business of editing and distributing *Femmes*, she'd go along, but at such times, on their return trip, they preferred to walk back along the hillside. They loved walking in the summer night. Once a week, when the latest issue of *Regards* had gone to the printer, Pali would return with the midnight train, and at such times, she'd go to meet him at the bottom of the hill in the moonlight or in the pitch dark. During our own nightly chats, she described these late-night walks, the weekends by the shore of the Marne, their summer vacations in Brittany, the enchantment of the French countryside, the Rhône and the castles along the Loire, in detail for my benefit, as well as her own.

When I first went to Paris, practically speaking, I did not need a map; I knew where to find things, because during these late-night chats, my aunt impressed everything on my mind.

As they headed back home, they engaged in quiet discussions about the day's events. They lived simple, cheerful lives, she adds. Whereas our personal misfortune began that year, or else sometime around those years, she writes in her next sentence, one that didn't turn out quite as it should have. In Hungarian, misfortune is a completed event and will not tolerate the verb *begin*. She feels the lexical awkwardness herself, because in the following sentence she writes about the barely perceptible hair's-breadth breach between them that grew with the passing years, increasingly distancing them from each other. Which isn't quite correct either, because for such distancing a hair's breadth will not suffice, it calls for something like tectonic forces. At most, the married couple act as if they were not aware of the action of the tectonic forces. Only decades later, when asked by a young physician, did my aunt first describe the changes in her husband's character she'd noticed during those nights in Asnières, and that's when the doctor confirmed that indeed, they must have been the first signs of her husband's illness.

And then, at seven in the morning of the third day of their two-day argument, the bell rang at the door of their Paris apartment at 22 rue Saint-Augustin.

It's probably the woman with the monthly bill for the milk, her husband said.

Or else the police, my aunt said.

Brandishing a search warrant, five men forced their way into the apartment. They turned the place upside down. Mostly young policemen from the countryside. They ransacked Georges's room, where they found only a wardrobe and a desk made from orange crates, but this is what they must have found the most suspicious of all. They didn't notice the cupboards hidden behind some curtains, thanks to which a lot of important documents escaped detection, including a manuscript by Mihály Károlyi, the former prime minister and president of Hungary, which he had deposited with them for safekeeping. They took my uncle with them. They had a warrant for his arrest.

Turn to the prefecture for information about him, they told my aunt, who, because of her husband's arrest, in her memoirs calls the years that followed wasted years.

Not that I believe that a person's life contains wasted years. Even his or her dementia is not wasted. Had they left Paris in hopes of setting up a vegetable garden, they'd have deserted the movement based on social equality, and their friends would have been justified in considering them traitors as well as cowards, and my Aunt Magda realized this. In this particular instance, she also realized the discrepancy between the logic of her own upbringing, meaning the promptings of her instinct to flee, and the logic of the movement. Still, she couldn't help thinking that after the war they might use their humble earnings to enlarge their vegetable garden, they might even buy two trucks and a small vacation home somewhere in Aix. Thanks to my aunt's knowledge and experience with growing vegetables, they might even establish a chain of vegetable farms, and once their enterprise grew large enough, they could buy a big apartment in one of the better districts of Paris and so on, until the trees reached the sky, in short, until perfect bourgeois happiness budded forth from its seed and blossomed in profusion.

It seems to me that it wasn't my uncle who had gone gaga; with her instinct to flee, it was my aunt whose judgment had become unbalanced, and not because such a parody of a brilliant bourgeois career was at odds with her destructive character, which it was, but because even once her book had gone to press, the practical ethical counterargument still hadn't occurred to her. She did not acknowledge, she did not notice, that in his trusting or, if you will, dotty way, my Uncle Pali decided against sanity in the name of honor, and he did so for both of them. This is how the drama was tailor-made for them. And they did not waste the years to come, in which, due to the conspiratorial leaning of the Communist movement, there is an abundance of blind spots and uncertainties, to be sure; on the contrary, they spent this time engaged in honorable and undoubtedly courageous resistance because, after a while, the pressure that history had exerted on them purged the idea of flight even from my Aunt Magda's soul.

My Aunt Magda was one of the most intelligent human beings I have encountered during the course of my long life. But there was a slight fault in her character. She did not always succeed in bringing her emotions and her intentions, her sense of reality and her ideals, under a common banner. She wanted to get even with her husband, and she had such raw emotions with respect to him and with respect to her son, and even with respect to me, that they dampened her ability to make sound judgments and undermined her innate sense of ethics. One might say that she wanted to get even with the man she loved after he was gone, and she wanted to do it in her memoirs, for all eternity. And she wanted to do it not because her husband wouldn't buy her a button factory, and not because she and the man she loved didn't start a garden center on her hated father's Gömörsid estate, and not because he introduced her to a political movement of which for a long time, a very long time, she understood nothing, even though she diligently repeated, parrotlike, its slogans, and not because, in line with the desired model, they had to live in privation for decades, and not because they had to accept the secret support of the well-off members of the family, or when they were really hard up, she had to go beg them for money, and not because the world movement they chose finally turned their lives into a complete and irreversible fiasco; she wanted to do it because, despite all their mutual love and devotion, without the slightest sense of guilt, Pali cheated on her right and left, and she refused to face up to it until it was too late. She suffered the torments of Tantalus; throughout her life she pretended to have noticed nothing; she put up with it, for one thing, because of her upbringing, and for another, because she loved him.

At the same time, I see from the notes and writings she left behind that my suspicion had not been unfounded, and she gave in to her physical urges at least once and at some length herself, and for long clandestine months she cheated on her cheating husband, who, in keeping with the laudable habit of all cuckolded husbands, suspected nothing all the while that he collaborated, on the friendliest of terms, with his wife's lover, the handsome and upright writer and activist Frigyes Karikás, when they were translating Hašek's *The Good Soldier Švejk* into Hungarian together. But there is no doubt that toward the end of his life, this man, whom she loved more than anyone, this charming and truly clear-thinking man, Pál Aranyossi, became dotty, and along with his memory, the last traces of his charm, too, were also gone. For at least ten years, my aunt had to keep an eye on him, to prevent him from doing something crazy. To be precise, he had fallen prey to the mental derangement of old age combined with premature hebetude, in short, dementia presenilis, but while his personality was disintegrating, and along with it the most marked aspects of his character, he was still cheating on her, he cheated on her to the very threshold of complete dementia. He was already soft in the head, but he still cheated on her in the ugliest of ways, and in order to bear it with dignity, my aunt told her women friends about it amid shrill bursts of laughter.

You'll never guess who Pali, that nasty piece of work, cheated on me with.

He'd grown completely dotty, he didn't even realize anymore that he'd shit in his pants, but with some curious automatism, as if heeding the call of some erotic urge independent of him, he was still grabbing the maid's breasts and backside, he was still feeling her up, grinning as he pawed, I saw it with my own eyes. From which it will be seen where this urge is located inside a person; by all odds it functions independently of his character traits or, put another way, as long as these character traits are functional, he can at times hold his raw erotic urges in check. When Marika went by, he grabbed for her. He grabbed Marika every chance he got. It was amusing rather than rough or scary. He slapped her behind in a sweet way, full of yearning. He grinned like a mischievous child who knows he's being naughty. Luckily, the maid, whom in line with her liberal principles my aunt called a domestic yet treated as a simple servant, had a heart of gold, and took the side of the sick man against his unbearable wife. Marika came to Budapest from Kistarcsa to get away from her husband, who had earlier sent the police after her. He beat her regularly, hardly a week passed when he didn't beat her black and blue. He was a guard at the infamous internment camp at Kistarcsa and he was born in Kistarcsa, like Marika, but he was at least ten years older than she, and nature had endowed him not only with brutality, but with a hefty dose of pathological jealousy as well. When the camp was closed and the inmates were assigned to various prisons, her husband was transferred to the prison at Vác, and at this point, Marika fled with her little son once again. When my uncle shit in his pants and the lady of the house made a terrible scene, shouting at the poor old man, you shit in your pants again, you shit again, why didn't you say, you shit in your pants, she shouted until Marika came running with a washbowl of lukewarm water she'd brought from the bathroom, and she silently cleaned him up. Now and then the poor old man realized what had happened, and then he'd burst into doleful tears. The doleful tears came not because he'd shit in his pants, his brain may not have actually registered the fact, it had lost the ability to do so, even his own stink did not make him realize his situation, the tears came because his wife, the idolized grande dame, was shouting at him again for something he did not understand. Meanwhile she stood over him, a towering figure in full cognizance of her might, and screamed and shouted like a shrew.

In company, she had to make her husband stop talking, quickly and with humor, so the others shouldn't notice what she'd known for some time. God forbid. And yet they'd surely noticed that the brilliant and spirited Pali is no longer brilliant, but stares uncomprehending into space, and now and then says something that makes no sense. She had him admitted to various hospitals, she had him taken to various sanatoriums, just so she shouldn't have to see him and witness his decline, and so she wouldn't have to keep a constant eye on him and make sure he doesn't wander off and cross the street and get run over. Or disappear without a word in the crowd and traffic on Teréz Boulevard, or wander off from the garden of their house in Leányfalu. So she wouldn't have to make sure that the door of their apartment is locked at all times, and both garden gates, too, locked with a key. And never ever leave the key to the apartment door in the lock, because he might open it.

How often must I tell you.

Because, now and then, if we left the key in the lock, he'd leave the house in his pajamas and dressing gown, without knowing where he was going. I brought him back myself more than once from the sun-drenched country road leading from Leányfalu to Visegrád, where I found him trekking along in his pajamas and slippers. The rigorousness of our family customs, based on rationality, didn't make my aunt any more forbearing toward him. She couldn't forgive his infidelities and she couldn't ignore the sadness she felt over her own life. She couldn't forgive him the fact that because of him, she had to forgive herself her own father's vehement nature and her own mother's opportunism, both of which she'd inherited, and which lasted until the day she died.

I had to hold myself in check, too, so I could forgive my friend Miklós Mészöly for the turn his own fate had taken, and in fact I couldn't have done it had Magda not put me to rights.

But on this leg of my trip, I looked out the train window in vain, there were no mountains to be seen anywhere, even though my uncle had written in the notebook that has survived him that the craggy mountains rise haughtily all around in a half-circle, white, blue, crystalline, sparkling when the rays of the sun strike them, or when the sky is gloomy, they tower over the camp in massive chunks of brown and black, much like in a nightmare. These are his words from his Vernet diary. The icy chain of peaked tips, camel humps, bear scalps, dog heads, and buck backs shaped the country's frontier to the side, these are his similes. On this side of the frontier is France, which has succumbed to war, beyond it, dark and threatening, the mighty Spanish prison, this is his description of the situation. And they huddled between the two in this putrescent mousetrap.

When he wrote these lines, the camp at Le Vernet, and with it the entire world, couldn't have been anything else for my uncle than a gigantic mousetrap, and he was not far off in his assessment. He still favored the literary striving for similes shared by writers and journalists alike, similes never before seen or heard. The writers of the day considered the use of simile the greatest literary achievement. Camus and Beckett, on the other hand, did not look for simile, because they did not favor pathos. In the second half of December 1940, meaning just before Christmas, when the snow veritably battered them from the direction of the Pic du Midi, they were lice-ridden and filthy. They squatted and shivered because, as he writes, the unusually thick, wadded quilt of snow did nothing to warm the unheated barracks. This, too, is his simile, this wadded quilt of snow. Such a mass of snow made the walks they took for their health along the paths that divided the various sectors and exchange of views extremely difficult, because the snow would not stop falling. The heavy snow forced the study groups to abandon the sunnier nooks of the yard in favor of the dark barracks, making their free university training in linguistics, philosophy, history, and political science, which they pursued, if peripatetically, meaning during their walks and as they talked, more difficult. Nonetheless, their prisoner-students followed their prisoner-professors faithfully along the snow-trodden paths.

These two notebooks from the camp at Le Vernet have survived, simple school notebooks, as well as dozens of notebook sheets torn from God knows where, and also a couple of printed forms filled with writing, including a *Demande d'entrée en Suisse* form, meaning a petition to enter Switzerland, which is also filled with writing on both the printed and unprinted sides. With regular, if somewhat angular and tilted, charming if somewhat difficult to read letters, my uncle writes in French that there are no known layers, levels, or segments of society, no religions and no views that are not represented among the three thousand prisoners. There is a particular concentration of German, Spanish, Hungarian, and Yugoslav journalists, writers, artists, actors, and dramaturgs. He often sees colleagues with pen and notebook in hand walking along the paths of the camp engrossed in what seem to be monologues, abruptly stopping in their tracks to jot something down. With his two school notebooks, my uncle was surely one of their number.

The two notebooks have badly faded terra-cotta covers. On the front cover of one, a voluptuous, barefooted goddess is perched atop a Doric column; she is holding a lute in one hand, while with the other she is reaching for a rose to pluck from the rosebush hanging profusely over her. The notebook even has a title: *Le Floréal*. The back cover bears practical information for students; there's a *Table de multiplication*, a *Division du temps*, a *Signes abréviatifs employés en arithmétique*, and a *Chiffres romains*. They used to print similar things on the backs of Hungarian notebooks, verb conjugations, multiplication tables, a chart to decipher Roman numerals, and conversion tables for various units of measurement. Inside the terra-cotta cover there are two original graphic works that have been pasted in showing the daily life of the camp. I don't think that they are by the same person, still, they both evidence the practiced if not professional hand of a graphic artist working for the papers. Also, they are both India ink drawings. One illustration, with lines strikingly applied by a thick India ink brush, depicts the murky interior of a barracks with a close-up of the middle level of a triple bunk bed where, half sitting and half reclining, his peaked cap pulled over his eyes, a man who has sought refuge from the cold outside is shown huddled in his military coat and trembling. Above the empty part of this bunk bed is a tiny window shedding some reflected light from the snow outside. The shimmering light falls on a suitcase lying on the bed, exactly as Bruno Frei describes in his memoirs, *ich stellte meinen Koffer an das Kopfende der Bretter*, I installed my suitcase at the head of the boards, *wobei es schwer war, zu verhindern, daß er beim Fensterlock hinausfiel*, although it was hard to prevent it from falling out the open window lacking its glass pane. There is also some sort of material in the picture, it is rolled up, it might be a pillow, it might be a blanket, and near the wooden ladder that leads to this middle bunk there is a prominently placed, gleaming empty plate and a glittering spoon, sober images of persistent hunger. There is also a ladder leading up to the third bunk bed, and above it is depicted another window with the glimmer of the snowy crags streaming through it. The small picture is signed. I tried to find out who might be behind the "CS 1940" signature, but unfortunately, I came up empty-handed.

The second illustration is not signed and is more like a caricature of the hygiene conditions at the camp at Le Vernet d'Ariège. In front of the Hopit, meaning the building bearing a red cross and the sign Hopital, whereas it was an infirmary at best, and even then, a poor imitation of one, stands a French gendarme in a heavy winter uniform, berating, questioning, issuing orders, and hurrying along a group of shivering internees to the hospital. There is a small child in shorts and mules in their midst; he is walking with one hand raised to his eye and crying, although I have not come upon any mention of children or adolescents being kept prisoner at Le Vernet d'Ariège. Still, it can't be ruled out, it is possible, and besides, we must accept the picture as an authentic representation. Behind them is a young man with crutches, one leg missing, the other with no shoes, who is supported by a bearded man in a Spanish peaked straw hat; he at least has ankle boots on his feet; and next to him hurries a man, his cheeks and jaw wrapped in a rag against toothache; he is shivering, his hands are sunk in his pocket, and he is wearing a vest that is clearly not suited to his bulk, but at least it keeps him warm; behind them is a man with a mustache, his head heavily bandaged, wearing a military jacket, and also a man in working clothes and a peaked hat, his arm in a makeshift sling; and bringing up the rear is a figure with a beret on his head, his hands sunk inside his threadbare winter coat, a long scarf artfully wound around his neck, on his feet city oxfords, the sole intellectual in the company.

This notebook is written in three languages and contains my uncle's notes on the tempest-tossed fates of the other captives as well as German poems with numbers, and also some lines of poetry translated into French. A name on the first page of the notebook makes it more than likely that the poems were written in the camp by my uncle's camp mate, comrade, and friend, the well-known poet Rudolf Leonhard. We know from the colophon of *Regards* that along with Anna Seghers, Theodor Plievier, and Arthur Holitscher, Rudolf Leonhard was also one of the magazine's German correspondents. The Soviet correspondents were Fedor Gladkov, Vladimir Pozner, Vsevolod Ivanov, and Valentin Kataev. To this day, no editor could wish for a better bunch of correspondents. John Dos Passos dispatched reports from the United States, Egon Erwin Kisch from Czechoslovakia, while Mihály Károlyi, former prime minister, then president of Hungary, was in charge of reports from his country. The magazine's board of directors was no less impressive; it was composed of the likes of Romain Rolland, Maxim Gorky, André Gide, Henri Barbusse, Charles

Vildrac, Eugène Dabit, André Malraux, Isaac Babel, and Vladimir Pozner.

Still, I couldn't make heads or tails of the numbers placed between parentheses. The poem entitled "Schwalben," or Swallows, bears the number 501. "Krähe," or Crows, bears the number 253. "Braut," or Bride, the number 190. "Vorsicht," or Attention, the number 394. Since these poems, written in German, must have been composed in one of the dark barracks or during their long walks between barracks, they can't be page numbers from a printed book. But they might be the numbers from a book written by hand. The cycle of poems Leonhard composed in the camp, entitled *Le Vernet*, was later published, if not before then certainly after his death, in one of the four volumes of his collected works.

Arthur Koestler provided the most objective picture of the hutments or barracks themselves. They were constructed of wooden planks, he writes, covered with some sort of waterproof paper. Each was twenty-six meters long, and each housed two hundred men. Its furnishings consisted of two lower and two upper platforms, also constructed of planks, running along the two long walls and leaving a narrow passage in the middle. The space between the lower and upper platforms was one meter, so those on the lower planks could never stand erect. The rows were divided into ten compartments by the wooden poles supporting the roof. Each compartment, he writes, contained five men and was two and a half meters wide, thus each man had a space of half a meter to sleep on. This meant that all five had to sleep on their sides, facing the same way, and if one turned over, all had to turn over. The boards were covered with a thin layer of straw, and the straw was the sole movable furniture in the barracks. The most dramatic picture of these straw-covered boards is provided by Bruno Frei. He writes that after his arrival, a guard shoved him inside and said he should present himself to the head of the barracks, who would assign him his place. But once he was inside, Frei lost his sight and hearing. He felt as if he'd plunged into a pitch-dark shaft, where the noise was infernal. The air was heavy with the summer smell of drying straw, and just like in a mine shaft, there came the noise of shouting, grating, hammering, and pounding. As I slowly felt my way, he writes, I found myself in a narrow corridor, on both sides of which stood three-tiered board compartments. Some men in the half-light that stretched into the distance were busy nailing crossbeams to the supporting boards of the sections, which would have to serve as chicken-roost ladders of sorts leading to the two upper bunks. They didn't have hammers to drive in the nails, so they used shapeless stones instead. A gendarme who stood in the middle of the narrow passageway was just tearing a bale of hay apart with both hands as the desperate inmates, their faces distorted with their curses, were literally fighting over the smallest bunch of hay. If you want hay, you'd better get a move on, someone shouted in Bruno Frei's ear. He didn't know what he was supposed to do and why he should need the hay. He understood nothing at all, he just wanted to lie down somewhere, this was his one wish, and let events run their course. Just then someone from behind hugged him, and in his strong voice whispered in his ear, so then you're here, too, comrade. As he spun around he met Mario's eyes, tears flowing from behind his glasses, trickling down the deep grooves of his face. I felt that the last vestiges of my self-control were gone. We hugged each other for all we were worth. This is the section for criminals, Mario whispered. I thought I was stuck with these good-for-nothings, but now it'll be easier to bear. He hugged his friend once again, when a gendarme's shouts put an end to their mutual display of affection.

The poems and their translations in the two terra-cotta notebooks afford us a view of the strictly and rationally organized lives of the Communist resistance in the camp. Later, in this barracks for criminals, Bruno and Mario, too, organize their own small Communist resistance cell. My uncle doesn't just make notes for his own benefit, he doesn't just make mental preparations for the next issue of *Regards*, which had recently fallen victim to the war, we also see him occupied with the camp's present, translating the poems of his camp mate, meant to be read out loud, into French or Hungarian. He writes "important" next to the poem entitled "Das Jahr," but why it is important or for whom, we have no way of knowing. Be that as it may, it is to his credit that he found solutions for prosody both in Hungarian and French. Besides the poems, poetic fragments, and translations, the notebook also contains entries in French and Hungarian describing various parts of the camp, the hospital, the hygienic condition of the inmates, their catastrophic health care, their illnesses, the helplessness of the desperate inmate doctors, they don't have medicine, they don't have bandages, those with tuberculosis are not isolated, *salle des tuberculeux pas séparée*, he writes, he describes the kitchen, the various foods, their quality and quantity. He records all this without a trace of sentiment or emotion. Just once does the journalistic text shout out at us, in the midst of a description of the hospital food and the lack of medicine. Gangsters. Gangsters who steal food even from the gravely ill, who will not allow the new consumptives to be isolated from the other sick inmates, who won't even give a glass of milk to those with chronic illnesses, or some aspirin, at least. The nurses drink the milk. Then he continues the description of the food rations in his usual objective, descriptive style, saying that they're just barely enough to keep the inmates from starving. But he does not write like a man intent on letting future generations know all these details; he merely resorts to the words of a decent journalist who is working on his latest article.

I know of only one other equally objective report from the twentieth century about hygienic conditions and nutrition in the camps, the book by Leonardo De Benedetti and Primo Levi entitled *Auschwitz Report*. Levi's list of publications does not contain this admittedly nonliterary work, whereas the two authors provide anthropological observations we won't find anywhere else, and they do so with the admirable objectivity of the Turinese circle. Turinese objectivity lacks ideological components, and as such, it is a refreshing oasis of sorts in the landscape of the various European takes on objectivity. The work of the two authors provides an admirable instance of European rationality as it adamantly reaches back to humanism and antiquity, its two intellectual sources. The French edition was published by a small Parisian house, Éditions Kimé, in 2005. It was translated from the Italian and was by all odds originally written in Italian. De Benedetti was a physician, a surgeon, and Levi was a chemist, a fortunate combination. A couple of days after they were liberated, they wrote down their observations about the hygienic and physiological conditions in the camp on request from one of the health officers of the Red Army. Like Levi, De Benedetti had also been dragged off from Turin, or Torino, by the Nazis, both men arrived by the same transport and returned to their native town, which enjoyed a special place in the intellectual life of Italy, and where, after writing his major works, Levi committed suicide by jumping out the window of his apartment. Even in this early analysis, completed in 1946, they treated the obvious question, how can people survive under physiological conditions that otherwise make survival impossible. When summing up his own experiences in Le Vernet, Arthur Koestler writes in *Scum of the Earth* that in those days the European continent had already reached a stage where a man could be told without irony that he should be thankful to be shot and not strangled, decapitated, or beaten to death. Under these circumstances, complaining seemed frivolous and inappropriate. The scales of sufferings and humiliations were broken, and the bearable, too, had lost all recognizable limits.

My uncle's other notebook had almost completely fallen apart, though it probably wasn't complete to begin with, or else he tore out some single or double pages as he needed them. It had originally consisted of one hundred pages. On the cover of the depleted notebook, in art nouveau letters it says 100 sheets. The cover also bears his name in ink, written in small, humble, engagingly intelligent letters. Aranyossi. Bar. 7. Meaning, barracks number seven. This incomplete notebook contains a one-act piece written in French containing five numbered scenes, some of them worked out and meant to be accompanied by music and interspersed with songs. It is entitled *Flamenco*. The notebook contains another piece entitled *Bolero*, undoubtedly also meant to be accompanied by music; it is a dramatic sketch with five numbered scenes, some of them complete. Any way we look at it, *Flamenco* is impressive. It stands apart from his later works because it lacks propagandistic intent. Except for his slightly propagandistic documentary novel, *Who Killed Wilma Montesi*, which he wrote when he was already ill and which was published in 1956, *Flamenco* is surely his best work, even though he wrote it on commission and thought of it as his contribution to the Communist movement. The suffering must have been striking and universal, and he wanted to breach it. He was a professional journalist who wrote every one of his articles and books on commission, some on commission from the movement, and almost always, his commitment to the movement appears between the lines. He couldn't work without a commission and a deadline, I saw this with my own eyes; he fidgeted around, busying himself with odds and ends, he went for drinks or something to eat with a village acquaintance or an old friend, for instance, with Prime Minister Ferenc Münnich or another good comrade; he went looking for anyone at all, a neighbor or their own gardener, or else, retreating into the depths of an armchair, his glasses pushed up over his forehead, his face expressionless, he'd read for hours on end as if he'd just meant to look something up, as if he were looking for information, and then he'd get up and go about his business. Without a commission, he was lost. Both as a writer and translator, he wrote with an easy hand and a yielding pen, gleaning his words from repositories of language lying at great distances from one another. He wrote in French, he wrote in German, and also Hungarian, and even in Swedish. In the case of *Flamenco*, the commission may have come from the international Communist group working illegally in the camp.

The secret Communist organization in the camp consisted of various national cells. The Spanish and the German cells were the most populous and the strongest as well. We know from the memoir by Dezső Jász, brigade commander of the Republican army, that Árpád Haász was the first Hungarian he met in the internment camp at Le Vernet. He was the same Árpád Haász who took over György Nádas's post as secretary of the Galilei Circle and who, on April 27, 1917, in a shocked and outraged letter, informed my grandfather that at an extraordinary directorial meeting of the Circle, a decision was made that their library should be named after their friend and comrade György Nádas. In his memoir entitled *From the Hungary of Councils to the Pyrenees*, Jász provides a list of Hungarian Communists with whom he shared a common fate in the camp. Jász was the cousin of a certain Magda Bán, who was walled up in the illegal basement with my father and uncle. The first person he mentions, without the aristocratic embellishment to his name, is my uncle, Pál Aranyossi; other people on his list include the prominent Communists László Rajk, Imre Sebes, Sándor Sebes, Sándor Sziklai, András Tömpe, István Tömpe, and Ferenc Münnich, who, even if they failed to do so to universal approval, nevertheless short-stopped the centuries-old feudal and capitalist march of postwar Hungarian history. Rajk was later killed by his own best comrades, Sziklai was killed by rebels on October 26, 1956, in Budapest because he wanted to protect the dictatorship of the proletariat from the proletariat, while on December 15, 1971, Tömpe, a leading figure of the Party, committed suicide over his disappointment about what he saw as his party's betrayal of the proletarian dictatorship in favor of a shift toward a capitalist-style market economy, in which he was not mistaken.

In the illegal Communist group of the camp at Le Vernet, Árpád Haász was responsible for agitation and propaganda, and it is likely that he had asked Aranyossi to write the play while they were in barracks number 7. They had known each other as well as Dezső Jász from the Galilei Circle.

Any way we look at it, the Galilei Circle was the pith and marrow of the antifeudal, anticlerical, antiauthoritarian, leftist, liberal democratic strivings of the first two decades of twentieth-century Budapest, and despite the dramatic circumstances of its suppression and the trial of its members, its influence continued for another fifty years. Not only György Nádas, who later committed suicide, but his younger sister Magda Nádas, his older sister Eugénia Nádas, as well as their younger brother, István Nádas, were all members of the Circle. The girls met their future husbands in the fourth-story hall in Anker Köz, or else in the adjacent library, Magda, the journalist Pál Aranyossi, who at the time still spelled his name Aranyossy, and Özsi the physician and researcher László Mándoki, whom she later divorced because she realized that he'd been cheating on her, and once even found him in flagrante with his secretary. The promise she and Magda had made to each other one night while talking in bed, namely, that the men to whom they would open their hearts would have to be short, fragile, soft-spoken, gentle, and above all unprepossessing, they were thus able to keep, even though I never thought of either Aranyossi or Mándoki as especially unprepossessing. But in the eyes of the girls, they certainly weren't handsome studs like their feudal and bourgeois father, my grandfather. Theirs was the first generation who in the wake of the revolutions and disenchantments of the nineteenth century made no demands either on the king or on society, they just wanted to lead different lives, and did so. They didn't just want to discard their girdles or, as they said back then, corsets, they didn't want to be subjected to anyone anymore, not even to their parents, they wanted emancipation in many senses of the word, national, religious, sexual, they wanted social emancipation and universal suffrage, but they did not want war, they would not tolerate exploitation and the destitution of the masses any longer. Also, till their dying day, they hated the idea of charity. Nietzsche, who exercised a powerful influence on their generation, imprinted his own principle of the will to power on their minds, a basic principle about the world that with his weak psychic makeup proved too much for György Nádas, just as it proved too much for my Aunt Magda. We must will things, this is how their generation saw themselves, and if there's anything man is capable of, it's willing. When they fell for these strong-willed bourgeois girls, Aranyossi and Mándoki were already good friends; they were both pacifists and socialists, they had both fought at the front, they had both been seriously wounded, and in the last two years of the war, they both served in the hinterlands. Aranyossi was then treated for his bronchitis in the clearing hospital set up in the royal palace in Gödöllő, while Mándoki became the physician, the head of the laboratory, and finally the chief physician of the resort hospital turned military hospital in Turnau.

When they couldn't meet in Budapest, they exchanged letters.

My good old friend, Mándoki wrote from Turnau in Böhmen on November 23, 1916, I hear from Eugie that you have safely reached Noah's ark in Gödöllő, where you are angry with me for not having written to you. I make amends with this letter, and as for your safe harbor, congratulations.

Even though they had not considered marriage, my Aunt Eugie

and he had been in love for a year by then. My grandfather wouldn't hear of the lanky young man. He was not about to give the hand of his daughter, celebrated throughout town for her beauty, to a penniless doctor serving at the front. Özsi had a knack for drawing, and after she graduated from the famous gymnasium of the National Society for the Education of Women, at the time the only gymnasium for girls in Pest, which had opened its gates in 1869 thanks to the aristocrat Mrs. Veres née Hermina Beniczky, who was also its first director, and which differed from the gymnasium for boys only in that the girls were not taught Latin, Eugenie decided to attend the Applied Drawing School, officially known as the Capital Town Municipal Applied Drawing School, because she wanted to acquire the skills needed to become a metalsmith. To acquire, this is the term the people of Pest used. Also, the school enjoyed strong personal and professional ties with the Fachschule für Zeichen und Malerei and the Kunstgewerbeschule drawing schools in Vienna, to which it bore a striking resemblance. These schools took the feudal privilege of furniture design and interior decorating and applied it to middle-class life. The Applied Drawing School issued master's certificates in various branches of the fine and applied arts to its students, who hailed mostly from decent middle-class homes; in short, it offered the sort of vocational training that spared them their peevish apprentice and assistant years. My Aunt Özsi met Margit Gráber, with whom she became lifelong friends, in this school. In her memoir entitled *Book of Memories*, Gráber writes that the street where it was located has since been renamed and the school itself has become a high school for the arts yet everything remained the same as it had always been. When she was last there, she writes, the same young girls inhabited the halls as back then, and they were being instructed by the same male teachers with the same long legs with whom young girls invariably fall in love.

In this school they did not have to sit on benches. Rather, they sat around the model. They bent over objects. They all enjoyed drawing, but no one supervised them, they could skip a class whenever they felt like it. When winter was gone at last and good weather had suddenly made an appearance, they hurried out to the nearby Danube to take a short boat ride, or they went to an exhibition, or out to City Park to row on the lake. The propeller was a small white boat that conveyed passengers from one side of the river to the other. Still, whatever can be learned about painting in a school, this is where she learned it, Gráber writes. They had good teachers, Manó Vesztróczy, the well-known painter, was among them, a privilege for any art student. She learned to appreciate pictorial relationships from him, and also pictorial construction, color relations, and many other things besides. She especially liked to remember his landscapes painted with sparkling greens. But at night, her two brothers, who were attending college, took her with them to lectures at the Galilei Circle.

On March 15 of each year, the Circle held a big celebration at the Vigadó in Pest. Each time, the celebrated poet Endre Ady sent a poem for the occasion. As for Margit Gráber, she had the honor of designing the cover of their gala program for 1912. Gráber played a major role in the formation of my own attitude to pictures, while the tradition of the former Applied Drawing School played an important part in my training as a photographer. I mention all this merely to show the reader how the various layers gradually settled on top of each other in my life. It is like an alternate rhyme scheme, and generally, this is how things work.

After the siege, the former school opened its door as the Fine Arts Lyceum, and when in 1950 it was turned into the Gymnasium for Fine and Applied Arts, the art faculty was moved into a dismal-looking house in Práter Street. Nevertheless, teaching retained its former professional standards and focus on art. Here, too, no one bothered with who was present and who was absent. I was working as an apprentice in a photo studio on Kossuth Lajos Street at the time, but twice a week, in the morning and the afternoon, for two whole days, I went to this proletarian-looking apartment house in Práter Street to study photography. I studied optics, chromatics, and photo chemistry and composition from two art historians, Mrs. Rózsa and Lajos Végvári; the former lectured on art history from antiquity to the present, the latter taught the history of photography along with all its photorealistic and veristic schools. This took three years. The school's curriculum was set up in line with the tradition of the former Applied Drawing

School, because in addition to offering instruction in the traditional applied arts, rug weaving, tapestry making, coppersmithing, art glass-making, gold and silversmithing, furniture making, wood carving, marquetry, and porcelain painting, the former Applied Drawing School was the first to offer training for photographers that included lectures in art history, thereby raising all these professions out of the morass of artiness and pure business practice. Also, just like in Margit Gráber's case, this was my first and surely last school where I didn't nod off all the time from sheer boredom. If a student couldn't pass the tests in the theoretical subjects, he couldn't get his assistant's certificate. There were no other restrictions. At last I understood what it was all about, what was related to what, and how I could best utilize what I had learned. The year when Margit Gráber was busy designing the cover of the gala program, the last year students of the photography class were taking pictures of Özsi, the most beautiful girl in the school, for their art exams. Of these, seven portraits, more precisely, seven half-length pictures, have survived from the hands of seven different photographers, but using identical techniques. The photographs were taken in a studio, or possibly in various studios, but without artificial lighting effects of any sort, meaning, with the use of diffused light and with seven different lenses.

Diffuse light deprives the photographer of the simplest means of creating character, since he no longer has a means of emphasizing or obscuring the features of his subject. After all, everything concerning photography is in fact about drawing with light, the relationship of light and shade.

Given the circumstances, it couldn't have been more difficult to portray the model's features. For lack of lighting effects, the camera placement takes precedence over character, the distance from the object and the placement of the subject within the photographic frame becomes more important than the person of the sitter. But then, a picture invariably answers the abstract question of how I see an object, or else it answers the concrete question of what an object is like intrinsically. These pictures have preserved seven versions of my Aunt Özsi's youthful beauty, and each reveals a humble beauty. Also, in two of the pictures, we see two different perspectives of her body that could hardly be reconciled with the contemporary ideal of beauty. On one, her slender body, wrapped in a striped cotton dress, hovers over us, the cubist peaks and broken lines of the striped cotton fill up nearly the entire pictorial space, and they do so with such ambition and determination, as if they meant to force the sitter out of the picture, while on another the slender body seems angular as it veritably bursts through the soft cloth and is positioned in a striking *contrapposto* in relationship to the head, while her profile is like a sparrow hawk's. I am familiar with my aunt's striking facial features and can safely say that the positions dictated by the photographers serve to reveal her character. She had the self-assurance of a monarch, but was never demonstrative. She did not engage in arguments over details, she waited until those engaged in the argument tired themselves out and lost all sense of how to resolve anything. At such times she always stood ready with her own decision, which, because of her previous silence, seemed more like a timid suggestion. Her decisions were based not on logic or emotion, they were based on her sense of form, and for this reason, she never justified herself.

There is also a portrait of her that presents her habitually reserved expression, her lack of smiles, and the captivating sensuality of her body as the two contradictory sides of her being. This photograph, along with some other family photographs notable for some other aesthetic considerations, has been hanging on the wall of our bedroom in Gombosszeg for many years. Özsi is turned toward us, but with her huge, beautifully shaped eyes she is looking somewhere into the distance, well below the picture's horizon. Her glance is sad, it reflects a certain fear of life. This, too, was characteristic of her. With her fine, unsmiling beauty she remained a mysterious woman, but there was nothing spiritual about her. With her, everything was grounded, tied to earthly forms, and surely no one had unraveled the strings of her hot-air balloon, ever, though obviously, she didn't think too highly of earthly things either, nor was she interested in owning things; at most she was interested in the aesthetics of earthly existence. In this photograph she is wearing a nearly matte, cleverly tailored, light-colored, sleeveless silk dress with piping, shot with material of a darker hue and draped over the shoulder, and surely conceived in the so-called princess style. Also, she has a mink stole nonchalantly flung over her shoulder. The barely visible gold chain around her neck bears a medallion the size of a plum, an antique cameo, and on each of her perfectly shaped naked arms is a double-stranded bracelet of very small pearls falling over a golden bracelet. One hand is laid lightly on her lap, and she is holding something with two fingers, maybe a closed fan, maybe a very light ladies' handbag. The other hand is steadying the mink stole on her shoulder, as if she were afraid it might slip off, whereby her two naked arms frame the portrait, and her hair is lost in the even darkness of the background.

She was curious, eager to learn, and naïve, Margit Gráber writes about herself, and since her parents meant for her to pursue a career that would ensure her a steady income, they enrolled her in the Academy for Applied Arts, where my Aunt Özsi followed her for two years. Gráber was two years her senior. It was around this time that they first admitted women, much to the chagrin of the male students, who let the young ladies in on the confidence that they needn't exert themselves, because only a man is capable of creating real art, which was the prevailing opinion of the time. But not only were they not put off, they laughed at these silly boys. And when the war seemed likely, thanks to their pacifist leanings gained by attending the Galilei Circle, they still hoped that the organized workers in Germany would never be convinced to participate in the coming war. And when the general European folk festivity, the mobilization began, they all knew, Gráber writes, that their happy days were over. Her brother enlisted as a garrison artillery runner the very first day and protected the Dalmatian coast until the final day of the war. Gráber, whom her girlfriends lovingly called Médi, studied glass painting at the academy, and when the head of her workshop also joined the army, she began designing stained-glass windows for public buildings and apartment-building staircases in Budapest; she painted medieval ladies and knights on glass until, at the Palace of Arts, she came face-to-face with a painting by Béla Iványi Grünwald that became the talk of the town. She immediately signed up to study at his school. She wanted him to be her teacher. As soon as summer arrived, she took off for Kecskemét, eager to study with him at the artists' colony. When she showed up with her small suitcase, Iványi Grünwald was sitting on the sunny steps of the building with the painter Vilmos Perlrott-Csaba, who was wearing his usual elegant suit, but no shoes. The young Médi had never seen anything like this before. People did not appear in public when not fully dressed. In higher circles, it was not done even at home. The two barefooted men, each impeccably attired in a three-piece linen suit and tie, were flinging coins, or as people say, pitching pennies. By all odds, this lack of manners must have had a strong erotic appeal, because soon after, Margit Gráber and Perlrott-Csaba, many years her senior, became an item, and as Médi later bashfully said, at the dawn of their love affair, neither of them bothered to ask for parental or any kind of official permission.

As for my grandmother, she mutely approved of my grandfather's decision that, come hell or high water, he'd never give his extraordinarily beautiful daughter to the impoverished military doctor László Mándoki. My grandmother approved nearly all his decisions. She approved as a subordinate, and she approved as an opportunist, for which her daughters couldn't scold her enough. Why can't you say no, Mother, why can't you put your foot down, just once. Still, my grandfather made a number of rigid decisions that with quiet diplomacy my grandmother was able to divert from their catastrophic denouement. She managed, so to speak, to humanize his insane ideas. Meanwhile, poor Grandmother and Grandfather had no idea what their other daughter, the destructive and feckless Magda, was up to, and that because of her, they'd have to confront an even greater good-for-nothing, an unemployed, wounded, weak-lunged French translator or journalist or whatever, when he'd come to ask for their daughter's hand in marriage. A scandal of staggering proportions was brewing in the family. Aranyossi had known Magda for about a month and a half and they'd been exchanging letters, something that the two sisters discussed between themselves, but kept from their parents. There's a remark in one of the letters to the effect that Özsi had informed Mándoki, then serving in the heartlands, of the happy circumstance, namely, that his friend had fallen head over heels in love with her younger sister.

Özsi was aloof and reserved, she was always on top of any situation, while Magda was passionate, aggressive, loud, prone to easy laughter, and ungovernable.

Since the outbreak of the war, he's had a theory, Mándoki writes to the same friend, also a member of the Galilei Circle, he first thought of it in Galicia while experiencing the bloody trials of their first retreat. In short, his theory is that a person, if he wants, or better yet, if he is capable of it, will group the objects of the visible world within himself, the trees, the shrubs, and in fact, the image of burned-down shacks with the decaying carcasses of fallen animals, so that they will form some sort of harmony. When he was cold or starving, he tried to comfort himself by doing just that, and he'd certainly have managed it, if only everything were not far more terrible than one can imagine. In short, he doesn't just want to make excuses for not having written to his friend, he wants him to know that since the retreat, he's run out of energy, he is empty inside. He locks himself in his room, or as they say at the front, he goes into *Deckung*, he takes cover, he hides in a ditch and lives as if in a cocoon. A person can't be productive in a cocoon, which goes without saying. The unyielding, boundless monotony of the hinterland does not allow a person to come to terms with terrible events.

As for his daily chores and circumstances, Mándoki continues, by now his friend probably knows that because of his by now pathological loss of weight the medical officer took pity on him and put him in sick bay, not that it will help. He has basically nothing to do as a doctor, which is one of the reasons he welcomed the offer. He is wasting away, going off the deep end, losing his mind. He waxes nostalgic about his busy days in Budapest, when going out to a nice place made him feel free as a bird, though not alone, he writes, by which he is referring to Özsi once again, or possibly the company of loose women, a pleasure and distress he shared with his friend in the times they had spent together. Along with Eduard Bernstein, Oszkár Jászi, Zsigmond Kunfi, Ervin Szabó, and György Nádas, they too were not only attendees but lecturers as well during the winter and summer semesters of the Galilei Circle.

According to the contemporary printed programs, György Nádas lectures on the laws of price change, László Mándoki on the penchant of the natural sciences to overgeneralize and judge, Oszkár Jászi on the tension between nationalities and peace between nations, Eduard Bernstein on the inevitability of war, Zsigmond Kunfi on the relationship between pacifism and socialism, Ervin Szabó on free exchange internationally as a guarantor of lasting peace, and Pál Aranyossy, who at the time wrote his name with all its aristocratic appurtenances, the double *ess* and the *y*, not an *i*, lectured on French socialism and Jean Jaurès. Given his idle hours, Mándoki writes to his friend, his intellectual inactivity is torture, and his wartime wounds will never heal. He must spend at least four or five hours in his ward, but he does so only out of mere courtesy, since there is nothing he can do for the patients. He chats with his colleagues. He's reading Dostoyevsky's last novel, *The Brothers Karamazov*, and these are the most valuable hours of his life. He spends half his nights with it, he can hardly put it down, it is an amazingly beautiful, extraordinary book. Thanks to Dostoyevsky, he is concerned with the question of the tragic consequences that the most commonplace notions might have on a person's life. For instance, let's take the concept of God. It's something they rarely brought up between themselves. He rarely thinks about it, whereas it prowls quietly around him both as a concept and a problem in quest of a solution. The question is not whether God exists. Since he got bored of praying when he was in high school, the existence of God hasn't interested him in any obvious way. And therein lies the problem, because even those who believe in God don't believe in him as unequivocally as Christ's teaching would demand. A great many people believe in him, but if they believed in him the way they should, there would not be a war today, and it takes a staggering event such as a war to make people stand up and reflect, otherwise they make excuses for themselves by appealing to "the struggle for survival" and other similarly banal catchphrases. And should they come face-to-face with something out of the ordinary, they don't dare strain their logic, even a bit, they don't dare go to the end of the line, they don't generalize, lest they discover the conclusion before they're ready for it. And yet, what do nonbelievers do, and what do I do, he asks his friend and he asks himself. There is no man who does not call out to God in a moment of utmost distress, if only once, one single time, in his moment of utmost agitation. On the other hand, what is a person who is used to scientific order and logical thinking to do when he finds himself in the midst of such a run-of-the-mill war situation. When he takes a good look around, he can't very well accept God as an organizing principle. It would be unscientific and it wouldn't do him any good. In which case he is reduced to accepting the sordid, servile nature of his soul. How can this be helped, he asks his friend in the letter. By not allowing these shocking events to materialize in the first place, he adds. But can we hope for such a thing, he asks, is so much determination and intelligence possible. Then with a single life-affirming gesture he puts an end to his reflections and calls his friend my good old friend once more, and asks him to write as soon as possible and let him know if there's anything he can do for him. Surely, he is asking as a doctor, with reference to his friend's state of health. And he sends his love until he hears from him.

Where was their shock and disappointment over the First World War by then, their youthful hope and revolutionary enthusiasm. They couldn't very well entertain any such hopes in Le Vernet. But if, considering its defeated state, the Communist movement still had anything to offer, it was the determination not to let its members' spirit lag or fall prey to depression and despair. The Communist group in the camp managed to organize the daily activities of the inmates in a way that endowed their lives with a semblance of normalcy. At any rate, they managed to do so in those barracks where the Communists outnumbered the criminals. They even set up a top-secret military group headed by Dezső Jász. They organized counterintelligence, they exposed or kept a close eye on the informers, they kept in touch with members of the camp guard who cooperated with the resistance, and they organized the systematic education, instruction, and extended training of the inmates, because they considered intellectual curiosity an elemental condition for survival. Which of course meant that they had to concern themselves with survival once again, and once again, the eventuality of an independently organized life slipped from their grip and into the far-off future.

In all probability, they staged the play my uncle had written.

The harshly critical comments, written in small letters by an unknown hand on the margins of the sheets in French, brief and to the point, indicate as much. Rewrite. Expand. Work out. Elaborate. Elaborate. This speaks of a professional director who would later discuss with the writer the changes he feels must be made. My Uncle Pali follows his suggestions very cleverly. There is no dramaturgical difference in quality between the deleted and the inserted dialogues, the overall quality of the text is not harmed by the deletions and insertions as he works even more nuanced considerations into the text, but these are by no means considerations with an eye to the Communist movement or Communist propaganda. He made the insertions on the same finely lined note sheet as the text, and for lack of glue, affixed them with the serrated edges of postage stamps. In this manner, he created manuscript pages that could be folded over and opened up. The deletions are at first insecure, but then he goes over them with a surer hand, something that I can sympathize with. A professional knows that at times he must cross things out and might even have to destroy the result of several days' work, but he also knows that he might not be able to come up with a better version, and so he crosses something out once and for all only when the new version is ready.

The drama takes place in one of the barracks of the camp at Le Vernet, and judging by the description provided by the playwright, he had scenery as well as some sort of makeshift curtain at his disposal. The scenery must have depicted the back of a barracks in the back of the actual barracks, a brilliant scenic design idea. Instead of forcing the viewer to confront the reality of the barracks, there is a painted barracks, which rescues him from the place where he happens to be, and which is stinking with filth. It is a baroque idea, a profoundly French idea, inspired by *peinture grisaille* and Poussin's illusionistic depiction of space. We're not in this barracks, we're in *a barracks*. We're not in this palace, we're in *a palace*. At the time, Europe was in fact one big penal colony covered with a web of penal colonies. There was an empty barracks in the camp, number 32, and the camp command must have given permission to hold the performance there. Before the prefect of Ariège dismissed the too-humane camp commander, they even held weekly film screenings in the empty barracks. The prefect of Ariège cast a long, dark shadow over the camp and the inmates waged a war of liberation against him, meaning against his newly appointed camp commander, in which they were assisted by Gaston Delache, the commander of the guard. The Communist resistance used this empty barracks as the last base, the jumping-off point for escapees, and it may well be that the criminals helped them in exchange for payment. According to Dezső Jász, they helped more than thirty comrades escape in a single year. Gaston Delache was a member of the Armée Secrète, the secret army of the French resistance, and so were several of the guardsmen who didn't see what they were supposed to see when they were supposed to see it. The criminals also used this empty barracks to organize their nightlife, which was quite impressive from an anthropological viewpoint. We know about this phenomenon from the German photographer Erwin Blumenfeld's *Einbildungsroman*, a memoir written in the caustically bitter style of Thomas Theodor Heine and Georg Groß. For reasons of its own, the French administration endowed him with the great good luck of assigning him the barracks reserved for those criminals who'd previously been inmates of all the possible French penal colonies, whereby Blumenfeld found himself in even more grueling conditions than Bruno Frei and his Italian comrade, Mario of the deep-seated lines and eyeglasses, whom Koestler also mentions in his book. Here, in barracks number 31 of Section C, no lesser personage than the prince of Andorra was in charge of organizing their lives. The prince's suntanned, pockmarked face was covered with signs of old wounds, and one eye had been knocked out at a penal colony, possibly Devil's Island in Guyana; he wore a black monocle, but out of regard for his fellows, this dandy, a stranger to fear as well as pity, as Blumenfeld characterizes him, hid his face with a Panama hat tilted to one side.

By contrast, his white tennis shirt was open to the navel so that the princely crown tattooed on his chest should be there for all to see. He never wore the same pants twice. He wore patent leather shoes and kept slapping his calves, or else anyone who might be on hand, with a dog whip. The criminals had been living in the barracks for a year. They'd been living according to their own laws when Erwin Blumenfeld arrived with the other German internees. It was in the interest of the guards that the criminals should live by their own laws according to principles that were not far removed from the principles of the authorities in charge of the penal colonies. They were mostly Spanish and French criminals. When the German internees arrived and tried to get their bearings, these Spanish and French criminals refused to answer their questions. They held all Germans in contempt. The camp commanders tried to hold them in check by allowing them to indulge their chauvinism, and they also turned their backs on their black-market dealings with members of the guard, but at the same time, they did their best to disrupt their unity by placing dangerous elements, meaning Communists, in their midst.

On one of the first days Blumenfeld was in the camp, a young Spaniard went missing during the morning roll call. It was said that he hanged himself because of his unrequited love for the prince, and as a matter of fact, they soon found him dead in the barracks. The privileged internees of barracks 31 kept carefully shaved young men as their lovers. But as soon as they cut this particular young man's rope, the rope too became the object of lively commercial dealings. A hanged man's rope brings luck, and so the demand outstripped the supply. The prince's men cut the rope into pieces and sold them off. The lucky owners wore them over their hearts as talismans. According to Blumenfeld, the prince of Andorra never lost his composure. He showed no emotion even when not much later, during another morning roll call, another Spanish lover of his, to whom he gave the pet name El Greco because of his leanness, suddenly stepped out of line, and in front of the others ripped his belly open with a carving knife, then, in keeping with the rules of seppuku, threw himself on the knife. After he died in front of their eyes, the camp guards carried the body away. The prince of Andorra seemed oblivious to what had just transpired, and when the morning roll call ended, he lay down on the cot set up for him on the lawn to sunbathe, as was his custom, while his subjects manicured his hands and pedicured his feet. In his uneasy, constrained, jocular style, Blumenfeld continues to weave the thread of his narrative by mentioning that he had a copy of *Harper's Bazaar* among his belongings that contained some of his photographs, and he was so proud of it that he brought it along and would now and then take a look inside. In order to make contact with the prince of Andorra, he sent the cherished copy of the magazine to him. He was motivated by his journalistic curiosity, but I can't help thinking that he would have liked to enjoy some slight privilege or other. He was called to an audience that same afternoon, but he couldn't approach the prince directly. Instead, one of his adjutants ordered him to sign this precious copy of the magazine for the prince, and in exchange, he'd be granted permanent entry to the casino. Blumenfeld thought that he'd become the victim of a wicked joke. But that night he was led into the empty barracks number 32, where it turned out that the privilege should be taken literally, and where he was stunned to see the secret life of the camp, something he'd never even heard about before. It was in full swing. The prince's chamberlain, who stood above the adjutants in rank, had a key to all the barracks, and used it to bring their criminal mates from the other two sections of the camp to the empty barracks to partake of the privilege of gambling with the prince, and here they played dice, baccarat, and *chemin de fer* for high stakes. They knew how to pass through the high-voltage enclosure that surrounded the entire camp and availed themselves of this knowledge to visit brothels or bring back girls for late-night revels; they also knew how to procure cocaine, silk underpants, cigarettes, foie gras, fine wines, and distilled liquor. Also, getting around the camp censor, they sneaked in the mail of the Communists from the outside world for good money, or for the same good money were not above denouncing someone for these same crimes.

My uncle's drama has six characters. Rodrigues, the main character, is between forty and forty-five years of age, badly worn down but energetic. His chess partner is of indeterminate age, cheerful and lively, a bit absentminded, but of upright character. There's also an on-looker, a kibitzer of sorts, who never leaves the side of the chess players, a handsome man of forty, rotund and quiet, who can't do without others but is of little consequence to them. The fourth is Sanchez, the eternal go-between, a busybody who is also around forty. The fifth is Juan, younger than the others, though he looks older due, in part, to his suntanned skin. According to the dramatist's characterization, one might call him beautiful. In Hungarian, we would bashfully call him handsome and I should translate this beautiful as good-looking, but I will leave this beautiful as I found it. If a man is beautiful, let him be beautiful. All the same, his face betrays his anxiety, his exhaustion, and the terrible experiences that have taken their toll on him. Last, there's an Andalusian peasant with a guitar who appears in scene three and accompanies the performance with his songs. The dramatist characterizes the Andalusian peasant as slightly older than the others, around fifty years of age, his clothes revealing all the miseries of flight; half soldier, and more than half the overseer of the pack mules that accompany the Republicans' marching columns. He carries a joint stool around with him to sit on, and when he's not strumming on his guitar or singing, he busies himself carving a big bone he'd fished out of the soup kettle. This Andalusian makes his first appearance in scene three, and from that point on, accompanies the play with his guitar.

The play they performed is a rather ticklish story concerning jeal-ousy. I don't think it's based on a concrete event known to everyone in the camp, because that would have meant stigmatizing one of their own. But it is such a well-conceived drama of jealousy that it touches every man to the quick.

Sanchez informs Rodrigues that a new Spanish prisoner has arrived at the camp and would like to talk to him. The newcomer is Juan, who had once been Rodrigues's best friend and had seduced his wife. Rodrigues, who until then had spent his time amiably playing chess, now turns into a raging wild animal. Pushing Sanchez aside, he's determined to kill Juan, except he's been placed in a barracks at the farthest reaches of the camp. The camp is divided into sections, and though from time to time the criminals and the members of the Communist resistance manage to sneak into one or another section, it is a risky undertaking that requires careful planning. You can't just take off. And so, killing someone posthaste is out of the question. In this first, passionate scene, the dialogue threatens to become the libretto of a comic opera, but my uncle follows the tradition of French drama so faithfully, he doesn't fall into this dramaturgic trap, and in this unresolved situation, he concentrates on the differences in temperament of his characters. One might say that in order to delve into their temperaments, he derails the scene. In the erupting chaos of emotions, he attunes his monologues and dialogues to the structure of classical music. One can veritably hear Corneille and Racine telling him to break a leg before the performance. In the meantime, Juan, the former best friend, has become a traitor, while there's a chance that Sanchez, who is no less underhanded in his dealings, has offered his services to the guards whose job it is to spy on the inmates, and this is why he wants to bring Juan over from the other section of the camp. For all we know, the woman they both love has in the meanwhile betrayed the revolution in the interest of family peace, and is not only his friend's lover, but a Falangist as well. From which it is clear to me that when my uncle wrote the play, he had his own wife's attempted treason in mind, and he may have also been thinking of his cuckolding from before the war, meaning my Aunt Magda's lover's revenge. And when he reaches this particularly dangerous and dangerously paranoid stage of male thinking, my uncle goes one step further and enhances the drama by having Juan enter the barracks without previous notice.

The former friends must now engage in frontal combat. An encounter such as this ravishes the soul of every male, shakes his body to the core, making its effect felt down to the marrow.

Good God, what is going to happen here.

Murder, no doubt.

In the postwar years a rich harvest of memoirs about Le Vernet were written by important writers, memoirs that were largely ignored by bourgeois historians, and no wonder, because it would have meant opening a chapter in bourgeois historiography. It is interesting to note that when my uncle writes about Le Vernet in Hungarian, he calls it an internment camp, but when he writes in French, he calls it a concentration camp. When he writes in French, he automatically follows the expression current at the time, which came to the occupied French from the Germans, though later French historiographers corrected this and started using the concept of internment camp, reserving *concentration camp* for the German camps. Still, the history of the internment camp at Le Vernet reaches back to the colonial wars. Its early history lacks rich memoiristic literature, and it has no historical literature; at least, I have not found any traces of it. What we do know is that in the late nineteenth century, the abandoned brickworks was used to quarter the Senegalese units of the French army. According to some sources, before that, colored collaborators camped out under the open tile roofs, men whom their own people would have surely killed, had not the French extricated their orphaned souls from the grip of the colonies. In the weeks following the outbreak of the First World War, it was used to hold Austrian and also some Hungarian citizens, and soon after, the prisoners of war of the Monarchy, with plenty of Hungarians among them. When in the early 1920s the last of the prisoners returned home, the camp was converted into a military depot.

I set out from Toulouse around noon, it was Tuesday, it was warm, and the indigenous wind, the *vent d'autan*, also known as the *vent du midi*, the wind of the geographic south that blows mightily under the heavy clouded sky, shaking and tearing at the trees, not letting them go, bringing the maddening mood of the desert with it, and when it stops, in five minutes the rain is upon us. This is what the old song says about this wind; at any rate, this is how I translate it, ignoring the metrics. Except, there was no rain, just this merciless, dry African wind. The railway carriages were packed with high school students. An Arab girl with striking features sat across from me, engrossed in reading a book. Her expression became careworn; surely, something she'd read was beyond her grasp. She took out her small, round CD player, put the earplugs in, and was soon transformed right before my eyes. She became radiant. After a couple of seconds, she gave me a flirtatious glance, bewitched and bewitching, which surprised me, to say the least. Clearly, that look was not meant for the elderly gentleman sitting across from her, nor was it meant for me. But just then, terribly embarrassed, she realized what she was doing, and she turned down the flame. Her radiance had been addressed to the stock of memories that the music she was listening to evoked.

I looked out the window, like someone who tries to impress every last element of the landscape into his memory. I mustn't forget. Yes, this was the landscape. No two ways about it, this was the branch line over which, between June 1943 and July 1944, the six transports passed so that after their long journey they should arrive with their load at their final destinations in Dachau, Mauthausen, or Ravensbrück. The transports were first taken from Le Vernet d'Ariège to the desecrated synagogue in Bordeaux, or else to the fort Caffarelli in Toulouse, built of terra-cotta brick. The last transport, which subsequently became known as the Phantom Train and which was carrying internees cramped into nearly one hundred cattle cars, was expected to arrive at Dachau in three days. But because of a blown-up bridge, the transport was turned around at Angoulême and sent back to Bordeaux, where at night, locked inside the cattle cars, the prisoners lived through the bombing of the train yard, those that survived, that is. Many wagons suffered damage, and one wagon burned down along with the people inside it. The prisoners experienced all the other bombings, too, locked inside these cattle cars. The Allies preferred bombing the bridgeheads, they targeted the train stations from low altitudes, while the maquisards preferred blowing up the tracks, this was their *bataille du rail*, their transportation battle, which caused the transports carrying the prisoners to stop where they were and remain stalled there for days. This meant the prisoners had no air inside the bolted wagons.

Sometimes the prisoners were able to signal to low-flying Allies with their white handkerchiefs or pieces of light-colored clothing not to shoot, at least, not them. They may have been hoping that the maquisards would set them free. It later turned out that there were in fact such attempts, but they all failed.

That morning they herded the prisoners into the synagogue, where yet more transports had arrived from other neighboring camps, from the Fort du Hâ, the camp at Souge, where just the day before they had executed fifty prisoners who had attempted to escape. They were then herded into cattle cars once again, at which point, with the new arrivals, their numbers had swollen to seven hundred, including sixty-two women. On this last and hottest summer of the war, they were constantly tortured by hunger and thirst. They had nowhere to relieve themselves. The dead and those who lost their minds were sometimes locked up with them for days on end, along with the urine and the excrement. Sometimes they were let out of the wagons for a couple of minutes, when in the extreme heat their train was directed to a side track to make way for the Wehrmacht transports.

The French railroad workers would also attempt to prevent the trains from moving, because they were hoping the approaching Allies would liberate the prisoners before the transports guarded by the German camp police reached the German frontier, and they nearly managed it, thanks to their attempts at sabotage.

The transport set off from the main railway station of Toulouse, the Matabiau, on July 3, but on August 17 it was still in the Rhône Valley, where because of the bombed-out tracks at Roquemaure, they could proceed no farther. The prisoners were herded out of the wagons and were forced to march the seventeen kilometers to Sourgue, where, with the help of railroad workers, thirty-four prisoners managed to escape. The rest were herded into wagons again. The journey lasted eight weeks. Five hundred and sixty-three prisoners made it to Dachau alive, but the women were immediately sent on to Ravensbrück.

Of the prisoners of the Phantom Train, 176 people survived to see their liberation.

But even before that fleeting episode with the young girl, at noon, back in Toulouse, as I was waiting for the bus for the Matabiau station, I experienced another such misconstrued glance, but this time, the glance was mine. A person's life is full of emotional and sensual flare-ups; in literature, Constantine Cavafy was the first to describe the phenomenon. As if the promise of eternity were revealing itself through a person's instinctual life. Anything could happen at any time, and in his guts and in his glance, it does happen. Man is a creature who must always take everyone into account, there is no end to man's promiscuity, it is not hindered by gender, his attention is animalistic. Unconsciously, his glance disregards those who are out of the question, the ugly, the old, the weak, the ailing. It is at such times that man's innate lack of courtesy is most apparent. But just as surely, his glance will alight again on all those who satisfy his animal desires, as well as those he regards as potential rivals, and he will instantly decide on a plan of action. Who he must toss with his horns without delay in any manner at all, or disarm or banish, for that matter. In the dry, strong south wind, under the open sky, a young haggard-looking Arab woman, to whom life had obviously not been kind, was waiting at the empty stop. I glanced at her, then looked away. It was clear to me that this was not me, meaning that it was not the consciously controlled self, and it was also clear that the physical attraction was immediately accompanied by social rejection. Both reactions were functioning on the level of primal instinct. Later another white man came, well-groomed, plumpish, around forty, a decent gentleman who must have lived in one of the villas of the neighborhood, he wished me a good day, but he did not wish the Arab woman, to whom life had obviously not been kind, anything; on the other hand and on the animal level of the senses, with this gesture he cemented the racial unity between the two of us, white belongs to white, something we would not have felt between us without the presence of the Arab woman, not to mention the fact that as far as blood is concerned, I should be much closer to an Arab than to a pudgy Frank infected with Occitan, Provençal, and Anglo-Saxon blood, who proceeded to sit down, then immersed himself in the study of a bunch of papers and sketched maps he drew from his briefcase, but he must have been thinking about something completely different, perhaps his tiresome wife or their awkward night together. He might have been a salesman, a real estate agent, a land surveyor, a CPA, or I don't know what. Later still, an Arab man, thin as a reed, who couldn't have been much older than the Arab woman with the difficult life, joined us, but the bus had still not come. I was impatiently pacing, and once, as I suddenly turned around, I couldn't help but notice that a couple of seconds sufficed for the two of them, and their eyes were alrcady lockcd into cach other, they were already holding each other with raw strength, my Lord, how far they'd gone. Which could also be understood as meaning that in no time at all and without impediment, the Arab man had elbowed me out of my rightful place. Or that the Arab woman had already let him occupy my place. I had surprised and unsettled them with my unguarded glance as if, with my scandalous instincts, I'd come between them on purpose, as if they couldn't forgive themselves either for my having seen them together like this. This confused muddle surfaced among strangers in the blink of an eye. In the blink of an eye I laid waste to their all too brief happiness.

The station where I eventually got off became deserted in the blink of an eye, and the entire neighborhood, too, was just as quickly deserted.

I found an information board, but I did not find the name of the place where I was headed. But in line with the instructions from my ignorant hosts, I knew that I must go to Le Vernet and not Venerque. By the time I finished studying the board and the map, the high school students were gone, too, from the vicinity of the station. I now had no one to ask for directions. Out on the square, two black African men were busy painting white signs on the newly laid, fresh-smelling asphalt, shouting, enjoying themselves. They looked at me as if I were an apparition, they didn't understand a word of what I was trying to ask them. They were looking across at me from another continent, perhaps another planet, and had no idea what this awfully famous *camp d'internement* might be. There was nothing about the station building either to serve as a reminder of what had transpired here seventy years before. An old row of plane trees led to the town, and I set off along it. After walking about a kilometer and a half, I found a tiny village center at the other end of the hedge, along with the usual shops, a bank, a beautician, a grocery store, even a florist, but everything was shuttered, just like everywhere else in the French countryside at noon. A sign on the square indicated that I'd find a fortified seventeenth-century church nearby. I suspected that St. James's famous pilgrimage route led somewhere through here, the Chemin de Saint-Jacques de Compostelle, on which tens of thousands march each year, taking their classical faith in Providence with them. I later came across the humble signs pointing the way at every turn. Their fortified church was one of the stations of their pilgrimage, but I couldn't have cared less either for their fortified church, or their pilgrimage, or their faith in Providence.

I don't know what is leading me, and I don't know where it is leading me. It is not curiosity. As I approach the end of my life, there is little curiosity left in me. Surely, my present state is not unlike the state of the pilgrims of long ago that induced them to embark on untrodden paths to do penance for their sins. I, too, must do penance, except I must do penance for sins I have not committed, nor do I intend to commit. In which case, it makes no sense asking the Lord that I shouldn't want to commit them, just as it is no use asking him to protect my soul against the regressive anthropological reality of the perpetual and large-scale massacre and torture of man by his fellows.

Sober recognition has no appointed route of pilgrimage. Doing penance for having survived, though my survival is by no means my own merit, it is no merit, and as it has no meaning either, I can't even consider it a boon. Walking in silence to places where people suffered and died, for reasons we do not know, has neither sense nor function, yet we cannot avoid asking why they died. Whoever avoids asking it will not only incur damnation, whatever that may be, but will toss humanity farther on the path to perdition. This particular abyss has no bottom. Still, we are bound to confer the last rites, though neither in the secular nor the clerical sense of the word, no, by no means, and we are just as surely bound, in the name of the soul, to forget neither the place, nor the silent clamor of the dead, nor their persistence which hovers over the din that weighs heavily on our lives.

The place was not there, the *lieu de mémoire*, as the French historian Pierre Nora called it. I still had an hour and a half to look at that accursed and beautiful fortified church, to take a good look at the pagan devotional objects of the cult of Providence that was past its due date, before, enriched by yet one more mistake, I could board the next train back to Toulouse so that the following morning I should embark on the whole damned search all over again. But I did not turn back,

I continued on my way, I wasn't inclined to accept my hosts' mistake, which thus became a fiasco of my own.

A bit farther from the village center I found a boarded-up villa with an upper story and a tower, and I spent quite some time musing over its decrepitude. Its architectural style reminded me of the elegant villa up on Svábhegy, the former summer residence of the Perczel family from Bonyhád, where I spent six years with my parents as a child, and also my younger brother and my maternal grandparents, who moved in with us until first my mother, then my grandmother died. For a long time I referred to this villa as our house, our garden, whereas it was not ours, and yet with its garden, trees, and plants, and not least of all the changes in ownership that at the time were beyond my comprehension, it nevertheless determined, at the most fundamental level, my concept of ethics and aesthetics and my decisions with regard to them. I walked along the villa's once splendid and ornate fence, now in ruins, held together here and there with wire. It had a huge park run wild, much to my liking. With its ancient trees, its oaks, maples, and sycamores, it provided a pleasant shade for my ambling. It was one of those exemplary genteel villas from the end of the nineteenth century whose architectural character went unaffected by time, except the towers were gone, along with the ostentatious lifestyle that was pulled from under it, like a carpet.

Walking along the crumbling brick perimeter of the park I reached the turbulent Ariège River. In this particular part of Le Vernet, an impressive brick bridge with four arches conducts the busy traffic over it. In Bordeaux all the buildings are made of yellow sandstone, including Gare Saint-Jean, the main railway station, which had suffered major damage during the war but was rebuilt along with the freight terminal, also bombed repeatedly. In Toulouse and its vicinity, on the other hand, just about everything was built of terra-cotta brick, the public buildings, the cathedral, the elegant residences, bridges, and forts, including the forbidding citadels of the Foix counts built in the early Middle Ages. In 1125, the prince of Toulouse permitted the citizens to build a town hall, and before long, the huge brick structure started a fad, and conscious of their strength and independence, the citizens turned the town into a conglomeration of terra-cotta brick, from top to bottom.

La Ville Rose.

Toulouse.

They needed to fire lots of brick for their terra-cotta town. Possibly, later on this gave them the practical idea that the undesirable elements, strangers, prisoners of war, the politically persecuted, and the political refugees should be herded together under the roofs of the abandoned kilns and kept prisoners under the most dire of circumstances.

In the sad brickworks universe of Europe, the camp at Le Vernet d'Ariège is surely one of the first, if not the first.

I knew that the camp was gone with nothing there but the abandoned ground, if indeed I'd even find that abandoned ground. But the turbulent currents of the Ariège revived my imagination; I might be in the right place after all, and this Le Vernet is that Le Vernet. According to what I'd read, the Ariège passes right through it. At the moment, adventurous kayakers were making their way through its wild, roaring currents. At the same time, I couldn't find the unending flat plain where the brick kilns or the wooden barracks must have stood, and I couldn't find the water tower or the mountains either.

Bruno Frei offers a precise account of his arrival, strangely enough, they all do; he describes that certain meadow behind the station house and the rocky, snow-clad peaks and dark precipices of the Pyrenees. Frei also describes the fifty-hectare camp divided into sections marked A, B, and C, where he found himself among criminals. This locking together of Communists and criminals by the commanders was also a feature of the camps, so that the natural antipathy they felt for each other should take its appointed course. They did the same, and in the same way, at the Margit Boulevard prison in Budapest and in the German concentration camps. I couldn't find out whose idea it had originally been, and how the fiendish idea then spread through the constellation of the penal colonies of Europe. But Bruno Frei was definitely mistaken when he wrote that the camp was situated right behind the station. Koestler provides us with a more reliable account. From the station to the camp gate, the internees had to walk a kilometer and a half along the path that ran parallel to the railway track. Today the traffic is composed mainly of a succession of trucks whizzing by, making a horrendous din and creating huge blasts of air meanwhile.

At first I couldn't find the place, there was no trace of it, but when I did find it, there was nothing there. I had to accustom my eyes to the great big nothing that was Le Vernet.

Then, after two days, behind a clump of trees I caught site of the water tower resting on stilts familiar to me from my reading.

The water tower was much smaller than I had imagined from the descriptions I'd read. Today it stores bales of straw under and around it. A bit farther off, a man was working the soil with a harrow pulled by a tractor, the same soil that had once been the camp ground and before that had belonged to the brickworks. What does he unearth with his harrow, I wondered, and what does he sow.

The man's wife had just driven out onto the highway on her motorcycle when I got there amid the infernal draft created by the passing trucks. She was going to get their lunch when I stopped her, she even said so, I'm going to get our lunch, as if we were old friends. She rested one foot on the ground without cutting the motor, but shouting over its roar and the rhythmic chuk-chuk of the tractor, she readily gave me instructions, telling me what had been where, and what was where now, where I could find what. But with an easy shrug of the shoulder, she skirted the issue of her share in what had happened at the camp and thus her share in the history of the place itself. Emotions have no place here, you have to sow seeds for the crop and turn up the soil for the sowing. With her open crash helmet, her suntanned, more citified than country face, she was both personal and impersonal with respect to history. When she told me about the place, she was very near to making a distinction between personal responsibility and historical responsibility, but could not find the words for it. In all of Europe, hardly anyone had found them, hardly anyone had looked for them. With her accommodating ease, she at least let on that she is one of those people who do not deny other people's past and suffering in the interest of exonerating themselves, which was as much enlightenment and social responsibility as she managed to salvage for herself in face of the repeated religious and secular evil of the twentieth century, which is to her personal credit. We are all living under the brutal reign of the ecclesiastical and secular herd spirit.

By all accounts, the latrines had been where we were just standing and talking. Bruno Frei even tells us that their daily chores involved emptying the latrines, their own daily shit, with buckets. But they felt it humiliating that they should have to clean out the latrines of the gendarmes as well several times a week, then pour their own shit and the shit of the guards, which was always stale and more difficult to scoop out, into large buckets. Their aversion is understandable. They then emptied the buckets into large bins, loaded them onto trucks, and emptied their contents into cesspools that they had to dig themselves dangerously close to the Ariège, after which they had to carry the empty bins and filthy buckets down to the river and scrub them clean in the ice-cold mountain stream.

Sometimes, when the small water tower was out of commission, they'd haul water from the roaring river. I must have read this bit of detail somewhere else, perhaps Koestler, perhaps Erwin Blumenfeld or Rudolf Leonhard, Dezső Jász, Ferenc Münnich, or possibly Francesco Nitti, I don't know where, I can't find the passage. They liked carrying the water. The sight and the sound of the roaring river gave them back their freedom, a sentence I can't get out of my mind. It may have been my uncle who said it, who, after being held prisoner for sixteen months, in the summer of 1941 escaped with László Rajk and after various adventures both reached Budapest and engaged in illegal Party work. But their escape is not clear, the story would need clarification.

Some days later, on the main square of Le Vernet d'Ariège, where the sycamores were pruned into the same geometrical shape as in the other Le Vernet, or indeed on every single French square, I found some hefty photo albums in the small museum separated off from the local school's day-care center. A person has to ask for the key at the town hall, then he is free to spend hours all alone with the photographs and the documents stored here.

I was alone in the museum. As I was reading, turning the pages, making notes to satisfy my own pointless passion, on the other side of the thin wall, or rather, a stand-in for a wall, the school children were eating lunch, making a racket and rattling the tableware. In the tiny museum I could sense the smell of the food on the tables and hear every word the teacher was shouting. They must've been eating some kind of roast for lunch, possibly with potatoes au gratin. I tried to guess as I looked, aghast, at the photographs in the album.

This was on a Friday at noon, after I fought for the key at the town hall.

I first arrived in Le Vernet d'Ariège on a Wednesday afternoon, but the museum was closed. The slip glued to the glass door said that you could ask for the key during working hours at the town hall, but the town hall was also closed. Besides the main square, the community also has a market square and on it an ancient church. The sycamores with their tortured square shapes were just bringing forth their leaves, and there was not a soul anywhere and no shade. The shutters of every severe window of every small, severe house standing on the strictly appointed square were strictly closed. I sat down on a step, ate my lunch, and listened to the roar of the nearby Ariège. But not only the great Ariège roars and rumbles behind the gardens; a small, clear brook also trickles through the community, at times silently disappearing, at times mutely reappearing as fish, transparent as glass, leap from its waters. I'd been studying my surroundings for perhaps ten minutes when I realized that someone had been steadily watching me. On the opposite side of the square a man even older than I was standing at the open window of his house. He was leaning both hands on his walking stick, and he was eyeing me at his leisure, wondering what I was doing there, and whether I'd notice him and start up a conversation.

The pictures in the hefty albums I found in the museum had been taken by a professional photographer. He used a professional camera and professional lighting. He took two pictures of each prisoner, one in profile, one frontal, nice, proper portraits. The photographer was by all odds himself a prisoner and worked according to the rules of police photography, but also in line with his own fastidious requirements. He knew the prisoners and gave their portraits character, and he obviously enjoyed the two different perspectives. This type of artless, unsparing naturalism in portrait photography came into its own only later, sometime in the late 1960s.

The work of this illusion-free but warmhearted photographic forerunner filled me with amazement.

But on that particular Wednesday I hurriedly got up from the step where I'd eaten my lunch and headed for the old man on the other side of the square to ask him how I could get into the museum.

He said it was Wednesday.

For a while we each stubbornly held our ground, but failed to understand each other if for no other reason than because he'd just recovered from a stroke, which made it difficult for me to understand him. But more to the point, I had trouble understanding him because I didn't know that on Wednesday all public offices are closed in France, while he didn't understand what there was not to understand, even by a dim-witted foreigner such as I.

He kept repeating that it was Wednesday.

Fine, it's Wednesday, I know it's Wednesday, but what is that supposed to mean.

There came a moment when it occurred to me that this is not French and it's not a dialect and it's not a stroke, it's Occitan, Wednesday in Occitan means something entirely different, and not Wednesday at all, but at this point there was no backing out of our conversation. If it's Occitan, then I must understand what *mercredi* means in Occitan, a marvelous, nearly extinct language also known as *langue d'oc* that in fact never existed as such, because at all times it existed only in its various dialects; it was not a written language, not a literary language, but a language of the people with multiple variations; at one time the life of the Mediterranean people throbbed here to the rhythm of these dialects, and around these parts, the natives occasionally still speak it. Marc Martin, my French translator, can't speak Occitan anymore, but his parents spoke Occitan with their parents, or at least, they understood their parents when they spoke Occitan. Years later, it was thanks to him that I learned what Le Vernet, of which I found four communities in this southern region, means. It occurred to me that this word might also be Occitan. And so it is, it's Occitan, though there are not four but seven communes by this name in this region of the Pyrenees and in Provence. It means alder grove or woodland, and as we know, alder trees grow in wet, marshy lands. We have a copse of alder trees in Gombosszeg as well. In a document dating from 1373 written in Latin, it is mentioned as Vernetus; they Latinized the Occitan, and so this must be the first surviving mention of it.

I should come back on Thursday or come back on Friday.

Still, we had a nice conversation about his illness, something that, just like in the Hungarian countryside, served more as an excuse to study the other person. He was studying the same thing in my face and posture that I was studying in his. Talking serves to divert attention, it gives way to quiet speculation. Why did I come here, what am I doing here. This is what he wanted to find out by studying my face. This old and disgraceful history of theirs, why would it interest me. He wanted to learn from my face what business it was of mine.

I couldn't have told him the story all at once anyway.

Meanwhile, I studied his features, wondering whether he or his family might have been involved in the disgraceful history of the camp. Did he as a child see the gendarmes in front of the station sticking their fingers up the prisoners' rectums after they'd been ordered to strip naked.

He would have been the second person I'd have asked more or less openly, because on Tuesday, right next to the station, I'd already asked someone, a man the same age as I, but he ignored my question in such an unpleasant way, and he did something else besides, so that I hesitated asking the same question of the old man with the stroke on Wednesday.

He was a big boy by then, he said with annoyance, of course he knew, all his family have always lived here. But as for the museum, I should come back on Thursday. They hardly went as far as Perpignan, and to Toulouse or Foix only if they had to go to the court or the prefecture, but why would they have gone farther than that. And he repeated again that I should come back on Thursday. He kept repeating it so that he shouldn't have to say another word about the whole wretched story.

Fine. I stopped scratching at the festering wounds of the village. I stopped asking questions, though it was more like I swallowed my own questions back down. I realized that I couldn't ask him the questions I'd have liked in a stylistically acceptable manner, and so I wouldn't get from him the whole ugly story, which was his story as well.

I couldn't go back on Thursday, though, because on Thursday I took my leave of my hosts and moved from Toulouse to Pamiers, so I'd be closer to the place where the camp had once stood. My Aunt Magda had also stayed in Pamiers for a couple of weeks the first time she sneaked across the demarcation line; she had to cross the Cher River illegally, which was a difficult and risky venture, she was conveyed over it on a dinghy so she could visit her husband at Le Vernet d'Ariège. She had stayed there with her French comrades; the town was familiar to her from the time when they helped Rajk and Aranyossi escape. At least, this is what she told me, though I see that she wrote two other versions of the story at odds with each other, and there are two further versions, one meant for the public, the other as an addition to Party history, but neither version mentions anyone helping with the escape, or that she had had a hand in the escape. A further version came to light for the first time in a discarded written comment of hers from the fifties, according to which her husband escaped from Les Milles, and this in a highly confusing context, the facts that seem to be at odds, whereas this became the final version of her memoirs.

I went on Friday instead.

Pamiers was by no means unfamiliar to me when I moved there from Toulouse on Thursday. It was familiar to me not only from my reading, but also from stories I'd heard in the family.

After they left Paris, Ruth and Peter, the German writer Anna Seghers's children, were snuck across the demarcation line by a peasant, a complete stranger, out of the goodness of her heart. For her part, Netty, meaning Anna Seghers, was conducted across the border by a suspicious character for a hefty sum, since the good-hearted woman would not undertake sneaking three people across it. They had also come to Pamiers so Seghers could be closer to her husband, László Radványi, who was also an inmate of the camp.

At first my Aunt Magda stayed with them in Pamiers, but she didn't find Netty at home when she arrived in the small town. She found two starving children instead. Their mother had had to go to the consulate in Marseille to arrange for their travel papers to Mexico. It seems that it took a lot more time than she had anticipated. She had gone shopping and cooked something for the children, but when a couple of days later Netty returned, it turned out that the children went hungry not because she hadn't left them money for food, but because they wanted to put the money aside for their move to Mexico.

The two families knew each other from Berlin.

Later my Aunt Magda and Seghers met in Paris as well, soon after the war broke out, when my Uncle Pali was arrested. My Aunt Magda thought it best to leave their apartment, and Seghers and Radványi went looking for her on the basis of information they'd received from the underground until they found her in her hiding place on the rue Bellier-Dedouvre, in Butte-aux-Cailles on the Left Bank. They helped her and gave her money, too, until Radványi was also arrested.

My Aunt Magda told me the story along with other stories as she sat among her pillows.

If she fell asleep before midnight, an hour and a half later she woke with a start. Or else she couldn't fall asleep at all. Or if she managed to fall asleep and didn't wake up with a start, then she woke up with a start at daybreak, and as she told me, these early morning awakenings were the worst. When she woke with a start, she read with her back supported by pillows, or else we talked.

Tranquilizers and sleeping pills had no effect on her nightly anxieties. Meanwhile, I sat on the side of her bed or in our great-grandmother's armchair.

She hadn't been able to sleep for ten years by then, not since they arrested Minister of the Interior László Rajk on May 30, 1949, and a couple of days later, his wife, Júlia Rajk, whom in public she called a fine comrade, but in fact could not abide. She considered her willful, ignorant, and arrogant, a woman given to intrigue, a stubborn mule who in her ignorance accused her of terrible things, had shattered her career, and she forced herself to put up with her in public only because of László Rajk, but after András Szalai, who had been István Nádas's senior liaison in the resistance, was also arrested, a good night's sleep was out of the question, and also, a couple of days before that, on May 24, they arrested the Communist journalist Béla Szász, another person they knew from Paris, where Szász had been Jean Renoir's assistant, and would have made a name for himself in film had the Party not ordered him to return home, but they did, my Aunt Magda explained, and he let the Party lead him by the nose. It may have been July 5 when they arrested the Communist György Angyal, who also returned to Hungary to help the Party, and whose wife, Panni, came running to them, ringing their doorbell, because she didn't dare call. It was Sunday, at dawn on Sunday, at least that's how my Aunt Magda remembered it, this is what she told me, and that's how I remember it now, that it was Sunday, whereas in fact it was Tuesday. In any case, Aunt Magda and her husband said they couldn't help, and before long, most of these people were killed by their Party on trumped-up charges.

Still, they made some careful inquiries from people who undoubtedly were afraid of being arrested themselves. They also tried to talk Dajmirka, meaning Endre Nádas, into finding something out from the secret police, but Kató, meaning Kató Elek, wouldn't allow it, she wouldn't hear of it. They're not about to expose themselves because of some American spies. This is the good old middle-class word for it. To expose. I'm not about to expose myself. It sounded quite authentic like this. When they asked Dajmirka something, it was usually his wife who answered, while Dajmirka kept his eyes on Kató's lips, wondering what her opinion would be. On July 7, a Thursday, they arrested Károly Perczel, the architect who on the rue Bellier-Dedouvre organized their underground activities and, come Christmas Eve, plucked the tunes of the Internationale for them on his violin. They had no information for Panni Angyal even weeks later. A comrade, a really good comrade, told them that they'd be wiser to keep their mouths shut and not ask questions that wouldn't be answered. During the first weeks of the war, they were all living in the Angyals' small apartment on the rue Bellier-Dedouvre; in this district jam-packed with impoverished emigrants, they helped one another as best they could. They also found out from Vilma Ligeti, a friend of theirs who'd come back from Paris just a couple of months before the wave of arrests, that Ilona Kojsza, who had been Noel H. Field's representative in Paris before her return, had also disappeared from her home in Galamb Street without a trace.

I don't know, I don't know, please don't ask me anything, your ladyship. The superintendent didn't dare tell Vilma Ligeti anything about Ilona Kojsza's sudden disappearance. Such a thing would have been inconceivable in Paris, in Paris the concierge would have told her. Even twenty years later, Vilma still waxed indignant. Besides, Vilma was convinced that people would always tell her everything, and I do mean everything.

Meanwhile, in Prague the secret police had literally trapped, kidnapped, then arrested the American millionaire Noel H. Field and his wife after they moved there from Geneva, Switzerland, where through a Unitarian aid society based in Paris, they had been supporting the illegal Communist parties and the emigré members of the illegal Communist parties. They were brought to Budapest by plane in the greatest of secrecy, something my uncle soon learned about from Ilona Kojsza.

As if they'd found themselves in the crosshairs or stuck in a cobweb, my aunt and uncle wouldn't believe what they learned, because it wasn't believable.

Aranyossi had been general secretary of the National Association of Hungarian Journalists for two years by then, having been appointed in the spring of 1947 as the only candidate of the coalition parties. But where were the coalition parties with their mutual agreements by then. He remained in office for another year when, on the pretext of a cleverly orchestrated scandal involving sex and finance, he was removed. And as if that were not enough, they also arrested Pug Nose, meaning Géza Losonczy, who had been their senior liaison in the resistance. From which it became abundantly clear that they could not count on mercy either, that the spirit of the Stalinist purges had reached them.

My aunt and uncle learned about the arrest of the Fields in Prague from a Czech journalist who'd come to Budapest. By late summer they could feel the noose tightening around their own neck and couldn't understand why they hadn't been arrested yet. One by one all their friends and acquaintances were being arrested, people who after the siege had returned from France to Communist Hungary. Whereas the explanation was quite simple. Ernő Gerő, Rákosi's right-hand man, had called for their arrest in the Political Committee, and Gábor Péter, head of the secret police, had in his hand the trumped-up charges against them, but Rákosi repeatedly stepped in and prevented their arrest. If the situation called for it, Rákosi would let anyone be sent to their doom or would send them there himself, but he spared Aranyossi. Aranyossi had organized the *comité* in Paris comprising famous left-wing intellectuals who, though for quite some time they had not succeeded in orchestrating the release of Rákosi, who'd been sentenced to life imprisonment and was being held in the Csillag Prison in Szeged, nevertheless managed to receive on his behalf dedicated copies of books from members of the *comité*, who were all well-known editors and members of the editorial board of *Regards*. Thanks to my uncle's efforts, while he was in Csillag Prison, Rákosi received signed copies of books by Romain Rolland, Henri Barbusse, André Gide, Martin Andersen Nexø, and Henrik Pontoppidan. For some time, they made sure that one book a week should reach the prison, where the head warden handed the books over, despite the fact that, because of his recalcitrant behavior, Rákosi was in solitary confinement and was not allowed to read; he didn't have paper and pencil either, so he could neither write nor receive letters. Rákosi was thus left to rely on his memory and imagination if he didn't want to go mad. When he received the books, his joy must have known no bounds. Even before the books reached Szeged, Aranyossi arranged for the archbishop of Paris to send a special envoy to Rákosi's prison. The envoy was the respected Catholic politician Henri Lacaze, who brought Rákosi the archbishop's gift, a special edition of the Bible in French, bound in red velvet. When the envoy reached Szeged accompanied by a Hungarian monk, he rang the bell at the prison gate and showed them his credentials. Aghast, the chief warden sent for the prisoner, tortured by solitude, to come to his office, and watched as, in the midst of a lively exchange, the representative of the French National Assembly handed the prisoner the archbishop's gift.

The Aranyossis had forgotten all about this and couldn't understand why they hadn't been arrested yet. But they had other, more complicated, dangerous, and important missions. My Aunt Magda had spent months in the mining region of Pas-de-Calais, where she organized a women's group for the poorest proletarian women that served as small cells of resistance and solidarity. She also organized strikes. When a summary court sentenced the Communist politicians Imre Sallai and Sándor Fürst to death in Budapest, they smashed up the furnishings of the reception rooms of the Hungarian Embassy in Paris to pieces. Just two days later, Dajmirka organized a similar action in Brussels, where not only did they smash up the furnishings, they also threw papers and documents out the window. Dajmirka was arrested and deported without further ado, meaning that to the great relief of the French police, he was expedited across the border.

In their apartment on Teréz Boulevard, my Aunt Magda was startled awake by the slightest noise.

It was not a noisy apartment, its windows gave out on Szófia Street, the narrow side street leading to the Music Academy, and not the boulevard. She was especially startled when someone slammed the wrought-iron door of the elevator.

A couple of weeks later, though, my aunt and uncle finally understood the logic of the arrests. They understood ahead of the others that these were cleansing operations, show trials, and that the initiatives wouldn't end anytime soon. They finally understood because, back in the thirties, they had received reliable information about the logic of the Stalinist purges. Thanks to their knowledge of this offensive logic, it was clear to them that Rákosi and Gerő were issuing arrests not only for the Communists who had not fled, but the Communists who had returned from exile in the West, and they did so in the order in which they managed to extract, either by word or physical coercion, incriminating evidence against them. Their turn would come, if for no other reason than because in Paris Gerő and they disagreed on the question of whether the Party in France and the Party in Hungary should follow Moscow's directives to the letter or whether the Party in Hungary should remain independent. The cleansing operation was not going to spare them.

My Aunt Magda did not panic. At least, she insisted that she was not afraid. Instead, she grew weary, bored, trying to solve impossible tasks that tired her out, and she suffered from anxiety, which is different, after all, than fear. Anxiety has no object. The undertow was not about to spare them yet again. She had no more resources left, and since she knew she had no cushion, either physical or mental, to fall back on, the stress would not let her sleep. Meanwhile, Pali was sleeping like an angel by her side, because Pali never let anything upset him his whole life, but she lay wide awake, reflecting on their past, searching for anything that might be incriminating in the eyes of their comrades, then fabricated counterarguments in her head. In the silence of the night, she pleaded on behalf of the defense.

During the day she went about her business, but at night she could not stop herself from delivering these pleas. They stopped sharing a bed. She slept in Pali's study instead. She didn't want to disturb him with her sleepless nights. She could at least turn on the light. She made a pretense of reading. But she was not reading, no matter what she held in her hand, in her head she was still working on her plea for the defense. She felt that if they, too, were now to be accused by their own party of undermining communism, it would be more than their lives could bear, she'd go mad, she'd lose her sanity. Back in the thirties, they had to deny the very existence of the Stalinist purges in their papers, the *Regards* and the *Femmes*. They acted against their conscience as journalists.

Leaning out of our great-grandmother's armchair, I yelled at her in the middle of the night.

Why did you go against your conscience. Why did you have to deny the purges. You didn't have to. Why didn't you write about it if you knew.

I was an adolescent and unfair, and she ignored my yelling.

They convinced themselves that it was necessary, she continued without the least show of emotion, because she wanted me to understand that such a grave criticism of the Soviets would have weakened, even broken up, the antifascist People's Front movements throughout Europe. It was a practical decision, I should take it from her, given the looming shadow of the offensive politics of the Nazi empire, they could take no risks. This is why they fought a fierce battle with the great renegades of the Communist movement, Koestler, Gide, Orwell, Silone, and the others, though truth to tell, they all had their suspicions.

But still, why did you all lie, why did you have to lie. Despite my own sober reasoning, I couldn't forgive them their lies.

Later, I even found significant traces of their treacherous lies. *Regards* contained a steady column, "Nouvelles de la vie soviétique," News of Soviet life. Unlike other parts of the paper, this column was edited in the light of the struggle between good and bad, white and black. Soviet life, to them, was a question of dogma. They took the anomaly of French capitalism and presented it in sharp contrast to the life so brilliantly organized in the Soviet Union. I can't say that the contrasts or parallels were always false. Except, unfortunately, they went further than that. *L'Humanité* sent Paul Vaillant-Couturier to the Soviet Union for ten months as its correspondent, an assignment that he probably accepted in all innocence; from time to time he was editor-in-chief of the paper, but he also sent dispatches of his twenty-two-thousand-kilometer travels to *Regards*. My aunt and uncle often spoke about Vaillant-Couturier; they loved him, and for quite some time after the siege, kept in touch with his widow, Marie-Claude, whom the Pétain government's secret service exposed as working for the French Resistance and handed over to the Germans. She was then deported to Auschwitz and Ravensbrück, and later gave evidence at the Nuremberg trials; I even seem to remember her visiting us in Budapest. Paul Vaillant-Couturier was a lawyer, journalist, and the deputy from Seine-Saint-Denis to the National Assembly. He was a charming if irresolute man, or so they said. He often turned his back on the Communist Party, and just as often returned, repentant, to the fold. Even after so many years, people found this amusing; though they'd have never put up with this much irresolution from anyone else, for some reason they found Vaillant-Couturier's irresolution charming. The two Pauls, the editor and his colleague, must have been close not only because of their similarly charming characters, but also because of the dramatic turn their careers had taken. At the close of the nineteenth century, Marguerite Vaillant, Vaillant-Couturier's mother, was a famous French soprano. As a young man, her son lived the life of a proper dandy, he wrote, painted, and studied law, his poetry was published by anarchist as well as Catholic publishers, he turned the heads of one and all, but he was also called up into the army, and he set off for the front full of enthusiasm, but then, having experienced the horrors of war, just like my Uncle Pali, he returned from the front a confirmed socialist, as they said back then. Because of its naïveté, his impeccably written local report, "A Show of Purges," published in *Regards*, makes for even more staggering reading today than it must have at the time of its publication.

They staged a show for his benefit, and he took it for the truth.

I was familiar with two or possibly three bound copies of *Regards* from my childhood, each containing a full year of issues, and without me realizing it, as I turned the pages, the photographs left an indelible mark on the way I see things as a photographer.

They kept the bound volumes in the small dressing room of the apartment in Teréz Boulevard. It wasn't even a small room, it was more like a passageway, probably stretching between the bedroom and the bathroom, but as far as I can remember, it had a window looking out on the courtyard. Since Sándor Rendl's law offices were here before, this space must have served to store documents. If they had to take something off one of the upper shelves, if, for instance, my Aunt Magda wanted to take one of her numerous hats out of one of her hatboxes, she stood on these three volumes of *Regards*. Considering that the first issue appeared on January 1, 1932, and the last issue in September 1939, they wouldn't have fit. When Yvette retreated to this quiet place, I went with her to get away from the noisy grown-ups and to pore over these back issues, which brought news of her homeland into our hermetically sealed world.

Before I left for Toulouse in search of the place where the Le

Vernet camp had once stood, I visited the Bibliothèque Nationale every morning to take a thorough look at this newspaper, now lost in the mists of time, with my own aged eyes, soon to undergo surgery.

In the apartment we shared on Teréz Boulevard, the three volumes were stored in Georges's room for some time, in the back row of the bookshelf, among all sorts of Latin incunabula and elaborately bound lexicons put out of commission because the data they contained had become outdated. I remember exactly where they were, I could fish them out at will.

I went early in the morning, but I didn't go to the rue Vivienne, not to the impressive old library, but to the quai Mauriac, to the brand-new castle-in-the-air example of postmodern architecture partly situated underground, but with its four towers reaching for the sky; I went down its cinder-block shafts, into its cinder-block intestines. Sometimes, as I waited for it to open, I had to stand on line on its flat board-covered roof along with hundreds of people carrying umbrellas against the impending Parisian rain, all of us waiting to pass through security. I stayed until late afternoon, I stayed for a whole month. This building is the be-all and end-all of mannerist architecture. It doesn't have a single nook or cranny, ratio, or size that could be reconciled with rational thinking or its appointed function. On the other hand, it is unarguably aesthetic. And the books, too, managed to find a place in it. I had not planned to spend so much time in the library, I merely wanted to take a quick look at the back issues of *Regards*, but their content held me spellbound. I am not just a photographer by profession, but a journalist as well, and with all my experience working at various papers, I can safely say that *Regards* was admirably edited. And in this admirably edited journal, I found Paul Vaillant-Couturier's finely worded epoch-making self-delusion to be the blushingly naïve account of a perfectly innocent traveler. I am presiding over a cleansing committee tonight, Comrade Degott says to him one fine day, and asks if he'd like to join him. He's known Comrade Degott for some time. They have to travel a mere fifty kilometers. This Degott must be a pseudonym, it certainly doesn't sound convincing as a Russian name. With pleasure, he'd love to, Vaillant-Couturier says. And as an aside, he hastens to explain to the reader what he is meant to understand by cleansing, a feature of the Communist Party that serves to defend Soviet, meaning proletarian, autonomy. Then, as if out of a Russian classic, he describes an idyllic journey by coach through the woods near Moscow, the trees interspersed with lively lights and colors, until they reach the club-house of the agricultural combine of a place called Krashnat Preshina. Possibly, a place by this name doesn't exist; at least, I found nothing even remotely similar in any atlases within fifty kilometers of Moscow. It was a club where, just like everywhere else in the Soviet Union, the workers were their own masters, and they even decided about their own education and training. This is where two engineers, an older one and a younger one, will be appearing before the committee. The rows of benches in the club room are already filled to capacity. The younger engineer had been the secretary of the director charged with sabotage, and his name is Golitsyn. It seems that the director opted to sabotage the march of the counterrevolution, but the name is likely fictional; it is improbable that the director's secretary is an enchanted prince bearing the name of the last prime minister of the last Russian czar. When Vaillant-Couturier was searching for a pseudonym to re-place the real name of the young engineer, this well-known name must have come to mind. After the October Revolution, the Bolsheviks put Prince Golitsyn on trial, but because the charges brought against him proved to be unfounded, he was acquitted and released. He was exe-cuted by the men of the special branch of the GPU on Thursday, July 2, 1925, in Leningrad. Russian literature is full of Golitsyn princes, and Vaillant-Couturier may have taken the name from there; there is a Prince Golitsyn in Pushkin's novella *The Blackamoor of Peter the Great*, while in Tolstoy there are several, there is one in *War and Peace* and another in *Anna Karenina*. When Oblonsky walks into the hotel with Levin, the waiter informs them that they have just received fresh oysters, and if their Excellencies would like to have a private room, he could set the table for them there. Prince Golitsyn and a lady are in there now, but will be leaving shortly. Be that as it may, the younger engineer by the name of Golitsyn admits to having collaborated with the director, it was his duty as his secretary, and he further admits that they hindered construction of the research laboratory for agricultural machinery on purpose.

While they spent millions on it, Comrade Degott, president of the purging committee, interjects heatedly. How long did you hinder work in this manner, if you don't mind my asking.

Five months.

But how could you do such a thing, Comrade Degott shouts.

I didn't do it alone, Golitsyn answers, trying to excuse himself.

When the hearing is at an end, Vaillant-Couturier even sees the two engineers go back to their place. He provides a faithful description of the full scenario, though he understands nothing of the proceedings. He doesn't understand that it's staged for his benefit, though it's highly unlikely that his editor, who wrote a short introduction to the piece, doesn't understand either. He understands, and he does so at a time when the great purges haven't even begun, though news of them has reached Paris just the same. On the way back, Vaillant-Couturier asks Comrade Degott what is to happen to Golitsyn and his superior, will they be arrested. What an idea, Comrade Degott, president of the purging committee says, that's the last thing we want. They will return to their workplace and they will find their proper place in production. This is the way it's done under the dictatorship of the proletariat, where the workers are building democracy for themselves, Vaillant-Couturier writes, summarizing what he'd seen. Where are the torture chambers of the GPU, meaning the State Political Directorate, where the brute force, where the deception, he asks as the closing accord of his report.

News of the Molotov-Ribbentrop nonaggression pact didn't take my aunt and uncle by surprise either; at best, they didn't immediately understand why their own party would reach its long arm from Moscow to stab them in the back. But before the public, what's more, even to their closest friends, they tried to vindicate the treaty with the Nazi regime by arguing that the Soviets needed to play for time, it's just a diplomatic maneuver, and if they can prevent the war with this maneuver, then so be it. They lied, they made excuses, and they never forgave themselves for it. Their spurious arguments caught up with them when on the basis of a secret provision of the treaty Stalin's army invaded and annexed the eastern parts of Poland. This was a shock, and although it was dampened by the onrush of the horrors of war, the European Leftist People's Fronts did not survive the shock, a shock whose consequences, measured in human lives, was evident in the resistance movements as well. It meant that their credibility was a thing of the past. Even to my adolescent eyes and ears, it couldn't have meant anything else. I yelled at my aunt because of it, and in fact, she silently suffered it, because she knew I was right. Not only could they not forgive themselves, their friends could not forgive them either. In the late sixties, Vilma Ligeti was still up in arms if she remembered how brazenly Magda and Pali had lied, even to her. They are still lying. They are lying nonstop. Her anger was justified. The man she'd been living with, whose name I can't remember, also left the French Communist Party, then joined a Gaullist resistance group, and then, lying wounded in a hospital bed, was caught and shot by a Gestapo squad. Vilma was convinced that his former comrades had betrayed him, specifically, the nurse who was working for the Communist resistance.

But they lied to themselves and not to me. I didn't believe them. I didn't believe them for a second. The whole fucking lot brought about their own ruin, not mine.

There was no counterbalance, the story could not be rewritten, there was nothing anymore for which my Aunt Magda could possibly forgive herself. She could no longer separate her intentions or considerations from the mass murders. She did not know what would come next and what sense it would make, indeed, whether it would make any sense at all, but startled awake in the dark of her room that looked out on Szófia Street, as she kept her ear glued to the elevator, wondering if the just barely audible snap of the elevator door wasn't going to be followed by a persistent ringing of their doorbell, possibly even banging on the door, she knew without a doubt that she had come to the end of her tether.

The nature of her anxiety, the mechanics of starting awake from sleep, is something I am familiar with myself, even though the sources of our separate anxieties are very different.

She felt that she had made a mistake, she had ruined her life, though she couldn't have said how she had ruined it or with what she had ruined it, or when.

I couldn't answer these questions about my own life either. I only know that although it has a certain coherence, its coherence doesn't have meaning either. In any event, I have not been able to find it.

As far as the meaning of life is concerned, I have an advantage over her in that a life devoid of meaning from birth cannot be ruined.

Try as I might to ply her with questions during these long nights, to ask where she went wrong, she couldn't, or rather she wouldn't, answer the question, whereas she tried.

Just one French word emerged from her stammering, *cauchemar*, *cauchemar*, nightmare. Nightmarish visions and nightmarish figures woke her from her uneasy slumber and remained by her side throughout the night. The beautiful life-size portrait, encased in a modernist gold frame, of Vilma Parlaghy, my Viennese great-grandmother in her pink evening gown, hung on the wall of her room, and there stood the last Viennese baroque armchair from her informal salon along with the baroque chandelier and the huge baroque mirror on the wall, but again and again, the column of ghostly figures emerged from behind them and refused to leave, and at the head of the column stood the Communist Frigyes Karikás, the writer, journalist, and Party activist whose code name in the movement had been Comrade Flower, and whose code name my aunt pronounced with loving admiration. Mama Falus, Frigyes or Frici called her, Comrade Flower, she called him. They used their code names as their pet names. They affectionately endeared each to the other by doing so. Be that as it may, his comrades didn't make much ado in Comrade Flower's case either, and by all accounts beat him to death in Ljublanka Prison in Moscow on the night of his arrest near dawn on March 5, 1938, after they'd ordered him back from Paris to help build the first proletarian state. He could barely finish the first Hungarian translation of *The Good Soldier Švejk*. He had translated it for Monde publishers. The publishing company was founded by György Bölöni and Pál Aranyossi, and Count Mihály Károlyi not only obtained the starting capital for them, he also generously offered to be the publisher's guarantor, which later caused him no end of grief. They published and snuck across the border the Hungarian translations of first-rate literary works whose publication the Hungarian censors did not allow. Needless to say, my parents bought the first Hungarian translation of *Švejk*, which is how I came to read Jaroslav Hašek's novel for the first time in Frici's translation.

She hastened to turn on the light so Frici shouldn't come, or if he did, he should go away. Károly Garai, Albert Lantos, and Frigyes Friedmann, whom they especially liked, shouldn't come, and Pug Nose, meaning Géza Losonczy, shouldn't come either, with his determined stride, his indifferent expression verging on apathy, and his attentive eyes that were like two stroking hands, as my Aunt Magda said of him. Nor should András Szalai come with his broad smile. She had to seek refuge in her innocent readings. Also, Kojsza with her beauty and annoying narrow-mindedness should stay away. She nearly gagged when she talked about her, she hated her with a passion, it got on her nerves that I saw her now and then, when she would relate to me, in great detail, the story of her torture, which surpassed imagination; my aunt sputtered whenever she talked about her, about this Ilona Kojsza, whereas she couldn't help but admire her beauty, her bravery and innate elegance, which especially irked her. Ten years later, in the summer of 1974, quite by chance, I found and took a picture of the villa Ilona Kojsza had talked to me about; it had a tower and was located in the Buda hills at 48 Eörvös Street; it had been the nationalized villa of a Jewish baron of industry with fiendishly bad taste, where they were beaten and tortured in an effort to make them bear false witness. Kojsza, Rajk, and Béla Szász were all beaten in that house, and probably Cardinal Mindszenty was held prisoner there as well. Rajk first gave them evidence there. This is where they first confronted him with Béla Szász. Szász and Kojsza refused this ignominy, furnishing false evidence. Even though they had only the vaguest impressions to rely on for their descriptions, I found the house thanks partly to them and partly thanks to chance. I, too, call my sensual impressions to my aid whenever I describe something. Sounds, smells, there is nothing else. This is the common denominator between people. When they were taken away in the dead of night, their hands tied behind their backs and their eyes covered with a kerchief, there was nothing but the hissing and squealing of the tires and the scents of the summer night.

They didn't know where they were, where they were being taken, and what the next moment would bring. How could their minds record anything else but for the details and the smallest details of the details, what else was there to be stored in their minds as memory.

But above all, Pug Nose, whose fate shed more light on the voluntarily undertaken crime and catastrophe of the Communist movement than anyone else, he must not come, so she shouldn't have to think about him. When Pug Nose, meaning Géza Losonczy, was arrested by his own beloved comrades for the second time and thanks to them found himself face-to-face with the thug who had beaten the Communists as a member of Regent Horthy's political police before the siege, and whom Ilona Kojsza had mentioned to me by name, except his name went straight out of my head, the same thug who had also beaten the Communists at the far-right Arrow Cross headquarters on Andrássy Boulevard during the siege, and who continued beating them or giving orders for the beatings in the same place, now the headquarters of the Communist secret police, and who continued beating them and having them beaten even in '57 and '58, this, too, I know from Kojsza, in short, during his second arrest by his own comrades, he found himself face-to-face with the same thug.

Losonczy's mind clouded over from the very thought, the mere possibility of the beatings that would never end. His interrogators thought he was pretending. This is how he's trying to escape having to make a confession. Which would have had to be a false confession yet again, needless to say. And so, in their rage, they beat him to death. At least, this is what people in Budapest said back then, though I am referring here and now to a Budapest where there was no such thing as reliable information. Another version had it that he went on a hunger strike, and they killed him by force-feeding him.

Sunk between her pillows, my Aunt Magda closed her eyes to shut out the light. She was aware of these different versions herself, after all, they made their rounds in her circles. She didn't want to talk to me about these murders outright, even though I knew about them not only from her, and often not initially from her.

She hadn't known fear before, she hadn't felt it, she lived through twenty years of emigration, poverty, their nine expulsions from the Party, their false names and forged papers, their illegal return home, the German occupation, and the Arrow Cross terror without the least sign of fear or anxiety.

I could hardly believe it.

In her grande dame manner, she was more surprised than anything at my doubting her, and she laughed at me. On the contrary, she said, she was worried all along that there was something wrong with her, she must be suffering from some illness, because it's not natural that she should feel no fear at all. Which is probably why she collapsed twice.

She collapsed and remained unconscious for two days when they took Pali away from the National Casino, yes indeed, and Oszi Solt brought her around when he gave her a shot. Next she collapsed because of Pista. Pista collapsed in the basement, and she couldn't help him. It still hurts her to think of it. When she started telling me, she began choking on her tears. When she left him in the dim basement entrance with her tears, as she locked up the basement from the outside again, locked Pista in with her tears, yes, she broke into a fit of tears right there in the Pozsonyi Street courtyard, and she had to lean against the wall of the house, and that time her collapse lasted a whole week. They suffered this nervous collapse because of the kittens when Pista told her about them, but Pista could hardly get the story out, he just cried and trembled at the basement entrance, she said to me as she sobbed among her pillows. But Oszi was there for her again, he gave her a shot of something, maybe vitamins.

Probably this is how the fear she'd repressed all those years took its revenge.

Only your mother, Klári, could outstrip me in not being afraid. I really shouldn't tell you this, but I see Klári, too, many times. Klári comes, too.

On the nights when we sat in her room under the weak light of the baroque wall lamp, she was wrestling with some sort of final reckoning. Once she made the brief and striking statement that her heart was full of the dead. She meant that the Nazis, and especially her dearest friends, her Communist comrades, had killed too many people she loved. It is terrible to admit, but she learned fear from her comrades.

Still, she would not renounce them.

I reasoned in vain, I shouted at her in vain, I tried to convince her in vain.

My heart is full of the dead.

Despite our family's mandatory distaste for pathos, in this sentence of hers there hovered a heavy dose of self-pity, the last, hypocritical trace of self-pity, despite the fact that theoretically, hypocrisy, too, was taboo in our shared code of behavior. Our grandfather, their despised father, had played the game often enough to make them weary of it. But to my mind, the historical dimensions of her atonement, her mourning over her lost Communist passion, excused her behavior, to some extent, at least. Her suffering was proportionate to the mighty scale of the dramatic debacle and collapse of the Communist utopia deeply rooted in the historical current of Christianity. Stupid adolescent that I was, I was bent on saving her, though given my adolescent mind and hunger for knowledge, I actually welcomed her history-induced sleepless nights, I welcomed her restlessness and her weak heart, I enjoyed listening to her as I sat in the baroque armchair, the last remnant of my great-grandmother's informal salon. I found the measure of her atonement impressive, it satisfied the thirst for revenge I had to carry with me like so much dead weight because of my idiotic parents. I wanted to know about the dead in her heart, their fate, what became of them. What became of my dead father and my dead mother. I wanted to know and understand the history of the two great mass murders of the century, but first and foremost, the story of the Communist movement, which had remained a mystery to me.

In those years the Hungarian prisons were still packed with political prisoners, and I wanted to know how I should go about living my own utopia-free life as compared with them, how and according to what considerations I should reevaluate the things that knowingly or unknowingly they had stuffed into my head. There were months when the scale of my aunt's memories made me a little crazy. At the same time, she welcomed my attentiveness; the wish that she should pass her secret knowledge down to at least one charitable soul, her Petyonka, kept her going. With a change in my manner I'd managed to rid myself of this endearing name, Petyonka, and she was the only one who still called me that.

Since under the dictatorship of the proletariat the public is kept ignorant of the facts, what's more, knowledge in general as well as knowledge in particular are anathema, such knowledge should at least be passed down through oral tradition. Surely, this is what she must have been thinking. That we should at least preserve the minimum of accuracy necessary for an inert and inactive existence, it being the sole guarantee for the continuity of life.

Sometimes the sky outside the window, pierced by neon lights, was giving way to the blue light of dawn and the first tram had already rattled past, but I was still asking and she was still talking, whereas I had to get up early, I couldn't be late for work or for vocational school. I had to be at work by six, and luckily, at school only by eight.

Marika, the domestic whose last name I can't remember, try as I might, shook me awake. She made me eat my breakfast, she came running after me, just one more bite, Péter, while you tie your shoes, Péter, while you slip into your coat.

I wasn't late. I was late maybe twice, but my schoolmates, the girls, covered for me. Being an orphan had its advantages. People thought it romantic. But not me. I could never again be truly at home anywhere, and that was the harsh reality of it. Sometimes I'd show up at the photographer's studio in Kossuth Lajos Street, where I worked twice a week, at the last moment, or at the vocational school on Práter Street named after István Dési Huber, which I also attended twice a week, but I did show up.

If at night I got home from a party, a rendezvous, a concert, a dance, or a drinking bout with friends, or the movies, the theater, the opera, or my favorite haunt, the New York Café, where the motley crowd was comprised of dubious characters, good-for-nothings, pickpockets, poets, bibulous diplomats, former rabbinical students, unemployed journalists, dilettante prose writers and finely attuned philosophers, whores and lady-killers, gays and gay whores, alcoholics, a heady mix of people in which, practically speaking, no one had anything in common with anyone else, as if we were a pack of stray dogs, me included; in short, if, slightly tipsy, I went home to the big apartment we shared, provided that I went home at all and didn't spend the night somewhere else, and I saw the light streaming out from under my aunt's door, I'd barge in on her.

I had the impression that she was expecting it, that she'd been waiting for me and was happy to see me.

Back then Teréz Boulevard was called Lenin Boulevard, and our apartment was located in the house at 65 Lenin Boulevard, which had originally been 3 Teréz Boulevard, but the people of Pest invariably adopted the politically motivated changes in street names with a ten-year lag. For instance, instead of Bartók Béla Street, some people still said Horthy Miklós Street. In the language of Budapest, Teréz Boulevard shifted to Lenin Boulevard only in the late sixties, at the time that I had just left my job and the city, too, and found refuge in Kisoroszi, at the northern tip of Szentendre Island. And so, for me, Teréz Boulevard has remained Lenin Boulevard. In the same way, it would have never occurred to my Communist father to say Marx Square, and he invariably said, let's meet in Berlin Square.

Sometimes I would go to my aunt's room much the worse for drink, because there was a time when I drank to excess. I drank mostly slivovitz, the cheapest liqueur I could get; I drank Albanian cognac and Hungarian plum pálinka, I drank Polish vodka, I drank all sorts of fast-acting poisons. Given my age and physique, I drank way too much, but no more than I could afford from my apprentice pay and from what I made on the side. My friend Miki and I would take wedding pictures, what I mean is he went ahead, he acted as our agent, and equipped with an official-looking receipt book and a carefully sharpened ink pencil, but most of all, his glorious, ingratiating smile amply spiced with caustic humor, sensuality, keen insight, and bitter knowledge of the human species, he veritably cast a spell over the young couple or their relatives. He knew that it was no use offering our services as photographers to older women, meaning the mothers of the bride and the groom, because these women keep a tight grip on their fucking money and would not let go. Not a single fillér. Besides, they'd end up heading for the studio of a photographer they knew anyway. They say no to everything. It's a reflex with them. It's a no that no one will ever be able to talk them out of, and Miki knew it. He knew them like the back of his hand. He approached the fathers of the bride and groom who'd been in their cups, those who'd fought at the front, those who'd been prisoners of war. The poorer they are, the more unfortunate they are, and the more gullible they are. Subjects of their masters. What luck, sir, that we're here and that we're willing, at the last moment, to take snapshots of this beautiful wedding. Never such a beautiful bride, such a handsome groom. And once the scene was set, when, with uneasy incomprehension, eager to get this collateral unpleasantness over and done with, the victims handed him the advance, only then would I show up with my photographer's equipment. It had to be done quickly, before those awful women appeared, those old cows with their wavy hairdos, to put an end to everything and prevent us from making a little extra money on the side. We worked in registrars' offices and Miki gave the registrars a cut, so they wouldn't make us leave. There were many women registrars by then, and he swept them off their feet with his youthful, handsome looks. Meanwhile, the young couple, whoever they were, got properly taken photographs. I tried very hard to make them appear much more beautiful and handsome than the poor, hassled people they really were in their shabby rented clothes, I lit them as best I could, and I retouched them. In the evening, Miki delivered the finished pictures, and it was not always easy to make them pay what they owed.

I don't know whether my aunt noticed my drinking jags, because she never once mentioned them. My brother insists that she noticed, but was afraid to say anything. Those closest to us don't protect us from the real dangers lying in wait for us.

If I got home completely soused, I fell into bed, or else I stuffed myself with whatever leftovers I found in the kitchen. If she heard me, Marika would come to the kitchen, give me something to eat, turn down my bed, and help me out of my clothes, so I shouldn't sleep in them. Not yet eighteen, I was well on my way to becoming an alcoholic. There were no alcoholics in the family. There were plenty of lunatics, but as far as I know, none of them suffered an addiction. Fortunately, even when I was drunk, I was never drunk enough to keep from seeing the futility of my drinking. Alcohol was not the answer to what ailed me. Once, my aunt came home from Berlin, where she'd attended some sort of international conference of historians that was preceded by lengthy research at the local archives. The train from Berlin, where needless to say she met Netty, arrived late at night. I kept rum or brandy in my desk at home. When I arrived at the Nyugati station, I was dead drunk, but I went so she shouldn't have to carry her bags herself.

That time, she may have noticed.

Netty was a good comrade to her, and because of the way they'd been brought up, if for no other reason, they learned to turn their backs on anything awkward. They preferred not to notice lack of manners or lack of restraint. My aunt called her Seghers. She didn't mention or call her by the first name she used as a writer. She never said Anna, at most she'd say Netty, a leftover from her old, good bourgeois life. To her, Seghers was not the well-known writer but a comrade, a German comrade, the wife of a Hungarian comrade. They were of the same mettle, and they hailed from similar social backgrounds. An innate intelligence, an impressive knowledge of the humanities coupled with a secure understanding of society, both empirical and theoretical, these must have been the traits they shared. Seghers was beautiful, handsome even in old age, while even in her youth my aunt could at best be called attractive, though she retained a good portion of the self-assurance of a bourgeoise grande dame, never mind that the bourgeoisie was gone by then. Their bodies were burdened by the futility of their lives, and their intelligence, too, was burdened by it. My aunt suffered incessantly from her own unfavorable appearance. She's a *patte à puff*, she's made of puff pastry, she's an awkward figure best advised to see herself through the prism of her intellect. This *patte à puff*, a product of her harsh self-sarcasm, described her to a T. She paid close attention to details, she had a gift for understanding them, but she had no patience especially for the workings of emotion. She and the others could no longer see the future of their utopia, and indeed, it had no future. They had become impatient, and impatience affects the material world as well. They'd had it up to here with the Marxist conception of history based on Hegel's teachings, to which they had tailored their entire adult lives. They wanted to help history fulfill itself, to witness the demise of suffering and the relief of mankind, but at the head of the column of the countless dead they'd left behind, they saw only the specter of history, the emptiness and futility of their messianic striving, along with its speculative nature. In this world, there was no Hegel, and there was no Kant anywhere.

In accordance with their proper bourgeois upbringing, they wrapped their despair, incomprehension, complicity, and disillusionment, their daily penitence along with the assorted accusations of others, in silence. Proper bourgeois upbringing condemns accusation, and it condemns reproach. They knew perfectly well that they were ignoring reality, after all, they'd spent their entire adult lives with the intention of contemplating it with a critical eye, and now, as they were approaching the end of their lives, with their hopelessly warped consciousness and wholly superfluous critical stance they found themselves smack in the middle of a virtual reality. In the name of a utopia that was receding into a future that would never be, they had had to ignore all life that was authentic, to revise, again and again, to waylay and delude their own sense of reality. They also knew that their gloomy frame of mind had not only reproduced the general crisis and depression of the Communist movement, it had deepened it. A Communist is never depressed not because he is disciplined, but because he does not lose his faith in self-sacrifice nor his trust in the value of critical thinking. This is why, in his farewell letter, our poor father felt the need to beg his party's forgiveness. First he begged forgiveness for taking us with him, meaning that he wanted to stand over us and carefully aim a nice bullet at our heads or hearts, but when confronted with my younger brother's beauty as he slept he couldn't bring himself to do it, but then in a codicil he asked his party for forgiveness, because he was going to do away with himself somewhere out on the Danube's bank in Óbuda, and entrusted us to the care of his comrades and our own good luck. Which meant that even in their sorrow, racked by doubt and teetering on the brink of despair, they were not independent human beings. They were so much at one with their party, they couldn't see that they were the Party. They imagined their lives in a plural that could exist neither in the language they spoke, nor in their culture, nor anyone else's for that matter. What they imagined made no physical sense.

For half a century they lived entrusting themselves to their own unselfishness, whereas in their collapse, or at the end of their lives, they must have realized that their self-relinquishment and self-sacrifice had made no sense at all, nor would it be of any use to anyone at any time in the years to come. At most, their activities bore with a certain modest self-worth that, needless to say, had no bearing on the essence of the world, nor did it alter it in any way, nor would the world show any interest in them. The world had embraced the cult of self-realization and not that of self-relinquishment, solidarity, or empathy. Still, their actions afford us a better understanding of the structure of various forms of social change, as well as human monomania and egomania. They had freed solidarity in all its forms from within the magic circle of charitable deeds; they wanted to institutionalize it, to give it concrete shape; they placed the concepts of Christian love and social care within an administrative framework, and they laid bare the meaning of worldly asceticism, and this, too, is undoubtedly to their credit, but nothing more. They could not slow the march and madness of fascism, they could not deflect it, they could not stop it. But at least they gave it a try. This, too, is to their credit. On the other hand, there is no falsehood, lie, cheating, murder, and robbery thanks to which they could have forcibly introduced collectivization into the economy. Instead of creating plenty, they created permanent scarcity. They turned society into a congregation of dilettantes, and in these societies, where people learned to make a virtue of necessity, they thought that everyone should be an expert in everything and that anything could stand in for anything else; in short, one by one, they destroyed the ethos of every conceivable profession. Also, without aggression and repression, this system could not have been sustained for a single day, which made the whole thing laughable.

Sitting in the Viennese armchair in my aunt's room, I realized that such a thing could never be admitted by her. Still, I wanted to help my aunt, sometimes in ways that were harsh, but I wanted her to admit it. I believe that the honesty with which she spoke to me on these nights she'd never have risked with anyone else.

I was a raging adolescent, unfair and extreme, and I didn't understand why she wouldn't speak as openly as she did with me, at least with her friends, of whom she had plenty since she was young, Bori Fáy, Jolán Szilágyi, Borbála Szerémi, Gizi Révai, Panni Angyal, Bella Dobrova, Kató Gortvai, Márta Gergely, Anna Kara, Erzsi Perczel, Margit Pór, Blanka Pécsi, Dóra Járó, Margit Izsáky, Vera Földes, Vilma Ligeti, Sári Vadas, Bori Zsigmond, and so on, this was the old crones' club or chicken coop, as they called themselves. Each had a life more interesting than the next, but among themselves, they were like old sparrow hawks.

In my youthful fervor, I couldn't imagine what my aunt stood to lose, were she to speak to them openly one fine day.

Perhaps Stefike Dési Huber and Jolán Kelen were the two great exceptions among her friends, she could talk with them about lots of things without prevarication and in a normal tone of voice, but in matters of politics and morals, they too lied to each other, steadily and mutually, but most of all, they lied to themselves. Possibly Stefike Dési Huber was the only one among them who wasn't given to lying, and if she lied, it was out of regard for the others. She had snow-white hair and she wore it in a withered little knot. Her attention was unwavering. She listened to them with an air of benevolence, she reminded me of the acacia taste of honey, she was sweet, a sweet woman by nature, she remained aloof and she wouldn't comment, so she wouldn't have to judge them. The need to order the world theoretically or ideologically was not in her nature.

Due to her depression over the Communist movement, Seghers suffered from drink, while my Aunt Magda suffered from a bad heart. Because of her bad circulation, she had to stay in bed for days on end, staring at the wall. She preferred a bad heart to falling prey to depression.

Once I said to her, if she sees all this so clearly, what's her problem with Déry, Koestler, or Gide. Or if she now agrees with them, why does she harbor such undying hatred for the great renegades. What is her problem with Imre Nagy, Mrs. Rajk, Mrs. Károlyi, or Djilas. Why doesn't she tell it like it is, why doesn't she raise hell, why doesn't she cause a scandal.

After a moment of hesitation, all she said was, only my party can bury me.

I admit that her answer caught me off guard, her arrogant stupidity was like a slap in the face, it made me lose my temper.

You can't mean it when you say you'll be attending your own funeral. You can't mean it when you say that you're living your life with a view to your funeral. You can't mean it when you say that your funeral is more important than other people's lives. Who gives a shit about funerals. Why don't you shit on your own funeral right here, from the third floor.

She made no answer, she just looked at me, she just looked at me like someone looking through soft winter fog. I used such coarse language with her on purpose, I used words she'd never have let pass her lips, ever, because I was intent on provoking her. Whereas by then both of us were past every possible funeral, the exhumation and infamous reburial of the disgraced and the executed, we knew what such a necrophilic ceremony means, the be-all and end-all of hypocrisy, a parody, a farce, a perfidy, to say the least. It doesn't mean shit. The same people who had killed László Rajk then exhumed and reinterred him in an honorary grave.

Only my party can bury me, no one else, this was her proud

answer, and that I shouldn't talk to her in that tone of voice. And I should kindly leave her room. Whereas I'd have liked to drag this bald old wreck of a person from her bed so she'd do something meaningful with her life for once, to speak out and do so in public.

How dare you, she said with the sort of gentrified whine that she ridiculed all her life, even though she cultivated the style with her bourgeoise girlfriends, who were of like ilk. But the more disillusioned she became and the more she got on in years, the more adamantly her bourgeois use of words and her bourgeois manners resurfaced, as if she were still giving orders to a division of maids, butlers, cooks, and governesses, whereas everyone could see that she could at best order her few decrepit old women friends around.

Her grave heart troubles must have been a symptom of a grave historical depression, but she turned away the only possible remedy. She felt nothing but contempt for all those who, in the name of reality or justice, broke publicly with the Communist movement, and at times only this contempt kept her going. Unlike them, she chose a weak heart and sleepless nights over desertion.

She had met Ilona Duczynska on several occasions. They met in Vienna and they met in Munich, even I met her in Munich once in the late seventies, but she held her in contempt as well. She's a traitor, my aunt said.

She asked me to go with her when she went to meet Mrs. Károlyi. Strange that she should have asked me, because we weren't on speaking terms by then. She didn't even return my greeting when we bumped into each other in her vast apartment, because once, in the heat of one of our sudden, heated midnight tiffs, I happened to say that instead of selling their summer house in Leányfalu, they should give it back to the state.

What she sells or does not sell is her own affair, and it's none of my business.

How can a house she got from the state be her own business, I countered. The house had been the property of the people and has remained the property of the people, even if she has appropriated it. Why is private property so important to her all of a sudden, why did she lose her Communist conviction with regard to owning property all of a sudden. By what right. What does she base this privilege on.

I should leave the room this instant.

I got up and kicked my great-grandmother's baroque armchair from under me.

She demanded that I find myself an apartment and move out within the week.

I countered that if that's the best she can come up with, they should go fuck their house. And that I don't intend to move out of my own apartment.

And with that I left the room, headed for the kitchen, and had a bite to eat; I was satisfied, because with this exchange, I'd severed the last thread that bound us to each other. I felt free. I was no longer bound by my duty to the family. But I didn't ask myself what next. Freedom, for one thing, which is not always easy. Just then, out of the blue, there stood my cousin Georges. He was fuming mad.

What did you say to my mother, he yelled.

I said you should go fuck your house.

For an instant it looked like he'd either rush at me or faint.

Or give it back to whoever gave it to you.

And there stood, between us, the kitchen knife on the table, which didn't escape our attention.

I must say that for my part I wasn't upset, I didn't even stop eating.

Without another word he went back through my room and slammed the door.

My one excuse is that at the time I wasn't even seventeen; I was at the age when a person generally breaks with his family, because he feels that everything these awful people say or do is a lie.

My Aunt Magda asked me to go with her the summer after Aranyossi died. She said she didn't want to go alone and explained her request, which was more like an order, by saying that there was too much fuss around Katinka Károlyi, and she hadn't been feeling particularly well lately. We won't be staying for dinner, we'll just say hello to Katinka, a mere formality, nothing more. Neither one of them can afford not to meet, it wouldn't look right.

Meanwhile, both of us avoided the question of why she wasn't asking her son, because we knew the answer. When Mihály Károlyi, who at the time was Hungary's ambassador to Paris, learned about the arrest of László Rajk, who at the time was Hungary's foreign minister, he promptly wrote a letter to Rákosi, the head of the Party, demanding an explanation. But instead of handing the letter to his secretary to be dispatched posthaste with the diplomatic mail, he grabbed his overcoat and hat and hurried off to the rue Saint-Jacques, where the embassy's consulate and public relations office were located at the time. The writer, journalist, and historian Ferenc Fejtő was head of the office. But this time the Count, whom his colleagues called President, because in 1918 he had been the president of the first Hungarian Republic and accordingly, besides all his other ranks and titles, he had a title that a person can't lose, in short, the Count didn't go to the head of the public relations office but to Georges, his colleague, his comrade in arms, and Pál Aranyossi's only son, whom he'd known since childhood. If the Károlyis didn't happen to have dinner, nor money to buy dinner, they went to the Aranyossis with their three children in tow, and if the Aranyossis had something cooking in the kitchen, if they had onions, paprika, and potatoes, they also got some of the paprika potatoes.

I do not believe that the accusations that led to the arrest of our minister of foreign affairs are grounded in fact, the ambassador said, his voice grating more than usual as he entered Georges's room, *je ne crois pas à la véracité des accusations qui ont entrainé l'arrestation de notre ministre des Affaires étrangères.* I wrote a letter to Rákosi, *j'ai écrit une lettre à Rákosi*, in which I request a proper explanation, *pour réclamer des explications sérieuses.* And he asked Georges if he'd like to sign the letter, in short, *voulez-vous la signer avec moi.* Whereupon, hardly waiting for Károlyi to finish his say, not even thinking of the respect he owed this brave and unselfish man, he said that as far as he's concerned, it's for the Party to decide, *pour moi c'est la parole du parti qui décidera.* At least, this is what he wrote in his French memoirs. As if he didn't realize that in the months to come, it would be his official duty to parrot the shameful lies of a show trial.

I see, Károlyi said, and he left the room without further ado. Soon after, Georges was made head of the public relations office. Needless to say.

The Károlyis and Fejtő never forgave him for his betrayal.

We took the tram to the Rózsadomb Restaurant in Buda. The year of mourning was not yet over, my aunt, the careworn widow, was in black from head to toe, in the most conventional way imaginable. She wore a small black hat from which hung not so much a veil as a simple black net, a sign, which was only right and proper during the year of mourning; it framed her face to her lips, she wore black gloves to go with it, black shoes, black nylons, and not the sheerest, because it just wouldn't have been fitting, not with mourning clothes, anyway, and after more than a decade, this is how the two elderly women met again. The guests had not yet taken their places at the table, it wasn't even evening yet, there must have been about fifteen of them, mostly devoted feminists, I spotted Júlia Rajk, the widow of László Rajk, and Sára Karig, who was in charge of the Károlyi archives, but everything happened so quickly, I never got a chance to take a proper look around. They were standing around in three groups, I think, with cocktail glasses in hand. The big glass door of the restaurant was wide open. Mrs. Károlyi was standing in the middle of one of the groups, and as soon as we entered, she put down her glass and hurried to meet my aunt, who recognized her only after a time. No wonder. Mrs. Károlyi was wearing a black leather outfit that endowed her with a martial-like appearance, and in Budapest, which had been isolated from the world for decades, no one had seen anything like it, though the previous year, when she first visited Budapest after years spent in exile, she'd come to make inquiries, to approach, however carefully, those in power at the time, and so, as the invisible young photographer for *Nők Lapja*, I'd already seen her in the same outfit. She had meant it to provoke, I should think. I was with a group of journalists when, with the president's chief of protocol at the helm, she was taken to a brand-new housing estate, and the following day they took her up to Buda Castle, to show her some of the locations of her previous life, perhaps one of her former palaces. There was a restaurant located in the cellar of one of the palaces, they dragged her down there as well. Why would it have interested her. Nothing interested her. Not even her handsome young English secretary, whereas it was whispered behind her back that the young man was the elderly lady's lover. Some of my pictures made it into the paper. They were very bad pictures. Now I felt lucky that I could witness the faultlessly choreographed meeting of the two elderly women, the Red Countess and the Communist grande dame. They took hold of each other's arms, they held each other's arms so they shouldn't have to embrace each other. I didn't follow my aunt inside, I stopped short in the open doorway. By all accounts, Mrs. Károlyi offered her brief condolences, in the most formal manner possible; she must have offered a sentence or two about the deceased, of whom she didn't think too highly. She had warned her husband about Aranyossi, whom she blamed for her husband's closeness to the Communists. He'd tried to practice moderation, but thanks to Aranyossi, he got closer to them than he'd intended. Not only was Aranyossi's reasoning persuasive, he was a persuasive character to begin with. My aunt accepted the condolences with the expression of a bereaved widow, then with a single, swift glance, they took a quick look around and Mrs. Károlyi, née Katinka Andrássy, must have said something light, which Mrs. Aranyossi, who was slower on the uptake, found amusing, they laughed, then Mrs. Aranyossi must have said something cordial, at which Mrs. Károlyi shook her head lightly and answered with something similarly cordial, the only sincere fleeting moment of their encounter, I think, and to further pluck the irresponsible strains of their cordiality, out of sheer politeness, if for no other reason, Mrs. Károlyi invited Mrs. Aranyossi to join her at the table, a gesture that, with reference to her profound pain, Mrs. Aranyossi regretfully declined, which, for her part, Mrs. Károlyi said she understood, whereupon Mrs. Aranyossi expressed the hope that she had not kept Mrs. Károlyi unduly from her other guests, whereupon, tit for tat, Mrs. Károlyi saw Mrs. Aranyossi to the door of the restaurant, entrusting her to the care of the young man who, though he had been introduced to her once before, she obviously did not recognize. Then they took hold of each other's arms once again, they touched each other's elbows, too, for a moment, so they shouldn't have to embrace. There was no love lost between them.

My Aunt Magda couldn't get away too quickly, but just a couple of steps from the door, there was a taxi stand and we headed for it.

My Aunt Magda had nothing but contempt for those who in the name of self-sacrifice and in the spirit of confession in its theological sense staged one last scandal before estranging themselves from the redemptive, terrorist current of the European spirit. She was personally familiar with the hated renegades and found plenty of personal reasons, small faults in their characters, for why she should hold them in contempt. Except, this had nothing to do with so-called truth. She held Gyilasz, Spender, and Silone in contempt, she held Koestler and Orwell in contempt. At the same time, her conservative-liberal upbringing showed right through her contempt, this fine little distinction tempered her intellectual predilections. It took the edge off the most radical strains of her political scorn. She couldn't curse the way I cursed, the way my mother cursed, or her own wild peasant of a father, my Neumayer grandfather, for that matter. She considered. Her upbringing prompted her to consider and acknowledge the literary merits of otherwise treasonous works, as well as the positive intellectual capacities, character traits, and physical givens of individuals she otherwise held in contempt, so that, even with their manly good looks or poetic gifts, she should despise them all the more. Karikás was the secret love of her life, but even so, she was of the opinion that it is still better for someone to be murdered by his own comrades than for him to become a traitor.

This impressed me, it took my breath away. As far as she was concerned, there was no turning back, which meant that she had truly rebelled against her own liberal-conservative world, she wanted a new order, except she was incapable of rebelling a second time, she couldn't have created her life's path for herself, in which case it's best to be consequent, to stay in the assembly of liars and murderers. She lacked the reserves for any more reversals. Even as a rebellious adolescent, I realized this, but I was so intent on saving the aunt I loved and respected from an ignoble ruin that I couldn't forgive her for the weakness of her old age. I will not be a traitor, she said, though this, too, had a false ring to it; after all, she was a traitor many times over. She betrayed just about everyone; she rewrote her past as she saw fit; she betrayed her husband, and she betrayed Frigyes Karikás, the great love of her life; she repeatedly and shamelessly betrayed her own son, she disowned him, she slandered him, then because of his weaknesses took him back under her wing, all while she held him in the greatest contempt; and somewhat later, she betrayed me, too, repeatedly and in an ugly way; she sold what was left of our small inheritance without qualms; once I pulled out the bottom two drawers of the commode because I was looking for something among the silver, and the silver was gone down to the last piece, whereas she respected me, she respected my gift for analysis, she tended and pruned it like a professional gardener, and pruning it, she provided me with information, she pointed out authors and sources to me, she respected my gift for writing.

But she destroyed herself with her obstinacy. She lived to old age, and the more self-destructive she was, the more forcefully the basic genteel overtones of her upbringing came to the fore. Her ears must have retained it in Miss Jolán's own tones from the time she was their governess.

Haltung.

Contenance.

Seghers stayed in Pamiers with her two children in the fall of 1940, two years before I was born, and where I arrived on a Thursday, sixty years later. The foundations of a person's life are laid by others before he is born. The woman who gave them shelter, a certain French comrade whose name I don't know, I can't remember it, told her neighbors that Seghers and her two children were Polish refugees. My Aunt Magda even mentioned the name of the street repeatedly, except I can't remember that either. *Impasse.* This is all I remember, because it was a word I hadn't heard before, yet understood right away. In those years it was ill-advised to be the child of a German mother and a Hungarian father. In the language of volatile French nationalism, during the First World War Hungarian or German had meant stones, sticks, cudgels, broken heads, and spit mixed with phlegm, and during the German occupation of the country, the tradition just had to be revived. From the perspective of French nationalism, there's not a scrap of difference among a German, an Austrian, or a Hungarian. Damned *boche*. Filthy *métèque*. But for me, Pamiers was full of promise. I stayed at the best hotel. The best wasn't more, mind you, than the small, miserable hotel of an old town gone to seed. The French countryside can be very miserable indeed. It differs from the miserable Hungarian countryside only in that French poverty is orderly. Moldy corridors, sleazy little rooms, miserable but clean bathrooms. A wonderful, comfortably furnished restaurant with a first-class chef and delicious dinners, I must give credit where credit is due. They served the goose liver terrine in frozen Calvados jelly with a honey cake biscuit, an intimate introduction to a dinner fit for a king. And with dinner came the wines of the region blessed with their peculiar tartness and sweetness, one night freshly caught trout, another night partridge, and also lamb and local cheeses from the aromatic mountain pastures, the brutal *cassoulet toulousain*, not to mention the crowning glory that was the dessert. Mountain butter does wonders for a dessert. I doubt that my aunt and her comrades stayed here when they came to help certain prisoners escape. It would have laid them open to easy identification by the police, whereas, in keeping with the rules of illegality, they had to remain as invisible as humanly possible. Probably, they arrived separately, they snuck over the demarcation line separately, they took separate trains, and each of them stayed with a different comrade in one of the remote quarters of the town, a comrade who'd been notified through illegal channels beforehand about their arrival. Where and when they'd meet up also had to be arranged beforehand, and if they could not meet, they had to have another prearranged time set for the next meeting.

I immediately set off to find this proletarian district on the outskirts of Pamiers; I wanted to gain some idea of the circumstances of my uncle's escape, and to find the strange house of which my aunt spoke, but there was no quarter like it to be found, or else it was gone, or so I thought. I found it only days later, on Sunday afternoon, nestled in one of the steep bends of the rumbling Ariège, in the vicinity of the Pont du Jeu, at the northernmost tip of the small town. Here stood the former proletarian quarter with its abandoned or partly dismantled industrial workshops, and an ancient but well-tended ball court with the ubiquitous Sunday players who tossed wooden balls, *les boules de pétanque*, under the steady gaze of rickety old men and prepubescent boys. There was also a newly built paper mill that was in operation even on Sunday. In front of it all stretched a small, meticulous promenade with its shabby though perfectly clipped row of plane trees so typical of French poverty, crowded with Sunday strollers. That's where I found the passageway without a name, *impasse sans nom*, along with the house where, according to one of her midnight recollections, my aunt had probably stayed, and I marveled at their conspiratorial Communist inventiveness. The small house faced this proletarian promenade, it was unbelievably narrow, but it had two upper stories and a mansard room as well. You had to descend some stairs to reach the front door, and if at night the police should have come banging on it, theoretically she could have easily climbed out a back window on the ground floor that gave out on a meadow and fled along the narrow well-trodden path that ran along the bend of the Ariège so that, at a prearranged signal, she could perhaps return to her lodgings, or else her comrades would have found her another hiding place.

I found everything just as she had described it; after so many years there was still the window giving out on the meadow, there was the well-trodden path, but when I set off from the hotel for my first expedition, politely, though perhaps more insistently than otherwise, the concierge warned me that I mustn't stay out on the street after eight.

I thought I had heard wrong.

Why can't I stay out on the street, I asked in all innocence.

I'll see for myself, he said, I'm going to find myself alone with my white skin, this was his answer, and seeing how appalled I was, he put an end to our discourse and buried himself in his papers.

For the rest of my stay at the hotel, he never again acknowledged any comments of a personal nature from me. He did not forgive me, and in a couple of hours, I realized why.

A stupid stranger who, to add insult to injury, speaks hardly any

French, had the effrontery to rebuff his helping hand, to ignore his solidarity. On the other hand, how was I to know where I was and what I should take at face value.

Pamiers is the city of ancient monasteries and lyceums, of Dominicans, Carmelites, Augustinians, and Franciscans with their late-medieval brick walls and brick churches. The town has a brick cathedral, too, beautiful in its asceticism, but these buildings are mostly inert, empty, abandoned. Today this oldest part of the town is inhabited mostly by Arab immigrants, and by oldest, the inhabitants mean the eighth century. After eight in the evening, the larger squares are gradually taken over by old men in kaftans and fez, they stand around in groups or bunches or sit in a row, they play chess or just keep silent; without a thought given to the Arab youth and children making a racket around them, they talk as they count their prayer beads. Then to your surprise you realize that, all around you, you see only Arab boys and Arab men. There are no Arab women. In this architecturally European environment reaching back to a time predating the early Middle Ages, this is at once threatening and fascinating. Locked and boarded-up houses and empty shops, early medieval rows of houses caving in on themselves. The husks of a splendid old town. Now and then an imam in his beautiful kaftan glides past, or the shadow of a woman covered from head to toe in blue or black.

All around us, up on the solitary rocky peaks, stand the ancient ruined castles of the Albigensians, or the Cathars, the Good Men, as they called themselves. I was eighteen when I wanted to write a novel about these Good Men, and for years collected material for a book by this title, but nothing came of it, I abandoned the project.

Still, before I realized what had happened, by 8:10 I was so thoroughly alone with these Maghrebian Arab men and boys that I was first anxious, then downright afraid, and it was no use telling myself that I had nothing to do with the history of French colonization, and I don't give a damn about their French racism and the hard-as-stone Arab racism that accompanies it. It's none of my business. I'm just a tourist here. End of story. But what I was thinking didn't matter; brandishing baseball bats, the teenagers slaloming wildly around me on their skateboards and the motley groups of young men standing at some distance from one another forced me off the square they'd taken possession of for the night, and they did so with the orchestrated movements and the elemental joy of the hunt, as if they were coming at me with their skateboards only by accident. They were handsome, strong, and brutal, and they grinned at me with hatred that they enjoyed. Like all racism, this racism, too, expresses the delicate game of belonging. It is a typically masculine game, a profoundly erotic game, it is played by men between themselves with trust in their common strength, potency, and erections, a game that, need I say, given their frenzied drive to copulate and reproduce, women will gladly play themselves. It is up to them to turn these men, enamored of one another, to themselves instead. Racism is the ancient, collective worship of the erection. It functions in the layer of consciousness where magic dwells and is connected to the notion of multiplying. At first I told myself that it is an accident and my judgment played me false, the concierge's French racism had infected me, it's a paranoid thought, kindly shoo it away, but after the third attack, I couldn't very well trust myself to this thought. I was afraid that coming at me from the back, the side, or the front, with his strength and momentum one of them would sweep me off my feet; they came at me from all sides but did not hem me in completely. They were playing with me, by preying on my sense of safety they had me where they wanted me. I would have liked to leave, but as I hurriedly withdrew some cash from an ATM, my situation became even more precarious. How dare I do it without their permission. They jumped off their skateboards, their grins vanished, and only their fevered excitement, meaning their beauty, remained, something that in his own overly ornate language Jean Genet so audaciously wrote about, he let their beauty corrupt him so he could cause extremes of agitation in the hearts of his white-skinned compatriots. Because of them, he joined the ranks of anti-Zionist racists. With the same energy and led by the same magical instinct, he could have just as easily let himself be corrupted by the beauty and racism of the Zionist Jewish young men. The skateboards kept whizzing past me; as if they were threatening to chop off my legs, the boys reached after them with the soles of their feet at the last moment, they formed a tight circle around the ATM, they kept a provocative eye on me, as if wanting to learn my pin code, they did not budge, and it wouldn't have been surprising if just for fun they'd have grabbed my card from between my fingers, and my money, too. I didn't have enough money, though, to tempt them. I barely just managed to leave the proving ground of my good faith, the main square of this beautiful old town, when on a side street I found myself face-to-face with another group of Arab men. They, however, didn't so much as look at me, they quite literally took me for air all the time that they came toward me, leaving me just enough of an escape route to allow me to steal away by pressing myself against the wall of a house dating from the early Middle Ages. They made sure that I should have no option but to steal away. This cruel method of arousing fear, this erotic phalanx, why deny it, held me in thrall. They weren't playing the game for my benefit, they were clearly making a show of their strength and orchestrated potency for the benefit of one another. And it was no use trying to fool myself. They had in fact humiliated me. The combination of my awe mixed with understanding and the humiliation I suffered was unexpected and surprising. I ran down the deserted street because I felt I had to run, all the while feeling mortally ashamed for running away like that.

I was nearly at the hotel when I decided to go through the open door of a restaurant. The restaurant was empty. Then, after a while, the proprietor appeared from somewhere in the kitchen. His menu for the night did not include soup, but he said he'd gladly make one. What kind of soup would I like. This question made amends, a French restaurateur is making me soup, in which case I should feel at home after all. When he brought me my water and my wine and my soup was audibly simmering in the kitchen, a group of young sportsmen came in with their coach. They were loud and kept making grating noises as they moved their chairs about, but then they sat down at their usual table, and from then on, the restaurateur had more than enough on his hands. As he kept bringing out the wine, heady aromas emanated from the kitchen. He made me a truly original vegetable soup with lemon, thick and well seasoned, and crème fraîche. It took him fifteen or twenty minutes at most.

And then on Friday, when I took the train from Pamiers to Le Vernet d'Ariège and went to the town hall, they told me to come back in the afternoon, or on Monday, because it's lunchtime until three, and they're not giving me the key during lunchtime.

A severe-looking woman sat behind the huge official-looking counter. I didn't take her quite seriously because her sharp demeanor and dry looks reminded me a bit of my cousin Georges's daughter, Yvette. First I tried to reason with her, as I used to do with Yvette, who was two years my senior, saying that by the time she finishes lunch, I'll finish my business in the museum.

By the time you get back from lunch, I'll bring the key, I promise.

No, she protested, no, it's not possible, it's out of the question.

Why is it not possible, I shot back, as if I were hissing the reply from the soles of my feet or my groin, fully conscious of my rights, as Yvette would have done in my place.

Well, she can't leave the museum unattended, she hopes I understand, those are valuable documents.

I understand, I said, but I'd come thousands of kilometers, I'd come expressly for this, I was here on Tuesday and Wednesday, this is the third time.

She nodded with satisfaction, yes, she knows I was here before, as if she were proud that this *métèque* had come on a wild goose chase yet again. Probably, she must have gotten wind of it from the old man with the stroke, or the people I'd asked on my way here. I doubt that anything else had happened in Le Vernet d'Ariège the entire week. I was just another filthy stranger come to delve into their shameful local history yet again.

I said that she can't do this, I'd been trying since Tuesday to no avail, I don't want to have to come back again.

Well, there's nothing more she can say, she said, obviously enjoying the malicious glee that she nevertheless tried to temper with discipline. I should come back in the afternoon, or Monday, or whenever.

It's up to me.

This was too much, this last, angry outburst, this obstinate arrogance, which reminded me yet again of the obstinate French girl, my cousin Yvette.

Yvette and I got along splendidly, we were mutually patient and curious, yet at times we were at loggerheads because I felt that her stubbornness was not natural, that it fed on clichés, convention, the unshakable sense of her French superiority. That's how the French do it, she'd shout. At times I conceded that the French are right when they do something this way or that. But there was a line that she was ill-advised to cross, though accompanied by her malicious and arrogant little French smile, she nevertheless repeatedly approached that line, and at times underhandedly crossed it. She loved crossing lines, she couldn't do without it. If I reminded her that she was on forbidden ground, she gave the short, surprised laugh I knew from her grandmother, my mother, and myself; the family trait tempered her French arrogance, and then for a while everything happened in a way that I could find acceptable until, one way or another, she surreptitiously reinstated her own method of doing things in line with the French colonial ideal; she insisted on it, no matter what, meaning that the intelligent native will accept her order of things precisely because he is intelligent. An intelligent being must accept universal order as a matter of course. The universal order is Francophile, and the Good Lord himself speaks French impeccably as spoken in Paris and Versailles. All appearances and hearsay to the contrary, the French conception of order is much more rigorous than the German conception of order. It is not tailored with an animate group or an army in mind, it is not tailored with the herd instinct in mind, nor blind obedience, nor the ambitious royal strivings of a tiny Prussian state that can be proclaimed only in the Hall of Mirrors in Versailles. No, by no means.

I am not leaving until you give me the key, I said, because I was in fact ready to start a sit-in for my rights. This severe little woman just stared. How dare I, I'm just a stranger. And then I suddenly thought of a solution, a logical argument. Cool as a cucumber, I laid the last trump card on the table, she's going to hand me that key because it is not yet noon, it is five minutes to noon, so she must hand it to me for five minutes. I even nodded and pointed to the unquestionably precise official clock on her official wall. The clock indicated that the museum must stay open for five minutes more. At this, she handed me the key without a word. Her sharp little countenance remained frigid and severe, but not negative, not hostile. Cartesian logic renders one's features embarrassingly neutral. She may have even relented a bit, with my perseverance I may have succeeded in reaching her plebeian soul, because, with the utmost detachment, she merely said, if I finish before three, before she's back, I should leave the key in the school's kitchen.

Soon after, as I stood in the small museum filled with the noise and smells of the school cafeteria coming from next door, I found myself looking in the eyes of László Rajk as a young man. The Formica studio counter with which the photographer identifies the negatives, whether in Le Vernet d'Ariège or on Kossuth Lajos Street in Pest, said 043. So then Rajk was the forty-third individual the photographer had taken a picture of in the camp. In the pictures, each prisoner wears a uniform, a dark shirt, and fatigues in an even darker tone, though possibly, the prisoners were given this attire only for the sake of the pictures. Perhaps the photographer, himself a prisoner, wanted to be humane, and he didn't want to show the others in their shameful civilian rags. Perhaps he had a shirt and a jacket that he had everyone wear. In his memoirs entitled *Scum of the Earth*, Arthur Koestler paints a very different picture of his first impressions, and indeed, in the few amateur photographs that have survived, there is no trace of any fatigues or uniforms. Taken in summer, these photographs show the men naked to the waist, while their civilian trousers or underwear, as civil as they come, had been washed repeatedly until they resembled rags. Realistically, these men of skin and bone must have been almost naked during the summer months. There were about thirty of them, Koestler writes, and they carried spades over their shoulders, their heads were shaven, but their faces were stubbly, and they were clad in rags. Some marched through the mud in slippers, some with their toes sticking out of their shoes, some wore galoshes over their bare feet.

On the title page of his play, written in his notebook, my uncle paints a somewhat more favorable picture of their attire. In the play, Rodrigues wears a threadbare but neat Spanish uniform. His unnamed chess partner is in civilian clothes, but looks more like a vagabond, because he was forced to pull an old, ragged coat over his otherwise respectable golf suit against the cold. The kibitzer, who is also nameless, wears a cape over his overalls. Sanchez is in part-military, part-civilian clothes, but looks presentable all the same. Juan, a newcomer to the camp, is soberly dressed in clean, proper clothing, and he even sports a tie. On the other hand, the old Andalusian peasant's clothes, part-peasant, part-military, bear obvious traces of the vicissitudes of his flight.

In the photograph, Rajk is wearing a neat shirt and jacket, but neither his face nor his clothes have anything in common with Koestler's description, nothing that could bear witness to the horrible conditions and the humiliation, nothing to indicate that he is in captivity, or the humiliation he suffers. His suntanned thinness may be the only giveaway. It is undoubtedly the thinness of work done under privation, the day laborers' thinness and the road builders' thinness, the thinness of the servants on large estates, who for centuries, day in and day out, had just enough to eat to ensure their physical survival. The top button of his shirt is undone. He radiates calm and unwavering Communist resistance. Hunger could not break his posture or his spirit.

The album contains several hundred numbered photographs. There must have been a list somewhere to help identify the individuals on the basis of the numbers, but I couldn't find a list like that anywhere in the small museum, whereas I'd have liked to find my uncle's one and only good old friend, Antal Bieber from Bácska, whose face I could not recall, try as I might. The local Arrow Cross leader's big belly and shiny face, yes, but not his. I was also eager to find faces familiar to me from my earliest childhood, Györg Angyal, Imre Mező, Ferenc Münnich, and Dezső Jász, among others. Except, I soon realized that some of the visitors had simply taken the photographs out of their pockets; probably relatives, surviving comrades, and acquaintances had also asked for the key and had stolen from the album the pictures of the dead persons close to their hearts. I couldn't find my Uncle Pali's portrait either. But all the while that I was looking, I was tempted to steal the two pictures of Rajk, the one taken in profile and the one taken from the front. I reasoned that the numbered negatives must still be around somewhere; it was obvious that the enlargements were made much later than the negatives, probably in the seventies, and not before.

But I didn't steal Rajk's portrait after all; I wanted others to see the decidedly handsome features of this Communist, which in the later photographs show clear signs of suffering.

With experience of photography, the originality or age of the photographs and the era when the negatives and the enlargements were made can be ascertained with reasonable accuracy without having to resort to chemical or optical tricks. Starting from the earliest age of photography, photographic techniques were repeatedly modernized in regular ten-year cycles, and these changes can be seen in the photographs; even the different ages of the original negative and the copy can be ascertained. Rajk's photograph was probably taken in 1939, the year he was interned, or in the summer of 1940; his deeply tanned skin would make the latter more probable, but the copy kept in the museum was probably made in the seventies. Before that, only contact sheets may have been made for the police records. The era in which a photograph was taken can best be ascertained with full precision if you hold the negative in your hand and see the trademark on the side, and perhaps the serial number, while the reverse side helps you determine the circumstances of its developing and fixing. But the enlargement was made much later, I saw that the moment I pulled the picture from its pocket, because photographic paper of this type did not exist before the war, nor before the seventies. Which served as an argument for stealing it. That the curators were in no rush to replace the missing pictures served as an argument against stealing it. Rajk's execution and dramatic reburial seven years later was one of the greatest spiritual and intellectual trials of my childhood.

This is why I felt that I had a right to that picture. I might even give a copy to his son, who inherited the shape of his father's head, his prominent cheekbones and knotty forehead. The newborn Lacika was eventually placed in the bunting lined with the finest wool and made of the finest damask, adorned with a fringe made of Brussels lace, that my great-grandmother used for her own five newborns, first Klára, our grandmother, then Anna, Erzsébet, Béla, and Pál, followed by our grandmother's babies, Eugenie, György, Magda, István, Endre, Miklós, and finally our father, László. Later, my Aunt Eugenie's two babies, György Mándoki from her first marriage, and Veronika Rendl from her second, also spent their first weeks in the bunting, and between the two, Magda's newborn, György, who in France became Georges. Their second child, Bucika, was left out of the line of those who used the family's bunting with the Brussels lace, because she was born in Råsunda, a suburb of Stockholm, and died there as a newborn. I went looking for her grave but could not find it. Meanwhile, the beautiful family bunting remained in Budapest, and so I was swaddled in it, too, and then my cousin Kati, my younger brother, Pál, until one fine day during the recess of a meeting of some women's coalition, Júlia Rajk, who was expecting her baby just then, complained to my mother that she didn't know what to do, because she couldn't find a bunting. In that case, you'll have ours, my mother said, and the next morning she took the bunting to Széchenyi Street, thereby severing it from its family history. But as far as she was concerned, the populous family of Communists was a more authentic family than ours, and in this family, László Rajk was held in great regard, though I wouldn't go so far as to say that he was liked. People said he was obliging, but overly reserved.

Loving someone was not a criterion of Communist solidarity. If they were obliged to trust someone, they simply ignored what they felt about them.

My parents listened to the radio broadcast of Rajk's trial in profound silence. At this point, there was no room in their lives for me. My younger brother was better off because, ever since he was born, he'd scream his head off day and night, he always had some terrible problem in need of immediate remedy, not only the childhood diseases with their sharp fever bell curves, from which he suffered ever since infancy; the truth is that he could turn himself blue in the face from sheer stubbornness, which he and I probably inherited from the paternal side of the family; he howled until he couldn't breathe, thereby making sure that my parents, locked into their own world, would attend to him, in the technical sense of the word, at least. But for the duration of the Rajk trial, our parents weren't present even when we were in the same room. It was as if they had been buried by a landslide. In those weeks, we were entrusted to the care of Rózsi Németh, who watched us when our parents were away, but current events diverted her attention as well. Between September 16 and 24, 1949, Kossuth Radio broadcast the trial from seven to eight, and also between nine and eleven every evening. Rózsi waited anxiously to see what Apáka would have to say about it and what Anyáka would have to say about it, for these were her names for them. And also what they left unsaid. No one knew where Rajk's son, Lacika, was, much less what had become of the family's prized baby bunting. Sometimes they didn't listen to the trial at home, but would go elsewhere, I don't know where. When this happened, I listened to it alone, with Rózsi listening in now and then. She sent me to bed. Yet occasionally they nevertheless managed to blurt something out. My mother had been anxious over Lacika's fate ever since Júlia Rajk's arrest, though it would be more correct to say that her innate anxiety made her fretful, and it seemed to me that she tried to repress her feelings, she tried to quell her anxiety. I remember the quiet references to Lacika. These were not necessarily verbal. Dogs communicate like this. Lacika's fate upset me, too; in the mind's eye I kept seeing the little baby in his parents' prison cell. And since I knew that my mother was interested in Lacika's fate, I asked her repeatedly what became of him. As for the prison, I imagined it the way contemporary etchings represented the jail in the fortress of Kufstein with its Hungarian prisoners in chains, where, for a short time, possibly for only a couple of weeks, our great-grandfather had also been held prisoner. Sometimes I imagined Lacika being left alone in an empty apartment. Little wonder, since as far as I can remember, except for something resembling a bark, I got no other answer to my questions. He's fine. Or something to that effect. All the same, I tried to keep up with my parents by using my imagination. My mother's attempt to get the better of her anxiety left such a deep impression on my mind that when decades later I ran into Lacika, by then a young architect with a gigantic physique and a booming laugh, coming down the late-winter road on the forest's edge leading to our hut in Kisoroszi, his arm around the shoulders of a girl with a mop of curly hair, in the company of András Monory Mész, who was studying cinematography at the academy, I could hardly get a word out, I was so taken aback. Luckily, he wasn't concerned with me, he much preferred to wrestle with this girl in the forest litter, her name was Ági Zsigmond, and he had to use all his strength to wrestle her down. My historical silence, the senseless manifestation of my history-induced crisis of conscience over his fate, lasted quite some time. It lasted until Laci designed the scenery for the production of my comedy entitled *Spring Cleaning* in Pécs, though because of us, the production was banned while still in rehearsal. Years later, Laci redesigned the scenery for the production in Győr that was given the go-ahead.

There was no aspect of the wave of arrests and the strictly censored radio broadcasts of the great trial that did not affect my family. It was the third staggering blow from their party, and it was far from the last. While the trial was being broadcast, the city fell silent; as for my parents, they too fell silent, as if on the third Friday in September, when the trial began, they felt bound to accuse themselves of some offense they had not committed, or as if their knowledge of humanity had lost its validity. Or else the intentions of the trial may have been reasonable, except in their eyes it had no credibility. Though they couldn't have said why. They couldn't imagine their party making a mistake.

Later, the story of the family bunting took another unexpected turn that I feel I should relate, even if with a heavy heart. Much later, when tensions had not yet subsided, though life continued on its appointed path, and not in spite of but because the principal defendants had been killed, thereby putting an end, once and for all, to the dynamic period of the adventurous resumption of life after the siege, my Aunt Eugenie called our mother on the phone, saying it was time she returned the bunting, because Vera was about to give birth. I remember this phone call, and I also remember that it would never have occurred to my Aunt Eugenie that we didn't have the bunting anymore. Our mother admitted that she'd given it away. Well, she'd better get it back. But she wouldn't tell my aunt who had it. No wonder. At the time, our father was department head at the Ministry of Communication, and probably, he was responsible not only for the smooth functioning of the telephone lines, but also for the technical requirements for tapping them. And with this, the story of the family bunting took a turn fit for a legend. According to Vera, our mother asked Júlia Rajk's mother, Mária Földi, for the bunting, and thanks to her, she was able to place her son, Gábor Herczeg, in the same Viennese baby bunting adorned with Brussels lace that all the other newborn babies in the family had been swaddled in. Except, our mother couldn't have asked Mária Földi, László Rajk's mother-in-law, for the bunting. It took fifty years for me to realize that they weren't talking about the bunting at all, but about something else, except my mother couldn't tell others what that something else was.

An armed detachment arrested László Rajk in his Vérhalom Street apartment on May 30, 1949. It was a Monday. They did not arrest Júlia Rajk that day, but put her, with her baby, her mother, and their maid under house arrest. They came for her on June 6, which was the following Monday. They came to arrest her, but said that they were taking her in for questioning. Júlia later recalled that she had just breastfed her barely four-month-old baby, and as if she knew what was going to happen, she made her mother promise that she would never give the child to anyone else. The following day, Tuesday, they took the baby away from his grandmother without further ado, and threw the two of them, Júlia Rajk's mother and the maid, out of the villa without their belongings. There they were, with nowhere to go. In the only surviving family photograph showing László Rajk with Júlia Rajk and their newborn baby, Júlia Rajk is holding the baby swaddled in the same bunting in which in September 1948 I am holding my little brother in our family photograph. The following day they'd emptied out the villa to make room for Lieutenant General Sándor Nógrádi, the political chief of the Hungarian People's Army. And so, after four years had passed, my mother couldn't very well have asked Mrs. Földi for the bunting. Probably, they took the baby away in it. Which means that our mother must have known what had happened, and where the baby had been taken. What's more, she must also have known that despite her turning to all possible authorities, Júlia Rajk's mother would not get her grandson back. She must have known that they had stripped him of his real name and given him a new name instead. Consequently, she must also have known where to look for the family's bunting. I must have known something myself, because I spent years wondering what happened to the children of traitors, though I knew the answer, they were taken to an institution to carve decent human beings of them. My mother must have said it like this, she used the verb *carve* a lot, at least, that's how I remember it. I often wondered what would happen should it turn out that our parents were also traitors. What would become of us. Would I also get carved. And how would I react to the news. They'd carve anything extraneous off me, too, not just them. Our mother may not have known that Júlia Földi and László Rajk's son was given the name István Kovács, according to other sources, István Györk, but she must have been among the very few who knew where the baby had been taken, and thus, where she could ask for the bunting, unless, of course, Emmi Pikler's orphanage had used it until it had turned into rags.

Probably, Lacika's papers were ready by the time he was admitted to the orphanage in Lóczy Lajos Street. It had twelve wet nurses on its payroll at all times. Emmi Pikler, who had previously been Lacika's pediatrician as well as the doctor of the children of other parents who'd been arrested, was now in charge of the home. It is thus unlikely that Emmi Pikler would not have realized that the baby registered at the nursery as István Kovács or István Györk was in fact the son of Júlia Földi and László Rajk, both of whom were under arrest. Lacika's little body could not be mistaken, just as Lacika's silk batiste bunting edged in Brussels lace could not be mistaken. As disgraceful as it may be, the facts seem to indicate that our mother got the bunting back from her and not from Mrs. Földi. After the siege, she and Emmi Pikler built up the children's welfare system together, the network of nurseries and kindergartens, and they organized, hand in hand, the training of district nurses, as well as nursery and kindergarten teachers. Pikler was in command of the professional aspects of the operation, while our mother was in charge of organizing and supervising it.

As for Aranyossi, he had no choice but to attend the trial. One day in late summer when he was summoned to it by phone in his office, he stood up from his desk and just stood there. Theoretically, he couldn't have known why he had been summoned, and yet he knew. Out on Andrássy Boulevard, it was business as usual. His first thought was that he should have stayed in Paris. Their son and daughter-in-law, who was a local schoolteacher, and their two grandchildren, Yvette and Jean-François, lived in Aulnay-sous-Bois, one of the working-class districts of Paris, their grandfather first saw them when in July 1946 he returned to the French capital as the editor-in-chief of the weekly *Szabadság*, to send dispatches about the progress of the peace conference not only to his own paper, but to other Budapest papers as well. He barely wrote anything, which neither his colleagues nor his wife understood. In the letters my Aunt Magda wrote to him in Paris, she scolded him, she warned him, she was furious, and in her memoirs, she later put her husband's negligence down to the dementia that was taking hold of him. When I put the letters and notes he left behind in chronological order, I see that without his wife's knowledge he put out feelers to see how he might resume his life in Paris, and by the end of the first week, he saw that there was no real impediment to his doing so. His beloved city, which in the first days of the war cast him out, now welcomed him back. Meeting followed meeting, book contracts were signed, and he was appointed secretary of the Romain Rolland Association. I found nothing to indicate what had convinced him to return home after all. Along with the Hungarian delegation participating in the peace talks, he stayed in the grand Hôtel Claridge on the Champs-Élysées, and began to organize their joint future or his own future from there.

A messenger brought his visitor's card to the trial, he later told me, somewhat uncertain of himself due to the dementia that was seizing him before my eyes.

When I asked him something, when it was still possible to talk to him about one subject or another, his expression was that of someone trying to orient himself in the dark; there was a look of alarm in his eyes, oh, where will he find what he is looking for in his mind. Not here. Maybe there. Sometimes he couldn't find it, or if he did, it seemed to overwhelm him, as if he were incapable of separating the information that came at him in unmanageable chunks into its various components. Sometimes the onrush of information confounded his tongue for minutes on end. He couldn't very well say so many things at once. Several decades later, Miklós Mészöly's face showed the same symptoms when, standing at the abyss of dementia, he nevertheless attempted to answer my queries about his illegal activities for the Hungarian Collective.

The visitor's card was not only a privilege that went with my uncle's office, it also served as a serious warning. Except, he had no way of knowing what he was being warned about. At the same time, he couldn't have avoided thinking of the only possible historical analogy for current events. This is how the Holy Inquisition invited those adherents to an auto-da-fé who were themselves suspected of heresy. Let them see for themselves what happens if they don't relent and instead continue in their old ways. At the same time, even if they relent, the sentence stands, except they will be exonerated in the eyes of the Lord and will not incur eternal damnation. There are no accidents, there is no such thing as luck or mercy, we have invalidated them, these are the kinds of things my uncle said. The world is ruled by divine will. Time and again, I had to usher him back to reality. On the sunny morning in early fall when he was due to attend the trial, they had to get up early in their apartment on Teréz Boulevard, I remember this, too, they had breakfast together, my Aunt Magda saw him to the door in silence, as far as I can remember, they didn't say a word. There are times in your life when you feel that the air around you is tangible. My uncle had to go to the assembly hall of the Metal and Engineering Workers' Trade Union headquarters in Magdolna Street. He was among familiar faces. The well-known writer Tibor Déry was sitting in the first row, right in front of him, but no one spoke to anyone if they could possibly avoid it. They had to sit there, my uncle said, but

he doesn't think that there was anyone present who didn't listen to
the indictment without going into a state of shock. I am not at all
surprised that this is when the people around him discovered the first
signs of dementia in him. After all, not only Rajk, but he, too, had
been tortured at the jail on Margit Boulevard. According to the logic
of the illegal Communist movement, if he was tortured, he may have
also been recruited. According to the indictment, after the outbreak
of the Spanish Civil War, the Hungarian secret police had ordered
Rajk to go to Spain and report back on which Hungarian Communists participated in the fighting, and also, he was told to subvert the
Hungarian Rákosi Battalion. My uncle realized that after each of the
points in the indictment were read, he'd closed his eyes and bowed his
head. Where was the Rákosi Battalion when the civil war broke out,
he couldn't help asking himself, and from then on he couldn't ignore
his own answer. Nowhere. In Anachronia. He felt that his party was
sending him a message. No one treats facts this freely, and if the public prosecutor insists on this absurdity, it can't be a mistake, the Party
must surely need this lie. While he was translating, he'd spent lots
of time on philology, and no matter how he looked at it, none of the
assertions made sense. He talked about it with the indifference of his
advanced illness. I spent long hours with him in his room sitting in
one of the Rietveld armchairs. He would be lying on the couch in his
smoking jacket or sitting behind his desk when I surprised him with
one of my questions pertaining to history, literature, or linguistics
that could not wait. As if he were still searching for an explanation
to something for which explanation hardly exists. First his humor fell
victim to his illness, then his facial expression, until at last the fiendish disease deprived him of his gestures as well. The Spanish Civil
War broke out in July 1936 in Madeira, but the first group of Hungarian volunteers arrived in Madrid only a year later, in October 1937.
Rajk couldn't have had anything to spy on until then. He couldn't
very well have thought that the chief public prosecutor was ignorant
of what happened. Which means he must look for a secret message
behind his words. He wasn't ill back then, but probably the regime's
paranoia had taken its toll on him, and when he tried to tell me, I

listened with an awareness of the consequences, and received the information with this in mind. But there it was, in black and white, the next point of the indictment, my uncle continued, according to which Rajk didn't even wait for the defeat of the Republicans but sneaked across the French border, and this wasn't true either, this too surprised him, and first in the internment camp at Saint-Cyprien, then at Gurs, and finally at Le Vernet, he was supposed to have made the acquaintance of agents of the Yugoslav spy organizations that had infiltrated the camps. And then followed something in the indictment that he really didn't know what to make of, namely, that the first Yugoslav agent Rajk came in contact with was his good old friend Antal Bieber, whose name Public Prosecutor Alapi mispronounced, he said Bebler, or else they'd misspelled the name in his papers, because he was reading from papers. Or possibly Bieber wasn't called Bieber in the first place, but was really called Bebler, in which case this, too, was part of the secret message, my uncle thought, except he couldn't decipher it. So then Tóni Bieber had deceived him, too, he'd deceived everyone. Everyone deceived everyone. But how could he have deceived everyone, because in that case you couldn't have found him in Bácska under the Bieber name. You stayed with the Biebers, after all, and not at the Beblers'. You stayed where I put a word in for you, you stayed with Tóni Bieber. And also, the French secret service was supposed to have infiltrated the camp, along with the American intelligence service, which was directed by Allen Dulles and was represented in Europe by Noel H. Field. And hearing Field's name, my uncle said, stunned him. He knew that Field had been arrested, but he didn't know why. So that's why. This was his appointed place in the story. The difference, too, was interesting, the difference between how my Aunt Magda and my Uncle Pali related a story. They provided two different pictures even of the same event. When my Aunt Magda talked about an event or a person, I had no doubt, ever, that it was as she related it to me, despite the fact that she might have related it to others differently, because some consideration tied to the Communist movement or self-interest called for it. On the other hand, I invariably doubted the authenticity of my Uncle Pali's accounts, if just a bit; he, out of aesthetic considerations, always spun facts into tales, he rounded them off, he aimed for punch lines, or at least, I couldn't see properly behind the facade of his tales. On the other hand, he was a born gentleman, he wouldn't say anything really personal and remained chivalrous even in the face of his own movement's barbarism. He arranged the subjects of his stories as a philologist, he placed them in a historical-philological context, so we could see them from a humanist perspective or what we call Christian ethics, all while he avoided the question of where his own place was in this whole thing.

Rajk was also supposed to have been recruited by the Gestapo. It's true that the Gestapo visited the camp; thanks to the French guards, it was known in the camp even back then, and with the full agreement of the Vichy government, they began selecting and decimating the German emigrants, that's also true, but when would Rajk and the others have been recruited, given that even the French commander of the guard did his best to thwart the Gestapo's activities, and in fact, amid great shouting and cursing, the French had the Gestapo men fleeing the camp. In this first round, the members of the French guard simply froze them out. But Noel H. Field was supposed to have arrived at Le Vernet one fine day, and he was supposed to have told Rajk that by orders from his superiors, he would help him get back to Hungary. Actually, something similar did occur, but much later, and it was not Field who brought the message. Field visited the camp as a representative of the Swiss Red Cross, but he didn't do it to pass any orders on to Rajk. His mission was to free a Yugoslav Communist, whose name my uncle could no longer remember, with the help of a real Swiss safe conduct pass, he happens to know this from Ilona Kojsza, who was Field's assistant in Paris, my uncle said, and who had arranged for the pass in Geneva. Rajk and Field had never met, or else they put up a good pretense to that effect. But regardless of what happened and regardless of how it happened, the fiction presented on the first day of the trial no longer pertained only to Rajk's escape, it was also the story of his own escape; after all, they were both brought out on orders from the Party, in which case he feared that sooner or later they'd get around to him as well, accusing him of escaping with the Gestapo's help. However, my uncle said nothing to me about this; I learned the story of their escape from my Aunt Magda at a later date.

Every sentence of the indictment invalidated every other sentence. Also, my uncle couldn't figure out what the message aimed at him might be; all he could think of was that these people must be crazy if they read a text like this out to them. According to the indictment, another German deputation was supposed to have come to Le Vernet, which happened to be true; they'd come to take over the running of the camp from the Vichy government, and the head of the delegation, a Gestapo major, was supposed to have ordered Rajk into his presence and was supposed to have told him that he'd be sent to Hungary to work for them. There aren't enough footnotes in the world to help one understand the distortion. According to the indictment, Rajk was sent back home by the Americans as well as by the Germans. Many of their friends thought that this colossal blunder in the indictment must be the unfortunate outcome of an internal struggle similar to the one that had occurred between the Landlerites and the Kunists, and that several people had composed it at the same time, adding to it and deleting from it, but my uncle and his friends didn't think that this was a sufficient explanation or an apt analogy. If very early on, while he was living in illegality, Rajk, and we don't know when and we don't know why, possibly for a bowl of lentils, sold himself to the secret services of the imperial powers, to all of them at the same time, then they, too, are accomplices. Why are they sitting here as peaceful observers, why didn't they say anything. Your mother asked me very quietly, if what they say about Rajk were true, then why would she have passed the silk batiste family bunting edged in Brussels lace on to the child of such a guilty man. Why didn't we see it. Because we didn't. This was the great verifiable question. They would have seen it. That goes without saying. If they didn't see it, then they themselves must also be recruited agents, except they don't know it yet. Or else the accusation is false.

This line of reasoning could be followed with a sane mind only with knowledge of the inner workings of the Communist movement, meaning its conspirative system, but its sense couldn't be followed even then. It made no sense trying to make sense of it. It makes no sense trying to understand things that make no sense. Still, we can't very well ignore this spectacular historical show. This is why I thought of stealing Rajk's photographs, for the sake of better understanding, so that I might understand something about the Communists that can't be understood, and in the end I left them there for the same reason. I left them there so others may learn from them, that they should see his handsome, stubborn face as his conviction lifts him above his suffering. At the same time, I doubt that anyone except for me would be interested in this story, though without stories such as this, the history of the European social movements can't be understood. Seeing these evil deeds and evildoers, Europe's governing opinion turned its horrified back on its own centuries-old history, it basically excised the history of its workers' movements from its historical consciousness, denouncing it after the fact, and the likelihood that it might turn back from that path anytime soon is very small indeed, that it might reinstate it in the appropriate place of its consciousness.

I found nothing in the texts in the cases nor in the museum publications to indicate where the original negatives might be or how many there were. I assume that the negatives are stored in the archives of the Musée de la Résistance in Toulouse. If the negatives have survived, and why wouldn't they have, it must be an impressive collection. Between 1939 and 1945, and to the greater glory of the French state's rationale, the camp had forty thousand inmates hailing from fifty-eight nations.

Later I also found the camp's cemetery.

But now it was only Tuesday, and there I stood at the same rumbling Ariège, though I had to admit that I'm not there, this Le Vernet is not that Le Vernet. Farther up the shore a couple were walking their dog, who in its playful mood barked full-throated at the rowers exerting themselves against the current. The rowers barked back, which made the dog even more playful. A little later, when I returned to the small station and looked at the train schedule, I found the name of Le Vernet d'Ariège quite by chance. I needed to travel about forty minutes more on the same train to reach it, and I saw that the train would be pulling into the station in a couple of minutes. I was elated. So I found it after all. I went to buy a ticket. The railroad worker sitting behind the mute glass wall of the empty waiting room told me to go to the ticket machine; with broad gestures he indicated that I should go outside, walk around the building, and behind the building, there, yes, behind it, you'll find it, but hurry, hurry. I didn't have change and the ticket machine rejected my card. It said that it was mute. The adjective surprised me, *muet*, but at least now, in the last years of my life, I learned that in French, the concept of speechlessness or muteness can also be applied to a bank card. A bit farther off a young man was standing by his car, watching my antics with the card, and I shouted to him, asking if he could give me change. He couldn't. But I should ask the other man. I didn't see any other man. He's there, sitting in his car, he said, pointing. But I had run out of time, because the train had pulled in. I shouted back to the young man that we've missed the train, and I laughed, but he, as if bound to feel ashamed at our mutual failure, blushed and shouted back to me that I should go, run, I can make it and buy a ticket from the conductor on the train. I won't even have to pay a fine.

I ran over the rough gravel crunching under my feet, I reached the train and managed to hop on, and that minute the automatic door shut behind me. I waved a thank-you from behind the glass. He was clearly glad at our mutual success, and waved back, grinning from ear to ear. On that Tuesday afternoon, this was probably one of the smallest major events in the world. But the conductor did not come. I couldn't find one anywhere. I walked down the aisle and then sat down somewhere, provisionally, as it were. Though you're always just a bit wary of being caught out by a stern French conductor, caught trying to freeload, it felt good traveling at the expense of the French taxpayers. It wouldn't have been the first time I'd be given a dressing down by a conductor because I'd forgotten to punch my ticket at the station. This expression was also new to me. *Il est nécessaire de composter son billet avant de monter à bord du train.* Which means that after you buy a ticket at the ticket window, you must insert it in a machine that will punch the date and the hour on it, meaning that you will thus validate it. This word made me every bit as happy as the first French word I had ever heard. *Bateau*. Boat. So there you are, you board the train, just a bit afraid, and ashamed, too, the French are so helpful in this regard, and there you are, cheating, you're cheating the French taxpayers. Not only have you not punched your ticket, you don't even have one. Meanwhile you sway from side to side in the car, you hold on and in the late afternoon light take stock of your fellow passengers.

This was the light of the south, a southern light, dry and warm, the light of the Mediterranean. Despite its dryness, the air coming in through the window brings with it the scent of eternal snow. Its sharp edge. No more than an icy current mingling with the dry scent of the woods and rocky precipices. The sky was partly overcast and would not allow a glimpse of the nearby snowcapped mountains that your animal sense of smell has detected in the air. This is how we pulled into the station where I barely managed to get off the train. I had arrived at my destination. I saw the name of the station. I'd pressed the right button, but the door would not open. Then a tall boy who sat near the door with his legs splayed slowly got to his feet to help this helpless old man, he pushed the button, slammed it, as it were, at which it opened. He even showed me how to do it next time, and that I shouldn't be timid but use my fist, he said, *merde, putain*.

Erwin Blumenfeld writes about his arrival at the camp, that he'd never before seen the name of hell inscribed on a sign: Le Vernet d'Ariège.

Nowhere else in the war-torn country had he encountered such a bunch of assorted riffraff, meaning young French soldiers, as at this station. They started beating the exhausted new arrivals with their rifle butts as if the poor men could have put up a resistance. They had to strip stark naked in the light of day and stand there so the soldiers could stick their fingers up their rectums looking for gold, guns, flyers, he had no idea what, while with utmost indifference the inhabitants of Le Vernet d'Ariège walked past them, or waited apathetically for their own train.

But on that particular Tuesday, no one got off the train except for me. As I took a couple of tentative steps on the gravel of the desolate platform, the gravel crunched, marking out an infinitude of time with every step I took. Meanwhile, the train pulled away behind me, the sound of the engine receding into the distance. There was silence, the kind of silence that is saturated with sound, a deafening silence under the sky heavy with rain clouds, yet with the sun managing to break through here and there. The air was warm and oppressive, as if it were summer. The throbbing mating calls of thousands of cicadas hovered above the meadow, their calls penetrated only by the shrieking and screeching of birds I could neither see nor identify.

I realized only the following day that the shrieking that was louder even than the call of the cicadas and Route nationale 20, which passed not far from me, came from at least three types of birds melting into one musical medley. Across from me stood the silent and deserted neoclassical station building, its ground floor and upper story shuttered for eternity. No about-face in French history will bring the stationmaster back to this small station to live upstairs with his family, nor will a switchman and a telegraph operator do twenty-four-hour duty downstairs ever again.

Farther off, on the two sides of the closed building, there stood two huge, magnificent laurels whose perfectly shaped crowns and heavy boughs stretched well above the building's roof.

The following day I discovered that the sparrows I'd heard singing from across the tracks lived in the yellow-flowered bushes in strictly separate groups, and that the harsh, ascending call and raspy chatter of the magpies came from the peaks of the laurels. There was another bird screeching every bit as loud as they, but I couldn't identify it. I later encountered more of these screeching birds in Pamiers and even more of them up in the mountains, atop the rocks and the hollow, decaying remains of the Albigensian churches and fortresses, laid waste nearly a thousand years earlier. Up in the mountains, as I sat surrounded by the Edenic sounds of the Ariège, I decided that these creatures must surely need to screech and shriek so they can communicate with one another over the river's incessant roar.

I also spotted a clump of trees farther off, and under them a sort of asphalt turnout where some cars and a truck were resting in the shade, but a couple of minutes later, when I looked again, they were gone. Like ghosts, they had disappeared. I knew that I'd gone as far as I could possibly go, I'd reached the end of the road.

Consistent with the descriptions of former deportees, in the southern sky, amid the ominous, heavy clouds, I could also see the forbidding crags of the Pyrenees. The clouds, as if they were the eternal wrath of the mountains themselves, refused to budge. I caught a glimpse of the mountains in their full glory, their snowcapped precipices, when I moved to Pamiers. As for the station building, I didn't realize until later that it was not deserted, and that a young woman had taken illegal possession of it with her small child. I discovered their secret without meaning to while I was standing there, waiting for the train, and I saw the woman carefully opening the shutters of one of the ground-floor windows from the inside so she could lift her little boy with his small tricycle through it. Fortunately, she did not realize that I had discovered her secret. As soon as she put the child down she closed the louvered shutters. From then on, I tried to spend as little time as possible in the vicinity of the station. I came across them two more times. Once from a distance I watched the child merrily riding his bike under the trees of the rest area with his mother slowly trailing behind, yet despite the appreciable distance, she kept a wary eye on me. Have I left with the train yet.

That day I'd bought myself something to eat in Pamiers, I bought a hefty slice of headcheese pickled in vinegar, something I'd been meaning to try for a long time, to see what French headcheese tasted like, I tore a roll apart and stuffed it inside, and I ate this roll later that day under the shade of one of the laurels vibrant with the sound of the cicadas. I knew she was watching me and I felt a sense of relief when at last the train door shut behind me. However, on my last day, possibly the following Tuesday, when, following the directions the woman on the motorcycle beyond the still-functioning water tower had given me, I at last found the camp cemetery, which had been declared a national historic site, but something was wrong. The little boy was riding his bike behind the station, heading in my direction on the sidewalk. He smiled sweetly and broadly at me from a distance, and wanted to strike up a conversation. Except, I couldn't understand a word of his babble. I smiled back at him, but I was afraid to reciprocate his gesture of friendship. The child's frightened mother must be watching from behind the louvers, I thought. I could feel it. It made my hair stand on end. I'd rather miss the train, I thought, than stand here, and so I walked some distance away from the station. But in order to do so, I had to pass by another building that had belonged to the camp at one time, the commander of the guard had lived there, possibly Gaston Delache, who worked for the Resistance, had lived there as well. It was the place where, on my first day, a man of my own age sicced his dog on me because of an innocent question. When he heard it, the rake he was using to loosen the soil of the flower bed got stuck halfway, he called the dog by its name and must have said something like go get him. I don't know what words the French use to turn a dog on someone, and so I couldn't have understood.

There and back, twice a day I had to pass the fence of the former commander's building and the taller buildings for the staff. The dog did not forget. On every blessed day and every blessed occasion, as soon as he spotted me, he started raging behind the fence, and in his rage followed me along its full length. He raged even when I decided to walk on the other side of the Route nationale 20, in the stink of the gasoline and the noise of the trucks, to avoid this beast and his snarling bark, his bared teeth and clenching jaws.

Captain Gaston Delache may not have lived in Le Vernet d'Ariège, but in nearby Saverdun, through which the ample waters of the mountain river also rushed. I tried to find out but to no avail. The captain had two daughters, Jacqueline and Michêle, we know this from the unpublished diary that their friend Andrée Roou wrote in 1944. Jacqueline and Andrée are the best of friends. Their teacher is called Madame Dreuil, and the girls admire her because she is strict but fair. She arranged for those of their schoolmates who because of the restrictions and the small rations would have nothing to eat to get their meals at school, from noon until two. A woman by the name of Jannette helps serve their meals. She is a fine woman, Andrée writes, and they are close to sacrificing themselves for the sake of the children. The way this young girl writes her diary is nothing short of admirable. She begins with a historical summary, then in just a couple of sentences, presents a clear picture of the German-occupied region, the *zone libre*, with all its secret social and societal movements, a region that has lost any semblance of its former liberty. She saw the Germans march past with their armored vehicles and trucks to close the Spanish border. They have a third friend as well, Pierrette Rouziès, the daughter of the ever-shouting carpenter. Together they make up the girls' brigade. Their motto is secrecy, friendship, fidelity. Every day during recess, they meet the boys' brigade by the fence. The boys' brigade is led by Henri Maurette, Andrée's friend, who is two years her senior. The boys' brigade includes some of the older boys, too, because Henri has a seventeen- and a twenty-year-old brother, whose parents passed their farm in Piquetalent on to them so they could tend the soil there for themselves. André Saint-Martin, the gendarme's son, and Maurice Durin, the physician's son, are also members of the boys' brigade. Andrée's father owns a garage, while her mother is the superintendent of the post office in Saverdun. Christmas vacation is over, Andrée is getting ready because the following day, on January 3, which falls on a Monday, she must go back to school. She got an orange and some chocolates for Christmas, which she's reluctant to unwrap. At the fence Maurice Durin says that before he set off to school, he was in the room adjacent to his father's office and he heard a woman's voice, it was Madame Duffieux, the dentist's wife, telling his father that the Gestapo was coming to arrest him and their lieutenant as well. I saw your father, Andrée blurts at the fence, he came to tell my father that the Gestapo are coming to arrest him, but he saw that they'd already taken a part of his car to stop him from fleeing.

My father said they should leave quickly, he would take him wherever he wanted to go.

But who is this certain lieutenant, Henri Maurette, the others asked. To which Pierrette responded that the lieutenant must be her father, and she went white as a sheet. They came over to our house many times at night, and they spoke in a whisper. I saw it coming. Pierrette won't be coming to school on Tuesday.

On Friday, Andrée sees her approach and she hurries to talk to her. Everyone from the boys' yard runs up to the fence to ask about her.

She has no good news to share with them. She can't sleep at night, she says, she's too agitated. Maurice Durin says that when the Germans came to their house and found only his mother there, they started questioning her, but she kept repeating that she didn't know, she had no idea where her husband went, and they left her and rushed off. They came to our house, too, Pierrette says, at ten at night, eight Germans with a Frenchman. They questioned my mother about my father's whereabouts. They stuck a gun in her belly, but she just kept repeating that she didn't know anything. He must be in hiding someplace. Tell us where he is hiding. I don't know anything. Which exasperated the Frenchman, who slapped my mother's face with his gloves.

Oh, the pigs, the boys on the other side of the fence shouted, how can they strike a defenseless woman so she'll rat on her husband. Who do they think they are.

When I first arrived at the station of Le Vernet d'Ariège and got off the train, I really wasn't thinking anything. I stood in the unaccustomed silence of nature as if in the silent interval of history. I knew I had arrived, I'm here, this is what I wanted, I wanted to be here and I'm never leaving here again, and against my will and to my profound sense of shame, I began to cry.

For a long time, perhaps until I was thirty, but in any case, for a very long time, try as I might, I couldn't understand what anything meant in this vast shared history of ours. What does Le Vernet mean. Now I know. It means alder, alder wood. Also, it took a mighty effort on my part to keep up with who interprets what and in what way. I wasn't naïve. I knew everything as a child, just as these children from Le Vernet or Saverdun had known everything years before. What I saw back then, and the situation, too, had said plenty about the state of things, but for the most part, I didn't understand their words, I couldn't make sense of them as others clearly did, and this pertained not only to foreign languages because I couldn't even parse them in my own. To this day I must wage a desperate struggle to understand words that others use with ease.

For instance, for a long time, a very long time, when I was a child, the mystery of what goodness might mean gave me a veritable headache.

These wartime children standing by the fence know just about everything, things that theoretically they can't possibly know. They know that Pierrette's father, the constantly yelling carpenter, had hidden arms in the ground and that he and Dr. Durin may have sneaked across the Spanish border. They know that someone had been sent to Pamiers to conduct three young men across the border. They know that they can't be safe on the other side of the border, but they also know that they can't stay here. Louis Maurette, Pierrette's uncle, for instance, had to flee from Saverdun to Foix and from there to El Serrat and then on to Andorra, but as soon as he crossed the border, the Francoists caught him, they threw him in jail, then he fled to Casablanca, and from there to Algiers, and he'll be coming back with a liberation army. They will begin by dropping reconnaissance paratroopers. They listen to London radio, they know that they must wait for a single sentence. *Les mimosas sont en fleur.* The mimosas are in bloom. They know that a woman can't be weak, she can't admit anything even if she knows everything, not even if they torture her. Dr. Durin's wife knew everything, too. They came back and questioned her until dawn, and after a while Dr. Durin's mother, Marie, started screaming, leave her be, she doesn't know anything. She knows nothing. Meanwhile, in the adjacent room, Maurice Durin was crying all night because he was so afraid for his father, and he told the others at the fence about this, too. They argued over whether they'd throw only the men in jail and then drag them off to Germany, or the women and children as well, and then André Saint-Martin, the gendarme's son, bent on parading his knowledge, comforted them by saying no, they're definitely not taking the women and children, whereupon Jacqueline Delache, the daughter of the commander of the guard at Le Vernet internment camp, said that that's not what she hears from her father, they've already dragged off several women, they're being dragged off en masse.

I felt anxious, to say the least, I felt anxious whenever I thought about all the damage I'd be causing in the interest of my goodness. I must act like a hero, the sort of hero who will rat even on his parents if it should turn out that his parents are traitors. My anxiety was not unfounded, because they finally caught me out. But not for what I had expected in line with the rules of logic. Not when I was bent on satisfying one or another of my cruel little inclinations but failed or at least failed to control them to some extent, at least, and not when I failed to hold my stubbornness in check and this made me very happy; they caught me out when I held it in check, because I wanted to be good. For instance, they said I'm a coward that can't say boo to a goose, and why didn't I fight back. But I didn't fight back because I wanted to be good. Why don't I say what I think. How will I become a straightforward person. I can't let people beat me up. If one beats me up today, tomorrow they will all beat me up. I must fight for what I think is right. Except, I didn't understand this either, this straightforward person, but more so, this what I think is right, apparently, this right is my personal property, and also, how am I supposed to fight for what I think is right in a way that is right. I mustn't say everything I think, sincerity and openness have their limits. This, at least, I understood right away, except I was at a loss to apply it, because I didn't know where to look for the limits of a general concept. Being visual, I decided that such a limit can surely be gauged somehow. I don't necessarily have to lie, I can just keep quiet, they said. Be courageous, but not reckless, think before you act, but do not be a coward. Think first, weigh the consequences, and act only then. Know why you do something. You must know it even if you bang your head against the wall. And they laughed. At least, I understood their laughter.

You must account for your deeds and accept the consequences of your decisions with equanimity. And don't complain. Complaining is out of the question.

When they said that I must compose myself, I was again at a loss. I knew that a musician composes music. But how can I compose myself. This, too, puzzled me.

On this particular Friday by the fence, Jacqueline Delache also told them that the Germans had dragged off forty Jewish children from Château de la Hille to take them to a concentration camp in

Germany. At which, the corners of her lips were trembling with the effort to hold back her tears, Pierrette said that no one ever comes back from there. But why children, Lysou, the youngest girl in the group, asked. Because, the older children explained, Hitler hates Jews and wants to have all of them killed. But that's disgusting. Children can't defend themselves. Andrée Roou explained to her that the Germans are racists, they think they're perfect and everyone else is evil, but that the Jews are the worst of all. Lysou clearly understood the explanation, but asked in despair, is there no one then to protect these children from being dragged off. Yes, there is, Jacqueline Delache said. The director of the Château de la Hille came to talk to my father and the camp commander, they met all day, and came up with all sorts of tricks to stop the Vichy government from allowing the children to be taken to Germany and have them handed over to the Swiss Red Cross instead, but in the meantime, the director should be allowed to take her charges back to Pailhès. According to the diary, the children at the fence gave the director an ovation for not letting the children in her care be taken off.

Then the following day, on Saturday, Henri, the leader of the boys' brigade, met Pierrette and Maurice at the fence with the good news that they don't have to worry, their fathers were not caught, they're with them out on the farm in Piquetalent. The same day they learned that the sentence they'd been waiting for had been broadcast by London radio during the eight o'clock news.

The mimosas are in bloom.

I couldn't begin to imagine when and what I should be doing in the interest of my goodness. So I'd understand the nature of goodness, my father took me to the bathroom once and with the help of a rubber tube filled with water he demonstrated the law of communicating vessels over the bathtub. He may not have intended it as a lesson in ethics, but that's how I thought of it. If you raise it here, it will flow out there, it can't be helped; meaning that there's no action that won't have an immediate reaction and counterreaction. Or there's the time my Uncle Pista, the chemist, gave me an old chemist's kit for Christmas that was in a wooden box divided into two big compartments, and right away, my father showed me how two things in a test tube can conjure a third. On these snowy evenings and tranquil Sunday mornings, he dazzled me with his demonstrations, some of which made me feel as if I were being given the answer to how the love of two people would conjure a third. They'd explained it to me before, my mother openly, my father more circumstantially, but I never understood. Two people love each other and embrace. *Na, sag schon,* my grandmother Cecília Nussbaum would have said in Péterfy Sándor Street, you don't say, yet another thing whose meaning escaped me. They also explained that as a consequence of her love, my mother carried me beneath her heart. Which was supposed to mean that even before I was born, I was close to her heart. But on that Christmas Eve, I was very close to understanding it, conceiving of the physical and chemical similarities as if, the very next moment, I could understand the essence of the universe.

Grasping something infinite on a single Christmas Eve was a very strange feeling.

We started grasping the infinite by first understanding litmus paper. If I dip the litmus paper in a liquid of my choosing, it will indicate whether the liquid is acidic or alkaline, and do I know which liquid is acidic and which is alkaline. Soap is alkaline, vinegar is acidic. So now I know once and for all what a chemical reaction is. With the help of a color chart, we can determine whether the chemical reaction is weak or strong. Except, for the life of me, I couldn't figure out where the scale came from. How does the paper know what it is supposed to show. I had to accept that these values are based on experience, they're the result of common consent, positioning, and observation. Still, I was full of doubt, my self-respect rebelled, because it was as if I were accepting the arbitrary assertions of strangers. It hurt my desperate need for freedom.

You know that an iron stove is warmer than your body temperature, but you don't have to touch the stove every time you want to make sure the assertion is correct, do you. What an idea.

Clever as I was, I realized that I'd be better off shutting my mouth now and then, and not ask questions and put up a fight and doubt everything all the time. It's enough for me to pretend that I understand. I didn't understand, not a word, but I pretended that I did. On the other hand, because of the pretense, I suddenly understood. But this trick didn't always work. I pretended I understood, I kept nodding my head to get it over with, but I remained in the dark. Some chemical reactions happen only in alkaline and others only in acidic environments, this is why we have to check the pH level with the help of the pH test paper. Actually, the pH test paper was just blotting paper. Still, it had to know something that blotting paper doesn't, because people had put that knowledge inside it somehow. I didn't know what to make of the chemical reaction either when my father explained it to me. People in the family used it against those they condemned. Old reactionary. Reactionary Joe. Senile reactionary. The whole big reactionary bunch. But if every chemical change, whether alkaline or acidic, is reactionary, what am I to do. Without familiarity with their Latin roots, the identity of word forms had me confused. Furthermore, there are materials that do not participate in the chemical reaction, my father explained as we stood over the box bursting with dangerous treasures encased in various sized compartments, and still, a given chemical reaction won't take place without them. Quite by accident, this I understood. These materials are like poor but industrious people, I concluded. They're not pushy, they're not doing their job in hopes of being paid or rewarded. I felt a sense of commiseration and sympathy for the catalysts. We spent days in the bathroom working with these materials. The double decomposition was miraculous. It was even good hearing the word. And it was good carefully heating up the test tubes and flasks over the flames of the Bunsen burner, and measuring the solid materials and the liquid residues. There was also a miniature apothecary's scale in the kit, it had pans carved of horn. We have Lavoisier to thank for the use of scales in chemistry. The sum of the two measurements should theoretically add up to the quantity of the original material. I understood this, too. Except, it never does. I understood this as well. I was familiar with the Bunsen burner from Grandfather Tauber's goldsmith's shop in Holló Street. The esoterics of the metamorphosis and indestructibility of the materials was miraculous. I conceive of it as follows, that every action has a measurable effect. In which case, the weight of good and bad deeds must be measurable as well. But I couldn't ask my father about it, because he was unexpectedly called away because of some serious accident. Something happened somewhere, and he didn't come home for days, and I had to clean everything carefully and place it all back inside the wooden compartments.

But for a long time, a very long time, the various concepts confused me not only because they remained unclarified or because of their equivocal meaning. At times, only the identity in their morphology confused me. Or conversely, a glaring quality or emptiness remained in my interpretation and I didn't understand why others didn't notice or else why they're so credulous of an empty or arbitrary definition. At still other times, the need to decide didn't leave time to reflect. I had to decide right away about the subject or outcome of my decision, in short, the relationships involved in the process. If they strike you, strike back. It sounded simple enough, it was a clear order, but the consequences could not be foreseen every time. Or else they punished me for something I had not committed and had no intention of committing. When this happened, it was as if the whole world had suddenly collapsed on me, burying me underneath the debris.

András and I were supposed to have pulled off Yvette's panties so we could see her you-know-what, and she was supposed to have put up a fight, kicking and striking out at us, and I was strangling her, and I'd better own up, it's no use trying to deny it, her neck and arms are black and blue all over. Whereas we did not pull it down, we did not look at her you-know-what, I didn't even know I was supposed to be curious, how would I have known, and Yvette didn't put up a fight; I couldn't have held her down in the first place, and I didn't try strangling her, I never strangled anyone, ever. None of it was true, I didn't know where they came up with it, and I didn't know what I was supposed to do about my outraged sense of justice.

Yvette was sharp, sad, wild, flaxen-haired, and her hair was cut as short as a boy's. She was supposed to have received a mortal wound, which, except for me, no one took seriously, or couldn't. I didn't understand this for a long time either, this word, *mortal*. Someone who has been mortally wounded can't complain, or if they complain, the wound couldn't have been mortal. But this is how they said it, especially the girls. She's mortally in love. Her mother wounded her mortally by letting her leave Aulnay-sous-Bois and her siblings, while her father, whom the family called Georges, wounded her mortally by disappearing from their lives without a word. He didn't just desert his wife and children to take up with a perfect stranger and get her with child, but sent her here, to the end of the world, to this stranger-than-strange and hateful country, just so she shouldn't be a burden to him. The family said that the similarity between the two of us is especially striking because both of us take after our Mezei grandmother, Klára Mezei. Which explains why we love each other so much. This, too, puzzled me, this *love* was another word I didn't understand. It would have never occurred to me that Yvette and I love each other. I didn't understand what they meant. I don't know why, but I was nevertheless pleased that I looked like these two people close to me, though look as I might, I looked and looked, but I couldn't discover any similarity whatsoever. From what I knew of her, Grandmother Mezei was a worn-out, gray-haired old woman. She had birthed and raised seven children. In the old photographs she wore loosely tailored black dresses of silk. But by then she'd been dead for years. After her oldest son, György, who was studying to be an architect at the Hungarian Royal Joseph University of Technology, committed suicide at the age of twenty-two, she wore nothing but black for twenty years, until she also died. She didn't want to make a point of all that black, it's just that after the year of mourning had passed, she couldn't get herself to discard it. Obviously, she couldn't pretend that she'd forgotten her dead son from one day to the next, she preferred to push the year of mourning out in front of her until she died. She didn't wear her pearls and jewels anymore either, except for a double-stranded obsidian necklace that stood in for jewelry, dark and matte, its beads chiseled into the shape of octahedrons.

To this day, György's death throws the family into such a state of agitation that the mere mention of his name makes everyone cry;

after a hundred years, everyone's lips tremble, though they immediately swallow their tears, they repress them, which produces a yelping sound, a sort of family yelping reserved for grief. I inherited not only the agitated manner, the trembling of the lips, and the yelp, I also inherited the architect student's name as my second name. My Aunt Eugenie's son inherited it as well, and my Aunt Magda's son inherited it, too, but none of this helped. György Nádas was dead. I inherited his first name along with the obligation that I, too, should swallow back my pain, my tears should remain invisible, and I mustn't burden others by crying aloud.

As for the suicide, talking about the reason for it is taboo. It must be wrapped in silence. Worse comes to worst, if I can't help it I can make that yelping sound, but that is all.

My Mezei grandmother was an erudite woman, humble and soft-spoken, who suffered from her voluble, stout, and brutal husband throughout her life, though she did not suffer mortally; still, she never once complained, this is what the stories in the family suggested about her.

Why must you put up with it, Mother, her daughters kept asking. When they pestered her with their questions, their mother modestly lowered her beautiful, quivering lashes, offered a gentle smile, and wrapped herself in eloquent silence. She may have been in love with this man who as a youth had been exceptionally handsome and attractive all his life, which her daughters did not take into consideration, or else did not approve of. They felt humiliated for having so many brothers and sisters, and between themselves they called their father a stud. Although they got nowhere with their mother with their provocations and, compared with the boys, they survived their father's tyranny with lighter injuries. He didn't beat them. My mother kept the heavy black necklace with the double row of beads that my grandmother wore on the photographs in a bonbonnière with a silver lid that was decorated with Grandmother's curlicue monogram. Surely, this was the only curlicue in her entire life. If I asked why this uncle whom I never knew, this uncle called György whose name I inherited as my second given name, why he had killed himself, my mother's lips trembled, but she would not answer me. She was at home, she was just ten when it happened. She gave no answer, though just once she said, a broken heart. She didn't say that he did it because of a broken heart, she purposefully kept her answer brief. A broken heart. As if he'd killed himself for a mere trifle. This manner of answering me was identical to the manner in which my Aunt Özsi answered her daughter Vera when she, too, asked. A broken heart. Which meant, stop asking. So Vera also stopped asking. Nevertheless, whenever I saw my chance, I would ask again. Once my Aunt Magda avoided a straight answer by taking a different approach. He was a very strange boy, she said, a very withdrawn boy, and their father kept tormenting him relentlessly for every little thing. He did things that boys don't usually do. In any case, it was not customary.

But what did he do, what is it that boys don't usually do, I asked. Deep in thought, she turned her head, and because of the repressed yelp and the profound shame, even after so many years, her lips trembled as she answered. For instance, he liked embroidery, and I could tell that she'd never said this to anyone before, he liked sitting with Miss Júlia and our mother, and they did embroidery together. Our mother didn't mind, but if our father caught him at it, he flew into a rage. He learned to darn socks from our mother and he was every bit as good at it as she was. He helped our mother darn things. And she said all this with so much resentment, even after so many years, she said it with such disgust as if she were her own detested mother, and she shared the common view that a boy must not do something like that. A boy must not darn socks with his mother. As for me, from this I understood that they had killed him collectively, even though it took several more decades before I understood what had made them do it.

Yvette didn't look like Klára Mezei, our dead grandmother, at all. Or possibly just her chin and her thin, dramatic eyelids. By now I can see the physical resemblance among the three of us, but back then I couldn't. All three Mezei girls had the same chin and the same translucent, dramatic lids. Children see the essence and so they don't pay attention to individual physical characteristics, but rather to the person who bears them. Yvette was always up in arms, she raged, she was easily upset and was quick to take offense, she was not one to hold herself back from redressing an affront. She was much stronger and two years older than I, and nearly a head taller. Three times a week, she went from Teréz Boulevard for her swimming practice at the Sports Pool on Margaret Island. She went to do her laps, as she called them. At the pool she got used to fighting with boys stronger than herself. She told me to go out to Margaret Island, too, to do laps, this was the expression for it, to do laps, an activity I didn't trust, just as I didn't trust the expression, but I nevertheless went along once or twice, making sure that the expression should never slip my lips. Spit. Mucus. Whatever they coughed up, they spat in the pool. They pissed in the pool. They slammed their snot into the pool. In the shower room they even pissed on one another. When you went to Margaret Island, you went out to Margaret Island, but I wouldn't say that either, and so I went to Margaret Island. But once there, Yvette barely acknowledged my presence. I couldn't understand her. Why did she ask me there. As if I weren't her cousin. True, I wasn't her first cousin, because her father was my first cousin. As far as I was concerned, this first cousin was also a vague concept, there was something suspicious about it, not only because combined words were always doubly problematic for me, but because Grandmother Tauber always emphasized that Elemér, about whom we do not speak, was her first cousin, and that he brought great shame on the family when he ran from Kálvária Square all the way to Csepel. Also, Yvette didn't have a moment to spare for me before practice, because the big boys wouldn't leave her alone for a second, they chased her around the big outdoor pool in groups, they blocked her escape routes, but she adroitly slipped through their clutches, and once when they caught her all the same and forced her to the ground, with her wet body she managed to slip through their wet bodies like a lizard and ran up the steps of the bleachers.

When I went down to the pool the second time, this is how they said it, come down to the Sports Pool, I'll ask the coach to try you out and then you can come with me and do laps, she said, meaning for training, I can go with her for training, we met on these steps, but she ran past me without a word, and she wasn't even being chased.

How could I have pulled down her panties. But we did have one thing in common, though; she wasn't obedient either, just like me, and would cause mischief where and when she could, just like me.

I'm stubborn, how can I be so stubborn, my parents and my teachers asked, and Rózsi Németh, my godmother asked, too, but she laughed at my stubbornness, she was happy that I'd become an obstinate Calvinist, just like her.

Why must I always do the opposite of everything, I'm stubborn, obstinate, stubborn as a mule.

But that's just it. How was I supposed to know why I'm stubborn, why are they asking me. They're the ones who should know. Also, if that's the way I am, how can I be otherwise. Or how can both of us resemble Klára Mezei if they say we're nowhere as meek and patient as she was in her life, which was tailored to her willingness to serve. Yvette, at least, knew how to appear like a quiet young girl, easily hurt. Whereas she loved provoking others, except she went about it underhandedly. I felt anxious because of my stubbornness, while she relished hers, she laughed for joy. I couldn't make her out. How does she do it. She pretended to be the opposite of what she was. I, on the other hand, would have sincerely liked to be different, I wanted it wholeheartedly, or at least pretended so others would be satisfied with me, but the truth is I couldn't decide which styles of behavior I should choose in the interest of my aim, as if, in the interest of my goodness, I were free to be anything I liked, except I'm not anything, and so I must pretend. Pretend like my cousin. In my eagerness and especially in my need for love, which, let us admit it, is a basic human need, I began to try on various roles; in my imagination, I slipped into all sorts of other possibilities. Roles for girls, roles for boys. I tried out what I'd be like as an explorer, because as an explorer I could find a corner of the earth that hasn't been discovered yet. I packed up my small knapsack, a shirt, underclothes, a towel, and some snacks, but Rózsi Németh heard the cautious click of the front door and brought me back from the stairs. What would it be like if I were the boy Mozart, I tried this out as well. In a flurry of ecstasy I played on my aunt's piano in Dembinszky Street, until she came into the room from the kitchen demanding that

I stop, it's unbearable. What I'm doing is ridiculous. She'll gladly teach me, but I must promise I'll never give a repeat performance. Taken aback, I sat on the piano stool for a bit, but the effect of the scene stayed with me for some time. Probably, she wasn't worried about her piano, she was giving me fair warning in the name of her profession.

Yvette did not try on strange roles; on the contrary, other people's suggestions or objections clearly annoyed and irritated her. She puckered up her lips and, breathing through her nose, she said she couldn't care less, she said *merde* and *putain*, as her repressed rage nearly made her burst at the seams.

But Yvette could enjoy even her rage.

To reach the pool, she had to take the number 6 tram at the Oktogon, get off in the middle of the bridge at the entrance to the island, take the stairs under the bridge, and come up the other side, but she proudly said to me that she doesn't always do that, she sometimes violates her grandmother's strict orders, and from the traffic island where the tram stops, she runs to the other side, despite the traffic. She enjoyed breaking rules, and when she succeeded she was elated, she literally shouted for joy, or else, if she kept her emotions to herself, she blushed for joy. Actually, everything made her blush. I couldn't have pulled off her panties even if I'd wanted to. But I didn't want to, I didn't understand why I should have wanted to, or how I ended up in this awkward situation and why I should have to make excuses for something that never occurred to me, not in a million years. If this can happen, then it can also happen that I am not who I think I am. Or else it's the other way around, and my real name is on some false papers somewhere, and the name I have on my real papers because of my parents' lies is my false name, and that's not who I am. For a long time, a very long time, the thought that all these complications about understanding things have their roots in uncertainty tortured me. I am not who I am. How can I prove that I did not do something. I didn't understand this either. Something did not happen, I didn't do it. It would have never occurred to me at the time that my favorite cousin had made up the whole thing, that she'd been saying things to my favorite aunt about me that had no basis, and I do mean no basis, in fact.

On the other hand, why would Yvette have done it when she told me about every one of her grievances in detail, grievances that I couldn't understand, not even with the best of intentions. It wasn't my idea that we should be on such intimate terms with each other; it was her idea that we should have no secrets between us. Only girls would want to be this open with one another. It comes over them like a sensual tempest. Boys would never think of it, they're too busy with what they should hide from the other members of the species, and how they should go about hiding it. Boys act up in front of the girls, and they act up in front of one another as well. In front of the girls they pretend to be tame and gentle, and in front of the boys, they play rough. Even though I saw that I'm definitely not like the girls, I never considered myself like the boys either. For a long time I didn't even ask myself what gender I was; I didn't ask not because I was that dumb, but because it was clear as day to me that I'm identical with my gender. It had never occurred to me earlier that we have secrets to share or why we should have secrets, or why we should tell each other everything, and I do mean everything. It was clear that the word *secret* had some special meaning for just about everyone around me. When they told secrets, they lowered their voices and whispered in one another's ear. In the name of sincerity, they lied or distorted the facts. They knew that I knew, yet they said something different in front of me so they should preserve their great secret, which they would nevertheless eagerly reveal to others. Decades passed before I found the key to the fascination people felt for secrets and appearances. A secret is something like a family's bank account or a state's gold reserves or the silver coins hidden in a leaky pan in the earth, you can dig it up, you can use it for business and you can use it for blackmail, but only provided that the semblance of secrecy remains intact. People pretend they didn't know. Amid great vows of secrecy, Yvette even confided her great secret to me, that it's not me she's in love with. Again, I was baffled, though I said nothing because she was two years older and she was a girl, so she must know what she's talking about. It was up to me to figure her out and to figure out the reason she should have fallen in love with me in the first place, then change her mind. Her secrets surfaced from the depths of her being accompanied by some form of anger unfamiliar to me, anger that came hissing like a serpent from her very soul. She can't stand it that she's not allowed to wear a bra at the pool, and she has to appear without one in front of Andris Gönczi. It's bad enough that her parents banished her from their lives, sending her to this strange country where, except for her grandfather, no one, and she means no one, speaks proper French, and as for her grandmother, she gets on her nerves. And worst of all, they're assaulting her in her femininity by making her go to a barber instead of a hairdresser. Okay, fine, Vilma Ligeti speaks decent French. And it's no use protesting, Granny, please, not there, let's not cut it short like a boy, not so short. And she's forced to swim in a pair of knickers and run around the pool like the boys.

Boys don't take their pants off either to reveal their dicks, in which case, why can't she wear a bra, it's beyond her comprehension, she swears. *Merde*.

It made my head reel, *dick, prick, dipstick, balls*, it was remarkable that I first heard these beautiful poolside words in my mother tongue from her, and never before from anyone, I knew only *cunt* from before; at first I thought they were French words whose meaning escapes me. It took at least twenty years until I understood at long last what people mean by *balls*. The testicles don't look like balls, there are no testicles that look like balls. The use of the word *cunt* was no less a mystery, because they sometimes used it to mean ass, at other times the female genitals. I was truly at a loss, even though this is how they talked at the Sports Pool on Margaret Island. I had been teaching her Hungarian, but these words she'd picked up at the Sports Pool; she'd brought the words *prick, cunt*, and *balls* straight from the pool, and so, to this day, in my mind these words are related much more to doing laps than to the body parts that they signify. Still, I didn't like the fact that in their language, everything is *merde* and *putain*. Besides *whore* and *shit*, I was also familiar with *tough shit*. She'd hardly arrived, and by the following day we were standing on the bank of the Danube in Leányfalu under the weeping willows, where my Uncle Pali and Aunt Magda had a summer place that the Government Commission for Abandoned

Property had given them. At 3:20 in the afternoon the paddle wheeler *Petőfi* sailed upstream, but the people just called it the market boat because the market women of nearby Nagymaros and Dömös headed back home on it from Pest and Buda with their empty baskets. On the other hand, the real market boats didn't have names. I pointed and said *boat*, at which she gave a throaty shout, choking with anger as usual, no, no, her protest even made her cheeks turn red, *bateau*, and so on, each of us defending a single word of our own mother tongue to the last breath, *boat, bateau, boat, bateau*, until the sound of the approaching boat smothered our shouts. We enjoyed it, we laughed at each other's pointless emotion, we enjoyed knowing that the other's language is so infinitely stubborn and ridiculous. She learned Hungarian with ease, in just a couple of months, while I, in our great linguistic competition, learned barely any French. *Demi*, I did learn *demi*. We kept an eye on the clock, and when the *demi onze* approached, we hurried down to the river, eager not to miss the wake of the *Kossuth*.

We were allowed to go down to the river alone, but because of the current, we weren't allowed to go in more than knee-deep. But we went in anyway, we swam against the waves, we swam close to the paddles, it was wonderful, the clatter of the paddles was formidable, we swam into the backwash, even the strongest backwashes. I wouldn't have done it alone, but with her I'd do just about anything. She was brave without reflection, actually, she was reckless, and there was hardly anything that didn't make her rebel.

Fortunately, her grandmother never found out that her soft-spoken and fragile little granddaughter was crazy about currents and backwashes, and also what a wild woman she was. She looks for the largest and most dangerous currents with the older boys, and in Leányfalu, there were plenty of them to be found. She didn't insist that I go along. She went by herself or in the company of the older boys from the village. Though the water seemed innocent enough from the shore, the most dangerous currents swirled just upstream from the dock. The surface of the water veritably swelled in gigantic, oval patches, as if it weren't even water, but a thick yellowish gray, creamy substance bubbling up from the depths around the swells. You could spread it on bread. She let the swirling mass of water drag her down into the depths and pushed off from there.

I couldn't have been more than five when, in Balatonlelle one summer, my mother taught me how to swim and breathe evenly. I was a good swimmer, I swam impressive lengths without letting up, but I lacked daring. And so in Leányfalu I felt ashamed and gave the gigantic oval patches with the thick, yellowish gray creamy substance bubbling up around the edges a wide berth. Except, to really give it a wide berth, I had to swim out to the middle of the river, where the current and the river's depth were truly intimidating. Still, I found the current less intimidating than the eddy. Just once, I went with her of my own accord, and we swam right into the most dangerous part of the river, and then, in an unguarded moment, I came too close to the big swirling masses, because I followed her blindly and ignored the danger signs on the surface of the water. We were heading for a shallow just above the dock; this shallow was our great discovery that summer; we spent hours on this big shallow overgrown with patches of grass, but the current caught us and there was no turning back. When this happens it is best not to fight it, this is what the boys from the village said about the current, you have to let the eddy pull you down by the soles of your feet, this is what the oldest of the boys had advised. And indeed, the experience was phenomenal every time. The water sucked me in with a mighty force, as if I were slipping down the river's gullet, though not without trying to keep my dignity, but in the depths there followed a long, a very long pause. There was also more light down there than near the surface. This, too, puzzled me. Where did all the light come from so suddenly down there, a blond hovering gleam on the tranquil, sandy bed of the river strewn with rocks and pebbles. I can still see it all in this gleaming wave of bobbing light, the translucent seaweed swaying in the current on its edges, and the crystal clear, gleaming riverbed with the pebbles and larger stones, and against the soles of my feet the stony riverbed, a sharp collision, my body weighed down by the mighty mass of water. It was magical, it was ethereal, it was an eternity to which a person willingly surrenders.

I knew from these older boys that when this happens, you must push off with all your might.

The water mesmerized me. I gulped it down. I kept my eyes open. I had learned to swim before I was five, and for twenty-five years, until the Danube turned into a swill of blanket weed, I continued swimming with my eyes open. I hadn't seen her for some time, either on the water's surface or in its depths. Nowhere. I looked around for her in vain. I couldn't hear anything. Never was there such a silky flow of inarticulate silence.

At that moment I suddenly understood the older boys' strict warning. Do not stay with the water. Because I would have gladly remained there, the urge to turn into a fish was so overwhelming, or a stone, a blanket weed, the blond light, and be gently carried along by the current. Kick yourself free with all your might. Each of us must kick ourselves free of our own profound fascination with death. Or else remain. Yvette enjoyed it, too, she let herself stay underwater for a long time. She maneuvered her legs so she could stay there.

I never again did it on purpose and went to great lengths to avoid it.

Yvette was an avid reader, and so was I; she read all the time, she read on the tram, she even read standing up, she read everything she could get her hands on in her grandfather's impressive library in French, and she read a lot in Hungarian as well. The old man had amazing books; he didn't have to collect books, the books attached themselves to him; he read all the time, he translated, edited, reviewed. The books arrived in big parcels. We got our books in big parcels as well. We must have enjoyed some sort of buying privilege. In those years, both of us read an appreciable number of books, mostly classics. We were terribly fastidious. We fell for a particular author and not literature as such or even the act of reading as such, and if we found an author we liked, we hastened to tell each other about it. Our tastes, though, were miles apart. We neglected to take into account the two-year advantage she had over me, though the truth is that I made sure she wouldn't think of me as a stupid little adolescent. If an author fell into our net, we read every book of his we could find. We made a sport of it. I was ten when I first read all of Molière's plays in the Hungarian deluxe edition, though I wouldn't go so far as to say that I understood them completely, so when I finished them, I read them all over again. Each was an object lesson in human behavior. We'd inherited beautiful deluxe editions from Grandmother Mezei's and our poor Gyurika's library, partly in the original languages, partly in Hungarian translation.

I remember Yvette reading lots of Dickens, she was fanciful and enjoyed clever acts of evil, while I read all the Jules Verne and Walter Scott books I could get my hands on; in the former I enjoyed submerging myself in the adventures of knowledge, in the latter the raging forces of nature, but she thumbed her nose at these writers, she considered my interest in them so much boyish nonsense. For my part, I was bored by the monotony of human evil, which continues to bore me to this day. Just think of Molière and how circumspect he is in presenting evil and how he weighs things in the balance, even in Harpagon's case, how he portions it only so that he should then go all out, but by then he's not interested in the force of evil, but with man's obsession with objects, I can't think of a better expression, man's pathological object fixation. There is probably much evil in the world, Molière must have seen his share of evil himself, but literature never thinks in terms of singular objects and phenomena, it thinks in constellations. In any event, I am more interested in flights of the imagination and of science. I read Pushkin's demented late-romantic works many times, I couldn't get enough of them, we read them together, too, *Dubrovsky* and *The Blackamoor of Peter the Great*, though she much preferred the just-published *Eugene Onegin*. We were glad that Tolstoy had written so much. I still can't believe how quickly we finished reading the works of Gogol, Goncharov, and Turgenev. *Dead Souls* and *Oblomov* affected us greatly. Without their humor, I'd be at a loss to understand the majority of human behavior to this day. We both agreed on the value we placed on the insights of the classical Russian writers. Only by reading the Russians can one glean an understanding of the pettiness of man, his ridiculous ambition, his fear of hunger and ridicule, in short, his elemental need of his fellows. Only Flaubert and possibly Balzac can measure up to them in their understanding of human nature.

I recall only one instance when my father interfered in our mutual literary quest. I was about to launch into a novel by Dostoyevsky that Yvette had recommended, when, seeing what I'd taken off the shelf, my father commented that it would be more sensible to put it aside for now. If I remember correctly, it was *The Devils, Demons* in an earlier translation, and I think I chose it as my introduction to Dostoyevsky because of the title. I was put out by restrictions of all kinds. Why shouldn't I read it. Because not only would you not understand a lot of things, you'd think you understand, but you'd misunderstand, which is even more dangerous for your mind. It was not a prohibition but a comment about methodology, and besides, I was already well acquainted with the dangers of misunderstanding; I couldn't get my bearings in its labyrinths and mazes, and the more I wanted to find a way out, the more entangled I became, and so I left Dostoyevsky for later. We owned the complete works of Dostoyevsky bound in crimson cloth. I read the unedited translations, and at the age of eighteen or nineteen, I turned to them and devoured them on endless summer nights. Still too soon. Dawn was breaking. I had had at most two hours left to sleep. There I sat in the room of the apartment on Teréz Boulevard looking out on the yard with the last two sentences of *Crime and Punishment* playing in my mind. Namely, that the gradual renewal of a man is the beginning of a new story, the story of his passing from one world into another, where he will have to learn new forms of action, and so the writer ends the present story. Today I am sorry that despite the bad or erroneous Hungarian translations I did not read these books earlier. Had I read *Demons* despite our father's caution, had I read it with this title, perhaps I would have understood more of the Catholic roots and psychological forms that the international Communist movement took, more of the catastrophic group psychology awaiting the social-responsibility-minded participants of the twentieth century, and then my parents' broodings and battles might not have remained so distant and incomprehensible for so long, and perhaps I'd have understood their early deaths better, too.

Of the more recent writers we loved Gorky, Ostrovsky, Bunin, and Alexei Tolstoy very much, too. Tolstoy was Yvette's discovery. I also read every Mór Jókai I could get hold of and was dreaming about acquiring the old collected works, composed of one hundred volumes. But Yvette gave Jókai a wide berth. My parents wanted to buy me the hundred-volume collected works, but could find only individual volumes. Yvette preferred Kálmán Mikszáth and Zsigmond Móricz, and so I read all the Mikszáth and Móricz novels I could find. When we went for ice cream in the summer in Leányfalu, we rode our bikes past Móricz's well-tended apple orchard, and also, in spring, Móricz's former gardener, who was now working for Móricz's daughter, Virág, came to work for us as well. I knew that in the evening Jókai had played tarokk with our great-grandfather Mezei and Prime Minister Tisza; I even found our great-grandfather, who was also friends with Kálmán Mikszáth, popping up as one of the characters in his *New Zrínyiád*. Our great-grandfather was a colleague of his in the House of Deputies, and in the book, he is portrayed with forbearance rather than his usual sharp humor. This was an exceptional literary surprise that made me curious about the technique of writing novels, observing how the author's imagination distances itself from reality, or when and for what purpose he uses his own life, what he takes from it, and when. It was interesting to observe the various writers from this perspective as well, to see, for instance, how a real-life great-grandfather ends up in a novel.

It was done, I would become a writer, though I never let on. I prepared for it in secret. Also, it was flattering that my great-grandfather, her great-great-grandfather, was in *New Zrínyiád*, but that didn't make either of us like the book any better.

We were immersed in literature in other ways as well. We'd heard that this great-grandfather, Mór Mezei, who in this long-gone conservative-liberal Hungarian world was her great-great-grandfather and thus even more distant to her, also wrote several books with a political theme, but the family did not consider him a writer, just as they did not consider his younger brother, Ernő, a writer. Yet for a while Ernő was not only a politician and a writer on politics, he was also known as a writer of serious *belles lettres*, even poems. *Wanderings Under the Italian Sky*, his first foray into literature, stood among my parents' other books; it was bound between light brown, shiny fabric covers embellished in gold. Because of its intriguing title I started it over and over, and had to force myself to read it to the end. In the interest of aesthetics, Ernő strove for circuitous, overly ornate sentences that, however, defeated the sense time and time again. When I read *Wanderings* as a child, the one scene that stuck in my mind was when the young author looks up Lajos Kossuth, then living in exile in Turin, and they talk about urgent public matters, the Austro-Hungarian compromise, the debate over constitutional law that followed it, the participants in political life, and their feelings and passions. A certain Colonel Ihász led Ernő into the house and garden where the aging Kossuth lived. I was especially taken with the description of the rose-lined path that led to the house nestled in the garden's depths. Kossuth's rhetoric had also impressed me. I found his collected speeches among my parents' books and could recite some from memory.

For decades to come, I especially enjoyed reciting the opening accord of the speech he delivered in the House of Deputies on July 11, 1848.

Gentlemen! As I ascend this pulpit to call upon you to save the Homeland, the awesome gravity of the moment weighs heavily upon my chest.

Especially this weighs heavily upon my chest.

Ernő Mezei describes Kossuth as someone free of prejudice, and he is impressed that Kossuth is invariably judicious when faced with views and notions different from his own. Ernő Mezei's book also disappeared in all our moving about, neither could Mór's works of nonfiction and his political brochures be found, which is not surprising, since the moment had come in Hungarian history when the liberal spirit and striving for independence, passed down from generation to generation, disappeared once and for all. On June 16, 1944, on orders from Government Commissioner Mihály Kolosváry-Borcsa, they confiscated the works of one hundred and twenty Hungarian writers and one hundred and thirty foreign writers from the various libraries. This meant 447,627 volumes that made up the cargo of twenty-two freight wagons. The freight was taken to Csepel, where, under pomp and circumstance, in the presence of the government commissioner and the German cultural attaché, they were pulped. Even as children we knew that Mór Mezei's and Ernő Mezei's books were part of the shipment. *Pulped*, this word was also a novelty, and my father availed himself of the opportunity and explained to me all about paper mills, the methods of recycling used paper and rags, the cellulose content of a living tree, the manufacture of paper, the nature of hand-dipped paper and watermarks, and as he did so, he surely took the edge off the dismay he felt over the pulped books.

The confiscation and pulping of the books was successful, the list of titles has survived, but the books themselves can no longer be found.

Yvette even became personally involved with literature. The writer Zsuzsa Thury made her the model for the main character of her book *The French Girl*, written for adolescents. It was a bestseller for years. But Yvette couldn't have cared less, and this impressed me. I read it, and to tell the truth, there was not much one could say about it. On the other hand, I'd have liked to find out what was real in the story, and what was made up, but she shrugged it off. If it's a book meant for adolescents, it should be adventurous. She much preferred *Red Shoulder Straps*, the Soviet novel for young adults, which, despite my best intentions, I could not finish. Still, in order to please her I decided that just like the heroes in the book, I would enroll in a military academy, go to Moscow, and become an army officer. In the genre of the Soviet novel of morals, *Private Aleksandr Matrosov* was my favorite. The novel told of a young peasant lad who at the end of the story saves the lives of his comrades when he crawls to a German machine-gun nest and uses his body to shield them. His self-sacrifice surprised and fascinated me, it seemed Christlike. I read the Bible in secret, I didn't even tell Yvette.

My Aunt Magda, who, and I never quite got used to the thought, was at the same time Yvette's grandmother, wrote books herself. She wrote novels as well as history books. But Vilma Ligeti, her closest friend who was also a writer, thought as little of them as she did of the books for girls. All right, fine, so Magda writes, we mustn't overlook this little weakness of hers, but we mustn't take it too seriously either, it's nothing but journalism in disguise. However, she was mistaken.

They met in Paris when they were both refugees there, but after the German-Soviet Pact was made public, they screamed bloody murder at each other, which fueled their perpetual arguments about politics. My aunt and uncle didn't get themselves as worked up over these arguments as Vilma, who knew no bounds, because they thought that Vilma was actually a charming little woman, this is how my Uncle Pali characterized her, but neither he nor my Aunt Magda went further than that, preferring not to say anything about her intellectual gifts or lack thereof. The resistance movement brought them together again. Vilma was inordinately proud of the effortless construction of her Frenchified sentences, about which, with a dismissive wave of the hand, her friend Magda just said *pimf*, by which the people of Pest meant a shoddy affair, facile, beneath notice. If they said of anyone or anything that they're *pimf*, they didn't have to say it twice, there was no need to finish the sentence. But they were wrong. Vilma's style was a pleasant blend of the commercial and the quotidian portioned out with impressive musicality, even if the situations themselves were clichéd to their core, and so it lent a certain quality to her texts that couldn't be dismissed with a simple wave of the hand. Years later Françoise Sagan favored this commercial, music-enhanced, and masterfully mundane style of writing, though Vilma never rose to the heights of the ethereal *tristesse* for which Sagan was widely celebrated. In French literature it was bolstered by tradition and probably harkens back to Colette. Given the heavy-handed Hungarian literary tradition, it was a breath of fresh air. Later Magda Szabó also experimented with a similarly light mix. I was entranced by Vilma's use of punctuation; I'd never seen so many punctuation marks in a single seemingly endless sentence. With her interjections, exclamations, repeated questions, and heaps of linguistic reflections, she smashed the declarative rigor of her sentences to smithereens.

My Aunt Magda didn't take herself too seriously as a writer either, and she was right in doing so. Nevertheless, her novel *Five Young Ladies in a Manor House* is a decent piece of work. It could even have risen above the realm of quality entertainment if, out of political considerations, she had not ruined the end. If I had my way, I'd snip off this humiliating Red ending, which she threw in so she could atone for the joy and happiness of her bourgeois upbringing. As a child, I read it with great pleasure, if for no other reason than, thanks to this book, I was afforded a glimpse not only into the history of our family, the daily life of the Tiszasüly and Gömörsid estates, but, armed with the knowledge of our family stories and legends, I also got a glimpse into the precarious relationship of the poetic and the real, of fiction and real life, and this interested me more than anything. I must have been around eleven when I realized I'd devote myself to writing. When they asked me what I'd be when I grew up, I said all sorts of things, but I kept my plan to myself. It wasn't a decision, it was more like an awareness. It had no weight as such, but it was clear that I'd become the experimental ground of authors living and dead. I didn't just read, I studied the mechanisms of their sentences, and so I gained an understanding of what they were shaping into what and by what means, what roles they assumed, what they wished to achieve and what they failed to achieve, what ambitions they nurtured, and also the hidden substance of their writings, and what secret passions led them where and for what purpose.

Yvette's grandfather was a more flamboyant writer than her grandmother. In my opinion, his translations are beautiful. Thanks to the richness of his vocabulary, nurtured by Transylvanian memoirists, the precision and easy charm of his prose, he could compensate for the lack of depth and originality of his works. He produced literature on commission and on deadline. Or else he was busy with his translations. This was also exciting to watch. The way he collected his raw material, accumulating and classifying it, taking notes, and the way he discussed various subjects and writers with his friends and colleagues, and also seeing the messengers and office attendants from the publishers and newspaper offices bring the manuscripts and page proofs to be revised or reviewed, and later on, the printed works. I think I read all his translations as a child, the novels of Balzac, Victor Hugo, Flaubert, and Romain Rolland, and later, the books that Yvette had read in the original. He jotted down his translations in notebooks, he translated on the run, as it were, he didn't even bother sitting down at his desk, or else only provisionally, otherwise he wrote in a notebook he held in his lap sitting in a garden chair, and he also wrote on slips of paper and newspaper margins.

Whenever Yvette found something new in a book she was reading in Hungarian, something she didn't understand, a new expression, a phrase, or perhaps a love scene of a kind she had not encountered before, she'd call me on the phone. She could have asked her grandmother or her grandfather, and perhaps she did, but I think she reserved some of her questions for me. If she deemed a scene especially tantalizing, she didn't just call my attention to it, she hastened to read it to me. We read long passages to each other with the receivers held close to our ears.

Possibly, she was interested in all that lovemaking because of her father; she wanted to understand what her idolized and despicable father was up to with his lovers. What Grigory and Aksiniya are up to in the barn in Sholokhov's *And Quiet Flows the Don*. Even if she understood a bit more than I, she didn't understand, and I understood nothing, not a word. Some expression of passion had led to a scuffle. How could I understand what the brutality of the scenes meant, what it meant to each of the characters separately, what it meant to the author, what he intended with it, yet the strength of the sentences had us spellbound. Possibly, Yvette was really wondering what she should do as a woman to be more deserving of her father's love than her mother had been, what, as Aksiniya, she should have done for her Grigory. Or what the Cossacks were up to when they attacked the women in the stables of the recaptured villages. I couldn't make heads or tails of any of this, but it seemed to me that she understood something that I didn't. What happened in the barn emerged from a different circle of hell than the evil deeds in Dickens or Zola. Probably, her despicable father was doing the same thing. I knew that during the siege the Russians, and there had been Cossacks among them, had raped the women, but I didn't know what that meant. Yvette shared with me her suspicions, but her obsessive search for answers just exacerbated her pain. Also, we couldn't go into details because of ourselves. The thought that our father did this to our mother, and that I would have to do this to someone myself, frightened me. I couldn't imagine the act of lovemaking, even though I knew about it, I knew that there was something called lovemaking and that it was a bit like a scuffle. In my mind, what Aksiniya and Grigory did was tainted with the violence, the plunder, the murders and genocides I knew about. But I urged Yvette on all the same; let's follow the path that from all our reading had turned into a compilation of the various forms of human conduct, the terrain of open expression and concealment. There is another world behind the visible world where man's full countenance and figure shine forth or possibly, it can be seen only from there.

We found similar traces of brutality in Pontoppidan, Andersen Nexø, Strindberg, and Ibsen, evidence of a world beyond the visible world, or else, chaste references to it. Barring this detective work, we may not have read their excellent books and plays in the first place. Still, for a long time, a very long time, I haughtily told myself that I had nothing in common with this other world, except I must know about it if I wanted to be a writer. But for a long time, a very long time, its reality did not reach me, just news of it. Granted that upon the urging of others, a lot of things did happen, yet I couldn't accept what happened as my own, because in every situation I was too busy observing the other, the other human being. As if I had no passions of my own, I reserved my frenzy for the written word and the structure and rhythm of the sentences and the network of relationships that they revealed. I gladly assisted Yvette in her search, but mostly out of sympathy, so her father's conduct shouldn't cause her so much pain. I reasoned that if others do it in secret, if my parents might be willing to do such a thing themselves, it can't be that exceptional. People imitate each other, they repeat what they've seen, but all that imitation and repetition has nothing to do with me, because I'm different, I'm above such things. Yet I didn't prove to be as sensitive and noble-minded as I'd have liked to think, and when I realized the truth about myself, it came as a shock. When a certain author, a book, or a scene unmasked me, I became ridiculous in my own eyes. Innocent as I was, I couldn't help but admit it.

Rabelais. Master Rabelais was Yvette's discovery. I can't find the book, but I remember perfectly well that her grandfather had translated *Gargantua*, except he used a pen name or no name at all. We didn't know who Rabelais was, but he must have been a filthy pig, a monk who lived long ago, but how could a respected old gentleman like Yvette's grandfather put such shocking obscenities on paper. She lent me the book for a couple of days. Rabelais's raw strength mesmerized me, there was no ignoring him; his banter, his satiric wit and mocking humor held me in thrall, it swept me along into his vertiginous, mad adventures, I screamed with laughter, and as I did so, he exposed me for what I was as I, too, shuffled comically between my own hypocritical and overly fastidious life roles. Rabelais spares no roles we play in life, he spares nothing and no one, but not because he lacks mercy, but because none of the roles we play are healthy, we play no roles that are not false, and he tells us out of his love of mankind.

And right away, I found another volume of his among my parents' books, *Pantagruel*, written by Master François Rabelais, Mass Priest and Doctor of Medicine, translated by György Faludy and published by Cserépfalvi. Oh, I know him. Though to this day I don't know what a mass priest is. On the other hand, if they keep a book by Rabelais on their shelves, they must be great big pigs, just like him.

Rabelais turned the two of us inside out. We lay on my bed screaming with laughter. We read him in tandem, we read him over each other's shoulder, we punched each other and fell off the bed. And it's interesting that to this day my reaction to it has not changed, I still scream with laughter, and of course I now know what at the age of twelve I didn't know, or just intuited.

Also, back then, if I didn't understand something that was obvious to the French, Yvette flushed, she flew into a temper and said I was just a typical, brainless Hungarian. I didn't agree with her assessment of Hungarians, but I decided to be careful so she shouldn't really think of me as one. Also, I had my doubts about her innocence. I looked at her breasts, but she didn't have breasts. In which case, why should you wear a bra. She retorted that she'd never suffer such mortification in France. The French have brains, they wouldn't ask a young girl a thing like that. Each time she made a derogatory statement such as this, she puckered up her lips and huffed and puffed, and words that I could not understand issued from between them. These strange words spoken in a different language, I'd have liked to know what they meant.

How Man Turned into a Giant. I had a book by this title, a Christmas present from my father. It was a work on the history of technology meant for young readers, written to impress us with the heroic story of how man took possession of the earth.

There comes a time in every person's life when he must ascertain, time and time again, everything he thought he knew.

Boys, regardless of what Yvette called them, have pricks, but I couldn't find the answer to what use it was to them, apart from pissing, of course. And why they have one to begin with, when girls don't.

Once I asked my father. He had one too, what's more, his member kept surprising me with its insignificance. I kept looking for my chance to discover its significance. Once when I was in the tub, they promised me that mine would be just like his when I grew up, and they screamed with laughter. Which persuaded me that he must know what use it is to us when it's bigger. But isn't there some way to get rid of it. I don't want it. Why isn't it screwed on, because then I could screw it off. Or can't it be cut off. My father seemed surprised that his son should think such a thing. Actually, he was aghast. What's he to do about me, a half-wit like me. How can his son be so ridiculous, why should he have to concern himself with such rubbish. My question upset him, the lines of his face underwent a dramatic transformation. Such a thing rarely happened to him, and I was taken aback. I realized that I shouldn't have asked such a question. On the other hand, this made me conclude that family ties are no joke, they're not made up, a person's brothers and sisters are really his brothers and sisters. Whenever he felt put out, he was suddenly just like his brothers and sisters. We really are one family. The corners of our lips and the corners of our eyes quiver the same way from surprise and indignation, and we have to get control of our facial features the same way.

Quietly, a bit uncertainly, he asked why I'm asking such nonsense, how can such a thing even occur to me, why do I want to be rid of it, but I saw that he was just playing for time, because if he had his way, he'd slap me.

I have plenty of problems with it, and I told him so, now that I'd laid myself open with my stupid questions.

It presses against me, it bothers me, it's of no use, I can't find a place to put it in my pants, and it chafes me.

Material of all kinds chafed me. This was the most persistent suffering of my childhood, my shirt rubbing against my neck, my pants rubbing against my thighs, my shoes rubbing against my heels and toes. Of course, I didn't dare tell him that my prick or dick or cock, or whatever, sometimes stiffens from the rubbing. I was afraid that it was some incurable disease. It's best not to mention it, I don't want my parents to worry. When I die, they'll see for themselves anyway. Or can't something be done about it, that was the secret background to the question I asked my father, isn't there a way to be free, one way or another, of the persistent pleasure that resists logical reasoning and whose cause is beyond comprehension.

Don't talk nonsense, he said with a frown, as if, or so it seemed to me, he were declaring in no uncertain terms that he was not about to discuss such nonsense with anyone under any circumstance.

I tried to convince him, to talk him into it, because no matter how vigorously I shake it, the last drop ends up in my pants, and isn't there something that can be done about it, some way of turning it off. After all, girls get on very well without it. This was my final argument.

I wish I were a girl.

But my arguments were in vain; my arguments put him off, he froze, his indignation disappeared, and as if I were talking to the wall, he refused to answer me, from which it was clear to me that I was born a boy because of them, even though my mother says they wanted a girl, they lied to me, they lied, I'm a boy because that's what they wanted. Except, in that case, why did my mother say she wanted a girl.

Yvette very cleverly shifted the burden of her humiliation from her parents' shoulders and blamed it on the barbaric Hungarians, especially on her grandmother, who was the primeval mother and primeval cause of all Hungarian prohibitions and the sole physical impediment to all earthly delights, but whom, boiling over with a surfeit of hatred, she nevertheless idolized, and was hoping that once they're in Leányfalu again for the summer, she'd finally let her wear a bra. But she didn't. I didn't say I don't understand it, but I didn't. I also didn't understand why it's such a big deal, or why her grandmother won't hear of it.

On the other hand, I began to feel what she was feeling. When we ran out to the street, across the sunny road and down to the riverbank, because at eleven or three twenty the boat came, *le bateau*, she crossed her arms in front of her chest the way grown-up women do when they have to remove their bras in front of others. I saw my mother do it at the seamstress, and also the women in Göd when my grandfather and I entered the big changing cabin down by the river used by both men and women, and they started screaming when they saw us. At such times, they raised their upper arms with their hands clasped in a fist. Sometimes their shame made my own skin bristle, I got goose bumps all over from the feeling of vulnerability. From which I realized that I, too, am a girl.

If Vilma, silly little Vilmácska, or dumb little Vilmuka, as my aunt called her, was with us in Leányfalu, Vilma took pity on Yvette and tied a small red kerchief around her and made her turn around, she was happy, *c'est du joli*, she's so pretty *avec cette petite rouge*, with this small red whatever. But Vilma was not the only exception, Yvette didn't relegate her grandfather or her father either to the ranks of brainless Hungarians; after all, they spoke impeccable French, and so they must know as well as she that the universe, too, is French. Georges would regularly rake his mother over the coals whenever she made a slip in the heat of conversation. When this happened, it was written all over his face that his mother is simply not French, and how deeply and unrelentingly he despises her for it, even though he first learned French from her at the age of five in Berlin, which on the other hand gave him cause to joke that his mother tongue is not Hungarian but French, because he learned French from his mother. Meaning the little French she knew. From this I understood without having to be told that as far as they were concerned, I was on home ground, but Yvette was the one being humiliated, and it's my fault that she can't wear a bra.

When her parents came with her two younger brothers, Serge and Jean-François, to see Yvette in the summer, I spent days with them at my aunt's summer place in Leányfalu, so they shouldn't bother their parents all day and have someone to play with. This happened on my aunt's strict orders, and my parents agreed to everything that my aunt wanted. This embarrassed me at least as much as her boyish haircut or lack of a bra embarrassed her. If something happened out of my control, I would have none of it. This emotion was so overwhelming that when I was younger I often fainted with fury. My fainting spells became legendary, until Elza Baranyai came up with the saving idea that next time I faint, instead of calling her, my mother should give me two big slaps instead.

Don't fan him, Klárika dear, just give him two big slaps. And so it happened and I never fainted after that, and when my brother first fainted with fury, in line with the cure that had worked wonders on me, he got slapped, too, but in his case, the method didn't always produce the desired results. He couldn't breathe, he turned blue, and this frightened them more than my fainting fits. They didn't dare slap him. They started calling Elza Baranyai again, until she'd had enough and said to my mother, don't slap him after the fact, Klárika dear, slap him before the fact. The minute the child starts raging.

Which worked.

I wanted to hear nothing about duties and obligations. It's up to me to decide who I want to play with, when and where. I don't want to play with strangers, even if they're my relatives. I don't want to play with anyone.

I preferred to watch my naked brother in his crib eating his own shit with a healthy appetite. What can I say, I found this scene in Leányfalu edifying. He barely pushed it out and right away, he ate it. For decades they kept at me, why did I let him, why didn't I say something. Our parents were long dead, but my Aunt Magda was still at me for it.

You let him smear it on his face.

It was better when Vilma Ligeti was with us in Leányfalu, because we didn't have so many things we were told to do.

I already have a friend, András Vajda, and I'm not making friends with anyone else. I'd have preferred to have Laci Tavaly as my friend, but he was friends with others now. I didn't understand and he didn't explain. He probably didn't think he owed me an explanation. But then, this is why I liked Laci Tavaly. Everything that I found puzzling he thought was obvious. Things that took me decades to understand he understood right away. I was terribly hurt that he'd dropped me without an explanation. This became the elemental pain in my life, the model for pain. Or else he had such a serious reason for it, that he didn't tell me in order to spare me. After all, I didn't tell him either when his weenie was hanging out of his pants. Anyway, he was right not to tell me. A couple of weeks ago, I found the copy of a document among my parents' papers typed on thin indigo paper that sheds light on what happened. I'd first read it many years ago; the document itself was not new to me, but something in it that touched me personally had escaped my attention, because this document, I am ashamed to say, is a multiple denunciation, several people are denounced in it. The original was probably written on the letterhead of the Democratic Alliance of Hungarian Women. I know from this copy of the original that our mother had written the denunciation in both their names, hers and our father's, or had dictated it. She addressed it to the Greater Budapest Committee of the Hungarian Workers Party on Köztársaság Square. She writes that she is attaching a flyer found that morning, it being June 19, 1950, that was carried by the wind in Palatinus Court located between Pozsonyi Street and Újpest Quay. She writes that she suspects a direct link between the newly established basement chapel and the origin of the flyers. Late last year, about November or December, she writes, we heard sharp whistle signals coming from the court at night. Probably, the whistles signaled the approach of automobiles or other vehicles. At the time we assumed that the whistle signals were meant for thieves, she writes, and we called 123-456 to report it to the police. The whistles continued. Eventually, they felt that they had ceased. But a couple of weeks before, she writes, it came to their attention that a basement chapel had been established across the way, at 14 Pozsonyi Street and there is heavy traffic in and out. They have already reported this as well.

About the occupation of the premises, they have succeeded in finding out that a certain Dr. Lajos Szigeti, who resides at 13 Szent István Square, had founded a furniture storage company, and had rented the space for this purpose. The space stood empty for about six months, but the person renting it had paid the rent. They see a connection between the two things, and these must be closely related to the activities of the Basilica Parish. She must also mention, she writes, that during the German occupation, the superintendent of the house at 14 Pozsonyi Street, a man by the name of Szakonyi, wore a green shirt, and judging by his actions, was a member of the Arrow Cross. Even after the liberation, he made statements typical of the Arrow Cross. What's more, Emil Tavaly, the superintendent of the house at 12 Pozsonyi Street, also had to have knowledge of the goings-on in the chapel. He was originally an ironworker, she writes, but during the time of inflation, he stopped going to work, left his class, and through his wife's influence came under clerical influence. He is a member of our party, she writes, but in this he does as his wife dictates. In one way or another, both of them must be aware of what is going on in the chapel. Because they must open the gate, they are up late into the night, and during the summer months, they practically spend the night in front of the gate, they sit in front of the building until the early hours of morning.

A couple of days before, around one a.m., they heard the whistle signals again. Probably, it was our mother who went down to the street, though on the basis of this carbon copy it can't be determined who signed the letter. Still, it is highly unlikely that our father would have signed a letter on the letterhead of an organization he did not belong to. While she was downstairs on the street, she writes, the signals were not repeated, but as soon as she closed the gate, they resumed. Which I don't quite understand, because the tenants of buildings in Budapest did not have a key to the gate. She further points out that the basements of the Palatinus houses are mazelike and suitable for illegal activities. We had taken advantage of this earlier in our own work, she writes. It seems, she continues, that the enemy has also discovered this circumstance and is taking advantage of it. It now seems to them that the late-night whistles serve to mask the incoming and outgoing traffic needed for the printing of the flyers.

It worried me that it would always be like this, that I'd never have any friends again.

All the same, Yvette's two younger brothers, Serge and Jean-François, didn't interest me.

How can I be friends with someone I don't know. But at least I had a chance to observe them, and silent observation occupied me more than friendship, even more than Laci Tavaly's friendship. From what I could tell, the three of them understood one another perfectly, even though they were so different. All three of them, Yvette and her two brothers, were guarded, disciplined, with sober eyes, though in nearly every situation the lack of mimicry put one off. The obliging though sharp half-smile that sat in the corners of their lips invariably reflected something of their rejection of their surroundings. They had unexpected outbursts that reminded me of the French Revolution, when the angry citizens surprised the queen sitting in front of her mirror in dishabille.

They could fly into a rage readily, but this was always on purpose, which lent more strength to their outbursts, and more smoke, too.

I was not allowed to fly into a rage, while they were applauded for it or, at least, they did not have to hold themselves back. Their mother, Sonia, also indulged in horrendous outbursts of rage.

But that evening they accused me not only of looking at Yvette's you-know-what with András, but I was also supposed to have touched it, touched the thing that the grown-ups wouldn't have said out loud for anything in the world. They didn't say what I was supposed to have touched. I protested that I didn't touch anything of hers, but what that was supposed to be I didn't dare say either. It would have supplied my denial with an object, which would have made it sound like a confession. But I most certainly did touch it, my favorite aunt shouted, the one who was Yvette's grandmother, and who now turned into a veritable monster, a harpy, I most certainly touched it, I'm lying. My Aunt Magda rolled her r's, but now she also screeched. She might have thought that if she screeched like that, I'd stop lying.

But that's just it. I'd have lied only if I had satisfied her sense of justice by admitting to a sin I did not commit and had no intention of committing. I didn't even know that such a thing was possible. Should I lie now in order to satisfy her and put an end to the quarrel, or should I not lie, thereby insisting on the truth. The two demands made logical if not ethical sense.

It must have been late summer or early fall, it was warm and the windows were open, the lights were on. She'd taken Yvette home barely an hour before, and now she was unexpectedly back, screeching, with one of her colorful cashmere turbans on her head.

I knew her well, but she had never done anything like this before. I knew that this was an exceptional moment, and I was afraid that from now on, it would always be like this.

We lived at 12 Pozsonyi Street, on the seventh floor, and they lived on Szófia Street, on the corner of Teréz Boulevard, near the Oktogon, on the fourth floor. Yvette must have told her of her mortification on their way back on the tram, she must have shown her her black and blue marks, which she must have acquired at the pool when she was fighting with the boys, and in fact, they may have wrestled her to the ground, they may even have had their hands around her neck as they were looking at and touching her you-know-what. Or she might have expected me to do the same, to wrestle her to the ground the way Grigory did to Aksiniya, or the older boys at the pool. Or else I just didn't understand. I understood nothing. For all I knew, these older boys didn't touch her anywhere either. Anyway, in her anger and indignation, my aunt decided to turn back. She couldn't breathe. I didn't understand a word she said. If she maintains a thing like that, why doesn't she bring Yvette back with her. Even with her French arrogance, she wouldn't have dared accuse me of such a thing to my face. I was supposed to have hurled myself at her. My parents were standing aghast in the middle of the room, among the armchairs they'd hurriedly pushed to the side. Yelping half-syllables left their lips as they towered over me, and to my great surprise, they had no intention of protecting me from this furious demon who happened to be my aunt.

My protestations did not weigh in the balance against them, while they didn't weigh in the balance against her. Although they'd taken my side many times in the past and took my side even when I had done something really wicked, this time they didn't believe me. For instance, there was the time when I was guilty of the unspeakable offense of nailing a shingle to the front gate according to which I claim to have a doctorate, I'm a head gynecologist, my office hours are such and such, and Laci Tavaly's mother, the outraged wife of the superintendent, came out saying enough is enough. The landlord is beside himself. How can such a perverse and incorrigible boy live in his house. It took me many long years to realize that maybe they didn't allow Laci Tavaly to be my friend anymore because I was immoral. But they took my side against these lunatics even then; on the other hand, they couldn't stand their bourgeois pretense at outrage. Our son immoral. How dare you. They also took my side even when, earlier on, I'd committed an even graver offense.

I had shouted a string of obscenities to a lady in the apartment across the way, on the other side of Palatinus Court. They tried to calm her down, they explained, cutting each other short, they asked for her forbearance because of me, and they gave me what for only when that awful woman was gone. Actually, she was a lithe and wild blond beauty. And that was the problem. I watched her from the window of my room. I tried to remain invisible behind the curtain, or else peeked, wide-eyed, from under the windowsill, something I'd never done before in my young life. Catching a glimpse of her was all I could think of, I yearned to see her at least partially undressed, or if possible, in the nude, it didn't matter as long as she came to the window. Perhaps I just wanted to see as much of her beauty as possible.

Once she crossed the room naked. This early zealous waiting and yearning attached itself to all my later romantic passions. It wasn't directed at her nakedness, but the totality of her person or the yearning for totality, of which nakedness is merely one aspect.

I didn't understand anything, I didn't understand this either. It seemed that a relative is a person who can come into our home when-ever she feels like it, she can enter my life, she can enter our rooms, she can shout and accuse me to her heart's content, she can even hit me, if she likes, and they won't shield me from her wrath, even though they believe that a child must not be hit or beaten. My aunt was so out-raged by my refusal to admit any wrongdoing that she raised her hand against me several times. But then she relented, she couldn't hit the son of her youngest brother. It took great self-control on her part not to hit me for something I was not guilty of. No wonder I understood nothing of what was happening in this impossible situation.

A relative is a person who can hit me. A relative is a person whose you-know-what I can't look at even if I should feel like it. A rela-tive must practice self-control with regard to another relative in this, above all else.

This was the magical précis of the scene. The landlord wouldn't have been so outraged either had I presented myself to the passersby as a dental surgeon or a hairdresser, for that matter. On the other hand, when I think of it, the gynecologist adventure was not without precedent, no wonder the wife of the superintendent and the landlord said I was a confirmed sinner.

Had I been able to see what was happening for what it was, had I been able to see the connections between things, something that, needless to say, they saw, things would have been different. But at the time I had no clue about what was going on, and many more decades had to pass before I could understand something at least of what they understood, and also, how they understood what they understood.

I wanted to share with Laci Tavaly, the superintendent's son, a new word I'd learned. I can't remember anymore where I heard the new word first, I may have first heard it in kindergarten. They lived downstairs on the ground floor, at the bottom of the court lined with yellow tile. Anyway, the new word made me so happy, I was so en-thusiastic that as soon as they brought me home from kindergarten, I wanted to share it with him. Pressing my head against the window grating, I shouted down from the seventh floor, I called his name, I kept shouting his name until he showed up outside.

In such a deep yard, a shout echoes something awful. He called me Nádas, I called him Tavaly. The entire yard echoed with his name. I don't know why, but throughout their young friendship, boys called each other by their surnames.

What is it, he shouted back, and then he also shouted that you can't shout like that here and I should shut my trap. If I don't, he'll call his mother.

But I know a new word, I shouted, because this was more important somehow than either the house rules or the landlord.

What new word, he shouted.

Cunt, I shouted, and the yard echoed with the shout.

I know *cunt*, I shouted, because he didn't answer for some time.

What cunt, he shouted.

Girls' cunt.

You're an idiot, Nádas, he shouted, I learned it last year in Németlad.

But by then, the housewives had come out of their kitchen to the balcony, and they were soon followed by his mother and the maids, they were all shouting indignantly, but mainly laughing, saying that this is really too much. The landlord's dreaded maid also appeared on the third floor.

Will you stop, her ladyship will have none of your shouting.

What a scandal from a little boy up on the seventh. A scandal, a scandal.

I really had no idea what the scandal around Yvette's you-know-what was all about. After all, we'd planned to get married, because neither of us thought much of the circumstance that Andris Gönczi was the one she really liked. Also, she pointed out that we're only second cousins, and that clinched it. In France, only first cousins are forbidden to marry, and I'm her father's first cousin, not hers.

And then she said something I'd never heard before. She said that in France, incest is a serious offense. *Vérfertőzés* is what she said, like this, in Hungarian. Blood contagion. Pollution. Taint.

This Hungarian word preyed on my mind for some time to come. The pollution of blood between relatives. It took decades before I could make sense of this nonsense. I even kept having to repeat the names

of the various relationships in the family to get it right. Magda Nádas, my father's sister, was her grandmother. It wasn't the relationships
themselves I found difficult to understand or accept without reflection,
but the words pertaining to them. The son-in-law, the daughter-in-
law of the sister-in-law, and the niece of the godmother's son-in-law
in Törökszentmiklós. Also, I didn't understand how my parents can
be so sure that I'm really their child. Or what if they're lying and they
took someone else's child home from the hospital. Or they found me
under the ruins of X and took me home. Or what would have happened if Grandmother Mezei hadn't married the brutal Arnold Neumayer, who later changed his name to Nádas, but had married the
poet József Kiss, for instance. If Klára hadn't given the enamored poet
the boot. In which case, maybe I wouldn't even exist. Or else I might
also be a poet. I was mostly occupied with things that couldn't be
imagined. What would it be like if I were completely different. Or if
I weren't here at all, for instance, if I weren't anywhere yet, because I
wouldn't be born until later. Or if I looked like some stranger, and my
name wouldn't be my name. In which case, where would I be in the
meanwhile. The I that I am would be a different I. I wouldn't know
Yvette, because I wouldn't even know my own mother.

Yvette was driven so far from her home because of such family ties.

Yvette lied and said that her mother is ill, her lungs are weak, and
so she can only take care of her two younger brothers and bring them
up properly. Two children are quite enough of a problem. Fortunately,
I didn't call her to order and tell her not to tell such a colossal lie, or
that she shouldn't be taken in by her parents' and grandparents' un-
abashed lies. I didn't say it because there was another assertion making
the rounds in the family. We must be tolerant of other people's weakness or credulity, and so I couldn't tell her that her grandmother had
told Vilma Ligeti a very different story. Her mother, Szonia, doesn't
look ill at all, weak lungs, what an idea. She can't begin to imagine
why they feed this poor child such nonsense. At most, they found yet
another benign spot on her lung.

But Vilma protested. How can Magda say such things when she
knows perfectly well that Szonia is ill.

Szonia is playacting, my aunt countered.

Of the two, my Aunt Magda's words carried more weight, and so I willingly accepted her version.

Szonia is playacting.

Szonia was a big, bony woman who hit her children when they misbehaved, and her stride was so determined, you could hardly keep up with her. Certainly, you wouldn't think she would be prone to playacting. She was direct, friendly, and straightforward. Her children were never disciplined enough for her. Georges had left her because he didn't love her anymore. Georges had the same stride, determined, each step as long as hers. It was interesting to watch them walk next to each other in Leányfalu, Szonia and Georges. Yvette had the same stride, though she was a bit bowlegged. That's not how we walked. Szonia can't keep the house in order, everything's topsy-turvy, it's chaos, *un bordel*, everything in their house is dirty, you saw for yourself, Vilma, and still, you argue with me.

Georges never loved her to begin with. Besides, Georges can't control himself. Georges knocks up every woman the first chance he gets, and then wants to marry them right away.

Georges doesn't love anyone.

See, that's why she had Georges knock her up, so he'd marry her.

So someone, anyone would marry her.

Which was a great big lie. After fifty years, having seen the letters that Szonia wrote to her mother-in-law from the sanatorium, I can safely say that this was a great big lie. From Szonia's letters, full of tenderness and written painstakingly, we even get fleeting glimpses of the sensitivity, empathy, and tenderness with which my aunt answered the gravely ill woman, how eager she was to help her daughter-in-law who was so anxious about her children's future.

My mother spent lots of time on the phone with her younger sister, her older sister, her brothers-in-law, but especially her sisters-in-law, and so there was probably nothing of these family stories that they kept telling each other, reshaping and embellishing, that I didn't know about. Szonia was not just ill, she was gravely ill. But they didn't talk about this, they talked about her not washing the dishes. My mother discussed everything with my Aunt Magda, and she discussed everything with my Aunt Eugenie, and also with Aunt Teri, Teréz Goldmark, who one fine day married my chemist uncle, István Nádas, in short, Pista, though she didn't discuss quite everything with her. As for my Aunt Irén, Irén Tauber, she'd discuss things with her only with a certain forbearance, because Irén floated a bit above the ground, she gave you the impression that she didn't quite understand anything, not fully, and that perhaps she was just a bit off in the head. Which was the truth. Irén understood nothing of what other people called reality, but like me, she hovered and bounced uncertainly back and forth between their assertions. But my mother was even more sparing with my Aunt Bözsi, Erzsébet Tauber, because Aunt Bözsi's volubility put her off, she was too loud for her by half. On the other hand, she discussed just about everything with Dajmirka, meaning Endre Nádas, *qui ne peut pas dire dormir*, not that it made any sense, seeing how Dormirka was not interested in anything whatsoever, and regardless of the topic, he barely grunted an answer; it was all too obvious that he couldn't have cared less, he hemmed and hawed and restricted himself to clichés; and to his wife, my loudmouthed Aunt Kató, whose maiden name was Katalin Elek, she spoke only for the sake of appearances, and made sure to remain allusive. Pista may have been the only person she'd talk to freely, but with him, she discussed subjects of a very different nature. As for Arnold Tauber, her own father, it was no use discussing anything with him either, because Arnold Tauber was utterly indifferent to family matters. Oh, dear child, please, he'd say to my mother timidly in order to cut her short. But she told my father in detail what she'd discussed and with whom, and then the two of them would go over the same family matters between themselves, and since they were so full of each other and paid so little attention to anyone else, they spoke freely, they didn't button their lips, more often than not, they didn't care if I was there or where I might be, and did I hear the intimate family vignettes, a circumstance that actually made me happy, because I learned from them that there are different ways of looking at the same thing, though today I am more inclined toward István Nádas or Arnold Tauber's view, because these details, repeated again and again due to their essence, interest me only up to a point. They interest me only until I come to understand their function. I should have realized much earlier that these stories, which appeared to reflect reality, in fact had nothing in common with reality, and yet when I read Szonia's exceptional and beautifully written letters, their light-years' of distance from reality caught me off guard all the same.

Of course, the apple doesn't fall far from the tree. Pali, too, the things he does. But that's what the Aranyossis are like. Though only the men. Irma or Nusi would never act this way, they're bona fide, respectable mothers. Poor Magda, too, the things she must put up with. At least, Pali doesn't want them to marry right away. Magda goes to her seamstress with the new fabric that Pali brought her from Paris, she finds the door open, and what does she see, you won't believe it, Pali with the seamstress on the table among the patterns and the materials cut to shape.

And it's not just Pali. Their father, Gyula, he knocked up all the women in Kolozsvár, and he left five other lovers behind in every other town.

Many long decades had to pass before I understood what had happened that evening.

I probably loved András Vajda more than I loved her, this is what Yvette must have been thinking, and she was probably right, though I loved him in a different way, I loved him for a lot of things. I loved his reserved little smile, his dark skin tone, his thick black hair, the rainy scent of his hair. And I also loved having a friend again, someone who was exclusively my friend. Seeing that Laci Tavaly was no longer my friend. Fortunately, I didn't know yet the difference between love and being in love, I didn't know why people who call themselves grown-ups are so eager to differentiate between the two, between loving and being in love, but I loved him, and as far as Yvette was concerned, this was the only hostile reality she knew. I must have felt, even if at the time it didn't register with me, what a smart little boy András Vajda was. I realized it only when, years later at the High School for Chemistry, we ended up in the same class again. But his intellect, to which

I gave no thought back then, nevertheless weighed in the balance, and probably, accompanied as it was by his indulgent, knowing little smile as he listened to others, it must have impressed me more than anything else. Which must have hurt Yvette very much. Not that I had anything against any of Yvette's own intellectual capacities, even if these were mainly receptive.

She tried to manipulate our games so that we should join forces against András Vajda. I, on the other hand, didn't want to, not because I was so decent, but because András wouldn't have understood our underhanded little games. His brilliant intellect stopped short at such wickedness. He was helpless against it. Underhanded tricks should be aimed only at underhanded people, and I couldn't understand why Yvette didn't understand this. Gogol's Chichikov wasn't amusing because he tried to hoodwink everyone, he was amusing because of how all the landowners attempted to hoodwink him. Neither one knew what the other was thinking, all the while they were each thinking of hoodwinking the other.

I couldn't love Laci Tavaly anymore, though it would be more correct to say that I did my best not to love him. Yvette had no cause for jealousy, though his strength and cleverness, his meek, milky-white beauty still made me think more of him than anyone else. Also, he knew more than I did, whereas he was neither smarter nor older than I.

Because I was in love with him, for many long decades I was under the impression that Németlad, from where Laci Tavaly and his family had moved, was a magical corner of the universe where people know everything better than anywhere else. For instance, not only did he know the word cunt before I did, he also knew what rye ergot looked like and how it was collected on the stubble field after reaping. He always had one over me. I couldn't even begin to imagine these ergots, the stubble fields, or the reaping itself. After all, I'd seen stuff like that only through the window of a train. I didn't even know why the ergot fungus should be gathered on the stubble fields.

Yet everything was not right with my denial because once, when we spent the summer in a big, somnolent house the size of a villa,

my grandmother, meaning my maternal grandmother, Cecília Nussbaum, ordered us into bed after lunch with my cousin Márta, Imre
Szántó, and Irén Tauber's daughter, and drew the curtains and told
us to be quiet, so she could have some peace at last, and then Márta
kept pestering me, she wanted to rub up against me, and though I kept
pushing her and drawing away from her, she kept moving closer to me
under the blanket, she held me in a vise with her ankles and would
not release me, as if it weren't warm enough under the blanket in the
first place. She whispered that if I show her mine, she'll show me hers.
The local boys down by the riverbank all showed it to her. Márta was
short, lively, with an easy laugh; she now lives in São Paulo, in Brazil,
the number of her gorgeous Brazilian grandchildren is infinite, by
now she even has two Brazilian great-grandchildren, but back then
she kept drawing near and there was no getting rid of her. As a rule, she
was effervescent, her good cheer knew no bounds, and that's the only
reason she wasn't a burden to me.

She thought I was laughing with her, whereas I laughed mostly
at her.

She always talked a bunch of infernal nonsense to her little
girlfriend Jutka Lombos, she chatted and twittered with no end in
sight, she screamed with laughter from the sheer pleasure of her own
exuberance, and she used words that didn't exist and had no meaning.

I knew that I was being wicked and that I should check my wickedness, but I laughed at her all the same.

But this time, she frightened me. I didn't understand, I just glared,
trying to defend myself, because this time there was no trace of gaiety;
on the contrary, she was determined, grave, obstinate, and aggressive.
She'd seen her father's, too, and her father's was bigger than my father's. And she wants to see what mine is like. Except, I had no idea
what I was supposed to be showing her, what I should be displaying
for her benefit.

In that case, she's going to show me hers first, and I should look
under the blanket.

When perhaps a bit later Laci Tavaly showed me his because he
wanted me to show him mine so we could compare them, anyway, at

least by then I knew what he wanted, even though I honestly had no idea why this would be good for us, this comparing of the two.

Márta really did pull down her panties in Dömsöd, she kicked off her panties under the blanket of her own accord, but I didn't see anything. I didn't know what she was up to, what this whole thing was good for, because they pulled our wet bathing suits or panties off us several times a day down by the river and put us in dry sun suits, which is what they called the impeccably ironed pieces of clothing with halters in which we were not allowed to go into the water, and then everybody could see everything. No wonder that I didn't understand what we were supposed to do or what good it would do us. Besides, it wasn't even just in Dömsöd that everyone could see everything, but earlier on, too, in Göd, where Grandmother and Grandfather took me along for the summer, and her parents brought Márta along with Jutka Lombos in the sidecar of their motorbike.

My parents would never have gone to Göd. They couldn't stand this bourgeois wallowing in the mud, as they called it.

My grandparents had a small wooden house in Göd by the river's edge that bore the sign Tauber Villa. But it didn't belong only to my grandparents, because they shared it with some people who came down for vacation either before or after us. Besides, everything in Göd was shared all around. Anyone could take the bikes, too, and the families who were all friends went shopping together and they also cooked together. I thought that this was very nice, but my parents called it a bourgeois quagmire, a social democratic quagmire. In their dictionary, one was as bad as the other.

It was hot in Dömsöd under the blanket, the penetrating smell of the Danube had leached into us, the smell of mud got stuck on our hair and skin, the smell of the spent oil seeping out of the boats. Also, some light showed through the blanket. You should go lower, Márta said impatiently, meanwhile guiding my head until I reached her open thighs. She opened it with her little fingers so I could look inside. It was like raw meat in there, purple and like mucus, as if she were showing me a gaping wound. I thought it was pitiful and disgusting. But right away, my disgust frightened me because it meant that I felt no sympathy for her; on the contrary, the secret that had been imparted to me filled me with dread, the fact that she had this wound, and that I couldn't manage to hide my lack of sympathy.

Luckily, she did not notice.

Or else I managed to hide it.

And so, it wasn't such an open-and-shut case that evening either. I should have known what the grown-ups were talking about, what they were alluding to, and also the nature of their anger, but I didn't.

There were many things lodged in my consciousness by then, information of all kinds, but there was no live connection between them as yet. The structure was available, but its elements would have had to be connected by objective knowledge. My father threw lightning bolts of anger, my mother raged in silence, my aunt could hardly stop herself from striking me. Also, I should have known from Laci Tavaly that *cunt* is not just a new word that I'd brought home from kindergarten or whatever, and that in Németlad everyone's familiar with *cunt* and it's identical to the thing that girls have and that Márta had shown me one afternoon, a fact of which, in turn, Laci Tavaly was ignorant. Also, in Németlad they use it for something, which was another thing I didn't understand.

Even though I was in the right, even though I protested and pleaded that I didn't do it, that I didn't do anything, it was no use because they said I'm just making things worse by lying, and they're going to punish me for that, too. It was like the hand of fate. So then it's caught up with me. This time I'm going to atone for all the lies I've told, they're going to punish me for all my cheating and duplicities.

Or else they're putting me to shame for something I couldn't have known, because they didn't tell me. For instance, I had railed against the Jews for all I was worth because they crucified our Lord Jesus Christ. Those damn murderers, may they suffer until the end of times. Jews are God killers and their blood descendants are ready to commit murder without provocation. Which was so obvious, there could be no doubt about it. Our religion teacher explained in detail how they nailed our Jesus Christ to the cross in the company of two thieves, except we're not like the Catholics, who worship the cross, we hate the cross. I understood this, too, it was clear as day, we must hate the cross. We don't worship the saints either, we only worship Jesus Christ. He sacrificed his life for us. Our teacher even described how they drove iron nails through the palms of all three of them, and their feet, too, and he even showed us in detail. Except, I couldn't imagine these nails either, because I was too scared to imagine myself as a nail under the weight of a hammer as I'm penetrating a living man's palm. I studied my palm to see where a nail could be driven through with the least pain. How was I to know that by birth I belong to those murderous Jews and that I was born a God killer.

Whereas I should have known that my parents don't believe in any god at all, what's more, they're against anyone talking such nonsense, so why do I come to them with such idiotic talk.

For my part, as far back as I can remember, I couldn't do without imagining the existence of a divine being, even in spite of them, which was quite an ordeal for me. Doubting them and going against what they said was a risky proposition, and the cause of not a little anxiety.

Besides, the whole thing makes no sense, they said; after all, Jesus Christ, provided he lived at all, was also a Jew. So let's not say things that make no sense.

I was a Calvinist because I was baptized, this much I knew, I also knew that Albert Bereczky had baptized me at the Reformed Church on Pozsonyi Street, and that's why I attended Sunday school there. I even knew that he'd acted honorably during the siege. But how on earth was I supposed to know that I mustn't share in the elemental joy of Jew-baiting, that I'm barred, once and for all, from the great collective pleasure of belonging. I couldn't see through the historical maze of exclusion, and when decades later I could more or less see through it, what I saw excluded me more than ever from the basic human need to belong. I understood nothing of all this, I had grown used to not understanding, and decades had to pass before something of the meaning or significance of the collective vituperation and the collective adulation dawned on me. Meanwhile I gradually came to realize that in order to satisfy the requirements of goodness, one must not only encrypt the language of wickedness with the semblance of goodness, one must also be familiar with the hand-tailored opportunities for personal wickedness. This much they made me see with the help of negative logic. If I must be good and in the interest of my goodness I must ignore or destroy many things that otherwise could benefit me, let us see what must be kept hidden and when, and what shared experience must nevertheless be allowed a voice in the interest of shared experience.

When all is said and done, I wanted to be a good boy, and to that end I had to understand and solve very complicated things without understanding the expressions pertaining to them and without a place in my consciousness where I could deposit and store them.

It seemed that my parents and the others responsible for my upbringing didn't know what we could do about my cleverly hidden and moderated evil deeds. They left it up to me, thereby leaving me in a quandary. They didn't think clearly about the second step either, clearing away the dangerous toxins that go with being ethical, leaving me to sweep them under the carpet, to do with them as I pleased. I watched the faces of the grown-ups to see what effect my occasional good deeds, achieved with resort to cheating and lying, had on them, and concluded that they considered the mere intention of goodness to be goodness. I wanted to understand the differences and the clever little ruses that attended them, to understand how goodness can be goodness if it can't be achieved honorably.

It seemed that goodness must be achieved on an occasional basis, it is highly permeable and has only local currency.

After all, I reviled the Jews for all I was worth because I wanted my just and enlightened parents to approve of me, not so much my father, who had killed God himself and who, because of his bourgeois upbringing or innate indifference, was interested in social injustice at best theoretically, but rather, my God-killer mother, in whose breast the proletarian self-consciousness of justice burned with a bright flame, though this wasn't quite true either, because she nurtured the proletarian myth in herself from material she'd brought along, so it could then flare up at will. She was born into a petit bourgeois family, but they lived quasi-proletarian lives. I saw the difference, and it was obvious that things didn't add up. Appearance and reality could not be reconciled, the logic of their psychology was different and the logic of their ethics was different, and yet for decades I followed in my mother's wake, and wrote and said of myself that from my father's side I'm from a bourgeois family, but from my mother's side I'm from a proletarian family, whereas I'm not from a proletarian family, not even partly, any way I look at it. The fact that plebeian logic is as familiar to me as elitist logic is another matter. I might even consider them of equal rank. Still, my emotional makeup invariably privileges the plebeian over the elitist, because the empathy I feel for my mother pulls me in that direction.

A person possesses characteristics of which he himself is ignorant. If he has two parents, four grandparents, and eight great-grandparents, the social and emotional web that he should understand, process, and nurture is in fact impervious to understanding. In which case, goodness isn't exclusively dependent on intention after all. In the interest of being good I was supposed to have admitted that I pulled off Yvette's panties, but since I wouldn't admit it, it made me look bad in their eyes. No wonder I was confused. But I didn't do it, I didn't do it. So how could I have admitted otherwise. Or could it be that they knew better than I and that I had done it, I pulled off Yvette's panties. I was so confused and desperate that even this occurred to me. Could I be so perverse that half an hour after the fact I refuse to remember so I won't have to admit it. Did I in fact look at something that interested me so little that it would never even have occurred to me that I might be interested. Could I have wrestled her to the ground, could I have tried to strangle her, leaving bruises on her neck and arms. This self-recrimination without any basis in fact tortured me for decades to come. Why don't they tell me straightaway what it is we didn't see when András Vajda and I didn't pull off Yvette's panties. Still, thanks to the rational thinking I learned from them, something nevertheless occurred to me, namely, that some things that can't be seen must not be mentioned by name in front of others. There are things and events for which we have words, but these words must not be said. For my part, I don't tell Yvette either all the things that I know about her mother, her father, her grandfather, or who told me. Her idolized and despised grandmother told me, that's who. I don't want to tell her anything cruel, I don't want to add to her distress with these so-called truths, and this is the source of the great lie between us.

Or else grown-ups see and understand everything, in which case goodness itself is the mask. Grown-ups don't wear faces, they wear masks. But they don't wear masks in order to be good, in order that we should be good, they wear masks so that our well-considered and well-calculated wickedness should not stand in the way of our happiness. They must defend themselves from wickedness in the Eden of wickedness. Not that I would have minded. Let us wage war for the sake of lasting peace. When I grow up, I'll do the same. But until then what am I to do with the rigorous rules of conduct and the bombastic ethical rhetoric, if the words obstruct my understanding. Considering the deplorable state of our ethics, there was too much rhetorical hullabaloo, this is how I saw it, this was my impression, all while I kept an eye on their delicate balancing act. What could I have made of Aristotle, I ask myself now. Because if it is as he asserts, and everything and everyone in the world tends toward the good, then, in that case, there should be some indication to that effect, some record, some trace of evidence, at least with the passing of the centuries.

Also, there was no understanding the words because, for one thing, their meaning changed appreciably in line with their usage, and for another, their local value could have been understood only with the help of words that would have had to have generally ascribed meaning. The theory of relativity and the uncertainty principle are valid not only with respect to physical objects and physics, but with respect to language as well. And so, later, decades later, it was still a major concern of mine what to make of goodness. Not what to make of it in general, but what to make of it in a text, what to make of it in my own text. Even in the hands of practiced narrators, goodness often seems inane. A sentence will veer off track, thanks, first and foremost, to self-worship and the religious faith in the nobility of man. Which is just one of the many problems confronting the practitioner of narrative. The narrator must rely on material that all of us use every day, in short, words that have not only been chewed to the bone, but have also been derailed. Though at times it may save the text, bring about clarity or put it back on course, yet the narrator has the hardest time of all with goodness, and not because goodness is such a rare commodity, but probably, because the reflective mind conceives of goodness as a concept that is the opposite of evil or wickedness, in short, by proceeding along a negative track, and as a result, it cannot avoid stumbling over the high threshold that made even the Gnostics and the Scholastics stumble. They were excommunicated and burned at the stake, but that did not make the theological quandary about the conceptual duality disappear.

Others were no more successful in attempting to clarify where and in what the devil resides. The humanists and the adherents of the Enlightenment also came up against this problem and fell flat on their faces, and as for their latter-day followers, they relinquished, once and for all, any attempt at clarification when, at the end of the twentieth century, they put the entire affair, to wit, whether the world is consubstantial or multisubstantial *ad acta*, in short, whether we should take Communion at the altar in the name of the Father and the Son or in the name of the Father, the Son, and the Holy Ghost, and whether we should make the sign of the cross with two or three fingers. And also, how evil came to be part of Divine Providence, and so on. And if it's part of Divine Providence, if it got caught up in it and to the highest edification of ourselves and our fellows it is diligently bringing dividends, does the Almighty have power over it, and if so, how, and whether all the small individual dividends aren't putting man's one and only world at risk. Or if he, the Almighty, has no power over it, how can he be almighty, and what is he almighty in. Or if he doesn't exist and there is no higher instance than Creation and the separation of good and evil is not up to the individual, the Politburo, or the Sacred Congregation, because individual and congregational consciousness that would take the burden of Providence on its shoulders is nonexistent, the cosmos is for all intents and purposes neutral and the subjects living in the world of physical laws are equal; what's more, in the interest of universal peace it is expedient to retract the very idea of justice, but in that case, upon what common convention are we to base human coexistence or, for lack of such a convention, what can we expect of each other.

It was not a theologist and not even a philosopher, but two former inmates of Auschwitz, Rudolf Vrba, the legendary figure of the resistance movements in the Auschwitz death camp, and Primo Levi, preeminent among those writers who committed suicide, who provided the most immediate answer about how goodness works in the world, its incidental nature and local value.

Fifty years had to pass and I had to study the literature about the various holocausts and systematic genocides line by line, footnote by footnote, before I could at last see, along with Vrba and Levi, into the yawning abyss separating European theology, European humanism, European enlightenment, and European reality as it is at any one time. Vrba, who is a practical man, equates good with a single individual, the old and gaunt Isaac Rabinovic, who from under his wide-brimmed black hat is looking at those crowded into the cattle car as they approach an unknown destination. They don't know when they will arrive. They don't know where they are headed and to what end. Ever since they were crowded into the wagon and the train took off, old man Rabinovic has been huddled in a corner. He is silent. According to Vrba, the surprising conclusion he comes to after several hours springs neither from resignation nor from piety, but from the silent surprise that comes when, searching among his untested concepts, a person alights upon the only possible explanation for the irrational.

It is God's will.

As if he were saying that surely someone knows, my Father surely knows why this has to happen.

As for doubt, something that since Epicurus man's understanding cannot ignore, Vrba ties it to the figure of Moses Sonnenschein, he ties it to the self-consciousness of the pious son of a Polish rabbi who, despite the outrage and protest of the others, and possibly for his own consolation, keeps repeating that it must be like this because God wills it. It is his arm that Vrba grabs when, holding on to the side of a truck, they cross the camp at dawn. He, too, feels compelled to check the meaning of words, just as I was compelled to do so as a child, and now, too, when I reside in the antechamber of death. They see thousands of naked women in the freezing light of dawn. I wouldn't dare write it down without him, I wouldn't dare imagine it, but Vrba says ten thousand naked women. Armed with dogs and whips, their wardens are holding typhoid fever inspection in the *Frauenlager*. Some will be liquidated because of typhoid fever, others will perish from the early-morning cold within the next half hour.

It is God's will, this is Moses Sonnenschein's manic answer to Vrba's inquisitive touch.

The men are taken straight to the fiery ditches. They must go through the large heaps of abandoned clothes before they are disinfected and used again. The clothes of those corpses now burning in the pits, or that have already been burned to cinders.

Four negatives of the burning of the naked women flung into the burning pits have survived. Perhaps they were taken with a camera left behind in a cattle car by one of the deportees, and the anonymous photographer may have seen on the frame counter that there were four negatives at his disposal to take these pictures. The anonymous person took the four photographs on purpose, so we may learn, if we haven't already, what the naked women's last movements were before they were confined to the flames. This was as much goodness as he could glean from the moment. The scream slipping through their open lips. Their bodies incinerated under the open sky. We know it thanks to him.

When three hours later Moses Sonnenschein and Rudolf Vrba are transported back from work at the burning pits, half of the women selected are still standing on the platforms of some forty waiting trucks. And when the engines of the trucks start up, thousands of women start screaming. Vrba writes that the screams issue from the throats of many thousands of women. I don't dare imagine the escalating scream of thousands of naked women on their way to their annihilation, their lamentations, prayers, and supplications rising above the sound of the rumbling trucks. Some of the women hurl themselves over the side of the trucks. Let us not forget, these women are all someone, they are someone's children, wives, lovers. Also, they are afraid of death. At the given moment, this is all that remains of their chance for goodness. They are either shot or they can end up under the wheels of the trucks. As he passes by the wide-open gate of this theological paradise on the platform of a truck, Moses Sonnenschein is reduced to mumbling that there is no God.

The illusion is shattered. His five thousand years of trust in the concept of Divine Providence comes to nothing and his ethical self-control bursts apart from the overstrained tension of its spring. His defunct notions are now powerless to curb his frenzy, and he keeps shouting that there is no God. This is all that his personal goodness can muster. Having previously honored the long-held concept, he has now come face-to-face with its final and irrevocable refutation, and he must let the world know about it. Or if God exists, may he be cursed, he shouts three times in succession, may he be cursed, may he be cursed, may he be cursed.

I take it back, I take it back, Thomas Mann shouts through Leverkühn's lips as he is working on *Doctor Faustus* in the exclusive Pacific Palisades neighborhood of far-off California, in his exquisitely furnished home where the servants surely keep the silver well-polished, all the while that, in the interest of his work, he reserves his tears for the afternoon, when he will set off for his constitutional and will be looking forward to his five o'clock tea, which they will serve with canapés, *canapés au saumon fumé, fromage et au concombre*, but by then his tears will no longer make sense.

The writer and his protagonist retract the triumphal song of the bourgeoisie, the Ninth Symphony, whereas they don't know everything, not yet. This is as much goodness as the reigning European conception of God contains between work and five o'clock tea. It is as much as it ever contained.

On the other hand, the retraction can no longer be retracted. Every time the Ninth Symphony is played, especially its last movement, the "Ode to Joy," once played to shreds by the Nazis, it becomes its own retraction. The frescoes of the Sistine Chapel have nothing to do with theology. Nor did they ever. Documents offer plenty of proof of what Thomas Mann intuited early on, the elemental necessity of retraction.

Being familiar with the documents, I can't help but ask to what end I was born in sun-drenched Budapest on that certain Wednesday, October 14, in the accursed year of Our Lord 1942, when in the early morning the men of Einsatzkommando No. 9 drove the 1947 inhabitants of the Mizocz ghetto to a secluded nearby ravine. While they ordered them to strip naked, then mowed them down, then one by one, shot the wounded in the head, despite Heinrich Himmler's strict orders to the contrary, they carefully documented every phase of the proceedings from one specific camera angle, so that they could paste them into their family albums back home in Germany, and after their copious noonday meal spiced with loving affection, they could show them to the rest of the family, look, my brethren, see with your own eyes how we butchered so many people in the interest of our precious family happiness. Why didn't I get stuck inside the birth canal. Why didn't the umbilical cord wind itself around my neck. Or even before that, why did I have to be conceived. My mother knew the world she was pushing me into. She wasn't naïve, she wasn't uninformed, she wasn't the least bit stupid, nor was she unprepared or passive. Why didn't she stick a knitting needle up through her body. Why didn't she ask Imre Hirschler to abort me. Now, at the age of seventy-four, I say that I'd have felt much better aborted than I feel now as a survivor. By that time, Klára Tauber could have had no doubt whatsoever that Epicurus's hypothesis was correct. God is not almighty, he is not good, or else he does not exist. Or later, why didn't I have the strength to commit suicide. This, too, is a question begging for an answer. The interdiction against suicide makes sense only in a world in which Divine Providence is present. Why was I able to get the better of my damned inclination for suicide all the same. Why did it seem more sensible, when the effort to stop myself made no sense at all.

And yet goodness, Leverkühn, who is tortured by such questions of theology, says along with me for all to hear, he says it not so much because he is sure of himself, but because he hopes to ward off fear so that his voice shouldn't shake from his own oppositional stance, in short, he says that despite and independent of all forms of evil, goodness functions on a parallel track. They do not stand in a hierarchical relationship. At times, they are not in any sort of relationship at all. They neither inspire nor hinder each other. The photographs taken of the mass executions do not stand in causal relation to the domestic love and the killer instincts that make midday Christmas meals so special. They can be present simultaneously in a single person; there are no physical or emotional impediments to the autonomous functioning of good and evil; the functioning of both is based on the same anthropological given, something that surely we have brought along with us into our human existence in the form of instinct. In all cases, individual action enjoys primacy. I am compelled to act even against my better judgment or against our common future. There is no world apart from me. Not only were my mother and father at the mercy of their own urge to procreate, I was at the mercy of my own conception. We have an animalistic God who is at the mercy of our actions at all times. If it were not so, then, in the name of their own truth, the priests of the warring armies couldn't consecrate the weapons with which the two are about to mutually mow each other down. They would spit up bloody clots from their lungs, their hands would fall off when, in the name of the Serbian god, they would send the Serbs to massacre the Croatians. Such a thing would never occur to them.

The God we have will effectuate every act of every individual without the least scruple, and in this he is an almighty God indeed.

A person who serves this God must make sure of just one thing, that he should have no self-imposed ethical or psychological obstacles stand in his way, that the Irish Protestants should not be prevented from slaughtering Irish Catholics with reference to Jesus Christ, who themselves are slaughtering the Irish Protestants with reference to Jesus Christ, that there should be no obstacle to prevent the Croatians' own god from slaughtering the Serbs in the name of Jesus Christ. And lest we forget, according to Canon Law, the pope prays for the salvation of the murderers and not their victims, whereby he encourages the freedom of action of the survivors. The silent clamor of the dead has not yet reached his most holy ear; what's more, he must turn off his hearing with his consciousness, which he calls faith. European history progresses in the spirit of man's freedom of action. You cannot curb God's omnipotence at the expense of individual freedom. On the other hand, if you do not curb it, the number of the dead increases by leaps and bounds, especially among sexually mature young males. In the interest of serving their gods and churches, sexually mature combatants will overcome their fear of death so that they may annihilate other sexually mature combatants, in short, in the name of their convictions, they end up annihilating themselves. In which case, why should we forbid suicide when we should be condoning it.

Primo Levi ties his great theological question to a particular individual, prisoner no. 141565. His name is Elias, he is probably a Polish Jew, but beyond this, his fellow prisoners know very little about him. He speaks only Yiddish, the surly and deformed Yiddish of the Warsaw Ghetto. He might be twenty or forty years of age. He usually says that he is thirty-three and that he has fathered seventeen children. Elias has a resounding voice. He speaks to himself and to others at a volume and with an oratorical style better suited to addressing a dense crowd. Elias is a dwarf, he is no more than a hundred and fifty centimeters, but his muscles and strength are Herculean. His skull is not that of a man. The skull sutures under his scalp stand out immoderately. The nose, the chin, the forehead, the cheekbones are as hard and compact as those of a wild animal about to charge. It is not I but Primo Levi who describes him in this way. Elias is constantly in motion. Elias never rests, he is never injured or ill. He is skillful with anything requiring the use of his hands, and while he works, he sings without pause or declaims incomprehensibly. While others barely carry one sack of cement, he balances three on his shoulder. Levi writes something I'd never dare write, that he carries four sacks onto the scaffolding, and while he hurries along on his short, squat legs, he curses and accompanies his mighty effort with the terrible grimace of pleasure combined with pain. While the others starve, are wounded or sick, pass bloody diarrhea, their numbers decreasing, while they starve to death, he acquires food in some mysterious manner, frequently disappearing on mysterious visits and adventures. His exceptional gifts legitimize the camp's function as a death camp. He needs not fear being selected. His mere existence affirms that in Auschwitz everything is just fine, and there's no Auschwitz that a person can't survive with a song on his lips. The kapos, his fellow prisoners, and the guards are in full agreement on this and respect him for it. They are hoping to shed the bothersome veneer of humanity without undue difficulty, in which the road to the paradise of survival will be open to them as well. They look up to him, though they prefer not to look at his head or his face, because there is no past that Elias can remember, and there is no future to fill him with either hope or fear, and it shows in his expression. Two of his precious characteristics guarantee his existence, his madness and his bestiality. Levi, a chemist who hails from the humanist Turin Circle, says that except for insanity and bestiality, all other roads out of Auschwitz are dead ends. But he isn't just thinking of Auschwitz or Europe's past and present, he is thinking of human existence as such, of the grand experiment conducted by man to assign some higher meaning to his existence.

You see the speck in your brother's eye, but not the log in your own. I heard this from my parents and relatives, and I understood what they meant right away. They meant that if we are compelled to measure one another by a double standard, then, in the interest of our common future, let the other take the first step toward self-improvement. Clearly, a person can't very well take the first step, even with the best of intentions. At one end of the scale there are my former actions to consider, to block out, forget, touch up, hide, or deny; and on the other hand, in the interest of my well-being and happiness, I am bound to repeat my former actions tomorrow, too.

What's more, a reasonable man can't very well claim that he is imbecilic and bestial. For one thing, he can't claim this because of the miming of ethics needed for survival, but also, he can't claim this because in the majority of cases it would not apply. We endow human bloodshed and destruction with the adjective *bestial*, whereas even with our petty domestic sins, we damage the reputation of animals.

What's to keep us from annihilating others in the name of universal love, the common good, or equality, what is to prevent us. And if this is how it is, if this is how goodness is expressed, why should we take the heartrending sobs of mothers seriously. After all, they're the ones who send their sons to kill and to share in the spoils of their massacres. Though there is a connection between pragmatic and reflective thinking, there is no hierarchy between them, and above all, no coherence, whether ethical or conceptual, is to be discovered in their intermingling. It's what we're stuck with. Our God is such an incoherent and inconsequential god, and he is the only god we have.

Few people are capable of living in keeping with the requirements of reflective thinking. They would like to act in keeping with their imagination and their social and religious utopias, but having said this much, we cannot say that they can avoid or ignore their anthropological givens, or that in a crisis their actions are motivated by anything other than the laws of imbecility and bestiality, and no principle or norm of any kind can transform these into something noble. Goodness lacks pedagogical intentions, nor can it be shared or passed on. World-transformative intentions that spring from goodness and love lead straight down the path to annihilation; what's more, after a while it will be made sufficiently clear that such intentions were motivated by self-interest. When a person sees a problem, he will solve it under the guardianship of the same bestial and imbecilic, inconsequent and incoherent God he himself created so that he may serve him. And while he solves the problem or else gives the appearance of having solved it, he creates a hundred other problems. For one thing, if a person hopes to ennoble another person with recourse to philosophy or theology, he will end up debasing himself for a long time to come.

Goodness has no need of a single individual or of humanity as such in order to prevail.

With such conditions and givens, it is more difficult to capture in words the essence of human goodness than the details of a mass killing or a revolution, whereas these, too, are notoriously difficult to capture in words. Reflective action is not an option. But the sole source and aim of goodness is not action, it is perception and the simultaneous apperception of the mode of perception. The description of an evening, a copulation, a mass murder, or a revolution destined to fail is child's play; after all, it progresses along the triple track of identical situations, similarities, and differences, it takes cognizance of the relationship between quality and quantity, and these tracks are familiar to us all. On the other hand, in order to understand goodness, I must first note not the objects of perception, I must perceive the mechanism of perception as it reveals itself through even the greatest scandal. With respect to goodness, description is mostly helpless. It makes no sense to define goodness with an appeal to its quantity or quality, and consequently, the text, which can't do without quantitative and qualitative analyses, must forget goodness. Chekhov may well be the first and the last writer who nevertheless caught some of it in his net. And yet we can't say that since his death goodness has manifested itself only in the guise of wishful thinking or pipe dreams and intentions, or as an ethical requirement, or only just provisionally, momentarily, under a given set of circumstances, in certain given situations. You won't find goodness in contemporary literature. On the other hand, its absence is all the more glaring. Kafka, Beckett, and Camus followed the path of this absence. They followed the mechanism of the universe of perception along a negative path.

Or what is a text to do with happiness, this too is among the narrator's repeated concerns. What is it to make of the most important source of happiness, that of sexual pleasure. Eros, the great driving force, and Hermes, the great guide of the soul, have been trying for millennia to hold carnal knowledge in check, they make suggestions, put up stop signs, and standardize it so they can offer it up to lovers as a rite, lest, wrapped in each other's arms, they should plunge into the animal chaos of their mutual helplessness. And mostly, they plunge. But at least they should realize in time what is happening and seek solid ground, so that when the alarm clock sounds at 4:30 the next morning, they should be able to climb out of their paradisiacal abyss and go to work.

Or how are we narrators to handle the second most important source of happiness, brotherly love, which appears, if rarely, in nature; how am I to handle the Greek *philia*, the Greek *anthropos*, what am I to do with the Latin *caritas* and *humanitas*. Institutionalized religion spares no effort in herding these phenomena into their cultic yoke. Make no mistake. Secularization has not decreased but increased their power, meaning their conceptual tyranny. Let's see, say our imbecilic and bestial fellow men wrapped up as they are with their inconsequential actions and incoherent thoughts, let's see, they ask, left perilously to fend for themselves with their philosophical and theological questions, let's see whether there is a more noble form of love than the one that can dispense with sentiment directed at a particular individual as well as sensuality bound to a particular individual. Since we must kill with our consecrated weapons dispassionately, why shouldn't we love dispassionately. Except, divine love is dispassionate. Divine love cannot be neutral.

You've yet to be born, and they have already cast their conceptual web to ensnare you. Let brotherly love be exalted over love between two individuals. You shouldn't love the individual in a man, but the creature of God. If we were able to execute the operation of sublimation when told to do so, if at least our churches were successful at it, if the love of a man and a woman and brotherly love really shared a common substance thanks to which they could be separated from personal ties, possibly the other person's body or gender, cosmic understanding and foresight would in fact begin to function in a person, in which case the acquisition of divine love would become, as it were, a question of goodwill and good intention, and nothing would stand, ever again, in the way of its justification by faith. Surely, it would be highly desirable if such a thing could come to pass. But in that case, carnal pleasure and brotherly love would have to be the dual corbels of earthly goodness, meaning humanism and enlightenment. But this did not happen. There was always someone busying himself with an exact description of these basic existential concepts and attempting to find the best place for them in cultural dictionaries, thereby legitimizing them, but none have managed the project, neither the Gnostics, nor the Scholastics, nor the Humanists, nor the adherents of the Enlightenment. The institutionalization of goodness remained a destructive dream. Brotherly love and sexual pleasure are not perched on thrones of equal rank and importance, even if they function, despite the cultic measures and regulations. Hardly anyone places eroticism and philanthropy on equal footing, whereas they appeared hand in hand at the dawn of humanism. Monastic asceticism rendered them hesitant, tortured, and pale, while their drive for dominance made them brutal, and at the dawn of the Enlightenment they sneaked back through a side door. Today, we seldom hear of them, and what we do hear is mostly business news or fake news, pornography or sentimentality.

Yet because of this, who would dare assert that they are not fully and joyfully active, that there is no brotherly love, that there are no momentous encounters, or that there are no good people. The world would have perished long ago, were it not for the pleasure bestowed on the loins of others, or the various other manifestations of human goodness. The pleasure of the loins is the joyful and passionate consciousness of the world. But what's the sense in it when, in the language of narrative fiction, the world practicing goodness disappears or remains in the wings, and as for the created landscape, it is reduced to a vale of tears. At most, the shadow of goodness, the memory of happiness come through the text, and in place of the keen sexual pleasure the live pain, and the pleasure of pain and the pleasure of complaint.

What is goodness, what is pleasure, what is happiness, what is ecstasy. For strictly professional reasons, I must keep these questions as dry as gunpowder.

Who can separate love and being in love, the passion related to love and the need for love. And conversely, can being in love exist without love's passion. What is their essence, do they contain essence at all. Where is their place in Creation. Where is their place in a narrative. Are they modes of conduct based on innate capacities, or are they borrowed from magical and mythical models, or are they physiological and biochemical potentialities of the brain, emotionally contingent configurations. We know from experience that ecstasy and happiness have varieties, degrees, and quantities. But regardless of the system of comparisons we use, regardless of the measuring standard we use, who can tell how much room, in any specific instance, they can carve out for themselves from the commonplace Eden of cheating, temptation, seduction, deception, lying, betrayal, envy, scheming, cunning, thieving, robbery and profiteering, copulation, rutting, exploitation, hatred, and murder. This commonplace Eden is a sweet Eden, we mustn't underestimate it. Is the drive for profit or the drive for power, or possibly the drive for revenge, related to the sweet ecstasy of love. How could it be otherwise. And does ecstasy care whether its object is money, gold, wealth, position, possibly the attractive lines of another person's lips, or do we attain it through the most noble emotional and intellectual concentration. For ecstasy it is all the same. Goodness, joy, happiness, pleasure, do they evidence characteristics tied to gender, or else, is it the lack of such differences that reveal what in a man is not tied to the individual, and thus to gender. Are bestiality and humanity really contradictory, as Balzac thought in the introduction to *La Comédie humaine*. Are the subjects and manifestations of goodness, tenderness, happiness, pleasure, and love present in our lives only as colorful elements, or are they present as the preconditions of our emotional lives. Or do they function as intermediaries between cultures and religious cults, or as a Cerberus who, spotting the transgressor into the realm of culture, is quick to shout, stop, and go no further. Do they stand guard over hierarchy, where there is one, and do they stand guard over the lack of hierarchy, where people are prone to ensuring that there be no hierarchy.

On that evening in early fall when my Aunt Magda brought the accusation against me, I couldn't have been wholly innocent of their muddled conceits because I had been subjected to the shock much earlier; in fact, I had been subjected to a variety of intellectual shocks.

I must have been around six when they took me to the opera to see *Fidelio*, conducted by Otto Klemperer, who was chief musical director at the time. It must have been a special performance. We were sitting in the dark, golden gloom of a box, in the interior of a beating heart lined with red velvet and silk strewn with lilies. Theoretically, my parents should have torn the silk strewn with lilies off the wall, something that the students of the People's College had done with relish when they took possession of aristocratic palaces. They should have trampled the whole sickening petit bourgeois kitsch, the stuccos and gilding, into the dust. The footlights illuminated the expectant faces. All this must have happened in November 1948, after the Communist takeover. László Rajk was still minister of foreign affairs, and

Grandfather Tauber was barely on speaking terms with his daughter, and thanks to Prime Minister Lajos Dinnyés, our father, Technical Counselor László Nádas, was transferred from the Reparations Bureau to the Transportation Ministry. Except for me, everyone seemed satisfied with all that leftover ersatz pomp. Even though I understand why others consider all that fakery beautiful, I considered and still consider the two opera houses, the one by Charles Garnier in Paris and the other by Miklós Ybl in Budapest, built around the same time, ugly and ungainly, although I understand why others consider all that ersatz beautiful. Tense, with my bias held in abeyance, I watched the innocently watching faces of the people I was with, because I wanted to understand what was happening on stage. It was not easy to understand. Jaquino loved sweet little Marcellina to distraction, and because his love went unrequited, he pursued her with all the more vehemence. But Marcellina ignored him and fled from him. With all her heart, she loved only the new prison guard, Fidelio. She hadn't loved him the day before, she loved Jaquino, which soon puzzled Jaquino, not just me. Only Beethoven would have understood, because for his whole life everyone was always loving someone else, but presumably, no one ever loved him, or else the woman he loved didn't reciprocate his feelings.

How can something like this make sense to the sane mind or be forgiven. Also, I couldn't understand how so many people could tolerate such baseness. Marcellina now loved Fidelio, who had hoodwinked her just as disgracefully as she had deserted Jaquino. If only Marcellina knew how base Fidelio was, maybe she wouldn't love him. But she didn't know. Only we know. Or if Jaquino knew how disgraceful Marcellina was, why would he love her. They put a spell on each other and on us and everyone else because of their gullibility. Everyone could see their duplicity and wickedness, yet instead of protesting they praised their cleverness instead. How clever is this ugly Leonora who, in order to free Florestan, has dressed up as a boy and donned the mask of handsome Fidelio. Poor Marcellina, it's not her fault that she fell in love with a girl dressed as a boy, and that as soon as she sets eyes on the gentle Fidelio, she must leave the uncouth Jaquino. If a person sees someone better, they are bound to make the change. The entire world turned out to be a big, contractual, and infinitely complex set of perfidies, and not only on stage, but among the audience, and at home as well.

The point is that there was no Fidelio who slipped into boy's clothing, a woman in love and ready to do anything for her love's sake. The playbill gave her real name, and also the name of the singer. Leonora pretended to be Fidelio, but she was actually a woman called Anna Báthy, who went to the same hairdresser as Stefánia Klébinder, the mother of my Uncle Pista's new wife, and who also sang in the choir. As if indeed, because of the wicked deception, it behooves us to consider Anna Báthy the model of marital fidelity. After all, she's a famous and celebrated opera singer who is so famous and celebrated because she is capable of repeating these mighty deceptions in her ridiculous masquerade night after night. Pretending that she's the lithe and handsome Fidelio, who is really Leonora, who has brought deception to a state of perfection. Everyone could see that not only us, but Anna Báthy, too, fell for this nonsense. They believed together what they couldn't possibly have believed individually.

Even my parents did not make any critical comments, they did not protest, they were not in a temper. Whereas they should have torn down the building, set fire to it at its four corners, and poured salt on its smoldering ruins. I understood the wicked, fat woman in disguise who didn't love sweet Marcellina at all and didn't care about poor Jaquino's pain. How could I not have understood. Those men's pants nearly burst their seams on her colossal ass. For the first time in my life I learned that perception, too, can be perceived, meaning that I could step outside the scene even further. The experience in the looming light of the Budapest Opera box overwhelmed me. Even if Marcellina is in love and is stupid, she should still notice that she loves a wicked woman, that she loves a woman, but Jaquino didn't realize either who Marcellina was really in love with. She loves a woman with a colossal ass, a woman who of all things is also a singer, na ya, as Grandmother Cecília Nussbaum would say. Don Pizarro didn't realize either, and nor did Rocco. For some mysterious reason, the vile system of perfidy was not visible on stage. The audience didn't seem surprised, my parents didn't seem surprised, it was as if no one could see it. As a consequence, the perfidy that they called goodness on stage, and also in the reverential auditorium, cried out to the sky. I suddenly saw the universal system of mutual deception, but I couldn't have said how I could fight my way out of it, and I felt that I was suffocating.

Marcellina must be led astray, poor Jaquino must be driven to near distraction so that perfidious Leonora should free Florestan, who from his prison cell is fighting for the freedom of his people, a man who cares about nothing but the freedom of the people. Florestan was a professional revolutionary, a hero who didn't care about the feelings or pain of others even in the confinement of his loathsome dungeon, or else it is in the interest of the freedom of his people that he must pretend that nothing else interests him. And surely we mustn't notice all the perfidy ourselves so that he may succeed in realizing universal freedom, and that at least this one time we shouldn't betray him either. Meanwhile, Stefánia Klébinder was singing in the chorus of prisoners who were crying for freedom. How could I have helped but hear about such things from my Communist parents, about the present violated in the interest of the future. Still, this is how they saw their valued goodness at the time, which they must serve encased in the armor of their insensibility. There was historical logic to the story, there were worldly and religious models and analogies, it had a sense of adventure worthy of a novel for adolescents, heroism straight out of an epic, it had a concrete utopia, asceticism, and this is how I should have accepted it that night at the opera. Let's not say anything just yet, let's admit that the cause of universal freedom takes precedence over the personal happiness of others, because on this universal stage, the freedom of his people is even more important for Florestan than his own freedom and Leonora's honor. If someone is the champion of universal freedom, he must despair of loving others. Florestan doesn't love one person, he loves everyone, he must free not one person, but all persons at one blow. Why shouldn't Fidelio and Florestan have sacrificed this sweet little Marcellina and poor little Jaquino, this stupid goose and this uncouth blockhead, on the altar of a higher cause. Also, my parents had told me that Stefánia Klébinder isn't even singing on stage, just moving her lips, because she's not a member of the chorus but of the dance corps, and they put the dancers on stage only to make the crowd of prisoners look bigger, as if the big wide world were the image of an undefinable formation, a chimera, a system of impenetrable reflections. And why shouldn't they have used them, Anna Báthy or Stefánia Klébinder, considering that Marcellina's love was itself an ugly self-deception when she didn't even realize that she was in love with a woman, or when just the day before, she agreed to be betrothed to a man she couldn't stand, not even his smell. No matter where a person entered this single dramatic universe, he ran up against perfidy even if he had no knowledge of the Gulag, the show trials, or the woodsheds of secret villas in Buda where they tortured people to make them talk.

A fake, fake news, a fake precious stone in a fake setting. How shall I put it, only if we lacked ethical requirements with respect to goodness and faithfulness would it not have been fake. I was terribly upset. I was agitated, I was helpless and in a daze. I understood it but did not accept it, or, the other way around, if I accepted it, right away I didn't understand it. I was so upset that later, even after twenty-five years, when I heard the first bars of the overture to *Fidelio*, I felt sick. At Berlin's Unter den Linden, I fainted when I heard the first bars of the overture. Wolfgang Jöhling, the young poet sitting next to me, revived me; he thought that the first bars of the prelude made me fall asleep, and that's why my head fell over my slumping body. This happened on November 3, 1973, a Sunday. Not that I remember the date, it's the other way around, I've kept the program so I would remember the date of the performance, which was memorable in more ways than one.

There stood before us the unconsidered world scheme of deception.

But that evening, the worst was yet to come. The musical drama, which originally bore the title *Léonore, ou l'Amour conjugal*, premiered in Paris on February 18, 1798, ten years after the fall of the Bastille. Need I say, it was a resounding success. The piece combined the yearning for freedom and sensual vertigo with political and amorous intrigue, which proved to be a novel dramaturgical idea. It grafted the bloody revolution against tyranny onto a sentimental pastorale, thereby offering a master key to cheap success. It created a new genre and, in a certain sense, history. From then on, the French called pieces like this *comédie larmoyante*, and the Germans *Rührstück* or *Befreiungsopern*, or liberation operas, and on the basis of the German, the Hungarians came to call them *szabadító operák*, although tearful comedy is a much more apt term for the genre.

All the ethical and aesthetic gestures of these liberation operas were functionally incorporated into Europe's cultural consciousness.

The original version was composed by Pierre Gaveaux, a singer in Paris, and its libretto was written by Jean-Nicolas Bouilly, a lawyer from Touraine, neither one brilliant, nor a clever student of human nature. Monsieur Bouilly, or so it is said, did not come up with the story himself, and if that is indeed the case, then with respect to Jaquino and Marcellina, the story is even more damning. However, thanks to this, we get to perceive the emotional outpouring that, as opposed to his ideal, is man's true reality. I first saw *Fidelio* when I was six. The Rajk trial came a year later. The evening I was accused I must have been about nine. Opinion countered opinion, my Aunt Magda claimed, I denied, though actually I didn't even deny anything, there was no question of denial because that, too, proved humiliating, because my aunt wanted to force a transgression down my throat that not only did I not commit, there wasn't even a place in my consciousness where a fantasy like it could have existed. And at that point, my parents, goaded by my favorite aunt, decided to do something truly despicable.

The idea may have come from my father, who told my mother to call András Vajda's mother on the phone to see what András had to say about the situation. My mother was reluctant. Her reluctance showed in her body language, which I understood right away, but not so my aunt and my father. My Aunt Magda was indignant.

Not a week from now, Klári dear, but now.

You must do it.

Why should I, when you know her just as well.

And so she made the call.

During the siege, my mother refused point-blank to take in András. This was a cause of her reluctance that evening. She subsequently excused herself by saying that she had five children to look after, this wasn't the case yet. Today I'm inclined to think that the number of children needing to be saved grew gradually, and during the Arrow Cross terror, she gradually collapsed under the weight of her task. To engage in illegal activities and at the same time to save children is no small responsibility indeed, and the two can barely be reconciled. Still, until the last moment of her life, she had pangs of conscience because she had refused, her heart broke because she'd said no, she'd turned down her friend's request, and so she later gave András Vajda a wide berth. She may have told herself that because of her under-ground activities, she'd already asked Imre Hirschler for an abortion that summer, and now, because of another, she couldn't endanger the living, though she must have realized the weakness of her reasoning. Holding her son the same age as I in her arms, András Vajda's mother sank to her knees and cried out, Klári dear, I beg you. She probably had to go somewhere to save people, to bring them out of somewhere, perhaps her parents from a shtetl in the countryside. She flung herself on her knees on the modern-style Afghan rug that I later passed on to my brother. For a long time I didn't tell my brother what had hap-pened on the rug. But that rug began to hurt me as it had once hurt my mother. But my mother was so harsh with me and with herself that she repeatedly related what had happened on that rug, she beat it into me, she couldn't stop herself from repeating it. To excuse her decision, she even told me how Hirschler conducted an abortion, that it would have been a girl, she'd have been your sister, your little sister. I never wanted to see that rug, burdened with history, ever again. Fifty million people had been killed, but four years after the siege, my mother was still wrestling with that damned Afghan rug and my aborted little sis-ter. That rug became an obsession with her, and my little sister became a similar historical obsession and vision, much like my own with the small ankle boots and the feet of destruction in those handmade yel-low shoes. Every time she crossed the room, she must have thought of that woman begging her, and the fact that András managed to escape without her help probably did nothing to lessen the tension between the two women. As a matter of fact, not only did András manage to escape, he even managed to push his little brother out the fourth-story window, his little brother who fell on top of a parked car but, wonder of wonders, did not suffer so much as a bruise.

We ran down to Wallenberg Street to see the car. All the people in the area were amazed, they couldn't believe it. A couple of days later, they fixed bars to the window of the children's room in their home, and every time I passed their house, I felt compelled to look up to see if those damn bars were still there. My parents lost no time in affixing bars to our own children's room as well.

Now they were probably counting on the little boy who was far less headstrong than I to admit the wickedness that we did not commit.

When my mother picked up the phone to commit this ignoble act, I ran from the room, and no one stopped me. At the same time, I knew that with my escape I was strengthening the appearance of my supposed baseness. I can't own up to the fact like a man, meaning like an imbecile, at least, this was the almighty sentence of ethical mimicry in cases such as mine. But this was the old mistake, I couldn't have gotten myself to tell the lie that they demanded of me in the name of truth, even for their sake.

I have no idea what happened, what András Vajda's mother said, or what András didn't say. For years I was tortured by what they had imagined as I tried to imagine the crime we had not committed; I tried to imagine holding down Yvette's arms and legs, but her naked thighs and naked arms fell outside my field of vision; after all, we did not hold anything down. They never mentioned the incident again, they said nothing, nor did I mention it again or learn any more about it. But the mutual silence became part of the harsh reality of the people surrounding me. It was dictated by the bourgeois rules of etiquette. We always know more than we say, we know many other things as well, which is how it should be. Also, we kept silent in order to avoid burdening one another with unpleasant truths. Yvette never said that her grandmother may have made it up, and she never said that I had done anything untoward that had left its mark on her neck, arms, and thighs. And as for me, I didn't dare ask her why she'd done it and how, why she accused me instead of the boys at the pool, because I was afraid that what I might hear would be more terrible than anything.

One thing is for sure, I never again accepted her invitation to go and do laps with her. I loved her, I still do, but something irrevocable had come between us. Until I was forty-seven, I refused to set foot in the Sports Pool on Margaret Island.

András didn't ask anything either, but that evening our friendship came to an end. We met again only years later, under dramatic circumstances, when we ended up in the same class at the High School for Chemistry.

But back then I sat in the dark kitchen, and Rózsi Németh was moving about, groping about or sifting through some papers in the maid's room. She was probably writing a letter or preparing to write one. At such times she first read her old letters, arranging them on the small table in front of the window, and would start to write only afterward. She kept her letters in a big wooden box on top of the wardrobe, the wooden box Grandmother Mezei used in Gömörsid to hold the thread and yarn for darning. We had this box with its dull veneer for some time yet, but then it disappeared without a trace along with the sewing box she had in Pest that was a lot more ornate, with rich marquetry inlay and polished to a high sheen. Rózsi Németh's handwriting was awkward, and our parents didn't entrust her with keeping the journal recording my brother's development; instead, on the basis of her daily reports, my mother made the entries herself in her regular, beautifully fashioned handwriting, though there were days when Rózsi had to record this or that in the journal all the same. The truth is that when Rózsi wrote something down, she made lots of mistakes. *He went todderin into the korner. He was in hi spiritz and slept wel.* Her handwriting was not nearly as well-considered and orderly as she was; still, I recognize her immediately from her stoic entries.

She first carefully filled in every column for the day in the large notebook, from which we know that on Saturday, March 26, at seven in the morning, the seven-months-and-two-days-old child ate 100 grams, probably mother's milk that she brought from András Kepes's mother the night before, at ten he had milk, probably boiled cow's milk, at two in the afternoon boiled cabbage, and at six in the evening apples, which means that our parents weren't back yet on that early Saturday evening. I remember this apple well, it was grated apple, she grated it every single afternoon on an apple grater made of pressed glass. The apple grater had been put in service for my father's older siblings, and it was put in service for my benefit as well. What the difference is between pressed glass and cut glass, how glass is blown or cast in a workshop, I learned from my father on an excursion to the Zemplén Mountains as the digression to another explanation. Vágáshuta. We were walking along a small village nestled in a valley. It was called Vágáshuta. Glassworks. Yet another combined compound word. At times veritable explanation-floods came pouring from inside him, and every sentence of his explanation was enhanced by twelve further digressions and footnotes, and probably, this mass of information left a structural trace in my mind . . .

Sometimes in the afternoon, Rózsi Németh would grate an apple on the pressed glass apple grater for me, too, and she grated some cookies into it as well. My father used this old apple grater to show me how to identify pressed glass, he guided my finger along the sides, and he explained how the mold is made, and how the seam comes about where the two sides of the mold meet, and it can't be gotten rid of by filing it down. Can you feel it. She even let me have the core with the seeds. Eating the seeds was not allowed because they contain cyanide, even if in minute quantities, that's why the women in Tiszazug gave it in small portions to the husbands they wanted to get rid of. My father had told me about it once before, and asked if I remembered. As a result cyanide came into a perilous relationship to Zionism in my mind. Our father wanted me to realize how dangerous poisons were. If portioned out in very small quantities, the body begins to accumulate them, until the amount reaches a critical mass. At which those who heard this had a good laugh, the cleverness of the women of Tiszazug impressed them. It took the medical examiners fifteen years to understand the puzzling deaths among the male population in seven villages in the area. The body accumulated the cyanide until it killed the unwanted husband, and it didn't even leave any primary traces. The body is helpless against mercury and cyanide. And do I know that I have a relative among the homicidal women, Mrs. Majzik, whose maiden name was Júlia Nádas. When they dug up József Majzik's grave in Nagykörű, she was the first to be arrested. Poor man, he was a night watchman in his earthly life, and the pathologist found a large amount of cyanide in his organs. This took my breath away. Why my relative, of all people. At which juncture we found ourselves perilously close to an earlier joke of my mother's, which she came to regret soon after. It was Sunday, they were sitting in front of their filing cabinet on the kilim rug imbued with history, because they were looking for some document that they couldn't find. As I stood over them, with endearing indifference, my mother handed me an official-looking document over her shoulder, it was folded up, and it was the birth certificate of a certain Péter Kovács born out of wedlock, and it bore the date of my birth. For a second it even occurred to me that there's a Péter Kovács who was born on the same day as I, except in Tornyiszentmiklós. Then for a fraction of a second, I thought that the document must be one of their forgeries. But as she continued looking for the document she wanted, my mother added that actually, they'd meant to tell me before that I'm not their child, they found me on the street during the siege, and so they adopted me. I was sure that this Péter Kovács from Tornyiszentmiklós was just another cruel joke, and yet I couldn't ignore the possibility that what she said could just as well be true. And that moment I turned on my heels and, whether it was true or not, I left the room without a word. Once back in my room, and in spite of my best intention and my best judgment, I collapsed on the divan, I didn't want to, but I began to cry. I decided to gather some of my secret possessions from their hiding place and leave home that minute. Get away. A driving energy had been released inside me as if some fission, atomic fission, were erupting in my organs. But my mother, who doubtless understood this, came running after me, she threw herself on her knees by the bed, it was just a joke, a bad joke, she admits, and she hugged and kissed me repeatedly, but in response, the energy inside me forced some sort of animal cry out of me that I had never let out before, yet it wasn't even a full cry, because I managed to suppress part of it. At which our father appeared at the door of our room, clearly frightened, but as he always did in crisis situations, he preferred to stay outside, keeping his distance. Our mother and I cried and howled together for a while, but I couldn't get over this bad joke of hers to this day. I was helpless to quell my tears. They called the doctor, Elza Baranyai, and I had to take some medicine she recommended. At night, I managed to fall asleep despite my tears. While they were sifting through the documents, they were mutually immersed in each other. Because of their various duties, they rarely had a chance to be together as quietly as now. Probably, my sudden appearance broke up their duet, and the forged document my mother was holding served her desire to lock me out, at least for a moment. Now, of course, stepping over her own bad joke she called after me as quickly as she could, don't worry, don't worry, this Mrs. Majzik, she's just a namesake.

All the same, I ate the seeds in secret because I liked biting into them and tasting their bitterness. The women of Tiszazug wanted to kill off every single male. They wanted to have just one child each by these men, so they shouldn't have to divide their inheritance, that's how great the poverty was at the time, because there was so little good soil by the Tisza. Your great-grandfather, he owned six hundred and sixty acres of it.

At eight in the evening my brother got semolina with tea and lemon; the lemon was reserved for him. The rest of us drank our tea with Uncle Pista's lemon substitute. I remember that the semolina cooked in milk was thick, with big, swollen semolina bits, they cooked it with a tiny pinch of sugar, they let me lick the pot clean; first I scraped the sides clean with a small spoon, then I used my fingers. On this particular Saturday my brother had bowel movements twice, but Rózsi Németh didn't record his weight and temperature that day, she left the columns blank. Apart from the obligatory daily records, there was a column for comments, too. On this day Rózsi wrote in the comments that he was suffering from Sunday sickness. Meaning my brother. Meaning on Saturday. Sunday sickness was her own term for what ailed my little brother; it meant that there's nothing wrong with the child, except on those Sundays when our parents could spend an hour or two at home and were not called away on some urgent errand, possibly in two different directions, for days on end to unfamiliar places, my brother would howl from early morning to late afternoon. His baby logic was impeccable. He didn't howl when they left early on Monday morning, or when they left him on Sunday afternoon and went to the movies, the theater, or were invited to friends, because when they left, he was satisfied with me and Rózsi Németh, he howled when, out of the blue, they stayed at home on Sunday morning, and then he punished and threatened them by crying, he showed them how great his solitude was because of them, in short, he certainly had structural knowledge, the structure of unsatisfied possibilities stood ready in his consciousness, he knew about something of which he couldn't have had objective experience, no experiential knowledge. His sense of timing was infallible. During the week, when our parents could be counted on to come home at any moment, he gradually went from babbling to weeping, and by the time they walked through the door, he was howling, full-throated, and would not stop.

There was no calming him down. He cried like a pro. He couldn't breathe, he turned purple. He exhausted himself, then started all over again. He quietly tried out the rhythms and melodies of the possible variations on crying, he gave himself over to his life's bitterness, he worked himself into a frenzy, he's an abandoned child, he put all his resources at the service of letting his parents know that he lacks affection, and pursued this goal as long as he could breathe. On Sunday he would not eat or drink, and if he did, he threw up. Basically, he put his life functions on hold. He couldn't have known yet, poor thing, that according to Emmi Pikler's method, children should be left to cry. If they can't entertain themselves with their toys and are picked up too often, they will end up spoiled. As for their lungs, they are in need of crying and shouting. If our mother didn't slap him in time, he sometimes fainted from howling.

I kept quiet so Rózsi Németh shouldn't notice my presence and ask what had happened. Though she was never short on sympathy, she would have normalized the drama with her questions. Besides, I couldn't have said anything to her, because I understood nothing of the scenario. After a while they saw my Aunt Magda to the hall, that's all that happened, they talked by the open door for a while, they couldn't seem to stop, this is all that happened. I don't know what they were talking about. I no longer cared. I didn't want to hear. I wanted to hear nothing they had to say. I broke off with them, and it wasn't sulking or some childish petulance, nor was this my first serious break with them. Very simply, I didn't want to understand them anymore. Rózsi Németh realized early on that my little brother let our parents, my mother first of all, know of his dissatisfaction by crying, because our mother had deserted him in her eagerness to engage in her work of organizing nationwide networks. I had no problem with this, I didn't feel abandoned, because I knew that her time away from home was helping others, surely, many others, and this thought satisfied me. Her office in Széchenyi Street was huge. If I leaned way out the bulging window of the Inner City palace, I could see the Danube with the silhouette of Buda Castle and the entire burghers' town with its charred ruins. Still, after a while, possibly in the early morning, possibly late at night, and possibly based on Rózsi Németh's account of what happened that day, our mother was in charge of writing the journal. She couldn't nurse the baby anyway, so why should she stay home. Still, for a couple of weeks she tried nursing him despite the pain, and for a couple of days, they even tried to make her inverted nipples relent with an electric breast pump. But my brother couldn't have been six months old when she put him in Rózsi Németh's care. Sometimes she'd rush home from Széchenyi Street for a short time; it was near enough, just three tram stops away.

Today you are 1 year old, little Palkó. This is the only entry in her hand for August 24, 1949, a Wednesday. From then on, there are no more entries until October 1. From October 1, the entries were made by our father or Rózsi Németh. Our father's spelling did not stand on as sure a footing as our mother's, but his handwriting was just as beautiful. Probably, the entries were resumed because Emmi Pikler said that parents must keep strict records so that they can review the stages of the child's development with the pediatrician later on. Keeping records is especially important if there is a serious problem. They must be able to review the history of the child's development on the basis of facts. On this day, Júlia Földi and László Rajk's son had already been passed into the care of Emmi Pikler's children's home in Lóczy Street, he'd been there for the past two months with the alias assigned to him by the State Security Authority. When his parents were arrested, Mátyás, Éva Bozóky and Ferenc Donáth's son, was also sent there.

An entry written by our father reveals what happened in August to curtail the diary entries. Your mother went to school. This is what he wrote, it is in his hand. This was his way of explaining the month-and-a-half-long hiatus. It is not the only entry in the diary addressed to the second person singular, meant for my brother. Our parents used the diary to speak to my brother at some later date, when he'd be a grown man, as it were. On the basis of their diary, prompted by their enchantment with facts and written in accordance with their utopian ideals, today we even know that on Saturday, October 1, 1949, my brother had a runny nose.

But these two, Rózsi and our father, couldn't keep their conscientious diary entries up for more than a month and a half.

Before promoting her to a higher station, they sent our mother to the Party Academy for a six-month training period that she managed to cut down to four months. It was a live-in school. When she got her promotion, she moved from the palace in Széchenyi Street to a pretty little palace in Múzeum Street, where all the furnishings and rugs remained just as the previous owners had left them when they had to leave because of some wartime calamity or the appropriation of their home by the state. The original objects were still sitting on the mantelpiece of the white marble fireplace. I even remember that these homes and their contents were placed under the jurisdiction of the Office of Abandoned Property. They seized them and had the office dispose of them. This is how I saw the objects on the mantelpiece of the Carrara marble fireplace as well as the staircase carved of Carrara marble, and the walls lined with snow-white marble; I saw them with the enchantment of the name of the Office of Abandoned Property ringing in my ears. They were searching for the dead, they unearthed mass graves, they pulled dead bodies from under the ruins. They identified some people, they exhumed others, someone made contact from some distant corner of the world, someone stepped on a land mine. But, with blue and pink showing through the gleaming white, Carrara marble is enchanting quite on its own merits. It has a network of veins and red blood cells, as if it were a human body.

In recognition of their achievements, my Uncle Pali and Aunt Magda were given a summer house in Leányfalu. In accordance with the Political Screening Committee resolution, said Screening Committee having been set up in accordance with Par. 3 of Gov. dec. 13.240/1947, I hereby acknowledge your outstanding merits in the national resistance (resistance movement and anti-German freedom fights). At the same time, with the Instrument of Acknowledgment herein delivered, I am also notifying you of the above. The notification and the instrument of acknowledgment were signed by Prime Minister Lajos Dinnyés. At nearly the same time that the prime minister signed the documents, in a final resolution Dr. Jenő Sövény, general manager of the Land Office of Northern Pest County, notified them that he was entitling Dr. Pál Aranyosy, residing at 6 Teréz Boulevard, district VI, Budapest, to the furnishings of Károly Pintér's house in Leányfalu, said decision having been made after the county Real Estate Reassignment Council confiscated Dr. Károly Pintér's real estate in Leányfalu in accordance with its final resolution No. III/1946.18. For a long time, for a very long time, this is how I thought of this house, as a confiscated house, as if I were bound to imagine its former life, until I accustomed myself to thinking of it as their house and its furnishings as the furnishings of their house. The confiscation was made legally binding by decree no. OTT 379,750/148. II/2 and the use of the real estate was legitimized by decree 1946. IX.t.e. par. 16, and decree no. 18,000/1946F.M.Sz, par. 29. I have accordingly bequeathed said real estate to Pál Aranyosy of Budapest because said individual has verified that in the interest of the development of the People's Democracy, both at home and abroad he has conducted successful activities, has suffered persecution, and has thus merited his right to proper real estate.

The house could have been abandoned for any of a number of reasons. The owners may have emigrated, they may have been Nazis or members of the Arrow Cross who thought it best to abscond post-haste and with forged documents live their lives quietly in Tasmania or Chile. Or possibly the People's Court had sentenced them for war crimes, a sentence that was founded or unfounded. Or they were Germans, members of a national minority, and were loaded onto freight cars and forcibly resettled.

Probably, only my Aunt Magda was present when the property was officially handed over, because my Uncle Pali was just then heading a delegation of journalists who'd gone to Warsaw. They were put up at the beautiful old Hotel Bristol on Krakowskie Przedmieście, near the president's palace. Twenty years later, in May, when Minister of the Interior Mieczysław Moczar, whose real name was Mikolaj Demko and whom his comrades called Mietek and who during the partisan war became infamous for his exceptional cruelty, and who later adopted his name in the movement as his real name, and who, spearheading the anti-Zionist movement, led an all-out anti-Semitic campaign by fomenting mass hysteria with reliance on clandestine police methods, meaning provocation and disinformation, had managed to oust the last Jews, about thirty thousand or forty thousand Polish citizens, though according to some sources, nearly eighty thousand, I stayed at the Bristol myself. I went to Warsaw because I wanted to see for myself what was happening. I arrived as a journalist. I was working for *Pest Megyei Hírlap*, a small local paper but with a large circulation which, like all other papers at the time, was under Party control. At the offices of the *Życie Warszawy* I gave my hosts another reason for my visit, but back in Pest I told my editor-in-chief, Andor Suha, my real reason for visiting Warsaw.

Dear Heart, my Uncle Pali wrote to my Aunt Magda from the same beautiful peacetime hotel. I am writing this letter first and foremost because I have handsome stationery to write it on, but also, you will find my address on it, where you can reach me from the 12th to the 14th. We are leaving tomorrow at 7 by plane for our round trip, first to Gdańsk (Danzig to us), then to Gdynia, where we will spend three days.

I went to Gdańsk myself, where at the shipyard three workers told me in all seriousness that there was a meat shortage because of the Jews. They occupy the key positions at the foreign trade companies, and in order to create shortages and strained relations, they're selling all the meat to foreign markets. Later, the interpreter told me the same thing.

They said that this is where the largest agricultural cooperatives are to be found, my Uncle Pali wrote. From here we will continue on to Stettin, then down to Wrocław (Boroszló), where we won't wait for the exposition to open but will take an excursion to the mines of Upper Silesia, then continue on to Katowice, Auschwitz, and Krakow.

I visited these places myself when I was there.

We are flying back to Warsaw from Krakow on the 12th, my Uncle Pali wrote, from where we will be taking a side trip to Lodz on the 15th, but this time by train, we will be heading home at last. Our official welcome will be on our last days there, at the end of our round trip. We will lay a ceremonious wreath at the grave of the Unknown Polish Soldier—Révész, our ambassador, approves wholeheartedly— and that's when we'll be eating our official dinner, because now they're stuffing us to exhaustion only half-officially. Our ambassador, Révész, greeted us at the airport with the amusing news that a young couple are eagerly awaiting our arrival, because they don't want to get married without me. Well, try to guess who the young couple is. You'll never guess. Carine, the little girl from Brussels, and Feri Majoros, her infantile beau, who fell head over heels in love with her during the centenary in March. Carine now lives here in Warsaw, but she's waiting to go to Pest so they can get married before a Hungarian registrar.

My impressions of Warsaw. You saw the film about Warsaw. It is but a poor reflection of what accompanies and tortures a person wherever he goes. So much ruin and vandalism is more than anyone could imagine, and seeing it is a wearying and depressing experience. We saw the ghetto as well. Imagine for yourself Pest's seventh district sadly reduced to heaps of brick and rubble, under which, here and there, the remains of a beautiful wrought-iron gate stick out. Otherwise, there is no trace of life anywhere in the incredibly vast area, except for weeds that force their way through the ashes and embers in places.

Twenty years later, in that memorable May of 1968, I saw the ghetto as my uncle had described it, and not only the ghetto remained, as far as the eye could see, the old city also lay in ruins; the ruins of the presidential palace were fenced off by wooden planks. Only the white mass of the Bristol stood out from this desolation of ruins with its otherworldly elegance. At night its facade was illuminated, a white ghost that haunted us from a past that perhaps never existed. On the other hand, on both sides of Krakowskie Przedmieście, the lindens had grown a bit, putting forth their honey-sweet flowers.

I also remember well from those years that our mother left my one-year-old brother with a heavy heart when she was ordered to attend the Party Academy. Every single night she had to sleep with the others in a big dormitory of that damned boarding school, it was ridiculous, and she was terribly upset. She looked for excuses, she made up reasons for why she must refuse this great honor. With the arrest of Mrs. Rajk in June, the office of general secretary of the Democratic Alliance of Hungarian Women was freed up. They had their sights on Valéria Benke, who at the time was the secretary of the alliance in Budapest, to fill the post, but in the end, they appointed Magda Jóború instead. Benke had suggested my mother for her post, and her appointment would have meant a big step forward in terms of title, but she didn't have the necessary cadre training. At the time, the differences in rank occupied my mind in no small measure; after all, my parents kept talking about equality, the equality of human beings. If someone did not take human equality seriously, they said with derision that the individual in question was suffering from rank disorder. He or she is suffering from rank disorder. They said it as if they were determined to achieve full human equality, except something or someone was deterring them with their rank disorder. But I had a problem with their use of language. They didn't say that someone was going to the Party Academy, they said that they're going up to the Party Academy, whereas it was obvious that no one will climb up the Party Academy building just so that once they reached the roof, they'd be given a higher appointment. But that's how they said it, she went up to the Party Academy, while I was just going to elementary school and not up to elementary school, though actually, by then they were referring to elementary school as general school. I met Mrs. Rajk several times, I seem to remember meeting her once in my mother's office, in the big, empty room, and once my mother took me to see her, to show me off, I think, because the grown-ups kept showing their children off to one another. But I have only the vaguest memories of her from before her arrest. Once prior to some sort of street demonstration, she leaned over to talk to me. It wasn't her so much that made a deep impression on me but the way they talked about her behind her back, and I looked up at her with that knowledge, myself a bit mistrustful of her. I even knew that my Aunt Magda had to give up editing the illustrated weekly *Asszonyok* because of her, because they couldn't stand each other. They spoke sharply to each other, I noticed that, too, right away, even though they tried to show each other some respect. My mother did so not so much for Mrs. Rajk's sake as for the sake of her husband, the minister of the interior. Júlia Rajk was considered as mad as a mad hatter and just as unpredictable, a narrow-minded, stuck-up, hysterical woman, or as my Aunt Magda put it, a wife.

One thing is for sure, Júlia Rajk knew her own mind and she was impulsive, and there's no two ways about it, she rarely acted or reasoned the way her comrades expected her to. She gesticulated, she argued, but she did so impulsively and in a manner verging on the insulting.

Valéria Benke, who always wore a white blouse, I liked at first sight. I may have even been in love with her just a bit, the way little boys have crushes on grown-up women. Among these women, who had been beleaguered by history, and Mrs. Rajk and our mother were also among them, Valéria Benke stood out with her countryside looks, her hair worn in a knot on top of her head, her smooth, finely curved forehead, the dark beauty mark under her eye, and the sweet little dimple on her chin; she was unique, a fresh-as-peaches provincial woman from the Transdanubian Gyönk, who watered her fragrant flowers before setting off for Sunday mass. She was attentive, lively, sharp-witted, and soft-spoken, just like a rural schoolmistress. She stood out from the others in this, too, because the others were loud, harsh, strikingly urban, too clever by half, as if they were always wanting to talk down to the others, or silence them altogether. Each and every one of them. Mrs. Rajk, too, was always having her say, she knew everything better than anyone else, and she kept putting people in their place. These women wouldn't let the others get a word in edgewise. Benke was the exception. Which therefore made me wonder what a Communist was like. I never saw her agitated, though I did see her blush. She blushed even when she was older. I also remember her always smelling fresh; it may have been some kind of soap bearing the scent of spring flowers, or some cologne. She dressed simply, she wore a blouse and a skirt, and when the weather cooled down, a cardigan, but she somehow wore her clothes differently from the others. These others, these women of the Communist women's movement, had at that time renewed a dress code among themselves, I wouldn't go so far as to call it a fashion or a style, it was more like a women's movement fad salvaged from the turn of the century, a suffragette demonstration meant to declare not only their independence and equality, meaning that they're not one of those finicky, silly women you can pat on the behind or get them on a couch anytime then order them to abandon the kitchen stove and the kitchen sink and use them for representational purposes as comrade wives, no, they're not comrade wives, they're not going to be lapel pins in the buttonholes of the deeply honored male comrades, that's over and done with, dear male compatriots. You will kindly learn the new order. Officially, they addressed one another as female compatriots. We are, these women compatriots insisted, what we are. But they went even further. They meant their special mode of dress and behavior to act as a political protest against the women of the women's organizations of the various bourgeois political parties. Who do these gaggling geese think they are, these featherbrains, I'm not about to stick a peacock feather in my ass just to please them. Nothing doing. Forget it. No way, Jose. With their brutal manner of dress they veritably arranged themselves into a strict phalanx of the Communist women's movement and showed the gaggling geese adorned with peacock feathers that they might well be their female counterparts, but not their comrades, not by a long shot. They're seasoned warriors, equal in rank to their other warrior compatriots who, organized into a military order, will *épater le bourgeois* until there's nothing left in them to be *épatéed*. And if they don't like it, too bad.

The bourgeois parties continued to cultivate the tradition of charity, which, in spite of all the war damage, all the societal changes and the antisentimental reversal of the general mood that followed the siege, retained its particular bogus, representation-oriented, and most of all anti-emancipatory character. In their eye, a woman's only mission is to serve her family, meaning her children, and to help further the career of her husband. In the months following the siege, they were already busy with charity work, and in keeping with their beliefs they went about in their finery, their veiled hats adorned with silk flowers and plastic fruit, their kid gloves, cashmere turbans, fluffy boas, stoles and furs, their narrow skirts split way up; they meted out charity in pure silk and silk velvet, and aided the war orphans and disabled servicemen in elegant, wavy coifs fragrant with perfume. I loved them in these clothes, these impeccably coiffed bourgeois ladies as they went about their charitable work, handing out goodies, making appearances, attending the theater and receptions, and to the accompaniment of my mother's derisive remarks, getting in or out of their automobiles, or waving their gloved hands at the admiring plebs; I couldn't get enough of them, while in the eyes of Communist women they were nothing short of scandalous, what they were engaged in was pure hypocrisy, infamy, it nauseated them, but because of the government coalition, they had to grin and bear it. Their new manner of dressing was probably dictated by political psychology, and they had to reconcile their willingness to cooperate with their innate urge to protest. The way they dressed served as a warning to the bourgeois ladies that there's no two ways about it, this time we're going to be the winners. It may be democracy today, but tomorrow it will be socialism, and then we will have seen the last of your superfluous democracy. It's going to be over and done with. *Nyshta. Basta.* The end.

Right after the siege my Aunt Magda and my mother still dressed in the style of decent bourgeois ladies, and this confused me. I couldn't understand the inconsistency, what do they want, they never wore factory-made clothes before, they had their own seamstresses, milliners, glove makers, girdle makers, and the only difference between them and my Aunt Eugenie was that they had less money to spend on fashion; sometimes I went with them, they looked through fashion magazines, then consulted with my Aunt Irén, meaning Irén Tauber, who made their clothes, not that they ever bothered asking if she had the time. This silent saint spent her nights sewing for them. They exchanged patterns, had their skirts lengthened or taken in, or they had them turned out, they even knitted things or had things knitted for them. There were knitting women in those days, knitting women from the countryside, and embroidery women and crocheting women as well. They held crocheting and crocheting women in contempt, but they held folk embroidery in high regard, because it was done by peasant women.

While the antisentimental wave that swept the country after the siege startled the bourgeois women out of their neo-baroque good cheer to a point, not to mention the fact that it would have been difficult for them to fully restore the Horthyite neo-baroque in the first place, the promise of the new world order and the harsh reality of the present day held the Communists and the socialists in thrall. The Communist women couldn't very well go on their propaganda rounds in platform shoes, or make the round of villages in hats adorned with a veil and plastic flowers, or earlier, head for their health missions out on the isolated farms of the Great Plain, first in trucks, then in cars. Nor would they have had time to have their hair done. Hairdos were a thing of the past. Independent of party affiliation, the spirit of reorganization swept everyone along with it. The first dramatic change in fashion must have appeared in the fall of 1946. Women stopped buying high heels and they abandoned their bras. They did not wear jewelry. Perfume may have remained, but makeup, nail polish, eye shadow, powder, and lipstick were out. They filed their nails, but manicures were out, too, as were pedicures. At most, they'd have a corn removed or a bothersome callus, nothing else, nothing more. After the siege, this too was just like any other epidemic. Meanwhile, comfortable shoes were a thing of the past, while new shoes were not to be had. Most of the animal skins fell victim to the exorbitant reparation consignments that the Allies as well as Moscow had imposed. My mother applied colorless polish to her fingernails and her shapely toenails. If she had a bit of extra time, if she had a bit of patience, she let me polish her nails. This one vestige of elegance she insisted on, I don't know why. The women also gave up wearing silk stockings so they shouldn't have to get the runs in their hosiery fixed or have to wear their troublesome garters under their panties. Also, all of a sudden, they looked down on women wearing girdles. It was all right yesterday, but not today. I loved women confined in girdles, and I loved girdles themselves as objects, as works of art; they were constructed of elephant-bone plates and steel plates that could stand up on their own on the floor or the table. Sometimes I took my mother's old corsets out of the wardrobe, and there were also some from my grandmother Klára Mezei, what's more, one of my great-grandmother's corsets had also survived, it was made of fishbone and was snow white and light as a feather, and once, amid lots of laughter, our mother even took the measure of my great-grandmother's waist with its help. The finest pieces were those they wore under their evening gowns. Corsetry was once considered a top profession even if the majority of corset makers were ungainly, unsightly dwarfs, humpbacked, lame, bald-headed, and chicken-breasted. I couldn't say why these girls took up this profession. Women held them in the highest possible regard. They didn't work in noisy workshops, it was, after all, a very intimate profession, and no man could ever set foot inside one of these shops located in upstairs apartments and the backs of courtyards. Watching these strange, shabby little goblins as with their needles and marking chalk they busied themselves on these rich women's bodies in the pink of health left its mark on me. From one day to the next, the Communist women banished not only their girdles and garters, but their silk stockings, too, as gratuitous. Off with them, off with them. They wanted to be free of this burden once and for all. Garter belts kept coming apart, they came unbuttoned, were too loose or too tight, the elastic gave way, they didn't dry in time, in which case they had to put them on wet; they came undone, came loose, got stuck, the metal clip came off or broke or pressed against the skin, it pinched the skin, the nub came off, and so on. Always at the worst possible moment. When they had to head off in a hurry somewhere, or else wanted to sleep with someone without delay and would have liked to kick off their stockings and feel the other's nakedness, they had the terrible impediment of six or eight hooks to deal with first. Push the metal up over the button, unhook it. Sometimes I helped my mother or one of my aunts. The darn thing got stuck again, and if their nervous fingers freed one, another got stuck instead, and to make their chagrin complete, their silk stockings would get a run in them. And obviously, you couldn't very well go out on the street in stockings with a run in them, you couldn't appear in public like that. Not even a Communist woman comrade would risk any such thing. Besides, the proli women wore cotton socks as a matter of course. Only cheap whores, the worst of the lot, would go out on the street in silk stockings.

The solution to the great garter belt fiasco was hurried penetration, which they considered too high a price to pay, even though in the best of cases, or so I think today, haste can't lessen the joy of lovemaking.

They wore thick ankle socks and ribbed knee socks with their low-heeled shoes, their strictly flat sandals and awful moccasins. Needless to say, these socks would always slip down to their ankles because their ribs or welts would get stretched out. They wore whatever color was at hand and did not have a hole in it just then. They hated darning socks, socks with holes in them got their dander up. They also stopped coordinating colors. Take it as it comes. They wouldn't wear costume jewelry either, need I say. What for. They laughed at the beautiful clips and drop earrings. They mostly discarded their wedding rings, too. I'm no animal to be ringed. At thirty years of age they called themselves old battle horses, and that's just what they looked like, they were battle horses. I enjoyed their satiric self-reflections tremendously, but my eyes couldn't get used to my mother looking like a ragged, dowdy old warhorse. I felt ashamed of her.

Once, on her way out, by way of an aside as it were, she asked me what I would like for my birthday. This must have been my seventh or more like my eighth birthday. I asked her to put on one of her pretty dresses, meaning one of those dresses she hadn't worn for at least three years. And so she'd understand what I was thinking of, I hastened to add that she should also wear her snakeskin shoes and her pearls. She put on her black velvet dress, a boatneck with satin piping, it had long sleeves with black turned-out satin cuffs, each with tiny velvet buttons that she never thought of actually buttoning. This careless inattention lent a certain *je ne sais quoi* to the otherwise ascetically minimal tailoring. The pearl necklace was made of tiny pearls; she may have inherited it from Grandmother Mezei, because after Gyuri, meaning György Nádas, died, Grandmother Mezei wore only black. It was made of at least twenty strands of tiny pearls, just barely there pearls that she twisted a couple of times, though it was even more beautiful when it hung loosely, when she didn't twist it, because the character of each tiny pearl was then made visible. Once our father explained pearl fishing to me. Given half a chance, he explained everything, which means that surely, he knew a lot of things. My mother let me close the gold clasp, though it was really a rosette the size of a gold coin, and sometimes she wore the rosette up front and not on the back of her neck. She showed me what a clever clasp Grandfather had devised for it when she almost lost it once. According to the fashion of the time, the snakeskin shoes had very high, spiky heels. I helped her dress, and it was obvious that with ease she found her way back to these old pieces she had hoped to forget, what's more, she found her way back to the ritual of dressing, too. She didn't want to wear stockings to begin with so she shouldn't have to put on garters, meaning that she didn't want to pull down her panties in front of me, but then she wanted to wear stockings after all, so she wouldn't have to slip her naked feet into the shoes lined with creamy-white kid. Except, she'd gone so far in her rebellion against the old style of dressing that she couldn't find a single pair of stockings in her underwear drawer without runs in them. It was a marvelous drawer. The insides of Bauhaus-style furniture that had black, gleaming polish on the outside were lined with silky white birch. In the end she put on a pair of stockings in which the run didn't go all the way down. Meanwhile the doorbell rang and I went running. I thought my classmates had arrived, my guests, whom my parents let me invite for my birthday to eat milk loaf and drink cocoa with whipped cream. But it couldn't be my classmates, it was too early. Rózsi Németh also came from the kitchen, her face ruddy from baking the milk loaf. She made delicious milk loaf, twisted twice, high and shiny. The autumn sun came streaming into the hall. At first I didn't even understand what was happening. The light blinded me. Two delivery men had brought a package, a huge something, a ping-pong table, a proper green ping-pong table, a big one, and not discarded by someone but brand-new, and they brought the legs of the fold-up table separately, these were of a clever no-hassle design, they could be opened up or closed without effort, and the net in a separate big flat cardboard box, and also the paddles and the snow-white balls. They brought it straight from the shop. They said someone had ordered it. On the other hand, when Rózsi Németh asked, they didn't know who had ordered it. But it was paid for. Who could have paid for it. But there it was. They leaned the parts of the table against the wall and waited for Rózsi to come back from the kitchen with the tip. I thought that it must be my father's present for my birthday, but it was a foolish thought, an unfounded hope, because he'd never have bought me such an expensive surprise. He was ascetic. Considering his own father, tightfisted and spendthrift at the same time, he couldn't very well have been anything else unless he wanted to be just like him.

Our mother appeared in the hall only after the deliverymen had left.

Back then I had a classmate at the Sziget Street school who was called Fenyvessy, and who, theoretically, couldn't have been my friend, because Laci Tavaly was my friend, and a person can't have two friends; but when Laci Tavaly didn't want to be friends anymore, I didn't understand why not, even though I hung around him for a while longer, anyway, that's when András Vajda became my friend. But Fenyvessy had a younger sister, she was probably a year younger, because she started attending school when we were already in second grade at the Sziget Street school, though Fenyvessy attended Catholic and not Calvinist Bible class, and even though the Calvinist religious studies teacher always had some unpleasant remark to make about Catholics, I fell in love with this Catholic girl, his sister, at first sight. She must have been my first love, I think. I never had too many loves in my whole life. Psychologists say that a person can be in love no more than twice in life. To be sure, I was in love more than that, or who knows. Surely, it also depends on what we mean by love. No doubt, it was very different from what I felt for the young blond woman in the apartment across the street, for whom I waited day after day, hour after hour, so she should be fully naked again at long last and cross the room like that. My feelings for Fenyvessy's sister weren't as agonizing, they were more light and pleasant. For one thing, it never occurred to me that she could ever be naked.

I hadn't known before that such a thing was possible. The minute I realized that I don't know why, but I want to press my bare leg against her little bare leg and I want to keep it there to feel it, she must have realized that she wanted the same thing, except this made me feel a steady and bashful sense of shame, and it made her feel the same thing. It must have been spring and the weather warm, she wore a short skirt and I had short pants on, and we pressed our thighs and not just our legs tight against each other. From then on, I always wanted to visit Fenyvessy. That summer I wanted to play over at their house more than anything, and I did. On the other hand, everyone thought that I wanted to be friends with Fenyvessy, and I kept up appearances, even though he had his own friend, Berci Marthy. I worried that they might discover my scam. This became my ethical mimicry, my great big tearful comedy, the pretense that I want to be friends with Fenyvessy. For some unfathomable reason, I felt that I must not speak to anyone about the fatal and ethereal attraction Fenyvessy's sister and I felt for each other, and I do mean anyone, even at the price of violating the primary rule of friendship twice over.

My hypocrisy knew no bounds; I'd have gone to any lengths. I was Marcellina, but no, I was the cruel Fidelio. As I think back on it now, she must have been a rather ugly little girl. She had a slight limp, though at the time, bowleggedness from rickets, a humpback, or a pigeon breast were not considered rare deformities, and certainly not enough to prevent her limp from appearing all the more refined in my eyes. She must have been unhealthily thin. I liked that. A puny little girl. I liked that. What's more, these adjectives make me feel light and happy, even now. Her profoundly sad little face was wizened, like an old woman's hauling kindling from the forest on her back all day. In the language of fairy tales, a crone. Her dark hair, too, hung thin and graceless. In a folktale we'd say, like oakum. But I saw her differently than my own two eyes would have seen her on their own. Now, too, I remember her not through my former eyes, but through my lover's eyes. She was dark in a deep, velvety way, whereas her brother and her mother were strikingly blond and had snow-white skin, like the Irish or the English with the ring of freckles on their healthy cheeks. They were both strong, loud, fatty, assertive. It seems to me that their father was equally sinewy and dark, a sad and insecure aristocrat from the Great Plain, now the chief clerk of some high postal authority. In my eyes, his young daughter was dignified, except I can't recall her name, Ida, Ida Fenyvessy, Idácska, Iduska, it's just an idea, but I don't really know. She had an old-fashioned first name, a first name borne by aristocratic women. Ilma. Etelka. Imola. Ilonka. I'm just now trying to remember what it might have been. Her sadness and helplessness added to her dignified mien, and this impressed me. We didn't talk to each other, we may not have exchanged a single word that summer, what I remember is the silence. They had two small chairs in the children's room, and while Fenyvessy, whose first name I can't recall either, possibly Gábor or Géza, was making a racket with his own friends somewhere else, they went out on the balcony playing button football or went down to the yard, something I couldn't have cared less about, we sat silently next to each other on the small chairs and pressed our stockinged legs against each other. These Fenyvessys lived on one of the side streets of the neighborhood, possibly in Katona József Street, in a spacious and lavishly furnished second-floor apartment, where everything was carelessly flung down, thrown down, and would stay there for days, perhaps weeks, and I loved this, too. But their mother loved only her son, she felt comfortable with him, they'd shout to each other from the kitchen to the living room, or from the street or the yard to their upstairs apartment; she may even have held her daughter in contempt, still, she did not fuss with her, she left her to fend for herself. Amid all this great big, fatty, obese, and meaty yelling, the ugly duckling quietly wasted away, and so their mother lost no time trying to trap me, wanting to snare me for her daughter, so to speak, the ugly little duckling who had no one in the family to turn to. This calculated move was all too obvious to me; she kept inviting me, she stuffed me with all sorts of food, she asked me to stay longer, oh, don't go yet, stay for lunch, what's the rush, stay for dinner. Here are some nice dates, they came in a package, I saved them for you. And should she make me crepes with sweetened cottage cheese. This woman tied her own mimicry to her ill-begotten daughter, or her innate misogyny. Who knows. She pretended to be a caring mother, but she was mother to only one of her children. She begged me to stay. She wanted her daughter to have someone and she seemed not to care what the two of us were up to so quietly in the adjacent room. Whereas incredible things happened there. Or possibly, we just didn't catch her looking in on us. At times the little girl's leg, her thigh and arm and, for all I know, every part of her got goose bumps from this great pressing together of our bodies. Which made her attractive and repulsive at the same time. She made my hair stand on end. Also, it was at this point that a limit of sorts wedged itself between us, because I thought of her goose bumps as a faint ethical warning that I mustn't press quite so tight against her, that I mustn't do it. So possibly, it was the stirrings of self-control that made me shiver like that, too, or the fact that I noticed it, as if the good possessed a sensible rule, a limit, that I should honor. And when we opened the big cardboard box with our mother, we found a letter inside an envelope, and we learned that they, the Fenyvessys, had sent the ping-pong table to me for my birthday, with much love.

And I can't keep it, my mother said right away.

And I asked, I argued, why can't I keep it.

She didn't answer me, she just shook her head, no, no, I'm afraid not, it simply won't do.

I asked her what won't do.

It just won't do. We will now place the letter back in the envelope, back in this big box, Rózsi Németh said, and wait for Apáka to get home, and we'll talk over the details with him.

According to our mother's ethical standards, a present as expensive as this could not be accepted.

I think we shall solve this awkward situation, she said, by giving it to the school.

So far so good, except I didn't think it was right to give back such an expensive birthday present simply because it was so expensive. This was another reason why their fixation on equality, this great big fastidious hierarchy among equals interested me. It was a present to me for my birthday, I can't very well give it to the school. She saw my point right away and was quick to agree. She had no way of knowing that I was in love with Fenyvessy's sister and that they gave it to me so I'd marry her one day.

I should thank them in a letter, but must offer it to the school, and in my letter, I should find a courteous way of letting them know. If they take it amiss, that's their problem.

My mother, too, was in a quandary, this with respect to her new position. She knew perfectly well that she'd be given a lower position that she must accept, but pretend that it's of a higher order. But she couldn't talk about this to anyone either. She had no choice. They were stripping her of her role as national organizing secretary, and why would she have wanted to exchange a higher position for a lower one. Also, she considered the Party Academy a complete waste of time, whereas she was supposed to consider it an honor and take it in stride. Since the two things were happening simultaneously, my own involuntary silence made me understand her own hypocrisy.

Just as I can't show my true face, neither can she.

Up till then, she had organized and monitored several national institutional networks with the appropriate ministries, first and fore-most the Ministry of Welfare, though in a sort of commissar system, food for children, vacations for children, a women's aid network with Imre Hirschler and an infant aid network with Emmi Pikler, an eve-ning school network with Magda Jóború, and with Mrs. Aranyossi, née Magda Nádas, a network to teach illiterate women in the coun-tryside; she also organized, God only knows with whom, a network of school doctors, a mobile dental system, everything that in her view was necessary to support a new world. She traveled all around the country, supervising them, keeping her eye on them. She was also responsible for organizing the care of POWs, and later she headed not only the administrative department, but the department to aid the POWs as well, something that, if my memory serves, meant mostly the safe delivery of packages and letters; and she also supervised the aid to those left behind, and she thus came into contact with some senior officers and generals of the occupying Soviet army. Needless to say, they were all heroes of the Soviet Union. She enjoyed this tre-mendously, it appealed to her ego that as part of her duties she works, lunches, or dines with them at the former Officers' Club on Stefánia Street, which the Soviet army had taken over during the siege. If Hungarian companies lacked sufficient transportation capacity or had to expedite something to some impossible place, she made use of her Russian contacts and they would deliver the goods in their tanks. Once she took me along with her to the Officers' Club. She drank champagne with them and got tipsy and she told them how a Russian soldier from a fighting unit had slapped her in the base-ment of the house in Damjanich Street when they were searching for armed men who might be hiding there, and she was so happy to see the Russians, she nearly leaped into the arms of one, which this soldier misunderstood. She was also in charge of the welcoming cer-emony for the returning POWs, and she organized the various group actions and demonstrations of the national women's movement, and she took me along to some of these events as well. They demonstrated against black marketeers, they demonstrated against inflation and the devaluation of the forint, they demonstrated against anything that was contrary to Communist ideology or might have aided bourgeois restoration. They had initially coordinated their actions with their coalition partners, the Social Democrat, the Smallholder, and the Peasant Party women, at times they organized top-level coordination meetings in even wider circles, and that's why her office was such a big, attractively plain room in keeping with the neoclassical style of Pest, because this is where they held the big multilateral conferences. At least, this was her explanation when I asked her why, in this great big equality, a single person would need such a big room with such a big golden chandelier.

The Party Academy was located on Ajtósi Dürer Row across from City Park. The smell of freshly brewed coffee and freshly stenciled documents filled the building otherwise echoing with its own emptiness. The street got its name because Dürer's father, who was an engraver, came from Ajtós, a small settlement near Gyula. I must remember, we went to Gyula together, we went along with the health-care buses. Except, we weren't in the buses, we went after my mother in his official car; it was a sudden decision, first out to the farms near Szeged, but we couldn't find her there, it was the first time I saw farms and a farm center, then back to Szeged, then on the following day, after lengthy inquiries, we headed for Gyula. The king bequeathed Ajtós to the German merceneries. Earlier, the village was called by its German name, which was Türer. This is why Türer ended up in Nuremberg under this name, and that's where his son, Dürer was born. Ajtósi was his title of nobility, the Dürers from Ajtós were Hungarian nobles, as well as Germans. But not just his son. He was also called Albrecht. Remind me when we get home to show you his paintings. We did so. But our visit to the Party Academy was anything but successful. Our father wanted to surprise our mother. This was the first time in my life when I saw how a surprise can go wrong. We found the corridors empty, our steps echoed, the seminar rooms were empty as well, and so were the lecture rooms, but our father found someone in the building who told him that the students went on an excursion to Normafa with their teachers, and they will have their classes there. We'd come in vain. It must have been early autumn; at any rate, the school building stood before me in the early autumn light. We didn't go to Normafa to find her, where among the trees with their ample boughs on Eötvös Street we could at least have seen the villa with its tower where the Communists had tortured Rajk, Kojsza, Béla Szász, and the other Communists, and where before that they'd interrogated Mindszenty about nothing. The complex telecommunications and communications apparatus of the building, the remnants of which I saw in the early seventies when I found the building quite by chance, were probably designed and installed by my uncle, Endre Nádas, meaning Dajmirka, *qui ne peut pas dire dormir*, but at any rate, as department superintendent he had to be in charge of the operation. He had been a major, then lieutenant-colonel in the State Security Authority, the only boy in the family my grandfather never laid hands on but whom, because he was made an exception of, his brothers and sisters hated when they were children. As my Aunt Magda puts in her memoirs, they wished him dead. When in the tense summer of 1956 I called him to account for his crimes in State Security, he said that he was responsible only for technical and engineering matters, but his lips trembled.

But once, Rózsi Németh and I had a more fortunate visit with our mother.

I remember that it was cold by then, winter, but the sun was shining. We walked, or at any rate, when we got to Váci Street we walked, we pushed my brother's baby carriage along the brick wall of the Szabolcs Street hospital, past where I was born, then we crossed Heroes Square. My brother had on a short chocolate brown coat with a velvet collar that had a warm lining, and he was also securely wrapped in his small camel-hair blankets. When we crossed the square, I was allowed to push him, he babbled, pointed, explained things. At times he could be understood, and at times not. He fantasized, he conducted what you might call inner monologues and dialogues, though he didn't give the impression of someone not quite right in the head. I begged him, I snapped at him, but he wouldn't stop. He stopped his loud inner monologues and his loud inner dialogues with the world only when our father committed suicide. At the same hour. He never spoke out loud to himself, ever, after that. He also stopped wetting his bed. His hours-long ritual crying had stopped earlier, when our mother died. On the other hand, in the early hours of dawn, when my father had just killed himself, he started awake and woke me up, too, saying that our father hadn't come home, he must have been hit by a tram, at which I turned over, and told him not to bother me with such nonsense and let me sleep. Later, when he woke up, the grown-ups didn't dare tell him what had happened. Almost all of them stood up when he entered the room, as if the king had entered in his pajamas, and for some unfathomable reason, they looked to me to come up with a solution. And that morning, in order to take the burden off the shoulders of our aunts and uncles who were weeping and sobbing in the various armchairs, I decided that for now I'd tell my brother that our father had been in a serious accident and was taken to the hospital, and this is why they were all at our place, and also to decide what's to be done and who should take him to school that morning, and then someone volunteered, it may have been Teréz Goldmark, my Uncle Pista's wife, who tried her best to act as if nothing had happened. He mustn't see anything of the enormous shock that was held in check in accordance with family dictates. But the minute he climbed out of bed, half asleep, and tottered into the living room and took a look at the devastated grown-ups and saw that his father wasn't there, he knew for a fact what had happened, he saw it in their eyes.

Forty years later he told me all the things he knew when he looked at the brothers and sisters, husbands and wives dragged out of their beds in various parts of the city, now gathered together in haste. Forty years later, he still resented the brutal lie I'd told him, though at the time he accepted it without batting an eye and even got dressed on his own, whereas at other times he couldn't dress on his own because of his leg brace. The next day the little fraud even asked when our father was coming home, all the while that he surreptitiously looked out from behind his mask to see if the family lie that he was bound to accept was still in effect.

The day before the funeral, when I opened our father's wardrobe to choose a suit, a shirt, and some underwear to put on him and found the farewell note he'd written on blue airmail stationery, it was time to tell my brother the truth, and then my brother could cry at last to his heart's content, along with the rest of us. He cried just like my father had cried and just like our father's brothers cried. As he cried, he tried to be strong and swallow back his tears.

As we entered, a woman came out of the noisy dining room, with several other women in her wake.

There was nothing about the woman to indicate that she might be our mother and our father's wife. She seemed to have lost her former self during her long stay at the Academy, and she was just like everyone else. She'd turned into just another woman. A decent bureaucrat, a good comrade. Surely, this is when I saw our mother for the first time as she truly was, and for the last time, too; I saw her the way others saw her, as someone who was not my mother. She looked tired, much older than her years, but also cheerful, intelligent, and disciplined.

When they saw us, the people streaming out into the corridor seemed confused. Taken by surprise, the woman who was my mother also stopped in her tracks. She was not pleased to see us. On the other hand, the other women immediately grabbed my brother dressed in his brown coat with the velvet collar, they took him from the hooded buggy and passed him around from hand to hand. In the blink of an eye, we became Klári's two sons, and they gave us jelly rolls filled with homemade jelly. But the generous present, the ping-pong table that could be set up anywhere, I was not allowed to keep. Fortunately, we had no time to argue because the doorbell rang and my friends came in. Marthy and Fenyvessy immediately took charge, set up the table in the living room, and started playing on it as if the rest of us weren't even there.

Later, perhaps a year later, we unexpectedly moved out of the Pozsonyi Street apartment, and the fact that I'd be attending a new, unfamiliar school instead of my old school took me by surprise. I wasn't in love with that little girl anymore, whose name I still can't recall, maybe Etelka, Etelka Fenyvessy, or something of the sort; besides, I couldn't go to visit them anymore. Though I fought to keep the ping-pong table, the week after my birthday I had to go to the principal's office, where they were expecting me, they knew why I was there, and I had to make a ceremonious offer of the ping-pong table, along with its paraphernalia, to the sports club.

I would have liked to keep a paddle, at least, or a ball, but I had to give everything away.

It may have been January 6 when we moved; but it was definitely a Friday.

The city was covered in a thick blanket of snow and icy gusts of wind from the Danube battered us when our mother's official car drove us up the hill in Buda. The next morning my father explained to me how to get to school. There was a heavy snowfall outside. When I go through the garden gate, I should turn left until I reach the road crossing where I will see a crucifix by the roadside, and then I should turn right, that will be Diana Street, it is very steep, I can't miss it, I must walk up a ways, and when I reach the top, I will see the church and the school behind the trees. It won't take more than ten minutes. We practiced, this is my left hand, and I turn that way first, to the left, and this is my right hand, then he asked, just to make sure, which hand I write with. Which is the only thing I could remember from this right hand and left hand, the writing. I knew that my parents frowned on my insecurity with respect to directions, and just when I wanted to be a good boy. Sometimes I'd practice, this is the left and this is the right, but that didn't make me feel any more secure about it. The school has two main entrances, one is the kindergarten, it's on the left, the other is the school, that's on the right, it's written over the gates in big curvy letters, you can't mistake them. And I should take a look at the sundial on the facade. It is the largest and most beautiful sundial in all of Budapest, though it's not of much use in January, but we'll make one in the garden come summer, and then I'll explain it to you. Needless to say, I could hardly wait, and when summer came, I kept urging my father, let's make a sundial, let's make a sundial, but we never did. He had no time for explanations by then either.

It was difficult enough reaching the garden gate, the snow was so thick, the garden with its snow-laden ancient trees, shrubs and firs, was so enormous. What can I say, it was one and a half hectares. It was probably in the middle of an oak forest. It was as foreign, distant, and terrifying as if we weren't standing above the city that we left so precipitously but in some strange land. Out on the street, the wind swept up the snow and hurled it in my face; because of the great cold, the snow fell in sharp pellets. In the years to come, I even learned what type of snow belonged to what weather conditions. On this street they didn't sweep away the snow, there were no car tracks and no traces of human feet, at most a dog's or a deer's. My father had taught me to read tracks and not just the alphabet, he taught me on our excursions. A fox's tracks are easy to recognize in the snow because the minute its feet sink in, its tail also leaves a trace. So this wasn't a fox. I had to pull my visored cap down on my forehead, raise my scarf over my mouth, and I wore ankle boots with thick socks folded over my ankles. We bought my ankle boots the day before we moved. It will be cold, inside the house, too, they said. I could barely see anything and there was no sign of life, though I could just make out the outlines of the big villas nestled in the backs of the snowy gardens, behind the tall snow-covered fences, the barren trees and the snow-clad Austrian pines, here and there a roof, a veranda, a column, or a window apron and sill likewise covered with snow. In the silence I had not known before that filled the snowy landscape, I could hear things like the dry oak leaves knocking against each other, and the whispering wind among the pines. When I finally reached the weather-beaten old crucifix at the crossroads in the early morning blizzard and tried to look up the precipitous, snow-covered Diana Street leading to the top, a gust of wind caught me in the eye. In an attempt to shield my face, I looked back on Gyöngyvirág Street, where we had moved, I don't know why.

We had somehow managed to sleep through the first night in that strange, ice-cold house echoing with the sound of the enormous gusts of wind. We had nothing there. But on my way to school, I was sure that I'd been to this street up on Svábhegy before. I even recognized the simple tin crucifix that had once been painted in bright colors. Also, I knew that the tin crucifix had been painted by Masa Feszty, daughter of the revered romantic painter Árpád Feszty and granddaughter of the sober-minded writer Mór Jókai, who got carried away by religious fervor. But I didn't stay long in the snow driven off track by the wind, I had to head up Diana Street, lest I be late for school. We'd walked up this way with Sándor Rendl many times, and he'd told me about the two Fesztys, Árpád and Masa, and the tin crucifix on the mountain, and also Mór Jókai, the game of tarokk, the mamelukes and my great-grandfather Mór Mezei, though it would be more correct to say that he told me about them as well, but from a very different perspective than my father or my aunts. He'd been a clerk in our great-grandfather's law office, and so everything that he related in his exceptionally temperate, informative, but not didactic manner I considered a more reliable source of orientation than the stories I had heard in the family.

It was summer, but it must have been a cool summer and probably a Sunday. Sándor Rendl carried a hiking stick, and his light coat was draped over his arm. I even know what year it must have been. It happened just two years after the siege, in August 1947. He'd told me about Masa Feszty and the tin crucifix on one of our previous Sunday walks. We walked this way several times, I can't remember how many times. I checked with Vera if I remembered it correctly. I did, because Sándor Rendl's Sunday walks always lead this way. Before the siege he'd take his daughter Vera with him, and on one of our walks seventy years later, as we reminisced, we recited the two possible directions to each other.

When they didn't know what to do about us because they were busy elsewhere, our parents took us to my Aunt Irén, Irén Tauber. From there my cousin Mártika and I would go over to Dembinszky Street to my Aunt Bözsi, meaning Erzsébet Tauber, where my grandparents Arnold Tauber and Cecília Nussbaum had been living for a while in a room of their own. For some reason I was not familiar with, they had to leave their apartment in Péterfy Sándor Street. They probably gave up their independence because had they not come here to live, the city would have taken one of my Aunt Bözsi's rooms away from her and given it to a family from the countryside or whoever. However, we couldn't visit Aunt Bözsi whenever we felt like it, because she gave piano lessons on her big Bösendorfer. The whole street echoed from it, the house echoed when she demonstrated for her students how to play, while in her full-bodied, slightly raspy alto she shouted over her own demonstration. She gave lessons to my cousin Márta as well, or as she called her, Mártika. *Adagio, piano*, didn't you hear, but she didn't say it, she bellowed, *piano, piano*, how many more times must I tell you, *molto piano*, yelling as loud as she could. You're not paying attention to the score. Again. Mártika didn't have a piano at home, so she had to practice here every day. She could read a score before she knew her alphabet. Even when we were at the Dembinszky Street apartment, we weren't allowed to go into the living room. How can we be so scatterbrained. She earns her bread and butter from teaching, my Aunt Bözsi shouted in her deep, resonant, musical voice, her chest resonating along, she used it like a musical instrument when she spoke. She's not about to lose her students because of us. She was really good at furrowing her brow. This was her humorous way of letting us know how angry she was, though the truth is, she really was angry. She also headed a workers' choir at the Metal and Engineering Workers' Trade Union, where she let her voice out in earnest, and she also had a mandolin orchestra. When they rehearsed she didn't speak loudly at all, she plucked the chords of her syllables, just like they plucked their instruments. They were always rehearsing somewhere nearby, on István Street or on Bethlen Square. Our aunt was always on the go, she had to leave and we had to behave ourselves while she was gone, and if our behavior was not up to par, she said we got on her nerves. Which is another thing I didn't understand. She didn't want, for a long time she didn't want them to declare her husband, Miklós Nádas, dead. Nor should they declare him missing. What an idea. Her neighbor urged her to have him declared dead because then she'd be entitled to a widow's pension. In her neighbor's eyes getting a widow's pension was the be-all and end-all of good fortune, and it was a breeze. She had her husband declared dead. But not so Erzsébet Tauber, who continued making preserves every summer, peaches and pears, sour cherries and regular cherries, pickles and peppers, *lecsó* and pumpkins, the way Miklós liked them before the siege. Everything must be the way it had always been, everything must remain exactly the same as before. But whether she liked it or not, everyone who had disappeared was declared missing. But not for her. When Miklós comes back, he should find everything but everything just as it had been. She cut small stars out of carrots to decorate the sides of the pickle jars. They called each other my little star, my dearest darling, my little heart, my one and only. We weren't even allowed to push a chair aside. Miklós might show up at any time. I had my doubts, and yet I waited for this anytime along with her, waited for our little star to come home. And to prevent the rugs, the tablecloths, and the upholstery from wearing down before he came home, she covered everything with slipcovers, which became an obsession with her. To protect the slipcovers, she covered them with rag carpets, and to protect the antimacassars, she placed lace-patterned oilcloth over them.

I was allowed to go to Teréz Boulevard on my own as well. Before the siege, and for a while after the siege, Sándor Rendl's law office was located in an apartment there. Everything remained just as it had been, his filing cabinets, the glass-enclosed bookshelves, and everything had remained just as it had been in his study, too, along with the severe-looking deep armchairs upholstered in dark gray with black patterns, the bastions of law, in which the filthy rich clients in need of legal protection had no choice but to sit with their backs kept straight. They were protected on the severe-looking dark-gray sofa that made up part of the set as well. The arms were so high that they didn't even have to lower their arms. The entire spacious room whose windows looked out on the building of the Music Academy in Szófia Street was covered with a Smyrna rug woven of light colors, light blue, lemon yellow, silvery gray, coral, and pink. It veritably lit up the room. The walls were hung with János Kmetty's severe Szentendre landscapes, the darkest from his darkest period, and Bertalan Pór's lively landscapes from his most colorful early period. The mahogany writing desk covered in claret-brown leather and the gorgeous writing set of black marble and polished glass, with the seal, inkwells, the pounce, the pen tray, the letter tray, and the paperweight, all survived along with the razor-sharp penknife with its black marble handle, the badly worn antique coins in their black marble coin case, and also the wide-cheeked blotter that allowed you to slip the blotting paper under its black marble slab, and grabbing hold of the crystal handle polished bright as a rainbow, you could then blot your newly written letters. I loved blotting letters. I loved grabbing the blotter. What a word. In slang it meant to touch women illicitly. To grab. Paw. Throw out a feeler. Don't you grab at me, son, or you'll be sorry. The older girls said this to the younger boys. He grabbed her between her legs. The older boys said this among themselves. What're you, a fag, stop grabbing at my privates. The older boys also said this to punish one another for illicit contact.

When Sándor Rendl gave up his office and legal practice before they had a chance to take it away from him, he became legal counselor for the Hungarian Foreign Trade Bank and the Ministry of Finance, and his study passed into the ownership of Pál Aranyossi, along with all its contents. I don't know why, but my aunt and uncle moved into the abandoned apartment on Teréz Boulevard from Damjanich Street, and when for some unknown reason I once stayed there for a couple of days, my Aunt Magda made my bed on the severe-looking dark-gray sofa. The velvet pricked me through the sheets. They'd sheered this velvet into a bristly texture instead of a silky one. I loved falling asleep on the sofa of this huge room as I watched the light of the boulevard wander over the ceiling, and in the morning I loved waking to the shadows and sounds of the morning traffic on the boulevard, whereas it was not easy falling asleep on that bristly surface that stabbed me through the sheet whenever I moved. I was allowed to stay in the study even when my Uncle Pali was working, writing a letter or an article, or translating something. When he finished a page he called from behind his desk, come, you can grab and blot it. I was a respected person in this apartment. My picture was there in front of him on his desk, right next to Yvette and Jean-François, in a foldout red leather picture frame. At the time, his third grandchild, Serge, was probably not even born yet. Strangely enough, they didn't even replace my picture after Serge was born, whereas they'd sent us a picture of him. I kept checking the foldout red leather picture frame, but my picture was still there, as if I were the third grandchild, left over from the siege. While he worked, and he worked with conviction, he worked with such conviction that probably I learned all the small mannerisms of literary handiwork from him, I was allowed to read on the sofa, meaning that I mostly thumbed through albums of art and photography, not once and not twice, but again and again, which didn't bore me in the least; on the contrary, discovering new details and repeating those that were already familiar made it all the more interesting, the way my mother had taught me with the sinking sun over Balaton. Or else I looked through old issues of *Regards*, bound into volumes. I could take anything from the shelves, his beautifully bound old dictionaries with their full-page illustrations in color that could be unfolded. When I finished, I'd fold them up again and put them back exactly where I found them. Sometimes he'd let me take out his huge portfolio of drawings and, standing behind the tall coffee table, careful of how I handled the pages, I was allowed to leaf through the graphic works of Gyula Derkovits, János Nagy Balogh, József Nemes Lampérth, István Nagy, István Dési Huber, Béla Uitz, and Bertalan Pór. Again and again, I don't know how many times. The album contained Derkovits's entire series of woodcuts on the Dózsa-led peasant revolt that ended in horrible retaliation. I couldn't shake off the horror of it. Also, Béla Uitz's gentle female figures, János Nagy Balogh's pencil drawings of impoverished peasant rooms, István Nagy's charcoal drawings executed with a heavy hand and improbable self-assurance, his stacks, his ridges, his huts; in his work the sky afforded barely any light from behind the dark of the charcoal. Also Lampérth Nemes's turbulent India ink drawings of imaginary landscapes in which everything leans in the same direction as if the wind meant to force everything to the ground, and so on. There must have been other modern Hungarian artists belonging to the socially committed left, but they're the only ones I remember with assurance from among the pictures and pictorial details. There was also a finely detailed pencil drawing by Jolán Szilágyi of a kindly woman, her head wrapped in a kerchief. It was not a good drawing, but the woman's eyes mesmerized me every time I looked at it. She may have been a Russian woman, because her head was wrapped in the kerchief in a funny way. Or else Romanian. At such times speaking was out, it would have disturbed Uncle Pali in his reflections, but still, from time to time I asked him things and he'd give a brief reply. Otherwise, staring silently into space, he scratched his bare head, and there was always an Arcadian smile resting in the corner of his lips. Sometimes I scratch my head the same way. Or else he said that he's thinking. I never saw him at his desk casually dressed, meaning in careless or incomplete attire. He put on a suit in the early morning, a suit with a vest whose jacket, on the days when he didn't have to rush off somewhere, he'd exchange for a smoking jacket. He wore a tie as well, even in the morning, yet even in his conventional suits he remained a bohemian. Everything on him remained loose, comfortable, soft, including the knot in his tie. He made a big knot and didn't pull it down all the way.

I started writing myself by candlelight one winter afternoon when I was eleven. I sat at my desk, an old, ink-stained office desk nowhere as genteel as Sándor Rendl's. With the brevity of his answers my Uncle Pali indicated that fine, he'll answer me, but we're not going into details just now. The other members of the family had an impressive storehouse of knowledge as well, but his lexical learning in literature, languages, theater, history, and political philosophy was truly impressive. He had three strengths, his lexical knowledge, his gift for languages, and his gifts as a translator. His literary translations are as fresh as ever, which is quite a feat. He leaned his forehead on the palm of his hand as he concentrated on the next sentence. A person sees the sentence, he's put it together in his head, a word is a picture, too, and so is a sentence. What would happen if he were to change the word order or parts of the sentence. He must try. Not to mention the fact that he remembers when he first thought of a word, under what conditions, how he interpreted it and how he stored it. Also, in his mind every word has its special etymology, sometimes glaringly at odds with academic etymology. He'd also like to try how, if he reversed the order, the sounds would accrue to the sentence that came before, or the sentence to follow. And then he'd say the sentence out loud. Or what if he were to bring the next sentence up front, possibly the entire paragraph. Hungarian sentence structure is exceptionally pliable, and consequently, with just a bit of shuffling, it is capable of producing exceptional, till then unheard or unaccustomed shades of meaning. I sometimes do the same in my dreams as well, or to be exact, my dream consists of changing the word order and switching the order of the sentences. Which doesn't mean that behind the facade of morphology the dream isn't meant to convey an entirely different message about the previous day. Also, he'd suddenly stand and look up something in a reference book, or else he'd look for a better sentence in a book, he was sure he'd find it there, but when he held the book in his hand, he couldn't find it. Sometimes, while he was looking for something, he'd lose himself in the book. This often happens to me as well. Visual memory informs intellectual memory—on page forty of the book, on the left side, on the fourth line from the bottom I'm sure to find the sentence, and it is there, more or less. At other times, there's no finding it, it's not in the book I'm holding, either at the top or the bottom of the page, nor on any of the pages of any other book. Possibly there's no such sentence, it never existed. My imagination attributed the sentence to the author.

There are sentences, expressions for which I've been searching for decades because I seem to remember them, I know that they must be somewhere.

Or else he stopped by the window with a sentence he found by chance, allowing his attention to wander. He may have noticed something that caught his attention, or something out of the ordinary may have occurred behind a window of the Music Academy through which issued the sound of a piano, a flute, violin, or drums, and then he'd forget about the book in his hand. His study was full of books, newspapers, and journals he'd left open all over the place, intending to return to them later; some of these he'd take to his desk to copy some sentences into his manuscript. Or else he compared two texts, the original with the translation, checking the latter against the former, meaning that he was correcting, editing, or reviewing someone else's translation. At times he didn't write things in notebooks or manuscripts, but in the margins of typed manuscripts he'd folded and cut in two. I must have learned this paper-saving method of notetaking from him; though I'd forgotten it for a while, I took it up again later in imitation of Miklós Mészöly's similar habit. You recycle your old manuscript pages, or else in response to new knowledge, you refresh your former knowledge.

Sometimes while he was writing he'd raise his pen and then jot down some words on one of the note sheets to remind him of something, then he'd get caught up with his notes, and for a while, he'd be writing something entirely different. In one of his surviving notebooks I see that he must have meant to write about our mother, Klári Tauber, but I can't find the manuscript, if there ever was one. Just now I can't find the notebook either. He'd asked some people about our mother and made a list of those people he still had to question. They must have been close, though I believe that she must have been one of the few women in his life he didn't sleep with. Or so I've told myself. As if after so many decades I was still trying to protect our mother from him, whereas it wouldn't make much sense protecting her, especially in retrospect. This Pál Aranyossi, he was an interesting man, invariably considerate with women, courteous, reserved, but the minute he saw them some strange merriment sparkled in his eye, the joy of the game, it never sparkled quite like that any other time, puns came pouring out of him, jest followed jest, but he was never overbearing, he was never improper. They excited him, though I never saw him giving them the eye, meaning eyeing them, subjecting each part of them to scrutiny, their backsides, their legs and breasts, like other men who practice this quality control of the separate parts demonstratively, making a spectacle of possessing each part separately. This is why the gestures that his dementia brought out of him ten years later were so striking. He wasn't shrill when the other men, Oszkár Orody, Oszkár Solt, and Ferenc Münnich, discussed their adventures with women while they drank out on the veranda in Leányfalu, or earlier, when they went to the Hangya or Hableány pub, where my aunt would send me, dinner's ready, go, bring back those good-for-nothings.

They weren't big dinners. She made a salad from whatever she found in the garden or the pantry.

After he became prime minister, Münnich may have even preferred the topic of women to politics. Possibly, it had to do with age.

As they age, men are more prone to gossip. My Uncle Pali kept at a proper distance from the subject even in the company of men; he listened, he was interested, but he did not join in. Münnich's shrillness came from his vehemence. If he didn't drink he was not shrill, he was soft-spoken and reflective, as if he were waiting for something, except he liked to drink. His wife had lost her mind. He did not abandon her, though we never knew for sure whether she was in a mental institution or in their former home. He did not divorce her, he visited her, but he lived with a much younger, slender athlete, Eta Berényi, who had been my mother's student at the workers' athletic club. When Münnich was in his cups, he talked too freely in the company of men, but his jokes were not rough, he kept to the anecdotal manner of a jovial country gentleman. He talked about his earlier conquests just enough for the others to laugh at his anecdotes, but no more. As for me, I listened closely, wondering what these entertaining events had to do with Eta Berényi, whom I considered a much stronger person than this declining old man, who got tipsy quickly, then kept on drinking. I never saw him drunk, unlike my Uncle Pali, whose capacity for drink was enormous; he'd drink nice and slowly, keeping it on an even keel, but he drank a lot, until his face suddenly crumpled, and from then on he'd talk a bunch of nonsense. Jocular nonsense, but nonsense all the same. Sometimes he had to be dragged into bed. He laughed and laughed, we didn't always know why he laughed, but his laughter was contagious, and we laughed along with him. But my Aunt Magda was irritated all the same, and berated him as she laughed. When she was undressing the helpless, laughing man, you could tell how much she loved him. They drank only good wine, wine that they acquired under the table, or wine sent to them from various wineries in crates, mostly from Sopron, Szekszárd, Eger, and Tokaj. I watched my uncle's behavior so closely because I couldn't understand how such a fine man could turn into a Bluebeard, or how, with his obscene jokes, Rabelais could make his appearance through him.

You could tell by the settled yet concentrated expression on his face that he had a built-in compass to these reference books and the vast piles of note sheets and slips lying all over the place, and he also had a built-in map to go with them. He could find them with his eyes closed. Sometimes he would say something, and not necessarily in Hungarian, and at such times I knew not to respond. He was talking to himself. He listened to himself constructing a possible sentence, considering it from the point of view of rhythm. If the phone rang, he put down his pen right away, whether he talked at length or waited to be connected long-distance, and sometimes he spoke in some foreign language, mostly French or German. For a time he was a correspondent for the Swedish Communist daily *Ny Dag*, and then he spoke Swedish. But these breaks in writing clearly didn't upset him. As soon as he put down the receiver, he continued writing; he first looked at the sheet from a distance, as it were, then he continued where he'd left off. I loved our shared silence in the midst of the clatter of the trams on the boulevard, the honking of the horns, the rapid scales of the students practicing their music across the way, the chagrined or triumphant shouts of the music teachers and the yelling and cursing of the haulers coming from the coal merchant in the basement. I loved them passionately. Being silent with him was not difficult. Sometimes he glanced at me over his glasses, and at such times I could tell that he was proud of me, he was grateful to me for keeping my mouth shut for so long. When he started to write for the Swedish paper, on Friday, July 12, 1946, to be exact, under the headline the editors of the paper let their readers know that from that day on a man whom the veterans of the Party remember well would be working for them. He'd fled to Stockholm after the defeat of the Hungarian revolution, and had spent sufficient time there to learn Swedish.

When the Swedish paper mentioned the revolution, it was referring to the event that we call the dictatorship of the proletariat, but in more cultured circles they had earlier referred to as the Commune. He later moved to Paris, and for many years, until the great inner Party conflict of 1929, he was a correspondent for *Folkets Dagblad*. In this sentence, on the other hand, the reference is to the inner conflict of the Swedish Party. Many will surely remember his brilliant reports. Later he edited a Parisian weekly, then headed an international news agency based in Paris, while his wife, Magda Aranyossi, edited a major French women's magazine until Hitler came, and with him Pétain, and Aranyossi was interned at Le Vernet d'Ariège. He managed to escape, he managed to return to Hungary, he managed to experience torture inflicted by the Nazis in his own country. He is presently editing the popular Hungarian illustrated magazine *Jövendő*, but has promised to find the time to send us many more reports as interesting as the one below . . .

At the start of summer, Yvette and I set off from here, meaning Teréz Boulevard, we took the tram to the dock at Bem Square, and from there we took a boat carrying market produce to Leányfalu, or sometimes one of the big boats, the *Kossuth* or the *Petőfi*. Sometimes my Aunt Magda gave us extra money, and then we had lunch in the elegant restaurant on one of these big boats.

Sometimes they took me with them to Dobsinai Street up on Orbánhegy in Buda, where at times I stayed for a whole week. This was the house at number 12. And here, too, I had to go alone; fortunately, my brother could not come with me. The tall villa on Dobsinai Street was designed by János Beutum, an architect schooled in the Bauhaus style who was not just an architect or an art-architect, as he was called back then, but an interior designer as well, and so the villa was furnished with objects of his own design. The family of our father's older sister moved into the house in the spring of 1933, and it was confiscated in the spring of 1944. They had to move out leaving just about all their furnishings behind. They had just three days to pack up and leave the premises. They managed to move some objects and pieces of furniture to my Uncle Sándor's office on Teréz Boulevard, which was in turn confiscated, along with all its furnishings, a couple of weeks later, though the furnishings remained untouched. In secret, they passed the antiques and all the movable objects into the care of Catholic friends and acquaintances, the valuable rugs, their jewelry, silver, including my great-grandmother's silver service for twenty-four, along with the various silver trays and serving pieces. The undertaking was risky for their Catholic acquaintances, considering that decree number 1.600 M.E. issued in 1944 by the Hungarian Royal Ministry pertaining to the reporting and confiscation of Jewish property, which deprived Jews of their right to dispose of their fortunes in any form whatsoever and called upon all Jews and non-Jews who, regardless of the pretext, were in temporary possession of Jewish valuables, to report it. Of these, every single object survived the siege without injury and was returned to them. In those years, this was far from self-evident. Just one runner got badly damaged in Catholic safekeeping as a result of heavy shell fire, and we had to cut a big piece out of it. It must have been repaired by an outstanding weaver, the shop was there for some time yet on the corner of Veres Pálné and Reáltanoda streets; for the next seventy years, during my lifetime, hardly a scar remained from the operation, and though worn, it is still in my possession. They mended the injuries to the rug with strips taken from the piece they'd removed from it.

The confiscated house in Dobsinai Street burned down during the siege under circumstances that have not been clarified to this day. Only its functional frame and charred walls survived. The windows along with the window frames, made by the best carpenters, the doors along with their frames, the parquet floors, the staircase, everything but everything was burned to cinders, all the interior furnishings of the house that could burn, along with the artworks that were left behind. It was all gone. By the fall of 1946, with slight alterations to the basement and the staircase, it was rebuilt and refurnished, even though it was the second time in their lives that they seriously considered leaving, leaving the city, leaving the country, getting away from here. They first considered leaving seriously in the late thirties, after the German annexation of Austria, meaning the Anschluss. As if the heavens meant to help, Sándor Rendl received a flattering offer from the Bank of England to take over the legal management of the bank's Near Eastern branch, including all the legal problems of the successor states of the defunct Ottoman Empire. Haifa would have been the headquarters of the branch. They embarked on a round trip of the Near East. First they went to Egypt, then on to Palestine, then Lebanon and Syria, but they were most intent on visiting Haifa. My Aunt Eugenie felt that life in Haifa was too chaotic for them to settle there. They'd have had to move from a seriously threatened city to a village in a state of war where, without any Zionist or religious convictions, they'd have to live among Jews fighting the Arab inhabitants. Even if the Bank of England had assured them of certain extraterritorial, colonial rights, they'd have had to live smack in the middle of a civil war zone. They didn't leave their house in Buda. What's more, after the siege, they moved back in a second time, whereas in the days before the Communist takeover, before they hermetically sealed off the borders, Zoltán Vas very generously offered members of the plenary committee of experts working on the introduction of the forint, and thus, Sándor Rendl as well, free passage, along with their valuables. They recognized the necessity of such a step, but Sándor Rendl also recognized that his declining health would not allow him to start a new life in a new, unfamiliar land. Only Minister of Finance Ferenc Gordon availed himself of the offer.

Again, they stayed, and they had to abandon their house once again in the spring of 1952, this time without hope of return. To his great good fortune, Sándor Rendl did not live to see the day.

When the villa was rebuilt, my Aunt Eugenie made some changes to the original furnishings. Of the prewar furniture, only two armchairs survived the siege in the Teréz Boulevard office, whose style reflected the radicalism of Gerrit Rietveld's famous red-and-blue chair, which she and Beutum made more comfortable, better to sit on, by the addition of pillows. The post-siege redesign of the house dispensed with the avant-garde radicalism of the original and followed a more restrained modernist trend. The new furniture was made by Sándor Heinrich's firm, which primarily manufactured office furniture. Heinrich's shop was located in Párisi Street; he'd made my aunt's furniture before the siege as well, and he had an admirable feel for the artisanal details that went with simplicity and seamlessness of design. The furnishings were now even lighter in color and even more pared down, if possible, and even more apparent to the eye in all respects. Probably, in the rigorous aesthetics of the new furnishings it was not my Aunt Eugenie who followed Beutum's cue, it was Beutum who followed hers. Though Beutum was a staunch proponent of the architectural principles of the Bauhaus and the de Stijl group, he was a versatile architect and worked in many different styles in his lifetime. He even designed a bridge. This is why the cooperation between the client and the architect was seamless, even though it ended with battle cries.

There was a businessman by the name of Manó Balassa, I can't remember what business he was in, and he was also one of Sándor Rendl's clients, and he was so impressed by the Rendls' brand-new house that he ordered a copy from Beutum on an empty lot he found down the street. Except, he wanted everything to be even bigger. This was his only wish and his one stipulation. And Beutum not only built the enlarged copy of the house on the corner of Dobsinai and Fodor streets, he also copied its furnishings one by one, without consulting with my aunt. For decades, my Aunt Eugenie, whom I'd never before seen upset, remained profoundly shaken by Beutum's conduct. When I asked her about it, she couldn't even breathe. The structural solutions and interior furnishings of the building were the result of their collaboration, it was their shared intellectual property, and Beutum had sold her most intimate possessions to a stranger, meaning that he had shamelessly betrayed her.

Seen from the southeast, the unity and articulation, symmetries and asymmetries and deconstruction is truly striking, and the copying of it is clearly shameless. And so, my Aunt Eugenie's ire is understandable, but at the risk of bringing her ire down on me from the other world, I must admit that the Balassa Villa on the corner of Fodor Street is better still, even if the intention of its builder was fired by the need to show off and surpass his neighbor. Surely Balassa must have been one of those individuals who want everything to happen faster, to spit farther, to leap higher, to piss in a wider arc. But Beutum's architectural imagination reached its ideal proportions at what we might call a grander scale. Simply put, the cube is bigger, the deconstruction more convincing. Still, the relationship between the outer form and the interior spaces was more attractive in the house commissioned by Sándor Rendl and his wife. I visited the Balassa Villa, too. The Rendls' house remained humble in every respect, humble in its size, too, though far from cheap; after all, they used the best materials available and employed the most up-to-date architectural solutions. As a child, I didn't think of the deconstruction of the cube-shaped building or the proportions of the interior spaces; it was the precision of the whole that caught my attention, the way the three things, the interior space, the furnishings, and the lifestyle, were in perfect harmony. The villa was rich, to be sure, but there was nothing ostentatious in its richness. It was dominated by the spirit of understatement; in short, it had something to be modest about. Modesty is not mimicry but an intellectual stance. I never discovered a single object or action in the spaces of their house that appeared by whim. Whatever had a place invariably remained there, objects were not removed, nor did they pile up. Yet despite the strict planning, the spaces were not sterile, which, I think, must have been due to the colors and the materials used.

When they finished breakfast in the dining room, or in the summer on the dining room terrace, which I especially liked, the breeze, the persistent little struggle of their hands with the edge of the damask tablecloths and damask napkins so the breeze shouldn't blow them atop the honey or topple the cups, the chauffeur brought the car from the garage situated on the lower level to drive Sándor Rendl to the office. Before the siege it was a Pontiac that he'd bought used from the American ambassador, and after the siege, a Mercedes. In the interest of a better understanding of those years, the story of the Pontiac is worth relating. When a Hungarian Jew could no longer rent or own Hungarian land, when all his money and possessions were registered and his assets frozen, and he could no longer dispose of them as he wished, when he could no longer travel by train or bus, when he could no longer attend the theater, the movies, or concerts, when a Jewish child could no longer wear a school uniform, when a Jew could leave his home only during certain hours of the day and could visit a public bath only during certain hours of certain days, when the written works of 114 Hungarian and 34 foreign Jewish authors had already been taken off the library shelves and were delivered up for the price of scrap paper and pulped, Prime Minister Géza Lakatos signed decree no. 3.520 M.E. of 1944 disposing of the goods on hand in Jewish shops and other Jewish valuables. Theoretically, other Jewish valuables could cover anything. With reference to this decree number so-and-so, Sándor Rendl was called upon to remove the four tires of his Pontiac automobile and deliver them to a specified headquarters of the army at a specified hour of a specified day under criminal liability. He removed the four tires and surrendered them and was handed a receipt. A couple of days later he was required to surrender the automobile as well. He tried to clarify the situation and ask for the return of the tires in order to get around the obvious nonsense, which would not be in the interest, first and foremost, of the homeland engaged in a life-and-death struggle with Bolshevism. However, headquarters insisted that the maimed automobile be surrendered. Despite the difficult terrain, he had to move the automobile that had been propped up on a lift out of the garage at his own expense, need I add. They lifted it atop a special truck and transported it to the specified address, where they said that he should take it back, they can't use it without the tires. He had it taken off the truck's platform, again at his own expense, but left it in the yard of the barracks in the company of other dispossessed vehicles.

Every single morning the same thing happened in their home, and every single time without haste, which impressed me a great deal. Before the siege, her mother accompanied Vera to school, and from there she went shopping, or as the people of Budapest said back then, she went commissioning. Which meant that she went on her errands. She went by taxi or tram, or as they said back then, she took a taxi or took a tram, she went to the farmers' market on Fény Street, or she went to Kovács on Andrássy Boulevard. At times I went along, Kovács was a huge grocery store on the corner of Dalszínház Street next to the Opera, stocked with all available earthly goods, and here she picked out the foods they needed for the next couple of days according to a list she compiled with the cook; these items were packed in boxes and baskets and sent to their home that morning. From there she went to the Inner City, from where we got home at noon, sometimes with all sorts of scented parcels. On Christmas Day of 1949, Mr. Kovács's grocery store was all lit up, to my surprise. He somehow managed to survive the first wave of nationalizations, he must have enjoyed some privilege in acquiring his stock. I remember this vividly because Vera, who was in her third year at the College of Technology, was getting married that day to another student there. His name was Tamás Herczeg, and he was a tall young man with an engaging personality and an infectious laugh, blond and bursting with health, who was studying to be a mechanical engineer, and at noon, the members of both families were invited to a reception to be held in Dobsinai Street. Though the young couple had no idea when they met, the two families had actually known each other from before. Tamás Herczeg's maternal grandfather had been an architect, his name was Ármin Hegedűs, and he commissioned our grandfather Adolf Arnold Nádas to dry out his buildings. He built the Hotel Gellért at the foot of Gellért Hill, and my grandfather did the drying. Their children vacationed together, sometimes at the manor house in Gömörsid, sometimes at their estate in Iharos. I'd never seen a reception before. The word itself was a novelty, and the phenomenon was a novelty, too. I even remember that they served the consommé in cups, and my aunt and uncle had to host another reception the same day, because the young couple had invited their friends for the evening. On November 24, 1956, after we said our good-byes the day before and our father gave them useful advice about what they must take with them, the entire friendly bunch left the country together. There were thirty-four of them and they all left, and on January 4, 1957, they were all on board when their boat docked in Halifax.

When after a while my Aunt Eugenie and Gizi saw that this or that would be missing for the evening reception, because they had miscalculated how much they'd need of this or that, she went behind the buffet laden with the remains of the mountains of food with a slip of paper and the phone to call Kovács, asking that he should send over so much of this or that, and I followed excitedly behind. I was hoping that we'd go together to Kovács for this or that. But during the first few months of the following year, they closed his beautiful shop. There were no shops left in Budapest whose shelves were not empty, and this I remember even more clearly.

The chauffeur's wife acted as the parlormaid, she served the food and she also helped clean the house. They lived on the lower level in the basement, they had a separate entrance, and their quarters faced south. The cook's quarters, her name was Gizella Mrázik, must have been down there as well, at least, as far as I can remember, except her room faced west, not that she ever invited me to her room. Once I had to go downstairs to fetch her. I wasn't even allowed to enter the kitchen without her permission. My presence irritated Gizella Mrázik no end and I remained skittish with her. Gizella Mrázik didn't like grown-ups either, but she hated children with a passion. Beutum had raised the basement windows just above ground level to let the sun into the servants' quarters. This raising of the basement windows conferred a certain dignity on the building, a certain stately quality. The floor above the basement level was dominated by two spaces of impressive proportions, one was the living room, which at the time the house was built they still called the salon, and the other was the dining room. With its bay window, the salon shattered the geometry of the planes. The window panels placed along the curve were fitted to an upper bracket and worked like a harmonica, which allowed the six-paneled window to be opened all the way, the panels slid into one another, and the whole thing could be slid inside the wall. When they opened the window all the way in the spring or summer, the view of the city beyond the gardens afforded a splendid panorama that seemed like an extension of the interior space.

The salon continued into the dining room without any architectural fuss; this, too, was an innovation over earlier architectural styles, when they'd never have employed an open-space architectural concept such as this. Be that as it may, with the dining room we're back to geometrical purity. Its corner windows faced east and south. From here you could step out on the terrace and from there walk down between the shrubs and perennials of the rock garden to the big garden itself. Needless to say, the garden was tended by a gardener. When at noon Vera came home from school or later from college, and her father was driven home from his office or a law court, they served lunch. There was always an expectant silence before a meal. The table was laid in advance, and only very rarely did sounds issue from the kitchen. The kitchen was situated on the western side of the house behind the dining room, and it could be approached through a connecting corridor, and the cook handed the food to the room maid through a sliding panel above the buffet. Gizella Mrázik insisted on it, and the dining room was built this way expressly to satisfy her wish. She didn't want the guests to see her.

This is why she quit as cook at Baron Bornemisza's residence across the street; she'd had enough, or she'd had enough of people.

The hall was not big, the stairs led from here to the upper part of the house and also down to the lower level. I should say that everything was in proportion, but in that case I would have to say what that everything was in proportion to. It was in proportion to the body of a human being. This is what the Bauhaus, operating with functional forms, dictated. Don't insist on proportions larger than the design of the human body calls for. Perhaps only the terraces were oversized, if that. The largest terrace, what they called the roof garden, was located on the flat roof of the house. Sometimes I sneaked up there on my own, but my aunt didn't like it. The children's room and the bedroom upstairs had terraces looking out on the city. The three horizontal rows of stainless-steel tubing that served as bars on the terraces imparted a horizontal rhythm to the house. The bathroom and the dressing room were also situated on this level. The latter, with its window looking due north, was designed to be big enough for the lady of the house and her seamstresses to do their sewing. They preferred to work with my Aunt Irén, Irén Tauber, more than anyone, because they considered her a brilliant seamstress, to say the least.

The window of the dressing room gave a view of Svábhegy, of the spot where we'd be moving one snowy day in January. And so, Gyöngyvirág Street and its surroundings were already familiar to me from our Sunday walks with Sándor Rendl. We walked from Dobsinai Street to Fodor Street, which ran along a bend of the Danube, and from there we headed for Orbán Square, then started up Diana Street, which at the time was more like a gully. When we reached the tin crucifix on the corner of Gyöngyvirág and Diana streets that Masa Feszty had painted with plain bright colors, we stopped as if on cue. This was where the steepest part of the slope began. Later, too, it played a major part in my life because on my way back from school, this is where Gábor Baltazár, my next-door neighbor, and I parted ways with our classmates, Csider, Székács, and Piros, because they were going to Lóránt Street, though Székács lived a bit farther off. Csíder's and Piros's fathers belonged to the guard, but the boys were not allowed to know what their rank was or what they were guarding. This is where we continued on to Gyöngyvirág Street. We passed Aunt Róza's apple orchard, then Gábor said good-bye. Sometimes his mother was waiting for him at their living room window that looked out on the street. Gábor lived with his younger sister Éva in the villa next to ours. Their father had gone to Venezuela, I don't remember where anymore, and I never figured out why. It seems that he may have had to leave the country in a hurry because of some muddled post-siege affair. I looked to see where Venezuela was, it was very far away, though today I rather tend to think that the matter was probably financial in nature, and from what little Gábor told me, he hadn't abandoned them, he just couldn't take them along, because it was safer for him to flee without them, but he was planning to get them out later. An automobile would come for them, and maybe it'll help them flee. But Gábor couldn't be sure about this either, and the planned escape may have been pure fancy, childish fantasy, his way of hoping to see his father again, his way of rationalizing the situation. And come morning, this is where we were waiting for the others, at the crucifix painted in pure bright colors.

The two of us, Gábor and I, the first time we laid eyes on each other, we didn't need to get closer, we were already closer to each other than to anyone else. He was much taller than I, a strikingly handsome boy with long limbs, dark hair, and dark eyes. Their mother was a true beauty, every part of her, her every gesture proportionate; I'd never seen anything remotely like it before, only in the movies, and he had inherited his mother's physique. If I think back on it now, if I now try to unravel the secret of this closeness to her son, I would say that perhaps it was not so much their physique that was similar; it was Gábor's confidence and self-assurance that was similar in nature to his mother's, and this is why he felt that there was nothing he couldn't tell me.

Sándor Rendl had a bad heart, his blood sugar was high, and so was his blood pressure, and as a consequence, his red and blue capillaries were visible on his cheeks and nose. From a distance he looked like a ruddy English gentleman who'd eaten his share of roast beef in his long life. He was seriously ill, though he gave very few signs of it, but on these carefully hidden signs I was able to study the fragile interplay of semblance and reality. I still enjoyed watching from up close the arteries and veins as well as the alterations in them. Some years later, in the days just before he died, some of the small capillaries may have even ruptured on his nose just under the skin. Or God knows. It may have had something to do with his high blood sugar. The area seemed about to spill over, the skin was full of wounds, edematous scars and infected scabs, and the scabs fell off, leaving small lesions that would not heal. This look on the faces of older people was not uncommon back then.

The doctor recommended long walks. Make that heart of yours work as hard as it can, let it work, this was the doctor's advice, let's not spare ourselves, do you understand.

This is why we stopped by the tin crucifix on the corner of Gyöngyvirág Street, so he could catch his breath without being caught at it, and we continued on our way only then.

On the third level of their house, there was a very small room facing west that had once belonged to his stepson, György Mándoki, who died in forced labor. Sometimes they let me have it. No one except for the cleaning lady and the parlormaid were allowed to enter it, even though the fire had destroyed everything except for the bare walls. Still, during that first post-siege year, when they rebuilt and refurnished their house, they were still hoping for his return. The cleaning lady came early in the morning and left around three in the afternoon. She may not have come every day, but they dusted every day. When I lay down in that small room to sleep, I was as awed as an unwelcome pilgrim in some holy place. I think they must have thought something similar, because they had me sleep in this small room only when they gave a dinner party downstairs. They had to give many dinners in honor of Uncle Rendl's clients from home and abroad. This is how they said it, in honor of. This, too, was a new expression, one of many new expressions. Two walls of the salon were lined with bookshelves, but there was a cozy nook next to the entrance that the bookshelves framed, so to speak, and when there were no guests around, they made my bed in this upholstered nook intended for leisurely reading.

My Aunt Eugenie's aesthetic preferences tended to the modern in all respects. She hardly worked as a metalsmith, a trade she had learned in school, she may have lacked a sense of mission, she didn't become an artist, she became a wife, for which her younger sister Magda, who according to her birth certificate was really called Ida Magdolna, looked down on her just a bit, to the extent that a big, *patte à puff* woman is capable of looking down on a beautiful, svelte, and elegant older sister, the quintessential wife who has made her pact with being enslaved to a man. But had she taken up her trade in earnest, probably she'd have been a modernist, just like her schoolmates who became decorative artists, or her artist friends, the period's modernist painters and sculptors. To be sure, they had very few objects in their home, but these were carefully selected and just as carefully coordinated. They had a rather large, slightly translucent chrysoprase goblet, whose color was as exceptional as its form, cut, and polish. It was uniformly pale apple green without impurities, qualities that theoretically can't be expected of a semi-precious stone. Its shape seemed to have been achieved through cracking and splitting. The edges were sharp, almost razor sharp, and the slightest bit of light made them shine. The apple green was most brilliant at dusk, it shone right through the dusk. There were also some original faience bowls and faience vases, old majolica ware, fine tin-glazed pottery from Faenza in Italy with scrolling Renaissance patterns painted in blue and terra-cotta on a lemon-yellow base. I tried to familiarize myself with the relief patterns that decorated them by running the tips of my fingers over them, and these reliefs are at the tips of my fingers to this day. The upholstery and drapes came from Éva Szabó's workshop. She and Ernő Schubert were the most important Hungarian textile artists of the time, and she had studied at Sándor Bortnyik's private graphic design school, the Workshop. Bortnyik was the grandmaster of Hungarian avant-garde modernism, and in his school they followed Bauhaus principles, as a consequence of which it was commonly called the Hungarian Bauhaus. Later she studied weaving and textile design in Munich and Berlin, then finished her training with the great Viennese architect and designer Josef Hoffmann, at the Wiener Werkstätte. She opened her first weaving workshop in 1931 in Budapest's venerable Bálvány Street, which has since been given a variety of other names, and a year later she opened a shop in Kossuth Lajos Street, at the time one of the most fashionable streets of the Inner City. Needless to say, the street's elegance is now a thing of the past. Her rustic upholsteries and drapes, woven of cotton, wool, linen, and hemp, were used by the prominent Hungarian architects and interior designers of the day. She worked not only for Beutum, but also for Lajos Kozma and Farkas Molnár, both of whom far outstripped Beutum in prominence. She drew on a treasury of forms from early Christian, Renaissance, baroque, and folk art for the textures and patterns of her handwoven designs, she placed the motifs alongside each other in strict geometrical order, repeating them over and over. Even though in her workshop everything was handmade according to original designs, this was nevertheless the re-petitive gesture of mass production. It was this confrontation between pattern and production that was admirable. The pillow on the divan of the salon on which I rested my head for my afternoon naps was made of black woolen yarn worked in relief on a gray cotton base interlaced with yellowish orange hemp threads running lightly through it, and it sported symmetrically arranged stylized birds, peacocks, lions, hens, trees of life, miracle stags, tulips, rosettes, and knights in shining ar-mor with falcons precariously perched on their arms, all of which was treated with a light, humorous touch in infinite numbers, the lines running off the sides, as it were. The identical handling of the dia-metrically opposed motifs taken from a variety of sources would have satisfied even the aesthetic principles of my master, Miklós Mészöly.

I don't know if he was familiar with Éva Szabó's work, but it was certainly my first encounter with this modern aesthetic, and when I first read Mészöly's writings, probably this is why I understood him. They made these relief patterns on looms suited to the production of materials with large patterns, and they used three different threads, cotton, wool, and hemp. The method, called Jacquard weaving, originated with Joseph Marie Jacquard, the master weaver from Lyon, who developed the earliest programmable loom, in the early nineteenth century. Sometimes I tried to count how many peacocks, knights, horses, and hens there were on the pillow, and sometimes I fell asleep as I counted, and sixty years later I saw in Lyon, where the dirt-blue Saône and the sand-yellow Rhône gently flow into each other under a hazy blue sky.

Szabó took her inspiration for the upholstery for the pillow resting on the divan of the salon from old Hungarian-Transylvanian cross-stitch embroidery. The fabric was called Transylvania, and it could even be washed. No wonder. Easy maintenance was also one of the strict requirements of the Bauhaus. Éva Szabó also left her mark on real Jacquard textiles. Vera's room upstairs was decorated with grass-green upholstery woven of fine cotton and rough woolen thread, but the Jacquard cretonne pillow thrown over her divan had leaf-green motifs on a bone-colored base with baroque motifs. In this case, instead of miniaturizing her motifs, Szabó enlarged them. There were two armchairs in the room, they were also upholstered in the same cretonne fabric, also bone-colored. In my young life, these objects and materials were my introduction to the *Neue Sachlichkeit*, the New Objectivity. The Jacquard prints were named after Erda, the earth goddess of German mythology, though clearly, the plant motifs had more in common with the ash, the tree of life of Scandinavian myth, or the curlicue plant motifs of Renaissance tapestries, than with Wagner's thunderclap operas. I would imagine that on one of her frequent visits to Scandinavia, Szabó must have seen the illuminated initials of seventeenth-century manuscripts whose dull yellows, browns, blues, and pinks she hastened to apply to her cretonnes. Furthermore, the cardboard boxes that lay on the shelves of the spacious dressing room that opened from Vera's room were covered in the same material as the armchairs. It was miraculous sneaking in there and surreptitiously opening the tops of these boxes, and it was even more miraculous when my cousin, who was studying architecture at the University of Technology, was choosing from among her fine underwear or was getting dressed. And it was especially miraculous that she didn't mind my being there. I remember every curve of her body, and from various angles, too. She said that compared with her waist and hips, her breasts were too big, she had inherited Grandmother Mezei's breasts. While their house was being built, she was sent to live with our grandmother in Pannónia Street. I'm sorry I never knew our Mezei grandmother, Klára Mezei, and Pannónia Street, but Vera loved her more than anyone. She said her grandmother was wonderful, and my mother is perhaps the only other member of the family she loves as much. At night our father would tell her tales in the Pannónia Street apartment, because he was still a young man at the time and lived at home. This was entirely new to me about our father, I could hardly process it. Our father never told tales to any of us at night. Perhaps once. But even then, it was really a sermon for our edification dressed in fairy-tale garb. It bored me the minute he launched into it, because I could tell from his intonation that a moral would follow. He was profoundly disappointed in me because I wasn't the way he'd have liked me to be. After our mother died, he may have told my brother stories now and then, parables with my brother's spiritual ennoblement in mind. He wasn't quite so disappointed in him. I, on the other hand, was profoundly disappointed in my little brother, I don't know why, thereby perpetuating the inheritance of the fathers, the endless dissatisfaction whose legitimacy was justified by blood relations. It was my great good luck that Vera let me choose the most appropriate shoes for her. She had a pair of white platform sandals, I even remember the name of the leather, suede, and I loved these white suede sandals more than any other of her shoes, and from the way my father behaved, I realized that I should not concern myself with such things, I shouldn't even show an interest in them, after all, I'm a boy, but in secret I even tried on Vera's platforms, I wanted to know what it felt like for a woman to walk on pedestals made of cork.

Éva Szabó also made unpatterned, monocolored upholstery, and these were also important works, even if later on her admirers mostly ignored them. The texture of these monocolored textiles was almost rustic and thickly woven. She left the longitudinal threads knotty, and since the knottiness was irregular, the surface would have been uneven had the transverse cotton weft or the rustic hemp yarn not imparted a certain regularity to the weave. These strong textures were rendered middle class thanks to their unique colors. From the point of view of the avant-garde, Éva Szabó's art might be considered opportunistic, and so it was. In order to satisfy the taste of the upper circles, she abandoned avant-garde modernism in favor of classical modernism, and I thoroughly enjoyed her opportunism.

Éva Szabó did not use pure colors, but she did not use pastels either. She used earth colors and plant colors. The colors of the earth muted under a hazy sky. This, I think, is the right term, they were muted colors, she probably added a bit of black to the coloring made of natural ingredients. My Aunt Eugenie chose the upholstery for her house from this type of hazy material. A rustic weave created from a unique blend of pale terra-cotta and pale orange, as it stood out from the hazy brown of the walnut furniture, dominated the salon. The dining room was decorated with a combination of dull gray and dull terra-cotta textures tending to orange. They were made of cotton cloth reinforced with hemp and a mix of cotton and wool, though Szabó also worked with silk, brocade, and muslin. My Aunt Eugenie gave these a wide berth. On the special request of Her Serene Highness, Mrs. Miklós Horthy de Nagybánya, née Magdolna Purgly, Éva Szabó designed the handwoven brocades for her Hungarian-style court costume, the *díszmagyar*. But she also designed for the Church. She made a large silk tapestry for the new cathedral in Pécs. Still, she was one of the few privileged individuals who could keep their independence even after the nationalizations; she had to turn her workshop into an artisans' cooperative only in 1952, and remained its artistic director until her death.

As an adolescent, I'd regularly make my weekly rounds of the nationalized antiques shops, since paintings by the Hungarian avant-garde and classical avant-garde were not to be found anywhere else. They were hardly ever exhibited, and as the painters said, they were relegated to the warehouses of the Hungarian National Gallery, thereby disposing of the work of two generations of Hungarian painters as if they had never been in favor of the engaged naturalism they called socialist realism, a sure way of guaranteeing the reign of dilettantism all around. But in these antiques shops, one located in the Clotilde Palace on the corner of Kossuth Lajos Street and Liberty Square, the other, which was larger and was located on the corner of Falk Miksa Street and Leopold Boulevard, these pictures, rejected for exhibition, were displayed for sale, even if they were mixed in, without a second thought, with the nauseating petit bourgeois kitschy fairground garbage and the masterpieces of Austrian and Hungarian landscape painting that had survived from nineteenth-century bourgeois homes. The paintings of the artists of the Nagybánya, Szolnok, Kecskemét, and Szentendre artists' colonies could be had for peanuts, these were artists I had known personally or had heard about, those whom the living were still mentioning with admiration; and so I went looking for them, because it was improbable that these works would be available for viewing ever again. On these pilgrimages, invariably and without realizing it, I stopped in front of the window of Éva Szabó's workshop in Kossuth Lajos Street. Now and then I would even go inside. There was hardly anything new in the shop. Though she made designs for so-called houses of culture, union resorts, and Party headquarters that differed slightly from her previous work, though she got off the high horse of her previous standard, and her repetitive style moved closer to the requirements of the prefab apartments of the new housing estates, becoming clichéd and didactic, she did not abandon her insistence on handwoven fabrics and the classical modernist style inspired by historical motifs, which, however, did not seem to bother the official preferences of latter-day Rákosism and early Kádárism. The sales ladies of the older generation may have liked the crazy adolescent gradually growing into a young man who I was and about whom, I don't know from what source, they knew that I was an orphan, they even knew that I was a student apprentice at the nearby photographer's studio, and they saw that for some strange reason, I couldn't get enough of the handmade textures and hazy colors.

The metalsmith's objects in the Dobsinai Street house were all made by Margit Tevan. As I see it, Tevan united two trends in her art, two periods, the early Christian, though not necessarily Roman, perhaps at times she combined the pure forms of the liturgical goblets, cups, and bowls of Byzantine ecclesiastical art with the rustic ornamentation of folk-art carvings and embroideries with their rich storehouse of symbols and motifs. We owned several books on Tevan, designed by the best Hungarian modernist typographers, first and foremost, György Buday. Margit Tevan herself came from this exceptional family of book lovers from Békéscsaba. Her work had much in common with Szabó. The materiality of her objects, made of brass, copper, and tin, stood in contrast with the crowded hand-hammered world of symbols she took from tales and legends. It was thrilling to see this combination of the unique and the multiple, the pure and the rustic, the smooth and the crowded together like this. I learned to understand and appreciate this branch of Hungarian modernity tending to the classical and to the conservation of value, which, by the way, was no less politically dangerous than the mainstream avant-garde, in my aunt's home. I found the clever way these objects confronted the old and the new entirely convincing. Not only did the stands of Tevan's bowls, plates, and goblets decorated with caryatids and the mythological plants, animals, beasts, trailers and tendrils, stars and planets parading along the friezes of her cigarette boxes and ashtrays speak to me, I followed them with my fingers, I felt and smelled them. The cigarette ashes left an odor on the hammered metal that I could not have felt anywhere else. My Aunt Eugenie did not smoke, though sitting in one of the armchairs of the salon she would now and then light a cigarette, which looked handsome between her fingers and had a pleasant smell besides. No one except for her ever smoked in the family, though from time to time, my mother would join her for a cigarette. There was also a bronze table bell that they used in the dining room, it must have been an antique, a lady in Renaissance garb and headdress, with the clapper hidden under her uniformly pleated skirt.

They hung their paintings at a distance from each other on the bare walls, so they shouldn't interfere with each other. There was an early Egry, which I later sold to a collector for peanuts when at seventeen I broke with my family once and for all, with everyone, in fact, and I literally had nothing to eat. To this day I regret having sold it. In Dobsinai Street, this painting was hung in our great-grandmother's upstairs bedroom furnished with antique furniture and art objects. There was also a Kernstok with his splendid horses and even more splendid riders rendered with confident lines. The riders had wide, manly shoulders, their waists were well-tailored and narrow, but their backsides on the horses were as round as any female's. There were also several paintings and drawings by Szőnyi and several others by Margit Gráber and Vilmos Perlrott Csaba, and also several pastels by them, as well as works by Kmetty, Márffy, Vaszary, and Czóbel. The sculptures were by Pál Pátzay, and I think the heavy medal paperweight was by Ö. Fülöp Beck.

Though at the time art books were rare in domestic households, I nevertheless found one of Ö. Fülöp Beck's works among their books. They contained mostly a thematic selection of works meant for the public, the female nude, children in art, the art of drawing, flower still-lifes in Hungarian art, Hungarian metalsmith masterpieces, art of the Netherlands, sculpture of the Italian Renaissance, drawings by Leonardo, Michelangelo's sculptures in Florence, and so on. There were also exhibition catalogues. Later I had a big collection of exhibition catalogues of my own, until one day a chronic lack of space made me throw almost all of them out. It felt good touching the sculptures, to follow their shapes with my fingers and palms, their cool surfaces, their depths and edges instead of the radiant bodies. What a nose is like, what an ear is like, how they relate to the face, how the shapes interact, what reliefs they produce. What the relationship is between the face and the skull. I don't know what else to say, it was from this feeling of the surfaces that I came to understand the human head and the landscape of the face. A literary text is especially challenging if it is called upon to describe that landscape. In this case it was not about the body made of flesh but about something more, something else that is simultaneously related to organic and inorganic nature. I held a bronze skull between my palms before I did a human skull.

Sándor Rendl's law office specialized in international financial law, but on occasion, it represented artists who belonged to the circle of Rendl's wife, and sometimes instead of paying in currency, these artists paid in works of art that his wife chose or commissioned from them. In turn, and in the interest of family unity, Sándor Rendl also represented his wife's Communist sister and Communist brothers to the best of his ability if they were under arrest or facing trial, and despite his personal convictions, he did so to the best of his ability. However, from them he accepted neither money nor art. Their relationship was cordial, if distant. He and they suffered from significant otherness. I might call it a physical otherness. Also, it happened more than once that his wife had given them substantial sums again without his knowledge, although he'd begged her repeatedly not to do so, or else he had to go to one of the jails or prisons again to find someone whom, in the interest of their release, he had to bribe with appreciable sums of money.

You wouldn't want it weighing on your conscience if you didn't do it, would you.

Sándor Rendl did what he had to do, but each time there was a deep and lasting tension between him and my aunt and they had loud arguments. Supporting a political ideology that he considered confused and chaotic at best and socially dangerous at worst is not something that my Uncle Sándor could square with his conscience. Before as well as after the siege, he had voted for the Independent Smallholders Party. My parents considered them a bunch of reactionaries.

In Dobsinai Street, my aunt and uncle had three works by Pátzay, the life-size portraits of Sándor Rendl's parents, Sámuel Rendl, the box manufacturer, in his old age and his aged wife, Irma Grünberger, both impressive works that portray them without hiding anything unexpected or misshapen, a flat nose, stuck-out ears, goiters; they were loving yet ironic, and as such, they were probably inspired by the psychology and views of naturalism that characterize Houdon's portraits of Voltaire. The old couple depicted with love and irony later disappeared in the jungle of our family history. I saw them last in the pantry of my Aunt Magda's apartment on Teréz Boulevard, meaning in the apartment we shared, on the lowest shelf of the tiered stand, exiled into the company of discarded preserve bottles. They also had a bust, possibly even larger than life, of my Aunt Eugenie, which is surely one of the best examples of modern Hungarian art, now forgotten, from the years between the two world wars. It belongs not to the avant-garde but to the neoclassical modernist movement, to its intimate classicist trend instead of its resounding politically committed one. Avant-garde modernity is left-wing. Neoclassical modernity is conservative, so much so that in the years between the two wars, it not only allied itself with the officially preferred Catholic political current, it flirted with fascism, and some of the artists even stepped into it with both feet. For its part, avant-garde modernity not only flirted with communism, but became openly and belligerently Communist, and mostly suffered as a consequence. In Margit Gráber's studio or in a precariously creaking little pub built atop a raft on a tributary of the Danube where painters went to eat dinner, unfortunately, I can't recall the name of the pub, they had an ingenious sentence for this precarious political act. As if he'd quietly stepped into it. If someone became a politically committed artist, whether fascist or Communist, he could go hang his art on a coatrack. Like someone who has quietly stepped into it. They didn't say that he stepped into something, dog shit, no, but quoting Karinthy, just that he quietly stepped into it. This was their summary opinion. They knew this from before, they knew it from experience, and as for me, as a child, I took it to heart for a lifetime. They didn't waste further words on the actions or the individuals who took the primrose path to hell. Like someone who had quietly stepped into it.

The bust that came out of the school of neoclassical modernism was generously conceived, aloof and elegant, just like its model, my generous, aloof, and elegant aunt, who was never known to laugh. Tevan's works were inspired by early Christian religious art, Pátzay's sculpture was inspired by King St. Ladislaus's reliquary bust. My aunt's bust is covered by a dress draped lightly around her body, while

St. Ladislaus's bust is covered by a mantle. That's the only difference between the two. Plus the five hundred years between them. St. Ladislaus's reliquary was made around 1420, during the reign of King Sigismund, but it is not only a piece of sculpture, it is a reliquary to hold a skull placed inside a container secured by gothic bands that is in turn placed inside the reliquary, the real skull inside the bronze skull. It goes without saying that the bust had to be somewhat larger than the actual bust. My aunt's bust, too, was larger than life size. I saw that whenever she passed it, and recently, I even measured it. Pátzay's ecclesiastical reference, on the other hand, does not lack irony. What's more, his St. Ladislaus reference must have been dear not only to the heart of the official Catholic leanings of Church and state, but to Pátzay himself, who, considering his role in the proletarian dictatorship of a few years back, had a lot to atone for if he wished to receive commissions to create statues for public spaces, though, at the same time, the reference to St. Ladislaus's reliquary bust was also an obvious reminder of my aunt's abandoned profession, that of a metalsmith. This was Pátzay's hidden dedication. The bust was made in 1928 and it was exhibited that same year at the Venice Biennale under the title *Portrait of Mrs. Sándor Rendl*. According to the certificate issued by the Esposizione Internazionale d'Arte della Città di Venezia, it bore the inventory number 1450. I don't know how well the young man from the countryside and the young lady from Pest may have known each other previously, I have no available information, but their date of birth is the same, and in their youth, both artists frequented the same leftist avant-garde circles, which they later left, and from which they distanced themselves politically, and so it is almost inconceivable that they had not met before Pátzay fashioned my aunt's likeness.

Today, my Aunt Eugenie's profane bust with its perennial little antique smile in the corners of her lips is standing atop Grandmother Mezei's Biedermeier writing desk in the downstairs living room of my brother's house.

Whether they knew of the depth of the religious, art historical, and sociohistorical content of the bust or not, one thing is for certain, I was aware of it. I first saw photographs of Houdon's marvelous, wrinkled

Voltaire depictions in my Uncle Pali's study, when he was working on a book about Voltaire that was never published, and I found a photograph of St. Ladislaus's reliquary in one of my Aunt Eugenie's art albums. I think I first saw it on the cover of a small book on the metalsmith's art, and I couldn't understand what a portrait was doing there. As a matter of fact, it took me decades to understand it. This bust that they call a reliquary is puzzling, and to this day I can't figure out why they commonly call it a herma, or herm, when to the Greeks a herma is the body of a young male with an erect penis. Be that as it may, St. Ladislaus's bust is both man and formal structure, which can't be left out of the equation, if for no other reason than because, not too obligingly, Pátzay brought out his sitter's male characteristics, man's genetic makeup from a female head. The neoclassical modernists were more than happy to do the opposite. They discovered the body's feminine lines in pronouncedly masculine shapes. Of them all, Béni Ferenczy went furthest in this play with sexual identity. It couldn't have been difficult for him, considering that Béni's physique was pronouncedly feminine, while his younger sister Noémi's physique was masculine, as if nature had in fact exchanged their gender-specific proportions, and this is reflected in their art. I didn't know them, but I saw them several times at exhibition openings. At times Ferenczy constructed a brutally manly pair of female breasts, as if he had it in for them. He slapped the clay on, a great big handful, he rolled the nipples between his fingers, pushed them inside, and left them like that. Painters such as Szőnyi and Kernstok, influenced by classicism, tried their hand at something similar. We see the transfigured asses of Kernstok's gallant riders as they float above the backs of their horses. As soon as they plop back down on the horse's back, they won't be so ideal anymore, they will spread out in two directions. Kernstok doesn't want this, he wants to see an ideal ass. Without their ideal postures we'd no longer see their feminine behinds, their roundness. For some reason, we find this form attractive. To my great surprise, Miklós Mészöly, whom I loved as a father and respected as my literary mentor, and who was endowed with all the gainly and ungainly masculine attributes, had an ass with the same feminine shape.

He had the athletic shoulders and feminine ass of Kernstok's riders. The first time I visited him at his apartment in Városmajor Street and we'd been talking and talking for three and a half hours intent on each other's glance, he jumped up, let's go have a drink, he yelled, and threw off his clothes, and strangely, his underpants, too, then he pulled some clean underwear from a drawer and slipped into another shirt and another pair of pants. It is a true challenge for a painter to see the father in a woman and the mother in a man, and I've been discovering such latent shapes and energies in real-life women and real-life men, what we might call genetic inevitability, ever since. These artists taught me to see when I was an adolescent, which means that a person is capable of perceiving something he doesn't yet know about, something he is not yet familiar with. Ferenczy's treatment of the huge feminine buttocks was the direct opposite of Kernstok's treatment of male buttocks. He enjoys letting the feminine backsides come to rest on the pedestal, though at times he alleviates the crudity of the meeting with draperies, but without ever meaning to resolve it. It must have caused them immeasurable joy, immeasurable excitement around the groins when they could say, I grabbed it where it counts. I got a grip on it. Unless I am much mistaken, I have just hit the bull's-eye.

My aunt and uncle had a fourth statue by Pátzay, a small bronze no taller than 32 centimeters including its base, the young nude David in all his glory, at the moment he's lost hope. It's over, he's defeated, he might as well give up. This is what his raised hand seems to say. Everything is lost, irrevocably lost. The crystal axle of the universe is broken. Still, it's at this same moment that David discovers the five shiny stones in the riverbed with which he will change the course of history.

We see the adolescent David in midstride. I've had the statue since I was an adolescent myself, it is my panacea, and it has been standing on my various desks or shelves ever since. It was with me through my lifelong voluntary exiles, Kisoroszi and Gombosszeg. For decades, David shared my privations. He was the sole witness to my botched attempts at suicide, the shame, the humiliation. A good statue sees and is not just seen. The artist must have made several casts with varying success, because the one in the National Gallery is far inferior to mine. It may have been cast from a sketchy clay mold. To my great good luck, I've been looking at the perfect cast for sixty years now, even if, as far as that goes, it is not as exceptional as the statue of my aunt.

Pátzay's model must have been a proletarian boy with a shaven head, and as such, it has found a very good place with me. Still, I can't say that I am thoroughly familiar with it, because I discover something new every day. It is an inexhaustible subject of study. Then after nearly sixty years of getting acquainted with it, I was sitting one fine day immersed in the Deutsches Literaturarchiv's impressive photography archives in Marbach, where Friedrich Schiller was born and where the Neckar continues to flow and overflow its banks; I'd been sitting there for days, working eight or, if I was lucky, ten hours a day in the photography archives, looking through the photographs left behind by hundreds of dead colleagues at the archives' request; I'd been given a week, an absurdity, when suddenly, on several large amateur photographs from Harry Graf Kessler's legacy, there was the likeness of the youthful David before me, racked with doubt and forced to do battle.

The photographs were taken by Harry Graf Kessler in Maillol's wood-beamed studio, which was apparent at first glance, because in one of the pictures there stood the artist with his sparse beard intent on modeling the youth's foot. Maillol was probably showing Count Kessler the rough clay model, and he pretended to be working on it for the sake of the photographs. There is even a bit of unworked clay on the wooden modeling stick. Artists frequently do this favor for photographers, especially if they happen to be their clients; for the sake of the photograph they dip their brush into a bit of paint from their picturesque palette, or scoop up a bit of clay for their wooden modeling stick. In some other photographs, the nude model stands by the statue in the making.

When I saw that photograph, I knew that Pátzay must have been familiar with Maillol's *Narcissus* when he positioned his own sitter. I hurried to tell Professor Frank Druffner of my phenomenal discovery. At the time Druffner was in charge of the paintings, sculptures, and photographs in the Marbach archives. He listened intently, yet a bit like someone listening to a madman, though he must have understood what I was talking about. After all, archival and preservation work consists of nothing if not the carefully arranged mass of infinitesimal discoveries and completely inessential data. After a while he stood up and brought me the passages from Harry Graf Kessler's diaries related to the photographs. A preservationist can store incredible amounts of data in his head. On Monday, June 24, 1907, Count Kessler writes in his diary that Maillol sent a little bicyclist to him who was in fact a jockey, and he's called Gaston Colin. Maillol wants the young man to model for the relief and the *Narcissus* that the count had commissioned from him. But since Maillol pays only 5 francs and it's hard to find a decent model for that sum of money, the count gave the boy the rest. Four days later, on a Friday, Kessler writes in his diary that he'd dined with the Maillols in Marly for the first time. I came rather early, he writes, around six thirty, since Maillol had not fixed a time, and I visited his studio before dinner, where he uncovered the relief for me. The youth is almost done. He took as the model the little Colin, for the nude the young Gaboriau from St.-Germain, a roustabout, prizefighter, football captain, pastor's son, retired ship's boy, painter, and a student of Maurice Denis. I told Maillol that I thought that it was *plus près de la nature* than his earlier works. Kessler was bilingual. He mixed languages in his diary. He thought in German, he wrote in German, but did not translate the French into German. At this Maillol said, *Mais ça n'a pas d'importance, ça!* But that's not important. What's important is the presence of feeling. There are delicious primitive things and these are not at all close to nature. He works and works until he can express the feeling, until he can express the essence. *Le sentiment remplace la science.* Sentiment replaces science. Listen. When I begin work, I grope in the dark, even when I work without a model, trying to find my way, but I persist until I reach those things that express the feeling I'm after. Then he showed me the nude studies of the little Colin for the *Narcissus*. I will shorten his legs and reinforce his arms, but the chest and the back are very pretty. *Regardez, c'est curieux, il a des seins comme une jeune fille.* Look, it's curious, he has breasts like a young girl.

By the time my uncle and I reached the roadside crucifix to stop and rest, out of mere courtesy I felt I should explain to my Uncle Sándor how my parents and their friends would rig the upcoming parliamentary elections, and at the age of five I even knew that the falsification was being organized and directed by Minister of the Interior Rajk. It never occurred to me that I was giving away a top secret.

After a while, as we walked along Diana Street on our Sunday walks, up the treacherous incline, my Uncle Sándor spoke less and less and breathed with more and more difficulty. These roads were irregular, with gullies, and the pointed end of his walking stick kept knocking against the stones and making squeaking sounds.

My father had taught me early on how a person should take part in a conversation. He does not interrupt when someone else is speaking, and he also told me when he should ask a question and when and what he must not ask. How he should take over and how he should change the subject. And so, from a sense of duty, I wanted to tell him something new so he shouldn't have to do all the talking, but my colossal sense of duty went awry yet again.

By the time we reached the Clock Villa, I had basically told him the whole secret story, and I went on talking because he'd turned silent, his silence was strange, and the color of his face, too, seemed to change several times. I glanced up at him. Perhaps his blood pressure was up, or perhaps he'd had enough of me.

The Clock Villa stood on the ridge of a hill. Years later I visited a schoolmate there, he insisted that I take a look at the button football board that his father had made for him. They lived in an annex of the villa that at one time must have served as the barn. Years later I saw the inside of the neoclassical main building as well, whose pediment is supported by the sort of squat columns typical of houses in the countryside, giving it an imperial air high up on the hill. When it was built, the stately porch overlooked a vast vineyard. The villa was named after the clock on the pediment. When my uncle and I took our Sunday walks, a barren hole gaped where the clock had been. During the siege, someone had removed and taken away the clock. I think that later I was in the former dining room that looked out on the columns maybe twice, because the democratic opposition held some of the lectures of its flying university there. The philosopher Mihály Vajda was the lecturer on democracy. Each lecture was held in a different place, with the informers in tow, of course, and so the fact that I had attended was recorded in the secret service files. In a summary signed by Dr. Attila Izsó, I was even put on the list of those individuals who needed further investigation.

According to the definition provided by the "Targets Dossier," opened in February 1981 but never closed, and which bore the number 11-OD-4884, those individuals were considered first-category observation targets who besides attending the so-called flying university lectures took part in other forms of opposition activity as initiators or organizers. The primary targets of the secret investigation included János Kis, Erzsébet Vezér, János Kenedi, and Ferenc Kőszeg. In the top-secret dossier, I was ranked as a second-category target. These second-category individuals participate in other opposition activities as well, Dr. Izsó wrote, but they are not initiators or organizers. According to the definition given by Dr. Izsó, the major motivation for the group's activities is to establish contact with first-category individuals being observed for intelligence purposes. Thus spake the good doctor. They observed László Rajk, László Rajk's son, whom his mother, Júlia Földi, took out of the family bunting edged in Brussels lace to nurse him for the last time, and a photograph has even survived in which Júlia Rajk is holding the baby in the bunting, with László Rajk looking lovingly on for the sake of the photograph. Lacika, who in the meantime had grown up, must have given a lot more work to the informers than I; after all, he sold samizdat in his apartment, which they very bitterly referred to as the samizdat boutique, and from where they dragged off Ilona Kajsza even before her father's arrest, so she should give evidence against him. The detectives had a harder time with me, because I'd gone into involuntary exile more than ten years before, when, having given up my job, I turned my back on my native town and moved to Kisoroszi, a somnolent little town situated at the end of Szentendre Island, where an agent would have found it difficult to observe me in company without causing suspicion. A small artists' colony came into being there, more by chance than design, because there was hardly any similarity in our views on art, or any other matter, with which we could have inspired one another. Most of us followed István B. Nagy, the painter there, whose father was the local physician, though for my part, I went there because of Lajos Sváby, then Miklós Melocco showed up, and later Péter Melocco, who was a teacher, and so on. There was also someone called Tamás with his high-spirited girlfriend, an excruciatingly weak sculptor, a sweet, stupid man. By fall everything fell silent as the artists moved back to town for the winter. Only I remained. I sat in my rented room. At most, I'd go visit the Mészölys, who commuted between Kisoroszi and Budapest; we went on long walks, or else I visited the local Reform minister József Tóth, who had a big family. For the first time in my life I took Holy Communion with him, on condition that I learn the Heidelberg Catechism and profess my faith. I have no idea who was watching me, whether one person or several. On these Kisoroszi summers, there was much socializing, but after the first few autumn days, there was only silence. I still have no access to my personal files, but there were plenty of indications of the flattering eye of the security forces. Sometimes they even made sure that they should be noticed, it was meant as a final warning, but with teeth clenched we took no notice, ignored who was watching whom, when, and why, and how many more times the final warning was still to come. About what, I wonder. If a person bothered with such things, the dictatorship would have split the nucleus of his personality apart and he'd have begun to rot from within. The other negative outcome of his fear of being observed would have been him being snared in the net of the regime-specific paranoia of the time. Ignoring the secret police was a matter of our freedom, our autonomy, the God-given freedom of the senses.

My friend and mentor Miklós Mészöly and I decided that we would steadily ignore being watched, though we were aware of it, needless to say. We couldn't help but notice that in our absence strangers had been in our rented rooms and some objects and furnishings had been moved from their original place. I've been going through my papers like a maniac ever since. The bastards took some irreplaceable notes, and I can't believe it, even now, they took them because they thought that they were coded. They wanted to decipher them. I illustrated the structure and working mechanism of consciousness on some colored sketches, and to this day I don't want to believe that they made off with them. Probably, the explanation lies with the fact that these illustrations were in color. The agents worked with black-and-white film in their miniaturized cameras, but since they were convinced that the colors on my illustrations had significance, they had to have them. I studied descriptive geometry for two years at the High School for Chemistry, and I used all my knowledge and all my intuitive powers to illustrate the structure of consciousness. They were mad illustrations, I admit, visionary illustrations, they were born in a state of grace in the summer of 1971, I made them at the crossroads of a botched love affair and an adventure with drugs. Mészöly, on the other hand, had a lot more to ignore than I, because they wiretapped him twenty-four hours a day, both in his apartment in Városmajor Street and in the various rooms he rented in Kisoroszi, and then in the big wooden vine-covered house up on the hill. His files are also unavailable, but the files of the other members of the opposition indicate that he was being watched for several years, possibly for a decade. When we saw that the other's attention and imagination were focused too much on the informers again, we warned each other. We refused to talk about who in our group might be an informer. Either he stopped me, or I stopped him, but together we never entered into a conversation of this sort. Since we had reliable information on the disinformation campaigns of the various secret services, we opted for self-censorship. Their disinformation campaigns sometimes produced tragic consequences. We couldn't tolerate the humiliation of being duped by possible disinformation about someone. We wouldn't allow the other to harbor suspicion. We forbade ourselves and each other

any sort of suspicion. Innocence was our only remedy, our only anti-
dote against dictatorship. Who is likable is likable, who is dislikable
is dislikable. We relied solely on our ability to feel, to sense things.
If we don't feel like talking confidentially to someone, we don't talk
confidentially to him. At the same time, we realize that our freedom
can lead us astray; after all, there are likable informers, it's a professional requirement, more or less, and also, we're not infallible. Let our
senses work, we give our senses free rein. Seeing how the dictatorship
has wreaked havoc with everything, let our perception, our sense of
things, be the only thing, the last thing that it can't contaminate. I
now see from the documents that the informers also had to report on
Ági Zsigmond, the exotic-looking girl who, among the fallen autumn
litter in Kisoroszi, wrestled with such enchanting vehemence with
Lacika, who in the meantime had fortunately grown up. Dictatorship was helpless against pretty young girls wrestling with handsome
youths among the fallen autumn litter, and they could go to hell with
the reports of their agents, now and forever, amen. In this second category they were also watching Iván Pető, the historian and archivist,
who after the change in regime of 1989 became president of the Alliance of Free Democrats. They also kept Ambrus Oltványi under strict
surveillance; he too had been placed in category two, which couldn't
have been easy for the agents, because he kept strictly to his room,
as did I. Oltványi had suffered from polio as a child and struggled
with its consequences for the rest of his life, but he became a man
to be reckoned with all the same. For a while he lived in the same
house in Városmajor Street where Miklós Mészöly and his wife had
an apartment. Miklós would sometimes take me downstairs to visit
him; he sat by a small Biedermeier desk in the middle of his gigantic
library. The whole apartment was one big library. In December 1956
he was arrested by the Soviet military authorities for circulating illegal pamphlets, and while he was inside, that's how they said it back
then, inside, he was taken inside, he was held inside, his mother had a
nervous breakdown and committed suicide. There was also a category
three to be surveilled, made up of those individuals who attended the

so-called flying university, the jocular name of the unofficial lectures held by the opposition but who, as Dr. Izsó explained in his top secret analysis, did not engage in any other suspicious activities.

Compared with how I remembered it from my childhood, nothing on the building had changed when the flying university lectures were held there, except that the spot where the clock had been was now plastered up, a botched job, and the condition of the protected monument, too, was showing signs of decay; some parts were pulled down and others added, they did all sorts of things with it that they shouldn't have. Hungary had become a nation of shanties, a nation of lean-tos, a nation of bunglers and botchers, a nation where no one is an expert on anything but will engage in everything and anything for the sake of survival. The mud was knee-deep around the former servants' quarters and the stables, and junk lay all around, if for no other reason than in the dictatorship everyone collected everything, they stored all the junk they possibly could, it might come in handy in a shortage economy, as a result of which the confused heaps of junk grew by leaps and bounds behind just about every mansion, villa, or country house, as well as the lobbies, balconies, and stairways of the apartment houses.

I heard the story of the house from my Uncle Sándor during one of our first Sunday walks. In May 1849, during the so-called spring offensive, in the critical period of the freedom fights against the Habsburgs, the Clock Villa served as the headquarters of General Artúr Görgey's council of war, he directed the siege of Buda and recaptured it from there. The house, which the chocolate factory owner Ferenc Heidrich had built as a summer place for his family, was still quite new at the time. The war council met in his dining room, and a hundred and twenty years later, the democratic opposition held their free university lectures there. At the time the southeastern slopes of the chalky mountain chain were dotted with vineyards and their accompanying villas, the mountain peaks and the northern slopes were replete with oak woods fragrant with vegetation, and the mountain was inhabited by German vintners the locals called Swabians, they spoke only German and drove their swine out to the oak woods to feed on acorns. Later vacationers from Pest moved there for the summer, but German persisted as the language of the neighborhood. Families moved up for the summer with their entire household, such things were not uncommon; for instance, come summer, our Grandfather Neumayer relocated to Pesthidegkút with his seven children and servants in tow, though later they'd sometimes go to Gömörsid, where the move wasn't so complicated, because the household there was kept up.

Sándor Rendl visited my grandfather's estate in Gömörsid as well when he was hopelessly in love. Pál Aranyossi also visited as a young man, when the family still held out hope that they'd prevent his engagement to my Aunt Magda from becoming official. Thinking he was being very clever, our grandfather offered Aranyossi an appointment, and asked him to tutor the young Miklós and Laci in French. The lovers had a good laugh at this offer, which my grandfather had meant to be a rebuff.

By the time we reached the top, Sándor Rendl was usually silent, and this made me feel that I should do the talking. Though he tried to keep up appearances, his gasps for breath were audible, and so were the sound of our steps and the way his walking stick hit the rocks, but nothing else.

The soil of Orbánhegy and Svábhegy is dry, it crumbles easily, limestone crumbles easily, the hill had hardly any roads that were paved. Possibly, Istenhegyi Street was paved. Under the cool, cloudy, Sunday sky tending to rain, no one walked along the washed-out paths. Cleansed by the rain, the larger stones stood out from the yellow clay mixed with white limestone chips. As I looked at him askance, it seemed he'd have liked to slap me, whereas nothing was further from his mind. He never raised his voice. Regardless of the situation, he remained courteous and considerate. He praised his wife in the same considerate manner, he was in raptures over his daughter's every word and gesture, but even in his rapture, he remained aloof. He retained his courteous reserve with the servants as well. But now he must have been raging inside. He obviously cared for me, he wanted to make sure I felt at home in his house. He asked me to accompany him on his walks even shortly before he died; his manner had not changed, we talked like two grown-ups about a variety of subjects. From the top of Svábhegy, where my school later stood, we took a more circuitous route back to Orbánhegy. We made a detour to Költő Street, where we admired the house with the twisted chimney every time, it was considered a rarity in chimney design, a masterpiece, an eccentric actor from Pest by the name of Károly Benza had built it for himself, then we looked at the writer Mór Jókai's garden next door to Benza's house, the villa's gate was always wide open, and I wanted to see for myself where my Mezei great-grandfather went on summer nights. The villa was now inhabited by Masa Feszty, Jókai's granddaughter, and years later I visited her studio here, when I was asked to acquire something for the collection of Jókai documents for my literary society in school.

Masa Feszty did not trust me, she'd have liked to throw me out along with my request, but in order to avoid it, she pestered me with her latest paintings. Would I like to see her latest paintings, she asked. As if I'd seen the others. As far as I can remember, they must have been religious pictures, the miraculous deeds of saints and their even more miraculous appearances, halos and all. Needless to say, she gave me nothing from Jókai's estate for the literary society. She said she'd get in touch. I waited for years. I blamed myself for giving in to the urgings of the teacher heading the literary society. I gave in because she was persuasive, tall, with heavy bones, pale, with an impressive storehouse of knowledge, a nun whose order was disbanded from one day to the next; they were forced to disrobe and were sent running. It must have been a teaching order. Uncle Sándor and I continued along Csorna Street, crossed Fodor Street, and were then back in Dobsinai Street. These were mostly steep streets that weren't even paved with stones; they were more like gullies covered with weed, untrodden, inaccessible to automobiles, and mostly uninhabited.

I don't remember the words I used to tell him the exciting news about the elections that I pieced together from my parents as they discussed them between themselves as well as others, but I remember my excitement as I told him the story, because I thought he'd be just as pleased as they. I remember telling him that in its bid for power, my parents' party revised the electoral law so that the votes should be in its favor. I also remember telling him about the blue slips that allowed people to cast their ballots in districts where ostensibly they had a temporary address. I thought this clever trick would please him as much as it pleased my parents, who talked about it in great detail and with obvious relish. And that's when he nearly struck me.

But by the time we reached Gyöngyvirág Street to stop by the painted crucifix for a rest, my excitement had vanished, my wanting to show off was gone, this I remember perfectly well. Also, my glancing up at my uncle's face and figure. He wore three-piece suits, in the summer light-colored, but in the winter, more like gray. There was nothing showy in the way he dressed. An immaculately appointed gentleman with a light overcoat draped over his arm, and in his hand a walking stick. At most, the cut of Sándor Rendl's eyes was exceptional, smooth, Mongolian, a bright round face with hardly any lines to define it, perhaps two small furrows in the corners of his lips, and two small furrows under his narrow eyes. His face was tight, and this tightness gave it its character. Not so his suits. In spite of all their perfection and being so well cared for, there was an innate looseness about his clothes. His wife and daughter spared no expense on their wardrobes, they dressed according to the latest fashion, compared with them he dressed soberly, and during our walks he wore mostly well-worn suits.

It didn't occur to me that I was in fact reporting on a violation and that he must first find the moral and pedagogical position suited to the intellectual capacities of a five-year-old child, and that he'd have to wait for his anger to subside. I don't think he considered what I'd told him the product of my childish fantasies. He must have put two and two together and realized what the Communists had been up to, something that even the opposition couldn't piece together, judging by their parliamentary speeches at the time. With their cheating in the elections, they're going to smash democracy to smithereens. So that's why they canceled the official residence registry. So that's why they introduced the blue slips they called register extracts. With these slips printed in numbers far exceeding the number of voters, anyone could cast their ballot anywhere, as they did. So that's why they'd deposited this little boy in Dobsinai Street, so they could go on their trucks and cast their ballots in two places, five places, who knows how many places, without having to worry about him. Sándor Rendl had nowhere to deposit the outrage and anger he felt toward my parents, this is what I felt on my skin, literally on my skin.

The shell of forgetting cracked open in spots, and now I understand the situation, what's more, I even remember the details. That Sunday must in fact have been the day of the National Assembly elections of August 31, 1947. Before breakfast, his chauffeur drove Uncle Sándor to his polling station on Némvölgyi Street, but my Aunt Eugenie didn't go along, she said she was in no hurry, she'd go in the afternoon. I also remember that the cook, Gizella Mrázik, had the day off and my Aunt Özsi was preparing breakfast, or she was getting ready to make lunch; in any case, she was standing in the kitchen. It can wait, she said, the cat won't drag off Némvölgyi Street, she said. My uncle and I set off for our walk after breakfast, after he'd cast his ballot, and he clearly didn't seem half as concerned as I, and that's why I got so excited, and probably my need to tell him what I knew came from his seeming lack of concern. Seeing how he's unfamiliar with the great secret, I must share it with him.

He was not active in politics, he was not a member of any party, but he had pronounced political views.

In the years following the siege, there was nothing that was not missing from households and the economy, but the reparations transports had to be launched the day after the signing of the cease-fire agreement, meaning that within six years $300 million worth of industrial products and agricultural goods had to be expedited, and the Reparations Bureau, which was directly responsible to the prime minister, could oblige any private industrialist, industrial concern, or agricultural unit to produce and deliver finished products and materials needed to satisfy Hungary's reparation obligations in the specified quality and quantity, within a specified time frame and at a fixed price; as a consequence, the balance of the postwar market, already struggling with shortages, was upset, the black market flourished, and within the framework of unprecedented inflation, by the spring of the following year, the pengő began to crash. The reparations law was published in *Magyar Közlöny* on February 12, 1946, and by early July the pengő collapsed, and a new currency had to be introduced with the fragile backing of the new fledgling economy. This was tantamount to finding the philosopher's stone or squaring the circle.

At this juncture, along with Zoltán Vas, the Communist president of the Main Economic Council functioning under the supervision of Prime Minister Ferenc Nagy of the Smallholders Party, my Uncle Sándor also became a member of the advisory board that assessed the chances of introducing the forint, and the two of them drew up a plan for introducing the new means of payment. My Uncle Sándor was appointed a delegate by the Independent Smallholders Party, and though he was not a member, this party was close to his heart. It was up to him to clarify the international monetary repercussions related to the introduction of the forint. And now he had to learn from a mere child what the Communists had up their sleeve, and why, for months, they'd been busy undermining the largest coalition party, the Smallholders, which he'd been supporting with his expert knowledge and his vote. He supported it because the Smallholders represented the principle of the inviolability of private property most strongly, while my parents represented and worked on behalf of the principle of the complete and irreversible liquidation of the same. In their eyes, theirs was the firm Archimedean point from where they'd frustrate the further advance of capitalism and liberate mankind from its gravest ailment, the insistence on ownership.

When we continued our ascent up Diana Street, my Uncle Sándor switched his stick and overcoat to his left hand and took my hand with his right. The overcoat also indicates that it must have been the last day in August, the Sunday of the parliamentary elections. On cooler summer days, gentlemen wore sand-colored overcoats just like his. In the years preceding climate chaos, on the early afternoon of St. Stephen's Day, meaning on August 20, a cold front reached the country and crashed head on with the sweltering heat that lasted approximately a month and which was alleviated only by sudden showers. It arrived with a thunderous sky, stormy winds, and lightning, it brought a dramatic change each year, cool, rainy weather that started to warm up again only in the first days of September.

I couldn't decide if my uncle took my hand to steady himself or to reassure me. He rarely did it, except when we had to cross a major crossing, Böszörményi Street with its heavy traffic, or Fodor Street. Just like other members of the family, he dealt very gingerly with physical contact; it is part of my own family inheritance, and I've been trying to shed it for a lifetime. I keep on doing things, all my life I've kept doing things that went against the dictates of my emotions. Emotions belong to a person's makeup, and not his upbringing. While he held my hand, he told me quietly, as if an aside, meaning in his own conservative-liberal manner, using descriptive sentences, how parliamentary democracy works. He informed a five-year-old boy about the mechanism of parliamentary democracy. He also talked about how it doesn't work. And how it can be paralyzed. Not a single sentence remained in my mind from his lecture, just words and fragments. Which doesn't mean that I couldn't follow what he had to say. I also heard about constitutional putsch and military putsch from him first, and they never caused me difficulty after that. At most, the similarity between *putsch* and *punch* bothered me. I always hankered after punch cake and punch ice cream, but they said that they contain rum and wouldn't let me have any. Specific gravity was a concept I had to learn anew every time, but not putsch. On the other hand, whenever I hear it, I have to exile punch from my thoughts. Come to think of it, I didn't need anyone to explain *mirage* to me again either.

The subject and tone of my uncle's lecture have survived intact in my mind. The sentences have been lost, submerged, but the structure, along with its meaning, has survived. I remember the national network of polling stations because by way of example, he even told me that this area has another polling district besides the one on Német-völgyi Street, and its polling station is located at the school on Diana Street. Years later, when we were living on the hill, I knew from this previous information where my parents were going to vote, though by then I had no illusions about the outcome of the elections.

It was clear to me that this was my uncle's measured and thoughtful response to all the things I'd told him with such enthusiasm. His explanation was not meant to judge or qualify, it did not contain an opinion, instead, it bolstered my belief that I shouldn't consider my parents' views absolute.

We hadn't reached the top of Diana Street, but he was panting yet again, and so, if for no other reason, he had to curtail his say. We were standing in front of a neoclassical villa looking down on the valley. It was built somewhat later than the Clock Villa, though in the style of baronial mansions rather than rural country seats. Five years later, I passed it several times a day on my way to school, sometimes as many as four or six times a day if I went shopping or to stand on line, or to the school garden, and I saw the romantic, English-style garden of the miniature palace gradually take on a wild, unruly aspect. I was attracted to abandoned gardens, I liked their wild aspectness. The statues, the shell-shaped flowerpots and chalices carved of stone had fallen to the ground. They lay discarded under their pedestals in the leaves; no one straightened them up in our own garden either; they were covered in snow, and in a couple of years were overgrown with ivy. The surrounding woods reclaimed the walking paths, and the weeds broke merrily through the tiles of the terraces. Their owners had abandoned them, or they were taken away from them, and the owners themselves were forcibly relocated outside Budapest. Only the caretaker and his family remained in the annex of this villa adorned with a pediment, I knew them, the younger son of the former caretaker was my classmate, though I can't recall his name. The caretaker had come back from a POW camp in one of the last POW transports, I remember that, too, and also that when he returned, they didn't recognize him. Later, he tore down the front gate to build a pigpen in the back of the mansion.

We brought hardly anything along from Pozsonyi Street, we didn't give the movers much work. The villa that we moved into was confiscated from the Perczel family of Bonyhád, who'd built it as a sort of summerhouse during the late nineteenth century, judging by its eclectic style. Mór Perczel, the general of the 1848 freedom fights, must have been an old man when the house was built. As they said back then, he was an old warhorse, a grumpy, unapproachable man. As a young man he was a success with the soldiers, but as a general, he was a complete washout. There was a reception hall in the house accentuated with half-columns of green marble, though subsequently it turned out that the marble half-columns and capitals decorated with acanthus leaves were only cleverly painted stucco, while along the full length of the reception hall there was a winter garden of irregular shape constructed of iron framing and glass tile. After these came all the other spaces, one after another, that a genteel home such as this needed, a spacious dining room that could accommodate twenty-four guests, and where, after dinner, the guests could go out to the terrace decorated with Turkish mosaics, and from there, in the company of chatting ladies, they could all walk down the steps decorated with carved planters out to the park, or else the ladies could join the gentlemen in the smoking room adjacent to the dining room. And as could only be expected of a genteel home, a short passage led from the smoking room to the bedrooms situated on the northern side of the house. There were two, but no, perhaps three, and they were very spacious, but I can't be sure anymore of how many there were. I was more interested in the former life of the house than in the number of its rooms. But the two most beautiful rooms of the empty house were the gigantic kitchen and the unusually spacious bathroom, which was covered with hand-painted delft tiles, and the kitchen where, to my great surprise, the tiled stove stood in the middle, just like the round heater in the bathroom, which was also covered with delft tile. However, the red brass lining had a hole in it, and in order to mend it, the delft tiles would have had to be removed. The blue hand-painted tiles, probably also fashioned by hand, had Netherlandish landscapes, and at the back of the landscapes, miniature folk scenes, perhaps five motifs in all. There were thistle fields with cows, and farther off, two young shepherds, and also a field with willows, on the edge of the field a windmill, and on the path in the distance, a lone wanderer carrying his meager belongings on his back. I also recall skaters on a frozen canal seen from the bridge of a sluice, a fair or market with its stalls and booths, and a muddy road meandering between ramshackle thatched huts with an approaching cart in the distance. It was all exactly as I'd see it years later on the perfectly flat Dutch countryside. The various motifs were painted almost identically, but the painting was done by hand, and so the identity of the tiles gained a new meaning. This, too, was a discovery, twenty years later it turned into a literary theme, a single reality and its ever-changing variations. The porcelain fittings, the bathtub with the soap dishes, the size of the toilet bowls, the generous curves of the sinks, the size of the bidet's basin and its many jets, the small bench in a niche, the industrial size, perhaps two meters long and one meter wide, of the kitchen sink on the elephant legs cast from porcelain and adorned with blue ornaments, the curved sides of the sink to make standing by it comfortable and safe to lean on, not to mention the size of the taps to suit the size of the basin and the old-style lettering on them, exquisite, exquisite. As if they'd built the kitchen and the bathroom for indolent giants, giant servants blessed with giant arms and for the giant behinds of genteel savages. All this was smashed up eighteen months later, smashed to smithereens and carted off as debris. They might as well do it in one go. For a long time, a very long time, we didn't have hot water in the bathroom. By then there were no craftsmen either, they were forced from their workshops into the nationalized branches of industry. If something in the nationalized houses needed repair, at least three people showed up from FIK, the FIK is coming, I can't find anyone, but the FIK will come, don't worry, there are no more bona fide repairmen, the FIK isn't coming, we're waiting for the FIK to show. This was the newly founded Fővárosi Ingatlankezelő Vállalat, the Municipal Real Estate Management Company, a drunken, ignorant, brutal bunch of flunkies who in the next twenty years ruined everything in the nationalized houses that was still in working order and couldn't fix anything properly. First they stripped the bathroom heater of its delft tiles so they could patch up the holes in the red copper cylinder. But what any ordinary tinkerer could have managed, they couldn't. They removed the cylinder and never brought it back, the MÉH, the By-product and Debris Utilization Company, paid good money for red copper. There was nothing to replace it. Now we didn't even have cold water in the tub. We didn't have water for about eighteen months, when they smashed the tub, along with the bathroom. Until then, we warmed water in a big washtub. Now a rubber hose attached to the bidet carried the water to the tub. None of this bothered me. While I sat in the bathtub with the bit of hot water, I studied the hair's-breadth differences and variations in the delft motifs. The former smoking room became the children's room, the former dining room became my parents' bedroom. The rest of the rooms stood empty, or nearly so. Having experienced the siege, I took things in stride, things are the way they are because they can't be any other way. Every new moment is cause for celebration, because yesterday and tomorrow do not exist. I don't recall having asked any questions. The house remained cold even though we heated it, three days, even a week later it was freezing cold. For five years we lived within cold walls. It warmed up a bit only when spring made its miraculous appearance and we could open the windows at last. I don't recall being put out by the cold, but I do recall the warm spring air coming through the windows.

The boiler room was in the cellar, but to reach the cellar in the early morning in the relentless snowfall, you had to clear at least one path all around the house. That winter the snow wouldn't stop falling. Our father cleared a path through the fresh snow late at night, so he'd have less shoveling to do in the early morning. But although he kept shoveling the snow, the wind swept through the empty house, the snow shook it all night, it whistled over the eaves, it hissed through the pines, it howled under the night sky. We heated the boiler with brown coal from Nógárd, and so our father lectured us on the types of coal as well, the heating values of the various types, diamonds as the highest degree of the process of carbonization, graphite, which doesn't have a solvent either, and so on, all the way down to our humble brown coal from Nógrád, which, to add insult to injury, contained too much slack, because only the lowest grade was sold at home, the rest was sent abroad as part of the country's reparations; and then he explained lignite and peat as well. These two words, *lignite* and *peat*, are his gift to me. The coal dust could easily stop the smoldering. For some reason, this had no effect on me, even though I had to fire it up again and again. I had to start it up again, so what. When I come home from school at noon, I should see to the boiler first thing. Sometimes I had to shovel the snow at noon, too, at least the snowdrifts. I saw to the boiler first thing. There was an old, hand-carved snow shovel, we found it when we moved in. Now that I think back on it, it must have been the work of a gypsy trough carver, he carved it out of willow wood, now I know that he carved it from a single willow trunk with a tool designed for this purpose. On our outings in early spring or late fall, our father taught me how to start a fire in the stoves of the tourist hostels. Meanwhile, we reviewed the boiler chamber, the chimney, the draft, the draw, burning, all the necessary conditions for full combustion, the combustion by-products, ash, the alkaline chemical reaction, iron stoves, tile stoves, the firebrick lining of the stoves, and so on. I don't know why, but he dwelt a great deal on firebrick, it must have fascinated him. We repeated everything, repetition is the mother of all learning, that's a Latin saying. And I, a true survivor, followed him in his thoughts, I followed him in his thoughts as far as he'd let me. Only the emptiness of the rooms and the winter garden fascinated me, the reflection from the snow fascinated me, I don't know why. It was like a theater performance. It may have been the first time I paid attention to the transformation and the shifting of light on the walls of the empty rooms, the window recesses and the wings of the doors, the first time I realized that these were the play of the outside world, of the clouds and the parts of day, reflections, effects, outcomes, secondary.

The house must have been newly whitewashed before we moved in, it was freshly painted, and in the cold, the smell was especially pungent, you could even smell the stinking glue in the paint, and there was also a strange unaccustomed smell through which I gleaned the lives of all those who had lived here before us, the life of the house.

If the fire was not glowing, just flickering, I had to add logs or kindling to the fire and wait, and when the sides had caught fire and the coal, too, was glowing, I added some of the coal dust, but be careful, for God's sake, don't put out the fire, my father warned. These were the last intimate moments with my father, when he taught me the efficient use of the furnace; I also had to check the pressure on the manometer, clean out the system, open and close the chimney, if the water pressure fell, add water to the system and wait until the spill channel on the roof engaged, and check all the radiators in the house upstairs to make sure the valves didn't leak; he also explained the manometer, thermal expansion, and thermal expansion coefficient without a thought to sparing me. On Sunday, he cut kindling and wood shavings to last the week. He taught me how to do this as well, but would not let me use an axe for several more years. When the coal did not glow anymore and the cinders had cooled, when the fire could not be revived, I had to clean out the cinders and start a new fire. The people who'd lived here before us also left the cinder rakes behind. Every small object left behind made a deep impression on me, and in this big, strange-smelling silence, I followed in their wake with my fantasy. My fantasies more or less made up for all the things that were missing. There were four rakes and I gradually realized that they served four different purposes. One could be used to scrape the slack off the side of the boiler, the other to smash the hardened bits of cinder, the third to coax the cinders out into the iron container placed under the furnace cheek, the fourth to gather up the cinders that had gathered in the corners of the boiler lined with firebrick.

At times I discovered that I was not alone. The day before, a fox had wandered into the cellar and I inadvertently locked it in, but it got out and ran away, causing the hair on my head to stand up. Another time I discovered a hedgehog nestled within a mound of sawdust.

The four wrought-iron tools may have belonged to the Perczels, serious handiwork, probably made by a rural blacksmith, but it's possible that Márton Horváth's caretaker had found them at a flea market.

Márton Horváth's former caretaker lived at the bottom of the garden in the caretaker's house, so come morning, he had to clear a much longer path for himself in the snow. The caretaker's apartment was a pretty little house situated between the tennis court and the greenhouses, but you couldn't see it from the windows of the genteel villa. Trees and thick shrubs hid it from view. But it was no longer a genteel villa and there was no longer a caretaker, he went to work somewhere else. The Horváths left the house in early fall and moved to Rózsadomb or God knows where, and they took the services of a caretaker with them. The Municipal Gardening Co-op sent us the bill for last summer's tending of the estate. Our parents wrote a letter to the Municipal Gardening Co-op informing them that they had made the payment but do not wish them to see to the garden in the future. The sum would have been too large for our parents to afford. Horváth belonged to a small circle of Muscovite Party chiefs that consisted of five persons, Mátyás Rákosi, general secretary of the Hungarian Communist Party, Ernő Gerő, leader of the Party, Mihály Farkas, minister of defense, József Révai, minister of culture, and Márton Horváth, and unless my memory misleads me, the Party jargon of the time called them the Five-in-Hand. I remember it perfectly well because as a child I couldn't understand why such an important person had to move away from Rákosi's side, and how we ended up replacing him. Horváth was a member of the Politburo and editor-in-chief of the Party's daily paper. In the Political Committee or the Central Directorate, the opinion of the Five-in-Hand was law. *Szabad Nép* didn't call itself a daily, but the Party's central daily, which is an apt definition because it wasn't a run-of-the-mill daily, but the coded daily gazette of the Central Committee of the Hungarian Working People's Party, a newspaper in which even the most run-of-the-mill news was translated into thieves' Latin, but so that even those familiar with thieves' Latin shouldn't understand it. To this day, the language of *Szabad Nép* is the etalon among the languages of Communist conspiracy. It is at least on par with the language of *Neues Deutschland*, but the French *Humanité* and the Italian *Unità* are not even in a class with it. Today, *Szabad Nép* has no sentence that doesn't need a footnote, but if you try to write one, it turns out in midstream that the sentence makes no sense. Horváth wore small round spectacles and he was unpleasantly fat, and his epitaph was ready on people's lips. Here lies a pile of shit, known as Márton Horváth while he lived, which qualified not only his character as a human being, but his ability to write as well. Our parents considered the head of the Party paper an arrogant bore and a careerist. After his dramatic downfall, he even wrote a novel. When our parents called someone a careerist, it was like calling him an adventurer or a robber baron. In their special vocabulary, I might say a vocabulary based exclusively on Communist ideology, not only did *careerist* carry a distinctly negative connotation, but so did making good, getting ahead, and the concept of career itself.

A Communist had to act according to the dictates of logic, at times he even had to do something for logical reasons that went against his making good or his getting ahead, what's more, what went against the law, proper conduct, good taste, or public opinion. They laughed at anyone who acted in order to make good or to get ahead. This left such a deep impression on me that I avoid the use of the concept of career to this day. And not just in Hungarian. If it can't be avoided, I say working life instead, even in German, because to this day there is no situation in which it wouldn't carry a negative connotation for me. On the other hand, it was exactly for rational reasons that the question of whether Márton Horváth is an arrogant bore or not left me cold, because for a long time I couldn't decide how reality related to ideals in my parents' language, in short, I couldn't decide if in a given case they're talking about the ideal or the real, but by the time we moved into this unfamiliar house, I could figure some of it out with an appreciable degree of certainty. I cleared out the cinders. There were other epitaphs as well, making the rounds. Here lies Mátyás Rákosi, six feet under, may he stay there and not wander. Here lies József Révai, a Central Committee member, may he lie here forever and ever.

At first, the highest Party echelons were of the opinion that for consipratorial considerations, the highest circle of the Party echelons, meaning the Five-in-Hand, must live in the same place. Probably, they wanted to keep one another under surveillance. To this end, they confiscated nearly all the villas on Lóránt Street that lay between Istenhegyi and Diana streets, they had the inhabitants move elsewhere, or had them deported or arrested, or sent to internment camps. For some reason, though, they didn't take the Székács villa away from the family. I couldn't understand back then, and I still don't understand today. The Székács family had owned several mills in Orosháza that were later nationalized, and they also owned stock portfolios, which had the exact same value as those of the members of my family, Anna Mezei in Duna Street, Erzsébet Mezei in Benczúr Street, and Sándor Rendl in Dobsinai Street, meaning zero. Yet they kept the certificates in case the Americans should return and take the country back from the Russians. I didn't throw them out either. The Communists dissolved the shareholding companies and added the money to the state budget or, as the elderly ladies said, the Communists confiscated their fortune, meaning their own nephews and nieces confiscated it. They considered it an affront. They shook their heads in disapproval, because if they objected to something, they were used to their servants and minions putting it right.

For some reason, Géza Székács and his ill or hypochondriac mother were allowed to remain in this environment that was becoming stranger and stranger to them. But Anna and Erzsébet were exiled from the countless rooms of their large apartments to the service quarters in the back of their apartments in Duna and Benczúr streets. Erzsébet, meaning Záza, was very lucky, because she could keep the kitchen next to her small room overlooking the yard, half of the hall leading to the kitchen with the servants' toilet, as well as the maid's room, where her lady's maid lived, though probably this was a lie to spare us. One half of the hall was separated from the other half by a wardrobe; the area beyond belonged to the co-tenants. You could hear every sound they made. When I think back on the two elderly women, I get the impression that the feminist lady of the house and her lady's maid must have lived together since their early youth. In Duna Street, Aunt Anna, meaning Aunt Baby, didn't fare as well as her younger sister, Záza. She was allowed to keep only one room of her apartment with kitchen rights, which for some reason tickled her imagination. She found it amusing that she was allowed to use her own kitchen and her own kitchen utensils, and now others could use them too, those who had occupied her rooms, along with her furniture. Something childish had surfaced in her. She'd never picked up a pot or a pan before, why would she now, she didn't even know where they were stored or how many there were, but to her great good luck, she didn't live much longer. Záza outlived her by years. Her lady's

maid died first, while she died smack in the middle of the revolutionary upheaval.

We visited Záza for the last time just before we moved. We went
to see her on January 1, a Monday. I don't know which relative's idea
it was to surprise her with this New Year's visit in the single room she
now occupied. On the first day of the year the Mezeis always gathered together at noon, they had to arrive at the sound of the noonday
church bell, and needless to say, the youngest member of the family from the branch of the Nádases, the Kövérs, the Mándokis, the
Rendls, the Aranyossis, the Taubers, the Goldmarks, the Herczegs,
and so on joined in, always at someone else's place, provided they had
enough room for such a large crowd. They wouldn't leave it out for
the world. I prepared for these gatherings well in advance. The noise
and the coming and going was tremendous, the families brought the
children along, and naturally, there was no hot food, meaning that
there was some hot food, a richly laid out buffé with all sorts of delicacies was waiting for the guests, this is how they said it, buffé, like
the French, but my brother and I loved calling it buffet, just the way
it was written, piles of plates stood on the sideboards and piles of cake
on the platters. Somewhere on the corner of the Körönd and Fer-
dinánd Street we found a small florist that was open despite the heavy
snow, and our father bought primroses for our Aunt Záza. This was
the last bouquet of primroses in the shop and I could feel how lucky
we were. But we took other gifts as well, boxes full of cakes, because
this was a surprise, Aunt Záza was not counting on us, she had not
prepared for it; they discussed everything in great detail on the phone
beforehand, the surprise and who will bring what, or else who will
order what from where, but not sooner and not later than the noonday chiming of the bells. Everything and everyone must arrive at the
same time. There were two of them in the neighboring street, Vilma
királynő Street, an Evangelist and a Catholic chiming of the bells, and
they started pulling the ropes just as we got there. Needless to say, not
everyone arrived precisely at noon for the chiming of the bells, there
were some notorious latecomers, the Aranyossis, they hadn't come in
time for the surprise, but we were there, and I was allowed to stand by

the door of the former kitchen and hold the primroses freshly divested of their wrapping. The illustrious family members were growing in number behind me in this great noonday ringing of the bells, and then my father rang the doorbell. For a while, nothing happened. I'd never experienced such an awkward situation in the family before. It was not proper to ring again, *nicht möglich*, not possible, so there we stood, all of us, waiting with due ceremony. This was an outside balcony of sorts covered with glass, and we were standing in front of a door with glass panes. Someone whispered, why don't you ring again, Laci, maybe they didn't hear. Our father rang once again, this time a bit longer, so the impossible had happened after all, at which the small glass pane set in the door opened a crack, and through the crack we saw Záza's lady's maid with her disheveled gray head of hair, wearing a silk robe just barely gathered around the neck. She closed it right away. The bells had fallen silent by then and we stood abashed in the sudden silence.

But soon everything turned out just fine, the nieces and nephews shouted merrily, let us in, Záza, let us in, Záza, until Záza slipped into her robe, and everyone pretended not to have noticed that the bed in the room Záza was allowed to keep was still unmade and that both women had been sleeping in the same bed, and then the members of the family got busy, they laid the table, they arranged things, they took over for the two women, until, their hair arranged, the two elderly women appeared from somewhere and surprise, surprise, I handed them the primroses. A couple of hours later, when we left them with the ruins of our New Year's Day visit in the room looking out on the yard that they shared, they were happy.

Géza and I became close friends. Géza was a serious boy, heavyset, strong, with friendly brown eyes; we'd visit each other, and we planned to go far away together and become world travelers, and to prepare for it, we read lots of Jules Verne, and decided that in the summer we'd go on a trial run as far as Orosháza. Székács said that they demolished some of the villas and filled in the foundations, while others were left empty, or they brought the families of the guards up here from the countryside. My classmates Csíder and Piros had also come from the countryside, and Margit Leba, too; they were put in these big empty houses with their meager belongings, and they lived in big empty rooms, just like us. They put up barriers and sentry boxes at both ends of Lóránt Street, they declared the zone off-limits, and let the impenetrable forest repossess it. The guards almost always let me through the barrier, go on, scram, just make sure they don't see you. Meaning that their commanders mustn't see me. Not that they cared about us children. And if they wouldn't let me through, there was a good reason, but no one spoke about that. Still, they kept an eye on me from a distance, lest a watchdog attack me.

We knew what the good reason was, but we didn't talk about that either. Within half an hour Rákosi would be coming with his entourage. The watch had received the alarm on the G-line, the G-line was the conspiratorial name for the so-called special government telephone network, and the use of this special network was among the greatest of privileges. In Budapest about five hundred people, in the countryside only one hundred people had access to it. Traffic through it was kept strictly separate from the normal telecommunications network, and so it was not at the mercy of faulty connections, it was not overloaded at the busiest times of day, and an outside source could not listen in because, theoretically, no one could get on the line from outside. Which was not completely true. When he needed to use the G-line, our father turned his back, he hid the phone from me, so I shouldn't see the trick, he tapped the cradle according to an agreed-upon rhythm, it would ring briefly in response, and he could cut in if he had to talk to someone without delay. Once, during one of our interminable chats with Yvette, a stranger cut in, listened for a while, perhaps waiting for us to finish, then, to our mutual alarm, the unfamiliar voice broke in and said, stop talking, I need to call your father, then he put it down without another word.

In accordance with the decision of the Prime Minister's Office brought at its meeting of May 26, 1949, and further, in accordance with transcript no. 7. 904/1949 of the Minister of Transportation, we hereby notify the Minister, meaning Ernő Gerő, that the office of the Prime Minister requests the installation of five G-lines. Immediately after the prime minister, the second on the list is their senior connection, Pug Nose, meaning Undersecretary of State Géza Loson-czy, he still has two years before he is arrested. On the other hand, Rajk has only four more days when the Ministry of Foreign Affairs requests that the minister of transportation install a main station in his office and a substation with series connection at his residence at Vér-halom Street 27/b. Just one month later, in an official document dated June 28, 1949, countersigned by Ministerial Department Chief Dr. Kálmán Kovács in the name of the Secretariat of the President, meaning the office of the ministry of transportation, which had grown to hydrocephalic proportions by then, our father is informed that apart from the central administration, in both ministerial sections, meaning the railroad and the post office, meaning in the buildings located at 75 Andrássy Boulevard and 12 Krisztina Boulevard, in the rooms equipped with surveillance apparatus, they are setting up a secret administrative unit to be overseen by individuals to be delegated by the various departments, and are herewith appointing Technical Advisor László Nádas *úr* a member of the secret monitoring committee charged with overseeing the administration of the above. Back then, government institutions still addressed people as *úr*, or gentleman.

When the guards were notified of Rákosi's approach over the G-line, we ran silent and excited to Istenhegyi Street to watch the convoy hugging the curves in the road as it approached at a dizzying speed, tires screeching. Two huge ZIMs flanked an even more majestic one; it had white tires, and its windows were covered with white lace, as if it were headed to a wedding. The boys knew that the Russians had copied the ZIM from the Pontiac. But I'd never seen white lace curtains in a car before. The boys said that the car with the elegant white lace curtains was carrying Rákosi. They said that the car was armored and that it was custom-made for him. But they also said that sometimes they just pretend that Rákosi is sitting in this armored car, when in fact he's being taken to Zugliget in a junky Pobjeda. He has a house there, too. Or else they pretend that the convoy is headed for Zugliget, but half an hour later, another convoy brings him here. It's done to trick the enemy. They come up with new tricks every day, because you never know. There's a big assassination plot afoot, so we have to be on our guard as well while we wait and watch the approaching convoy, so the secret police won't take us for assassins, because if they do, they don't ask questions, they just shoot. They must expose every single assassin. They shoot them. Or they get rid of them. Don't you worry, they have plenty of ways to deal with them. There was no knowing if there were people sitting in the three big Russian vehicles, because the other two also had thick curtains, real Russian curtains. Stalin's car has curtains just like it.

They did away with a street that was more like a gully, steep and unpaved, which had once connected Adonis and Lóránt streets, though it didn't have a name; it had been used by the German vintners when they came down it from their vineyards spread over the southeastern slope, or else carried the water needed for irrigation; at times their carts were laden with heavy barrels, and later the rains would leave deep grooves in the land from the wheels. When it rained up on Svábhegy, the water rushed down the grooves, it came sweeping down from the mountaintop, and once the grooves, now ditches, were full, the rain as it swept down carried the road along with it. They surrounded the enclosed area with a high wire fence and secured the fence, doubly reinforced with barbed wire, to a motion sensor that sounded the alarm for the watch stationed in the villa at the corner of Istenhegyi and Lóránt streets. Csíder lived upstairs, the guardroom was downstairs. They trained spotlights on the endless fence from sunset to sunup. Actually, these spotlights gave off only a faint light. But the moment a breeze made the wire fence tremble or a bird settled on it or a fox sniffed at it, if anything at all made it so much as tremble, the lights came alive, they turned blinding bright, then went off, then were blinding bright again, rhythmically frightening one and all, and the signal bell in the guardroom screeched to the same rhythm. The guards then unleashed some large terrifyingly silent German shepherds inside the fence, but the timing here, too, seemed ad hoc, so no one would be able to anticipate it. The enemy mustn't sniff it out. Because I'd better believe it, enemies are everywhere, sniffing things out. At such times we never saw people, just the dogs. Csíder and Piros told me that the dogs were trained to attack people. Even though I detected in it the linguistic attempt to show off, the expression, trained to attack people, filled me with dread.

The dogs recognize the guards and their families, but they leap at strangers, they force a stranger to the ground, they don't bite his arm or neck through, but they don't release him either until the guards show up.

Later the top Party echelons decided that for safety reasons it would be best if those belonging to the uppermost circle of the Party, meaning the comrades who made up the Five-in-Hand, don't all live in the same place, and for reasons of subterfuge they should have a second house. In case of insurrection all members of the Party leadership should not be put at risk. I'd never heard the word *insurrection* before, I first heard about insurrection from these boys. At this point they moved the watch, the guard boxes, the fence, the checkpoint, and the dogs farther in along Lóránt Street. We still had five years to go before the insurrection. Needless to say, except for the children, no one knew about these things, no one spoke about them, in those years the grown-ups buttoned up, the cat got their tongue; no wonder, they thought the dictatorship would last forever, but even the boys spoke in hushed tones, because they were forbidden to talk about anything whatsoever.

Since so much of the area was off-limits, I wandered the empty rooms instead. I stood around in the glaring light of the winter garden. There was nothing for me to do in the empty rooms. I merely went from room to empty room, then back again, retracing my steps. These empty rooms occupied my entire being, they've defined all that I once was and all that I am. This is what I am made of, these empty rooms. Day after day, I felt compelled to look at them and listen to their silence. Each room was silent in its own way. Each spoke to me in different words and different sounds. I was alone with the house, the sound of the eaves, the falling snow, the cellar, the attic, the furnace, all the cold and empty spaces. Our father turned off the radiators in the empty rooms, but that didn't help either. The rooms we used, the kitchen and the bathroom, were no warmer than before. The draft came in through the cracks in the doors. In a matter of days, the uninhabited part of the house around the inhabited spaces turned ice cold.

When the sun was out, it was warmest in the empty winter garden, but in the empty hall at night, the water froze in its glass. This made my parents laugh. Klári, can you believe it, the water froze in its glass. Even so, our father couldn't have turned off the radiators entirely, in the empty rooms of the former summer residence, because the water would have frozen in the pipes, bursting them apart. There was no coal. Our parents did not think of the lack of coal or the lack of all the other things, for that matter, the constant lack of basic food, as an anomaly of the planned economy, because they said that we can't very well have coal when the coal is needed for the forges, the foundries, and the ironworks so that the new planned economy, based on heavy industry, could get off to a good start. The country needed to break with its agrarian past and be transformed into a modern industrial state. It's the least sacrifice they can suffer in the interest of our future. I didn't ask and they didn't explain, yet I could see the connections. Actually, the boiler shouldn't have been heated with brown coal, because it was a coke boiler. Except, obviously, if the Soviets, the Yugoslavs, or the Czechs, to whom we had to pay reparations in accordance with the Paris Peace Treaties, requested brown or black coal from Pécs, then it was brown or black coal that we had to send them. They didn't have to explain this to me. The Paris Peace Treaties were tantamount to orders, military orders with deadlines. There was no room for maneuvering; at most, one could present logical arguments now and then, and only through diplomatic or military channels, but such maneuvering did not bring relief with respect to the Hungarian economy as a whole. They didn't have to explain this to me either, because they were always talking about dispatches and indemnities. If it's lignite they wanted, it's lignite they got, but we also dispatched industrial diamonds from our reserves. On Pozsonyi Street, my father also explained industrial diamonds to me. You couldn't substitute or exchange one thing for another. When the bit of coal from Nógrád that we found here in a carefully arranged pile was gone, we had no more coal. *Et voilà.* For my father's sake I pretended to be interested in this whole heating business, after all, I'd be in charge of it, but it didn't particularly affect me. Why deny it, at the age of nine it took quite an effort to shovel the coal, it was difficult to slip the shovel under the coal, the handle of the shovel was too long, it was difficult lifting it without some of the coal spilling over, but it's only now that I think of this, at the time I ignored it, I couldn't very well say that I'm just a child. After all, I did manage to shovel the coal, didn't I. In the morning, one of our parents would take my brother to kindergarten in an official car, and one of them would pick him up at six in the evening, again in an official car. But he'd been at it for at least an hour by then, screaming and howling for all he was worth. My brother had an inner biological clock. He cried on schedule. For decades to come I didn't have the faintest idea about telepathy, yet it seemed to me even then that in some manner he was tied to both of them in a way that I was not. His whimpering and blubbering turned into howling just when they were about to go fetch him, and even when some unforeseen business held them back and they were late coming home. Our parents and I had a good laugh over it. I looked at the clock when he switched from whimpering to howling, and when she was back, Mother asked about it. The two times always coincided. He started whimpering at 4:30, and he worked himself up into a state, he cried until his crying turned into one huge gigantic pain, and he greeted our parents in this pitiful state. By five the kindergarten teachers felt that they'll never hold out till six. Sometimes they sent my brother into the corridor, so his crying shouldn't affect the others.

Oh dear, Nádas is crying again.

Luckily, the kindergarten corridor was heated.

But if his crying affected the others, then they cried in a chorus, without knowing why they did it.

When I think back on it now, I must say that these great crying jags in unison were the laudable manifestations of human empathy.

Sometimes my worried mother would call from Múzeum Street that she couldn't find our father on Krisztina Boulevard, it's nearly six o'clock, and I should run and get my brother, because she's stuck in a meeting, I should dress him properly and take him home. When this happened, I ran headlong through the woods, then up a steep path with rain-swept gullies; I took it because it was the shortest route. When he saw that it wasn't his mother and it wasn't his father come for him, just me, he was so furious, he stopped breathing. Something broke inside him, his pain got stuck in his air sacs. I had to smack him on the back, the kindergarten teachers shook him to get him to breathe, I massaged his small limbs, his chest, but as soon as he could breathe again, he gasped, he flew into a frenzy, he pushed me away, not you, not you, he resisted letting me dress him, and when I managed to get him into his clothes and his street shoes all the same, he kicked out with both legs as I tied them up, and out on the street I couldn't even hold his hand, not you, not you, my presence pained him, in his mind the connection was direct, and on every day of every season he howled all along the snow-covered, windswept, sunny, misty, cold, or sweltering hot Diana Street alongside me in the self-imposed solitude that was his own punishment. If I took his arm or grabbed him by the collar, he screamed for me to let him be, leave him in peace. For four years straight he screamed like this every afternoon, but only until the day our mother died. Once we got home, he filled the big empty house with his hysterics. I didn't particularly mind, I didn't have to be told why he was acting like this. I understood, but what on earth was I to do with my understanding. I had to concentrate on it not bothering me. But sometimes I ran out of patience. On the other hand, sometimes he ran out of steam, but only to fall back on his hysterics again forthwith. He refused to eat or drink. He was not about to be sidetracked. Sometimes the prolonged futility of it all drove me to distraction. I knew that it wouldn't make him stop, yet I hit him, smacked him on the head, I couldn't stay in our room a minute longer, I couldn't do my homework, I couldn't read, I spanked him, thrashed his bottom, and strangely enough, this never surprised him, it's what he was expecting, and he upped the volume, which just added to the noise and to the futility of our lives in that cold and empy house. Try as I might, there was no diverting his attention away from his screams and his pain.

If I attempted anything of the sort, or else, the other way around, if I started screaming, too, imitating him, mocking him, making a monkey out of him, he turned into a spitfire and went purple with hysterics. Leave me alone, he screamed, though he screamed the same thing even when I pointedly ignored him and wouldn't even look at him.

Under no circumstances would I have them take me to school along with my brother. For one thing, I couldn't have gone to school with Géza Székacs and Gábor Baltazár then. Also, on one of the first school days, I made an interesting discovery.

Some of the children were brought to school by car, either their parents or a driver brought them, but the others hated these children and held them in contempt. After the siege, there were hardly any intact automobiles in private ownership. In our class only one boy was brought by car, Konkoly-Thege, it was a Hudson, if my memory serves me. He lived in Konkoly-Thege Miklós Street, and his father, the astronomer Konkoly-Thege, was the director of the observatory. My classmates took exception to him being brought by car, to say the least. They couldn't have cared less that his father was a famous astronomer, or that the street where he lived was named after his grandfather, and it was no use pointing out that he lives farthest from school, and his father is not a Party member, but an astronomer.

Just look at Konkoly-Thege, they sent a ZIM straight from Parliament to fetch him today. Yesterday he seemed quite satisfied with a Tatraplan.

Why bother with a car, when Vadász would gladly carry him on his back.

A horse's ass, that's who, and not me.

Every morning, Konkoly-Thege had to pretend that he didn't hear anything of what the others were saying. Every morning, he sneaked into the classroom with the look of someone expecting to be beaten up, it's part of the package, just as long as they don't hit him on the head. But he did not stop coming by car. Or maybe his parents made him. As for me, the very thought of the Tatraplan made my stomach quiver, because deep down I was actually proud that my father was driven to his office or out to the countryside in just such a dark blue rear-engine Tatraplan, a real dive-bomber. Because of its noisy and foul-smelling rear engine or because of its streamlined design, the boys called it a dive-bomber. Obviously, I was well advised to avoid such a special status in the eyes of my classmates. The fact that there was no avoiding it was another matter. In this new school, too, I had to stand up in front of the class and tell them what position my parents held, what their profession was, and how much they made. Which finished me off for some time. The next morning, I refused to get inside their car and wouldn't even give them an explanation. For their part, they didn't seem concerned, they took it in stride.

Or maybe it had to do with my age. I don't know. I had stopped asking them about anything or anyone by then, and I didn't tell them anything either. But it didn't hurt, and it still doesn't. Anything I wanted to find out I found out some other way, or found out only later, much later, or never, in which case, it's fine just as it is. Except, being so exasperatingly and shamefully short on information, I am now reduced to going through archives with a fine-tooth comb. It's not that I didn't love them, just that I didn't care anymore what they had to say about anything, anything at all. What a bore. I already knew. At most, I asked tag questions.

It was not a question of them not loving me. I had accepted the fact that I'd get only so much of them and no more. They didn't even have the time to tell me to do something or to offer guidance. And I didn't care when I saw that my tag questions embarrassed them and they prevaricated, or for some reason I could not fathom, they lied, they lied through their teeth and in sync with each other. They cast furtive glances at each other. No way on earth are we going to tell him that. As if I were an idiot who can't pick up on the glances they exchange.

With our sudden departure from our former home, something came to an end that had actually ended earlier. Asking questions no longer made sense. It wasn't worth it.

For all I know, the night when they accused me, Rózsi Németh wasn't preparing to write her usual letter at all but was packing. She moved out way before our own move, perhaps a year before. She moved into the nursery school teachers' training school that bore Amália Bezerédj's name. But this didn't hurt either, because by then the prohibition on complaining had filled up my universe. Get it through your thick skull. You are not hungry. Complaining is the bad habit of others, not us, except I had no idea what they meant by us. There's no one to complain to, unless the Good Lord via pneumatic mail, as my mother was fond of saying. This is why I struck my brother. Why is he crying, there's no one to hear, it's time he realized it. The little idiot was out to blackmail them. He didn't realize that they couldn't be blackmailed because they were too caught up in the problems of the nation.

In the next two years we visited Rózsi Németh several times in the stable, as they called it. Her companions, young women from the countryside like her, insisted that they could smell the horses in the dorm. We sniffed around, too, to see if it was true. But they weren't complaining; if anything, they were proud, they loved sleeping in a count's stable. Whether they felt it or just imagined it, the pungent smell of the count's horses had settled in their nostrils. To be perfectly frank, Rózsi actually said that the smell of the aristocratic horse piss had settled in their nostrils.

Our mother and I had been to the horse stable earlier, when it was under construction. We took our mother's official car, a field-gray Pobeda, an ordinary unprepossessing automobile. My mother inspected the construction work with the architects, except she neglected to mention that Rózsi Németh would be leaving us to study there and become a nursery school teacher so she wouldn't have to serve strangers all her life. Later we also moved to a new place, but I didn't ask anything. I wasn't obstinate, and I wasn't stubborn, I was not even indifferent, it's just that I knew I'd find out eventually anyway. Some bit of news or some circumstance would provide the answer. It wasn't a decision on my part, and I wasn't offended or angry, though I didn't want to spare them either, it's just that there wasn't one concrete reason for our move, nor a variety of reasons. Something had changed way before we moved, but what that something was I haven't been able to find out to this day.

Now that I think back on it, the first conscious break in my life actually brought a sense of relief. Ask no questions. In the end, I started to occupy myself with the subject that would interest me for the rest of my life, the mighty overlap between appearance and reality, even though, despite my best efforts, I never managed to define what reality is in relationship to semblance, or appearance. The truth is that reality is one of our most nebulous concepts, certainly in the languages I am familiar with. There was no reason anymore to pester them with my questions. It was all too obvious that like others, they too were prisoners of appearance. I couldn't let my feelings interfere with my research. I wasn't interested in the shape that appearance and reality took, I was interested in the way they were used as concepts, and the formal concepts they relied on to integrate the semblances they had created for themselves into the sphere of tangible and visible reality, meaning, how they created the semblance of reality from elements taken from reality and how they then fit it all back inside reality, which is thereby based on the system of appearances.

Crazy as it may sound, from the time I was eight years old, I preferred lexicons to asking questions. At the same time, I liked plying strangers with questions. I also liked putting questions to my Aunt Eugenie, who gave brief and mostly very disappointing answers, and also my Uncle Pista, whose first response to my questions was one of alarm, as if he were hearing something distressing, but his second response was inevitably considered and academically fastidious. Still, I liked putting questions to my Aunt Magda the most, because she invariably surprised me with her wondrous, adventurous, and lengthy answers fit for fairy tales. As for my parents, I much preferred thumbing through the *Révai Lexicon*, the *Pesti Hírlap Lexicon*, but first and foremost, I liked the *Social Lexicon* with its sixteen colorplates and its many illustrations and diagrams, and also its chronicle of social movements that served as the appendix, published by *Népszava*. Until I grew out of adolescence, this social-democratic lexicon was my constant companion; I took it out, opened it, read the entry that interested me, provided I found it quickly, just like Pál Aranyossi had done when he wrote an article, edited or translated something at his black writing desk, and he had to stand up suddenly to find some missing data or check a fact.

By that point, up on Svábhegy, my parents could no longer reach me with the explanations they felt they owed me. My mother's constant moralizing bored me at least as much as my father's constant talk of physics. I knew beforehand what they thought about things. I paid attention not to the subject of their explanations, but rather to the purpose behind them, not what they said, but why they said it. As a result, because of my devotion to them and my childish love for them, I was full of anxiety. It hurt me that I was deceiving them. I'm being devious. I'm not listening, I'm quasi-listening. Up until then, being a proper autistic child, I quasi-listened reflexively, I didn't even realize I was quasi-listening, but from the time that they accused me of something of which I was innocent, and I had nothing at my disposal to prove my innocence as I stood before them at the mercy of our mutual insistence on goodness, I had no other choice but to figure out what proof they had for their accusation, and what they were relying on to hide what, what others think of the same thing, what I am to make of their intention, and where I should deposit all of this in my consciousness.

Back then they took my brother to nursery school from Pozsonyi Street early in the morning. It was located in the same house on Leopold Boulevard where I had attended kindergarten after the siege, and from where I sneaked off and nearly stepped in front of the wheel of a bus with my ice cream cone; this happened in front of the house at number 3, where during the siege the Arrow Cross had tortured and killed people in the cellars. The nursery and kindergarten were just across the way, at number 2. So now, at eight years of age, after Rózsi Németh had left, I found myself alone in our Pozsonyi Street apartment. I learned self-reliance on the days when I had to go to school in the afternoon. I could not afford to lose myself. For the first time in my life, there was no one to remind me of the time, and I had to keep track of it on my own. I had to warm up my lunch in time, I had to find everything I needed and stuff it in my schoolbag, and I had to make sure I didn't forget anything; I had to lock up in time and deposit the key in its secret hiding place, though once it fell out; and I had to reach school in time and not stand open-mouthed out on the street, but keep my penchant for gaping in check. For a long time, I couldn't reconcile the seemingly infinite amount of time at my disposal all morning with all these restrictions to my freedom, and I still can't reconcile the two. They were irreconcilable not practically, but conceptually, and I had to find the solution and the explanation for this as well through my own devices. Without the infinite there is no freedom.

Once our parents told me to take a stranger, I was told what he looked like, into the living room, and only the living room and not the bedroom and not the children's room, because he's going to look at the furniture from Gömörsid that we have in the living room. I waited, but he didn't come. And then, one winter afternoon, perhaps at the end of November, I was headed home from school, it was already dark, bluish black in the winter sunset, the yellowish lights were burning on the street and also burning in the shops and apartments, and the number 15 tram was also lit up as it rattled along the road paved with yellow ceramic tile; anyway, as I reached the corner of Sziget Street, I saw that the window of our living room upstairs was lit up as well. I found our parents in the midst of cleaning up. They had emptied the living room of its contents almost completely that day; they hauled off the fortified castle, meaning the buffet from Gömörsid, and they also hauled off the dining table from Gömörsid with its carved legs, whose infinitely long top was supported by carved gods with carved wreaths comprised of flowers, shells, starfish, and fruits and on which my mother and my father played so happily with me, it must have been right after the siege, my father gave me a shove, which made me fall on my belly and slide across the table until my mother caught me at the other end and quickly turned me around to push me back, and I enjoyed this so immensely that I couldn't breathe from laughing, and so even after seventy years, it makes me feel a boundless sense of joy, the kind of joy that Imre Kertész must have felt in Auschwitz, the scandalous, unadulterated joy of being; and they also hauled off the intricately carved dining room chairs, with just two battered armchairs left from Grandmother Mezei's salon set, now kicked to the side. I didn't ask why they left them behind, or where they took the rest of the furniture. They thought it was highly amusing the way these able-bodied men struggled to haul the fortified castle down from the seventh floor, and how they kept getting stuck on the landing. I didn't ask who these able-bodied men were. We're not about to drag it around with us all our lives. I didn't ask where we're not about to drag it with us. In the days to follow, they packed the contents of the buffet in wooden crates they'd brought up from the basement, the tableware, the kitchen utensils, and then the books bar none, their papers, the summer dresses, the bed linen, but then for a long time, nothing happened. They didn't say why it wasn't happening, or what wasn't happening, and I didn't ask, but they'd hardly finished packing and now they had to unpack the crates, because they needed things, and from then on, their lives were taken up with going through the crates, looking for one thing or another. They laughed when they couldn't find what they were looking for, and they laughed when they found it. For nearly a year, the open crates stood in the empty living room with piles of temporarily retrieved objects all around them. There was no light in the living room, because our father had climbed up on an enormously tall ladder and had taken the awful-looking ugly chandelier from Gömörsid down from the enormously high ceiling. He said we'd sell it to the first junk dealer that came along. This is how I found out that the able-bodied men were junk dealers. Junk dealers, or bone-grubbers as they were popularly known, were generally called to the house, though some junk dealers stopped down in the middle of the yards below and started crying from there. The rag-and-bone man is here. The rag-and-bone man is here. Whatever's up for sale I buy. Whatever's up for sale. Used clothes, pots and pans, paintings, rags, paintings, rags. I'll take it off your hands. This paintings, rags, sounded especially sonorous coming from them. The rugs were gone, the huge handwoven Torontál rug in the children's room with its geometric design was gone, I missed it, I loved stepping along it, looking for a system even in the asymmetric design.

The Persian rug was gone from my parents' bedroom, and the crates, too, were gone, along with the tableware from Gömörsid. After so many decades, I am just beginning to realize how many things have disappeared, all the things I didn't care about in the first place, all the things I never asked about again. Perhaps the brothers and sister had divided these old things, the last remnants of the Gömörsid inheritance, among themselves. Perhaps this is how the first era of our shared family awareness came to an end.

There was no Christmas tree that year, and no Christmas tree ornaments. I didn't ask why not. Uncle Pista's men didn't come from Törökszentmiklós, which was also Rózsi Németh's village, anymore either, because his chemical plant had employed twelve men, and any enterprise that employed more than ten workers was nationalized and shuttered. But he didn't seem to mind; the decree hadn't even gone into effect, when he closed the plant, an insane gesture that reminds me of myself. The only thing that surprised me was the row his wife, Terézia Goldmark, kicked up because of it at one of our family gatherings. She rolled her r's, she screeched. She couldn't understand what made Pista do it. They explained it to her. I think she wanted the others to convince Pista to change his mind. After all, she had a point. She had married a well-to-do engineer from a good bourgeois family, and now, from one day to the next, she found herself in the midst of a bunch of penniless, mad Communists.

Rózsi Németh had called our mother at her office to wish her a blessed Christmas. Our parents found this highly amusing as well. But the atheist reserve in their laughter was seasoned with an appreciable amount of love. They had nothing in common with this blessing, they neither wanted to receive nor did they wish to confer a blessing, but they appreciated that Rózsi Németh wouldn't let their atheism get in her way, in short, that she was a free spirit.

I couldn't attend Christmas mass in her church anymore either.

But that winter, I went skating. Sometimes I'd even go to the rink in the morning and again in the afternoon. From three in the afternoon, they played waltzes and foxtrots over the loudspeaker. I felt that it was a risky undertaking to spend so much time skating of my own free will, even if it's a school break, but I couldn't resist. I did whatever I pleased; there was no one in the empty apartment to stop me. Once they said I shouldn't go anywhere in the morning because a man will be coming to fix the phone, and he actually showed up with his small square kit with all his tools inside, a man with curly blond hair, who was whistling as I opened the door for him, and now I read in the papers in the archives that this transpired on March 29, 1949, a Tuesday, and since I can clearly see with my mind's eye as I open the door for the whistling repairman, I know that the weather was warm that morning, but the sky was overcast. Though entire batches of documents have disappeared from the archives, a small handwritten official receipt has survived in which the whistling repairman informs his superior that he has installed 1 pc. service signal alarm bell in postal service apartment station 124–185, because that was our telephone number on Pozsonyi Street, and his report is officially countersigned by four officials. From further files, written records, reminders, and transcriptions I also see that the orders for installing the alarm signal came directly from Postal Director General Pápai, who in turn received his orders from Minister of Transportation Ernő Gerő. The paperwork was seen to later, meaning that they backdated the documents against the rules, and the actual installation of the alarm had taken place a week and a half earlier than the administration date pertaining to the orders. The signal bell later gave me no small food for thought because, try as I might, I couldn't see what my father was doing or how he operated it, either when they called him, or when he called them. If someone was in the room, he hid the phone behind his back and very quickly manipulated something on it, and used the cradle and not the dial to make a call. He used these special signals to let the telephone exchange know that he had come home or else to inform it when he'd be leaving and where he was going. He had to be on hand twenty-four hours of the day. He could call people over this same exchange, but only by giving their code and not their name. But he made sure I was not within hearing distance and couldn't see his hands. I don't even know what section of the Party membership this communications system was reserved for. Judging by the calls and the subject of their discussions, it must have been a rather wide circle, including professional subordinates as well as the highest government circles. Sometimes he gave orders, at others he received them.

I had a weekly pass to the ice-skating rink, and they punched it each time, just like my tram ticket. During Christmas break I sometimes didn't even go home for lunch, to avoid getting my pass punched twice in one day. I could buy buttered rolls or buttered croissants in the warming room for twenty fillérs, or for thirty, with mortadella. For another twenty fillérs a man screwed on or removed the skates from my ankle boots. I ended up spending as much as forty or fifty fillérs, which also made me very anxious, I was afraid I'd run out of my pocket money. My parents gave me my pocket money for the week on Sunday night to buy my pass and buttered rolls, but I had to give them strict accounts of my spending. What bothered me more than anything, though, was having to listen patiently to my father's admonitions about frugality, or his outbursts against extravagance. But it was worth it because the older girls liked skating with me. They taught me to make circles. It was all very serious, as if we were practicing for a performance, except we didn't know when and where the performance would take place. While they practiced their pirouettes, or whirled around and around on their toes and took some terrible falls, I had to circle around them with a stretched loop all the while I increased my speed, drawing what they called a wreath around them until the circle was quite tight. At such times we sometimes bumped into one another and fell down on the ice all in a heap. The older boys would then show up, adding to the size of the heap. This put me off just a bit because the weight and damp smell of the human heap, this whole experience of cramming together and squirming, was not exactly pleasant. The big girls considered our show a success only if their page, meaning me, executed the smallest possible circle just as their ballet turns were completed, and then, with a bow, their page, meaning me, could help them finish their show with a curtsy.

The older boys were reluctant to do it, they were not about to be the page to any silly girls. I felt a bit ashamed that I hadn't thought of this myself, because if I want to be a big boy, it's something I should think about, and yet it was then that I made up my mind that I'd become a dancer, I'd be their page, and after a while, I'd lift the big girls up in the air. One Sunday morning we saw *The Nutcracker* at the opera, I had a horror of these matinées, the rumpus the children made, but that same year they also took me to see Gabriella Lakatos and Viktor Róna in *The Flames of Paris*, but this was at night, it was a performance at the outdoor stage on Margaret Island. With its Narodnik passion and plebeian strength, this story held me in thrall, and right away, I wanted to be Viktor Róna, meaning a handsome and tall revolutionary, just like him. As opposed to the bourgeois hypocrisy and petty complications of *Fidelio*, the revolution as depicted through Viktor Róna's body made me happy, something that I now understand more or less, because these ballets were the work of the renowned Russian choreographer Vasili Ivanovich Vainonen, a dancer born in St. Petersburg who studied with the Imperial Ballet, and so he brought the two-hundred- if not four-hundred-year-old tradition of theatrical dance to my native town, Petipa, and not Petipa's spirit, but his person, because dance is a highly concrete genre, it nurtures the steps of *pas à pas* Petipa, several people's simultaneously, Marius's first and foremost, but also of his brother Lucien and their father, Jean-Antoine, who in 1848 left the Madrid Opera for the Imperial Opera, as well as all their pupils' steps, Nijinsky's and Fokine's, the entire St. Petersburg and Leningrad school along with Diaghilev, in short, the classical as well as the modern dance traditions. When it comes to dance, this is a great achievement. I later took photographs of Gabriella Lakatos and interviewed Viktor Róna, and by then I undertood, more or less, why, apart from my father's pronounced homophobic feelings, I couldn't become a dancer. I regret it to this day. Everything in my life turned out just fine, but this I regret. Had I been as persevering as Viktor Róna had been as a child, I would have succeeded. He was also short of stature as a child and wasn't too tall even as an adolescent, and his ballet teacher made it clear that it's not enough for him to dance well, he must also grow in height. If he failed to grow during the summer, he'd throw him out of his class the next year. That summer he grew as tall as a pine. The following year we saw *Swan Lake* and *The Fountain of Bakhchisarai*.

But on the skating rink, these older boys I admired cared only about increasing their speed, they weren't interested in anything else; it is a shame that I never got a chance to try to see how they managed this great speed, because the big girls competed for me, arguing over who I should skate with next.

For a long time, a very long time, I had forgotten all about these little ballerinas in their tight pants, their Norwegian-patterned pullovers, their little cheeks ruddy from cold and excitement. The images were buried deep inside me.

That first morning on Svábhegy I found the school with ease despite the snow. I also found the principal's office with ease, because the janitor showed me the way. The principal was called Mrs. Halmágyi or Harsányi, I remember her name only vaguely, which is not very nice of me, because she must have been quite a remarkable principal. She gave the impression that she was so benevolent and attentive so she wouldn't have to share the immeasurable burden and suffering that weighed on her shoulders with others. I never knew what that suffering might have been. Perhaps, prompted by her own suffering, she made a safe haven for those among the teaching staff who had been driven away from someplace else, where their lives were made intolerable. Tamás Bánky, the choirmaster and music teacher, must have been one of these people, and also Judit Benkő, the biology teacher, who started tending the school garden with us, it had fallen into ruin during the siege, and Lóránt Ferkay, the fastidious and stubborn art teacher, too, and József Gulyás, too, must also have been like that, the handsome, sad, and cruel math teacher with the cleft in his chin. I assume that he'd come back from a POW camp. There was something on the faces of the former prisoners of war that you didn't see on anyone else, a unique blend of cheer, surrender, and lethargy that nothing could dispel for the rest of their lives. Erzsébet Galgóczy also sought refuge among the teaching staff, she was our Hungarian teacher, she wore her gray hair braided and put up in a wreath, and so did the nun who wore grayish green dresses with white collars and sometimes striped aprons and heavily ribbed cotton socks, and our Russian teacher, too, whose name escapes me, I was afraid of her, she scared the living daylights out of me, she was a distraught, unkempt, ill-mannered little woman, nervous, high-strung, who'd fly into a rage during class, her rage veritably made her burst at the seams, she went berserk, flailing her arms and screeching, we had no idea why, or else she sat apathetically and didn't care what we were up to or what we were talking about among ourselves, and also, sometimes she'd storm out of the classroom and not come back, or else she'd come back, her eyes swollen with tears, and she spoke many languages, but Russian she couldn't manage. She may have reviewed the day's lesson just before class, though we had a feeling that she hated doing so. She turned into one of the principal characters of my recurring dreams, a woman who expects me to solve something that she herself is incapable of solving. In these dreams she's at the head of the examination committee, her hair is disheveled, her dresses hanging in disarray, and she's screaming something at me in Russian.

The principal had no shape, she was poorly dressed and she slouched as she walked and wore a hunted expression behind her glasses. She was the mother of four children who also attended our school, but they gave no sign of suffering. They had no reason to fear their mother. Even her glasses kept slipping down her nose, and under her worn-out sweater her breasts hung and swung all over the place just like the breasts of the women of the women's movement, and so in my mind I ended up equating her with them. She sat lopsided at her desk, as if it weren't her desk at all, nor her office either, but the minute she looked up from her papers, she showed an immediate understanding, which unsettled me all the same, because despite the suffering, there was also an ironic glint in her eye. At times it looked more like sarcasm. Real humorists are heavy with suffering and bitterness.

She grabbed her sweater, stretched out from all the washing and wear, your class is not in this building, come along with me, my dear, I'll show you the way, your class will be in the barracks, my dear boy. Anyone who was born in this city and who has lived through the siege in this city knew what a barracks was. *Barracks* was the word used by those who had returned from the camps, though it could as well be the barracks of a military camp or an annex of a main building that survived the bombing, a warehouse that was put to a different use in a city reduced to rubble, or it could be a hospital barracks, there were plenty of them in town. She called everyone my dear boy or my dear girl, but there was no insincerity in it. This slovenly dressed woman gave the impression that she knew every one of the students in her school individually and loved them individually, too. The minute anyone came into her presence, right away she loved them, and the truth is that there was nevertheless something deeply offensive about it. That's why we were afraid of her ironic gaze just a bit. Hospital barracks were wood-frame structures that could be erected quickly and they stood mostly in public parks or in the gardens of general hospitals. They were put up posthaste to accommodate the wounded of the First World War and to serve as pavilions for contagious diseases when the general hospital wards, the private sanatoriums, and the mirrored palace halls had no more room for additional sickbeds. Our own barracks stood opposite the church on the fringes of the public park located on the corner of Felhő Street, it was a tidy little building painted an unprepossessing grayish-green. The two wards opened from one long corridor. The barracks had been built for soldiers with pulmonary diseases, and though in my memoirs I try to rely only on data that can be verified and have no undocumented information and resolve that before I die we should be able to separate semblance from reality and reality from fantasy at long last, still, I found nothing to substantiate this. On the contrary, the records indicate that the school was built by the municipality of Budapest and handed over to the public in 1926. Still, I don't think that that's how it was. Probably, the city restored it and said that it was new. Up on Svábhegy, people said, with not a little disgust, that during the First World War, they brought pulmonary patients up there who could not be accommodated by St. John's Hospital, but they also brought there the demented patients who'd recovered from their lung diseases but had suffered from gas attacks, so they should at least breathe fresh air. There's nothing else they could do for them anyway. The poor things had wandered in the park among the trees all day long. And in fact, there was a memorial for the heroes of the First World War that had perhaps less kitsch to its credit than usual, right there, in the park.

Mrs. Halmágyi or Harsányi pulled her sweater over her head as we hurried in the falling snow along the tree-lined path that led to the church until we reached this small, gray military-looking structure, and as soon as we entered, I felt a strange weight descend on me, a weight that would not relent for decades to come. There was a blazing fire raging in the big, ornate cylindrical stove. I now know that the weight is called anxiety. I had never encountered anxiety at the scenes of my previous life. Intense anxiety makes you feel as if your body has a greater weight and expanse than it actually has. Your body loses its shape, it breaks through its confines, it disintegrates. There was a horrible stink in the classroom, the characteristic stink of decay. I knew I couldn't get away. Besides, the principal laid a gentle hand on my shoulder and kept saying, dear child.

Dear child, you will sit in the last row.

I couldn't have explained why I wanted to get away, even to myself.

All those strange faces looking at me.

Besides, there was no room anywhere else.

There was nowhere I could seek refuge.

It stinks. He's telling us it stinks here. He says we stink. The little snipe from town, his delicate nose can't take the carbon monoxide.

The little idiot thinks I'm farting, when I'm just stoking the fire.

What're you staring at, little fart.

I wanted to flee but could find no rational reason for doing so. Thanks to my upbringing, it was just such a situation whose legitimacy I could not accept. I couldn't very well break free of a gentle hand on my shoulder. I couldn't do something that made no sense. From then on and for a long time to come, I didn't know what to do about myself or the outside world, how to be free of its weight, how to reconcile the two. How I should piece together my limbs, all out of whack, and make myself whole again. How the finite and the restricted could be transmuted into freedom.

Later I learned all about the ingredients of this stink, and the subject of my learning became, at the same time, the sociology of the place; the two were one and the same, though at first I was aware only of the preponderance of the carbon monoxide and the anxiety. I knew what carbon monoxide was and what effect it can have on the composition of the blood and what carbon monoxide poisoning consisted of because by then my father had relentlessly hammered half of the physical world into me, and if he had the time, he made me repeat it again and again, we repeated it together so I'd memorize the specifics of the physical world once and for all, if it was the last thing I did. But I knew nothing about anxiety. He even explained the properties of the cobweb to me, and also the cocoon, and how raw silk is made, and China, the Silk Road, the court of the Chinese emperor, the Forbidden City with its women whose feet were bound, and so on, he also explained and had me repeat how the spider attaches the two supporting strands of its net, considering that it can't fly, but how was I to know, I'd never felt anxious before, I don't remember being anxious before, or how the caterpillar wove a cocoon, use your head, it's really simple, I couldn't figure it out even if it was simple, he explained it, but he also explained the metamorphosis of caterpillars and worms, the composition of the saliva of worms and spiders, the concept of metamorphosis, which we should understand in its figurative sense only, like in mythology, and then he told me about the superstitions and beliefs attached to such notions, of which, need he add, we must beware, like the devil bewares incense or the vampire garlic. The reference to the devil and the vampire made my parents laugh and they said all sorts of things that were way beyond me, because it must have been some erotically charged reference between the two of them, until in the end, they screamed with laughter.

The classroom was hot and cramped, there was no escape, no turning back, and water was dripping down the windowpanes. I could hardly find an empty hook. The coats smelled. My classmates smelled. After the siege, the number of inhabitants up on Svábhegy grew by leaps and bounds because they moved families whose homes had been destroyed by bombs into the deserted villas and the spacious houses of expelled local German peasants, sometimes several families into a single house. Up on the mountain, because that's what the locals called it, the mountain, there were many empty servants' houses and servants' quarters as well, not to mention the caretakers' quarters, the abandoned gardeners' quarters, sturdily constructed sheds, shacks, empty stables and granaries, and so, when after the siege the industry of the capital city began to absorb the countryside and the local population increased, locals as well as newcomers moved into these structures and made them their living quarters.

I had to sit in the last row next to a weird-looking boy. It wasn't a small classroom and it was bright from the reflection of the snow outside, but they crammed too many benches into it. It took me a while to realize that our breath was dripping down the three windows looking out on the park. From time to time, the janitor came from the main building and added coal to the fire. As soon as I sat down next to the weird-looking boy, the smell of garlic toast, boiled bacon, headcheese, and sausage came pouring out of him, also, they ate it with onions and pickled pepper. For a long time after the siege, people could still keep animals up on the hill, cattle, horses, pigs, chicken, geese, ducks, sheep, and goats. In Törökszentmiklós I saw them make boiled bacon, the liquid in the cauldron murky with fat, they threw garlic, savory, bay leaf, salt, and pepper into it, and they boiled the bacon cut into large chunks, the headcheese, the sausage, the blood sausage and the liver sausage, in that order. They then removed the garlic with a skimmer, and in a big bowl combined it with salt and paprika, poured several ladles of piping hot lard over it that they had melted in another cauldron, then quickly spread the lot on both sides of the boiled bacon, and as a final touch, rolled the blocks of bacon in paprika. Next they hung it on hooks in the cold under the eaves, where it attained the desired texture.

The dry-constructed, timber-frame temporary barracks put together with impregnated gypsum slabs in which they accommodated the first two grades of the school barely had a foundation, sometimes they didn't even dig down to the frost line, and this was the clever structural contrivance, they laid the floor joists on a layer of sand or slag, and they nailed the rough-hewn floor to them. They applied oil so it shouldn't decay or, at least, the decay shouldn't be visible or felt. They didn't clean the floor with water but, year after year, with sawdust mixed with oil. The stink of used crude oil hovered in the air, it grew rancid, it fermented. The wall of the structure was not damp, because the impregnated gypsum slabs cast off the water, and in theory they didn't conduct sound or heat either, but in practice, the cold was coming from all around, it came pouring out of the walls, it radiated from the floorboards, and the hot stove was helpless against it. Also, I was sitting close to the window. There was a draft and I could see the frostwork forming on the windowpane. Also, the structure's wooden frame grew fungus and mildew merrily as it rotted away in the eternal mist. I hadn't experienced the prevailing odor of the Hungarian countryside before, that foul, musty smell. Also, I had no idea that all told, this was a village school, where I soon learned to distinguish the various stenches; there was the local musty smell, meaning the musty smell of the barracks, and there were the imported musty smells. Each of the children had his own musty smell. Besides, most of them never took a bath. An apt expression would be that they were scruffy. Not only did they not bathe, they didn't even wash. I saw what they did. At most they washed their hands and face, they splashed water on their face from a washbowl, but not their necks, their shoulders, their chest or underarms. They had to be told to do it. At night they fell into bed just as they'd come from their wandering and ball games. They slept in the same silesia underpants and undershirts that they wore during the day and changed them once a week at best. When decades later we lived in Kisoroszi on the tip of Szentendre Island, where we had no running water and we had to bring water from a well, my friend Miklós Mészöly insisted that the skin cleans itself and so he didn't wash either. A week later, he also smelled. After a while, a person doesn't smell his own stink. I'm sure that after a couple of days, I also took my own musty smell to school with me.

The weird-looking boy I sat next to on the back bench was called János Tót or József Tót, his father was the school janitor, they lived in the road mender's hut in Felhő Street, in a small service apartment that was later demolished. But he disappeared from our lives way before that. I wondered about his disappearance for a long time. I don't know what happened to him. The janitor's son was a pale, skinny boy, he went around in absurd baize clothes, street sweepers had uniforms of the same dark gray fabric, his father may have been a roadworker earlier, and probably, his dark gray silesia clothes were retailored at home from his father's former uniform, and he looked out of them into the world with big, dark eyes. He was grimy, just like the others; even though he always wore a white shirt, by midweek his collar was thick with dirt. You could tell that he understood nothing of what his teacher said. We were the last in line during gym. I didn't understand anything either, but at least I tried. As far as I remember, he was shorter than I, but his autism was more pronounced. This little boy was locked airtight inside himself. Our teacher, whom I can't recall, try as I might, but it was definitely not a woman but an older man with an unpleasant smell, wanted to transfer him to the auxiliary school for the retarded, but he didn't do it because of the janitor. Everyone was terrified of the janitor and even the unwieldy principal kept her distance, because the janitor ratted on people. The janitor was sly and underhanded and, needless to say, he was arbitrary with us as well, and though he acted quiet and humble in front of the teachers, he ratted on them, down to the last man. Years later, when we were going to school in the main building, he once informed on someone with horrendous results. The ÁVH state security forces came with sidecar motorcycles and at least fifteen men at the ready and raided the place. They blocked off all the exits of the school building, no one could enter and no one could leave. The corridors were empty and silent. They took samples of everyone's handwriting. They made a list of all the absentees, whom they interrogated in their homes, because the janitor had found a ditty on the wall of a stall in the boys' toilet.

If you're up to here in shit, hang on to your standard of living for a bit, say Comrades Stalin and Rákosi.

This is one reason they had the forbearance to put his son on the back bench. Tót didn't have to listen, Tót could do anything he wanted, as long as he didn't keep the others from learning with his feeble-mindedness. His teacher never asked him anything, and he was never called up in front of the class. I found Tót intriguing. If he said something just like that, to himself, and I inadvertently answered him, or I happened to say something to him, though I rarely felt the urge, he fixed me with his big dark eyes, his lovely lips opened a bit, and he looked as surprised as if I were the eighth wonder of the world, an apparition, as if my question made no sense. Not that he didn't understand. He understood. Our teacher had it all wrong. He wasn't dim-witted by any means, it's just that he wasn't there and there was no knowing where he was and whether he could bring himself back to the world we know. At most he looked out at it and wondered at the way things were, but he could not leave the place he inhabited, nor did it occur to him that he should. Whereas all day long he busied himself with something entirely profane, and he did so compulsively. He got hold of clean writing sheets or empty notebooks from somewhere, whereas paper numbered among the major shortages, it was portioned out, perhaps the janitor stole it for his son from the faculty room, because as long as he had paper, he was sure to behave, or God knows, and he filled it with his own name in intricate lettering. Nothing else. János Tót. Or József. But this he wrote in the most intricate, ornate letters. He kept experimenting with new ornamentation. He kept writing until the sheet was completely filled up with his name. Once he said that he was practicing his ministerial signature. I didn't ask. He wasn't talking to me. He said it to himself, he said that he's practicing his ministerial signature. From which I understood that every single day, my bench mate was preparing for his ministerial appointment. When the day comes, his signature must be mature and self-assured, because he'd have big batches of documents to sign. I wonder that while I sat next to him, and I sat next to him for a year and a half, how many times he must have written his name as his ministerial signature, a hundred thousand times or possibly a million, I don't know. He hoarded his signatures somewhere because once he said I should go home with him, he'd take them out of their hiding place and show them to me and we'd pick out the one with the most eye appeal. When he spoke, he chose his words carefully, as if he were already a top-ranking official. He read old Hungarian authors, Jósika, Eötvös, Zsigmond Kemény, I don't know where he got these books with silver- and gold-embossed binding made of shiny canvas or leather and smelling of mildew. I first heard this phrase, eye appeal, from him. If I wasn't careful, he'd take my notebooks or books and fill them with his name. I don't know why, but I never took them away from him, I let him fill them with his name; it felt good watching him write on an empty page in one of my notebooks or one of my books until it was of no more use to me.

Sometimes I started to write my name like he did, but I quickly got bored with it. I tried being elaborate but found that curlicues were unsuited to my name.

When you entered the main school building and walked up the five steps leading to the landing, the janitor's booth was to your left. The main building had central heating, but the janitor heated his booth with an iron stove and the heat and the stench were staggering. It didn't look to me like the janitor could be the father of this János or József Tót. Perhaps he was his stepfather, perhaps his real father perished at the Don. This is how they said it, he perished. If the janitor so much as opened the sliding window of the booth to threaten someone, to give someone a key or to yell, be quiet, be quiet already, the heat and the stink came pouring out. In the road mender's hut where they lived, the smell of burned lard filled their kitchen. They used the one room only to sleep. I visited them once when János or József Tót had been absent for a while, he was sick and he was sitting in his parents' big bed writing his name in a notebook that was already filled up with his name. He turned the notebook upside down and wrote his name in the empty spaces. I was supposed to tell him what we learned in the last couple of days and what homework he needed to do, but he didn't care. For a while he listened, spellbound, or rather, he looked, he watched me talking to no point, then he turned back to his notebook and continued writing and writing and writing János Tót. Or József. Today I'd say that I felt a tender affection for this grimy little boy with his grimy white shirts, I couldn't help but admire his beautiful lips and pitch-black eyes.

Theoretically, the houses of the local Germans and the villas of the gentry were built with a lot more care than the adobe houses in the Hungarian countryside, but for lack of proper city sewers, after the shortest rain, up on the hill the water came pouring, streaming, cascading down, forming small cataracts, and after torrential rain it came gushing in torrents from the hilltop and the peaks, forming veritable waterfalls, while on the first spring day it gushed forth from under the snow in yellow streams, noisily carrying crumbling fragments of lime paint sediment along with it. There was hardly a house or lordly mansion on the hill with one room, at least, that wasn't damp and smelling of mildew. The Baltazár villa next door also smelled of mildew. I thought of it as gentrified mildew, because their mother's perfume sweetened it. This exquisite young woman was the most beautiful of any I had ever seen, and so in my mind I exempted her smell from the stink of their rooms. The smell of mildew is warm and dark. The smell of mildew has a higher temperature than the soil or the air, it smells of decay and combustible products. The Perczels' villa with its impressive size was built into the hillside and faced southeast, and so instead of looking out on the park, its northwestern front faced the retaining walls constructed of rough quarry stone. These retaining walls never dried out, and even in the heat of summer, beads of water glistened on the white stones. Big fat purple slugs and bluish rat snakes inhabited the crevices, but the lizards kept away, enjoying the sunshine at the base of the bone-dry southern walls and the rock gardens. Our beautiful kitchen with the delft tiles faced these wet northwestern stone walls, and the empty maid's room, the pantry, one of the empty bedrooms, and the bathroom adorned with delft tiles also faced this wall. All the rooms had a pungent smell, the tiled ones less so. The rooms and the reception hall remained relatively dry and free of odors, but the empty iron-framed winter garden smelled to high heaven. Its floor, covered with loose and perennially shifting Turkish tiles, reflected how the entire house was shifting, sliding and precariously balancing as it sat atop the veined limestone. As soon as the snow melted, our father dug down in various spots, measuring, studying, explaining, the winter garden lacked a proper foundation, the iron frame was placed atop a foundation wall made of just five rows of brick, and even that's not properly insulated, the thin concrete layer under the brick was surely cracking, sinking, rising, but the mighty weight of the iron framework kept the shifting soil in check. It won't come crashing down on us. But this dark mildew smell ate its way into all our clothes, our hair, our skin. I felt how pungent it was especially when we went down to the city, or over to Dobsinai Street, or when we got damp from rain or when we entered a strange apartment, and then all four of us smelled. We smelled at the cinema, we smelled at the Cserépfalvi bookshop on Váci Street, which they had taken from its owner by then and where we sometimes met the Aranyossis until they shut it down, but most of all, we smelled at the theater and the opera.

I assume that they weren't aware of it, they certainly never mentioned it, or else they thought it best to keep silent about it, like they did about so much else.

I have nothing to go on except for secondhand information about why on earth we had to move from Pozsonyi Street, considering that our move had no rational necessity prompting it; at any rate, to this day I certainly can't find traces of any such necessity either in our papers or among my memories. It was only years later that our grandparents Arnold Tauber and Cecília Nussbaum had to move in with us because my aunt, Miklós Nádas's wife, née Erzsébet Tauber, who was officially declared a widow after all, wanted to marry Gyula Nemes. Or why our planned move had to be delayed by nearly a year. At the time I didn't suspect that our parents had been singled out and would now be projected several rungs up the Communist hierarchy. But even if this was so, they didn't concern themselves with it, they kept the news to themselves, they were not fired by ambition, on the contrary, even the thought would have been shameful in their eyes, odious. A Communist has work to do and must work steadily, a Communist does not build a career. A Communist works wherever the Party puts him. Still, on the basis of surviving documents, the narratives of acquaintances and friends as well as my own memory fragments, I must conclude that this is what had to happen. As I see from the documents I've put into chronological order, we moved up to Svábhegy in January, and in March the president bestowed one of the highest possible decorations on my mother. The troika, meaning the Five-in-Hand, must have had plans for her, and so had them move up to Svábhegy.

One thing is certain, our parents reached the peak of their careers in the four years after the siege. In his or her own way and in accordance with the system of values of the Communist movement, both of them must have worked to the full satisfaction of their party. Probably, their line of duty must have suited their constitution, our mother with her cheerful disposition and her outstanding gift for organizing on a national scale, and our father with his expert knowledge and dogged perseverance. One was dynamic, open, high-spirited, the other as insistent on objects and procedures as if he identified himself with them. Little wonder if their comrades in the screening departments took notice and said, let's have them be this or that. Even their self-sacrifice is unostentatious. And that's when the proverbial fly must have landed in the ointment, some miscalculation or some constitutional anomaly, theirs or someone else's, a bolt of lightning, a storm, I don't know what, a break they must have suffered just before our move.

The next couple of years, the last couple of years of their lives, they changed before my very eyes; one fell prey to illness, the other collapsed under the weight of what was happening to him and lost his sanity, except they didn't take him away, and we had to put up with him. They silently plunged into darkness. I didn't plunge, just nearly, I was bolstered by the garden, the plants, the animals, the aquarium, the terrarium, the girls, and the school garden most of all, which they established in Felhő Street in the early years of the twentieth century; and also, my nursing and household duties bolstered me up, but my brother very nearly plunged with them. He must have been saved by his innate strength.

During our first summer up on Svábhegy, they gave me a little dog they must have found in the neighborhood, and I busied myself with him.

Panic-stricken by the hair-raising logic of what was happening to them, they persisted in their silence even as they crashed. Suddenly, their childhoods, pervaded by the diseases of the body and soul, showed from within the silence. What was left of their infantile selves. But as long as our mother lived, meaning as long as, joking and laughing, she was dying, our father never once complained. He collapsed in silence while he laughed along with our idiotic mother. They were in fact under enormous stress, that's true, they were irritable and unresponsive to the needs of others, that's also true, and they became even more distant, unapproachable, which affected my brother more than it affected me. He didn't understand. I understood, and chose to ignore the problems I had with them. I had my good manners to fall back on, and as for my mean streak, I could practice it on my brother and my grandmother Cecília Nussbaum. I stopped attending to my parents in the hopes of finding something out about them. It was better not knowing. On the other hand, if I put two and two together and considered our new residence on Svábhegy, the size of the villa, the spectacular size of the rare trees in the park that served as the arboretum, the condition of the tennis court and the well-tended greenhouses, which I discovered only in late March when the snow had melted and I could finally see where we were living and all the things at our disposal with my own eyes, the greenhouses, a red clay tennis court with the posts and the net, because my parents wouldn't waste half a word on their new environment, if that, and if I further considered that the head of the Party was living next door to us, that the restricted area was separated from our villa only by a fence, not that they ever mentioned the restricted area either, they never said a word about it, and so I had to discover it for myself, whereas it was a risky undertaking; in short, if I take all this into account, I can't ignore the possibility that one of them must have been counting on an appointment greater than what was suited to them, a promotion beyond their station. In those years, as indeed in all years of renewal, even if it invariably came as a surprise, this type of promotion unsuited to the individual was not considered a miracle. But I have no way of knowing what that appointment may have been, or which of them would have received it. Possibly both. I have no information to substantiate it. I searched and searched, but came up empty-handed.

The truth is, our mother knew just about all the Party leaders, and she must have known all their little secrets, if for no other reason than that she worked with their wives either on various occasional projects or as their colleague, and so she got wind of their daily domestic

315

conflicts, which she then discussed with our father or with my Aunt Magda over the phone. For instance, they knew that Mrs. Rákosi couldn't get pregnant, they knew that she was healthy and capable of conceiving, it's obvious who told them, Dr. Hirschler told them that Rákosi wouldn't hear of having his sperm count checked, and they even knew why not, which made them laugh in a way whose meaning I could not decipher. Or else she knew them from illegality, as they called their covert activities on behalf of the Communist Party from before the siege. To know someone from illegality, to know someone from the movement, this was to be understood according to Hegelian and Marxist concepts. They imagined history as a striving toward transcendent fulfillment through organic development, taking the human race along with it, and they worked hand in hand with history, they thought of human history as the worldly expression of the coming of the Messiah or Christ; Marx had called the heaven of fulfillment communism, which they could foster, or else hinder, one way or another, with their deeds, in which case they'd been foul reactionaries, the toadies and sycophants of the bourgeoisie. On the other hand, there was no turning back the wheels of history.

Several written sources indicate that in his own development our father was assisted by no less an individual than Ernő Gerő. Whatever title he bore, whatever title he held, minister of transportation, minister of finance, minister of the interior, Gerő invariably gathered around him a group of experts made up mostly of younger men, and for lack of expertise of his own, he relied on them. Even when he was put in charge of occasional technical matters, he remained the chief administrator of their party, and needless to say, he needed experts in this capacity as well. He surely made good use of our father. In his official CVs Gerő was called an economist, but he had not been trained as such. He studied medicine, but finished only two years of medical school in Budapest, when the illegal Communist movement swept him off his feet and he eventually landed in the Party.

The experts he gathered around him were known as the Gerő Boys, an indication that the functionaries of whichever ministry Gerő happened to be in charge of hated these smarter-than-thou shadows who stood in Gerő's service or followed in his footsteps, and they made fun at their expense. In short, our father was surely one of these hateful people, one of the Gerő Boys. The Communist nomenclature generally used people with upper-middle-class backgrounds, in short, bourgeois backgrounds such as he had for just the sort of backup work he was good at.

Probably, they must have come into contact during the first years after the siege, when Gerő was put in charge of rebuilding the bridges, and in this capacity, he was also an important tool in the hands of Party propaganda. Gerő the Bridge Builder. Killing two birds with one stone, they not only succeeded in equating Gerő with bridge building in my own mind, but in the minds of the people of Pest and Buda, separated for lack of bridges, they also succeeded in equating the idea of bridge building with the beneficent and heroic endeavor of the Communist Party as such. After the siege, Buda suffered more from its separation from Pest than Pest suffered from its separation from Buda; on the other hand, without Buda, Pest was deprived of Buda's hills, woods, freedom, and fresh air. Clearly, our father had to attend the inauguration of the rebuilt Margaret Bridge because of Gerő, and not in any official capacity. In this ancient layer of my consciousness, the memory of the bridge inauguration is bound up with Gerő's name, but the sharpest image as it emerges from the dark depths of my mind is of the bridge fallen into the Danube, the quay strewn with dead bodies, the grime, the damaged objects, the wartime radiance of the coldest winter of the century, a frozen radiance, they are all nestled in the deepest layers of my consciousness, the construction of the caissons with the heroism of the workmen and the noise, similar to but more penetrating than the sound of pile driving, and Ernő Gerő, the valiant bridge builder, may the end rhymes in his name proclaim his fame.

In my mind Gerő's name is also bound up with Gerő's person and the attendant feeling of immediacy carrying warm overtones. Chances are I must have met him at one time. In another layer of consciousness, this link was probably strengthened by the fact that Ernő Gerő, with his rhyming name, wore a suit of similar or identical wool fabric as my father, and this must have strengthened my emotional identification with this stranger, even though by then I knew that earlier in Paris, before the siege, during their time in illegality, during the time of the illegal Communist movement when they were both working on fostering historical inevitability, he came into conflict with my Aunt Magda. He was originally a Landlerite, but in Moscow he became an adherent of Béla Kun, for which the Aranyossis never forgave him, even though they knew that in Soviet Russian emigration betrayal was a condition for survival. There was no other option. Simple dishonesty did not suffice. Also, they couldn't forgive Gerő his wife. Erzsébet Fazekas, that gaggling goose. That accidental writer, that quack and professor who has no knowledge of any subject whatsoever. That born schemer, that petty functionary, that milkmaid, that dilettante. How can someone be so incapable of separating their family life from their work in the movement. By which they meant Gerő, he was the one who couldn't separate the two. My head was reeling with such sentences. Which meant that this Gerő is a weak, easily influenced namby-pamby, an unprincipled individual, a worm, no better than an amoeba.

Consequently, in the uppermost layer of my consciousness, the sentiment leaning toward sympathy based on the fabric of his suit and the judgment whereby he is a weak individual and his wife has emerged from a pile of caca, would have had to fight it out. To this day, my feelings for Gerő depend on whether I think of my father or my Aunt Magda in relation to him; after all, I loved my aunt no less than my father. And since we're involved with such microscopic details of my mapped consciousness, I might as well add that this was a sporty fabric, it was always made of two different-colored woolen yarns, they called it *mille point* because it was made up of thousands of small points or dots, but in order to make the suit's fabric even more interesting, they wove little colored knots into the darker yarn, red or green, to give it a rustic texture that stood out from the basic color of the men's or ladies' suits at uneven intervals, from the brown, gray, or black. Only members of the upper-middle class and possibly the aristocracy wore suits made of this wool fabric, and at times also the sports ladies, or as they said in their circles, the *sportif* ladies, who preferred it for their English tailored suits. When the ladies and gentlemen went hiking in their mille point suits, they also wore a peaked cap of the same material.

Gerő insisted on keeping his advisors when, with an appeal to professional or political reasons, the various bureaus or institutes were bent on separating them from him. From what I can glean from the archives, because of his work at the Reparations Bureau, our father must have been in touch with Gerő personally. Within the Hungarian Communist Party, at one time Gerő was in charge of the Department of State Policy, meaning that he supervised the plans for the new national budget. When in order to meet the reparations quota the Standard, the Eliwest-Priteg, or the Telephone Factory manufactured, by a strict deadline, some very expensive piece of equipment that demanded thousands of working hours from hundreds of laborers and required a great many imported parts all of which they packed up piece by piece and waterproofed, each piece accounted for, all according to assembly specifications, including an entire transmitting station, let's say, an entire telephone exchange or a railway command center, those who put in the reparation order would sometimes cancel it out of the blue, and order something else instead. Capriciousness such as this threaded the Hungarian national budget with *in puncto* collapse, as they called it back then. Their whimsy had a certain logic to it, and based on the files it seems that my father understood this logic. The Budapest representation of the Czechoslovak government made objections or gave suggestions only with regard to technical details at most. On the other hand, the Yugoslav government would also change its order in midstream, or repeatedly cancel its order. As they said back then, they made a habit of it. The level of their industrial production was low, and where that is low, planning, too, lies low on the horizon; besides, the partisans were in the majority in the government and they made sure to oust the experts who'd been left over from prewar times, and in line with the interests of the Communist movement stood public administration as well as administration in general on its head. Our parents might have recognized themselves in this epoch-making battle scene, but people under the spell of radical political views seldom recognize themselves in anything. They specialize in selective blindness, and this is why they should beware of dictatorship. Our father negotiated with Belgrade several times, and each time he came back saying that the Yugoslavs are hopeless negotiators. Ante Pavelić had fled, Mihailović had been executed, but they wouldn't stop their underground war. The Chetniks against the Communists, the Communists against the Ustasha, the Ustasha against the Chetniks. When the Titos paid their first official visit to Budapest and the Aranyossis and my parents were invited to the reception given by Prime Minister Lajos Dinnyés, they were awed by the bravery of the former Yugoslav partisans, while my mother was veritably swept off her feet not only by Tito's masculine strength but Jovanka's beauty as well. She and my Aunt Magda praised her beauty, cutting each other short in their eagerness to praise her. They knew that Josip and Jovanka were living in what they called a reckless union, meaning out of wedlock, yet this didn't stop Kata Hegedűs, Dinnyés's wife, from meeting Jovanka within the framework of a women's program and accompanying her to the best Inner City fashion house, despite the fact that although it was said in Budapest society that Jovanka is an attractive woman who knows her own mind, and though she lacked diplomatic experience, she'd learn, they were quick to add that alas, for now she more often than not behaved like a hand on a dairy farm, a scullery maid, which caused Mrs. Dinnyés terrible embarrassment more than once. But we must make allowances. They took great pains to explain the meaning of allowances as well as the difference between being legally wed and living out of wedlock, but I still didn't understand. For decades to come, I wondered what wed and lock had to do with each other and how two people could live outside of it. They made allowances for her clumsiness, but the mentality of the South Slav Communists was more than they could fathom. Perhaps they were stumped by their own selves as seen in the distorting mirror. When they said that a person is an impossible negotiating partner, meaning that the individual is incapable of reasoning or making compromises and is bent on dictating the outcome, they could hardly have said anything more damning. It meant that the individual in question was not suited to a position of any kind. The members of the Yugoslav reparations delegation are good comrades, but they are unsuited for their positions. At least, they knew the reason for the fault-finding of the Soviet government representatives, the key to it, and so were not averse to it. In Yugoslavia, on the other hand, there were nothing but shortages, and what ends up where or doesn't, in Zagreb or Belgrade, was always decided by the momentary balance of power of centers acting independently of each other. There was no discernable logic to it, and also, they suddenly found themselves face-to-face with the illusions that they themselves harbored with respect to the logic of the Communists' exercise of power.

There could be no doubt about the competence of the Soviet delegation, except their secret service was pressing for the installation of strategically important parts that the British- and American-owned telecommunications companies, in line with orders from their own secret services, couldn't deliver even if it would have been in their commercial interests to do so and in accord with the peace treaty. The Cold War was brewing, it was taking shape, it was coming to a head. When the Russians wouldn't accept an order or if they canceled it, the Hungarian telecommunications companies, struggling with serious financial issues to begin with, were in danger of closing down. My father was of the opinion that such leftover equipment should be put to use in developing domestic networks. The domestic telephone network was not on par with current requirements, but it was worth saving. He had to cooperate first and foremost with the functionaries of Gerő's ministry, and together they set up expert committees to study the technical and financial conditions for acquiring the now superfluous, half-finished or finished equipment, and to make suggestions to the minister. When Gerő later transferred our father from the Reparations Bureau to the Ministry of Transportation, he also changed positions within the committee of experts, and from then on represented the ministry as against the Reparations Bureau. As for Gerő, he probably had no idea, nor was he told, that my Aunt Magda, the hateful woman in the turban who had quite an extensive network of connections within the French Communist Party, was a Landlerite, meaning that with her anti-Moscow views she intrigued against him until, as a result of the conciliatory arbitration between the French and Soviet comrades, he would be forced to resign and be ordered back to Moscow, a city by now silent from all the purges, in short, that this turbaned conspirator was my father's sister. I don't know what kind of man Gerő was, vindictive or forgiving, but I do know that he'd gladly have gotten the Aranyossis out of the way, if Rákosi, because of his own partiality, had not prevented him from doing so.

Even if in vague terms, still the files of the Reparations Bureau provide some sense of my father's duties. I can't imagine a file that could have influenced my life more than the one I found in the dossier of the Reparations Bureau bearing registration number XIX-A-11 and dated between 1946 and 1952. In some cases there can be no doubt that he had filed them, I recognized his handwriting, his signature, his calculations and marginal notes. He always used a pencil for his marginal notes. He had wonderful Koh-i-noor, Hardtmuth, and Eversharp pencils, thick and thin, soft and hard. Probably he brought these back from his negotiations in Prague or Vienna, I still have one of these, and also his slide rule. I don't know why. He must have also brought my red plastic desk lamp with the red oval shade, under whose light I began to write when I was eleven, back with him from one of these trips abroad. I have no idea when it disappeared from my life along with the red light it cast. Later I did my writing in the morning, and not by lamplight.

My father requested and received standby reports from Standard, the Telephone Factory, and Eliwest-Priteg, they played for time, they reassured, they urged, while with cooperation from the Planning Office, the Ministry of Industry, or the Ministry of Transportation, he helped resolve the short-term financial problems of the companies under contract to deliver the reparations.

Foreign subcontractors, the British, Austrian, and Swiss companies, kept raising their prices, postwar shortages throughout Europe had to be alleviated, there was great haste and great demand. In order to meet delivery dates, the ministries had to stand surety for short-term loans, which the minister of finance agreed to with more than a bit of annoyance, and no wonder; after all, because of the reparation shipments, the deficit was growing at more and more ministry departments. With his wonderful pencils, he invariably made his own careful calculations on the accounts rendered, and asked the companies to correct their faulty calculations. Which was the reserved diplomatic expression for a general problem. After all, it was not a question of the business manager or chief engineer of a company not being able to count, but of the symptomatic ongoing argument between the Chief Economic Council, the Allied Commission, the Ministry of Finance, the National Materials and Price Bureau, and the various companies involving multipliers, and the conversion keys of the various currencies. It was mud wrestling. A gigantic battle. The cease-fire agreement gave the grand total of the shipments in pengős, the peace treaty accepted this sum, and so the reparation shipments had to be accounted for to the Allied Commission in pengős. But by then the pengő was a thing of the past. After the introduction of the new currency, the forint, the minister of finance had to come up with a multiplier that would balance the difference in the money market margin between the forint and the pengő. The multiplier was 3.00. On Sándor Rendl's recommendation, the Chief Economic Council accepted the multiplier temporarily, which was only natural, since they couldn't predict how the forint would fare in comparison with other currencies, and so they couldn't commit themselves to something over which they had no control. But regardless of how the forint fared in relationship to other currencies, in just a matter of months it was clear that the minister of finance had pushed the multiplier down too low. If the foreign-owned companies obliged to satisfy the reparation shipments rendered accounts on the basis of this conversion key, they suffered serious losses, and the British and American companies couldn't very well be expected to carry the burden of the expense of the Hungarian reparations. On the other hand, the minister of finance had to insist on the multiplier. His job was to keep the national budget deficit that plummeted because of the reparation shipments as low as possible. But very soon, the multiplier swept the telecommunications companies, the Telephone Factory, the Eliwest-Priteg, and even the strongest of them, the Standard, to the brink of bankrupcy. Had they gone bankrupt, they'd have taken the domestic subcontractors with them or would have become insolvent in the face of the foreign companies, and as a result could not have acquired more raw materials, and the Hungarian state could not have satisfied its reparation obligations. Telecommunications was just not one of many as far as the reparation shipments were concerned; in volume, telecommunication shipments were third in place after only steel and mining. My father had to guarantee this third place. I keep writing my father instead of our father here, because my brother hadn't been born yet. It seems to me from the archival documents that he understood and accepted the concerns of all the parties affected and did not favor any one of them over the others. He mediated between the representatives and the industrial plants in Hungarian and French, but mostly in German; he negotiated and corresponded, he did what he had to do. At the time French was the international language of telecommunications and railway transportation and not English or German, but communication with the Yugoslavs and Czechs was best facilitated by the use of German, the common language left over to them from the Austro-Hungarian monarchy. Because of the high stakes involved, his work was surely anything but monotonous.

As I was going through the files at the National Archives, written in the usual impossible jargon, I remembered my father, the technical counselor, floating in a bathtub filled to the brim with water; this was on a Sunday morning in winter, and he kept submerging himself, then reemerging, and laughing with pleasure. This image, along with all its shimmering details, is from the bathroom of our apartment on Pozsonyi Street; up on Svábhegy none of us bathed in a tub filled to the brim because, for one thing, there was no hot water, and for another, my father's playful good cheer and his self-satisfaction, too, were a thing of the past by then. My father had become a hunted animal. But that Sunday morning, as he floated in the tub filled nearly to the brim with hot water, he was just explaining the basic principle of proper money management to me. Have your cake and eat it too. Or as he put it, the goat eats its fill, while the cabbage remains.

Though he undoubtedly spared no effort in his work to satisfy this principle floating atop the water in the bathtub, he chuckled at the sight of his son trying but failing utterly to make sense of what he was telling him. I hemmed and hawed as once again I failed to explain all the things I didn't understand; what's more, the principle of the goat eating its fill while the cabbage remains infuriated me. Also, I didn't really understand it. It was the law of metastasis and the conservation of matter, which he'd explained to me not long before, and even gave me examples of it so I shouldn't forget, that prevented me from understanding. It remains as matter, but can't be made use of as cabbage. And since in those years everyone in Europe suffering under their wartime burdens tried to resolve the anomaly by recourse to this popular wisdom, the negotiators passed the buck, maneuvered, and probably laughed at it, too, within their own circles. All parties concerned would have liked to pass the shortage or the responsibility or both on to someone else. In his famous Fulton speech, Churchill was the first to pass the buck in a spectacular manner. France and Italy were experiencing one government crisis after the next, and as for Germany, the Marshall Plan *hin und her*, for at least two decades, in the interest of its own survival, it swept the financial, material, and intellectual dirt of the war under the rug, and it could do so because it was in the primary interest of the Western Allies that Germany should recover as soon as possible and become a power to be reckoned with. To this day Germans honor Hermann Josef Abs, the chairman of Deutsche Bank who in 1952 headed the West German delegation to the London debt negotiations; after all, thanks to his clever negotiation tactics, he managed to reduce his country's external debts, which, if they had to be paid in full would have threatened to undermine the national budget; how clever of him, he passed the buck, thereby managing to leave the countries they had once robbed of astronomical sums in the red once again to the tune of the same astronomical sums.

The general anomaly at passing the buck had its own humble experiment locally as well when the business managers of the Hungarian telecommunications companies in foreign ownership found allies in the functionaries of the National Materials and Price Bureau. They suggested a multiplier of 3.888 as a realistic value margin, and the telecommunications manufacturers found this multiplier not only satisfactory, but profitable as well; in short, they torpedoed government intentions. Although a draconian degree issued in haste by the Ministry of Industry wreaked havoc with their calculation, it did not push them to the brink of bankruptcy. Consequently, in his registered letter addressed to General Manager Nándor Lenkei at the Standard's Fehérvár Street headquarters in Budapest dated December 13, 1947, my father expressed his regret at having to inform the general manager that he was not at liberty to compensate for the countervalue of their reparation shipment with the 3.888 multiplier provided by the National Bureau of Materials and Prices. Though according to rescript number 10,029 of the Chief Economic Council the three-fold multiplier is merely temporary, paragraph 5 of decree 150,150/1946 IM directs that in the case of reparation shipments, only a 5% profit can be reckoned up, and so if the multiplier supplied by the Bureau of Materials and Prices is applied, the profit margin would be appreciably higher than the law allows. Then in the following paragraph he writes, using the more impersonal official plural, that General Manager Lenkei and they had agreed in mid-October that they would settle on final prices. Standard should have made an offer within a short deadline, in which they'd have added the profit prescribed by law to the cost price. Yet in spite of repeated requests from the Reparations Bureau, the quotation had not been received. Accordingly, they must uphold their previous position on the matter, to wit, they can expedite payment exceeding the 3 multiplier only in the event that Standard tenders its calculations in accordance with the profit margin. In the end they paid using the five percent profit margin, the last year that Standard could still show a profit, however humble.

Files, memorandums, transcripts, and reminders like this were not necessarily signed by my father but by Technical Chief Council Ferenc Pikler, head of the Reparations Bureau's Department of Industry; he was a mechanical engineer, yet the fact that his name appears on the file as presenter, council, or technical counselor indicates that he wrote them. What's more, we even know that the typist of the files was a certain Mrs. G. She must have been identical to the woman who on the sixth floor of the office building on Rumbach Sebestyén Street gave me paper and colored pencils to keep myself busy by drawing, whereas I didn't want to occupy myself with drawing, I was much more interested in the nature of their relationship. Despite my mother, my father was drawn to this woman, whom I also found attractive right away and, because of my mother, also hated with all my heart right away. Today I'd say that I must have noticed the shared promise of an affair.

My father was immediately under Chief Counselor Pikler. He stood in fourth place on the list of salaries of the general department. On July 4, 1947, General Department Chief Pikler took home 1,200 forints, Deputy General Department Chief István Szabó took home 1,000 forints, Chief Engineer Miksa Villányi took home 700 forints, and Technical Council László Nádas took home 600 forints, whereby his salary was twice or three times that of his colleagues. Their salaries had been approved by Zoltán Vas, the Communist president of the Chief Economic Council. Pikler had also returned home from exile in France; he had lived in Marseille, where he joined the opposition and fought against the German invaders as a maquisard.

At other times my father's name appears in a dossier as a reference, saying that so-and-so discussed this or that with him at such and such a time, or that they are hereby answering his letter about one thing or another. But by the following year he could no longer put the liberal disposition he'd inherited from his family to good use, it was no longer a year of reconciling views or drawing up compromises, and he was no longer as cheerful as before, even if he was still more or less the same. The yawning scarcity left behind by the war, the reparations, and the country's reconstruction made itself felt in the Hungarian economy as well, except Hungary had no one to whom it could pass the buck. Even those nations with substantial colonies, meaning that theoretically they had a place they could rob just as they'd been doing for centuries, now found the circus spectacle of passing the buck difficult to execute to perfection. They'd hardly made the attempt and right away they came up against armed independence movements. In the years to follow, my father was not the only one who didn't get far with his wisdom about the persistent presence of the goat's appetite and the cabbage. Probably, this wisdom worked only in the happy bygone years, when a debt could be passed on to the serfs or the Negroes, or a country could say, we're not paying the Jews, and if they don't like it, we'll organize a nice little pogrom for them, which will make our people happy in the bargain. Despite this, our parents' party felt that the yawning deficit could work to their advantage. They wanted to make up for the yawning deficit through a sweeping nationalization program. They felt that this was only right because they saw that the division of the land, which should have taken place centuries earlier, the division of the great Church and feudal estates, had worked out well, the great mass of destitute and illiterate peasants and seasonal workers who lived like serfs now had land of their own, land, land, as Móricz wrote, and agricultural output grew by leaps and bounds. They were given land with a certificate of ownership, as if they'd been knighted. Such certificates of ownership were issued on the basis of government edict number 600/1945 M.E. pertaining to the abolition of the system of great estates and the right of the people of the land to own it. It was dated March 15, 1945, Debrecen, the temporary seat of the National Assembly, and it was ordained by the Provisional National Government. The certificates of ownership were signed by Minister of Agriculture Ferenc Nagy, and they were made out to the name of the claimant by the local Land Claim Committee, indicating in which bulk of land, and under which distribution number, how many acres or how many square hectares of land the new owner could take possession of. I found one such blank form among the papers I have kept from my parents. The certificate of ownership compensated the victorious paupers, and not the Communists.

At the same time, the British and American owners ran up debts because of the reparation shipments, but kept the big factories in operation for reasons of marketing strategy, and they did so despite the fact that they were fully aware of what was to be expected of the general nationalization fever sweeping through the entire region now under Soviet control. The Hungarian government didn't just attempt to minimize their corporate profits in every possible way, it wanted to push them into bankruptcy, then nationalize them at the lowest possible price. In our parents' party, they did not mince words when discussing the issue. At the January 19, 1949, meeting of the Hungarian Workers Party, Gerő said that the policy of attrition of foreign-owned companies and those mainly in foreign ownership must be practiced with due caution considering our important production goals and the difficulties of foreign trade negotiations. It was not absurd to think that with the undervalued nationalization of foreign companies they would be able to make up for the yawning national budget deficit. They drove Eliwest-Priteg and the Telephone Company into debt without any difficulty, and the state bought them at a low price. Standard was the most important telecommunications company in the region and the last that was still not nationalized. Gerő and Rákosi had every intention of nationalizing it along with all the others, except the Russian secret service wanted to obtain as much strategically important information as possible from the products they manufactured for the reparation shipments. The American intelligence organization, the CIA, and the chiefs of staff of the American army, however, were on guard and prevented Standard from building strategically important innovations into their equipment. The anomalies with respect to the reparation shipments to Russia had their own rationale, and the team of technical experts at the Reparations Bureau were aware of it. The Russians came up with excuses, they hastened shipments, they blackmailed, then they criticized and refused to pay, they didn't accept the installations they'd ordered as reparation shipments because they couldn't find the innovations they were eager to get their hands on, especially in aero technology and air traffic control technology. They needed these to sustain their strategic advantage.

Researchers of industrial history are familiar with a memorandum written on both sides of a sheet dated February 26, 1948. It was found in a dossier of the Department of State Policy of the Hungarian Communist Party. Researchers consider it the earliest document in which the heads of the Communist Party are considering the possibility of nationalizing the Standard factory. The memorandum concerns the symptomatic problems of the factory that were caused by chronic lack of capital. The memorandum was written by someone intimately familiar with the factory's technical and financial indicators both from the inside and the outside, someone who could furnish data on it in the utmost detail and who understood the relationships among all these factors. In our home, the Standard was a constant topic of discussion.

It is my impression that my father wrote the memorandum at Gerő's request. I'd even go so far as to say that at the time, no one else could have written it. Archival documents indicate that our father was transferred from the Reparations Bureau to the Ministry of Transportation at Gerő's request. At the time the post office and communications as well as the railways and public roads came under the jurisdiction of the Transportation Authority. In subsequent years, it was at times disassembled, at times reassembled, and our father's position shifted accordingly among division chief, special branch chief, special branch deputy chief, department head, group leader, and deputy chief of division. He was veritably bandied about. Be that as it may, we know that he'd prepared comprehensive plans for the latest reorganization of the ministry. Comprehensive reorganization stood everything on its head, but in a way that ensured that everything would stay the same. It is clear from the plans that they were prepared in haste and were immediately approved by the Transportation Council on September 20, 1948. Corruption, too, must be eradicated by the proper appointment of managers. The thought that something should be eradicated must have been a real novelty in the vernacular of state politics that had been carefully elaborated during the Monarchy and neutral to the point of the death of language. In this senseless and useless fever of reorganization, Gerő must have needed individuals, chess pieces whom he could easily replace with other individuals, knock them down, individuals with whom he could checkmate other individuals. Probably, he intended to put our father in someone else's place, but something must have come up, I have no idea what, and Gerő himself was soon removed from the scene. But I have found no information about what actually happened.

The information from the archives would have been reliable only if the original documents related to his appointment as chief department head, dated November 4, 1948, had not been removed from the archives of the ministry sometime later, but they were, and there is no information about who had removed it, or when and why it had been removed. This information was left undocumented on purpose.

However, we know something of the appointment procedure. For example, simultaneous with the appointment, the appointer, in this case the prime minister or the minister of the competent department, was bound, in line with the monarchic official procedure, to initiate an action related to the determination of the rank and classification of the appointed individual. According to the Prussian, meaning the monarchic order, an official had not only a position but an official rank as well, the Office of Finance had to initiate proceedings to determine the salary of the appointee. The procedure to determine my father's official rank was initiated by Chief Postal Counselor Dr. Árpád Honéczy in an undated proposal, and judging by other dates, this proposal must have been written after November 4, but no later than November 16. In the proposal, Chief Counselor Honéczy requests the permission of the Honored Committee of Appointments and Employment for the minister to appoint Counselor László Nádas as Chief Superintendent of Postal Services with the no. 9 postal salary classification. The document, signed by Minister Ernő Gerő, also tells us that László Nádas, who in his position as technical counselor and according to his official rank as presenter tendered service in the Reparations Bureau between June 5 and November 3, 1946, and was accordingly placed in classification 3 of salary category VII of the national system, was then transferred to the ministry according to the Prime Minister's directive no. 11098/1948.M.E.II/A of November 4 of the same year. At this point we might sit back and relax, thinking that we have now learned something concrete about the appointment, if only the paragraph of the proposal did not contradict the previous entries in the archives registry bearing earlier as well as later dates. The last paragraph does not say that the minister appointed László Nádas chief of Department no. IV of the Ministry of Transportation, as it says in the registry; the proposal says, in consideration of László Nádas's political history and professional qualifications, the Minister wishes to appoint him deputy chief of section of the Ministry's Department no. IV. After so many years, I couldn't care less whether the prime minister or the minister wished to confer a position and of what sort on our father, but the minister must have known about the appointment the prime minister had conferred on our father and why, for more than a month, his various papers were registered in the book like this and not some other way. I tried to find the document pertaining to the department chief appointment in the protocols of the Council of Ministers because on the proposal of the competent minister, such high appointments had to be approved by the Council of Ministers or the prime minister himself. I found nothing in the protocols regarding the council's decisions. There was further confusion around the proposal pertaining to László Nádas's official rank.

If the Prime Minister and the Minister wish, it goes without saying that they can appoint László Nádas to whatever position these ministers wish, they can appoint him the Archbishop of Esztergom, for all that, this was their obligatory opportunistic phrase, their cynical phrase, the chinovnik phrase that these bureaucrats, fastidiously observant of formalities, knew and recited. Which, it seems to me, means that certain individuals must have slowed down the procedure, they set the defensive and cautionary mechanism of the apparatus in motion. They may have known that the minister would be dismissed, in which case he can take his protégé with him, for all they care, and not leave him behind. The Smallholder prime minister would also be dismissed, they knew this, too, and an alarmed peasant, a farmer, would be put in his place as a puppet, the alcoholic István Dobi, who is not as dumb as he looks, but dumb enough so the Communists can do with him what they like. At such times, officials don't make decisions, they wait it out.

As a slip affixed to one of the files I found nevertheless reveals, my poor father must have been wholly ignorant of the complications involving his appointment and classification when his mentor was already backing out of it.

What my father's division was doing on the sixth or seventh floor of the post office headquarters I learned only half a century later, after the in-depth study of some beastly boring files. The place was called the Telecommunications Directorate General. My father suspected nothing of what was happening in the background, if for no other reason than because he headed the directorate for about six months without an official appointment, but in keeping with the prevailing bureaucracy, the Finance Office gave him his salary classification along with his salary as chief of division. So why would he have suspected anything. Probably, the three procedures went along their appointed paths parallel and independent of one another, they did not cross paths; what's more, in line with the bureaucratic procedures left over from the Monarchy, these procedures were bound to ignore one another; at most they had the right of inspection after the fact. The Office of Finance received the document pertaining to my father's appointment as chief of division and was bound to concentrate only on what it was given. On the other hand, the procedure of the minister's secretariat could not interfere with the procedure of the Office of Finance until it concluded its own two further proceedings.

It is clear from the documents that not all the subsidiary offices and not all the special departments had been informed that the minister finds he doesn't know himself why on earth he'd appointed László Nádas, or since he'd done it, what could stand in the way of his classification as division chief; besides, they didn't want to ask anyone why the original appointment had to be revoked just a couple of days later in such secrecy, or why, for six months, they didn't inform said László Nádas that his appointment had been revoked. But it is understandable why the administrators couldn't have acted other than they did. Because in that case, the minister, with recourse to further transcripts and memoranda, would have first dismissed the poor man, in short, with recourse to some pretense, given him the boot and appointed him special branch deputy chief instead, though even his rank as chief technical counselor of postal services would have been too much, and they'd also have had to start this procedure from scratch on another level; in short, bureaucratic chaos and madness would have gotten the better of them, whereas bureaucratic order must always win the day over any single official document. They were teetering on the brink even so. They had no choice but to quietly remove the original documents from the archives.

Except, I must admit that resistance from the apparat would not have sufficed to create administrative chaos of such dimensions. Something must have happened that the files do not mention, because it happened higher up. But whatever may have happened, in order to facilitate a solution they removed the files pertaining to the division chief appointment on orders from the minister.

I've been to both Dob Street and the post office headquarters on Krisztina Boulevard, and I remember clearly, there was no stove in either place. There might have been a stove in the ministry's building on Andrássy Boulevard, a tile stove, as I recall, but they'd transferred my father there only toward the end of his career in the ministry, where he was in charge of the department involved with telecommunications. I would imagine that they tore up the files and threw them in a wastepaper basket. Wastepaper baskets reserved for this purpose, I remember this, too, were taken away by two men of the Department of Classified Information. They always came in pairs. Probably, they came in pairs because in this way they could keep an eye on each other. On the basis of my own experience with bureaucracy in my parents' offices and secretariats, I even know that the faulty or unnecessary files were thrown into specially marked wastepaper baskets. For instance, I couldn't throw apple cores into them.

The secretary called for them to come and get it, and then the classified information handlers came in pairs. They also came after working hours. By the time the cleaning lady showed up, there was not a stray slip left in the specially marked baskets. Any of them.

The handwritten marginal comment with an illegible signature on a note that once accompanied one of the files also tells us that originally my father's appointment as division chief, along with the attendant rank and salary classification, should have been temporary to begin with, and so there's no reason to bother about either László Nádas's salary classification or his rank, wrote the chief bureaucrat with the illegible signature in the margin of the file. László Nádas is up for a more important post that the Prime Minister will decide about. I have no idea what this more important post that the prime minister didn't decide about or about which he changed his mind in midstream might have been. In any case, that's when the young man with the blond wavy hair and the sunny disposition must have installed the equipment they called a signal bell in our apartment on Pozsonyi Street. Ernő Gerő was still the minster, but not for long. Lajos Dinnyés was still prime minister, but not for long. With the help of the signal bell our father could get in touch with the various telephone exchanges, and even interrupt a telephone conversation. I found this very exciting. Clearly, he was talking with his colleagues or superiors, excuse this interruption, please, but I need to discuss something with you posthaste, and then a hair-raising sentence followed. Or the other way around. They called him. They interrupted our chats over the phone with my cousin Yvette twice, I remember this, too. Both times, I was flabbergasted. Someone had listened in, waiting for the end of the sentence, then said, I want to talk to your father. Yes, of course, what can I do for you, he'd say. I've studied the plans and I must call your attention to the fact that you need to work more on the blueprints of the throttle valve hookup with respect to the amplifier stations as well as the junction points. Kindly excuse me, but the last time I neglected to mention the number of loading coils for pupinization. I think we need more. And please don't forget that the sound frequency part of C2-D section must be completed independently of the corrosion inspection, but the sound frequency part of section B-C 2 must not be seen to until after the results of the corrosion inspection are known. Also, kindly remember that you must finish laying the cable conduits along the Chain Bridge and the southern bypass rail bridge by December, because we can't move the work up to the new plan year.

I loved standing behind him and listening to these completely unintelligible sentences.

Sometimes he waved me off. To make myself scarce. At such times he was talking to high-ranking military and secret-service officials. I snuck away, but I remember the specialist vocabulary to this day even without the meaning of the words. Twisted pair cable. I have no idea what twisted pair cables were, but it sounded good. Culvert. That's even better. Water needs a culvert, so why couldn't wired cables have culverts. Now I know what it means to connect something to the Lorenz machine, because I did some research. Kindly connect it to the Lorenz machine, if you don't mind, I'll obtain permission later. Which meant that they should tap a certain telephone line and, if need be, decode a telegram or the coded conversation, which meant that our father had had certain things connected to the Lorenz machine. I had no concrete knowledge of it, but it was no secret to me that a clandestine world of administration was working behind the visible world of administration, and that my father was also helping this invisible world function, and also, that it was clearly a lot more important than the public administration. I knew something that others know nothing about. No wonder I was curious, especially after my Uncle Sándor had given me a highly effective booster shot. The question was what secret knowledge our father had and against whom. For instance, in their language, accomplish meant you can go ahead and do it illegally. I'll bring the legal permission from the interior minister or the defense minister later. They were working with the German cipher machine whose coding and decoding function was cracked by a group from the British secret service in London prior to the bombing of Coventry, and from then on, the Nazi military had no secrets from the Allies. The Soviet secret service had the good sense to cart off the Lorenz machines from the territories they'd invaded right away, though after the Communist takeover, they may have returned some of them. And so, the division responsible for telecommunications was responsible not only for building up and operating telephone exchanges and telephone lines, it was also in charge of coding and decoding secret messages and tapping suspicious telephone lines. I see from documents that a top bureaucrat of the Interior Ministry whose name is not indicated and a certain Major General Béla Berczely of the Ministry of Defense must have issued orders to tap telephone lines that had come under suspicion and to decode telegrams and letters that seemed to include mysterious content. On the other hand, I don't know what boundary marker may have meant with respect to setting up telephone lines. In the secret service, they mark the place of a secret message with a boundary marker or on a boundary marker. I don't know what the technical difference is between a main station and an extension or substation, what cable earthing is or what on earth pupinization might be. I know that they place the coils underground in these impregnable containers, but I don't remember why they needed the coils.

Sometimes, when my father finished his say with the words whose meaning were a mystery to me, he'd ask if I understood, at other times he'd ask if we understood, which didn't make much sense, except this annoyed me no end, and I repeatedly called our father's attention to this anomaly; he listened, he reflected, he understood, and he was so well behaved, he tried to avoid this bad officialese habit, but then would revert to it again and again, and eventually I stopped asking. Of course, we should know that in this earlier world, the railways, the postal delivery services, and the telecommunications system were organized along military lines, and in line with the Prussian, meaning the monarchic order prevalent in state administration, its language of command was likewise military, which meant that colleagues were on friendly terms with one another only within the hierarchic circles; also, they called their work service, they'd gone into service, they'd come from service, they carried out orders; they used the familiar or formal mode of address with one another depending on their rank, meaning that those of equal rank used the familiar form of address with one another, while those under them addressed them formally.

A superior's decision was as good as a standing order.

Regardless of how it happened, I doubt that our parents moved out of Pozsonyi Street because that's what they wanted, meaning that they moved to the edge of the off-limits area, of all things, where only select people could go, of their own free will. The people of Pest called the Hill of Roses Cadre Hill and Pasarét Cadre Strip, but Svábhegy was so high up, the sarcastic vernacular of Pest couldn't even deal with it. They were probably moved there in the expectation of their upcoming positions, but in the last moment before they moved, like lightning out of the blue sky, their party changed its plans for them.

Our father wasn't appointed God only knows what after all, and they even canceled his present appointment, temporary to begin with.

It's even possible that in this great unexpected shifting of scene it wasn't our unpleasantly impersonal father who was to blame, but our mother with her popularity and her suicidal and dangerous sense of justice.

All this is merely speculation, of course; I'm working through the possibilities in public, whereas I know next to nothing about this great last act of their lives together.

Around this time a celebrated Soviet professor visited Budapest. I found this out, too, much later, because, confused by their sharp mood swings, I'd stopped asking my parents questions. He was an orthopedic surgeon, one of the illustrious heroes of Soviet science, as they said back then, which was not just a flurry of speech without a basis in fact, because these people bore the title Hero of Socialist Labor. I should remember the surgeon's name, but I don't, nor have I been able to discover it. He visited Budapest to introduce his Hungarian colleagues to his revolutionary method, how they should peform surgery on a dislocated hip, how they should replace the faulty hip bone with all sorts of irons and attach these to the hip bone with all sorts of bolts. He'd come for an exchange of ideas, one might say, and the exchange of ideas was an important aspect of the comradely concourse between the friendly nations. My aunt twice over, and almost my mother, the widowed Mrs. Miklós Nádas, born Erzsébet Tauber, had been lying for months in great pain at the orthopedic clinic on Karolina Street. As for the hero of advanced Soviet medicine, he demonstrated the surgery on her painful dislocated hip that for some time to come would be celebrated as a Soviet miracle of sorts.

When our mother and I visited her at the hospital, my Aunt Bözsi was radiant, she couldn't believe her good luck that this should happen to her. She was the talk of the hospital. Even Professor Zinner came to see her several times a day.

They may have offered a furnished villa to my parents at first, and perhaps that's why they got rid of just about all their belongings. There could hardly have been any other justification for their actions. Several of their acquaintances, friends, and comrades had already moved into deserted or confiscated villas. They'd take me along to see some of them, but I don't remember who. We went to a villa in Délibáb Street, and later to one all the way up on Sashegy that looked like an owl-haunted castle an industrialist must have built on the wild crags to look haughtily down on the city, and these comrades must have had at least three children, one of them was a boy with a shock of thick blond hair, the same age as I. He wanted to be an architect. At the time I couldn't decide whether I should become a dancer or an architect, like him, but be that as it may, we decided we'd study architecture together and set about designing a building right then and there with the building blocks his parents brought back from Moscow. Later he really did become an architect, except I don't remember his name. While I was attending the Lajos Petrik Technical High School, he attended the High School for Construction in nearby Szent Domonkos Street, which by then had been rechristened Cházár András Street, in honor of the former champion of public education. Sometimes we met and talked on the street or on the trolley. We also went to a neo-baroque villa in Fodor Street up on Orbánhegy, next door to Sándor Rendl's modern villa, where the neo-baroque came with a full staff of servants. The cook who'd stayed on with them was making them something amid a huge cloud of steam, she was boiling dumplings with parsley in a pot of water, she let me look inside, and with our hosts we also inspected the apartment of the caretaker, who'd stayed on as well. My parents were taken aback and protested meekly, but the new owners wanted to show us everything, they were inordinately proud of all the things that they now had. The comrades divided up among themselves what was left of the old order, its real estate assets as well as its other physical assets that they'd set their sights on or, if need be, confiscated. Our mother was averse, she felt squeamish and said so, in their circle, such things were not talked about. They opened the full linen closets and showed them all the things that the previous tenants, who fled their home in terror, had possessed. But our mother not only felt an aversion to the things that the new tenants were given by the Office of Abandoned Property, everything but everything according to the strictest inventory, as their hosts stressed, our mother voiced her disgust out loud, she made an aggressive show of it. I don't know why she didn't object when the Aranyossis moved into their house in Leányfalu in the same way. Guided by the herd instinct, people will tolerate a lot of things from those close to them. I don't know which sentence broke the camel's back, because I was at some distance when all hell broke loose. You enjoy putting your greedy hands on other people's belongings, our mother yelled. I don't know if they ever talked about such things with the Aranyossis. Possibly, it was her hosts' ostentatious display that irritated her.

Klára, dear, you're disappointing us. You shouldn't take everything to heart like this, Klára dear.

I'm sorry, but this makes me sick.

I'm going to ignore that, Klári. They were rotten bourgeois, Klári, tell me, why should I feel sorry for them.

We left Fodor Street without waiting for lunch. We left after the argument with the lady of the house ratcheted up in volume, when everyone was shouting, because the other guests, both the men and the women, tried to calm down the two warring factions, or at least hold them back a bit, because they were both screeching, and the others were afraid they'd fall on each other; red as a lobster, our mother was choking with rage, you could tell that her blondness was actually close to red, then she grabbed her coat and literally stormed out, and as for us, amid the indignation of our hosts and the other guests, shamefaced and silent, we followed in her wake. But I must admit that those dumplings looked fabulous in the pot as the water boiled along with them. To this day I am sorry I did not get to taste them.

But it's possible that our parents were supposed to serve abroad, and that's why they got rid of nearly all their possessions, and as for our Tauber grandparents, they may have had to give up their independence around that time because they wanted to move in with their daughter my Aunt Bözsi in Dembinszky Street to take care of her because, thanks to modern Soviet medicine, she could never walk again, and they either removed the pins from the irons or they put them back, or else they put new irons in some other place, ad infinitum.

They affixed the new iron to the old. This marked a great change for me, because they didn't take me to Péterfy Sándor Street anymore, but to my Aunt Irén in Damjanich Street, and my grandfather Arnold Tauber now took me to his sister in Wesselényi Street only on rare occasions, or to City Park, where he went to meet his friend.

Or possibly, my parents were merely acting according to the new Communist puritanism when, while waiting for a change, they decided to get rid of all their former possessions, thereby ridding themselves of the last telltale vestiges of the large Gömörsid estate that had the oppression of the poor to thank for its existence. They wanted to be true to their principles, and that was truly fair-minded of them. Except, their new surroundings proved excessive, at odds with their puritanism. They couldn't adjust. There they were among the rose beds and arbors, among the flower beds with their withered annuals, there they were among the blooming rock gardens in an extravagantly planted park crowded with botanical rarities, and they didn't know the names of the plants and they didn't know what they should or should not do with them. They didn't even have the necessary tools, and for some time, had no idea where they could get them.

Our father assembled a doghouse, and we lined it for our little dog.

Felhő Street also became important to me with time because the school's botanical garden was located there. The botanical garden had greenhouses. Outside the snow was still ankle-deep, but inside it was warm and misty, and I started my career as a plant cultivator, an interest I pursue even today, sowing seeds and separating young plants during my second winter on Svábhegy.

First I learned how to mark out a line and with what, how to work the soil, how to plant the various seeds, in which type of soil and how deep, and also how to hold them between my fingers, and also how they germinate, what a seed leaf is, how we should thin out or fill out the rows, and when the first real leaves appear above the seed leaf and when they are hardy enough, how to pull out the seedling and plant it in its new place so it can grow into a proper plant, and also, which plant likes being replanted and which suffers as a result. What should be sowed in place, and what should be grown from a seedling or planted outdoors as a small plant. The janitor came and said that anyone who wants to join the biology circle should go see our biology teacher, Judit Benkő, in the school garden after class, and this interested me a lot more than the literary circle. I had never seen Judit Benkő before. No one else volunteered except for me, and I don't know why I volunteered myself. I usually volunteered only when no one else did, to save the honor of the class, as we said back then, because I wasn't the volunteering type otherwise. I saw Judit Benkő for the first time when I opened the door of the greenhouse and she looked up at me. She waved a hand for me to come closer, and from then on I attended mostly to her hand and smile. She worked swiftly and to the point with that strange little smile on her lips, though sometimes she slowed her pace so I could follow what she was doing. She taught me how to handle a plant, and to this day, I work in our garden as if with her hand. She was a young woman, when I look at her former face as I'd stored it in my mind, she couldn't have been more than thirty, probably living on her own, and her solitude, as I look at her image, must have had its roots in history, I picked up as much with my sixth sense even back then. The siege remained an indelible experience. She wore a threadbare blue smock, under it ski pants, and she had on hiking boots with a pair of hiking socks folded back over them. During the post-siege winters, many people did the same. Even though she hardly spoke, Judit Benkő was not mute, except she rarely launched into explanations. Her silence reminded me a bit of my tight-lipped Tauber grandmother. She didn't speak unless it was necessary, she didn't say more than she had to, and I felt comfortable with that. She preferred to watch how I did things, everything I did, and if she wasn't satisfied, at most she showed me again. She was quiet but not timid, hers was the sort of quiet that one can't help but attend to. During class, too, her explanations were quiet, and I don't remember anyone taking advantage of that. Even the most wicked boys were a bit awed in her presence and behaved themselves. That little smile always perched on the corner of her lips, a smile that was painful and wry at the same time. She came in quietly and she left quietly. The children were somehow moved by her, and not just in class, but everywhere; she carried a strong aura with her in the corridors, we were under the spell of something that none of us understood. But let's not forget that the concrete always has less meaning for the mind than the abstract. They didn't talk about her behind her back either; no one knew anything about her, and it seems that no one dared make up stories about her either. Then after a while there were several of us in the gardening circle, perhaps six in all, mostly girls, but we didn't go every day, just several times a week in an established order; sometimes we'd even take turns and go on Sunday. The girls had to be on duty in pairs so they wouldn't be alone in the greenhouse or in one of the shacks. But the boy on duty could go to the school garden on his own. The greenhouse had to be heated twice a day, every day until March, in the morning and late afternoon; I volunteered to see to the heating on Sunday, saying that I lived nearby anyway. But sometimes the others would show up as well, or else Judit Benkő would unexpectedly show up from town. The manure had to be gathered by Monday. The water temperature had to be checked, the rows of saplings had to be carefully watered and sprayed, and this or that had to be pulled out making sure that the roots of the saplings shouldn't come free of the soil. I sat in front of the boiler, tended the fire, and listened to the silence.

Then at five minutes to eight I ran from there to school, and I must say that these early mornings before teaching began were miraculous.

My little dog sat in front of the school garden, and he ran home only when I entered the school building. He understood everything, there was no need for explanations.

The others could have had no idea of these miraculous early mornings, the development of the plants and their maturation, not even our parents.

Sándor Rendl died in February of the following year, when we were just about to start sowing. I was in the greenhouse, shoveling the fresh compost onto the raised beds. Our father came to fetch me and said I must go home on the double. I spotted him as he climbed up the steep hillside, emerging from the woods, I didn't understand what my father was doing there with that frightened expression on his face,

343

I didn't want to acknowledge him, I wanted him to go away, the fresh compost was more important, we made the compost ourselves, to this day I make compost the way I learned in the school garden, hasn't he got anything better to do, why won't he go away. But he didn't go away. Instead, he walked along the long garden path. He and Judit Benkő talked briefly and I could tell that he liked her, and that made me feel good. Sándor Rendl had suffered two angina attacks in quick succession, he was taken to St. John's Hospital, which we could reach even by foot along Diósárok Street, but according to the death summary, cerebral embolism was the direct cause of his death. Back then, they rarely succeeded in treating it.

In the evening we walked over to their house up on Orbánhegy.

But before I relate what happened there, I must first talk about all the things that happened to them two years previously, in the fall of 1950. Our parents told us only in part, sparingly, in code as it were; they couldn't keep it to themselves altogether because, after all, it happened in the family, which upset them, they were ashamed. Vera Rendl's father-in-law, Uncle Feri, meaning Ferenc Herczeg, at their apartment in Nagykorona Street which by then they called Alpári Gyula Street in honor of the Communist politician, and my aunt Magda Aranyossi was already busy collecting material for the monograph on Alpári she'd be publishing in ten years' time, when my brother and I had been placed in her care as our guardian and we shared an apartment on Teréz Boulevard, but there were still several months to go before after a late-night conversation I was to make a final break with my family once and for all, and when Teréz Boulevard was already called Lenin Boulevard and the house numbers, too, had been changed, though the people of Terézváros continued to call it Teréz Boulevard, by which I do not mean to imply that everything is related to everything else, but at this point in the text, history gets bunched up in my mind, it's like when they boil milk and it suddenly sticks to the bottom of the pan, because one thing is certain, namely, that on Lenin's recommendation, at the Third Congress of the Communist International, Gyula Alpári was appointed editor-in-chief of the official journal of the Executive Committee, the journal was first called *Inprekorr*, then *Internationale Presse-Korresppondenz*, then later, under the name *Rundschau*, it functioned as an international press agency and photography agency, meaning that it functioned as a cover organization; and Alpári edited it in various places, first in Berlin, then in Zurich, and finally in Paris, until in the tense weeks following the outbreak of the war he surprised Pál Aranyossi by suggesting that he hand over the editing of *Regards* to someone else, because the Party had redirected him to the French Communist Party, and that Aranyossi should take over the editorship of *Rundschau* from him, which from a professional viewpoint was not a favorable offer, but as orders from the Party, he had to accept it, and they consoled themselves by jocularly saying that he'd taken the baton passed to him by Lenin, until one bright morning in September 1939, he was arrested in the midst of a thorough search of his apartment only to be deported to Le Vernet d'Ariège; as for Alpári, he was arrested a year later by the Gestapo, he was conveyed straight to the concentration camp at Sachsenhausen, where they demanded that he describe the inner workings of the Comintern in writing in accordance with the Nazis' liking, but no living person would undertake anything of the sort and so he denied it and was shot, and later the men of the ÁVH, the Hungarian State Security Authority, showed up at the Herczegs' in the same apartment that had earlier belonged to Mór Mezei when it was still known as Kronengasse or Nagykorona Street to search the apartment, and his wife, Erzsébet Hegedűs, was not at home because she happened to be sitting at the National Theater with my Aunt Eugenie, where they saw Shakespeare's tragedy *Macbeth*, which had premiered that spring, and when just past eleven, Erzsike took her leave of Özsi, with whom they'd been friends since they were children, and she got out of the cab, and Özsi continued on her way to Dobsinai Street with the driver, she saw that the concierge had left the gate open, except he hadn't, he was sitting in the apartment as a witness to the house search, and by then, her husband was nowhere to be seen.

Ferenc Herczeg was first engineer of a textile factory. I'd met him perhaps twice, possibly three times before his arrest. As it later turned out, he'd been arrested because a high-pressure furnace had exploded at the factory, and they were investigating the possibility of intentional negligence or sabotage. Whether there were enemy powers behind the sabotage. But they talked about these enemy powers only for my sake, to put my mind at ease, but I saw that they didn't believe it themselves. Though his wife, Erzsébet Hegedűs, and his son, Tamás Herczeg, made inquiries, they never found out where he was being held or who had arrested him and why, whether he had a toothbrush and pajamas and what he was being charged with. Weeks went by. He was accused of sabotage, but no one in the family knew that. Dajmirka, *qui ne peut pas dire dormir*, may have known, and also his multilingual wife, Kató, both majors at State Security. Using his old police and public prosecution connections, Sándor Rendl also tried to find out what he could, except connections, or nexus, as they called back then, by which a murky business such as this could be clarified, were now a thing of the past. Back then, the sentence I fear you're mistaken, I have no nexus of any sort anymore was often heard in good bourgeois circles. Before his death, this may have been Sándor Rendl's last quiet attempt to save someone's life, but he was able to obtain only some bitter experience, if that, namely, that either he is mistaken, or the world has buckled around him. The network of relationships that for centuries had turned a place into a city no longer existed. The Communists had replaced the entire state apparatus, and so he couldn't obtain confidential information anymore. It was clear to the family that it was not a police case. There was no prosecutor and no legally appointed advisor. The public prosecutor would appear from behind the scenes only when the sentence was ready to be announced. But only if Uncle Feri were still alive. It was obvious that they should be looking for him at the ÁVH headquarters on Andrássy Boulevard, which was now called Stalin Boulevard, and not Andrássy Boulevard, in honor of the former Hungarian statesman and foreign minister of Austria-Hungary. They may be preparing a conspiracy trial against him like the conspiracy trial against Imre Geiger, the general manager of the Standard, and his alleged accomplices who had not conspired against anyone or with anyone, just as the

Communist Rajk had not done, nor Pug Nose, nor did they sabotage anything. Geiger was sentenced to death and executed.

They must approach their brother Dajmirka, Endre Nádas, he's sure to find out.

No one knew exactly what he was doing at State Security, because Dajmirka, *qui ne peut pas dire dormir*, never talked about it, *jamais, jamais*, as if he hadn't heard their questions; our father may have known because as I see now, their fields of specialization were connected here and there, but I know this only after an in-depth search of the archives; one thing is certain, only our father knew Dajmirka's official phone number and he could not share it with anyone in the family, this I remember perfectly well. He didn't tell Pista, because Teréz Goldmark was untrustworthy in their eyes, that bourgeoise goose gaggles indiscriminately, they said. The telephone number of Dajmirka's apartment on Verpeléti Street was also classified. If anyone in the family wanted to speak to Dajmirka during working hours, they got in touch with our father. The more loquacious members of the family assumed that Mrs. Endre Nádas, née Kató Elek, had her gift for languages to thank for her rank of major, and they snickered behind her back that her ladyship the major would end up learning Mongolian, too, in which case she might even make it to general. She was an impossible woman, that's for sure, an underhanded schemer, what's more, *noch dazu*, a coward. She was forever quacking, fuming, she was exasperated twenty-four hours of the day.

My Aunt Eugenie would never let on about how and where the meeting that went amiss occurred between them, and whether Kató was present, meaning, whether she wasn't the one to be blamed for the odious business, but we do know that Dajmirka, *qui ne peut pas dire dormir*, turned his sister away in no uncertain terms. He was not about to make inquiries. He was not about to ask anything of anyone. Surely, they had good reasons for arresting him, it's no use him making inquiries after a man like that, and he's not about to compromise himself by attempting it. He hopes Özsi understands. I can't think of too many things that my Aunt Eugenie wouldn't have understood. She could take the most absurd things in stride without batting an eye. Only their Aunt Záza, Erzsébet Mezei, could manage the same in the family, and their father, Mór Mezei. On the other hand, Ernő Mezei's slightest emotion showed on his face. The faces of the Nádases didn't remain neutral in such situations, their facial muscles trembled, the lines gave it away; their ever-present fear of what they saw as the state of the world etched itself into their gaze. My brother reacted to dubious or unpleasant news in the same way. On that particular evening, Dajmirka, the favorite son of Adolf Arnold Nádas, a major of the ÁVH state security forces, the little Hercules *qui ne peut pas dire dormir* whom his siblings hated so much when they were children, because of his privileged position they wished him dead, on the afternoon when our father came to the school garden to pick me up, went even further, if possible. When he learned about Sándor Rendl's death from our father, he immediately called his older sister from the office, and they exchanged a couple of neutral sentences regarding the death and the upcoming funeral, then Dajmirka asked his sister, he said as if as an aside, when he and Kató go to pay their condolences at Dobsinai Street that evening, Tamás, Vera's husband, shouldn't be present, so they shouldn't have to shake hands with him.

Given their position, the two of them, he and Kató, couldn't very well afford to make personal contact with the relatives of a person under investigation.

Which took gall, saying a thing like that. After all, Ferenc Herczeg was not under investigation, he was being beaten and tortured, they wanted to extract a confession from him about crimes he had not committed and couldn't have committed, he was supposed to confess to dealing with foreign powers, to divulging military secrets of which a gentleman living an ordered middle-class life could have had no inkling, and in order to satisfy these absurd requirements, in the end he implicated his best childhood friend, who had emigrated to Australia in the meanwhile, Australia was a good distance away, his bearing false witness couldn't hurt his friend there, but when the authorities realized that they must make do without recourse to foreign powers, that there are no hostile foreign powers and they hadn't succeeded in bringing a charge of sabotage against him, because he is so obviously innocent of the explosion, then, without officially bringing charges, without a court hearing and a sentence, they transferred him to the internment camp at Kistarcsa for an indefinite period of time, and it was from there that the family first heard from him after a full year had passed.

He promises, said Major Endre Nádas, whose job as head of the technical division was to supervise the proper functioning of the technical and engineering aspects of the diversified secret service organization, and as far as I can tell from the scant number of surviving files, he was in charge of the smooth-running of what you might call the operation, which is no small thing, in short, he promised they will keep their visit short.

He hoped his sister understood.

Eugenie answered, and perhaps for the first time in her life she said that she did not understand, and she couldn't expect her little brother to come and endanger their careers by visiting, but if they should do it just the same, naturally she'd see to it that Vera and Tamás were not present, she'd do it not for the sake of her little brother, but for their sake.

The grass was growing like mad, we didn't have a scythe, of course, and our father had seen men mowing, but he couldn't do it himself.

It's interesting, now that I think back on it, that although in a couple of years I learned the basics of growing flowers and vegetables and I also learned to inoculate and prune fruit trees, I learned to dig, rake, hoe, weed the lawn, fertilize, use compost, plant, replant, thin out, spray, pick the produce at the right moment, dig up roots with a spade, what's more, I even knew how to grow rice, and in my Aunt Magda's garden in Leányfalu, I got to practice gardening to my heart's content and on summer mornings I sometimes worked alongside her, and she was truly an experienced if reckless gardener, yet up on Svábhegy it never occurred to me to uproot the soil with a hoe, to pull out a recalcitrant weed, or pick up a pair of pruning shears. I can't even remember if we had pruning shears at home; theoretically we must have had because we had lots of roses, sweetbriars and shrub roses, we even had a rosc arbor that our parents hated so much that they disassembled it. I watched with stupifying indifference as this arboretum, planted according to no particular design, gradually fell into decay; in short, unflinching, yet not without a touch of curiosity, I watched my parents' desperate goings-on in the garden. They'd decide to launch into something, which for lack of gardening know-how or time they either never started or if they did start it, they immediately ruined everything, or else they couldn't finish it, in which case, whatever they'd started was sentenced to perdition.

All I know is that Rákosi ordered our mother to appear in Akadémia Street for a closed meeting. The meeting was about introducing a law on family planning, though those invited weren't informed beforehand. Rákosi greeted our mother with exceptional cordiality. He inquired after her sons. She had been awarded the Gold Medal of the Order of the Hungarian People's Republic during the spring of that year. It was one of the highest state awards. Possibly, they wanted to appoint her to a higher office, or her along with our father, I don't know. I don't know the exact date of the meeting either. Decades later, I learned from Valéria Benke, who was also invited to the meeting, that it took place years before the Draconian law that later became known as the Ratkó law went into effect, and I also learned from her that it was summer and very hot. At the meeting Rákosi told those present that the comrades in the Political Committee were dissatisfied with the birth rate, and he presented the dire consequences of the low birth rate for the national economy. Point by point, he also presented his demands for labor management. There was one striking absence, though, that of the minister for public welfare, Anna Ratkó, the aunt of Jóska Ratkó, the poet about my own age, and a bona fide cadre of the people. Her ministry was represented by one of her deputies. But it was soon clear to those present that because of the low birth rate the comrades were dissatisfied not only with Ratkó's activities as minister, but also with her person. Comrade Ratkó had no children either. Rákosi meant this as a jocular example, and he added that our best comrades don't take the dramatic decrease in the birth rate and its effect on the national economy seriously, and the members of the

Political Committee felt that this was not a proper Party attitude on the part of certain comrades. Which left no doubt in the minds of those present that they were planning to pull the ministry out from under Ratkó's feet, or may have already done so. As in so much else, there was no knowing now either what Rákosi was hiding behind what, or what he was compensating for with what. After all, those at the meeting knew that Comrade Rákosi's wife couldn't conceive either, even though they were doing their best, and they did it on the days on which Comrade Hirschler said they had the best chances of success, Comrade Rákosi even accompanied his wife to Comrade Hirschler for treatment personally, but to no avail. It was also clear to those in attendance that the members of the Political Committee, well versed in Marxist ideology, were embarrassed by the concept of public welfare. Social welfare was necessitated by inequality. But if the objective basis of inequality disappeared, after all, the means of production would now be in the hands of the working class, there was universal employment and unemployment was a thing of the past, in short, the regulation of questions pertaining to public welfare must be answered within a new framework, and the competence of the ministries must be reexamined accordingly. Hearing this, our mother was aghast, though the others in the room didn't catch on yet to what Rákosi was getting at. Valéria Benke, wearing one of her usual white blouses, was sitting across from our mother at Rákosi's long conference table on the second floor of Party headquarters at Akadémia Street, where, after his circuitous preamble, at last Rákosi presented his suggestions with respect to rigorous birth control. The number of medical abortions must be reduced to zero, the number of medical interventions must be reduced to zero, the use of contraceptives must be regulated. Until age forty-five, every woman capable of conception must not curtail her pregnancy. The only exceptions may be a health risk attested to by a doctor, or a direct risk to life. For the sake of the national economy, women had to bear children. If we don't make a law to this effect, and keep this in mind, Comrades, then we can't build communism, Comrades, because there won't be anyone to build it, Comrades. They also knew that Imre Hirschler had suggested that

Comrade Rákosi should have a sperm count, because in the interest of a proper diagnosis, we need to know, Comrade Rákosi, said Hirschler to the head of the Party, whether Feniochka is capable of conceiving, but we must also find out how things stand with Comrade Rákosi's own capabilities. From the point of view of treatment, we can't neglect the question of whether the sperm ends up reaching its destination. If they're too lazy and don't reach it, then it's no use treating Comrade Kornilova, Comrade Rákosi's dear wife, because she, Feniochka, will not conceive.

After Hirschler's third gentle coaxing, Rákosi very quietly asked the doctor what he needed to do, at which, without mincing his words, Hirschler said nothing could be simpler. He'll give Comrade Rákosi a special cup, Comrade Rákosi must take it to the bathroom and come back with a sample.

But how can you even imagine such a thing, dear Comrade Hirschler, Rákosi said, turning red as a lobster.

He'd rather not imagine it, Hirschler said, laughing, but surely, Comrade Rákosi has heard about such things before. Let's just say that you need to do it with your own hand. Touch and drain.

When decades later Hirschler related the story to me and said that he was the only person on earth who could talk to the Party chief like this, leaning out from behind the protective cover of his profession, he was overcome with elemental joy, infantile joy, infernal joy.

When Comrade Rákosi reached the end of his presentation and asked the participants of the meeting to kindly offer their opinion and Benke saw our mother's color rising, that she was losing her self-control and would cause a scandal as usual, she kept kicking her under the table, waving and signaling for her to hold her tongue, shut up, wait for her turn, our mother ignored her, and when Magda Jóború, her immediate superior and after Mrs. Rajk's arrest general secretary of the Democratic Alliance of Hungarian Women, finished her dip-lomatic circumlocution, our mother reached the end of her rope, as the otherwise very quiet Benke related it to me in the late seventies in the library of their house in Orló Street, and she enjoyed the tell-ing inordinately, I must say; in short, our mother, fuming with rage, literally shouted that in line with the simple folk saying and with her simple folk thinking, all she could say to Comrade Rákosi was, first the pigsty, then the pig.

At which point a profound silence ensued and only the noise from the square in front of Parliament could be heard in the meeting room in Akadémia Street, tram number 2 stopped, another started; because of the heat, the second-story windows had been left open.

At first, no one understood what this infuriated woman was talking about. Who was she, and besides, how does a woman like her end up here. No wonder they didn't understand. How were they to know that in the simple language of the folk, to which our mother had just referred, the bald-headed and obese Rákosi was referred to as a pig or a fattened pig.

What a thing to say.

Actually, Comrade Rákosi may have very well known what words the simple folk used with reference to his person.

How can anyone say a thing like that.

And by the time they understood what she meant and realized that they'd known the infuriated woman from way back, it was too late, the brutal sentences could neither be retracted nor blown away like a puff of smoke.

But what do you mean, dear Comrade Nádas, Rákosi asked with his shiny, obese, and sweetest possible smile once he caught on; after all, though he gave no sign of understanding her, he was a village boy himself.

Valéria and Ernő Havas's house was like one enormous library. I didn't go upstairs, but likely the upstairs, too, was filled with books. The evening I visited her, Benke was clearly still enjoying every one of my mother's onetime sentences. There was even some strange tremor to her voice when she repeated them, but it hadn't come with age. Her articulation was unusual. Possibly because when she was young she had to get rid of her dialect, though I can't be sure about that. It seemed to me that her enjoyment and great respect for our mother was tainted with the fear that never left her in all those years.

What I mean, Comrade Rákosi, is that we should approach the

task the other way around, first we must have a sufficient number of nurseries, kindergardens, and schools, we need lots of day-care centers, and in these day-care centers we need school kitchens, and in the kitchens potatoes, and we also need bunting and we need diapers, and they must first be manufactured and a steady supply guaranteed, first we need all the things we're missing, the pediatricians need sterile spatulas, Comrade Rákosi, to check if the child's little throat is inflamed, but they can't check now, because there's not a spatula to be had in the entire country, there's no ointment for their little bottoms, we need rubber panties, Comrade Rákosi, but for a population increase of this magnitude, first and foremost, we need plenty of accommodations, midwives and childbirth assistants, but first they have to be trained, and we need to organize a network of health professionals, district by district, because we want to see a decrease and not an increase in infant mortality, we need vaccines and production capacity, and definitely not the other way around, Comrade Rákosi, that's what I meant, Comrade Rákosi, and I must insist on this order, Comrade Rákosi, at least in the name of the Budapest organization, she said, raising her own lobster-red head in defiance. The lack of care and supply centers is especially glaring in the countryside, the number of children's accommodations are not even sufficient to allow women to go back to work now, in the bigger cities, at any rate. Apart from the rotten cabbage, the rotten turnips, and the rotten tomatoes, more is called for in the school kitchens, Comrade Rákosi, and not only at the Party resort in Aliga by the lake, she said as Benke related it, because the Party resorts annoyed her, we should be able to supply the nurseries and kindergartens at least with fruit and vegetables, who among the comrades have seen a single lemon and when, if so, kindly raise your hand, unless in the buffet downstairs, and then I haven't even mentioned the right of women to self-determination, which I would be loath to leave out of the equation, dear Comrade Rákosi. If we leave the right of women to self-determination out of the equation, the angel makers and medicine women will be back in a flash with their hot baths and long, big knitting needles, but we mustn't play with women's lives in this irresponsible manner, must we.

In which case I understand now what Comrade Nádas meant by the pigsty and the pig, Rákosi cut in, seeing that our mother would have gone on and on. At the time, people like her were convinced that the problem was that the dictator didn't know about this or that. The news of the anomalies hadn't reached him yet. His evil advisors kept it from him. He has to be given it straight. Unless he is mistaken, Comrade Nádas feels that the law is somewhat precipitous, Rákosi said to our red-cheeked mother as he smiled steadily, but that's why we're here, Comrades, then he ordered a recess so the comrades could reflect on these serious questions together and come up with concrete suggestions for a solution. *Concrete* was his favorite word. With him, everything always had to be concrete. The comrades had to concretize their reflections nonstop so that they could give concrete shape to their prevarications and fatuous approvals. Our parents didn't understand this for a long time to come, but I understood early on that in their language, concepts don't always mean what they mean. That's why he asked them, he didn't ask them to come with complaints, he didn't ask them to sing arias of complaint, but to speak openly, like comrades, about concrete matters that the Political Committee had already discussed in detail; but then, nothing must stand in the way of comradely discussion. Let's examine what is to be done, Comrades, concretely, let us be concrete.

As soon as they got up from the table, the others chided our mother in no uncertain terms. They scolded her, they hissed like serpents, how could she do it. Zealous secretaries had opened the large French doors by then and there stood before them the richly laid table in the adjoining room. I could tell anyone at any time what was on a table like this. The sight must have been the straw that, so to speak, broke the camel's back. Not only could our mother not look at a richly laid table ever again, she had become constitutionally averse to the forms of continual prevarication around her, she didn't know what to make of the forms terror had taken. Her body warned her that there was no continuing on this path, and it rebelled. She was literally full of bile, her gallbladder pained her, and so did her back.

In the language of the movement, they called terror and all its small, hellish dictates voluntarism, which had nothing in common with the word's original, theological meaning, but as far as that goes, concrete didn't mean what it meant either; as opposed to those who opposed terror *en bloc*, they thought of it as revolutionary terror, thereby using the spirit of Jacobinism to legitimize the dictator's every wish. Without Marat and Robespierre, the flames of revolution would have been extinguished. One might say that she couldn't stomach Comrade Rákosi's radicalism, in short, the form terror had assumed, even if basically, she approved of his intentions. These were the two millstones offered to our parents. They were free to be ground between them. They wanted something, but never like that. They considered the error of the system an error in style. They wanted the same things, but they wanted them differently. They took their historical samples, their storehouse of concepts and analogies, from the wrong place, and they were judicious and unselfish. They insisted on their revolutionary asceticism. But they should have looked for partners for their admirable demand, which I can only approve of, in free nature, and since they found no such partners even in their most intimate circle of friends, after all, such people do exist in free nature, except they are as rare as a blue moon, our mother's behavior became more and more erratic. As a child, I didn't understand this. Later I thought that their ideas were shortsighted. But neither of them was shortsighted. None of us can ignore the idea of social equality. Without ideals and utopias, a person will perish. Once he can't do with his rationalism and pragmatism anymore, he might regress and turn to mysticism and magic, but his path back to the animal world is now cut off. Also, there hovered in front of them the myriad of individuals who always want more for themselves than what they can possibly consume, and admittedly, it would be a daunting task indeed to create a universe of equality with people who not only insist on private ownership, they want more of it. They kept referring to the masses of whom their party was supposed to be the embodiment, but these masses also kept wanting something different all the time than what their party wanted. The recess, too, seemed to drag on.

A disconcertingly long time had passed, but Comrade Rákosi did not come back, everyone felt awkward, and then Ferenc Donáth, who led the general secretary's office until, just a couple of months later, he was arrested for conspiracy, appeared in the corridor, and as he passed by, and as if by way of an aside, he told one of the comrades who happened to be smoking out in the corridor that Comrade Rákosi is sorry, he is otherwise engaged, the meeting is postponed, and he continued along the empty corridor with his empty fate. His wife, Éva Bozóky, was locked up in the internment camp at Kistarcsa, their child was conveyed to Emmy Pikler's orphanage in Lóczy Street.

The deadly silence was fixed in place around our mother when the participants of the meeting emerged from the Akadémia Street building and their drivers pulled up to collect them and to convey them back to their elegant headquarters, and so they stopped berating her. I witnessed similar scenes at their various headquarters, theater lobbies, and the opera. When their drivers showed up, the comradely mannerisms were suddenly finished, there was no more diplomatic double-talk, there were no more smiles, laughter, and playacting among the comrades, they were on guard, and if the smallest mistake occurred, they turned into pillars of salt, because from the order of their departure, the hissed orders and interjections from the attendants, the make and date of the manufacture of the cars, everyone understood where their place was and what they were entitled to or not entitled to within the nomenklatura, and also, what they must do not only to keep the power they had, but to forge ahead, up to the top. It was obvious to everyone that under the circumstances, if she continued to insist on equality and fraternity while serving the strict hierarchy of which she herself was a part, our mother was the crazy one, and not they.

My consciousness rejected this manner of self-deception; for years to come, I didn't know what to make of these scenes or experiences, where to deposit them in my consciousness; I witnessed them, but failed to make sense of them. Our mother wanted to behave differently in situations such as these, except she couldn't, because there was just one reality, and not one for them and one for her.

Small planning committees, near-invisible people, light little women and swarthy men, were in charge of the proper order and rhythm of the leave-taking, which was not easy, because for reasons of security the cars either had to head back to the Party garage in Kárpát Street or, isolated and without attracting notice, wait on one of the side streets. Her ugly and insignificant little Pobeda came for her, too, and conveyed her to the small white marble palace in Múzeum Street. She insisted on this, that it shouldn't be another car, just this ugly little Pobeda, and later an even junkier car. She put up with the silence of her exclusion with good cheer and discipline, but to her dying day she could not break through the wall or alleviate the tension that she herself created between her ideals and her experiences. Meanwhile, they had removed Anna Ratkó from her post, they pulled her ministry out from under her when smack in the middle of ever-growing mass poverty, they got rid of the Ministry of Public Welfare, but she was given the Department of Health, where she was free to realize her party's dictates with respect to birth control.

Possibly even more people were now enthusiastic about our mother, and they were even more enthusiastic than ever before, though they couldn't have been on really close terms with her; they appreciated her keen intellect and said that she could always be relied on to find the key to any situation; also, she was forthright and determined. Still, they were guarded when they called her; they had no intention of slamming the door in her face, but tried to keep their distance, and in their truly humble manner, the two of them, our mother and our father, opted to retreat into the profound emptiness that now surrounded them. From then on they did not visit Valéria Benke and Ernő Havas in Lóránt Street for tea or coffee, and Benke and Havas did not come over to our place in Gyöngyvirág Street, and their oldest friends kept their distance as well. Kari Tóth, Sanyi Kerekes, and Jani Asztalos called from time to time to arrange a meeting, but they never managed to meet, the spirit of the terror that they called Jacobin hovered over them, the frightful ghost of being accused of factionalism hovered over them, the heavy load that they'd salvaged from their time in illegality hovered over them, never to be fended off. In order to keep up certain relationships, they'd sometimes send us to celebrate the birthdays of their friends' children, which I hated, but my brother entered Creation happy with everything in it and so we could hardly drag him home from these obligatory dates; or else these friends took us hiking with their own children, but our parents didn't go along, they didn't want to compromise their friends. It was all so shameful, enough to make you want to cry. Factionalism would have wreaked havoc with Party unity and would have made it possible for informers to wheedle their way into their ranks, and for the enemy to cause contention among them. This was the basic formula that they carried over from their time in illegality underground, this chimera of contention. They had to beware of factionalism just as a priest had to beware a deadly sin or the Devil's holy water. Satisfying their basic human need for human contact, the political community or alliance of like-minded people, was out of the question, once and for all.

Our mother's funeral may have been the first quiet political demonstration, possibly an early barely perceptible instance of a political demonstration that could be understood as such, if only among her comrades. But among them, definitely. Her comrades understood. They must have known what had brought them to our mother's funeral. They couldn't very well say that it wasn't the death of this particular Klára, they wouldn't have dared admit it even to themselves. The personality of the deceased must have surely played a part, but this many people couldn't have known her that well. It must have been the news of her openness, the reality of the loss of openness and honesty smack in the middle of the dictatorship that had brought them together. The real reason that brought such an immense crowd to the cemetery at Farkasrét with their immense number of wreaths, bouquets, and solitary flowers was declared publicly in the region only thirteen years later, when a small group of Czech and Slovak intellectuals began envisioning socialism with a human face, and Mrs. Dubček was busy packing in Bratislava so they could move to Prague with the new slogan and so that at long last Alexander Dubček should be able to say the unthinkable in public. This was the last great attempt of the Communist world movement to save itself. Dubček wanted to make the Russian comrades understand that we honestly didn't want anything else, Comrade Brezhnev, all we want is socialism with a human face. Fools that they were, they didn't realize how scandalous their statement really was. Taken literally, socialism with a human face meant that the socialist societies as we know them were inhuman and Comrade Brezhnev was a colossal ass. And then, at the secret crisis meeting held in the presidential railroad car on a siding in Čierna, in order to give weight to his counterargument, Comrade Brezhnev gave Comrade Dubček a horrendous slap in the face. Comrade Dubček and his men had forgotten to take their slogan out from under the magic spell of their own thief's Latin. On the other hand, it couldn't have been done. Had they succeeded in doing so, they'd have had to call for free elections, in which case, they, along with their human-faced socialism, would have drawn the short end of the stick and the breach in the dike would have flooded them with a free-market economy or, as Marx put it in his excellent essay "The Eighteenth Brumaire of Louis Bonaparte," they'd have remained in the same old rut. They even managed to realize, though truth to tell, only the philosophers of the New Left realized, that Marxism does not provide an exegesis of the world and it is not a philosophy, Marx himself had protested against any such thing, he didn't want to be turned into an "ism," may God forgive him; nor does Marxism provide an anthropology or an ethics, despite the fact that Engels entertained some thoughts on the origins of the family while Lenin came up with a truly half-baked idea about human eroticism that he wrote about to the unhappy Rosa Luxemburg; probably, Marxism is a viable market theory, it describes the basic characteristics of capitalist economy, but its methodology is incapable of providing a description of socialism even as we know it, because it describes neither the inherited nor the acquired characteristics of the individual, and as for mankind's orientation toward the mythical and magical, it leaves this out of the equation altogether. Our mother had no theoretical insight at all, she would have been incapable of it, her education was very limited, her rhetorical gifts were solid, that's true, but she did not find, nor could she have found, a clever slogan for her humble, basic human needs. The public at large was not affected by what they were cooking up with their friends or between themselves in the language they had fabricated during their time in the illegal Communist movement, meaning all the things they were keeping from each other for decades, and how silence had become an organic part of their communication. Even if they were fed up with the brutality of their mutual silence, it was always the other's silence they were fed up with and not their own; they kept accusing, judging, slandering each other, because they thought that if this week they could still regard the error of the system as personal error, they would be able to salvage their ideals and utopias for yet another week, and so they were quick to find a scapegoat for everything. The serial murders and mass killings, kept under a taboo and later referred to as illegal actions, were not to the liking of most, that's true, and yet they kept quiet about these as if they'd done the deed themselves. They didn't talk about it, or else, they talked about it only metaphorically. They had plenty to keep silent about. With the putsch against the rule of law, they had opened a new chapter in the history of inhumanity and continued writing it with their terror. To the letter, this was their slogan, they must follow the orders of their infallible party to the letter. They'd have had to shake themselves free of something that they had done themselves, because without terror, their conceptions could not be realized.

Time and time again, our mother gave me colorful demonstrations of this absurdity.

Regardless of when Stalin died, in the morning or in the afternoon, when I heard the news, for the first time in my life I had a comprehensive image of the world, a daydream, a vision about the state of my own consciousness, a sharp, concrete image of the earth's surface with its forests and fields and rivers as seen from above, perhaps from an airplane. I must have seen aerial photographs in old newsreels, especially aerial warfare and explosions down below seen from fighter planes, but back then, aerial photographs were rare. When I heard the news, Moscow with its illustrious dead suddenly appeared in the center of the magical foldout map in my head. Budapest was in its place, and Paris, Prague, Stockholm, and even fabulous Luleå were in their proper places on the foldout map in my mind, and so were Rome, Belgrade, and Warsaw, and Madrid, too, with its civil war siege, and Le Vernet with the Pyrenees, and Buchenwald, Sobibor, Theresienstadt, and Oradur-sur-Glane, and Lidice, Hiroshima, and Nagasaki; we could get Lisboa, meaning Lisbon, on our big broadband radio now and then, but despite the fact that I'd read in the *Social Lexicon* that the Portuguese colonies came under the influence of British capital and that's how Lisbon lost its former significance as a colonizer, it had no place on the universal map in my mind, and despite the fact that I also read in the *Social Lexicon* that without its colonial empire, London disappeared the same way in its own thick Dickensian fog, a terra incognita in terror's geography, London too was missing; but the map contained all the small human nests, habitations, and local government seats approachable only through trackless wastelands or lying under a relentless cover of snow, Tomsk, Kursk, Tula, Kaluga, Oms, Kazan, Vologda, Tobolsk, and so on, whose names in Russian literature the authors would sometimes indicate only with an asterisk or a single letter, from which it is immediately clear that the author is about to relate a secret story about magical places where in his flower-printed tailcoat Chichikov would arrive in his britchka with his peculiar-smelling gentleman's valet to spend the night in a smoky and noisy inn where you couldn't see the pattern on the peeling wallpaper because of the fly droppings, and also far-off Kamchatka, they were all there individually, Kolyma was not yet on it with Varlam Shalamov, who wrestled with the mightiest of the gods, but the universe of the Gulag was on it with Solzhenitsyn, and also Kistarcsa, where they'd taken Tamás Herczeg's father, and as an even darker spot, Recsk, whose name was synonymous with death, and where they'd taken the poet who had translated Villon's poems into Hungarian, and whose translations my cousin Yvette and I couldn't admire enough, the poet's name was György Faludy, these were the Hungarian internment camps people knew about from hearsay. I didn't know what was happening in the camps, and when I heard the news, I broke into tears, though it would be more correct to say that I broke into tears because of the daydream, my witnessing the breadth and width of the universe. Stalin can't be dead, the universe can't be wounded like this. Our mother looked on aghast. She didn't say anything, she didn't touch me, but there was something compelling in her silence. I couldn't understand what she wanted. She wanted to stop me. Our father, as helpless as ever in face of any strong manifestation of emotions, watched me cry with something more like curiosity. You might say that I found myself alone in the family with my shock over Stalin's death. My Grandfather Tauber, Arnold Tauber, also remained as neutral as possible in face of what had happened. I asked Grandmother Tauber, Cecília Nussbaum, to give me some black material, she must have some in her rag bag, because the school's bulletin board was red even the following day. It can't stay like that. She found only an old black slip. I cut this slip into pieces, I picked out the stitches and removed the lace trimming, and covered the school's bulletin board with it. I seem to remember that I even wrote a short piece about Stalin's death. No one said anything, but our father's countenance seemed to indicate a modicum of satisfaction because of my crying, good, his son is crying. Our mother acted as if she were averse, as if she were disgusted by what she and my father had inculcated or conjured in me. This was the great quandary of their lives. On that day and the days to follow, and finally, on the day of Stalin's funeral, the same quandary made its appearance among my classmates. No, the wheel of time had not stopped in its tracks, the event was not quite as seismic as I had imagined. The clocks continued ticking to the usual rhythm. The visible world acted out a ritual around the dead man, but the world's axis did not break in two, and probably, the earth would continue to revolve around the sun, in which case there is something not quite right with the profound depth of my alarm and vision, its hypocrisy, mimicry, in which case there's something here once again that I fail to understand. I was being confronted with my own hypocrisy. Some of my classmates had said even earlier that Stalin was guilty of post office robbery, but I had no way of checking the trustworthiness of their contention; I wouldn't have dared ask my parents or anyone else if Stalin had in fact robbed post offices in his younger years, but I saw with my own eyes how they enjoyed trumpeting it abroad. Thief. Thief. They said the word with something akin to sensual pleasure, thief, that the post office thief has finally bit the dust. Whereas the simplest solution would have been to ask my parents. Of course he robbed post offices, they'd have said, how else would he have gotten the money for the Bolshevik movement. Because of this post office thieving I read two books that I've kept to this day. One was an official biography written by a whole workers' team, the other was an oversize book, *Stalin's Life in Pictures*. There was no mention of robbing post offices in either of them, nor could I find any mention of it in the *Social Lexicon*; on the other hand, they said that Stalin had attended a Church school, which puzzled me. If he's a Bolshevik, how can he be attending a Church school, whereas their answer would have been very simple to this as well; today I'd answer myself in my mother's voice, saying the only way he wouldn't have become a Bolshevik is if he hadn't attended a Church school. Otherwise, he may never have realized that their explanations about the world were false. It's that simple. But then, that's just why I didn't ask them; I didn't want to hear an answer whose logic was just fine, and yet I wouldn't have known what to make of it.

Still, I cautiously asked Székács where he got this idea of the post office thief from. He shrugged and said, it's common knowledge.

And by the time I caught on to what I didn't understand before, the colossal mimicry, our mother had had her first surgery; they'd amputated her breast in the middle of September, she lay in the surgical ward of the hospital on Kútvölgyi Street until October 3, and I walked along Diósárok Street to the hospital with the dry biscuits I'd made for her from sponge cake. How I managed to get eggs to make the sponge cake is another story. She hadn't quite recovered yet when in the first days of the New Year she was asked to organize the May Day parade, which she considered a great honor. From that moment on we didn't see her for months, and my brother could cry and howl to his heart's content. Our father didn't see her either. Proceedings were already under way against him in the ministry for misappropriation of funds, embezzlement, he literally broke down under the accusation, his bad back stooped under the weight, his nose grew to a point, he looked at the world with terror in his eyes. He remained like that until he died, he kept losing weight, he grew thinner and thinner, his body increasingly angular, tense, but he still had to scrape through 365 days of at least five more years. Embezzlement, this is all I could make out of their earlier whispered exchanges. At times they blend into one, at others they stretch into the infinite. *Embezzlement.* Just this one word. And once again, I didn't understand anything. And to tell the truth, I didn't want to. In my mind, embezzlement did not belong to any naturally occurring phenomenon or concept. I sensed its sinister content, I was familiar with the phenomenon from literature, but with respect to my father, I had nowhere to shove the thought of embezzlement down in my mind. I also realized that his friends were turning away from him, and he couldn't defend himself on his own. He became manic in the clinical meaning of the word, he became manic in the way the Greeks represent manic behavior in their mythological stories; the gods punished him with never-ending restlessness and gave him no pause, and from then on, with the exception of our mother's illness, he cared only about his truth, only his truth. He went in its wake. He called Kari Tóth to no avail. He called her again and again. Which he had never done before; after all, his upbringing was really good, but now he was a burden on everyone, he shoveled the food into his mouth so he could get it over with as soon as possible and be free to go in pursuit of his truth, seek justice for himself. Berczely would not see him. Bebrits would not see him. Go see Gerő. Gerő is sorry, he is otherwise engaged, says Kerekes. Gerő wouldn't see him. He chewed loudly, he chomped wildly at the table, eager to swallow his food so he could go write his appeals. He leaned into his soup so he could shovel it in as quickly as possible, then raised the plate to his lips so he could quaff what was left, he threw etiquette to the wind so he shouldn't have to waste time with a spoon. As a result, my brother's table manners couldn't be kept on the straight and narrow anymore either. Theoretically, this too would have been my job. They kept complaining that I wasn't paying enough attention to my brother. You're the older one, it's your duty. I couldn't live up to it. He followed in the wake of our father, who was no longer himself, he wolfed down his food, he slurped, chomped, while our mother seemed oblivious, she seemed not to have seen or heard what was going on. Kerekes said he'd call him back, but he didn't. Dedics wouldn't see him either. Today Jancsik yelled and told him that he shouldn't fuck with him. Nádas, stop fucking with me. No wonder I ran away from home one Sunday afternoon when it suddenly hit me that people were talking to my father like this. Jancsik, his superior, said to him not to fuck with him. Where else could I have gone, I went to the movies, and Géza Székács and Gábor Baltazár came along, and his younger sister Éva came along, too, and others, too, lots of people whom I can't remember anymore. There were more and more of us as we headed for the cinema. Not only did my dog come along, but other dogs as well. Gábor Baltazár also had a dog. Back then, no one on the hill would have thought to curb their dog. Up on the hill the dogs ran off wherever they wanted. I later saw a similar miracle in Rome, but that wasn't the Rome of mass tourism yet. During the mating season, they sometimes formed packs and fought horrendous battles. They may have been competing for the female of the species, but at times fighting fever got the better of the pack, and the female dogs would slink away with their tails between their legs or else they also got caught by the fever and joined the fray.

There was much snow that winter as well and howling wind and biting cold as we climbed up over the Swiss Steps to the top of the hill. They were showing a stupid Soviet movie that day in the hot and smelly movie house, a comedy, possibly *Kossacks of the Kuban*, I'm not sure, some nonsense. They were continuous showings, the show didn't let up, the lights were not turned on. When the last reel had wound down, they right away started projecting the first. It was great fun watching films like this. You could go in at any time and you came out when you got bored. You could do it for the price of a single ticket. Smack in the middle of the revolutionary terror, this was the be-all and end-all of freedom. The others had gotten bored long since, they'd left, but I was still sitting there watching that shit, because I didn't want to go home, ever again. I wanted to run away. I was going to see this film one more time, and then I was running away. I had my ankle boots on anyway. Possibly, that was the first time I noticed how precisely memory retains visual images. Even this shit didn't bore me because I could discover details in the visuals I'd already seen repeatedly, details I hadn't noticed before, and this experience made me realize the infinite character of discovery and research.

The cinema was up on the top of the hill, it had formerly been on Melinda Street but was now on Rege Street. This is where the city with its last lamps ended. Then came the snowed-in forests, the rapid slopes under Normafa, the Observatory and Bell Meadow. I'd have had to take just a couple of steps to disappear from their lives. I watched the film three or four times from beginning to end, I was preoccupied with discovering still more details, and it must have been near midnight when I reached home in the snowstorm, frozen half to death, but satisfied. I hadn't run away today, after all. I'd run away once the snow had melted. All the lights were on in the house. As soon as I entered, I found myself face-to-face in the hall with my mother. She struck me. You animal, I shouted back at her. By then my father had also appeared. He struck me, too. He hadn't hit me before either. But this first slap of his turned out so horrendous that I literally flew into the air and slid across the hall. In mid-flight I knocked over the small telephone stand and crashed against the wall so that all the objects on the stand fell on top of my head. I screamed and screamed, you animals, you animals. I found out only years later that they were about to call the police. I didn't tell them, and they didn't know that I had left, they didn't know when I had left, they didn't know where I'd gone, they called everyone they could think of, they noticed my absence when they put my brother to bed, they couldn't find me with anyone they'd called, the cinema had never occurred to them, possibly, they didn't even know that I spent my pocket money every week going to the movies, they'd walked all over the snowy neighborhood, they'd shouted after me in the stormy dark, they became alarmed because a couple of months previously a sex maniac who was later caught and hanged was running amok in parts of Buda. Needless to say, news of this nature was kept back by the official news agencies and was spread through hearsay, if that, though even if I'd known about it, I wouldn't have understood anything; for a long time, the word *sex* meant nothing to me, even when I read it in a poem; the last sex killer in my consciousness originated with coalition times; also, my parents told me that thanks to communism, all crime would disappear.

Besides, they never objected before if I went anywhere on my own. I went to the school garden in the early morning when it was still dark to heat up the greenhouses before school started, and theoretically, this could have been dangerous as well. Our mother also left early in the morning, first she went for radiology and a blood test, she went for a probe, catheterization, draining, or God knows what, they removed the drain, they inserted the drain, they drained her because she wouldn't heal, her damned wound kept filling with pus, they kept changing the dressing, after which she disappeared in the labyrinths of organizing the nation, she went to Csepel, she went to Csongrád, she went to Szeged, she went to Székesfehérvár, she went to Sátoraljaújhely, she didn't even come home the next day or as her own shadow, only late at night, sometimes in the middle of the night. Sometimes we'd see her again only on the morning of the third day. Our parents were like shades, like spirits. My brother started wetting his bed, which made our lives even more miserable. Every day a new sheet. A rubber sheet, but the urine ended up all over the place, either the duvet cover got wet or the duvet soaked it in. His mattress smelled. After a while, our room smelled as well. It was no use waiting for our parents to wash the duvet and the duvet cover, I washed them as best I could, I hung them up, I dried them on the lukewarm radiators, I gave him new sheets and duvet covers. If his loud moaning reached my consciousness, it was best to wake myself up that instant. When his moans startled me out of my sleep, it was best not to ignore it but to leap out of bed as quickly as possible and take him outside, because at such times the poor thing was struggling with his urinary reflex, he must have been wrestling with monsters in his dream, basilisks, pythons, he let out horrible groans, and if I failed to jump out of bed into the ice-cold night, if I failed to reconcile the useful and the unpleasant in my mind, I went back to sleep right away, and it would have been no use climbing out from under the covers later, he couldn't hold it back that long. I realized that the trick was to jump out of bed and grab him before his last moaning or groaning. It seemed best that I should sleep half awake, and eventually I accustomed myself to sleeping like that all my life. But it wasn't enough to take him outside, because he didn't wake up from his sleep. I had to face this brand of sleepwalking every blessed night. If I didn't pull down his pajama bottoms when we reached the toilet bowl, if I didn't hold or put his weenie into his hand, if I let him out of my hands by his bed or in the middle of the hall so he'd go on his own, if I didn't hold his shoulder, his arm, his neck, if I didn't support him, or just stopped talking to him, if I stopped nudging him, let's go, let's go, don't stop, if I didn't explain, we're heading for the toilet, Palika, we're still in the hall now, just hold it in, don't let it out, then as we walked, in his sleep, he peed into the big wide world, meaning that it started running down his pajamas. Which means that on some level of consciousness, he knew what was happening, he even sensed what he was supposed to do, yet whether he stood still or was walking, he slept seemingly unperturbed. I've been a light sleeper ever since. Still, from time to time I had my revenge. I wouldn't leap out of my warm bed, the house was freezing until the summer, it was sweltering outside but ice cold inside, I'm not getting up, let him pee in his bed for all I care. I'm going back to sleep in my nice warm bed. Except, the blissful revenge came with a hefty price tag. The next day I had to wash his pajamas, his sheet, his rubber sheet, the mattress cover or the mattress itself as best I could, and even so, the room we shared smelled awful.

It takes urine just a few hours to sour. But learning to sleep lightly had its advantages. Had I not learned to sleep lightly as a child, then after a decade and a half, in Kisoroszi, I couldn't have performed and successfully completed my own Freudian and Jungian self-analysis. It had one condition, that I manage to do three things simultaneously in my sleep, to dream, meaning that my consciousness should proceed along its own natural system of connections in a spontaneous and uncontrolled manner while I make note of it, meaning that I follow the workings of my own natural system without any adventurous literary demands and remember the incidental elements and occasional points of reference, and let's add, these added up to thousands of elements and points of reference so that the natural system of connections got all jumbled, in short, this was the structural diagram that constitutes the upper layer of dream work, the topography of the dream venture or, to resort to Freudian terminology, the dream edifice. This structure functions as a waste heap, throwing a barrage of images our way every night. Some of its components are neither objects nor linguistic elements but emotions, affects and abstractions, in short, objective references to the elements of the psyche. Forms. I needed the light sleep so that after waking, I should be able to examine this mass of objective and abstract apparitions with all their attendant visual and symbolic elements, in short, so that the process of dreaming should be available to the conscious mind. As a child and a young man this is the road I embarked upon, or happened upon; this was the only way I could remain in this world, or to put it another way, this analytic path saved me from the nagging and profound urge to kill myself. My life has had no meaning. At least, I haven't found it to this day. In my case, light sleep became the sole condition for satisfying the life instinct. It is a human faculty we all share, except we don't always make use of it. All mammals sleep lightly. We learn to surrender to the luxury of deep sleep only thanks to civilization. If it is called for, anyone can take advantage of light sleep, in which case the order of importance is switched around. The more intelligent a person, the easier it is for him to sleep the light sleep of beasts.

By then no car came to pick her up, she always hurried to the Gyöngyvirág Street stop of the cog railway in order to catch it, and so we walked together in the early morning dark for a short stretch, because after we parted, I continued on through the Braun Woods so I could start heating the greenhouses before school began and maybe also see Lívia Süle in Felhő Street. Hédi Sahn also lived on Felhő Street, the girl who mercilessly snatched me away from Livi Süle, this is how they, the girls, put it, though I hardly noticed the subterfuge and the attendant dramatic change, the snatching away, this great leap in my love life. Hedvig Sahn was not as shy as Lívia Süle, and so I had no qualms about her either. We talked for each other's sake the whole day. If she wanted me to touch her beautiful breasts, I touched them, if she wanted me to comb her hair and kiss her neck, then I combed her hair and kissed her neck.

I found out only decades later what pain I caused Lívia by doing so.

As I now conjure our mother's tired gray face, her shrunken, sagging figure, I also see that this may have been the mightiest effort of her life, it wasn't tailored to her, it wasn't tailored to anyone, but despite her illness, she was bent on solving something entirely on her own, despite her illness, she wanted to save communism by organizing this upcoming May Day parade, whereas it couldn't have been unearthed from its ruins even if her friends had not deserted her and she hadn't been left alone with her heroic but ridiculous endeavor.

On the day of the parade she organized that year, the entire country was on its feet at dawn. Which sounded good. This is how the papers put it, this is how the radio put it, but it was obviously untrue. The eager beavers, the demented, the bootlickers, the ass lickers, were on their feet, the careerists were on their feet, the opportunists were on their feet, or those hundreds of thousands whom the draconian rules of their workplaces coerced into attending the parade, they too were on their feet. Members of the parade management, meaning the temporary staff under our mother's direction, drove them on like cattle. To make sure they'd get up in time, with the exception of Sváb-hegy, in the rest of the country loudspeakers attached to the tops of the buildings or to poles blared forth movement songs and military marches. They echoed, they crackled, they stretched out the sounds, they made the melodies viscous. In the countryside, they called these battered objects, sometimes sporting bullet holes from the war, tin whores, I have no idea why tin whores of all things, but that's what they were called. Once a month, they held siren tests as well. The siege had stayed behind with us. We were up and about early as well, up and about when it was still dark, she took me along and I was glad to go with her to meet my destiny. A car came, I don't know what make anymore, and we drove like mad from one assembly spot to the next, from one train station to the next, the decoration workshops, the parade ground on Dózsa György Street, the various onsite stations of the Municipal Sanitation Company and the National Ambulance

Corps, until the cool early morning hours. The cool early morning hours made me happy. I was even happy feeling how hungry and thirsty I was, I was glad that I could go along with our mother and see everything and watch everything, and see how seriously she was being taken, and how attentive and temperate she was with everyone. She had an operative staff, the organizing guard with armbands; it must have been made up of a lot of people, I couldn't really see them all, and if we went inside someplace, she'd talk to them over the phone or else they left messages for her.

Marchers from the countryside came on time by special trains, trucks, and buses to prearranged spots, the county delegates came separately, the town delegates came separately, they had to be met, directed and redirected, this too was part of the prearranged schedule, though naturally, nothing happened exactly as planned, in which case my mother had to improvise and direct them to the assembly places over another route, where they were given their decorations, after which they had to be herded along prearranged routes. Let's not tarry, Comrades, keep in step, Comrades. If the marchers didn't show sufficient enthusiasm or didn't pay sufficient attention and a bottleneck developed as a result, the voice turned threatening in the blink of an eye. The people coming from the rural areas were up all night traveling. The police were especially weary of congestion, but if it occurred, it was they and not the organizers who had to step in. They had to prevent congestion at all costs, they had to stop it from happening. And once, after several hours of standing restlessly in place, the column in City Park started moving at long last, the parading units had to be kept loose, thus ensuring the continuity of the march by keeping the order that had been set down in the original schedule and synchronized with all the other factors, while at the same time the escape routes had to be kept free, leaving streets and routes empty, and the marching units coming from various points of the city had to be started on their way while making sure that they wouldn't interfere with one another. The units had to make big detours and endure long waits, lest the working people of Szeged get entangled with the marching workers from Beloiannisz. Who wouldn't have gotten fed up with this unnecessary circus, when he didn't feel like participating in the first place. We also made detours in our car. The marchers from Budapest were organized by districts, and within the various districts smaller gathering districts were appointed, and the marchers from the outer districts had to be brought to the center of town according to a predetermined schedule. By this time Budapest was not the city I'd known, it was no longer my native town, but Greater Budapest, a city reborn from the ashes of its wartime hibernation with all its agglomerations. They'd annexed the surrounding settlements to it, Újpest, Sashalom, Rákosszentmihály, Cinkota, Kispest, Pestlőrinc, Pesterzsébet, Budaörs, and so on. Then after the parade, these huge crowds, there on orders and after several hours plagued with fatigue, had to be led out of the city, which called for specially scheduled buses standing at the ready. Furthermore, the official May Day entertainment in City Park couldn't be attended by just anyone to drink beer, eat hot dogs, or get on the merry-go-round or swinging boats. Only the outstanding workers and stakhanovites could enter with their families. I saw with my own eyes how the two groups organizing the parade, the police and the guard, cooperated. There were dispatchers dressed in leather gear, and they had motorbikes with sidecars that made awful puffing sounds, they went back and forth between the main gathering spots and the main supply centers and would convey all sorts of things in their sidecars as needed. There were also dispatchers with simple motorbikes in charge of maintaining the smooth functioning of the operation, and there were dispatchers with motorbikes and dispatchers on foot responsible for sustaining the operation, and also dispatchers on foot in charge of keeping the marching groups moving apace, and dispatchers with motorbikes and dispatchers on foot who synchronized the group responsible for the food with the other groups involved in organizing the parade. The marchers had to eat, or at least have a bite of something, and they also had to drink and relieve themselves. The lack of one thing or another was forever threatening the organizers, there'd be a bottleneck, commotion, and extra supplies had to be ready at all times. The banners, the placards, the flags, the *tableaux vivants* had to be dispatched from the decoration depots to the assembly spots on time, and the first-aid stations, the doctors, the nurses, along with the bandages and other supplies, had to be at the ready. They had a big map that they'd sometimes spread out on the asphalt and they'd kneel around it. We inspected all these places. The organization headquarters, our mother's temporary office, was located on the fourth floor of the Party Committee headquarters in Mérleg Street, but we went there just once early in the morning. Here everyone was loud, people were running back and forth with papers, others made phone calls, but mostly they just acted important. It was clear to me that our mother's element was moving about, dealing with several things at once, making decisions based on her ability to comprehend the big picture and her understanding of men. She was very much in her element. As the time for starting the marchers approached, anxiety mounted among the organizers. I felt the anxiety myself. But not so my mother, she wasn't anxious, she was excited, thrilled, electrified. Still, the anxiety was so great among the organizers that her own levelheaded confidence was helpless against it. No one said so, but they were all afraid of a possible mass accident, they feared a catastrophe, they feared provocation, they feared something that could not be counted on but would be deemed a provocation, and then they'd all end up in jail, and so they were grateful for every passing moment, good, good, we're over that, too, we're still here, and I also realized that it wasn't the march itself that was dangerous, but the subsequent withdrawal, when after so many ill-spent hours people felt free at last and wanted to leave as quickly as possible. Why don't they leave them alone. It's about time nobody limited their actions. But it's because of the threatening chaos that they can't go. It was up to the police and the organizers to restrain the crowd leaving the parade ground. Consequently, the organizers directed the largest police forces to be on hand for the retreating crowds, meaning that they were sent to Andrássy Boulevard, which by then was called Stalin Boulevard, and also to Podmaniczky Street, which by then was called László Rudas Street in honor of the Marxist philosopher, and where the headquarters of the Freemasons was located and where, in prehistoric times, they celebrated our great-grandfather half to death on the occasion of his eightieth birthday. The marchers had to be directed all the way to the Oktogon, which by then was called November 7 Square, and the crowds had to be kept in marching formation all the while, which would have been a nearly impossible task if terror had not reigned supreme in the whole country, and indeed, in the European region as a whole. They nabbed anyone trying to sneak away, they brutally wedged him in or simply shoved him back in line. The Hungarian police didn't have rubber truncheons back then. They turned a deaf ear to all requests and pleading. On Teréz Boulevard, which by then was called Lenin Boulevard, they could head only toward the Margaret Bridge, but the crowd wasn't allowed to form a bottleneck here either and the people were driven on; in this retreating phase of the parade, no one called them comrades anymore, let's go, let's go, don't stop, damn you, get a move on, or else, stop already, don't jam up, for crying out loud.

Accordingly, after the march began, our mother turned her attention to the empty streets where the marchers would gather and march off after the parade, and she checked the readiness of the medical tents and the ambulance service. Before the marchers were sent off from their assembly spots, we first quickly checked the tribunes on the parade ground where they were expecting the special guests. She was in high spirits, full of energy, she was loud and shrill, she would outshout anybody's fit of temper or hysterical outbursts or else laugh it off, she could get the better of anyone's petulance with her own exaggerations, but peace would last only a moment, and the next moment, anxiety reared its ugly head once again. Men were working on the tribune constructed of pine beams and planks, fixing, trimming, hammering on two sides of Stalin's huge statue until the last moment. Their work echoed in the empty early morning square. We climbed up on the main tribune. We even went out on the balcony of the huge base of Stalin's monstrous statue, where Comrade Mikoyan and Comrade Rákosi would be stationed with members of the Political Committee. There was a pleasant breeze. But it was also the only place where her steady cheer was of no use to her. She just wanted to see if everything was clean and if the special kitchen staff had arrived with the waiters from Nádor Street. The edifice made of red quarry stone and decorated with the red reliefs designed by Sándor Mikus had a rather uncomfortable interior, a steep stairwell and a small room with a skylight halfway up, where they laid out the proverbial buffet for the comrades. The buffets were always laid out well out of reach, people knew of their existence but they didn't know about all the things that made the buffet tables sag under their weight, all they knew was that they sagged. I only saw it myself for a moment, but I didn't see all the things that were laid out. In every small nook and cranny of this rustic red stone interior soldiers stood in full regalia and ceremonial helmets, fully armed. We could hardly take two steps without them holding us up, so our mother and I made a quick retreat from the place. She acted as if she'd rather not acknowledge what she'd seen. There we stood in the early hours of morning in the deserted parade ground, swept clean for the parade. No wonder I thought I was standing with her in eternity, in an eternity swept clean of everything. We crossed the square. How could I have known that in another two years the city would disgorge raving crowds onto its shores in the pleasant warmth of the evening light, while trucks would come from another direction, and from still another people would bring iron ropes and cold chisels and they'd pull and tug at Sándor Mikus's enormous statue of Comrade Stalin standing on its sandstone base until it would break just above his boots and like Humpty Dumpty come tumbling down.

As we crossed the square, technicians from Hungarian Radio tested the loudspeakers. Groups of men were attending to their business in the temporary sound studios that had been set up in haste behind the glass walls of the modernist Union Headquarters, that's where we were heading, both of us had armbands that allowed us to cross the police lines; they knew our mother just about everywhere and lost no time in barraging her with problems in need of immediate solution. Okay, let's try again, microphone test, one, two, three, sounded the command on the empty square, where are you, Gyuri Bán, get a move on and, and you too, Józsi Varga, wake up, Józsi, let's greet the workers of Red Csepel; every little sound richocheted through the empty square, and along with them, along-along with them—with them, we take great pride-pride-pride in greeting-ing-ing-ing the laborers of the Mátyás-mátyás-mátyás Rákosi Works-works-works, at this point, Jani, we're switching to music, and then Gyuri-gyuri-gyuri, don't forget-get-get-get, long live the Party-y-y-y, long live Rákosi, long live the Party-y-y-y, okay, boys, it's a wrap.

On this day at noon, the church bells did not sound anywhere in the city, and we were way past noon when amid all the loud noise and music our mother dispatched the last column on István Street to close the parade. They had to finish at 1:30 on the dot. If my memory serves, she started the march with the gymnasts and Red Csepel, meaning the parade of the workers of the Csepel factory, and I seem to remember that she finished it with the second-largest workers' district of Angyalföld from Pest. I also seem to remember that this last group of marchers had to be especially colorful and happy. You could tell that they were anything but even before they were sent off. The last sparks of good cheer were gone by then; after all, the more we force a pretense the more quickly it cools. The marchers were tired, hungry, and thirsty, they'd had it up to here, they'd have liked to break ranks on the first side street they came to and get home as quickly as possible, seeing how their day off, along with the rest of their lives, had gone to the dogs. The sky, too, had turned oppressively gray by then. Our mother may have noticed little of this; she must have been pleased; after all, they'd got off without a catastrophe, the crowds didn't panic even once, the wind didn't start up, there was no provocation and hardly any accidents, there was no hail and they've seen something through after all, and no one went berserk, except with this last mighty effort of hers, she saved nothing from its ultimate earth shattering annihilation. Her excitement, too, was gone by the end of the day, she wasn't sparkling anymore, she turned ashen from her effort, and the color typical of people suffering from cancer appeared in her cheeks once again. Also, come to think of it, she couldn't have been entirely innocent of the mood of the last column of marchers after all. She had the foresight to finish the parade of the workers from Angyalföld with gymnasts, to make it more spectacular.

The last column of marchers had just dragged themselves in front of the tribunes. If anything, it was amusing to hear Józsi Varga or Gyuri Bán shouting into the microphone on the other side of the square in their endearing sonorous tones, long live the eternal and indivisible friendship of the Soviet and Hungarian people, hurrah, hurrah, but regardless of what they shouted, the square gave back only their beautiful and slightly off-key voices, once, twice, five times, because no one from the apathetic mass of humanity that made up the last marching columns answered them, and I do mean no one, not a single soul. I couldn't have received a more striking lesson about the world of real people, I'd have had to be deaf and blind not to understand.

The gymnasts came on six gigantic lorries pulled along the square by six Zetors to the accompaniment of horrendous noise and stinking clouds of gasoline. The gymnasts stood in pyramids that were surely meant to be symbolic, tossing hoops and clubs about. They waved their banners. When, to finish the march, the Zetors drove one by one onto the square from István Street to stand next to one another so that the gymnasts could form pyramids in what you might call a military formation for the sake of the great men standing on the tribunes, our mother took me by the hand. The two of us followed, pulling up the rear, you might say, and after us came no, not the flood, but the emptiness, complete emptiness. The Stalin statue was a long way from István Street, where we were. Or at any rate, after such an exhausting afternoon, with the burden of such a realization, it seemed quite a journey for a twelve-year-old child. We walked on and on with the bored gymnasts in front of us, and the tossing, the waving, the puffing of the Zetors, and the gas-oil clouds, and behind us, the emptiness. The houses of Ajtósi Dürer Row had their empty glass eyes trained on us. Our mother had no further reason to playact, she nearly collapsed, she could barely walk. But I was taken up with the emptiness gathering behind our backs as it grew in magnitude. A vacuum like this would never materialize in a city that is alive. As we approached the obscene Mikus statue of Stalin towering over the tribune and we could already see little Rákosi, little Mikoyan, little Mihály Farkas, and little Ernő Gerő, the bridge builder, who refused to see our father, along with all the other little formidable strangers and acquaintances, the emptiness gathering behind us seemed to irritate her, because she couldn't understand why I kept turning, what I was looking at, or possibly she understood better than I, and when she, too, turned around to see what I was looking at, she made one final effort to get the better of the emptiness of her life, and in order to please the comrades on the tribune, to galvanize herself into action, she pulled her hand from mine, and though she must have seen that up on the tribune her comrades in their awkward Russian coats and Russian hats too big for them were getting ready to leave and were impatient for this hoop-twirling and Indian-club-hurling workers' movement gymnastics to pass, she ripped the armband from her arm and began waving it at the tribune, you wave too, wave, she shouted, amid the stink and noise of the Zetors and the echoing sound of the brass bands and percussionists, flailing her arms about, she shouted, the only one to do so, long live Rákosi, long live the Party, long live Rákosi, long live the Party, with hysterical glee, but I was the only one who heard and saw, and probably, no one else but me, and I don't know why, but I couldn't get myself to wave.

She shouted what, in the rhythm prescribed by the terror, my classmates shouted at school celebrations as long fart Rákosi, long fart the Party, long fart Rákosi, long fart the Party, that's what it sounded like to me. Long fart Rákosi, long fart the Party. The principal walked along the rows pleading, do it right, do it right, but she didn't say what they should do right, because she saw how happy they were shouting what they were shouting. Life would have been a farce if only it hadn't been a tragedy.

A good thing no one saw what my mother was up to. I looked around for a place where I could hide my shame, but there was no stopping her, she was too desperate.

A good thing no one saw what I was up to, because for a split second it occurred to me that out of solidarity, so she shouldn't be so alone with her waving and shouting, I should also wave and shout with her, except I couldn't have raised my arm and no sound would have left my lips, and so I just kept looking to see where I could hide, how

I could leave this particular mother of mine to her own devices, how I could free myself of this horrible scene of my young life.

At that moment my heart bled for my idiotic mother. It was lucky, truly very lucky, that though they'd amputated her breast after her cancer had made its merry way to her liver, and despite all the radiological interference, she was able to continue her work. For about a year the doctors lied to her and told her that she had gallstones and that's why she had no appetite and that's why she couldn't digest anything she ate, and I do mean anything. I made her some nice chicken soup, I don't remember where I got the chicken from, no, I remember, from the other side of Gyöngyvirág Street, from the German farmer, but I wasn't allowed to say, because it was a secret slaughter, I made her soup from a secret slaughter, I made my soup thickened with roux, I made it like my Tauber grandmother, Cecília Nussbaum, had made it in her kitchen in Péterfy Sándor Street.

They said that there were thousands of people at the funeral, and it must have been just as they said. There were so many people that they got stuck at the cemetery gate. The platform in front of the mortuaries was packed with mourners in black, and under the angry sky the paths, too, were black from the great mass of silent and in some way angry crowds; this was also in May, the May of the following year; I couldn't begin to imagine who these people were and where they'd come from, our heads lowered, we made our way among them, my brother and I and our father, until we reached the catafalque surrounded by a flaming candelabra. There were people as far as the eye could see standing shoulder to shoulder as the workers' funeral march came creaking from the loudspeakers, as far as I could see, they were everywhere under the May sky laden with threatening clouds.

The day after the scandal in Rákosi's meeting room, her superior, who was herself a distinguished member of the circle of women congregating around my Aunt Magda, and who was also called Magda, though no one referred to her by her first name and she was more what you might call an acquaintance, they kept missing her presence, where on earth is Jóború, what's keeping Jóború, Jóború should have been here by now, because she had great ambitions, and let's admit it, she couldn't have spared the time for meeting friends, anyway, this Magda Jóború, who was almost as self-assured as a man, sharp, cultivated, and astute, ordered our mother to kindly leave her little white marble palace in Múzeum Street and come see her in Széchenyi Street.

Not tomorrow and not an hour from now, Klári dear, but right now.

She was relieving her of her post effective immediately, she said when our mother entered Júlia Rajk's former office, and she was sending her to the Party Academy at the first opportunity.

That same day at home, I already knew that she wouldn't be going to the Party Academy.

What the Party wants from you, Klári dear, you can't refuse, Klári dear.

I know I can't refuse, she answered, still, I'm not going.

Why on earth not.

It's very simple. You see, it makes no sense. I tried it once before, and it made no sense then either.

You must do it on a higher level.

You want to send me to Moscow, I take it.

It's a great honor. I hope you know that.

I'm not going.

In which case, there's nothing more to be said.

I do what the Party asks. You know that. I will go wherever the Party puts me. I have always gone wherever the Party put me. But I will not hide what I think.

That's why you must go to the Party Academy. It's the wish of the Party.

I am not going to the Party Academy. The Party Academy can't solve our present conflict.

You can't have a conflict with the Party, Klára dear.

You know perfectly well, Magda, that at the Party Academy, fools teach fools foolish things. My conflict is not with the Party, but with people. But as long as there's someone among you willing to listen, one person, just one person, I will go on expressing my opinion. In fact, I will express it even if there's no one left to listen.

It went on like this for weeks, face-to-face, as well as on the phone.

It was bad enough that she'd refused once before, except back then they made her see the light, one might say. And now she said no to Moscow. You can't make such a big mistake in this party, Klári dear. Her worry was understandable, she couldn't very well pretend she didn't know, she was under obligation to report it, and if she didn't, repercussions would follow. That is what they called Party discipline. Magda Jóború turned to Magda Aranyossi. Magda Jóború was sorry but she couldn't not report what had happened. My Aunt Magda was the only person who didn't try to talk my mother into attending the Party Academy in Moscow. She said to Jóború that alas, Klári was almost always right, even when she spoke nonsense. And when our mother told her the story herself, she listened attentively, then said only that she was worried.

I'm worried, Klári dear.

I hope so. But I hope it's not because of me.

Because of you, too.

My Aunt Magda must have been thinking of her own career, which had floundered on Júlia Rajk's stubborn resistance, the dialogues she'd conducted with her that were strikingly similar to the ones with my mother and just as futile.

A couple of years before, she had written Júlia Rajk, asking her to relieve her of her position as senior editor of the women's weekly *Asszonyok* that she had founded. She also wanted to be released from her bond to the Women's Association. Only a typed outline of the letter has survived, but she had related the story on the nights when I sat by her bed in my Viennese great-grandmother's baroque armchair in the apartment on Teréz Boulevard; the room was lit by the baroque sconces, and my great-grandmother was looking down on us from the life-size portrait of her by Vilma Parlaghy. In the surviving document, she gave three reasons for her request. She was tired, even though the complete physical she recently had could find no acceptable explanation for her fatigue. Except, an amusing Freudian slip in her next sentence reveals the cause of her fatigue. Probably, she meant to write that her general bad mood prevented her from discharging her duties, but she wrote that the general bad mood prevented it. She couldn't attend to her work as well as she would have liked. And so her next sentence took on an even sharper cast; in it she wrote that the spirit that had come to dominate the Women's Association was alien to her, she was not at home in it, and as a result, she couldn't sustain the relationships necessary for her to do her work. In fact, she was thinking of the conflict of two irreconcilable attitudes. During their more than two decades in emigration, my aunt and her husband were used to a different working method, friendly cooperation, correction and self-correction, an exchange of views and compromise. It wasn't first and foremost Júlia Rajk's authoritarian style she couldn't abide, because Rajk had screamed at her once, but she screamed back at her so that Júlia fell silent on the spot, it was Júlia's subordinates she couldn't abide, along with the constant commotion they caused, their officiousness and overzealous attitude. And she couldn't abide it not because she was too fastidious herself, because she wasn't, she couldn't abide it because it didn't deliver results, it made no sense, a person couldn't edit a paper under such circumstances. In the highly temperate style of the draft she writes that she feels that the constant lack of trust with respect to the paper is in fact addressed to her person, and she hopes that another senior editor will be able to convince Júlia and the board that she and her colleagues had done their work responsibly.

Júlia Rajk was happy to accept her resignation, yet as was her wont, she didn't fail to retaliate.

At which, my aunt's colleagues wrote Júlia Rajk a petition.

We, the staff of *Asszonyok*, have brought the following decision and ask you, Júlia, to pass it on to every department of the Hungarian Women's Democratic Association headquarters as well as every one of its department heads so that everyone takes note. It has come to our attention that unidentified persons are spreading tendentious and malicious gossip about Magda Aranyossi, our former editor-in-chief and department head, that she had to leave her post because her unaccommodating nature served to demoralize her colleagues. We, many of whom have worked with her from the first hours after the siege, are outraged by this rumor. Not only is it contrary to the truth, but the opposite is true, namely, that with her outstanding abilities as well as her unimpeachable ethics and compelling personality, her tact and goodness, yes, her goodness, Magda Aranyossi was the binding force that kept us together at all times. She imbued our daily tasks with a sense of mutuality and solidarity. We learned this, too, from her, we practiced it together with her. While we consider it imperative that in response to these malicious rumors our declaration be acknowledged by every single co-worker of Association headquarters, at the same time we hereby declare that if we learn who is spreading these rumors, we will initiate disciplinary proceedings against said individual.

When our mother told my Aunt Magda the story, which my aunt had already heard from Jóború, and they had a brief discussion about it, with the grande dame imperiousness one had come to expect of her, my aunt changed the subject, saying, you can't talk sense about nonsense. This was her summary opinion.

I liked this approach very much.

Although for a long time to come I had no idea what it meant to relieve someone of their post, it was certainly the first time I'd heard the expression itself. It was an event momentous enough for me to remember it. It had never occurred to me before that my mother had a post. Also, I couldn't understand why she would refuse to attend the Party Academy in Moscow if it was such a great honor. I, for one, would have loved to go to Moscow to study at the Lomonosov. Or to a military academy. To spend the summer at the Artyek Pioneer camp. But I didn't ask why she didn't want to go. Failure came pouring out of her every pore while my father watched her with wide-open, frightened eyes, and it was useless for our mother to laugh, to wax loud and pretend cheer with a vengeance in face of her life's bankruptcy. She was not about to come out the winner, she would not be able to give meaning to her life. My Aunt Magda knew this and never recovered from the knowledge. This surprised me so much that I never dared ask anything, ever again. At least it may have been some consolation that in the meantime Rózsi Németh had successfully finished the nursery teachers' training school and was heading straight for Paris, in which Georges also had a hand, and she'd be leaving the following week. As a newly minted nursery school teacher, she was going to take care of the children of the embassy staff. They considered this making amends of sorts. Rózsi was going to Paris, Rózsi needed new clothes. In the morning, our mother's official car, the ugly gray Pobeda, didn't come to fetch her. This, too, was something new. It would have made no sense asking why it wasn't coming. It was safer to watch and gather information. Who called, who came to convince her of something that she was adamant about, who left in a huff, who agreed with her, you're so right, Klára dear, who got arrested on charges of conspiracy or sabotage, and whether they, our beloved parents, weren't involved in conspiracy themselves. And should it turn out that they were serving foreign powers, would I report them. When I so much as thought about it, I nearly fainted, and so I preferred not to think about it, but I couldn't pretend that the thought hadn't occurred to me, because the great question of those years loomed, to wit, what would happen if. On the other hand, I had our mother's saying to calm me down, what would happen, what would happen if I had four wheels, and we could laugh along with her and finish the sentence with her, in that case I'd be tram number 6.

Still, she took out her Russian language books in secret to refresh her knowledge of Russian, I think she must have taken them out in case she had no other choice. My poor, poor idiotic mother. This was the sensitive point through which one could glimpse the depths of her infinite naïveté. At this point, her legendary sense of reality failed her. After all, her comrades had wasted no time in giving up on her, why would they have bothered with her if they couldn't use her. At first she didn't go anywhere, she prepared breakfast, she cleaned the house, then out of the blue she went down to town, she walked down Diósárok Street to the Fény Street farmers' market, and she returned on the cog railway; it started from Városmajor, then came St. John's Hospital, then the Lilac Grove stop, followed by the Forest School and the Gyöngyvirág Street stop, then Városkúti Street, Eötvös Street, Melinda Street, and last, the Széchenyihegy stop. She brought fish, carp, she later came to love taking the cog railway, because it gave her a chance to talk to people. Once she brought back a duck. People were glad to talk to her, and so she learned a lot of things that she hadn't known before, or possibly, she didn't want to know; she was going to make Serbian carp, she said, she bought tomatoes, potatoes, onion, and paprika to make it, she insisted that she enjoyed being a house wife, which I didn't believe, not for a second. In this matter her own mother, Cecília Nussbaum, had been right. Your mother is unsuited to play housewife, I tried teaching her, God is my witness how hard I tried. I could teach Bözsi, I could teach Irén, but not your mother. Now she was elated that at long last she got to see real life with her own eyes. Which was supposed to be a jocular reference to her comrades. Just you wait, Comrades, I'll tell you about all the things that are out there, on the shade side of life. Which left me baffled; after all, none of them knew anything, and I do mean anything either about what was out there, or what was in the shade; and sadly, our mother didn't know either, even when she took the cog railway and the bus rather than her official car. Or were they so innocent that they could have had no idea that other people thought differently, I don't know. But I didn't ask. Except, who was going to smash the carp on the head. By noon she had our lunch ready for us. The duck had such a penetrating odor that even though it had a beautiful red color and was crunchy, none of us wanted to eat it. She should have smelled it and soaked it in water and vinegar. When I spotted her Russian language book for the second time somewhere in the apartment, she offered an explanation; as if to excuse herself, she said that she was refreshing her ignorance. She even gave a bashful laugh. For a while I didn't have to pay for my school lunch, which was a truly lucky change in my young life, and I was grateful for it. It wasn't so much the food that disgusted me but the tin utensils that were always greasy, the greasy tin cups we drank from, the greasy tin plates we ate from; the edges of the spoons were as sharp as knives, while the knives couldn't cut through anything, and the tips of the forks were so pointed, the boys used them for fork-throwing contests, and effortlessly they could lodge them in the bulletin board, except my schoolmates and their tableside horseplay disgusted me as much as the greasy tableware.

The infernal noise and turmoil they called lunch was beyond belief, a bunch of brainless beasts falling on one another and their food while their teachers screamed for them to stop, whereas they couldn't care less. Only the two poor cooks who made these inedible lunches made it all worthwhile; no matter what they did, no matter where they went, no matter where they carried their bewitching indifference with them, they fascinated me even as I felt revulsion at the sight of them, and even if I had to drink from a greasy cup because of them. The cups reeked of paprika fat. Two giants. Two giants and the scullery maids washed the dishes with baking soda, but doubtless there wasn't enough soda and there wasn't enough hot water. There was nothing. Never before or after did I see such colossal women. The sight of their naked arms as they dipped the cups in the paprika water. They must have been twins. They carried their enormous bodies around on elephant legs. Their eyebrows were missing, there wasn't a single hair to be seen. Every day they drew big arches on their fatty foreheads with an eyebrow pencil, but needless to say, these arches were never the same the next day, and they painted their puckered little-girl lips with bright red lipstick. They were both strong, their skin was stretched to extremes and gleamed with fat, they hoisted immense pots and pans and carried the crushing weight of flour sacks and potato sacks of even more crushing weight, if possible, they rolled barrels of sour cabbage and mixed pickles. They didn't serve, they didn't portion out; they took their big ladles and slammed the food on our plates, then pushed them at us over the counter. Potato noodles. Semolina noodles. Cabbage noodles. These were our school lunch staples. There was no knowing which was which, because not only did they look the same, they were made the same way. They slammed the roast fatty bacon on top of the foul-smelling potato or carrot dishes, provided there was roast bacon to begin with. Then they slammed the greasy gravy on top of that. They made the gravy from fat, flour, and onion. They drenched just about everything in it. It was no use saying, one child wanted it like this, the other like that, one was asking for more of this, the other less. They ignored humble requests of this kind. They slammed it down, they slapped it on, they dashed it on, they chucked it on. They were our everyday reality, something we had to go up against day after day. As soon as they could, they sat down with their legs spread apart. The red lipstick beaded the skin above their lips, it got smeared or disappeared altogether from all the wiping. Beads of sweat rolled down from under their thin head of hair put up in a knot. Sometimes I caught a glimpse of them going to church. They had to sit down quickly, though it was more like slumping down. They couldn't close their legs. They had to think twice about where they sat, because not everything could take their weight. The two scullery maids kept picking things up for them; if something fell off their tin-lined table, they didn't even attempt to bend down.

In the morning, they took the cog railway up the mountain from town, and given their huge behinds, they couldn't sit on two seats, they needed four. I followed the movements of these behinds with such fixed attention, sometimes from up close, that I nearly fell over. They wore light dresses even in winter, and coats on only the coldest days. Their backsides moved in unison. They wore thigh-high lace-ups, but they could barely get their feet even into these, and they couldn't tie them properly. I followed them every chance I got. It took them quite a while to reach the school in Diana Street from the Városkút stop along the treacherous slope. They gasped for air. But it wasn't just the climb that did them in, the icy descent, a frozen clump of snow was an even greater challenge. They couldn't just step over something like that. They did everything together, but they never held on to each other on the way up or down the hill. Luckily, they didn't have to enter the school through the main entrance, because in that case, they'd have had to climb the steps up a floor then down to the basement; they reached the kitchen through the back entrance on Felhő Street. The kitchen gave access to the wretched dining room through a wide sliding window, where we sat on camping benches by long camping tables, and where every single noon the forks were stuck in the bulletin board. Their smell was invasive. They carried all the food they had ever cooked on their skin.

They never spoke, either to each other or to other people, no feeling or passion of any sort was ever apparent on their round, gleaming faces. But once I caught them speaking to the feeble-minded verger as he came out of the church.

If anything was left at the bottom of the kettles, one of the scullery maids would shout through the sliding windows, seconds, children, who wants seconds.

Those who were hungry, those who would eat anything, shoved each other aside for the seconds. They'd eat hobnails, people said about such children, for many of whom this was the only meal of the day, but no one ever talked about this. By mid-morning, the hungry children were so hungry, they stared the food you'd brought for your mid-morning snack out of your mouth. I was always hungry myself, but it would never have occurred to me that hunger was anything out of the ordinary, that it was not part of Creation. So it shouldn't happen to me, so the others shouldn't stare the food out of my mouth, I gave half my snack, which never consisted of more than a piece of bread with butter or pork fat, to Tót. I never said anything, I just handed it to him. Basically, he didn't talk to me, though he didn't talk to anyone else either, he lived among us like a small animal, but he always had his eye on half of my mid-morning snack. Though he tried to check himself, sometimes he wanted me to give him the whole thing. With a gesture typical of him, he just took it out of my hand, and I didn't protest.

When I got home from school in the afternoon, our mother would sit in an armchair near the window, darning socks, something she had never done before, not anything remotely like it, a good thing that her mother, Cecília Nussbaum, kept at her, saying it was apparently beneath her, but at least I taught her something. I taught everything to each of my girls. In the evening she laid the table and we talked in the kitchen, carefully and mutually avoiding anything that mattered; as far as she was concerned, the world could no longer be set right, and as for me, her problems were way over my head, though I had no idea what people meant when they said something was over their head; but I understood that we talked so we shouldn't have to talk as we waited for our father to come home for dinner, and if my brother wasn't carrying on and screaming. One would have thought that my brother would never leave our mother's lap and would have to be pried off her neck, but no, he ran after the others like a little animal, or else kept himself busy playing with his toys on the floor as long as our mother was nearby. All of this was so new. We didn't have enough chairs for our shared dinner. Our mother sat on a crate left over from moving house. Needless to say, there were no more white tablecloths, no more white batiste napkins, nor were these proper meals now, because they lacked table talk, because they'd have had to talk about embezzlement and suspension in front of us, and so we ate in silence, and even the silver napkin rings they'd saved I found only years later in a drawer, and I looked at them as if they were spiritual reliquaries. No one bothered to polish the silver; the tarnished family silver we'd forgotten all about lay jumbled at the bottom of the black chest of drawers lined with white birch. She placed the pot in the middle of the table with the ladle inside it. At our table, nothing of what my father had lectured me on etiquette was in evidence. For instance, the ladle was inside the pot. They must have been so stressed that their concern over us consisted of catering, more or less, to our most basic needs, that we had hot meals again and clothes to wear. Other than that, they didn't care about us, and when they did, their concern came out of the blue, as it were, in fits and starts. I didn't mind. I accepted that all my previous knowledge was now superfluous. Our mother satisfied her desperate need to be always doing things by unraveling some pullovers. We made the skeins together, then we rolled the skeins up into balls, and then she started knitting from the cotton and wool thread, and it would have been nice if only, in order to spare each other's feelings, we didn't reduce ourselved to talking about inconsequential things. I had no idea that she knew how to knit. My Tauber grandmother, Cecília Nussbaum, used to scold her, saying she couldn't even crochet, I couldn't even teach her to knit. Or else, she can knit, except she won't, she'd rather pretend. She'd first knit a handsome vest for our father from the most meager store of leftover wool, and I'd be next in line; she made up her mind, she'd knit me a pullover with Norwegian design, woolen, with a turtleneck. There were lots of old sweaters she could unravel. But this lasted only a very short time, a number of weeks, two months at most, at which point my pullover with the Norwegian design was left unfinished. I waited and waited, until the remnants of my naïveté, without which, probably, one can't live, went up in smoke. I suspected that the cancer must have spread in her body in this state of grace, though we saw few signs of her mood having changed. A woman who knew her mind, with both feet on the ground. She woke up in good spirits, she went to bed in good spirits, though now and then she'd be as angry as a peacock.

In those days, I don't know why, but I was most interested in Lívia Süle, who attended the girls' class and was in the same year as I. We kept each other bound with our eyes. It started at some sort of co-ed gym celebration, where we all kept looking around so we wouldn't die of boredom. Neither of us would have dared approach the other, there was no cause, but with our eyes neither of us let go of the other ever again. The only thing I ever asked in school was where is Lívia. For a long time I didn't even know her name, neither her first name nor her last name, and to be honest, I didn't care. It never entered my mind that I should call her by her name or that we should be talking to each other. At the same time, our mutual silence began to to hurt. I couldn't get enough of her attention. Also, it bothered me that her classmates were snooping, keeping an eye on her, girls whom I hadn't even noticed for a long time because of her, they're onto the way we're gazing at each other. I was almost as preoccupied with the thought that my classmates, the bigger boys, would beat me to a pulp. When this came into my head, Lívia went straight out of my mind. While I was sitting peacefully on the locker-room bench, intent on tying my shoes, someone whispered in my ear, don't you worry, I looked up at him, what was he talking about, but they knew my whereabouts, they knew what I was up to, I couldn't have any secrets from them, they knew I was just waiting for that silly little girl, that Lívia Süle, but I was not going to take Lívia Süle and snatch her away from the boys from Mátyás király Street, I could bet my life on it, they were going to lie in wait for me on a street corner, they would wait for me when I least expected it, she was under their protection, they were going to put a sack over my head to keep me from crying for help, and I'd better not count on getting away with anything. All this was new to me. My head reeled from everything I had to make sense of. Slowly, calmly, in the friendliest manner, the kid in question let me know that I was as good as dead. Try as I might, I couldn't remember the boy who sat down on the bench next to me as if we were friends and relayed the message of the older boys for my benefit. You're as good as dead, little brother. He must have been one of the boys in our large class, there were forty-six of us, I think, whom I hadn't met before. But afterward, other boys confirmed the threat more than once, boys I knew, saying that I shouldn't worry but prepare for the worst, enough is enough, if I didn't disappear from school pronto, this was their school, they were going to beat me to a pulp. Prém, for instance, said he was giving me fair warning out of the goodness of his heart. Which was another linguistic puzzle to occupy my mind. After all, no one ever said unfair warning. In which case how was I supposed to know what fair warning was. My sense of language couldn't accept that fair warning was really a threat. I had the same problem with heartfelt condolences. When grown-ups said that their condolences were heartfelt, it was written all over them that they felt nothing of the sort, try as they might to hide it. I don't remember his first name either, Prém's first name, but the texture of his hair, like a brush, his eyes, his sweet little smile, his fine limbs I remember perfectly. He was like a lively little brown bug. Or loach. Or pixie. Forcing his way onto the bench beside me. I made room for him to prevent him from touching me, because he was one of the local mountain boys stinking of decay, but our bodies touched, and I felt his stink, though not my own. He said I should stop polluting the air here in school. Apparently, I hadn't noticed that the whole class stank because of me. He couldn't imagine why I was here to begin with. There were enough schools elsewhere. It wouldn't kill our esteemed parents if they had to drive us someplace else. You think we haven't noticed, he asked menacingly, you and your brother being driven around in two separate cars, your old man and your old lady come to the kindergarten for your brother like some delegation. As a matter of fact, the two of them may have run into each other in their separate cars. And with that, Prém raised his ass off the bench and farted loud enough for all to hear, and then the boys sang out in chorus, here's a ditty, sweet as a lily, addressed to you know who, he sent the fart to my parents who came with two cars, and I could tell by his expression that he'd saved it on purpose, he'd held it back for them, and he was expecting me to protest when the stink reached me. The air all around you stinks, he said, you stink enough to make a polecat puke. This, too, was one of their sayings, meant to be the last verbal act of provocation. Meanwhile, greedy for action, the others were looking on, but I would not be provoked, I wouldn't fight; I never asked myself why, or what ethical consideration might provoke me to use my fists, or in the name of what ethical consideration I was refusing to fight, seeing so much everyday wickedness, when even my parents had urged me more than once not to back off but stand up for myself, except I could find no reason to fight back. Also, I saw that my indifference toward the provocation virtually paralyzed the others, and they either snuck away in silence or turned their back on me as they continued to threaten and abuse me.

As if I could forget, though how could I have forgotten, when sometimes I got my daily dose of threats on slips of paper. I'd find these slips in my coat pocket, the drawer in my bench, or in my notebooks. I racked my brain trying to figure out what to do and what I'd done to deserve it, or why I should leave the school, or where I could go without my parents noticing. I planned one morning, without telling anyone, to go over to Orbánhegy, down Dobsinai Street to Németvölgyi Street, and go right inside the bear cub school, where two bear cubs carved out of stone watched over the school entrance.

I didn't want to burden them, though I wasn't that considerate out of the goodness of my heart, it was just that I thought I should solve the situation first, and tell them about it later.

Until I figured it out, because being aware was not the same, there was nothing I could tell them, and try as I might, I couldn't figure it out. Besides, they'd just listen to my babble, oh dear, the poor child and his laments, our mother would say. Beat them up. Don't be such a pushover, such a shit-in-the-pants, or you might well end up being the number one martyr in the family. But it was no use trying to figure out why this was happening. But for the fact that I was among the smallest, there couldn't be anything conspicuous about me. I hardly spoke to anyone, I hardly left my school bench, I hardly left the garden. I didn't feel the urge. I read nonstop. At most, I watched Lívia Süle on the sly, that's all that happened, and I couldn't understand why I should stop, or how they noticed in the first place, or what they could object to, and so I kept doing it, despite the fact that they familiarized me with all the synonyms for what they were about to do to me. They were going to let me have it. They were going to tear into me, thrash, pummel, and clobber me. They were going to knock me out. Knock seven bells out of me. Pitch into me. Lay into me, beat the living daylight out of me. Kick the shit out of me. Just don't you worry. How could I have not. They were going to throttle me. Wring my neck. Knock my teeth out. Knock my kidney loose. Beat me to a pulp until I spit blood. I had no doubt that they'd do it, except, no matter how hard I tried, I couldn't understand why they should bother. Out in the garden, I trembled at the slightest stirring of the breeze. I was close to fainting. But I couldn't restrain myself from wandering about with my books, because its plant and animal life fascinated me, and so did the many writers with their many fascinating stories.

I even knew by then that there were two gangs, they were going to fight each other, and the actions of the two gangs were in some way related to beating or hounding or killing me. There were the boys from Mátyás király Street, and they wanted to beat up the boys from Diana Street. In theory, I was familiar with this childish nonsense, this tribal warfare, from my school in Sziget Street, but even back then I didn't understand, nor did I give a hoot about their conflict with the boys from Pannónia Street. I didn't care about their victories and defeats or the outcome of their button football matches and running races, which was not entirely true, because I attended them, how could I not, because I'd wanted to understand what pleasure they got from their constant, ostentatious display of vanity, this showing off, the tribal warfare and the need to win. Somebody would stop in front of the other and ask, you got a problem, buddy. Whereas he was the assailant, he was the one with a problem and not the other, but it didn't take much to get his dander up, too, because the first boy's provocation provoked him as well, and now they were both worked up and fell on each other. I studied these great human dramas with awe. Apparently, they needed this verbal warmup before their fight. But if one made certain nasty comments about the other's mother, then the one whose mother was thus maligned lost no time throwing punches. According to our parents, I should have done the same. When they called each other's mother names, there was no need for the warmup. The clash between the two parties seemed to be the emotional climax they were aiming for as the others looked on and cheered. Even back in Sziget Street or at the ice-skating rink, I refused to honor this half-baked duty to fight. What're you pushing me for, they shouted as they pushed the other so hard he lost his balance. I stayed out of it, thinking that by doing so, they'd ignore me. Except, I was wrong, because up on Svábhegy, the rivalry between the young males of the species had some social content that the rivalries in Sziget Street had lacked. It was not easy for me to understand the social significance of the power maneuvers and warring because it had some sort of topographical law behind it. The boys who lived on Városkúti Street, Diósárok Street, or Béla király Street on the other side of the cog railway tracks, or even farther up, all belonged to the Mátyás király group, but some of the boys who lived here on Istenhegy or on Kis-Svábhegy also belonged to the Mátyás király gang and not the Svábhegy gang. For a long time I didn't realize that the grown-ups of the area, who also divided themselves into sharply differentiated groups, had passed on the grudges they'd brought with them from the countryside, where the upper end of the village feuded with the lower end, and the servants railed against their masters, except the traditional structures of belligerence ran up against the new inequalities and other types of strife. And so, even though someone lived on Költő Street, Lóránt Street, Normafa Street, Evetke Street, or Tündérhegyi Street, in some cases he had to join the Mátyás király Street group. The overlap between the topographical and social stratification also confused me. Furthermore, only the boys counted, the girls didn't belong anywhere. According to her place of residence, Lívia Süle should have belonged, if in theory only, to the Diana Street group, but it was the Mátyás király Street group that took a collective interest in her, which was more than I could fathom. The secret war was inherited strictly along male lines. Also, you didn't have to join one or the other secret group to belong, which was yet another thing I couldn't make heads or tails of, but it seemed that the boys from the Diana Street gang took an interest in me. Given my ferocious need for freedom, I couldn't have imagined that this might happen, much less accept it. I did not join any group, and yet I belonged to the Diana Street boys, because the Mátyás király Street boys threatened all of us with a final reckoning. There was also their personal reckoning with me. Sometimes they spoke to me in the plural. They said that they'd come when we least expect it, though for a long time I had no idea what the use of the plural meant in their language. It occurred to me that there must have been some logical or some other connection between settling accounts with me and settling accounts with the others, because when the threat to my person was very great, in a whisper so his mother, who was waiting for him every day as she leaned her elbows on the windowsill, couldn't hear, Baltazár said as we parted that I shouldn't worry about their threats, the group would defend me. They'd agreed. Which came as a complete surprise, I felt grateful to him, there's no other way to put it, grateful, because I had never mentioned to anyone that I was being threatened, yet Gábor knew, he'd noticed. He'd agreed with the other boys behind my back. He did it for me, that was clear, but he did it behind my back, and I didn't like that, and I didn't like my own feeling of gratitude either. Except, they later threatened us and said not to worry, they'd slaughter, decimate, annihilate, and depopulate the whole bunch for taking me in, because, and we shouldn't worry, they happened to have a miracle weapon, and they were gonna set fire to the whole area. I wasn't born yesterday, I emerged from the hundred and two days that the siege of Budapest lasted, it wasn't my mother who pushed me out of her womb, I came into the light of day from a basement lair in Damjanich Street, so they didn't have to explain to me what a flamethrower was for. Vadász had promised them the flamethrower; he lived on Melinda Street, and so theoretically he should have belonged to the same group into which I was drafted without my knowledge, and accepted, too, the group in whose name Baltazár said I shouldn't worry because they'd protect me, and yet Vadász belonged to the Mátyás király Street group. Consequently, the boys in both groups talked about weapons all the time and collected ammunition; they removed something from the mines. Needless to say, they all had slingshots, and the size and quality of their slingshots was also a constant subject of conversation. One night our father turned my brand-new slingshot out of my pants along with my carefully collected small, round stones, confiscated it, and said he was going to throw it out; I pleaded with him to return it, because he'd already confiscated my blowgun with which, let's admit it, we could cause serious eye injuries to each other, but I didn't want to have to tell him that he had just confiscated my last means of defense.

He'd stopped explaining things a while back, but I was still afraid that I'd have to listen to yet another of his explanations that I wouldn't understand. I kept reaching out for my slingshot and he kept slapping my hand as he laughed. I tried butting him in the stomach with my head. He grabbed me by the shoulder and shook me so I'd come to my senses. I couldn't even decide if the boys weren't just blowing a bunch of hot air. They said they sent scouts to the other camp's field. I doubted this until I saw the scouts in our garden, searching our greenhouse. There were four of them, I saw them by chance as they sneaked about. I ran into the kitchen, it had a door leading to the garden, up the steps and out on the street, all the way to Baltazár for him to come, but by the time he understood and we got there, the greenhouse was empty. They must have come from the direction of Aunt Róza's apple orchard, we found the hole in the Baltazárs' fence, this was the only one they could have gotten through, because the other two sides of the garden lay adjacent to the restricted area. A couple of days later I saw that they'd smashed in all the windowpanes on the side of the greenhouse facing the fence. This was a terrible loss. In those years, there was no glass to be had at the glass dealer, just as there was no meat to be had at the butcher. They must have done it with tools. Then on

Sunday, Mr. Szabó, the former caretaker of the estate, told our father that they later smashed the glass panes of all our greenhouses as well. Mr. Szabó now worked in Csepel, where Elemér had once run amok naked, and if I didn't behave myself, if I didn't behave like all good boys should, and I saw clear as day that I couldn't behave like that, the same thing would happen to me. The destruction was staggering. Not only did they smash every single window, they smashed the beautiful recessed furnace made from adobe brick along with the lined heating duct. Baltazár said that they were searching for our weapons in the heating duct, and when they couldn't find them, they smashed all the windowpanes in their rage. The first time was just a warning that the war was not far off and we should prepare ourselves. There was a small shed in the back of the Baltazars' garden, and we hoarded the stones for our slingshot as well as some larger stones with which to protect ourselves on its slightly sloping roof. Csíder came along, but Piros didn't, because he said he'd be scared shitless.

Mr. Szabó told our father that he'd heard the racket late at night, got out of bed, and went outside. They discussed whether they should report it to the police or the guard in Lóránt Street. Which just spun me farther along the fear spiral.

I needed to get my hands on a new slingshot. I exchanged something for two machine-gun shells that I hid under the bed every night and put back in my pocket the next morning. I must have taken them with me wherever I went for perhaps a year, but when Rózsi Németh came back from Paris and they let me stay with her on Stefánia Street, which by then they called Voroshilov in honor of the Soviet marshal, anyway, as I was getting ready for bed, she saw me looking for a place to hide the shells, and told me to kindly take off my pants, and I did so, carefully so they shouldn't fall out, but she was keeping an eye on me, and quickly turned my pants upside down and shook them loose. She said that she would not confiscate the shells and she wouldn't say a word to Anyáka and Apáka, but we'd strike a deal. I could rest assured that she wouldn't say a word about it to Anyáka and Apáka, but I had to promise not to touch shells or explosives ever again, and if others fool around with them, I must move away.

But while I still had those shells, not only was I obsessed with the thought that I'd go to the school on Németvölgyi Street and without attracting notice sit down behind one of the desks, I was also obsessed with the thought that I must find a machine gun somewhere for my shells. So even as I hurried through the Braun Woods, making my way to Felhő Street to catch a glimpse of Lívia behind the fence of her house, because she was sometimes sent outside to hang the wash to dry or take the dry clothes off the line because it was about to rain, and besides, for some reason, on Gyöngyvirág Street I knew when she was outside, I could feel it on my skin; anyway, even as I ran through the woods, I attended to every snapping and cracking sound under my feet, but I didn't find a single abandoned machine gun. Gábor Baltazár and I made a new slingshot to replace the one that was confiscated. There was a competition among the boys to see whose slingshots carried farther, the ones with elastic bands or the ones with leather straps. The question occupied me as well, but it never occurred to me that I was a boy or that I was one of them. Which is the better ammunition, stone or lead, this too was a major topic of contention. They shot down birds with U-nails. They made their own lead ammunition. Trembling with a mixture of fear and hope, I studied the undergrowth in the oak wood to see if anything moved, if I could find the barrel of an abandoned gun as I ran, or to make sure that they hadn't set the woods on fire with a flamethrower so that I'd burn to cinders, but I couldn't find a gun for my two cartridges, try as I might. The abandoned German defense lines were still intact, along with their ditches and cement bunkers, in the thickets and woods up on Svábhegy, Orbánhegy, and Istenhegy. It was no laughing matter, we had to act; we knew that the Mátyás király group had a bunch of hand grenades. They were keeping them in a cave, but not only did we fail to find the cave, to our great shame, we didn't even have a cave of our own.

During the afternoon, we'd lie on our bellies on top of the Baltazárs' shed, waiting for them to attack us.

I said nothing, whereas it kept wanting to slip out, take me out of this horrible school and take me to Németvölgyi Street, take me anywhere, just don't leave me here. My mother noticed that I had a problem, and she kept questioning me, but I wouldn't say what I was thinking, because a similar discussion had ensued between us earlier, when I asked if I could go to the Gorky school on Ajtósi Dürer Row instead; it was a Russian school, and Szása Hámor went there too, because the Hámors had returned from Moscow and Szása was born there, but my mother just lowered her head, she was very angry, and I saw that asking such a thing was bad manners. I also saw that she was trying to hold herself in check and not turn on me, she didn't want her turkey-cock temper to get the better of her. After a long silence she just said, your name is not Szása and not Volodia, even though they're nice names, but even if it were, you couldn't go there. A Hungarian child must learn Hungarian literature in Hungarian. I didn't quite understand, but a person will more or less accept just about anything from his mother. Actually, it wasn't Szása I wanted to follow there but the boy with blond curly hair with whom I'd eventually study architecture, but whose name I can no longer recall. My mother's prohibition was similar to the time we met Zsuzsa Leichner at the Hold Street farmers' market; she was living in Washington, D.C., because her husband, Emil Weil, was Hungarian ambassador there, a hungry Hungarian, ha-ha, and now they were back home only for a short visit, and in all innocence, Zsuzsa Leichner happened to ask my mother whether we'd come by car. You've come by car, Klárikám, and as she said this, it was something between a question and a statement of fact, she somehow managed to stretch out this car, and it sounded like cahhhr. At which our mother said, no, Zsuzsa dear, we don't come to the market by car, we come by wheelbarrow. Which wasn't even true, because her ugly gray official car was parked on the other side of Hold Street, and next to the car was her chauffeur, waiting. Poor Zsuzsa Leichner stood there dumbfounded, after all, she asked out of mere courtesy. Their villa was on Istenhegyi Street, we'd been to their place many times, and it wouldn't have been a burden to take us home with our packages. So now she didn't know what to make of our mother's response. There was also the time when upon seeing me, a lady, her name was Ilona Vígh, asked her in the small white marble palace on Múzeum Street what she gave us for breakfast, because her two small sons were tired of cocoa with whipped cream. In that case, give them roux soup, Ilona, though it won't be easy getting your hands on eggs, our mother said and left that stupid, affected woman to her own devices. You couldn't buy eggs or whipping cream for years at the time. It was a shortage item, that's what they called it. And milk could be bought only with a coupon, I had to stand on line for it on Svábhegy, and it happened more than once that by the time my turn came and I'd been standing there for some time with my empty can or glass jar, they'd run out of milk. Or else, I'd get the milk home and find that it was sour and it clotted up when we boiled it, and this made me feel as if it were all my fault. Maybe I hadn't rinsed the can out properly again. But I had. Except, how am I to prove it. Sugar, too, was dispensed against coupons. Flour was dispensed against coupons. Meat, too, would have been dispensed against coupons, except there was no meat. There was nothing but lard at the butcher, and come winter, some clever butchers took the pork lard and carved a hammer and sickle or a Stalin and Rákosi bust out of it, then decorated these with bright red and green cherry peppers, red, white, and green, proof of their national pride, and an even greater proof of their love of the Party, which left me puzzled, because it was tantamount to high treason, yet people pretended they hadn't caught on to this perfidy, but when there was no more lard in the unheated shops, or when the warm weather set in, they took the lard statues out of the shop window, they weighed them, and wielding their knives, they cut pieces off Stalin's and Rákosi's fat heads, which the customers enjoyed in silence, another thing that, because of its proportions, was not easy to follow with a sane mind. This stupid Ilona must have bought the chocolate or the cocoa powder in the shop reserved for the privileged. There was no cocoa powder or chocolate anywhere else in the city or indeed the country, only in these secret shops. An ersatz cocoa replacement called Morning Drink was available, my brother liked it, I didn't. For a long time I couldn't figure out where these shops, where women like her buy such delicacies for their children, could be found. Our mother turned purple as a peacock, she huffed and puffed because of such women. It was because of dumb women like her that I couldn't go to a Russian school. Some strange new irritability settled inside our mother, we could no longer ask her anything without fear of reprisal, we couldn't say anything, or ask for anything. She hated the privileged with a passion. The children of the privileged attended the Russian school and were taken to Crimea for their summer vacation. Szása Hámor told me all about it and said I should go along next summer. But it was out of the question. Once I cautiously mentioned that if I did well at school, I would volunteer for the Pioneer Railway. Forget it. You're not volunteering for any bootlicker training school. She hated them with a passion, she saw that with their quest for property and their egoism, these idiots were ruining everything.

Basically, I agreed with her, except I couldn't understand how come she hadn't noticed that we were every bit as much members of the privileged class, and it was no use being so inordinately proud of their great big equality. I could not count on protection from them, I could not hope for explanations either; they were unsuspecting, ignorant, it wasn't their fault, I even felt a certain sympathy for them. Our parents knew nothing about the things brewing under the surface, the profound silence, breaths held back, then the short cough, a pair of eyes looking to connect with another pair of eyes as the butcher sliced open Stalin's head, and with a deadpan expression asked, would you like the nose as well, madam. They knew nothing, nothing. For instance, you couldn't slaughter a pig without permission, but the peasants on the mountain slaughtered pigs just the same, late at night or early in the morning. In summer they piled up the haystack so that they'd mute the squealing when they slaughtered the pig. They engaged in black slaughter, as it was called. Anyone caught engaging in black slaughter either went to jail or to the notorious internment camp at Recsk. Also, every single egg should have been reported, but people didn't report half. Had they done so, they'd have starved to death. They sold the eggs on the black market. When the shop ran out of milk, I bought it illegally from the peasants living in the area. And also cottage cheese, as well as butter and eggs when I baked sponge cake for our mother. Of course, I didn't say where I got it.

I lied and said that I used egg powder, or that they were dealing it out against egg coupons, because that's how we said it. They dealt this or that out. I don't know why they believed me, when they must have known perfectly well that I wouldn't tell them the truth. When anything arrived at a shop, good neighbors shouted to each other over the fence that they're dealing this or that out. They're dealing stuff out.

There was a clandestine world out there with its clandestine system of relationships, its own self-protection societies and defensive and offensive alliances, there were the Arrow Cross men, the local Germans, or Swabians, there were the Greater Hungary parties and the monarchists, each with their supreme truth, and each group up in arms against anyone and everyone who was still alive and kicking, everyone, themselves exempted, with their pictures, the treasured symbols of their strivings and ideals prominently displayed on the walls of their rooms and kitchens, their Virgin Marys and Queen Elisabeths, their Lajos Kossuths, the corpse of King Louis, drowned in the Csele Spring as he fled the Battle of Mohács, there they were, these warring factions, with their seething hatred and clandestine bartering that crisscrossed religious and ideological barriers, if you'll give me this, I'll give you that; thanks to the other children, I couldn't help but get a glimpse into all this. The Baltazárs got something in a package that they then bartered for something else at the other end of town. They sold half the milk black, while the other half they watered down, and so the inspectors turned a blind eye, they gave them some sausages from the fresh black slaughter. This clandestine world, which eventually grew into a full-blown Hungarian black market and put it on a sure footing, fascinated me every bit as much as our parents' strange ignorance. I was interested in the system and logic of these relationships. Our parents lived in another reality, in fact, they lived cast out on its farthest reaches, but in a surprisingly short time, in just about a year and a half, I knew the reasons for all the tension, I ferreted out the nature of the social stratification of our new environment. I never met with such blatant stratification in my hometown, either before or after. In those days up on Svábhegy, the traditional feuding between the former lords and the former servants, the field hands and the day laborers, the vacationers and the permanent residents, the peasantry and the gentry was further complicated by the subterranean feuding between the local Germans, the Hungarians, and the Jews, all of whom were at variance, and the situation was still further complicated by the feuding between the Protestants and the Catholics, and the struggle of the lesser nobility and landed gentry to defend the nation against anyone and everyone who managed to survive, themselves exempted, even against the pro-royalist aristocrats, this was the most bitter and also the most futile struggle of all, and there was also the struggle of the nouveau riche captains of industry who were pushing for modernization, a battle they kept losing over and over against the self-made gentry and landed gentry, arm in arm with the pro-royalist aristocrats, and then there was the persistent language of war waged by the local German peasants against the linguistic assimilationist strivings of the Hungarian-speaking Hungarian nationalists, and then we haven't even taken into account that all warring factions kept changing fronts, depending on their momentary strength, and from time to time they'd appear in a new guise against the others and would abandon their allies, either as a group or individually, they appeared on the scene in surprising new roles to wage a subterranean war of self-defense against the Bolsheviks, the Russians, the Soviets, the Ruskies, collectivism, the proletariat and the Communists of the world, an effort that united them as never before against a bunch of foreign forces that, as a terrible aftermath of the lost war, were now unleashed against them in the shape of the muscovite tyrants and collectivization, they knew this would happen, and so it had. There's your shared cauldron, go stuff yourselves. I saw into the depths of their anticommunism boiling over with hate even when I didn't want to. I became the one enemy they held in common. By degrees my situation became clear to me, though for decades to come I couldn't admit to myself what I had managed to understand all the same and what I hadn't, because I couldn't very well have chosen any of the possibilities before me. All I knew was that I wanted no part of this underground warfare, I would not accept any role in this underground warfare, I didn't want conflict with anyone, nor did I want to come out the winner in anything, nor would I run to our parents to take shelter behind them, nor would I rat on anyone or implicate them, on the other hand, I wouldn't be a victim either, and for all I cared, they could go and fight their wars among themselves, if that's what made them happy. I wouldn't have gone quite so far as to say lick my ass, because I understood them too well for that, and also, I had plenty of reasons to be afraid.

The siege provided me with ample visual evidence of the nature of violent death. If I didn't have luck, then I didn't have luck, and if I couldn't protect myself, then I couldn't protect myself.

In my mind, the frozen corpses with their bullet wounds that my parents carried on the sled they'd brought back from Gömörsid needed no further elucidation.

Everything was okay just as long as I came home from school with Gábor Baltazár and Géza Székács, they were the exceptions in this environment silently seething with hatred, grievances, and violent emotions; they probably came from the same conservative-liberal biotope to which I was bound by family tradition, or else I ended up there thanks to my own intellectual inclinations; also, I went to school with them, and Piros came along, too, the sweet, uncouth son of field hands, and Csíder, the sly, lanky son of proletarian parents, but basically a meek person, almost a gentle soul, the pockets of each of us hiding our slingshots with nearly a handful of pebbles or lead bullets, because we belonged to the Diana Street boys, even though I was the only one multiply disadvantaged among them, who didn't want to identify even with his own gang, I even had a horror of sporting events, if people were rooting near me, I moved away so I shouldn't have to see and hear them. Even as a small child I preferred long-distance running, just so I wouldn't have to race anyone short-distance. My situation changed for the worse when I had to pay for my school lunch, and from then on I went home on my own. The sum we had to pay for our lunch was commensurate with our parents' incomes; below a certain income, lunch was free, and so it came to light that our parents had the highest monthly income of anyone.

Our father's was two thousand, six hundred and thirty forints, our mother's two thousand, three hundred and ten, which was considered an astronomical sum back then. The others couldn't understand why the hell I stayed after school for lunch. I was the odd man out once again, and given my interests, this just added fuel to the fire. What I read was foreign to them, what I listened to was foreign to them. In the afternoon, those of us who stayed after school were given a slice of bread and an apple, or else a slice of bread and a slice of fruit jelly. The Mátyás király Street boys ceremoniously confiscated mine every time. They even said what they were doing. We will now take the fruit jelly. They swiped it off the top of my bread. I whipped my head around, to catch a last glimpse of the fruit jelly. It felt good the way the taste of the bread transformed the taste of the apple in my mouth. To this day I often catch myself feeling for the two tastes on my tongue. Sometimes one of the bigger boys, sometimes another would snatch the bread from out of my hand. They must have drawn lots to see who got to do it. It was part and parcel of the spirit of the place.

One of them even went so far as to make the grounds for the confiscation crystal clear. At home you probably stuff yourselves like animals anyway.

Our mother was given a new post again that they didn't talk about because she considered it beneath her dignity, meaning that she considered it utterly senseless, because it smacked of charity. She became head of the campaign and propaganda department of one of Budapest's districts, meaning that she had to make others accept or at least justify, in the name of good sense, the decrees and laws against which her own sense of justice rebelled. My Tauber grandmother would have said she was a meshuggener, *ein Nichtsnutz*. She accepted it, she did it without a word of complaint, and in the meantime, she consoled herself with the thought that the fifth district is an important district, most of the ministries are located there, though admittedly, the same Ilona Vígh was her superior whom she had put down in the white marble palace on Múzeum Street because of the cocoa with whipped cream.

Meanwhile, in our father's post, an even bigger problem was brewing. They whispered behind my back something embezzlement.

If after lunch, I don't know why, I didn't have to stay after school, I simply left and snuck out through the back gate, the one on Felhő Street, though we weren't supposed to use it, and besides, sometimes it was locked, in which case I'd use the gate in the back of the building for those who stayed after school, though sometimes this gate was also locked; in short, sometimes I had to climb over the fence and run through the woods as quickly as my legs would carry me, so I wouldn't be caught. But the boys found out somehow, listen, after lunch the little Nádas hurried along the Brancsi alone, panting, because this is what they, the boys from Mátyás király Street, called the Braun Woods among themselves, because we're not Germans to talk German, they said, because they're real big Hungarian patriots, that's what they are. It also got around that twice a week, at four in the afternoon, little Nádas took piano lessons in Felhő Street with Aunt Lehel, meaning Mária Lehel, whom every child feared, and not just those who took piano lessons from her or stole pears from her prized pear trees. This Mária Lehel had marvelous pruned pear trees, she brushed their trunks with lime, she wouldn't tolerate vermin in her garden. There was hardly any light in Felhő Street, so I never lost sight of the three light poles that I had to reach as soon as possible when I turned the corner into her street. In the winter, by four in the afternoon it was getting dark, and by five, when I left Mária Lehel's house, it was pitch-dark, and I couldn't get from one sphere of light to the next without having to transcend my own abject terror. In my dreams, this is how I stagger between the illuminated circles and my fear to this day. I know that I won't make it to the next circle of light, they are going to grab me first.

Such a thing would have undermined my self-respect, they'd picked me out for the role of victim, but I refused to be their victim and stoically kept up appearances, as if I understood nothing, knew nothing, knew no fear, and suspected nothing.

In those days it would have been irresponsible of me to burden my parents with such childish nonsense, and so our shared universe was mutually inhabited by our mutually unspoken problems. I couldn't have reached them with my problems even if I had hounded them. They understood nothing, nothing at all. For instance, they didn't understand when I said that they're offering ballet classes at school. Instead, in just two days they found a piano teacher for me who lived close by; her name was Mária Lehel, and she beat her students, she smacked their hands and heads, she had a stinging conductor's baton, or else she used her scores, and beat her students with those. She grabbed my hair, beat my head against the piano keys if I struck a wrong note, or if I ignored the time signatures, or got the key wrong. It says minor, damn it. Her piano trembled as she said this. They found me this cruel Mária Lehel, just so they wouldn't have to enroll me in a ballet class, which is what I really wanted. When I finally got up the nerve to ask for the money, they said no. It was so awkward as it slipped out that even I was ashamed of the sentence. Give me money because I'd like to pay for the ballet class. That was the sentence.

They looked at each other, started laughing, what laughing, they screamed with laughter, which in emotional terms meant that I was shut out of their symbiosis, but they, the two of them, seemed to know something between them when, in fact, they understood nothing. Their heads were stuffed with psychobabble. Their ignorance was outrageous. The two of them saw eye-to-eye on just about everything, which, needless to say, had its own aesthetic, it had elegance, and also a pronounced sensual content. I couldn't help but feel its attraction. Their mutual and mutually conceived sentence sounded like this, do they want their son to turn out to be a so-and-so. I had never heard the word describing what would become of their son due to the ballet, and after I'd heard it repeatedly and in various contexts, even then, for a long time, until I was about thirty years old, I had no idea where I should deposit the word in my consciousness. It just didn't fit. Their synchronized laughter filled me with awe, all the while that I couldn't see it any other way except that they were laughing at my expense, I was asking something ridiculous, which I understood less than I understood my classmates and why they were going to lay into me, beat me to a pulp, and beat the shit out of me. And then, as if they were shouting it in unison, but for each other's benefit, no, it was the last thing they wanted.

Meaning, they didn't want their son to become a fag.

It wouldn't be a good investment. They had no intention of financing my faggotry. I should go shovel snow. Earn my way toward it. It was winter recess. Early next morning, when it was still dark, I set off. The Public Sanitation Company started hiring people at its local office on Felhő Street at 5:00 a.m. Never in my life, either up on the mountain or anywhere in my native town, did I ever see the likes of the people gathered there. I waited with them for the foreman, and as we stood around waiting, they kept looking at me, sizing me up, wondering what I was doing there, and when it was my turn, the foreman sent me home, saying he had no need of children.

They're hiring from the age of sixteen, son, a woman shouted after me.

I didn't understand the word, but I understood investment, and so I thought that some financial complication stood in the way of my ballet lessons. On the other hand, at the end of the month, they gave me money to pay the piano teacher who loved beating me; also, I was surprised to see that the sum was much, much greater than what they'd have to give me for ballet class. Once again, I couldn't keep up with them in the labyrinth of their thinking. It was clear to me that it was no use trying to understand this gradually receding world of theirs in which I had to take expensive piano lessons instead of the inexpensive ballet class, whereas I wanted to dance and not play the piano. However, I realized at last that I mustn't embarrass them with my own ideas.

It wasn't so dark anymore, the days were getting longer and warmer. The thick blanket of snow was bathed in sunlight, emitting light clouds of mist, and as the sun set, as the temperature slid below freezing, the mist above the thick blanket of snow grew increasingly dense. As I came out of Mária Lehel's house with my scores and music books and the mist veritably rustled around me, a hard snowball struck me in the face, right on target, blinding me. And just as I was about to whip my head around in the direction of the park to see where it had come from, the next one came, and then the next, not all of them were on target, but one had a stone inside it. The impact made me drop the scores and the music books, the pages scattered along the icy surface of the snow, so the boys must have been satisfied with themselves. I caught only the faintest glimpse of them, mere shadow shapes. They confirmed their victory with laughter and war cries. One of them gave a whistle, it must have been a signal to another standing at an even greater distance in the mist. Their clumping footsteps receded somewhere along the row of trees leading to the church. It was suddenly quiet and I could hear the gentle rustle of the mist once more among the trees. I stopped and wiped my face, some of it had gotten into my neck and right away it started to melt, all of which I registered with a strange alertness; it happened to me, no question, I leaned over to shake the snow out, when I saw something dark dripping onto the snow. The stone had broken the skin above the temple. The skull bleeds heavily but briefly. Because of the previous day's attack, the next day I was fair game in their eyes. Prém tried to trip me up, a bunch of the boys stood around, bracing for a good laugh, but I managed to dodge his trick. I must have been ready for anything. During gym, while we were running, Prém pretended he was limping, sir, I sprained my ankle, he sat down on the side bench and watched indifferently as we made our rounds, but I was prepared, he couldn't fool me, I knew what he was up to, and once again I managed to dodge the foot he'd slid so breezily in front of my own. But back inside the gym, as I was about to flip over the box, Vadász kicked it out from under me. Had I not caught on to him in the split second before I flipped, I'd have landed on my spine. But in the middle of the episode, I managed to slow myself down just enough so that my now superfluous momentum landed me on the edge of the gym mat, which would have made them laugh, if only they didn't have to scream with laughter over Vadász's failed attempt. The gym teacher, whose name I can't remember, though I do remember that he was very attractive, a sadist, this too I stored in my mind as something awaiting an explanation, why someone must turn sadistic in beauty's paradise, grabbed Vadász by the hair and, screaming like a madman, started shaking and hitting him, he kicked him repeatedly and forced him to the floor.

Vadász squealed like a stuck pig, please don't hurt me, please don't hurt me, I won't do it again.

Not hurt you, you shit, you filthy shit, goddamn you, you piece of shit, not hurt you, I could end up in jail because of you, and he kept kicking him once he was down. Fucking hell, you're gonna land me in jail. This, too, surprised me, that the gym teacher, instead of taking my part after the fact, was concerned only with saving his own attractive skin, as if what had happened had happened to him, whereas it had happened to me. He even slammed the medicine ball into him, because it was at hand, he managed to hit Vadász's ribs, as he was busy shielding his head, hitting him so hard that he remained sprawled on the floor, unable to breathe for minutes on end, while the handsome offender ran screaming with rage from the gym, but not because he was sorry, but to find something else with which he could beat the filthy piece of shit within an inch of his life.

When he returned brandishing a broken javelin, the boy was still lying there, just as he'd left him.

And yet the next day, Prém whispered in my ear not to worry, I'd get what was coming to me, because the gym teacher beat up Vadász so bad that he didn't come to school, and it was all my fault, and the boys weren't about to take the affront lying down, and I'd better not show my face in front of them again. Instead of Vadász, Vadász's mother came to the school that day, and she lodged a complaint with the principal against the gym teacher, who a couple of days later disappeared from the school on Diana Street for good. I'd get what was coming to me, and I wouldn't have to wait long for their revenge, Prém said. Meanwhile, he smiled sweetly, as if he were whispering an endearing compliment in my ear. Prém could be incredibly convivial. In a sense, I thought of him as an exceptional phenomenon of nature. He managed to transform his helplessness, along with his seething thirst for revenge, into a lasting game, which rendered the game all the more cruel. Basically, he was demanding that I lay myself open to their every whim without a word of protest, no matter what they might do to me. And like one who'd accomplished what he'd come for, he moved on with beautiful, rhythmic dancing steps.

For all I knew, the war might have lasted forever, if only Vadász had not turned on me one day out of the blue. I was just getting up from my school bench and he was standing facing me, barely an arm's length away. I had no way of getting around him. Besides, I suddenly realized that was part of their plan, they'd surrounded me with no escape route in sight. Vadász wore checked shirts, only checked cotton shirts, always. He had a red-checked shirt, a green-checked shirt, a blue-checked shirt, and nothing else; he was now wearing his green-checked cotton shirt. He was a strong boy with peasant features and he was much taller than I. I was especially fascinated by his skin, because his white forehead gleamed, and also his thick black brows, I kept looking at the strikingly manly black eyebrows gracing his white face.

If ever he came face-to-face with a filthy Jew, he said, he's gonna punch him in the face so the piece of shit gave up the ghost.

He hadn't even reached the end of the sentence, but I already knew what he was intending to say, just as I'd always known beforehand what they were planning and why, and I had no illusions about the balance of power either, but my hand shot out, and while I screamed, here's a filthy Jew for you, I slapped him so hard, though it wasn't me slapping him, it was my hand slapping him, and I was as surprised as anyone, all the latent life energy gone undetected till then ripping right through the inhibition, in short, I slapped him so hard that he staggered, though it may have been his surprise that made him do it, and he keeled over his bench, and like someone who'd been folded up, slid under the seat. And needless to say, he couldn't very well wrest himself out of there with dignity to beat the shit out of me. He became a laughingstock, whereas I was a lot more surprised than he, I didn't know what was happening, the life energy placed at my disposal came from somewhere deep outside me, as if against my will, and yet it was of a piece with me. I never struck anyone before or after. I hit my brother, once, though it was really symbolic, a reminder not to whine after our parents, because they weren't coming. It was time he understood that we were outside their sphere of interest. I hit Magda once, but that wasn't prompted by temper either, but by ecstatic considerations of love. If I couldn't reach her senseless anxiety either with words or the gestures of our lovemaking, I'd been trying for seven whole years, then obviously I couldn't persuade her through words that I'm not about to dictate, now or ever, under any conditions. She had no reason to fear for herself on my account. I had to pull her out of the current of her amorous shock, I had no other means at my disposal except to startle her out of the paranoid nightmare that brought forth monsters, out of the dream of the conscious mind, because she kept launching into the hysterical lover's litany that ended in tears and breakups, never again, only to continue, on Tuesday or Friday, just as it had been, but to this day, the strength of that slap fills me with horror. On the other hand, it proved effective. Though that doesn't necessarily mean it was ethical.

We cried our hearts out, which brought plenty of returns when we made love, and it broke through her constraints so thoroughly that we never had to mention it again.

It happened on the bed of a mansard room in Kisoroszi in September 1968, a couple of weeks after the Warsaw Pact troups marched into Prague, it was warm, the window wide open, and the two of us naked on an unstable iron bed. József Tóth, the priest in Kisoroszi whom the small colony of artists who'd gathered there called Titu, the nickname he had as a child, who knows why, anyway he was coming up the stairs, making lots of creaking noises as he ascended, to bring me the Word. He did this every Monday if I failed to attend mass the day before. He came to repeat his preaching for my benefit, but if I didn't attend Bible class on Thursday, he came on Friday as well, to tell me what they'd discussed about which passage of which verse of the Bible. He didn't just do it with me, he went around the village, he visited everyone who had failed to show up for mass, including people who hadn't set foot in his church in ten years but were nevertheless willing to hear him out. I had to call out to him to sit down and wait in front of the door, because he couldn't come in just yet. If he found me with Magda, or Magda and I went to see him, the poor man had a problem, he was at a loss. He saw that we loved each other, and he reasoned that clearly he couldn't very well ask us to stop loving each other, no man on earth has the right to do that; on the other hand, we couldn't expect him to condone sin. It was clear, he didn't have to say it, the third book of Moses, chapter twenty, verse ten, the man that committeth adultery with another man's wife, even he that committeth adultery with his neighbor's wife, both the adulterer and the adulteress shall surely be put to death. Poor Titu, he didn't know what to make of us, or of the whole thing, we ruffled his feathers. Or what was he to make of the Prophet Hosea, who advised that you should go on loving the woman who is someone else's lover and an adulteress, even as the Lord loveth the children of Israel, though they turn to other gods. And so, even though he didn't quite know what to make of us, he considered his love for us justified.

If he saw us separately, that was all well and good, but if he saw us together, his crisis of conscience wouldn't let him rest. After all, Paul the Apostle, Corinthians six eighteen, says to flee fornication because every sin that man committeth is outside the body, but he that committeth fornication sinneth against his own body.

I told him that I fully understood and appreciated his words, but I couldn't help him because we had not sinned against our own bodies, nor had we sinned against the other person's body.

No, of course not, he said, taken aback, and shook his big round head with the big wire-rimmed glasses, he knows I can't help it, he said, it was his crisis of conscience, and he had to solve it himself, God willing.

The others were equally helpless; after all, they intended to have a good laugh at my expense, and now here was this big gangling champion of justice, this Vadász, who was about to punish the filthy Jew, but instead he slipped under his own bench, and now they were laughing at him, humiliating him, they were laughing at the debacle of his plans. When he tried to climb out, it looked as if the others were helping him, but they pushed him back instead so they could go on laughing, whereas he had always carried the torch for them. Though I understood their little game, though I understood that for these idiots, raw strength and cleverness weighed more in the balance than their own dark ideas and intentions I didn't like it.

Then one bright and beautiful winter day, perhaps it was the next year, Titu came to us himself, all bright and smiling, saying that thank the Lord, he now understood, he studied the Holy Writ, he was elated that such a thing could happen to him and he could hardly wait for the morning, so he could come and tell me. It hit him like a bolt of lightning. It felt as if it had felled him, whereas it actually raised him up. After all, marriages were made in heaven, and so the priest has nothing to do but confer his blessing. As Paul's letter to the Ephesians says, that's five twenty, give thanks always for all things unto God and the Father in the name of our Lord Jesus Christ, submitting yourselves one to another in the fear of God. That's all he has had to say about the matter. And so he blessed us for real, whatever that may mean. When we think of his blessing, we find it amusing, we laugh, whereas there is nothing to laugh at, because we've been living with this blessing to this day.

The secret war of the two camps continued, but the war against me came to an end once and for all in this school. It was called off the minute I left them high and dry with their malicious laughter and walked out on them. That same year I played Csongor in Mihály Vörösmarty's verse drama *Csongor and Tünde*, which Bánky, our music teacher, taught us, and with the news and photographs of the production, we even made it into some horrid illustrated papers. Thanks to my short cloak decorated with frogging, my red velvet shako decorated with feathers, and my boots made of red morocco leather, I became, in the blink of an eye, the favorite of the girls at school, and especially of their mothers. For decades to come, I remembered the beautiful drama from beginning to end, including every role in it. From then on, they didn't snatch my apple from me and they didn't snatch the fruit jelly off my bread. Our music teacher, Bánky, a gangling man with a bright disposition, noticed my singing voice during rehearsals, and said I must attend choir classes. He had me sing soprano solos. In the other schools, the High School for Chemistry and the industrial school, a new war against me would have commenced, but by then I was on top of the situation. I showed my hand before they could aim their gun. With the quick naming of names, I ruined their collective fun.

But back then in the school on Diana Street, the sudden reversal in group psychology must have been so powerful that it didn't even give Vadász a chance to indulge in ritual tribal vengeance. Sometime later he asked me to visit them on Melinda Street to trade something for something else, I don't remember what, but it was obviously a ruse. They communicated with one another in the language of commerce as well. When they spoke what you might call honestly with one another, that too was part of their bartering, the strengthening or weakening of their dependence on each other, or an intent to corrupt, which is the foretoken of a striving for independence. They had to take the wind out of the other's sails. Probably, he was thinking about some sort of ammunition. Or else it may have been a cartridge fuse removed from some live ammunition that he said I couldn't do without, and in order to spare him, I didn't tell him that I most certainly could. This, too, was an interesting phenomenon, the peaceful commerce between the groups that were mortal enemies.

At the time when I was still being singled out, four boys from an upper class were waiting for me in the park, and it was obvious that they were now going to beat me up. I tried to get out of the way, but they kept calling my name, they followed me, they said to stop, no need to shit in my pants, what am I, a girl or a fag that I'm scared shitless, and when we reached the heroes' memorial, one of them managed to come around and face me. They just want to show me something, no need to shit my pants. You and your kind always shit your pants. And they know we're always interested in what they want to show me. By which time the others had formed a ring around me, from which I was supposed to understand that I'm not me, I'm just a Jew, a turd, just like all the others, the whole Jewish kit and kaboodle, which outnumbered the cockroaches, and that's why Hitler didn't manage to exterminate us all, they're sorry to say, but what they've got for me, it always gets you all worked up. Meaning the Jews. But I refused to react to their use of the second person plural. If they used the plural with me like this, I invariably asked, I asked even as a grown-up, what do you mean you, what you. I happen to be alone here. They'd said it often enough for me to know what it means and where they'd situated me in their circle, more or less. Never once did I get an answer to my question. I got this second person plural many times in German, too, I probably couldn't get it in French, I don't know, but I didn't get an answer to my question in German either. I was forced to ask older scientists and respected colleagues, too, more than once, who they meant by their esteemed yous, when they saw with their own two eyes that there was no army standing behind me, I was standing there alone. Now, snickering and neighing, these boys pulled a bunch of amateur photographs with serrated edges out of an envelope and tried to sell them to me for ten forints. But they didn't show them for any length of time, they just flashed them before my eye, then shoved them back in the envelope, then pulled them out again. The price was ten forints, which was a great sum. I could never have had ten forints. Rolls cost me twenty fillérs. To tell the truth, they actually seemed embarrassed by what they were doing. Probably, an older brother of one of the boys needed the ten forints. Still, they kept flashing the pictures in front of my eyes, it's not such a big price for these pictures, because there's so many things on them, if only I knew, and they have more where these came from, except they're not showing me now. My father would like them, too. But I better not show my mother. And they guffawed and brayed like donkeys. They'd have surely been surprised had I played along. I had no idea what these naked men and women from the lower class were up to on the disheveled beds and piles of bed linen strewn all over the place. I didn't have to pay for it right away. My first thought was that the pictures were taken in an insane asylum, because I'd never seen one. They'd just shown it to me from the outside. That's where the crazy people live. I could have the contents of the envelope on credit, I could pay for it later, but in that case, needless to say, it'd cost more. Or they could pawn it with me, but in that case I had to give them something valuable for it. They knew about my valuable stamp collection. They followed me for some time in the foggy park amid the bare trees hawking their wares, and probably, the whole humiliating scene would have never taken place had they not found out somehow about my parents' high income. Still, I stuck to my guns, I kept insisting that I had no need of their pictures. On the other hand, I really did have a stamp collection that my father had started when he was a child, and as a matter of fact, there were some gems in it. I just continued the collection. He explained everything to me about collecting stamps, how to soak and dry them, how to classify them, but now I told them that they were misinformed, I didn't have a stamp collection. I didn't say that I didn't have ten forints for such pictures, because I had no idea what they were. At the same time I could tell that I wouldn't get off that easily because they were under duress to sell them. For years I wondered what was on those photographs and why those untidy and agitated men and women in those miserable rooms with their dirty walls were supposed to be so tantalizing. And yet I knew perfectly well that the erect penis played a role in the coupling of the male and female of the species. I also saw the Baltazárs' beautiful black dog trying to mount our supposedly ugly little dog, and to do so he stuck out something red, but he couldn't manage it because he was too tall and couldn't bend down low enough with that blood-red thing.

Except, it's not like what you all need or what you all don't need, fuck you. If you don't buy it, we'll beat you to a pulp this minute. But I kept walking ahead of them, refusing to agree to their business offer, and somewhere near the home of the certified accountant, on the corner of Diana and Felhő streets, they stopped, and for once I was lucky, they didn't follow me, they just shouted after me, that they're gonna beat us so bad one of these days, we're gonna shit our pants. Except, this time the plural referred to the Diana Street group and not the infidel, filthy Bolshevik-capitalist riffraff Jewish hordes, who were all me wrapped in one person, because I was born a God slayer. Diana Street was off limits for the Mátyás király Street boys, and I didn't see Mátyás király Street myself until I was a grown man. In the end, I went to see Vadász on Melinda Street.

Melinda Street was ours, it was all right, I could go there, even though Vadász belonged to the Mátyás király Street boys. Today I remember only the friendly crowdedness of their living room that opened onto the veranda, but nothing else. And also, how easily it slipped out that next time he should come visit us. This happened as I was leaving. I felt I'd gone too far, I meant it only as a courteous gesture, but a misplaced courteous gesture is in fact a discourtesy. No, it was not proper that I should have invited him, and as a matter of fact, he didn't come, which was best for both of us.

The builders, too, arrived unexpectedly, our parents didn't mention this to us either. When I got home from school, everything was wide open, strangers coming in and out of the house, I found no one else at home except these builders, strangers who ignored my presence as they battered the walls. As I approached, our dog came running from her house, she'd been lying low inside, she now came for me, I could see that now I was her only home, she was frightened, she didn't know what was happening. She was a wonderful creature, pure trust and goodwill. Only Gábor Baltazár's dog could measure up to her. They were knocking the Delft tiles off the walls of the bathroom and the kitchen and flung the debris out the window.

She was a marvelous dog, and we called her Cuddles, what else, she was a mutt, a half-breed, as our parents said with some scorn, another thing I didn't understand, why must a dog be a purebred, seeing how we couldn't abide racism; she was probably the fruit of the love of a dachshund and a spaniel, and my brother and I loved her. She followed us everywhere, she protected us; breathless, she ran alongside us, she came skiing and sledding with us, we couldn't have made her turn back or brushed her off even if we'd wanted, head held high, she followed us all the way to Normafa; she walked with a snappy gait, as if she were proud of our great big friendship, but she didn't come along with me to the ski slope in Harangvölgy. She watched my receding back for a while longingly from the top of the hill, but when I turned around, she was gone. She slunk away, dragging her tail as she ran home on her short little legs. She couldn't be shut in the garden, she dug a hole in no time and, triumphant, broke loose and ran after us, barking like the dickens. When she was happy, she'd often pee, sometimes she peed on my shoes. Which didn't bother me in the least. She came with me to the school garden, too, and she waited for hours at the school garden gate or down on the corner of Diana Street by the tin crucifix that in her religious frenzy Masa Feszty had painted in brilliant colors. If I waited on line at the food shop, the bakery, or the butcher, she waited on the other side of the street self-effacing, showing what a good dog she was, so people wouldn't chase her off or kick her aside. What was this ugly mug doing here. The ugliest dog I've ever seen. Who does this ugly dog belong to. She's mine and she's not ugly. If that dog isn't ugly, then you don't know what a good-looking dog is like, boy.

This dog was happy with us, and the two of us, my brother and I, were happy with her.

On the other hand, how was I to comfort her in the middle of the noisy goings-on around the house just then, what could I have said to her.

Besides, from that spring day it would have been difficult for me to say where our kitchen was or whether there was water in the house, or for how much longer we'd have to do without electricity in the dark hole with its small window giving out to the hall that would be our bathroom, because they'd taken their electrician somewhere and wouldn't bring him back.

Also, we were up to our neck with remodeling when we had to call it off because our grandparents, our Tauber grandparents, Arnold Tauber and Cecília Nussbaum, would be moving in with us as soon as possible, which meant that the remodeling would need to be reconsidered, otherwise we'd be crammed in. My Aunt Bözsi, the widow Mrs. Miklós Nádas, née Erzsébet Tauber, decided not to wait any longer, which hit us like a bolt from the blue, Miklós was no more, Miklós was gone, they killed Miklós, my one and only darling, the light in my eye, she was waiting to no avail, she was making his favorite preserves to no avail, every object in the apartment was always sparkling clean to no avail, and she dressed up as all up with her beehive hairdo unobtrusively gone gray from waiting, she tended to their apartment, their beloved nest that they'd built together to no avail, in which case she might as well have flung her widow's weeds to the wind and married Gyula Nemes, a widower for the same reasons. I'd met Gyula Nemes earlier in the Dembinszky Street apartment. Though my mouth didn't quite fall open upon hearing the news of the wedding, I was dumbfounded, to say the least. I'd never understood anything of the love lives of the adults, but now it was completely hopeless because I had no place to deposit this wedding in my consciousness, I'd understood nothing whatever, and had to go on staring at them openmouthed for the rest of my life. This Gyula Nemes was an amusing sight, everything hanging on him, not only his clothes but his big belly under his clothes, his buttocks, his breasts, his cheeks, his chin, his eyelids, his bushy brows, he must have been at least ten years older, I think, than my Aunt Bözsi, whose botched operation was followed by further operations, Professor Zinner and Professor Glauber at the Orthopedic Clinic on Karolina Street were bent on rectifying the results. They were both authorities in the cure of congenitally dislocated hips, and so they would not relent, they refused to give up, their professional ambition must have been overwhelming; the patient couldn't give up either, her pains were now constant, even when she was lying down. She couldn't walk, she couldn't stand, and admittedly, all previous efforts at correcting her condition had failed, but they could not fail, because just as the Party could do no wrong, advanced Soviet science could do no wrong either. And if advanced Soviet medical science failed this time around, they'd make some minor adjustments and corrections, so that everyone was satisfied with everything in the end. My Aunt Bözsi couldn't even go to the kitchen or the bathroom without her crutches. She taught her students mostly from her bed dressed in her lace bed jacket, propped up on small pillows edged in lace, her hair perfectly coiffed, her nails manicured, because even there, in excruciating pain, her good cheer never faltered.

If anything, she was louder than ever. She now had to outshout more than just herself.

For the life of me I couldn't figure out how Gyula Nemes came into the picture. He was slightly hard of hearing, his suits were shabby, oil and coffee stains graced his neckties, his dark jackets had dandruff on their shoulders. At times he was even seriously hard of hearing, and then, partly out of consideration for him, my Aunt Bözsi gave free rein to her otherwise penetrating contralto. When she was angry, she could make it crackle. The two of them were always laughing. She had to shout with Gyula, and they brought this to their guests' attention as well, Rózsika, go ahead, please, shout all you want with Gyula, as if you were mad at him, but even the shouting didn't always reach him, because the person's tone must have been important, too. They laughed at everything. There was no knowing what on earth the bride and groom, these victims of fate, could possibly have to laugh about. Gyula, please, don't think so loud, my Aunt Bözsi would say when Uncle Gyula passed wind too loudly, though he did so thinking that he was passing wind discreetly, because he didn't want people to hear, which made them scream with laughter as, taken aback, their visitors sat there holding their plates with cake, delicious compotes, and creamy tortes.

Our parents called our dog Green Coat, because the veterinarian and his assistant wrote on her vaccination certificate that the dog is green. Bitch, mongrel, green. How can such a beautiful animal, such a smart animal be a mongrel, who looks at me and the whole world with such sparkling eyes, and whom I love so much. I was hurt to the depths of my soul. That veterinarian wounded something vital inside me. I insisted that the dog's fur was reddish brown with black spots on her leg and her two ears. I insisted that they shouldn't write green on her vaccination certificate. Not green, sir, take a closer look. The doctor was surprised, not only by my tone of voice, for there was no talking like that to grown-ups, especially not those who had doctor before their name, because they obviously stood above the rest of humankind, but also, because you couldn't reason with a doctor either, so he was surprised by my choice of words. No one had ever told him to give something a closer look, much less a child. The schoolyard was full of dogs barking and howling like the dickens that at times lurched at one another or at humans, leaping, growling, snarling, gagging, and trembling; on the other hand, we provoked them by pulling at their strings, ropes, or leashes made from leather belts. Amid the loud groups of animal and humans, the doctor didn't have time for polemics. He looked at his assistant, who was querying him with her eye, then in a voice that brooked no contradictions, he pronounced the sentence, there's nothing we can do, my boy, the dog is green. They wrote it down. There it was on the slip, irrevocably. As soon as I was out on Felhő Street with my dog, I started crying. What crying, it was sobbing. I cried all the suppressed pain of my disciplined little life out of me. The dog was reddish brown and I would now shout it out to the gods of the universe. The thick fur on her back was like silk with some faint black stripes, and her reddish brown ears, her crooked reddish brown legs were speckled with small, beautifully wavy tufts. These lent her miraculous, gorgeous appearance and her snappy gait a decidedly amusing aspect, as if she were wearing four fluffy slippers. I loved the way she pranced about with them while her nails clicked against the pavement. But only my brother and I thought she was wonderful, everyone else thought she was an ugly, repulsive mutt. Still, despite all my despair, anger, and adoration, my eyes told me that to be sure, seen from a certain angle, and only under certain light conditions, a silky green tinge did appear, if just for a second, that no one had ever seen on a dog, and it moved along with her, waxing and waning, just like the silk shantung dresses of the women, from maroon to black, from brown to green. This color change, or *changeant* as the ladies of breeding called a certain material back then in what little French was left to them from the old days, *changeant*, I have a little *changeant* suit, what bad taste, going to a funeral in a *changeant* cocktail dress, what an idea, in short, I considered the *changeant* character of our dog's fur highly dignified, and now they stigmatized her with it, and our parents seemed inordinately pleased. She's a green dog. We said so. They were also pleased with the *changeant*. Our dog was a green *changeant*. They couldn't abide this wonderful animal who, hiding in the ruined heating vent of the greenhouse the Mátyás király Street gang destroyed, bore us six wonderful green *changeant* puppies. I'd been calling her in vain for at least two days by then; I called her name, I waited, I called her name again, I looked for her in the garden, but couldn't find her until I heard the faint, unfamiliar sounds, the interlaced whining of the newborn pups; I went in the wake of the unfamiliar sound, and I suddenly found myself looking in the wonderful eyes of my wonderful dog, who looked up at me, while the puppies were making squelching sounds as they tugged at her teats; she looked to see if I approved of them. She showed me how helpless they were; she licked and cleaned them so I'd understand. How could I have not understood and approved. In order to convince me she even licked my hand, she let me pick up one of the puppies, but meanwhile she gave me a pleading look, she was giving me instructions with that pleading look, oh, be careful with her, oh, not so hard, until I placed the blind, frightened little bundle of energy that smelled so good back between her teats. The pleasant smell that came from her was the quintessence of a dog's smell, the very idea of a dog's smell. I took Cuddles water and food every day until one day her puppies' eyes opened, and on one of the following days, she came scratching, whining, squirming, and writhing on our threshold, she demanded that I should go with her, except I didn't understand what she wanted, she slid on her belly, she slid along the sidewalk on her swollen teats, she beat her tail against the ground, and she ran back and forth desperately between the greenhouse and the house. Naturally, I followed. She was asking, she was demanding, that I do something in the interest of her puppies. She whined, she barked, she sneered at me. The heating vent was empty. I ran back to the house shouting and screaming. My parents said that Mr. Szabó gave the puppies to someone. But that wasn't true. It was a lie. Why must you lie all the time, I screamed.

They had asked Mr. Szabó to get rid of them.

I still can't understand why they did it, why they would have wanted to see them killed. They hated having such an ugly green dog, such a mutt, a cur, a playground mongrel follow them around, who wouldn't relent and go home even when they threw stones at her, and now bore them even more green dogs. When I yelled at them to stop, they said that they weren't throwing the stones at the dog, they were actually missing her on purpose, so she'd go home. This wasn't true either, it's just that now and then the dog leaped out of the way. But she followed them all the same. It's not easy being a domestic animal.

She followed them by hiding among the bushes or sneaking furtively along under the hedges. I understood the dog. She wanted to show them what a good dog she was. I submit that they may have wanted to get rid of her so they shouldn't have to kill more of her puppies. I found this abhorent, too. Letting someone else do the dirty work. They also had Mr. Szabó smash the carp on the head.

She contracted milk fever. She recovered from her terrible sadness even slower than I. I laid her in my lap and applied rags dipped in cold water to her inflamed teats. Despite the pain, she let me do it, and the compresses eased her pain somewhat. When a couple of weeks later she was running around again and was following all of us as before, my parents went to Dobsinai Street because our father needed to fix something for my Aunt Özsi. My aunt knew by then that this time around an ÁVÓ officer from the countryside had laid his eyes on the villa and they needed to do something to prevent it. On the other hand, what she and her husband didn't know was that the ÁVÓ officer would be nothing more than a sort of caretaker in their house, twice built and twice furnished according to strict Bauhaus architectural principles. They didn't know, how could they, that for years to come, the Counterintelligence Unit of the Ministry of Domestic Affairs would be using their house for state security purposes, they would use it for undercover work, all of which I learned from Gábor Tabajdi's book *Budapest in the Web of Intrigue*, and when the ÁVÓ didn't need it for this purpose anymore, they'd let it fall into decay along with the sheds and lean-tos they'd added to it in the meantime, and also the machine parts and oil containers scattered throughout the garden. Our father spotted all the structural problems in the blink of an eye and fixed them, making sure the house would be safe. The dog went with them, though it would be more accurate to say that as soon as our parents walked out the garden gate, she climbed through the fence and ran after them on her short little legs. That evening, they stayed for dinner at my Aunt Özsi's house. The dog took up her position in front of the gate. Their plan of action was to go to Böszörményi Street after dinner with the dog, where they would get on a tram, the dog would lose track of them, perhaps someone would take her in, or the dogcatcher would take her away. And true to their plan, they left her to her fate. But the dog was back home before them.

It was soon autumn, a wet autumn. I hadn't seen the dog for days by then. I can't say my dog, because she was at least as much my brother's. She was protective of him and stood at the ready to fight for him. When an older boy beat up my little brother, she made a horrendous noise and fell on the boy's ankle. When I went looking for her one Saturday, it may have been November, I looked everywhere that she'd accompanied me the previous couple of days. Perhaps I hadn't noticed when she'd left my side, and she was now waiting for me at a certain spot that I couldn't remember, I became obsessed with this thought. I simply couldn't remember when and where I had last seen her.

It was getting dark on that particular Saturday when I found her on the wet leaves under a barren bush near our house. But I found her only because she gave out a single, barely audible moan. She must have been running a fever.

I picked her up and took her inside the house. My brother and I made her bed in the hall. By then my grandfather Tauber and my grandmother Cecília Nussbaum were living with us, they occupied the room that our parents had originally meant for my brother and myself, and also, we had a maid again, a domestic servant, a wonderful sixteen-year-old girl from Pilisszentlélek, her name was Szidónia Tóth, and she had a long, thick braid of hair hanging down her back, and she was dressed in folk costume from head to toe.

The dog lay there just as I'd left her and wouldn't open her eyes even though we put food and water in front of her. There was no evidence of physical injury on her.

Grandfather stood above her for some time.

Yes, he said quietly, this dog is going to die.

Szidónia Tóth also came and stood over us. She unbraided her hair every morning, combed it, braided it again, and flung it over her shoulder. It was so heavy, it made a thudding sound as it hit her back.

If she won't eat or drink, she'll be dead by morning, we heard her say.

I took a piece of rag and dipped it in water. I wanted her to drink and I kept squeezing out the water into her jaw.

Without much conviction, but she licked her jaw.

You see, she drank, I said to Szidónia Tóth, as if the dog's life depended on words or my clever trick.

When I got up on Sunday, she was dead on her makeshift bed out in the hall. The whites of her eyes were trained on us, and her tongue hung out from under her fang, as if she were snarling. Her four little legs with their amusing tufts stood out, rigid, and her body was even more rigid, cold, lifeless, though the night before our parents had consoled us by promising to find a veterinarian first thing Monday morning, and we'd take her to him. Everything always turned out otherwise. When I heard Baltazár's sharp whistle, he could whistle by sticking two fingers between his lips, I always ran to the fence. We'd just buried our dog and their black dog kept visiting the spot, he sniffed around, scratched the earth a bit, then left. He was clearly agitated.

Szidónia Tóth said that we should place a heavier stone over the dog's grave to prevent the Baltazárs' dog from digging it out. My brother and I and some other children hauled the base of a statue that had fallen and broken in a storm to the grave. These pretty ugly garden statues of naked goddesses and fauns were made of yellow clay, but thanks to the beneficial passage of time, were blackened and covered with moss.

At the fence Baltazár told me that at dawn the previous day some men came and searched their home and they received a mandatory writ, and they were going to be forcibly resettled tomorrow, they could take a couple of personal belongings and household objects along, the rest they had to leave behind, and they were packing with Éva now, he didn't know where they'd be taken, but he'd write. He said this fast, in a whisper, he said it without any sign of worry or excitement. We stood for a while, looking at each other. We didn't know what to do or say in this universe of ours. Then we held hands over the fence. It lasted longer than a simple handshake. I watched his pleasant, slender figure climb the steps to the terrace, then disappear into the house.

That evening a very elegant car came to their house. Similar cars had come to their home plenty of times before and they weren't necessarily black, at times they were colorful, even cheerful, swallow tailed, turquoise-green, pink; they came for their mother at sunset and brought her back late at night, and all of them had special blue diplomatic license plates. They were limousines, some were even bigger; they were American cars, huge street cruisers, genteel barges from the time before the siege. Sometimes several such automobiles would come to the house, whole bunches of people poured out of them, a merry company with their lively chatter. At other times they sent something in a basket, a crate, a paper parcel, or their father had sent something through them, this is how they said it, to send something through someone, and at such times the liveried driver got out, walked up to the front door, and rang the bell.

I could see the red light of the cruisers from my window through the trees and shrubs, at times I even caught flashes of color, but from fall through spring, I saw the ceremony only in silhouette. When they sent a chauffeur for her, this woman, whose beauty and elegance surpassed everyone else's, soon made her appearance in her stunning hats or turbans and her dresses tailor-fitted to her pencil-thin body, at times she appeared in an evening gown, a light fur cape or stole thrown over her shoulder, or else a light coat. I also kept an eye out for her because if I saw her, I'd wait until it grew dark and the house was quiet, I'd wait for my little brother to fall asleep, and when the silence was total, I opened the window of our room, threw my shoes out into the garden, and my coat, too, if there was a chill, a child, the small child that I was, could easily fit through the window grill, and I ran just as I was, in my pajamas, and also wearing their pajamas, Baltazár and Éva welcomed me amid great ritual shouts of joy and tribal dances. By the time I got there, the rumba, the samba, the foxtrot, and the tango would be blaring from their gramophone. All the lights were on in the huge salon, the wall brackets, the standing lamps, the chandeliers; they built their house in hacienda style, which meant that it was accordingly large, their salon with its dark wooden beams was so big it needed two chandeliers to light it up, but the lights were also on in the kitchen and the hall leading to the children's room. Everywhere.

All these things were now at an end.

Early next morning I was startled awake by the unfamiliar sound of a truck passing the house. Or else I was just imagining it. It was just a dream, I should forget it and go back to sleep.

I ran to the fence, slipped through the hole that we'd enlarged to accommodate us, but by then their house was silent and all the shutters closed.

I waited for him at school. Maybe it was just a mistake, he's just late, they've let him come back, he'll show up with a written excuse, the resettlement authorities had made a mistake, the student was missing from the first couple of classes, it was their mistake.

I waited a long time for him to write, as he had promised. Possibly three decades passed, possibly four, when I found out that he was living somewhere in Venezuela or Argentina, I don't remember where, besides, it doesn't matter, and he also remembered me.

If there was no other way and there couldn't be any other way, you kept the other on a pilot light in your mind.

I wonder what became of their black dog.

For years their house stood empty, everything fell into decay, their pool in the garden had cracks in it. From time to time I slipped through the fence and wandered around their garden gone wild.

In those days Judit Benkő took us on short study trips into the Buda hills. It was a small gardening group, but I can't remember the others. It's strange, considering that we had to be a tight-knit little group, children who, along with me, were probably hateful little freaks as far as the others were concerned. I suspect this is why I didn't identify with them. I didn't want to be eccentric, the odd man out. I remember only one thing about them; if they said something, if it wasn't Judit Benkő who spoke in her soft, cautious tones, I was bored stiff. Even before they'd opened their mouths, I was bored. I felt an affinity only with Judit Benkő, but with her, the feeling was profound. I'd be at a loss to say why. We went on full-day Sunday tours with special equipment, hiking boots, windbreakers, we carried our food, haversacks and small knapsacks that contained our blankets and tools for collecting plants and insects, and also containers, and in our hands a carefully bound handbook of plants, for those of us who had one, at any rate, the Vera Csapody, almost everyone had that. From among Gyurika's books I took along Cserey's handbook of plants bound in oilcloth from the Pocket Library of Science published by Stampfel, with notes added by my Mezei grandmother. Sometimes I also took along the no less wonderful Jenő Nagy, the title was *The Birds of the Forest*, with 65 color illustrations and 26 charcoal drawings. I no longer have that particular copy, but I do have a copy that I inherited in Kisoroszi from Aunt Iduska, the widow of the local physician, Ferenc Nagy, during my first winter of voluntary exile there, along with a very beautiful Bible. She gave me Jenő Nagy's field guide to birds in three languages, Hungarian, Latin, and German, because I read it out loud when I first saw it on her table. This is the book Judit Benkő and I used. Aunt Iduska gave me the Bible in the early fall of the following year, when she left me alone in the empty house because she went to Debrecen to die at her daughter's house. She had lung cancer, I'm going to suffocate, she said. I should forgive her for telling me, but she had to tell someone. She wasn't going to tell her daughter. But why wouldn't she. Because she doesn't love her. In that case, why was she going to stay with her. Because she was hoping there'd be enough time for them to figure out how to love each other. The truth, which she didn't say, was that she wanted to die and follow her husband, and she did so. The truth is that she should have given the Bible to someone in the family because there was a very personal inscription on the inside flap, but we were very close. Iduska was short, lively, a mathematician, and I somehow equated her in my mind more or less with the idea of Protestantism, dry and hard, like a rock, devoid of sentimentality, just none of your namby-pamby, no histrionics. *To my Ferenc in memory of our engagement so he may always guide the path of our joint lives in its spirit*, she wrote to her fiancé, a student of medicine, in the Bible she gave him when she was still a young girl, and which she then gave me along with the guide to plants before she left for Debrecen. *With true love and devotion, Ida. February 22, 1930, Budapest.*

Judit Benkő and I always agreed beforehand who would bring which guidebook and tools with them.

Sometimes we didn't even go very far, just up the interminable Swiss Steps, all along Rege Street; we passed the Observatory, this stood among the ancient oaks where the asphalt road ended; we continued along the carriage tracks, then when we reached a tourist path with trail markers, we turned right and walked along a no-man's-land over hollows and steep slopes, up to a rocky peak where on a clear day you could see the hills of west Buda, and if you turned around, the flatlands to the south all the way to the misty extremities of the east. We didn't go because of the beauty of the landscape or for the sake of the excursion, but because of the plateau and the highly articulated slope to the south overgrown with scattered shrubs. This plateau and slope were incredibly rich in flora and saturated with enchanting, pungent smells. Once you'd gained a certain familiarity with plants, once you'd recorded the seasonal schedule of their growth in your mind, their germination and flowering, you could more or less get your bearings thanks to the smells in a stony plateau such as this. The crumbly, chalky soil was overgrown with clumps of rare grasses that could be found nowhere else and so were thought to be extinct, and also masses of bulbous plants all the way down to the valley. The sweet williams stood out prominently among them. I checked, the components of its smell haven't changed in sixty years. A person remembers smells, too, all smells, the smell of sweet williams among the spiked, dry grasses, just as he remembers tastes, but both need a bit of something for a person to remember them by. I learned to follow scents from Judit Benkő. She also taught me how to collect plants, how to press or dry them, either for my collection, or to obtain seeds from them, and also what to watch for with regard to plants, whether or not they could be collected, she didn't launch into explanations, she just taught me quietly on our excursions; for instance, she taught me that a single specimen should be considered protected until we find a second, third, fourth, or fifth, if there's just one specimen, it's best to leave it, let it breed, a person shouldn't damage the vegetation in his greed, we should mark the spot and collect samples next year, let's not satisfy our collector's passion at the expense of the vegetation. And since, thanks to the light western wind, this plateau and hillside were exceptionally rich in vegetation, it was equally rich in lizards, rat snakes, flies, spiders, centipedes, butterflies, and birds.

I don't know why, but under Judit Benkő's guidance, after a while I gave up collecting plants and I gave away my collection, though I can't remember who I gave it to, but from time to time I still find pressed flowers and grasses in some book I haven't opened in ages; I didn't think twice about using our books to press plants, and so I still find dried and discolored traces of my former hobby on the pages of old books, even scraps of dried petals. I placed them between tissue paper or blotting paper, but the juice from the succulent stems and buds stained the pages. I classified my collection according to plant groups, plant families, and types; I glued them to sketch paper and placed them in binders. Judit Benkő may have steered me away from plants because she saw that I'd touch frogs without aversion, and not just the pretty tree frogs or the brown-spotted green bullfrogs, but even toads; I dissected them, I prepared the muscles, and I'd even grab the various types of snails, lizards, and rat snakes without hesitation according to their anatomy, the instinct to lord it over animals is missing from my makeup; she saw that I wasn't bothered by the cool and slimy feel of reptiles and soft-bodied creatures, and I let a meter-and-a-half-long forest snake wind itself around my arm, and also the somewhat thinner, large fork-tongued whip snake with its striking patterns, the sunbathing lizards, the large ones, the green ones; I could even tame them for a second so they wouldn't get away, I carefully stroked them twice on top of the head between the eyes or under their turquoise throats that were throbbing from their heartbeat but only twice and no more, I worked this out for myself; Judit Benkő was especially thrilled by my discovery; in their surprise they stayed like that, with raised heads, watching with something like friendly interest, the way you look at a friend or your child, cheerful and trusting, even though they wouldn't tolerate me touching them a third time, and would then sneak away; on the other hand, this trick didn't work with the brownish gray Hungarian lizard that favored warm and dry places, the only one that didn't live in crevices but dug a hole for itself, and so was classified among the worm lizards, or the long-tailed, swift wall lizards. I also showed Judit Benkő that I could mesmerize the fork-tongued whip snakes by giving them the evil eye. At such times, the snake froze in mid-action, its eyes did not move, only its heart beat on its scaly side, but just as surely, you too were frozen into its whip snake being. It suspended your feel for time, it distorted your feel for space. It gave primacy to your hearing and sense of smell, thus depriving your senses of the millennia-long primacy of sight. Needless to say, I couldn't explain this to her, but she nodded with that faint little smile of hers. I had a large crowded aquarium, and I also fabricated a huge terrarium on our veranda, this is how they said it, I fabricate a terrarium, I fabricate an aquarium, I don't remember anymore who gave me the containers, possibly my father bought them or brought them from somewhere, I don't remember, the details are missing, but I do know that they were huge containers made of thick, heavy glass, they must have come from the time before the siege, and they were approximately a hundred and ten, possibly a hundred and twenty centimeters long and nearly fifty centimeters wide and at least as deep, if not deeper, they could be safely sealed with glass plates with holes in them, they stood on a heavy table on the veranda, I made a rock garden with caves in each of them, or grottos, as they were called back then, so the reptiles would have a place to hide, I gave them a thick cover of sand, they had strong trees made of dry branches, so they would have something to wind around, and I built a pond in one of them, which was actually a kidney dish, but I managed to cover its edges with moss and lichen; I also needed a third glass container, the terrarium had to be cleaned quite often, and then the animals needed a temporary place of refuge, there were crested newts in the terrarium, a small Hermann's tortoise, and for a couple of months a beautiful spotted salamander, I had to feed it with live bugs and small snails until, during one peaceful dinner, I let on to my parents that the salamander, when it's angry, secretes venom from its swollen glands which is spread, or as they say, diffused over the skin, anyone touching a salamander is as good as dead, which wasn't quite true, I wanted to scare my brother because he'd climb up on a stool, slide the cover to the side, and reach inside, but its secretion was in fact poisonous, I don't remember who I gave it to, a paper bag was the safest way of catching it; on the other hand, there were no lizards because they go berserk in captivity, they'd have died in no time, but I had snakes of various types, mature specimens, I had to feed them, I had to catch flies, insects, but I had to make sure the flies didn't perish, because the snakes would not eat dead flies, and so there was a period in my life when I caught flies, it lasted at least three years, Csíder and Piros helped me catch them, because there were more flies in the restricted area in Lóránt Street, the members of the ÁVÓ guard built pens in back of the houses where they kept rabbits, chickens, and pigs, thanks to which my bug collection, in which the beetles, the rhinoceros beetles, and the stag beetles took the laurels, grew to impressive size. I caught them in late May or early June, when they swarmed, advancing awkwardly and slowly along determined routes, they had difficulty landing and difficulty taking off, they lived among the foliage of oak trees, and so there were plenty of them on Svábhegy. If they weren't mature enough, I let them go, still, I killed many bugs for the sake of my collection. The best specimens we traded among ourselves. I also had leaf beetles of all shapes and sizes, and also saw other types of beetles and a butterfly collection; I had to send the butterflies and the insects to their eternal rest with spirits or ether. I killed them without a second thought so I could mount them properly on draft paper supplied with labels. Sometimes they woke up from their stupor in the middle of the night, and found themselves pinned down with pins. I had to kill them a second time. I also had to keep an eye on the propagation of the fish as well, because the guppies and the platties, the tiny newborn of the live-bearers, would have been devoured by the terrible cannibal fish, their very own aunts and uncles, or else the Mexican swordtails. I sat there for hours, even days, waiting for the guppy to give birth. I ran home from school to see if it had happened. Sometimes I managed to separate the fish about to give birth from the others. From time to time the reptiles shed their skin, and at such times, despite my best efforts at cleaning it, the terrarium stank to

434

high heaven. Every member of my family protested against the reptiles. I wouldn't say that I turned a deaf ear, but Judit Benkő was more important, she encouraged me to do what I did, and that was enough for me. I was the one using the veranda, and if the veranda smelled, then it smelled, people smelled, too.

Speak for yourself, our mother said, because I don't, and she screamed with laughter because, obviously, there was nothing I could add to that.

Once I moved my desk and bed close to the window by the veranda. I had to suck the algae-infested water out of the tank with a rubber tube, carefully, so the gurgling tube shouldn't suck up the small fish hiding among the vegetation at the muddy bottom, in which case I'd have had to retrieve them from the toilet bowl. I had an injured porcupine for a while that had the run of the house despite everyone's protest, it smelled, let out urine and stool. I found it while I was firing up the furnace in the coal cellar, probably it ended up there injured to begin with, and in its great need it wanted to hide itself under the coal; the silly animal didn't know that coal contains sulfur. It limped as it moved about, I cleaned up after it, and it never recovered completely, but it spent an entire winter with us in a big paper box at the bottom of a wardrobe, lined with pieces of cotton and wool. They had to put up with it, I wouldn't let them disturb the poor animal. When it woke up and began stirring in early spring, I opened the door, it crawled out, I gave it food, it didn't eat, but it more or less recovered from its lethargy, at nightfall I flung open the door to the veranda, the nights were still chilly, but perhaps the frost was gone, and still limping, if slightly, it walked out, and quick as lightning, it too disappeared forever. This porcupine had a personal relationship with me, but no one else. I also had a personal relationship with fish, though not with all of them. I could coax these personal acquaintances with my finger on the glass, the relationship mesmerized them, filled them with joy. The reptiles were used to captivity, but I had no personal relationship with them, not even when they slid from my arm to my shoulder, and probably would have liked to slide under my shirt as well. That summer I got a new dog from somewhere in the neighborhood, we called her Cuddles Two, so we shouldn't forget the first Cuddles. Except, Cuddles Two turned into a very different dog, more independent, wilder, with a pronounced sense of humor; she could tease and wind you around her little paw.

I may have been eighteen when I first looked into our father's papers related to the embezzlement, I barely sneaked a look, leafed through them, then put them down as if stung by a gadfly, intending never to touch them again. On the other hand, even this cursory look made it clear to me that there was no mention of embezzlement in my father's papers. Cheating on wages, or wage theft, as they called it, this was one of the concepts, violation of procedural rules the other. When a person suffers a grievance, he tends to exaggerate, and inevitably, our parents exaggerated when they talked about embezzlement and not wage theft in hushed tones among themselves, and this is how they related the terrible accusation leveled against our father to their friends. They protected themselves by resorting to exaggeration. But a person isn't happy when his father is a mere wage cheater. I was past seventy when I got up the nerve to check what had happened. I had to read all sorts of literature to understand the references in my father's papers, I visited various archives and libraries so I could comprehend the stupendous complexity of the various offices, bureaus, provisions, and rules. Even so, I couldn't keep the data pertaining to disciplinary proceeding no. 2882/1954. MH.K. initiated by the minister intact in my mind.

In order for the official story to remain on the surface of my consciousness, I needed to understand and keep in mind two things, the structure of the official proceedings of the time and the diametrically opposed intentions and logic of the two parties. I understood both, and yet my mind, I don't know why, wouldn't admit Chief of Division Comrade Jancsik into its confines, and it wouldn't admit Comrade Undersecretary Katona into its confines either, nor Comrade Minister Bebris, this despite the fact that Comrade Minister Bebris could boast of notable, what's more, highly amusing character traits, in fact, my mind balked at comrades such as this, it calls a halt, blows the whistle, enough of comrades, enough of *elvtárs*, how very apt, *elv* for principle, *társ* for mate, not as if I would object to the concept itself, if someone is someone else's mate, let him be his mate, for all I care, my main concern with this *elvtárs* business was always that they were not one another's mates and they certainly had no principles, they were careerists, selfish pigs, and consequently, they devalued the meaning of *elvtárs*, this common Hungarian word couldn't be used anymore as it was meant to be used, because the long years of lying couldn't be scraped off it anymore, and so it hurt, this too hurt, and furthermore, my mind wouldn't admit Mrs. Bujáki from the Labor Department, Pelesek from Accounting, Viktor Láng from the Legal Department, it rejected their hair-raising sentences with their official jargon. The most blatant characteristic of the eternal subject was that he couldn't even speak his own mother tongue. He resorted to thieves' Latin instead. I didn't want to be the interpreter of their sentences, I didn't want to explain what these people were thinking. They weren't thinking anything.

I've seen my share of intrigue, I've seen corporate intrigue, too, what these days we call mobbing, sustained psychological terror, but I don't remember ever being a party to this intrigue.

The intriguer took the first step, I dodged it. Iago didn't interest me, even in Shakespeare. Othello was more interesting, but he didn't interest me either. I'd rather have been a coward in other people's eyes than a fool in my own. I didn't take up the gauntlet. I realized every time that it would have been no use denying the fabrications of the intriguer, because his next fabrication would follow, the intriguer followed a monotonous system, he obtained pleasure from his fabrications, he wanted to roast me over a slow fire, he wanted to sink his hand into a live human substance, and if possible, to watch closely and enjoy the disquiet of the soul, the ungovernable protestations of the body and the bones, a cannibalistic joy. Iago was impotent. With the sight of my suffering, I offered him the most secret of all human pleasures, that of gloating over someone else's misfortune, because that was the only real place he knew. I felt sorry for him. After so many years, I still couldn't excuse my father for playing a role in a senseless upheaval the likes of which I avoided even in kindergarten.

If some official entity notices a transgression, what can it do, it must initiate proceedings, because an official entity is bound by law to furnish proof against the individual who has committed the transgression. But our father was set on proving that he acted in strict conformity with regulations. Except, in the dispute that dragged on for four years, neither party could agree with the procedural rules, nor with the subject of the dispute. They kept referring to two different regulations, when the two could not be reconciled, because the lawmakers themselves had not reconciled them. At times it seemed to me that my father was skirting the issue, at others that the authorities had gone mad. And while they were fighting each other, our mother ended up in the hospital again, this time at the surgical clinic on Üllői Street, where they prepared her for still more surgery. She was hunched over with pain and could take only a couple of steps, her hands pressed to her belly. Also, she had turned yellow. First the whites of her eyes turned yellow, then her skin turned yellow. Weeks went by with many examinations, but they did not operate. On the afternoon of October 29, 1954, when in the morning our father was dismissed from his position in Dob Street, the chief physician of the clinic had him sit down in his office and told him that he couldn't operate on our mother, it wouldn't make sense subjecting her to further trials, and he might discharge her in a couple of days. They were going to tell her that they'd decided to postpone the operation because the X-ray showed that her gallstones were badly positioned. Of course, she didn't have gallstones. The doctor told our father that in the terminal phase of their illness, patients suffering from cancer were happy even with obvious lies. At which, our father said, so my wife is incurable. Yes, answered the chief physician, who doubtless had meant just that, the course of the illness could be reversed only if we could perform liver surgery, he said, but we can't perform liver surgery. She may have a couple of small stones, though he doubted it, they could check, of course, and remove them, if they're there, but that could only worsen her condition. Our father kept quiet for a while, he wanted what he'd just heard to sink in. So then, the metastasis has reached the liver, he asked the chief physician. That is so, the chief physician nodded, but he wished to add, it is his duty, that Professor Korányi must have ascertained as much at St. John's Hospital when they first performed surgery on the patient, and from what he knows of the professor, and he knows him well, they're close friends, he'd made up the story about the patient's gallstones in the interest of her psychological well-being. He'd set his hopes on radiation therapy. But they were surgeons, they had to look facts squarely in the eye, the radiation therapy had some effect to be sure, but not on the liver. And then, along with a whimper, the foolish question left our father's lips, that in that case, how much longer would his wife have to live, but in line with the blueprint of the Nádas brothers that pertained to crying, he bit his lips and managed to stifle his sobs. He couldn't say, the chief physician answered, but he and Professor Korányi, too, would obviously do everything in their power to lessen the patient's pain as much as humanly possible.

At that point, our father left Üllői Street and went to Teréz Boulevard to his sister, my Aunt Magda, because he wanted to share the news with her, which for the time being made him forget the disciplinary action against him.

As my Aunt Magda told me during one of our late-night chats as she lay sunk in her pillows, she was just chopping onion in the kitchen, and she went to open the door holding the knife, and Lacika started crying, he'd hardly entered, he'd hardly said anything, and he was crying, not that he had to say anything, because he did say one word, *Klári*.

And on one of these days in autumn, when we should have been celebrating my birthday, though I'd stopped keeping track of my birthdays and it hit me only at the sight of the autumn fog that oh, my birthday used to be around this time, oh, my birthday was yesterday, on the day that the disciplinary proceedings against my father, who'd been dismissed from office, continued in Dob Street with hearings and witness testimonies, at home in the afternoon, I noticed that my brother had a strange limp.

I asked why he was limping, did they kick him during football, or what the heck happened, and he said he wasn't limping. So why don't you go play, they just called you from the street. He wasn't going. Why wasn't he going. Why don't I leave him alone, I'd better leave him alone, he yelled. Leave me alone. I left him alone, but he collapsed on his bed and, like so many times in the past, burst into inconsolable tears and kept calling for our mother. Her absence hurt me, too, except I knew more than he. I tried talking sense into him, telling him to stop and get it through his head, our mother was ill, she was in the hospital, we went to see her on Sunday, can't he remember, he kept screaming for me to leave him alone and continued crying bitterly on his bed, consoling himself with his tears, his tears may have been his only means of lessening the pain. He'd started school that year. The next day his limp was even more pronounced, when I helped him bathe in the evening, I saw that his left leg was badly swollen, but could find no visible sign of injury. I told our father, who took a look, my grandmother prepared a tartaric acid compress, but by the next day, the swelling had gotten worse, especially his ankle, he demanded that we leave him alone because nothing hurt. He was like a grumpy old man. Elza Baranyai sent them to the orthopedic clinic where they examined his leg, they touched it and had him walk, but he didn't limp, they had him lie down, held down his hip, pulled at his leg from the knee down, but when they asked, he said that it didn't hurt. Nothing hurt. Probably, he was one of the family's many fakers, refusing to acknowledge the obvious pain. Possibly, it was genetic code. To be safe, they sent him for an X-ray. Even to uninitiated eyes, it was clear from the X-ray that the globe of his caput femoris, meaning his femoral head fitted to the hip joint, was no more than a shell, a periosteum, cartilage, merely a bare shape that seemed only half-filled with ligament. He wasn't allowed to stand for about two months. Nor even sit. Our father carried him home from the orthopedic clinic in his arms and he and Szidike put him in bed while a taxi was waiting for him outside, and he excused himself, saying he had an important hearing to attend.

It made no sense. If the hearing was so important that he was leaving my brother in his condition, why didn't the dark blue Tatraplan come for him and why was a taxi waiting for him outside, but I wouldn't ask.

His disciplinary case was composed of documents from three different places.

The first batch was made up of personnel documents he received two years later, likely in November 1956 or possibly a little later, perhaps in January 1957. Part of the picture is as follows. The revolutionary councils demanded that the government eliminate the personnel departments that were functioning with the help of informers, their heads should be let go and the documents pertaining to persons in the records should not end up in the archives, no one should be given access, and they should be given to the individuals to whom they pertain for their own use. Only the administrative documents of the personnel departments should be handed over to the archives. No personnel records should be made that the person they pertain to cannot read. He must have the right to amend and correct every single statement. There were workplaces where the revolutionaries didn't wait for any law or provision, and in the first days of the revolution, they raided the secret administrative and personnel departments, threw the documents out into the corridors or down into the yards or the street, and people could take their own away with them. In late October, possibly on a Monday, when I'd been scouring the city for days to collect everything, flyers, newspapers, so I'd know what was happening around me, the collection that the secret service would take from my desk in about fifteen years' time, when they also took my notes on the structure of consciousness, in short, back in October 1956, I saw a bunch of excited men rummage through a huge pile of papers thrown out on the street, this was across from the Nyugati railroad station, whose glass enclosure lay in ruins, and the documents had been set on fire, their edges were singed. I went to join them. The light brown files must have been thrown down to the street in bundles, some remained like that, others were scattered, the pages skidding along the pavement from the impact. Many among the rummagers were in railway uniforms, some were conductors with their bags over their shoulder. From time to time they'd let out a shout and show the others what they'd found, and I started searching with them to see what they saw with my own eyes, they cursed, look what the pigs were up to, go ahead, take a look, it boggles the mind, if I didn't see it, I wouldn't believe it. Those standing farther off were arguing about whether they should pour gasoline over the pile of documents, because they wouldn't burn completely otherwise, or if they should give the railway workers who might be coming this way an opportunity to fish out their own from the debris. It was a sensible argument. Anyone could take a look at the unlawfully compiled confidential papers of complete strangers, and this just added to the danger of general anarchy, and during the first week of the revolution, almost everyone tried to prevent this from happening.

I remember perfectly well that in the Inner City Telephone Works, where our father was the general director, having been put there out of leniency after his disciplinary hearings, reduced in rank, humiliated, resisted the popular pressure at all costs, he first resisted the pressure from the rebels, who wanted to storm the office of the classified records and personnel, protected by iron railings, and when they couldn't prevail upon our wildly gesticulating and shouting father, they grabbed him by the arm, hoisted him up in the air, and they took him downstairs, a handsome line of steps led from the lobby of the eclectic-style Inner City building out onto the street, they carried him down the stairs, they carried him just as he was, without his coat, they didn't throw him out, they put him out, they let him go in God's name. This was the first day he'd come home since Tuesday, he came without a coat or attaché case in his wrinkled summer suit, it was Friday, a lukewarm morning, when a person could still do without a coat. That same day the rebels broke open the iron railings, but then didn't touch the documents. Possibly they had something better to do, possibly they recalled the arguments of the general director they'd thrown out of the building, and they left all that paper for the devil to deal with. But no sooner had he walked through the door than our grandfather Arnold Tauber told him that someone was just here looking for him, probably a good soul, but he wouldn't give his name, and said that the rebels would come looking for him. Our father stood, his feet rooted to the ground. It seems to me, son, Arnold Tauber continued

442

cautiously, because he'd have liked to wake our father from his stupor, that you should take the children and go. You still have a couple of minutes. Our father did not budge. But where should we go, he asked vaguely. We'll decide on the way, I said, taking the matter into my own hands. I took my small suitcase, threw in all sorts of quick necessities, told my father to grab his coat, we were about to leave, but he just stood there. He said fine, but our grandparents must come with us, because if they don't find him, they might take it out on our grandparents, but Arnold Tauber said said no, they're not leaving, but you go, go. Hurry. All of you. Even out on the street, our father didn't know which way we should go. We're not taking the cog railway now, I said, because I realized that, more than anything, we had to get away from our street. I decided that we'd go down the hill on foot.

Later, our father also stood up to the workers' council. I even remember his argument for the handling of the classified records and personnel documents; they're intern papers, he shouted, beside himself, that was the word they used at the time, intern, meaning for internal use only, but despite the logic of his arguments, his anger rendered his manners intolerable even at home as two contradictory forces clashed inside him, his class, which would brook no opposition, and his infantile soul, gifted to him and his five brothers by the terror that my grandfather Adolf Arnold Nádas exercised over them. He argued that anyone who ever used these intern papers knew that they had to be construed with moderation, you first have to check who wrote them, when they made them, and upon whose orders. His own personnel papers were also the spitting image of ignominy. But a sketchy version that someone had edited has survived, the intention of the person who ordered it must have changed in midstream, and someone in the personnel office had to revise László Nádas's character analysis so that no positive character trait should remain. If they're released, he shouted into the phone, if they're made public, these papers are so to speak incendiary, they will offend everyone to no purpose, they'll start a wildfire. Incendiary, they're incendiary, he kept shouting, as if it were his final argument. But then, because anarchy had to be prevented at all costs, and because he and his friends didn't want the occupying Soviet forces to put down the revolution, which, needless to say, they called a counterrevolution, and which he'd called an antirevolution even during the unrest preceding the uprising; in short, in order to prevent the unrest from becoming incendiary, he realized the necessity of applying the strategy of allowing certain things while prohibiting others, all while they spared no effort to negate the arguments of the workers' councils, to foment discord among their committees, to derail their actions through intrigue, to stop their strikes with strikebreakers, to eliminate the resistance groups and find arms even where people didn't have any, and consequently could not have hidden them, in short, my father realized that they had to make allowances, fine, everyone can take their own records home, and he brought his home as well.

The next batch of papers pertained to the disciplinary proceedings, the minutes, the memoranda, the reminders, the testimonies, the letters, the resolutions, the appeals, the reports, the statements, the acquittal and appointment documents, and so on. The official record dated October 23, 1954, containing the testimonies of eighteen people and our father comes to seventy-nine pages, but the same day they appended a letter to it addressed to a Comrade Sándor Jakab, a dossier labeled *Training Matters*, the handwritten draft of a previous disciplinary decision, the protocols of an examination and the committee's report on the inquest, and so the collection came to a hundred pages, and that was just the introduction to the full proceedings.

The smallest sheaf of documents contained his letters, petitions, statements, and memoranda. I have arranged the documents in chronological order. This way I get a better idea of what else occurred during this last act of his life, while the proceedings against him were carried out. When they brought our mother home from the hospital, she lay in one room and my brother lay in the other; by then, when my brother groaned in his sleep at night I couldn't take him out to the bathroom, because he could no longer stand on his feet, he was given a glass urinal, and I had to get him to pee in it. At which I rarely succeeded because I couldn't wake him up. The illness called Perthes disease, the consequence of inflammation of the hip joint in children that causes bone cells to die, is probably caused by an infection and wreaks havoc on the immune system as well, but I can't discount the possibility that our father's sustained nervous state, our mother's absence and illness, and the full-blown dementia of our maternal grandmother, Cecília Nussbaum, in response to the problems in the family may have also contributed to the shock to my brother's immune system; our grandmother would burst out of her room several times a day brandishing a mug, and showered terrible opprobriums down on our heads, though strangely, not on our father's, she spared him, but she yelled and screeched at her ill daughter, the neighbors, the maid, the whole world; she became a compulsive food hoarder, she hoarded bread heels and crescent roll tips, she was afraid of starving, and she kept the briefcase with the food remains at the bottom of our wardrobe; there was no talking her out of it, when there'll be nothing, don't you worry, it'll come in handy, she shouted when we discovered that she was also hoarding the dirty clothes at the bottom of the wardrobe because she wanted to save on laundry soap, her recriminations were a heady mix of the present, the distant past, and an auspicious future; our grandfather Arnold Tauber was the only one in the family who remained truly sane, he could even get his wife to calm down, he touched her elbow and endearingly called her Cili and put his arms around her, a gesture that was both aggressive and evocative of their former closeness, and if he was nearby, he hurried to my aid every time, he made our grandmother leave our room, and cautiously asked that I not vex her and not talk back to her, it's not such a big deal if she collects the dirty laundry, I shouldn't talk back, you don't have to talk back, and doubtless, all these collateral psychological elements must have strengthened my brother's urge to wet his bed.

On the other hand, my brother would not urinate lying down, and it was no use holding the urinal, and it was no use holding his weenie, and it was no use whispering wee, wee, the little boy is doing wee-wee, so he shouldn't wet his bed. This was the automatism of his previous nightly somnambulism, we had tied his reflex to pass water to a vertical position, once and for all, it seemed. But the minute I pushed the empty urinal under his bed and it knocked against the floor in the silence, the minute I got back to my own bed, the minute I turned off the light and slid under the covers, he moaned and groaned and wet his bed. Or else it happened once I fell back asleep. The urine soaked through the mattress and the duvet, they soaked up much of the urine, and Szidike had to start every single day with washing. She had to wash things that couldn't be washed, just dried. She rotated two cotton duvets that she rubbed clean with wet rags. She also rotated two different mattresses, rubbing them clean with wet rags, as well.

As far as I can tell on the basis of the documents, the wage fraud must have entered the official imagination, if we can call it that, in late July, a couple of days before that, and I don't know why, my father was called up for military service along with forty telecommunications experts from his secret department; within the framework of a top-secret military exercise, I don't know why, but it was top secret, they were ordered to show up for two months of reserve officer training, I don't know where. This information was also top secret. I don't know what this reserve officer training consisted of, but he'd discussed and prepared it in great detail beforehand with a certain Major General Berczely. I see from the documents that he went to the employment office to ask Mrs. Bánszky what the regulation said if he, because that's how he asked her, he didn't ask in the first person plural, he spoke only about himself, if he must show up for reserve officer training, how much salary was he entitled to, and how much subsidy was he entitled to. It was crystal clear to me that he wasn't thinking of himself, he was inquiring on behalf of his subordinates. Because of all that secrecy, he couldn't have done anything else. He had to know what the employment status of his men would be while they were undergoing military training; besides, he was entrusted with organizing the secret training itself. With others he was generous, with himself he was frugal to a fault. But there was no need for others to know this, after all, the question was how much he'd be getting, and what extras the regulations entitled him to receive. Mrs. Bánszky found the regulation and showed it to Nádas, or as it says in her testimony, she informed him that in case he was called up, he was entitled to 40 percent of his salary and all other allowances in the form of special aid. At which point Nádas asked her to also find out if the sum couldn't be raised considering that his elderly parents, who were Trade Union Social Security pensioners, lived in the same household with him. Needless to say, his elderly parents had been resting for more than twenty years in the Jewish Cemetery on Kerepesi Street by then, in a black marble family crypt built with foresight and rather good taste, Adolf Arnold Nádas had ordered it for himself, Eugénia Nádas had designed it, and István Nádas had paid for it, so Mrs. Bánszky or a certain Jolán Végh, who recorded the proceedings, had thoroughly misunderstood. Nádas's mother-in-law and father-in-law, Cecília Nussbaum and Arnold Tauber, were undoubtedly of retirement age, though I don't recall my grandmother getting a pension of any kind, and also, they were clearly living in the same household with us. Mrs. Bánszky promised Nádas that she would look into it. I think that during the summer, we'd have scraped by somehow with the fragment of our mother's salary, which had been reduced by two thirds by then, and which she received as sick pay, the 40 percent of our father's salary, and my grandfather's modest pension, they could have even paid the maid somehow, but he had to consider that not every one of the forty men in his care, called up along with him for the secret training, could make do on a fraction of their salaries. He made inquiries to see how this sum could be raised, something that in a head office such as this could all too easily be misconstrued. Mrs. Bánszky lost no time in contacting Comrade Jenő Bodó from Remuneration Accounting, and on the basis of the information he had provided, she informed Comrade Nádas via telephone that considering that his elderly parents were Trade Union Social Security pensioners, in case he were called up, he was not entitled to more than 40 percent support/aid. If for no other reason, our father couldn't have been satisfied with the answer because he was familiar with Defense Council Resolution 130/11/1953, which called attention to the fact that those called up for reserve officer training could not suffer financially thereby, in short, members of his top-secret officers' group were entitled to their full salaries, as he argued in the documents. Or if they couldn't be paid, he had to find some other clear title for the payment. In order to ensure success, he called up Major

General Berczely, the military head of the secret military operation, who confirmed that in the disputed case not the provision of the labor legislation but the resolution of the Defense Council must be considered authoritative. This was worth closer scrutiny, if for no other reason than because it made clear that our father's individual case was in fact symptomatic, it was regime-specific, which for a variety of reasons he couldn't have understood at the time. The Defense Council was the brainchild of the governing threesome of Rákosi, Gerő, and Farkas, who ruled through commissars' decrees, which meant that the decree issued by the Defense Council on March 10, 1953, overruled ordinary governmental decrees and laws. Except, with its no less hierarchic system of administration it had inherited from the Monarchy, the ministry apparatus had begun to consider the problem in need of a solution, and seeing their chance to be rid of our father, the schemers, too, must have put their heads together to see how they could turn this matter to their advantage.

I also know that Mrs. Bánszky, Mrs. Bujáki, and Pelesek gave their testimony on a Thursday. As I reconstruct it now, a thick fog had settled over the city, it was veritably dripping, and as I made my way home through the Braun Woods after my piano lesson, the thick fog reminded me that my birthday was the day before. My mind registered this observation with detachment, and so it is available to me even now. Still, I saw from the documents that on the same day, during her hearing at the Post Office Headquarters on Krisztina Boulevard, Mrs. Bujáki stated that during the month of August, she and Comrade János Pelesek, the head of her section, prepared their monthly work plan for September, the first point of which was the dispatch to Comrade Papp re. the supplement with regard to the stipends of the heads/employees of the conscripted/outfits. According to the transcript, this was how she read it from a piece of paper. The sentence made little sense; furthermore, the typewriter was missing some accent marks, and Jolán Végh, who sometimes hit the wrong key, also had serious problems with the rules of proper spelling. September 1 was the deadline given in the work plan, and Mrs. Bujáki and Pelesek were indicated as the supervisors.

The question of further remuneration was incorporated into the work plan for September on the basis of consultation with Pelesek, and Pelesek received orders for the incorporation from Comrade Nádas. Which, in the language of the head office, meant that Pelesek did not act independently in the matter of the stipend supplement, it was Nádas who ordered him to supplement the salaries of those called up for the top-secret reserve officer training with aid so that together with their military pay, the total should constitute the same sum as their normal monthly salary, which from the point of view of the office was according to regulation only if there was a regulation pertaining to it. As it happened, there was a regulation that made this work-around illegal; on the other hand, there was a regulation of a higher order that made it compulsory. The administrative apparatus of the ministry refused to recognize the Defense Council's decree, in which the opportunity for intrigue played a significant part; after all, for the past six years, they'd been looking for a way to rid themselves of this Nádas, though they themselves no longer seemed to know why. In short, in the name of the monarchic system they went against the system of the commissars' decrees, a circumstance that, being familiar with the nature of terror, I consider nothing less than amazing. According to the transcript, Comrade Nádas went to the office in early September and instructed Mrs. Bujáki that, starting September 5, she should send the pay supplements of those called up retroactive to the month of August, but they should make sure that they did not send the money to the same areas at the same time, so that too much money wouldn't be paid out to the families in the same areas at the same time.

We would think that our father had lost his mind, if only we didn't know that in these years marked by chronic shortages the number of money dispatches sent through the post office that went missing had swelled to such proportions that the domestic inspection system of the post office collapsed, and first and foremost, the Head Directorate had to investigate the investigation system itself, and that the number of complaints to the police had skyrocketed, something that, need we add, the mouthpieces called the press made no mention of. The mailmen delivering the cash also disappeared one by one; some disappeared because they had been killed along some village bypass because of the money, or else the mailmen themselves couldn't stand looking at all that money day in and day out, counting it, then handing it to other people, keeping nothing for themselves. They absconded with the money entrusted to them. While I was looking through the documents pertaining to this phenomenon, I was especially impressed by the story of a female postal worker who lived on her own and who, just as she was, in her uniform and with the clasped leather carrier bag on her shoulder that mailmen who delivered money carried with them, walked all the way from a village near Kecskemét to Nyíregyháza with the money entrusted to her, where she took a room in the only suitable hotel and stayed, eating and drinking, until her money ran out, then she went to the police and gave herself up. She told them where she'd left the bicycle and where she threw away the carrier bag, and that was where they found them. She told them where she'd bought herself new clothes, and indeed, that's where she'd bought them, she told them where she threw away her uniform, and indeed, that's where they found it. But not only such solitary heroines were at large; criminal groups were also privy to the tithes. If they saw that money was due from the same place to various addresses at the same time, they got hold of all the money, got rid of all the pertaining documents, and the committee sent to investigate the matter stood there like oafs, with nothing to report. And so Mrs. Bujáki turned to team leader Papp with Nádas's orders to find out what she should do, what was needed to send the money through the post office. When she was making her inquiry in Papp's office, Lantos called out from the adjoining room that the money in question couldn't be paid out through the post or in any other way, because the transfer was against regulations, which Papp also confirmed. Lantos was right. Various types of sums could not be paid out under a single entitlement. A person could be entitled to aid along with his salary, but if said person received a salary as well as military pay, he was not entitled to regular aid, because his military pay was considered his supplemental pay. This was so clear, even a school child could understand it.

At which the three of them, Papp, Lantos, and Mrs. Bujáki, had a good laugh. Their laughter must have been the turning point in our little family tragedy, evidence of the hand of fate. The trumpet of doom had sounded. Had Lantos not called out from the other room, chaos would have ruled the day, and that had to be prevented. On the other hand, this way, the regime-specific commissars' system clashed head-on with the monarchic system of the state apparatus, and the clash annihilated our father. Needless to say, none of the participants took note, because an era never sees itself, and regardless of how smart the players may have considered themselves, they were groping their way along dark corridors in the hope of finding a wall, but irrespective of their views, what had to happen happened.

Mrs. Bujáki looked up Nádas with the information she'd received from Papp, or else Nádas came to their room, and then she said, look here, Comrade Nádas, Comrade Papp told me that this payment is against regulations. Don't bother turning to Comrade Papp in this matter, because this is so obvious, there's nothing more he could say. These sums cannot be paid out either in cash or in the form of a money order. She was so angry that she told Nádas to his face that as far as she was concerned, from then on, she washed her hands of the entire matter, she knew nothing about it. At which Nádas said to her, in short, you won't take responsibility. At which Mrs. Bujáki confirmed that yes, in this matter, I will not. At which point Comrade Nádas took the pertaining documents away with him. At which, according to the transcript, Mrs. Bujáki had an awful suspicion. That Nádas, he took the documents with him like someone who knows what he's going to do with them. He wanted to get around her. Haven't they told him that it's against regulations. Nádas wanted to make her appear responsible for the illegal payments. When she first suspected foul play, Pelesek had already told Anderka that proceedings for a big illegal payout were under way, and Anderka knew that 21 million forints had been set aside by the ministry for this top-secret training as incidental expenses, my Lord, they wanted to take it from there, and did Comrade Jancsik know about it. How could he, considering that he was on sick leave. She didn't tell Pelesek, because in these strictly confidental matters she was bound to secrecy, but she lost no time in looking up General Manager Comrade Imre Dedics to report the matter, and asked his secretary for an appointment. She only told Pelesek not to mention the matter to anyone, she'd take care of it herself. When Mrs. Bujáki learned from Pelesek that Anderka was also an informant now, and that he also wanted to keep it quiet, it made her even more suspicious, she was truly horrified at the thought that Anderka may also have been part of the scandal and was covering up for Nádas, in which case they were conspiring together, because while Pelesek went to see Anderka, Nádas had already come back to her, ordering her to keep this supplementary wage matter under wraps. He and Anderka must have been in cahoots. And Anderka even told him, Pelesek told her, that Nádas had already talked to Mrs. Bujáki about this, telling her not to mention the matter to anyone. This is what Pelesek told her, in these words. Of course, she didn't tell Pelesek that Nádas had been to see her and had in fact said this, but she thought she'd faint on the spot. All right, it's none of her business, but to think of what's going on behind her back. The clever way they managed it between themselves. She then wasted no time in asking Erzsébet Jávor whether she'd seen papers pertaining to these payments, because Erzsébet Jávor had warned her earlier that the payments she'd asked for were against regulations, and now Pelesek knew, too, and Anderka knew from Pelesek, and in that case, she was going to inform Comrade Jancsik, Erzsébet Jávor told her right away, and Mrs. Bujáki told Erzsébet Jávor that it was high time somebody reported it, but she had to wait for Jancsik to come back from sick leave. At which Erzsébet Jávor informed Mrs. Bujáki that Jancsik was already back, but according to Mrs. Bujáki, this must have been mistaken information, because he was not back. This was where the element of dramatic delay entered the tragedy. The matter stood ready, though due to the dramatic mishap, the main schemer didn't yet know this.

Then in the course of the month of September, Mrs. Bujáki asked Papp if the supplements for August had been paid out, which they shouldn't have been, at which Papp said that they didn't come for the money, it seems that Nádas and the others had changed their minds. But at that point there was no stopping the wheel of fortune either with recourse to sane reasoning or petty arguments, on Krisztina Boulevard, Dob Street, or Andrássy Boulevard, rechristened Stalin Boulevard. The operational principle of the flywheel that I learned from our father still applied. They were going to be discharged at the end of September, it fell on the last day of September, a Thursday, and Mrs. Bujáki remembered this perfectly well even on the day the transcripts were drawn up, because on Wednesday someone from Anderka's team looked her up, saying that Nádas called because of the payment and he wanted to know if the actual pay for those who'd been called up had been clarified and Mrs. Bujáki had to compile the supplementary pay list accordingly and without delay. At which Mrs. Bujáki told this certain individual, whose name she was not familiar with, it was a man from Anderka's team, that she refused to be a party to this, the person even turned on her that she couldn't talk to him like that because he was just a messenger, but Mrs. Bujáki burst into tears and said they should take this matter to Pelesek, and Pelesek must have talked to someone about it, he must have acted on higher orders, because right away he said to her, don't cry, Mrs. Bujáki, and clarify the forint impact of the payroll classifications, and he ordered her to compile the supplementary pay list for two months on the basis of it. Mrs. Bujáki compiled the list, which came to around 35,000 forints, and she gave the list to Comrade Anderka. But why the remittance came to 40,000 forints instead of 35,000 forints she couldn't say for sure, she acted on orders, she just obeyed orders, but she noticed, on the basis of what Márta Milosits had told her, that the 5,000 forints were spent on the banquet expenses when they were discharged and for buying briefcases for the camp commander and Comrade Lieutenant Colonel Móricz of the defense ministry, and also pens and shaving kits for them. Mrs. Bujáki also heard from Márta Milosits that the pay supplements were paid anyway at the camp.

The documents also revealed that when Department Head Jancsik returned from sick leave and everyone informed him separately about what had happened and had sent him the files, and this important event at the main office had to happen in the days just preceding the discharge of the top-secret reserve officer team, he and Comrade Anderka lost no time in going to Nádas's office and opened the safe with the security key. The fact, which was not found in detail in the transcripts, to wit, that certain individuals had gotten embroiled in the wage fraud, was obvious to them. Besides other strictly confidential papers, the safe contained two envelopes with Nádas's handwritten notes. One contained Nádas's supplementary pay, Andorka counted it, it was all there, but Jancsik refused to count it, he didn't even want to look inside the envelope, and in the other envelope Anderka found the remainder of the incidental expenses with the receipts, and he counted the money that Nádas in his witness testimony on Thursday said he'd put there and not elsewhere so after his discharge he could return it to Principal Accounts along with the pay supplement due him. According to the transcript, he had done so. Except, Nádas could say what he wanted, it was no use, because Jancsik and Anderka testified that he paid it back only after he'd been found out. There was only one major scene at the head office left to be played out, in which Dr. Viktor Lang, head of the Legal Department of the Ministry of Transportation, as the representative delegated by the comrade minister, informed Comrade Nádas that the transcripts of Comrade Nádas's hearing of October 18, 1954, the morning and afternoon of October 19, 1954, and October 21, 1954, the hearing having taken place before the board of inquiry delegated by the first deputy of the minister of transportation, contained Comrade Nádas's statement pertaining to the matter at hand and asked Comrade Nádas whether he upheld what was set down in the transcript, and did he wish to add anything to the said contents of the transcript. Whereupon Comrade Nádas confirmed that he upheld the contents of the transcript, and insisted that he did not commit wage fraud. He was aware that because of its subject the matter was strictly confidential, but considering the disciplinary hearing, he considered himself absolved. His action was based on Resolution 130/11/1953 of the Defense Council. The money was issued on the basis of that resolution. Acting on behalf of the Defense Council Resolution meant that the financial repercussions of an officer's subsidiary training could not be borne by the workers, not even in part. According to the wording of the resolution, in complying with their duty, as well as in the preparation thereof, the participants were entitled to their basic pay without overtime or other supplements. He himself had no financial interest in the forty persons called up for auxiliary training receiving salary compensation. For this reason he considered it essential that Comrade Károly Tóth of the Secretariat of the Council of Ministers, the Secretariat of the Defense Council, and Comrade Major General Béla Berczely of the Ministry of Defense be questioned, furthermore, he did not consider it proper procedure that the delegated committee of inquiry should have discussed this matter with Comrade Berczely in the course of a brief G-line telephone conversation.

For the time being, he had no further statements to make.

It was an eventful spring to begin with, because at the end of March our parents went to the Mátra Mountains for a vacation, they wanted to get some fresh air, and they returned on April 2, because our mother was unexpectedly awarded the Gold Degree for Meritorious Labor, probably a final honor arranged by her adherents upon news of her impending death, to be presented to her at a ceremony in Parliament, this was a Saturday, but by the time they got back, Szidike Tóth had disappeared. All I could tell them was that when I returned from school and went to the kitchen to see what was for lunch, I heard her crying in her room. She was standing by her bed, she didn't pack properly, just threw her stuff into her suitcase at random.

I asked her what happened and why she was crying.

She'd received a telegram saying she had to go home without delay because they couldn't do without her at home, but I shouldn't worry, she'd be back by Sunday night.

This happened on a Wednesday, but she didn't come back by Sunday night.

She didn't come back on Monday either.

When I told my parents what happened, with my brother in tow, our mother went to take a look at the empty maid's room. The bedclothes were left just as Szidike had gotten out of bed, and she left behind other traces of her frantic departure as well. It wasn't a small room. Most likely, it had originally served to quarter several maids. In the back of the room stood a Biedermeier wardrobe with a beautifully curved pediment that we'd inherited from our Viennese great-grandmother's estate. Its two doors were flung wide open and it was empty.

Had I seen the telegram she'd mentioned.

Had our grandmother argued with her or shouted at her.

Had she taken her keys with her.

This question I knew the answer to, no, she had not taken her keys with her.

When I came home on Wednesday, I found the key was in the lock.

This is why I waited for her until late Sunday night. She didn't have a key.

And had she said anything else when she ran off, and would I please try to remember.

I realized that Szidike Tóth's disappearance was a more ominous sign for them than it was for me, and so, without thinking, I lied that no, she didn't say anything else.

I wanted to stave off any further questions. I lied that she didn't even say farewell, she took her shawl, she took her suitcase, and ran off.

She had to catch her train.

She couldn't miss the cog railway.

And in fact she had shouted back, she shouted it from the steep garden path as she ran up it with her suitcase, but back in the hall, she first hugged me for all she was worth, she hugged me with such force that I could feel the hardness of her body even through her big shawl and her skirts, she kissed my neck with her full, wet lips twice, which by then was not unfamiliar to me. In the intemperate love she felt for me, Hédi Sahn also kissed me passionately, with full lips when we found ourselves alone on her disheveled bed in the apartment in Felhő Street, she kissed my neck with a wild urge that we didn't quite know what to make of ourselves, even though our bodies stood ready. Szidike's embrace was hard, there was nothing spontaneous about it, she embraced me into herself, she kissed my neck, yet her body cast me off. Also, amid her tears, she twice panted into my neck that I was very good to her.

You were very good to me.

I had no intention of telling my parents about this whole thing, her goodness, the goodness, after all, I understood nothing of this whole goodness business, and also, since I didn't understand it, I couldn't very well have had a word for it. Such words were not to be found in popular novels. I still don't know what goodness is, the question has caused me no end of bafflement, but at that moment, in the company of a pain that was new to me, I understood that this was a good-bye, she was taking her leave of me forever. Of course, I had no idea what forever might mean either. Or why people said it, considering that it couldn't be forever, because in that case, a person would have to live forever. And yet I understood despite my lack of a word to help me, I understood perfectly well why she said it, why she let this goodness pass her lips, why she'd done it, and what my parents must have suspected, and why I couldn't tell them no matter what.

Before my brother fell ill, before he was confined to his bed twenty-four hours a day with his legs propped up on his pillows, and was not allowed even to sit up in bed, and it was up to me to make sure he didn't because I was older, and this was my responsibility in the family, I couldn't exempt myself from all the work, it wouldn't be fair to them and I'd better not forget it, or even later, when he got his brace at the National Artificial Limb Company on Mátyás Square, in whose repairs section the hands and feet were hanging from the ceiling, the pink artificial limbs left there for repairs, they used a long pole with a hook to hang them up or take them down, my brother was my responsibility, I had to attach his brace every morning, our father, needless to say, had no time for anything anymore, it was a complex task, the brace was attached to his ankle-high lace-ups that I had to clean and tie up, while the little fool took advantage of the situation and kept kicking me in the chest, the hinged contraption was used to take the weight off the thigh bone, I had to oil the hinged parts as well, because it creaked terribly otherwise, which he didn't even notice, but everyone else held their ears or screamed along with the brace to call attention to the unbearable sound, and in that brace he could do everything the others could with their healthy legs, for him it was far from unbearable, it was a given, he played ball and skied with it; and also, I had to attend not only to his nightly moanings, the brace, and tying up his shoes and cleaning them, but I also had to make sure his passion for peeping shouldn't get out of control. With his small brace he climbed up on the chest in the hall and from there to the top of a shelf fitted with sliding doors, this of medium height, from where, stretching to his full height, he could just manage to reach the small window from where he could see into the lit-up bathroom when our grandmother or Szidike Tóth was getting ready to take a bath or a shower.

I pulled him down from there several times; if anything, it was a dangerous venture, he protested, he hissed, a wrong move and he might fall down along with his brace and break his hip joint into a thousand pieces, and so I preferred to keep an eye on him, I was in his tracks, I grabbed him and stopped him from doing it, I berated him, for which Szidike was very grateful to me. This is what the goodness referred to and nothing else, yet in keeping with her religion, she turned it into something sentimental. At times she warned me beforehand and asked me to be on my guard so the little one shouldn't climb up on the shelf in the hall again, and needless to say, I was on my guard. But this could have had nothing to do with goodness, if for no other reason, because I stood in my brother's way, which for him was evidently cruel, and he answered every cruel act of mine of this nature with a tantrum, which was awkward, it hurt, his kicks hurt too, my own cruelty hurt, it hurt that I had to cause him pain, although I was the elder, I didn't know how to handle the cruelty I committed in the interest of my goodness.

As a result of all this, an unfamiliar complicity developed between Szidike and myself which, needless to say, my brother wanted to prevent, he wanted to take revenge on me, the little fool. I shouldn't be Szidike's little accomplice, but his accomplice. He tried to get me to join him on top of the shelf, and grinning, he said if I joined him, I could see for myself. I laughed it off, though his freedom impressed me. I witnessed something unfolding in this small child, something that wasn't there just a few weeks before. Had I not been interested in plants and animals, I may not even have noticed. He described the differences between the physical characteristics of our grandmother and Szidike with bright eyes and words that sounded highly convincing. I laughed at the little fool, but it would never have occurred to me to betray Szidike because of him, or even because of the sight he offered me, and this was one of the reasons I didn't tell my parents about Szidike's eternal good-bye.

They couldn't accept the girl's disappearance, they deliberated, they mulled it over. They had also learned what my classmates had told me, that there was a young man who waited for our Szidike on his day off down by Orgonás Street, and they headed somewhere together along Zsolna Street.

Margit Leba saw them, Éva Juhász saw them.

Also, by then my mother's head was reeling with stories of those women who bled to death on the filthy divans of genteel urban apartments or the kitchen floors of rural adobe houses at the hands of illegally operating doctors or medicine women, or else inserted a knitting needle or a piece of wire into their wombs as they squatted over a washbowl and died of blood poisoning, became invalids for life, and were unable to conceive, whereas they should have seen that what they were doing wouldn't serve its purpose. It turned into a veritable slaughterhouse, this is what she said about the new Ratkó Law with its severe ban on abortion. At this time, the bitter horror stories that made the rounds all ended up with her.

Kim Jang-soo saw it too, he saw the young man with Szidónia Tóth by the Orgonás Street stop twice.

She may not have gone home to Pilisszentlélek at all, but had run off with the young man.

The Korean children lived at the Forest School, one stop up the hill by the cog railway. The cog railway chugged along up the hill amid horrendous squeaking, and as it passed the Lilac Grove, the air was filled with the damp smell of oak trees, and you could see from the moving carriage that in the cordoned-off woods the girls and the boys lived in separate buildings, their classes, too, were on separate floors, they wore uniforms, had uniform haircuts, their teachers led them in separate groups and, so it seemed, they made sure that the boys and girls shouldn't meet. One group was taken along the upper path among the trees, while the other group was taken along the lower path, in the opposite direction. Their school was like a convent, and that's how they lived in the oak wood. As the cog railway cars ascended the hill, I could see that the groups, separated according to their gender, were taken separately even to the dining room. They first had to learn Hungarian at the Forest School, and only then could they go to a Hungarian school. The girls went to another school, but the boys came to study at the Diana Street school. The Korean War was still raging, which I'd been following on the radio for some time by then, and in fact, the children may not even have been brought to Hungary straight from Korea. We learned only later that, without exception, they were all war orphans. Back then, being a war orphan, a full orphan, or a half orphan was a familiar concept. The Korean children arrived when we were transferred from our temporary quarters in Felhő Street to the building in Diana Street, and I was seated in the first row instead of the last row, as before, because I was a good student, and obedient. A good boy, may the devil take all my exhausting make-believe. This is how Kim Jang-soo ended up sitting next to me. He knew a lot more than I did in every way, he knew everything, he was like the wise man of a village, he was a mathematician and artistic gymnast, though his Hungarian still left much to be desired. These Korean boys, because there must have been about six in our class, couldn't go to school for some time because of the war, and so they were perhaps two, possibly three years older than the rest of us. In my eyes, their orphaned existence, burdened with the continuous reports from the front, the victories and defeats and the attendant worries, their discipline, the likes of which I had never seen, either before or after, was like the continuation of the siege, and also, it strengthened my belief that on this earth the state of emergency among people is a constant, this is how it is, I must accept it like it is, all other ways of existence were just celestial notions, celestial visions, as Mihály Csokonai Vitéz, the student from Debrecen who later became a celebrated poet, wrote with his own gnosis in the language of his own romanticism, which I made a close study of at the time, in short, it is a world of precious ideas and evanescent ideals, and we are the prisoners of ideals and ideas, precariously caught between these parallel worlds along with the cruel godhead subject to eternal yearnings and the fallen angels and the Peace Council and the Peace Camp, and as for everlasting peace, it's the blah-blah-blah to fill up the space between two wars.

They were disciplined, and they clearly disciplined each other, they kept an eye on each other and wouldn't let each other cross the line. Behind which there lurked a cool cruelty. Their teachers brought them to school every morning with a special dispatch of the cog railway, and they took them back the same way, in silence and according to a strict schedule. Strangers were not allowed to get on these special trains. There were no exceptions. Their suits and coats were black, or else were of a dark blue that from a single step away looked black. Never before had I seen such dark blue material. Their shirts were checked or white, with a red Pioneer scarf, which we wore only on special occasions, but they had to fold it inside their military-style jackets, and there was no such thing as one wore one thing, another something different, nothing of a personal nature, it was either white or checked, but then they all wore white or checked shirts. The girls wore white ruffled pinafores over their black silesia dresses every day, and no one could deviate from this rule either. They held one another strictly in check and they also guided one another, from what I could see, and Kim Jang-soo must have been the chief supervisor of the group, he may have even been responsible for the boys in the other classes as well, though it took quite some time before I realized it. He could switch into a harsh mode so quickly, so out of the blue, that it made the others gasp. His sentences were brief and snappy, though his tone was subdued, characterized by the drawn-out, deep gutturals of his language. The next moment, there appeared on his face, the corners of his eyes and lips, his characteristic cheer, cheer that comes from wisdom. As if nothing had happened. I also realized that they answered questions according to a system of their own. Though I didn't ask, but others did, what is your father doing in Korea now. My classmates were wondering if their father was fighting and did he have a gun. But they didn't answer the question. Do you have brothers or sisters. And in order to be understood, they raised their voices, they explained, they gesticulated, older brother, younger sister. Where are they. What are they doing. Do you miss them. Do they send you letters. But they wouldn't aswer personal questions. Also, these Korean children could not be provoked. If, for instance, someone asked them if their parents were alive, they didn't say that they weren't. They just said that they were orphans. But to the next question, how did you become an orphan, what happened to your parents, where is your grandmother or your grandfather, they made no answer. Apparently, they were allowed to answer only questions of a personal nature that pertained only and exclusively to themselves. Once I learned to read their facial expressions, their differently habituated gestures, I saw that two interlaced structures were working within them, and only one stood under their teachers' interdictions. In the other system they were free to conduct themselves as they liked, they understood one another, it's just that we didn't understand what they understood and what they didn't understand, or else what they didn't want to understand, whereas they understood it perfectly. Also, there were things they didn't want us to know. For instance, it was no use asking if they'd come shoot baskets, because they wouldn't answer us, and not only did Kim Jang-soo not answer, Hu Jong-hwan, who always wore his heart on his sleeve, would not answer either, none of them would answer. It was more expedient to use the indicative mood and say, we're going with Székács and Ormay to shoot baskets. Which always got us an answer. I come with you to shoot baskets. But even when they couldn't come, they used the indicative, because they didn't have a word for rejection, and so they didn't have a word for it in Hungarian either. I must study now.

It was my impression that their teachers did not allow them to make friends with us, though there was a network of relationships among them barely visible to the naked eye that they negotiated among themselves to improbable shades and degrees, according to some given hierarchy that had nothing to do with friendship, meaning that they all had a predetermined place in the group derived from I don't know where, and also conflicts that came with their appointed place, about which they could not talk to us because of their teachers' interdiction. Sometimes they made one another cry, and once I even saw them fight, and it was much more fierce and tough than our own fights, but Kim Jang-soo intervened. And not only would he not allow fighting, he wouldn't allow tears either. They were not allowed to talk to us about what happened among them or with them. This, too, must have been one of their teachers' interdictions. They couldn't talk about their teachers either, and they couldn't even tell us their names. You could tell that they nursed their grudges for some time, but in front of us, they would put them aside. Some of these were furious. But when we were around, they didn't make faces and they didn't gesticulate, which made deciphering their feelings and emotions difficult to begin with, what's worse, with my European experience I couldn't see inside their dark irises, and I couldn't see inside their big pupils that barely left any white except for the two corners of their eyes. On the other hand, this made me feel that they could see through us with ease. The truth was that they looked down on us because everything we said or did must have been shockingly distasteful to them. On the other hand, they never said anything judgmental.

Kim Jang-soo did not look away, but if he did, it was clearly not an attempt to hide his feelings. He did not hide his face. He didn't have to. His ethereal smile was his impenetrable mask. Yet after a while, we nevertheless made contact from inside our mutual silences. His discipline didn't bother me. After all, my own was no different, and in this sense our meeting in the row of benches by the window was exceptional or fated. In any event, Kim Jang-soo was much closer to me than Székács, and even closer than Baltazár, whereas that was nearly impossible. Unfortunately, he couldn't come to our house, because after school was out, they had to get on line and were led away by their own teachers, and as for the Forest School, obviously, I couldn't go see them there, it was strictly off limits to us. However, we took it in stride, we didn't think of it as a prohibition but as a given. Kim Jang-soo must have especially enjoyed himself in the school garden. He understood plants and kept a strict eye on the development of those he was not familiar with, but he was not allowed to join the biology circle, he had to keep away from us. He even stayed away from planting rice, whereas Judit Benkő tried to get his teachers to make allowances, but there was no appealing, they all had to go back together. But the time we had at our disposal proved sufficient for our friendship, or rather, it would have never occurred to me that it might not be sufficient. There was tension, but that was the tension of our relationship, and what could be more natural. We were told that no one may set foot inside the Forest School without special permission. After nightfall, some idiots from the Mátyás király Street boys climbed over the fence regardless, but they couldn't spend more than a couple of minutes among the trees when, accompanied by urgent guttural shouts, they were driven out the main gate, and first thing in the morning, the police showed up at school. We all had to stand by our benches and raise our feet, first the one, then the other, as they subjected the soles of our shoes to strict examination. If they found someone's shoes suspicious, they took them out to the hall, but something must have come up, because they trooped off as quickly as they'd come.

Once, when we were talking about something, Kim Jang-soo said out of the blue that he will have look. At first I thought that he was making one of his usual grammatical mistakes, but not this time. He meant that he would have a look at our place, which was clearly out of the question. I don't remember anymore what I wanted to show him, or what we talked about that he could have seen only at our house on Gyöngyvirág Street. Perhaps the live-bearing fish, a guppy about to deliver its young. At that point what he wanted to look at didn't matter, what mattered is that he was going to violate a prohibition because of me. He wanted to see the house where I live, he wanted to see my family, what sort of people I am living with, though he'd never say so, I was sure of that. Anyway, I didn't bother my head about whether I understood Kim Jang-soo correctly, I just asked my sick mother to arrange the visit. Just this once, they should let Kim Jang-soo leave the Forest School. All I remember is that I had to tell my parents everything about the Korean children in detail, things that until then my parents knew nothing about. Then on one Saturday morning, Kim Jang-soo turned to me on our school bench, and in his quiet way said that he's coming over on Sunday. I come look Sunday afternoon. Our teachers consider matter. Your parents to us Koreans very honorable people. Which is how the resolution allowing the visit must have sounded. I could read his face by then and saw that the decision of the head teachers pleased him very much, that he was what we'd call bursting with happiness. Independently of the rigor of their political setup, they learned to preserve their dignity under all circumstances. Which meant perfect emotional neutrality. I have no idea what our mother did to make the visit possible. Before she was ousted from her position, the Korean and Chinese ambassadors invited her to official dinners more than once, or else gave a luncheon expressly for her and her colleagues. Perhaps this is the path she started out on, and that same week, succeeded. I didn't think about it at the time, but today it's clear why she succeeded so quickly. As soon as the Korean War broke out, my mother organized the antiwar rallies, the political rallies, and the protests with Valéria Benke, who was the secretary of the National Peace Council at the time. In the first months of the war they dispatched hospital trains to Korea, then, with Benke and Emil Weil, who acted as medical advisor, they also organized the construction of a military hospital, which was a highly complex task and we hardly saw our mother until they'd finished the preparations. Before Emil Weil left for Washington to present his credentials as Hungarian ambassador to President Eisenhower, we went with Benke to their home on Istenhegyi Street because Emil Weil had been to Korea to inspect the hospital and he wanted to share his experiences with us. Which was yet another reason for me to follow the daily reports on the war.

According to the Acheson papers of the Department of State, Weil first called up John F. Simmons, chief of protocol and assistant to Secretary of State Acheson, on August 1, 1951, it was a Wednesday, and the chief of protocol received him the next day. The Honorable Dr. Emil Weil, newly appointed Minister of the Hungarian People's Republic, called on me today at 2:15 p.m. to present copies of his credentials and to request an appointment with the President, Simmons wrote in his report on the following day. The conversation was of a particularly superficial nature, he wrote. Dr. Weil, possibly through shyness or lack of familiarity with the English language, said very little during the entire conversation, which lasted some five minutes. His contribution to our talk was so trivial, dealing with questions of weather and climate, that the chief point to record in connection therewith was his reticence. Emil Weil may not have been very talkative, I now add, but I don't remember him as being morbidly tongue-tied. Toward the end of his call, continues Simmons, I expressed to him the hope that, during the time of his incumbency as Minister to the United States, relations between Hungary and this country, which have certainly not been good in the past, might improve. Although Dr. Weil was accompanied by an Attaché of the Legation, Madam Zsuzsanna Szűcs, and an interpreter of the Department, Mr. Andor Klay, the latter two persons did not in fact take part in the conversation. Dr. Weil had a smattering of English, which he chose to use rather than rely upon the interpreter. No matters of a political nature were discussed.

Kim Jang-soo visited us on Sunday, but he could not stay for dinner. Our father took him back to the Forest School. I could tell that he was taken with Szidónia Tóth, he kept blushing, which couldn't have meant either more or less than what it meant, even on an East Asian face, and so, when he saw Szidónia Tóth with the young man by the Orgonás Street stop, it must have been like a stake through the heart.

They let him come see us several times on Sunday, but he always had to be back promptly.

We were also planning for him to bring Hu Jong-hwan, who wore his heart on his sleeve, I'd asked him to, because his excess of emotion made him an outcast among the other boys, who kept disciplining him, whereas probably he was older than they, my heart bled for him, whereas he had a way with him that I never could get used to, he drew me toward himself and kept hugging me, he pressed me tight every chance he got when the others didn't see, but when the others saw him do it once, he blushed to the roots of his hair, his head was aflame, they ganged up on him, they didn't talk to him for weeks, and he never hugged me again, still, Kim Jang-soo never brought him along, and perhaps it wasn't because they wouldn't allow it, but, or so I felt, because Kim Jang-soo himself was against it. I bet he had to work some magic in his own system so at least they'd let him come, because he almost always came unexpectedly. On the other hand, it was obvious that he hadn't come only because of me.

He saw Szidónia Tóth with the young man at the Lilac Grove again, and he wanted to tell us. He wanted to find out who the young man was, whether he was a relative, though he could have never asked outright.

Our parents made inquiries but could not find the young man. They wanted to speak to a certain comrade, who'd commanded Szidike to us, that's how they said it back then, commanded, and then that certain comrade might have known something about that certain young man. When there was no hope of them finding that certain comrade, my mother asked me to go with her one morning, and skip school, I really shouldn't make such a big deal out of it, it was just this once, because we were going to Pilisszentlélek.

It was a cold April, the snow had melted in March, and though up in the Mátra Mountains it had not yet melted, in the hills of Buda and the woods of the Pilis Mountains there were hardly any patches of white to be seen. When we came back from Pomáz or went up to Dobogókő, we walked by Pilisszentlélek many times. It was a lonely village nestled in a valley among the hills, its houses stood at some distance from one another, it had a whitewashed medieval church, Slovak and German inhabitants, and a large expanse of forest. In the villages of the Pilis hardly anyone spoke Hungarian, and when they did, they wreaked havoc with the language. The village was surrounded by woods, oaks and beeches dotted the landscape, and the impoverished inhabitants of the settlements lived off the forests. We had difficulty finding the house, it stood nestled snow white at the bottom of a gorge, with a wild mountain stream rushing nearby. It was like something out of a fairy tale, but inside it spoke of poverty the likes of which I had never before seen in my country. The door to the house stood open. As we descended along the muddy path, we saw Szidike kneeling on the ground, her skirts tucked underneath, her feet bare, and she was applying mud to the floor from a bucket, in short, she was plastering the earthen floor. It was hard work, and they did it twice a year in all the adobe houses. Years later, when I rented a room from her in Kisoroszi, Zsuzsanna Sághy taught me how to do it. This was the only way to preserve the condition of adobe houses for several centuries. They did it just before Easter, though in cooler places such as the Pilis, perhaps later, once it warmed up a bit, and again at the end of September, before the autumn freeze set in. They mixed chaff, cow manure, and soil with lots of loam, this is what they used to fill in the slits and cracks in the walls of the adobe houses, and when they added water and it turned either gray or yellow, they used it to correct the faults in the earthen floor of the kitchen, and this is what they called a house with a plastered floor or earthen floor. Sometimes they colored it. Once it had dried, and it took a long time to dry, the plaster formed a smooth layer, the cow manure functioned as a reliable glue of sorts. It wasn't the manure that smelled but the fusty and moldy walls that, in a valley such as this, can't be prevented. In the small house where Szidike Tóth lived with her family everything was immaculate, just as in Slovak houses in general. White and blue dominated. Their folk costumes were also white and blue. Szidike, too, had come to us wearing a folk costume, she had no other clothes, nor did she want any. These traditional costumes consisted of an underblouse, bodice, or camisole, which women wore next to their skin, the upper part also serving as a bra substitute, they closed it up with buttons or hooks, they were very tight and reached only to the waist, while the lower part, white but decorated with tambour lace and reminiscent of a skirt, served as a sort of half-slip. As a rule, they didn't wear panties. Over the underblouse they wore their pin-tucked shirts, or *pruszlik*, cut tight at the waist, on top of which were their skirts, on special occasions more than one could be counted, fifteen, even twenty, all of them pleated, but most of these served only as a sort of slip, on top of which was the outer skirt, patterned the same as the underskirts, and on top of the outer skirt an apron, though on weekdays Szidike didn't wear more than three or four skirts herself. First they sprinkled the plastered floor by making figure eights, then they swept it up, making sure that the sweeping didn't create dust. This house had a small veranda, meaning a stoop in front of the entrance, they called it a stoop because of its small size, and also, in case of rain, a beggar could find shelter under it. The army of beggars and the homeless wandered around the Hungarian countryside at regular intervals, even though in the 1950s they were officially labeled work-shy truants, and the police should have rounded them up. But generally, the local policemen were unwilling to do anything of the sort. They were willing to do many things, but not this. People knew when a certain beggar would show up at a certain house, on a Tuesday or a Friday, they would put the soup aside for him along with a slice of bread. Each house had its own beggar. Last year Uncle Géza still showed up at our house in Gombosszeg. His full name was Géza Pécz, he got his coffee with lots of sugar and bread, which he dunked into his coffee, because he'd lost his teeth; he also liked cottage cheese with sour cream, which he ate with lots of sugar and not salt and paprika, the way they ate it in our area; and we also gave him cigarettes that we bought especially for him, and matches, needless to say, and also some cash. He didn't know the value of money, but he expected us to give him some, it was part of our ritual. When he showed up, he'd also ask for books to take to the children. He called newspapers and magazines books, too. I have no idea who the children were, but he needed this little bonus. He also asked for a bag to carry the books. This meant anything in which he could carry them. Once he asked me to buy him a telephone, at which I asked, don't you want a church clock with a pocket chain as well, Uncle Géza. He laughed at this, but for years he kept asking for the telephone, despite the fact that he was unfamiliar either with the letters or the numbers. But this year he didn't come. He must be around eighty-three, if he is still among the living. He'd stopped coming one winter, but then he showed up, he'd been in the hospital. But not this year. Not yet.

At Szidike's house, the beggar ate the soup, but put the bread in his sack. The stream at the bottom of their garden was so loud as it rushed over the rocks that Szidike probably couldn't have heard our arrival, and we'd nearly reached the stoop when, surprised by my mother's voice, she turned around. There was a great deal of shouting and lamenting, this is as much as I remember of our visit, and not much more of their room and kitchen.

My friend Kim Jang-soo also came from an impoverished family of peasants, he told me once without having to be asked, but I could feel that he was trespassing on his teachers' interdiction; he had three siblings, the southerners burned their village to the ground, they made them dig a deep ditch and shot everyone into it to the last man, he climbed out of the ditch over the heap of dead bodies at night, he'd been wounded, but he wasn't alone, three of them survived, the other two were grown-ups familiar with the neighborhood who knew how they could reach their troops, the northerners, but one of them died from his wounds on the way.

A couple of days after our trip to Pilisszentlélek to see Szidike, when her pain became intolerable, our mother was taken back to St. John's Hospital. She put it down to her kidney stones; she moved about the hospital corridor bent over, with her palm pressed to her side. A couple of days later they transferred her to the surgical clinic on Üllői Street, where they gave her morphine, but they operated anyway for the benefit of the medical students. They didn't find any kidney stones, but the medical students saw that the cancerous tissue had destroyed her liver, which they told our father, along with the brief mention of morphine. Three days after her surgery, she felt a bit better, and when my brother and I went to see her on Sunday, she proudly held up the irregular stones that looked a lot like turquoise; they had her believe that they were hers.

During the last week of her life only our father went to see her, we could not go, and when she died early that Sunday morning, our father found only her dead body. She seemed so cheerful on Saturday afternoon. Probably, because of the increased dosage of morphine. A person knows what will happen, but death comes as a surprise, always as a surprise. Kim Jang-soo came to the funeral and stood at our mother's grave. He stood all alone and looked lost. I liked to imagine that in the midst of this absurdly large crowd he stood across from me at the open grave, thinking of his lost parents and dead siblings.

For at least two decades, every time I thought about him, I wanted to go to Korea to find him.

That summer, with my childhood now behind me, our father took me out of the lab of the Pharmaceutical Headquarters in Király Street, where I worked for the summer, and saw me to the Mátyás Rákosi Children's Camp at Balatonvilágos. He was wearing a linen suit he'd dyed black. He went to a dry cleaner's in Petőfi Sándor Street and had all his clothes dyed black. He wore a black tie. His two sons wore black ribbons on the lapels of their coats or the collars of their shirts. It made sense; despite my abhorrence, I had to admit as much. It indicated that here was a mourner whose heart had been rent, ritually reminding the world to spare him their jokes and rowdiness, at least for a while, except I hated all rites and formalities my entire life. Even in spite of my own better sense, I always considered it disgusting the way grown-up men and women treated birth, love, and death. I'd have liked to know the source of this loathing, but I have no idea. Our father even made sure that his white handkerchiefs should have black borders, that he should wipe his nose with these mourning handkerchiefs. Before we left for the children's camp, which had been opened a couple of years before so that in adjoining Balatonaliga, strictly off limits and heavily guarded, the comrades were be able to enjoy their vacation without being disturbed by their children, in short, that not only the outside world but the racket made by their own children should be put off limits to the holiday resort of the comrades, we first visited the cemetery. It was obvious that our father was taking me to the children's repository, which is what the comrades called the children's camp of the privileged among themselves. While our mother lived, she'd never have allowed it. Before we left, I gave away the fish from the aquarium and the turtle from the bowl and the newt from the terrarium. I let the snakes go free. They disappeared in the lush ivy in the blink of an eye.

I have no idea what my brother did that summer.

It was quite a challenge spending those three summer weeks with the other children my own age without them realizing that I was avoiding them. Their proximity was a serious punishment, not that they were to blame. There was an exceptional mood among the children in this camp, a mix of nonchalant cruelty and nauseating familiarity that I accepted as a given, but I kept my distance all the same. I made sure it didn't get under my skin, but they were so busy building and protecting their hierarchies that I don't think any of them noticed that I kept aloof. When the three weeks were up, one of the councilors surprised me by saying that I shouldn't pack my things, I wouldn't be taking the train back to Budapest with the others, and my father would visit me on Sunday, because I'd be spending another three weeks at the camp. And in fact, he came to visit me. He sent a wire saying he'd be arriving at such and such a time, he walked along the railway tracks in his black summer suit, all skin and bones, as I stood waiting for him at the fence of the deserted camp. I was allowed to go back home only in the middle of August. I had to start purchasing food, cooking, washing, cleaning. There hadn't been anyone in the house for some time to see to these chores. And when I saw that what I was doing was not enough and had to make more of an effort, I did a major summer cleaning in the house before school started, I was determined, I scrubbed the floor twice with the yellow tint and wax polish, using a floor brush affixed to my naked foot, making sure the brush was properly waxed, which still wasn't good enough, because the floor also had to be shined with a soft rag. That damned house, I was determined that it should shine. It shone with the paste and polish from István Nádas's former chemical plant. It took perhaps a week for me to finish with the house. It was a bona fide act of mourning. Cleaning has been right down my alley ever since. A work of remembering. I could get incredibly absorbed in every detail. Like one possessed, in my long life I have divested many a house, room, kitchen, pantry, and attic of its filth. I did it even with apartments and houses in which I was a guest or a tenant for only a brief time.

I truly hope that before I die, I can clean up wherever I am.

But I could not enter our grandparents' room with my cleaning supplies.

Cleaning required top-notch equipment.

I ignored the state our grandparents Cecília Nussbaum and Arnold Tauber were in after our mother's funeral, and it pains me to this day. Acknowledging their feelings probably surpassed what I was emotionally capable of at the time.

After Szidónia Tóth left us, our grandmother would have gladly resumed her former role in the household, but she was no longer in her prime, neither physically nor mentally; she got everything all mixed up, confused, and she forgot things in midstream. It seemed that my grandparents could take no more catastrophes at the hands of fate, whereas there were more to come.

I watched aghast what our grandmother was up to in the kitchen; it was nearly impossible to stop myself from making a comment, but it was no use doing so, because it would only end in a horrendous scene. Theoretically, it belonged to the realm of the impossible, but not only did she not know anymore what belonged where in the kitchen and she got the flour and the washing powder mixed up, and once actually used it to make roux, she even forgot how to cook. She heaped curses upon the woman at the grocery who sold her the bad semolina flour, whereas she'd told her she wanted pastry flour. It wasn't the first time that damned woman had cheated her. As God was her witness, it was the last time she would cheat her. Our grandfather ate what our grandmother put in front of him without a word. It wasn't always easy, but it wasn't impossible either. A tomato cabbage made with semolina roux was not the end of the world. Day in and day out, our grandfather sat on an uncomfortable chair in their room, whereas they had two comfortable armchairs; he placed his two palms between his knees, his posture was straight as a rod, with only his shoulder blades touching the back of the chair, but even that ever so lightly, he sat like this for hours on end, day in and day out, looking at the garden through the window. Trees and clouds in a person's eye were sufficiently eventful. He said nothing, he asked nothing. He may have talked with the garbage man when he came with his solitary horse, a big hunk of a man, he'd talk to him, I don't know why and I don't know what about. If my father asked him anything or said something to him, he gave one or two words by way of a reply, but he'd stopped talking of his own volition, and especially about himself, years before. Reed-thin, he was always immaculately dressed, a suit, vest, and tie, when he crossed our room, but we didn't dare talk to him either.

If he got up from the chair at all, he was sure to go out to the garden once a day; our dog followed him, she clambered around him, she'd have liked to jump up on him, but he didn't respond to our dog either. Unsure of herself, our dog sat down and looked after his handsome, retreating figure. She wanted to understand. But she didn't. Then, because that's what dogs are like, she took off after him.

Perhaps this time she would understand.

On the steep garden paths, our asthmatic grandfather wheezed and gasped for air. He could still drag the garbage bin out to the gate when he heard the garbage man's bell ring from behind the bushes at the far end of the street. He rang his bell as he led his horse along with a lead. For a while, our grandfather could still fire up the furnace, too, in the morning, and he chopped the kindling as well, but when I got back from school, I added the kindling to the fire to spare him that work. Out of respect and sympathy, sometimes I even joined him on his walks through the garden. He barely glanced at me, though there was attention in his glance, but he said nothing and I said nothing. After all, I was and have remained his grandson.

When my brother couldn't get out of bed and our mother, too, was confined to her bed in the other room, his teacher came over every single afternoon after school, which was far from routine. She took my brother's fate to heart.

She tried to teach him everything that she had taught my brother's little classmates that day, penmanship, critical reading, bunny rabbits, kittens, so he shouldn't fall behind. It was an exceptional sacrifice on her part. She was a certain Aunt Ica, but unfortunately, I can't recall her surname, and my brother doesn't remember it either. Now and then she and my ailing mother would engage in conversation, and now and then, if she could get out of bed, my ailing mother made tea for the two of them. My brother was much taken with Aunt Ica, he kept turning his brown face to her and batting his long eyelashes. The truth is, I was taken with Aunt Ica myself. My brother was so taken with her, he couldn't even pay attention to his penmanship or his reading, he preferred to watch the movement of Aunt Ica's lips as the two lips, painted fire-engine red, opened and closed. Even our grandfather Arnold Tauber was taken with Aunt Ica, and as for Cecília Nussbaum, who was sensitive to feminine beauty, she virtually bloomed and blossomed whenever she saw her in the afternoon. For about ten minutes, the pleasure in that beauty staved off the advance of her dementia.

Aunt Ica was pleasantly plump, as they said back then, she was the most beautiful pleasantly plump woman I ever had the pleasure of seeing. I have repeatedly sung her praises through the guise of my fictional characters; this praise is part of my life's confession. She was redheaded, dyed red or natural red, I don't know, but she was a red-headed woman with sea-green eyes, miraculous, miraculous, who, to her great regret, was a *femme fatale* only on the surface, which from time to time made her very sad. Almost everything about her was pleasantly plump. The gods on high provided generously for her, because her lips were full, her shoulders were full, her arms were full, her skin, need we add, was white as marble, but not any old way, because it was like both velvet and marble, and as for her buttocks, they were also plump, the curves enchantingly round, and even her calves were round. I don't dare mention her breasts here, suffice it to say that they were every bit as plump and round and gentle as her face. The Trinity is holy in aesthetics, too; the singular exists only in mathematics and theology. In nature, the singular is nonexistent. She didn't wear a bra, which during the reign of terror counted as an exceptionally brave act on Aunt Ica's part, and in certain situations, her tantalizing nipples, whose sensitive areolae must have been huge, showed through her dresses, she invariably wore dresses of a light color, lots of white, almost invariably white, but never pure silk, it wouldn't have suited her, she preferred rustic materials, pearlescent materials, satin, linen, hemp, white poplin blouses and shantung, and

I mustn't forget to mention her endearingly fragile waist, a wasp's waist, as they said back then, though I never understood this, considering that wasps don't have waists, and her knees and ankles, her gorgeous feet encased in shoes comprising only a couple of straps, her instep, her toes, painted blood red, like so many jewels, just like the fingers of her hands with their red talons, while her wrists were laden with colorful, clinking bangles. My brother learned little from this Aunt Ica, who was like a jewel herself, but probably, he learned to contemplate her beauty, to stare openmouthed, to understand and interiorize it. Besides, I don't think anyone could have learned anything from Aunt Ica. Aunt Ica was a patient teacher, gentle, smiling, easily given to laughter, a pure, self-sacrificing person whom no one took seriously because of her beauty. And that included me. When she laughed, the other person watched her teeth as they glistened with her sweet saliva, and not her, he watched the flesh, the bones, the body, what else, considering how depraved and lascivious man is. The edge of the teeth, as the lipstick left a blood-red trace on them. So much perfection can take this bit of imperfection. But why she was so cheerfully self-sacrificing or what she said in her tinkling little-girl voice, because everything about Aunt Ica, including her red hair and ocean-blue eyes, tinkled, few could have cared; the why and wherefore of her goodness sparked little interest in an ungrateful and shameless public, and so what my brother with his two dark gleaming eyes interiorized of her was no business either of the family nor the Department of Education. He wouldn't have been awarded special credit for it, as they said back then. And that didn't matter, because Aunt Ica smelled like heaven. As she walked around in her discerning and perfectly tailored dresses that sometimes sported a rather risqué décolletage, as she carried her scent with her around our room, the school corridor, the street, or indeed, when she stopped, she immediately snared the other person in the caul of her fragrance, because, after all, the other person was just a human being, and this was more than interesting, because at such times the other person regressed, he turned into an animal once again, he sniffed, he sniffed out the origin and component parts of her celestial scent, which was nonetheless a real scent, a blend of lipstick, nail polish, powder, and the perfume that descended from a seventh Oriental heaven, and only the gods on high could have said of what else.

After our mother died and my brother was already limping to school in his brace to attend second grade, he never cried again, he never whined again, because upon hearing news of our mother's death he abandoned the compulsory self-pity that came with his age, he didn't even cry at the funeral, whereas the mourners around him were all sobbing and sniveling, anyway, after our mother died, our father, who wore a black armband even over his black suits, accompanied Aunt Ica to the Városkút stop of the cog railway after a PTA meeting to discuss with her what was to be done, because Aunt Ica felt that she would fail my brother, and it might be best for him to start the whole thing from scratch with someone else, the two of them agreed that Aunt Ica should come to our house again three times a week to tutor my brother. Except, our father said that from now on she wouldn't be doing it for free, because he'd pay her by the hour. I'm not saying that he bribed Aunt Ica. Back then no one thought ill of such an action to save a child. Also, Aunt Ica wanted to get married. This was the issue that really weighed in the balance. There couldn't have been a man anywhere on earth who wouldn't have wanted Aunt Ica for himself. Yet no one had asked for her hand. I don't understand why not. Which clearly hurt Aunt Ica, at times it made her very sad. Aunt Ica must have been as dumb as a doornail, a fact that I considered of little consequence with regard to her. Aunt Ica was essentially an old maid by then. As I think back on her now, she might have been as old as twenty-five. I saw perfectly well what was going on between the two of them. With his bent back and his poorly tailored black suits, our father must have been like a scarecrow, and in her despair, Aunt Ica would have liked to entrust her life to this scarecrow, whereas nothing of his face remained except for two eyes grown gigantic with fright, his nose, now bone-sharp, and his two ears, also grown gigantic, that stood out on his bald head. My own ears stood out almost the same way. My foolish mother kept promising she'd tape them down, and then they'd stay like that forever. I looked to see what this gorgeous

Aunt Ica saw in our unfortunate father, whom she found bewitching. I wouldn't have minded having her as my stepmother so I could be close to her and stare at the roundness of her breasts, and my brother felt the same way, I think. As for our father, who was forty-six years old at the time and still had three more years left of his life, he noticed none of this with respect to Aunt Ica. Which was understandable. Still, our father not noticing caused me no end of frustration. Kindly notice her and marry her, and not Rózsi Németh, as our mother wished him to do before she died. And then their romance, or whatever, petered out, and one fine day Aunt Ica said that she had no more time to tutor my brother.

Our father's fate must have clashed dramatically with his makeup; his fate unexpectedly offered him something, but because of his makeup, he must have considered the offer frivolous. His obsessive visiting of our mother's grave dashed all our hopes of him marrying Aunt Ica. He remained faithful to our mother forever, even after her death, and he said so, which was a comforting thought, he wouldn't be bringing an ugly, demented woman to the house who was a total stranger, a wicked stepmother, but at the same time, I considered his declaration pathetic. It was a form of self-defense that did nothing to defend our poor father. The pathos meant that we must participate in her death cult even if it kills us, we must go to the cemetery twice a week and tend the grave, and the three of us must touch the headstone at the same time. Also, not only did we have no money to hire someone to manage the household, our father could barely scrape enough money together that year to buy at least half of the fuel for winter in advance. Worse comes to worst, come February, we'll be cold, but we'll install a small iron stove in our grandparents' room, and as for us, we'll make do as best we can. Spring was just around the corner anyway.

Just then, our grandmother announced that she was not up to cooking for us anymore, but she insisted that she'd cook for the two of them separately in pots and pans set aside strictly for their own use, and why not, considering that nothing was good enough for me, not that anyone had ever heard of a boy cooking, what an idea. May her memory be a blessing, but nothing that she made was good enough for our mother either, and if that's what I wanted, I could go cook for my brother and our father to my heart's delight. They'd go to their glory soon enough from my cooking. But I'd better keep away from her pots and pans. I couldn't even boil milk in her milk pot. It was obvious that everything, and I do mean everything that I cooked was filthy, odious treyf that only goyim would eat, she'd never touch it, it would kill her, and besides, she hadn't got the money to buy new pots every week because of my lordly whims when it came to cooking. At my Aunt Magda's place in Leányfalu I learned to make a *salade à la vinaigrette*, a pesto Genovese, or a pesto Bolognese, in short, how to make a tasty, substantial meal from next to nothing in minutes. With this new knowledge of mine, I got my grandmother's goat once and for all. She couldn't abide watching me cook. Though for a different reason, she would hardly ever let me do her shopping. She was determined to stand on line, though her legs could barely support her abundant weight. She knew right away what they were selling and where or, as she put it, what they were dealing out. I have to go to Széchenyihegy for sugar. Will somebody kindly tell me why Széchenyihegy of all places. They're doing it so those of us living on Svábhegy shouldn't have sugar, may the devil take them, along with their hill. Needless to say, no one was dealing anything out to anyone by then. The expression came from the times after the siege, when the Russians or the Americans gave bread or flour, sometimes chocolate or condensed milk past its shelf life, to the starving people of Budapest.

Summer may have been over by then, and we were probably attending school again, though I can't be sure, because except for our awkward visits to the cemetery, I retain only the vaguest memories from the days following our mother's death, but I do know that on that particular day, except I don't know which day, when I got back from school, I lost no time in seeing to things, doing the wash, cooking, or cleaning the house, in short, I set about my mourning ritual, as always. Anyway, that particular day I made meat loaf from ground meat. I soaked the roll in water, because there was no milk in the house. I remember the egg, that I had an egg. I remember clearly breaking the egg, but the egg, both the white and the yolk, was as if I'd never seen an egg before, as if I were looking at it through a magnifying glass, the egg lodged itself in my eyes, it burned into my eyes, I sprinkled salt and pepper on the ground meat the way I'd seen my grandmother Cecília Nussbaum do it, I kneaded it a couple of times, I tasted it, too, to see if I needed to add salt, but not only did I not taste the salt, I didn't taste the raw meat either. It was as if I were seeing ground meat in a bowl for the first time in my life, and the salt crystals, too, I saw each salt crystal separately. To this day, I could describe the shape and position of every single salt crystal on top of the meat. But no taste at all. Whereas I remembered that the tongue and the gums should feel something definite, even though I couldn't have said if it was my own tongue in my mouth or someone else's tongue. And in order to rid myself of this peculiar sense of something missing, a feeling as sharp as any excess, I took the bowl and walked from the kitchen over to the hall window, where I set it on the wide windowsill, where I continued mixing the meat, all of this in slow motion, or so it seemed, it seemed to take forever, so it shouldn't be too soft, I even remember wondering whether it didn't need an extra dash of breadcrumbs so it could be firm, or *fest*, as our grandmother Cecília Nussbaum would say; anyway, as I worked the ground meat into a firm mass with the practiced motion of my palm, I glanced out the window. I remember perfectly well that the sky outside was cloudy. As I now replay that old cloudy day, it may have been the first or second week of September. Before the window outside, our dog was rolling in the grass and jumping about. This sweet animal wouldn't stay still even when she was sleeping. Which reminded me that regardless of the strange things I was feeling and thinking, I must feed my dog. But at the same time, I could feel that I wouldn't have the energy and I wouldn't have the time even to shape and fry the meat patties. Still, I managed to wash my hands in the bathroom and I managed to give the dog something to eat. I don't know what. Then I washed my hands in the bathroom again, after all, I had stroked and playfully boxed with my dog so I'd feel something, and she returned the favor and licked my face, and of the threats we faced in the days after the siege, my mind retained my fear of getting intestinal worms. Yet I must have known that I was ill. I managed to make my bed. It wasn't easy, I had to raise the top of the bed to retrieve my blanket, but I didn't have enough strength by then, I had to prod it open. And yet I managed. I wasn't the one who managed it, but someone else who may have always been with me, possibly it was me, but now this other took over for me. This other managed to get undressed and get into bed instead of me, and to pull his blanket up to his head. As I think back on it, it must have been around five in the afternoon. I wasn't dizzy and I wasn't feverish, or else I didn't feel that I had a fever. Still, with this other person's eyes I managed to make sure that the outside world existed and it wasn't just me imagining it, that it wasn't me who'd imagined it up till now either, and also, that it hadn't changed in the meantime, and with these unsettling questions this other person opened my eyes to look out the window, just to make sure. The trees stood motionless under the cloudy sky, two poplars, their trunks covered with ivy, on the steep, grassy hillside behind the two windows. We were afraid that one fine day the weight of the ivy would made the poplars come crashing down on the house. This was the last image. When this other person closed my eyes the image disappeared, because the glare hurt the other person that was still me, and I even remember asking myself in this new dark why he was saying this, because I didn't understand who I'd be saying it to.

After that I did see some images, but no thoughts attached to them, because I probably lost my sense of time first, then my sense of space became confused, and then several long weeks had to pass in the real world before I could feel, by fits and starts, the presence of others or my own presence, for that matter, though I could not make out their gestures or their words, I saw them move their lips but couldn't understand their words, I could neither hear nor understand their words, my hearing and understanding returned only by degrees, and even then only to some extent, so that I could participate, to some extent, in the mechanics of sensing time and space that I had once shared with them, moving as they moved, hearing as they heard, when I could shape words, speak, and remember how to do such things.

It took even longer before I could separate my visions from the images that belonged to my newly if uncertainly recovered sense of space and time. Three and a half months passed before I managed to reconcile these relationships sufficiently to allow me to go back to school. This was just before Christmas. But I was back in this cold, snowy outside world for less than a week, it may have been the first day of Christmas break, when the visions returned, though where and how they caught up with me, how and where I turned delirious again, I can't remember, because I wasn't aware of it happening. I seem to remember that it was in the afternoon that I told my father as gingerly as I could, without upsetting him, it may have been on a Sunday, possibly Christmas Day, that I thought I was running a fever again, then there's a break in my consciousness, but then I see that I'm lying on my bed, I know that it's my bed and those are the two windows of our room with the ivy-covered, snowy poplars outside, but after that I remember nothing more.

On the other hand, I remember perfectly well what happened on that first morning in September.

I threw the ball up too high.

I saw the ball fly up to the sky and for a long time, a very long time, it was terrible, the ball wouldn't fall back down from the blue sky, whereas it wasn't my ball, and in the meantime someone was desperately shouting, no, not shouting, yelling, yelling beside themselves that I threw the ball up too high, you threw the ball up too high, too high, you shouldn't have thrown someone else's ball up so high, how many times must I tell you, it's too high, what a thing to do with someone else's ball, too high, and then, in a huge arch, the flight of the ball had already passed it, it passed the dead point up on high, and meanwhile this strange, never before seen painful sky that was clearly the ball's heaven clouded over, which told me how much time had passed while the ball was in flight, because I threw it up too high, whereas they told me not to throw it, the sky was still blue when I threw it up, too high up, the light was bright, the light hurt, the ball hurt, then the sky became overcast, at which the ball started to fall back down, except its fall came too late, I'd thrown it up too high, and now it didn't even matter anymore whether in this overcast sky it fell back down or not, you ruined everything, you threw it too high.

Meningitis, or encephalomeningitis, but for me its common name, brain fever, was more apt.

Probably, during the first hours of my illness, the symptoms were not evident to the naked eye, though our grandparents later said they realized that something is not right with this child if he makes his bed and lies down in the middle of the day. It was my grandmother who realized it. She told my grandfather, who later related it in the greatest detail. Ernő, please come, have a look at the child. Cecília Nussbaum always called our grandfather Ernő. I was sleeping. They touched my forehead, the two old people reached under the covers, they felt around, but neither thought I had a fever. They didn't see anything alarming in my breathing either. They couldn't understand why I didn't move, why I didn't stir, I was sleeping like a log, they kept coming out of their room to check, he was sleeping like a log, quieting their own anxiety each time with the same sentence, let him sleep. How were they supposed to know. Even if there was something wrong with him, let's leave him be, he'll sleep it off. Still, they were anxious for our father to come home, and when he went through the same motions, putting a hand to my forehead, reaching under the covers to see if anything was broken, I was still sleeping in the same embryonic position, and there was indeed just one worrying sign, namely, that I wasn't reacting to anything. He tried to wake me so I'd eat with them. But even that didn't wake me. At most, my breathing became irregular. Which calmed him. He had only the same wisdom to offer as my grandparents had offered each other, let him sleep it off. When our worried grandparents were returning to their room, he even cautioned my frightened brother, who was talking far too loud to them. In his fear, a person would rather not hear himself. He quickly removed my brother from the room and then out in the kitchen he saw that I had prepared and left the raw meat, he said that it was even shaped into patties and turned in the breadcrumbs, and they were lying in a row on the pastry board, ready to be fried, though I didn't remember shaping them and I didn't remember the breadcrumbs either. They fried them and ate them. They liked them. How fortunate. After our father gave my brother a bath and put him in bed, because he had to carry him from the bathroom, he wasn't allowed to use his leg without his brace, and I was still lying in the same position as before, he checked me once again, and when he reached under the covers by my feet, he didn't know why he did it, perhaps he thought he'd be able to judge by my feet whether I was running a fever or not, I moved, though I didn't change my position. Which meant that at the time, one of my reflexes was still intact.

This put him somewhat at ease, but he thought he should call Elza Baranyai, except it was too late, it was 10:30 at night.

First thing in the morning, he jumped out of bed to check on me, day was breaking, but in our room, shaded by the tall trees, the ivy, the laburnum, and the jasmines, it was almost completely dark. And when he came in, I sat up in bed, slapped my hand on the blanket, and said in a weak voice, Father, please, check. My blanket is full of stains.

Even if the blanket had stains on it, the stains wouldn't have been visible in the half-light.

Also, why would it have been stained.

He said something to the effect that he didn't see any stains, but by then I was shouting and screaming so loudly that on the other side of the street, in the bathroom of a villa that stood at the far end of a garden as big as ours, Major General Béla Berczely stopped shaving, and since the screaming didn't stop, or even if it stopped for a moment, it started up again without losing any of its force, he grabbed his robe, ran out to the street, and since he found our gate closed, he rang, he kept ringing and ringing, he kept pressing the bell, by which time everyone was shouting in our room as well, with the windows open. They wanted to take my temperature, but in my delirium I flung myself around, and though our father put his arms around me to restrain me, their attempt failed, they couldn't do it.

I knew all this from hearsay, I didn't have the faintest memory of it myself. I knew only that I threw the ball up too high. It wasn't my ball, I knew it then, and I know it now. I shouldn't have thrown that ball up so high.

Elza Baranyai sent for an ambulance, then took a taxi from the city to our house, but by then the structure of my delirium had collapsed, and for a brief moment I even saw them busying themselves with me, they even managed to take my temperature, though once again, I knew nothing about this. And the previous image was not accompanied by sound, this too is something I know. Probably, my fever didn't go up to 43 Celsius because the capillary of the mercury thermometer stops at 42. Elza Baranyai had me taken to the children's isolation ward at St. László Hospital which she headed, and which was the best possible place for me at the time. The instant she saw me, she knew it was meningitis, because when she slipped a hand under my skull, she couldn't bend my head forward, and this was coupled with hypertonia of the back muscles and rigidity of the spine. At any rate, this cluster of symptoms indicated meningitis, though later this became the basis of medical debate, because even after lengthy examinations, they couldn't decide on the type of brain fever it was. Perhaps the coherent sequence of images that has remained with me is attached to one of these examinations, though it's a deaf and dumb sequence of images. A sharp pain must have jolted me out of my delirium, though the pain didn't leave any traces in my storehouse of memories either. What remained apart from the mute sequence of images is something that in retrospect I consider an extraordinary danger signal coming from the body. Probably, they did a spinal tap, meaning that they took a sample from my cerebrospinal fluid, or else they detected an overly high degree of pressure and that's why they tapped the spine, as I now see from Géza Petényi's college textbook, *Paediatrics*, published in 1956. The pain made me see a wall covered in bright white tile. I see the wrinkles on the sheet of the examination table that I'd rumpled up with my convulsions, but as if they'd turned one of my goldsmith grandfather's magnifying glasses on it. Considering the rigidity of my neck and spine, it must have been very difficult to position my body so that they could proceed with the spinal tap. I see the tiles in one visual scale and the wrinkles of the rumpled-up sheet in another. I see several of them holding me down. I managed to free myself enough to change the picture, and now, at least, I tie this turning away to my free will, and then I saw a big glass wall, behind it fixedly staring faces, all strangers to me, probably a group of medical students, which makes me realize that this must be me. They called in Pál Kemény from the Tüzoltó Street Children's Clinic for a consultation. But on the basis of the test results, he couldn't say for sure either which type of meningitis they were up against, because it wasn't caused by fungi or parasites, it wasn't viral or bacterial, though they'd tested for bacteria very carefully. This was the best possible place for deciding questions such as this, because even during the First World War, St. László Hospital in Pest was the hospital for infectious diseases, an emergency care hospital with mostly hastily put up barracks that remained intact for decades to come because they were needed, but at the time they weren't as chaotic, filthy, and neglected as in the post-Socialist era. Neither the nursing staff nor the medical staff would have put up with it.

I retain no images of any of these examinations. They probably repeated the spinal tap, because my mind has retained an early sequence of images of it, very dramatic, and I also have a second sequence of images separate from this one in time, which is also dramatic, and in which I realize it's the last such test. I have also retained a couple of images of Elza Baranyai leaning over me in the ward, and I'm surprised to see that she's wearing a face mask. These are her two eyes, as for a moment I feel the cold touch of her stethoscope on my chest, and I see that this is a hospital ward, I don't know where I am, but there are other people in the room, and when I try to shift my gaze, I feel that my head won't turn as I've intended, though I don't know whose intention it is and why he can't look where he'd like because the stiffness of the neck and the stiffness of the spine are part of the group of symptoms, I can't see the people standing around me, but I see the huge glass window I'd seen once before, it's familiar, except there's no one behind it now, it's like a dream in which one room opens into another, and then chances are my delirium ended in a vision, because in fact, a room opened up from another room and I walked on and on, not on the floor, but without the least difficulty through the air. Probably this was just a hallucination, but it had a basis in fact, because when the images of the outside world became somewhat more stable, or at any event, images that people must regard as real, just as they must eat and urinate, seeing how they'd been brought into this world, they must feed others and help others vomit, and then I saw that in the building where I am, there are a row of cubicles separated by glass walls and every child is alone in his own isolated cubicle, as far as the eye can see. The reality resembled the hallucination, and not the other way around. At some distance from the foot of the bed, all the way down to the floor, there was one huge glass pane; I could see the park through it; the trees of the park entered my consciousness now and then through the most changeable weather conditions and parts of day, fall turned to winter, and I sensed the change as something tangible, a tangible difference, even though at the time my mind lacked the concepts of both fall and winter. My mind turned off the use of language for three months. These were crystal-clear images independent of conceptual clouds. Concepts didn't leave so much as their shadow in my mind. After a time, though I didn't know that time was time, and though it had no meaning, despite its chronology, hallucination was still dominant over reality as the delirium kept claiming me. And yet, despite the hallucinations, experience told me that there was a door behind my head, probably it opens onto a corridor, and that's where the people I'm unfamiliar with come from, and there has to be a light source, too, because they cast a shadow before them, and these shadows made me cringe with fear, I was terrified that they would perform another spinal tap. Elza Baranyai came through that door as well, and although she also lacked a name I tied her to a sense of familiarity, and there were others, too, I couldn't turn my head to see who was coming, but from time to time they turned me and stabbed me with a needle or something. Ten years later I asked Elza Baranyai what they stuck into me, penicillin, but why was it so terribly painful that it woke me, and it didn't just wake me, I cringed from fear the moment the door cast a shadow as it opened. The structure of the crystals as it entered the tissue fibers, she said. I saw them, they were talking calmly, but I didn't think I was supposed to hear, and only now do I interpret the contents of my former consciousness and think that they were talking calmly. I didn't know that there was something wrong with me, I didn't know what they were doing, I didn't know where I was, I saw the ward, to be sure, but I had no word to attach to it, nor did I miss it, I didn't know the place of this not knowing in the space and time of which I also knew nothing, yet it assumed a certain inner coherence depending on the type of pain the shadowy shapes caused, even though I had no idea where the back of my head was, or my thighs, and whether there was a difference or a distance between my spine and my thighs. Almost all of them have feminine shapes. When someone with a masculine shape came along with them, it wasn't him but one of the female shapes that made me panic because of the pain of which I didn't know it was pain, but my senses or the distinguishing mechanism of my mind was insufficient for me to know what made me panic, even though I saw what they were picking up from a tray. But neither the tray nor the syringe had a name. Whether the person caused me pain, or whether the person coaxed a sense of familiarity from my mind, like Elza Baranyai's masked face, no one and nothing had a name. I never saw faces over me, only the soft gauze masks of the feminine shapes and masculine shapes, but these shapes and masks shifted the image into a hallucination each time as imperceptibly as if they'd emerged just now from the delirium. Sometimes I saw the shapes in the white gauze masks bend over something, checking the coolness of their fingers or instruments, I think; they checked the progress of the tiny hemorrhages, like pinpricks, the symptoms of the meningococcal bacteria, on my belly and chest, which mattered to me only to the extent that I didn't have to be afraid of them, and as a result, they transported me from other types of hallucination into full unconsciousness, much like the shapes I feared.

Once I caught my father's figure behind the glass wall, but just once, whereas he was there every single afternoon for three and a half months, but even when I caught a glimpse of him, I could not tie his figure to the concept of father. It's only with my present knowledge that I know that it was my father standing behind the glass wall. He was standing outside in the park, he had to raise himself up on tiptoes so he could see my face because the bed was high, and then some kind soul stuffed something hard under my pillow, so I could see him from a better angle; he was wearing a coat and a black suit, which had become far too big on him as it hung over his now scrawny physique, but this must have lasted a short time. He even said something from behind the glass wall and waved, which I thought was amusing, because just then a pleasant, amusing feeling transported me elsewhere along with the other I and swept me along to still more amusing hallucinations. Sometimes my own loud laughter jolted me back to consciousness somewhat, and I couldn't stop laughing even though I should have. And then the tragic vision that I couldn't stop grabbed hold of me and took over. Those around me must have been aghast at these laughing visions, though I can't imagine how much could be seen or heard, because my sense of self was not functioning, I had no capacity for self-reflection of any kind. Probably, their frightened eyes were considering whether they should stick yet another medication in me and send it in the wake of the sulphonamides and antibiotics. Goethe's "Erlkönig" was not a romantic phantasm. Goethe gave a precise description of the various interwoven or fractured layers of reality as in response to outside forces they lean even more into one another, or else desperately attempt to resist one another to the extent that the pressure of the layers of consciousness allow. The child whom the horseman had picked up in his arm and galloped with him through the forest of the night was not ill, he didn't have a cold and he didn't have pneumonia, he had meningitis. The poet must have experienced it personally. I never thought of leaving my bed; everything just whisked me away from it and transported me to another world with ease or else brought me back, jolted me back from that other world.

I distinctly remember an improbably intense night when they catapulted me back into my life, even if they didn't supply me with a concept to go with it, and looking out from my bed I saw to my surprise that oh, it's night. I hadn't seen the night before. Not that I had a word for what I was seeing. There was no word yet to go with what had been my night. The apparition was the barren, luminous trees of the park standing defenseless in the weak, luminous lamplight, and no one came in the night and no one left, after many long weeks, I spent time in this dimension again, even if I lacked the conceptual awareness, because I lacked the words. And yet something made me happy, and the rising sense of happiness did not sweep me back into unconsiousness right away. This, too, was a great novelty. I could now be myself for a while, and the night could remain the night, and the temperature of the ward, lowered for the night, could remain the feeling of coolness; in short, they'd restored one of my sensory organs to me, they'd enriched me through the arrestingly beautiful reality of the lamplight outside, the circles of light alternating with those of darkness.

That night, as well as on subsequent nights, a sudden sense of joy kept washing over me, and I sensed that I was alone with it, though I had no words for any of these things, I am translating the sensation now for the sake of the details, to make my recollection complete. I didn't even attempt to search for concepts; rather, I sensed the things that I apparently gleaned for the various time layers of these nights or just this one night with a purely visual sense, and I was perfectly happy even without the attendant concepts.

Needless to say, when they first tried to get me up on my feet, I collapsed, if for no other reason than my sense of my own body had been deleted along with all its details, though I knew by then where I was and at lunchtime they gave me some nice soup, but I didn't know the difference yet between the body's prone and upright positions, or between my arms and my legs, or the spoon and my mouth. It was not the kind of knowledge that comes automatically. A great deal of time had to pass before I could manage the size of my body and the distance between my hands and my feet. I was back home by then, I knew the difference between my home and the hospital ward, and yet I still couldn't calculate the distance between things. Also, thanks to all the crystalline penicillin they jabbed into me, they destroyed the muscle fibers in my thighs and buttocks, as a result of which even walking with assistance caused me insufferable pain; it continued to hurt for a long time, a very long time, but for a long time to come I didn't know where the pain was coming from, since my sense of space hadn't yet been restored.

I have no idea how they got me home.

I lay in my parents' former bedroom; our father made sure that my brother didn't bother me, while he, for the time of my convalescence, moved to the maid's room, along with all his belongings.

I have no idea what we ate, what we drank, or who did what in a world that functioned in line with normal temporality. One thing is for sure, I could read by then, I was reading something in our parents' bed, though actually, I only pretended that I was reading, because I'd hardly read a couple of lines when, as they'd say in Russian literature, the scene would stand before me so vividly that I slipped into it, and the space was transformed and expanded into a frightful or comical vision, whereas I had a horror of visions. And possibly, I had a horror of comical visions above all. A vision like this was like the magic porridge in the Russian tale, first it swelled out of the pot so that it pushed off the lid, then it covered the top of the stove, then it swelled until it reached the room and then it seeped out the door and the window and slowly consumed the entire world of the tale. I tried to hold on to the narrative tooth and nail, but I slipped up unaware, I couldn't make myself focus on the simplest object of my imagination, imagination is imagination is imagination, it swept me along its well-trodden paths, the vision ran riot, it swelled, it grew by leaps and bounds. And then, when they took me home again after a month and a half, this time from Pál Kemény's ward in the children's clinic in Tűzoltó Street, where they called Professor Sárkány for consultation, winter was gone and it was early spring. But I remember nothing of that mild spring, just the feeling of weakness and physical helplessness.

You needed to cross the Sahara, but you weren't even dragging your feet because all that wonderfully furrowed yellow sand kept giving way, shifting under your feet.

I don't know what month it was when I could go to school again.

I didn't go to the school garden anymore, though; Judit Benkő asked me to go, we'll be flooding the field and planting rice soon, the seedlings are especially promising this year, because in the language of gardening, seedlings are not this or that, seedlings are promising, because, after all, who knows what might happen to them at the last moment, but I couldn't tell her why I couldn't go. How can you explain a sensation to someone, the feeling that you can't anchor yourself in this world, you can't be with the seedlings. You can't plant rice. About thirty-five years later, I received a letter from her, she surprised me with it more than I can say, after all, as soon as you're lucky enough to pass over the abyss of adolescence, a landslide buries your childhood under it, and the landslide is right to do so, I had plenty to bury, one day I'll write about that plenty, we were living in Gombosszeg by then and I was writing, I was assiduously writing this plenty, she wrote that she'd seen me on television, and though she read everything by me that she could get her hands on, she was happy to see me, and when next I was in town, she asked that I call her at the number she gave, she'd like to hear my voice, or I should write her and we'd discuss it in writing. I was happy to answer, and I promised. But then my writing, the plenty I was writing, meaning my work, which on the surface had nothing to do with our botanical excursions and the school garden, swept the visit underneath it for years, and by the time I realized I'd broken my promise, the number she gave me did not answer, and later even my letter was returned with that certain postal comment on the envelope.

I tried to pick up the threads of my old life. When I spotted a snake, I thought I'd build a terrarium and an aquarium again in the empty vessels that were still standing empty of their contents out on the musty veranda. Planning to start with snakes, I even prepared one of the terrariums, I spent long hours by what I thought were their hideouts, until I managed to grab one by the neck and force it to the ground, but when it slid up my naked arm, I released its head and tore it from my arm. To this day I have no idea what caused this transformation. Perhaps the process of sexual maturation brought a change in the system of attraction and repulsion to living things. As a result, the two terrariums as well as the aquarium remained unpopulated. I never again wanted captive animals near me, especially reptiles. Bánky, my music teacher, couldn't take me back into his wonderful choir either, where even those who had no ear for music sang like angels, because when I rejoined the group and he had me sing, it was supposed to be a soprano solo in some sort of cantata, but I was off key, I tried again, and he said he was sorry, my voice was changing, I must give up singing for a couple of years, I should sit down and listen to them and see how much they'd learned in the meanwhile, after all, my hearing was still intact.

That spring we also had to decide what school we'd like to attend next or what trade or profession we'd like to pursue. I would have liked to go to a teacher-training school. I didn't dare mention to anyone that I wanted to become a writer. We had a chemistry teacher, a small, attractive young woman possessed of the sort of whining mannerisms that make your palms itch, spoiled and wanting even more spoiling, who must have been the smartest daughter of the smartest older daddy in this best of all possible worlds, and needless to say, all the boys fell head over heels in love with her, just like their daddies, and so they all made fun of her and pretended to hate her, the little slut, what a whore, until they found a way of reconciling the hate and the adoration, and then they lost no time in wanting to marry her, her or no one else. The chemistry teacher was called Vera Hántás. But once a group of these overheated adolescent boys caught her with her equally ill-bred and very handsome husband, László Hántás, kissing and cuddling on the street, because the two of them lived somewhere up on Svábhegy. Because of their great envy, the kissing and cuddling in public spread through the school like wildfire, the boys even embellished it, played the tune with variations, and the rumors reached the girls, who giggled, until one of the boys said what Hántás did with the pretty little Vera when they kissed and cuddled, what a slut, a colossal whore she was, something that, to be perfectly honest, I didn't understand until years later. From then on, although they played up to this affectatious little Vera, they flattered her, they cozied up to her, as they said back then, yet they guffawed at the thought of all the things they'd do to Vera if they got under her skirt just once, and they called her Coochie behind her back. As for the kiss-and-cuddle Aunt Vera a.k.a. Coochie, when the woods came alive with sounds and everything burst into bloom and the birds chirped and cried, she didn't feel like holding chemistry class, and besides, she considered teaching beneath her dignity because her daddy said she was destined for better things, and so she didn't hold class but took us out to the nearby Braun Woods, where we sat down on the warm ground around her, I even remember holewort growing near me, and since the time had come to think seriously about our future and we were all fired up about it, though I'd already decided by then, she swooped down on us with her rather scant knowledge of psychology and told each of us what would happen to him, what would become of him. She named trades and professions, you will be this, you will be that, and also positions, you'll only make it to plant engineer, you're a gifted merchant already, you'll go into business, but Aunt Vera, you got me all wrong, I won't go into business, she didn't even hear us protest, you'll be a scientist, you'll be a boss, she named vocations, you're going to invent all sorts of things, you could become a renowned doctor, meanwhile she kept leaving me out of her gaze, and when her gaze settled on me, she said nothing, as if she were doing it on purpose. Even though I still had trouble assigning names to objects, ever since I recovered from my delirium I saw things more clearly. In her flippant self-confidence, she even said what would happen to the Korean children. For Kim Jang-soo she prophesied a future in chemistry. When she finished the dangerous game she was playing, which left me dumbfounded even in the stupor of my convalescence, and also because of her beauty, she mustered all the strength of her wickedness and turned to me. I truly wouldn't have thought that such beautiful grown-ups could tell a child's future. Which meant that a gift for prophecy was a by-product of her beauty. Or else certain individuals just knew, in which case she was one of those individuals. I was studying her face and girlish figure, looking for some distinguishing mark, a giveaway, when she turned her gaze back to me. And like someone who on a whim gives her intentional cruelty free rein and enjoys it, too, as if she were surprised, as if she hadn't noticed me until then, and you, you will come to nothing, she said. Nothing. It was surely not the prophet speaking through her, yet the sentence haunted me for years, and also, basically, she hit the nail on the head, because my father also rebuffed me without a second thought. No, I would not go to a teacher-training school, I would choose something tangible. I would not be a people's educator. He bristled at the idea. I couldn't tell him that it was only in preparation for my secret plan. If I could be a village teacher, which meant teaching the first four grades in accordance with a custom left over from the Monarchy, I could go to the countryside and get to know village life and the work peasants did, and later I'd start writing, with my accumulated knowledge. This was my plan. Which didn't happen that way either, but it almost did. After all, in the summer of 1968 I fled my native town and have been living in the countryside ever since. Since I'm interested in chemistry and understand chemistry, why didn't I learn chemistry, like my friend Kim Jang-soo. It would guarantee a steady income.

Given my convalescent state during those months and during the following decades as well, I did not argue with our father.

Once in the ancient past, when in his chemical works my Uncle István showed me what becomes what and how compared with the original ingredients and our father illustrated metathesis in the test tubes in our bathroom, I was really interested, back then it interested me, and if that's what he wants, why shouldn't I study chemistry, seeing how I won't be a chemist anyway, just as I won't be a village teacher. He wanted to keep me away from the Hungarian countryside with such vehemence that my compliance was far from irresponsible, it was the other way around, it was a sign of the responsibility I felt for him. He was completely out of his head by then, he didn't resemble his former self in the least, and I didn't want to upset him further with this nominal matter. He insisted that I have a steady income. He settled for nothing less. In which case, his insistence that I must not teach in the countryside was just an excuse, but it also bore with it a significance that I couldn't have understood at the time. I must learn a trade that would be needed even smack in the middle of a world conflagration. Clearly, everyone was expecting a calamity of universal proportions; in the wake of the nuclear tests on the Bikini Atoll, who wouldn't have expected the major powers to set the world on fire, and thanks to a chain reaction, burn it to cinders in the blink of an eye. But conflagration or no, our father must have been thinking that he must hold out until both his sons were ensured of a proper income. Considering my brother's age, he'd have had to hold out for quite some time. But he couldn't hold out, and our father knew it. He must have been thinking that at least I should have a secure profession, and not as a silly village teacher. He knew what he was talking about, he started school in Gömörsid. Also, in the course of our arguments over my choice of profession, he tried to make me understand that I was responsible for my brother. I mustn't be so indifferent toward him. I must help him, encourage him, the two of us would need each other. He must have been thinking about his impending suicide. This must have been his last hope, he must hold out a bit longer for my sake, he must succeed with this, the last and final mission of his life.

My illness had other than physical consequences, though. I lost my classmates and my so-called friends so thoroughly that I couldn't get them back. I also saw Kim Jang-soo's role of disciplinarian among the other Korean children with a sharpness that was unreasonable. Once I started up Költő Street, then walked on, without asking myself where I was headed, I reached the top of the Swiss Steps, but by then I'd forgotten all about the movie house, it was early morning in summer, there was hardly a person to be seen on the streets up on the hill this time of day, this was at Normafa, where in prehistoric times Laci Tavaly had slipped, he'd tumbled down the awfully steep hillside, my father and my mother ran like the devil, slipping down in his wake, but they couldn't reach him until he got caught on a shrub and burst into loud tears because the chestnuts he'd gathered so carefully and put in his pocket fell out and scattered on the ground, and then, there, up on the top of the hill on Normafa, I broke into a run, I don't know why. I had sneakers on. Ever since, and not as part of a sports routine, but just like that, for myself, like one running through a monologue, I traversed the various permanent and temporary scenes of my life, I covered about half a century, I even learned to run, more or less, from others and also I taught myself, I ran and ran until I ran myself into a heart attack.

But that summer I picked up another lost thread; I went swimming, though the only decision I made was that I wouldn't go to the Sports Pool, where Yvette was still going, though she didn't go there to do her laps anymore, but to the Lukács Baths, the haunt of lassitudinous city folk, as I'd done before. Before, boys of my own age would come with their prankish games, challenging me to do as many push-ups as they, and they could hoist themselves up on the bars fifty times, why don't I feel their biceps, and if not fifty, then how many times could I do, or they'd challenge me to race with them in the women's pool, except now no one turned to me with all that childish nonsense, though I didn't think about that either; probably, they were aghast at the very sight of me and gave me a wide berth, and they were right to do so, I thought it was just fine if I didn't have to participate in their silly games or join them on the terrace to ogle the girls.

It was definitely a Sunday, when the place was more crowded, but the so-called men's pool was all right, because people were not allowed to splash about in it. Also, the temperature of the thermal water was kept lower in the men's pool. The raggle-taggle, as the people of Pest gingerly called the common folk, could splash about in the women's pool. The lifeguard ordered anyone who didn't swim at the proper tempo and didn't keep in lane out of the water, with no appeals heard. Only the famous poet István Vas was allowed to swim as he liked. He wasn't swimming, he was fighting for his life as he kept sinking after every desperate flapping of his arms, because he breathed in reverse order, he inhaled when he should have exhaled. After swimming, I used the stairs near the women's pool to go up to the rooftop terrace. This winding staircase didn't smell as bad, because the men would sometimes relieve themselves on the landing of their own staircase, and the urine flowed down the stairs and smelled something awful. When the cabin attendants noticed, they carried big, heavy hoses up the stairs and, cursing and muttering to themselves, hosed off the filthy wall and the stairs, but the stink of urine remained.

At the side of the women's pool, a young woman was lying on her back. She supported her head with her hands folded under her neck, and she did so, making sure the movement would not spoil her hairdo while she took in the sun. She wore a pearl bracelet. She lowered her lashes and did not move. She wore a bikini. I'd never seen a bikini at the Lukács before. She also wore a choker around her shapely neck, also of real pearls of medium size, which surprised me no less than the bikini. It was a bit as if Gábor Baltazár's exquisite and impeccably elegant mother, who'd been forcibly resettled in a village by then, were lying there; it was exactly the way she used to lounge around on the side of their swimming pool, or it was as if the beautiful blond woman, whom I called ugly to myself, and with whom, for the first time in my shitty little life I fell head over heels in love, had suddenly appeared from Pozsonyi Street, where she used to cross her room naked as I watched from the window of my room.

I went upstairs to the sundeck, but even from there my eyes sought only the gorgeous woman lounging by the side of the pool with the string of pearls around her neck.

It was thrillingly clear that something was changing once and for all. Beauty, wealth, and elegance were the harbingers of this change. There were other indications as well, though these were more ominous, originating with doubts and containing within them anger and a certain bitterness. That summer, our father's friends came to visit, friends I knew from our excursions or from the time of the siege, Tóth, Lombos, and Kerekes. It was clear to me that they were bent on arresting with their bare hands the obvious political changes that were occurring, and that they would fail. János Asztalos came to visit, and Imre Mező came to visit, the two men were later lynched by the mob at the siege of Party Headquarters on Köztársaság Square, these were men I loved, even though their arguments had no effect on me, because along with the rest of Hungarian society, I too had long since turned my back on their inter-Party arguments.

On the other hand, the lab work I was doing interested me. I spent the summer working at a chemical plant in Király Street, by then rechristened in honor of Mayakovsky, who was by all accounts not a suicide but murdered; this was the Pharmaceutical Headquarters, where I first worked in its chemical warehouse, then in its quality control lab with the so-called experimental chemists, though I'd applied to study industrial chemistry. Vera Hántás knew this when she took us to the Braun Woods, and it must have riled her that this spoiled, ugly little cadre boy, this toad, would get the green light to attend the best chemistry school in the nation, even though he'd never become a chemist. When I learned that I had passed my entrance exam, whereas I didn't want to pass, it made me happy, because our poor hassled father was relieved. They'd canceled the disciplinary action against him around then, they basically rehabilitated him, though unsurprisingly, he was not given his former job back. On the other hand, they restored his rank of technical advisor and raised his salary. But he was not satisfied and insisted that he should be compensated. Kim Jang-soo went to study experimental chemistry, his school was in Zsigmond Street in Buda, and so I didn't see him for some time.

A couple of weeks had passed when one morning the principal brought András Vajda, my former friend from elementary school, into class and said that from now on he'd be attending, because his parents had transferred him from the secondary school for science to the technology school. I was glad to see him again, but he seemed taken aback, and from then on we avoided each other. He even avoided my gaze. On that particular Tuesday in the fall, they let us out of study hall early and told us to hurry home, because there was going to be a big demonstration. They made us promise that we wouldn't stop anywhere to watch, and if we hurried, we'd still make it home. Mag had to reach Csepel, Krasznai Soroksár, and Kiss had to go all the way to Kispest. It was obvious that our teachers were letting us go because they wanted to attend the demonstration and that they saw something inspiring as well as menacing in it.

But some of us decided to stay together just the same, though try as I might, I can't remember who the others were. I couldn't have gone home, even if I'd wanted to. It was impossible to reach Buda from Pest by then, because the bridges were crowded with people coming over from Buda to Pest. Public transportation came to a standstill, everything came to a standstill, just one surging, billowing blanket of people on the boulevards, they came billowing along Váci Street, and they came surging along Bajcsy-Zsilinszky Street, and we walked along with them; the empty buses and trams stuck out of the crowd like so many islands, but on the former Berlin Square, which everyone but our father called Marx Square, many people couldn't decide where to go next. Once they reached the bottleneck, the trams came to a standstill, with lights still on inside the empty cars. About eighty thousand people got stuck in and around the square, because they could join the other great surge of people only by forcing their way sideways, one by one, they sang, they shouted, they demanded, they offered visions of the future, they gave speeches. About half a million people had gathered in front of Parliament by then, many of them stuck in the side streets. They demanded that the Russians go home, they demanded that Imre Nagy speak. It grew dark by degrees, though the truth is I only realized it was now dark very suddenly. In the pleasantly temperate autumn night, I found myself standing in the midst of a massive crowd. I'd been out on the street since around three in the afternoon. They came from Buda over the Margaret Bridge, they came as an orderly crowd, they came over the bridges in wide columns, there were mostly students marching along Balassi Bálint Street with the emblems and banners of the various universities, and they came to the big square from Falk Miksa Street as well, but not Alkotmány Street, because it was jammed with crowds all the way back to Bajcsy-Zsilinszky Street, and they also came from the other side of the square, from Nádor Street, they came along the quay, there was almost no traffic by then anywhere in the Inner City because of the crowds, and the nearby Liberty Square, too, was now filled with people. They demanded that the red star on top of Parliament be turned off. Turn it off, turn off the star. And there I stood next to the Kossuth statue in the midst of the crowd with my very own sense of history. This history included Kossuth personally, and the square, too, where Mihály Károlyi announced the first Hungarian Republic in the presence of Grandfather Tauber. The people on the square did not pick up on all the demands, but they picked up on this one. Turn it off, turn off the star. They'd installed the star atop the dome just a couple of weeks earlier, and they did a fine job of it, to be sure. Except, it was the smaller version of the star taken from atop the Kremlin in Moscow, and there it was, shining bright and red atop the dome of the Hungarian Parliament. The square echoed with the cheerful demand, it roared with the common rhythm. But it seemed that there was no one around to make the decision, and no technician to satisfy the demands of the crowd as, silent, somber, and dark, Parliament reared its huge ornate bulk before us, refusing to concede the majesty of its subjects. There may have been some weak light burning in the rotunda. They may have heard the demand after all and were deciding whether to bow before the will of the people. But then they decided to turn off the lights on the huge square but not the light of the star. Now only the copy of the Muscovite star shone, there was concern that they'd storm the building and rip it apart with their bare hands, that they wouldn't put up with the provocation, whereas it's possible that the problem was purely technical, that the technician had flicked the wrong switch. The people on the dark square lost no time in illuminating it; they set newspapers and flyers on fire and raised them high above their heads, and as some lights died out, others lit up the square. The silence was now both solemn and festive, and for a brief moment the ephemeral beauty of the flames and experience of man's inherent pyromania had everyone in its spell. Still, there was something formidable about so much unchecked fire in such a huge crowd. I probably lost my drawing board and my T square around this time, but not just these, I also lost the descriptive geometry drawing that I'd made with the greatest care using both my soft and hard graphite pencils, which now needed just minor adjustments. Erasing was out of the question. Our geometry teacher noticed the slightest attempt at erasure. Besides, there was no such a thing as perfection in his eye. In religion and descriptive geometry there was only the attempt, and he even raised a finger when he said this, the attempt at faith, the attempt at description. And we should remember this once and for all. In his eye, erasing something meant that the student drew first and reflected afterward, whereas it should be the other way around, isn't that so. First use your head, if you have one, and draw only after. And then the light of the ruby-red star, the smaller version of the big, fabled Kremlin star, went out; the technician must have found the proper switch. The square was now still and silent. Yet another provocation, leaving the crowd in utter darkness. By then, the soft, warm autumn evening had a tart, sharp edge to it, and the metallic river smell of the nearby Danube permeated the air. Silence of this scale has a leaden weight. For some time the square couldn't believe that its demand would not be met and that it would be answered by yet another provocation. But just then, to the accompaniment of the crowd's triumphal shouts, the lights of the square were turned back on.

We won, we won. We won after all. Someone appeared on the left balcony, which no one saw because of the dark facade of the building, but he appeared, the news spread that someone had come out on the balcony, and the people cheered. He started speaking, but he couldn't be heard. The crowd shouted, we can't hear. We can't hear, we can't hear, the words rippled through the crowd. When there were so many people on a square, their combined shouting no longer echoed, and there was nothing more frightening than that. As if the people were thinking in unison, and they were literally thinking the same thing. Meanwhile the news that Imre Nagy was on his way spread through the crowd, because apparently, the person on the balcony had announced this. They began setting up the microphones on the balcony and hung a couple of big, funnel-shaped loudspeakers that had survived the siege along the facade, they tested them, tapped their fingers against them, microphone test, one, two, three, which echoed and reechoed as it bounced off the ledges of the surrounding buildings, and this made the people even more cheerful, and they laughed, celebrating their moment of triumph. But after a while it seemed that the sound engineers were just playing for time, god-damn them, that's what they were up to. Yet another provocation. I thought it strange that the people were using the Bolshevik expression, the provocation, but then the siege remained in the language as well way after it was a thing of the past. It is with us even now, except few people notice. A buzz went through the crowd, increasing in volume, the provocation made the crowd restless and frustrated, it ran out of patience with the adjusting of the loudspeakers, pockets of restlessness formed, groups, impatient speakers published their various demands, which was yet another new experience for Budapest, simultaneity and polyphony of an unfamiliar nature. There was no way of knowing what would come of all this, which demand would be taken up by the square and what that would lead to, because there was so much happening.

The event of local significance gained its universal significance from the energy of the crowd. Or not. Some things spread as news, others got stuck or remained solitary shouts. A truck overflowing with people rounded the bend from Szalay Street to the square, making room for itself among the crowd, as it were, but it came to a halt in front of the Palace of Justice. The people on the truck hailed the heir to the throne, they were monarchists, they wanted Otto Habsburg on the throne, the revolutionary crowds gathered on Kossuth Lajos Square wanted a Habsburg. Which made just about everyone gasp in surprise. The crowd stuck at the top of Alkotmány Street made way for them, let them go, let them go already. They carried signs, they even had a huge picture of Otto Habsburg. I'd never seen Otto's portrait before, but based on this picture, he really did look a lot like my cousin Georges, my Aunt Magda's son, who was mistaken for the heir to the throne at embassy receptions, in hotel lobbies, as well as on the streets of Brussels, Vienna, and Cannes. Some people wouldn't believe him and nodded, sure, sure, excuse me, Your Majesty, Your Majesty wishes to keep himself incognito.

Almost all the people on the square were strangers to one another, but you soon knew who came from where, because they told you, or else you could guess by their appearance, their faces; for some reason, this is what everyone wanted to know, they wanted to know where you were from. You also knew what the people next to you were thinking because just about everyone kept voicing their opinions, basically nonstop. This made even those who'd been silent up till then talkative. Some were disenchanted Communists. Some were students fired up by the clarity of Marxism. Some were democrats and Smallholders who'd been dragged through the mire, and also Social Democrats who remained faithful to the principles of their party. Some among them were religious people disgraced in their beliefs, others were conservative liberal atheists. There were steadfast anticapitalist laborers, and also small businessmen turned laborers by political necessity. There were students come up from the countryside, the children of humiliated farmers, who were partial to the idea of equality and capitalism. I remained the exception, someone who asked no questions and voiced no opinion; I remained an observer, though others of my age on the square were not as reticent or courteous as I. The strangers around me reminded me of the rural schoolteachers called people's educators, they said nothing about themselves, but instead tried to convince those they'd engaged in conversation that the whole thing happened because of the Jews. A young man had singled me out as well, and then a second and a third. Get the Jews out of politics, this was their suggestion. Where I was standing no one answered them, because these agitators caused at least as much consternation as the monarchists on top of the truck with Otto Habsburg's photographs. Some of them were former Arrow Cross, while others railed against the Jews because they didn't know that their Arrow Cross comrades had already made an attempt. I didn't answer them. Nor did the others. As if they were invisible, as if they hadn't heard. This had special significance on that first day.

And then the triumphal shouts rippling through the crowd gathered on the main staircase of Parliament were the signal that Imre Nagy had arrived. The square buzzed and boomed, Imre Nagy is here, Imre Nagy is here. He's here. Who's here, they asked. He's here. The square fell silent, it wanted to hear if it'd heard itself correctly, then it came alive once again, but as if sighing in relief. Someone even announced through the loudspeakers that he was here. Imre Nagy is here. From this point on, what I remember differs at certain points from what others remember.

When he appeared on the balcony, according to others he appeared at one of the windows of Parliament, they awkwardly turned an old movie light on him, and he tripped. Perhaps it was the high threshold, or perhaps it was the combination of his embarrassment and the high threshold that caused it, after all, this man called Imre Nagy, whom the crowd demanded for itself, had surely not spoken in front of so many people before, or else his character made him ill suited to such a role, he was a Communist intellectual, an ivory tower theoretician who lacked oratorical gifts. As I remember the scene, as he spoke, two people supported him by the arm at the balcony door. This is why the microphone was so far from him, and that's why it was so difficult to hear him, even though his words were passed on by the people in the crowd, as a result of which every one of his words could be heard several times on the square. As others remember it, two people were holding him steady by a window. But I insist on my own memory of the event. All you could see in this awkward beam of light was that someone stepped outside, tripped, his hat flew off, and for a second, he disappeared. The square laughed because it was in fact funny, a comic scene compared with what the crowd had been expecting, but not everyone laughed; the square laughed in pockets, or patches, but the silence of collective shame soon silenced the laughter. In a revolution there are no prearranged scenes. Though the city was waiting for you, though you're the Communist Imre Nagy, you're just like everyone else. On this mild evening in fall, all emotion was shared emotion, and thus, only the crowd could legitimize or suppress it.

I don't understand to this day why I wasn't hungry from three in the afternoon until midnight, why I wasn't thirsty, and why I didn't feel the urge to urinate.

His first word was *comrades*. The word would have bounced off the balconies of the buildings opposite for a while longer, but the crowd was quick to react and answered him with a round of whistles. We're not comrades. Not only did the crowd think alike, not only did it use identical words, its answer, too, was identical. And then, regardless of how strong Imre Nagy's Bolshevik socialization may have been, regardless of how strong his anti-Stalinist and anti-Rákosist feelings may have grown due to the Party's neglect of him, which brought him here on the back of popular anger, regardless of the fact that he knew of no just social order apart from the present Communist social order, he had to concede that it was pointless for him to try to placate the crowd by calling them comrades, it wouldn't work, it was over, it was past history, this many people couldn't be comrades. There was a traditional language of revolution left over from the nineteenth century, he should have resorted to it to begin with; my young friends, as a college teacher and an intellectual, he now attempted something along these lines, but the square wouldn't put up with this paternalistic attitude either. It grumbled in anger. Fellow citizens. This was rewarded with a shout of triumph, even though he could barely get the words out. For a man who had lived in Russian exile and who survived the Stalinist purges, doubtless because he betrayed many people in the interest of his survival, fellow citizens must have evoked some very unpleasant associations. But wouldn't you know, it came out of him just the same, we got him to use the Hungarian revolutionary language properly, he did it, and then this turn of events became part of that Tuesday night's sequence of triumphs. They've already turned off the star, and it's only Tuesday. Imre Nagy has shown up, and it's only Tuesday. We're fellow citizens, and it's only Tuesday. All this in just one day. We'd even reinstated the traditional language of the popular revolutions of the past. But from all the echoes and crackle of the loudspeakers, all the approval and disapproval from the crowd, all the joyous and antagonistic whistling, Nagy's speech could hardly be heard, nor do I remember any of it.

The initial, the one might say well-intentioned and congenial phase of the revolution that easily accommodated the mass desertions from the police and the military corps, the opening up and emptying out of the warehouses of the arms factories, the toppling, cutting, and ritual sawing apart of Sándor Mikus's shameful Stalin statue and the storming of the radio in Bródy Sándor Street, whose news reached us from the direction of Nádor Street that there's shooting at the radio, there's shooting at the radio, which was a great shift of emphasis that night from the congenial to the hysteria of the tragic, in short, the first well-intentioned, and let us add infinitely naïve phase of the revolution accommodated even these first serious shootings, and it took a bloodbath to put an end to all that naïveté and congeniality. This happened on Thursday in front of the Hotel Astoria when the crowd refused to move off the road. It stood in the way of a column of Russian tanks. This forced the commanding officer to show himself. What do you want here, why did you come, the demonstrators shouted at him. Why don't you go home; and not only did they shout it in Hungarian, there were people there who translated it for them, or else they shouted along with the crowd in Russian to begin with. The officer shouted back what those who knew Russian hastened to translate for the crowd, that the city must be cleansed of the fascist gangs. The crowd laughed long and loud. Where are there fascist gangs here, my friend. It wasn't difficult convincing the officer that there were no fascists around, and no gangs either. He should look around with his own two eyes. There were only unarmed students here, only laborers and civil servants, only people of learning. Don't you realize we're talking to you in your own language, they asked him, and they laughed, and he laughed with them. Of course he realizes. Desperate, he defended himself, saying that in that case, there must be some mistake, or else they've been had. At which the crowd celebrated the Russians, who'd been hoodwinked by their own, those bastards in Moscow who'd managed to hoodwink the entire world. They affixed Hungarian flags to the Russian tanks, something that, as a sign of their peaceful intentions, the confused soldiers and their officers allowed. Just then, with a mighty roar, another Soviet convoy of tanks approached along Rákóczi Street, and when the crowd saw that they were also flying Hungarian flags, joyful shouts of vivat, vivat, rent the air.

The revolution had prevailed.

Let's head for Parliament. They came from everywhere, because on that Thursday, the news that the Russians had sided with us spread like wildfire. The Russians have sided with us. On that Thursday, events were still happening simultaneously in various parts of the city. The Russians have sided with us. No wonder. They've been living here for years, even if the poor things weren't allowed out of their barracks. I can still recite the chronology of those thirteen days by heart, the romantic ravings, everyone's with us, the whole world is with us. You couldn't be present everywhere, but the news, the stories, and the miraculous legends reached everyone at the same time. Whoever heard these stories embellishing the fantasy used their empathic gifts, surely, this is why there are so many variations on the same theme. The first person plural belongs to the revolution, and while it excludes the first person singular, it encompasses it.

My friend and comrade in the army, the excellent bookbinder Gyuri Báder, followed the crowd to Parliament, but perhaps the story comes from someone else; anyway, they ran into Russian tanks there as well, and the people climbed on top of the tanks to celebrate themselves and to celebrate the soldiers. That's when the first volleys were fired. They opened fire on the people with machine guns from the tops of the surrounding buildings. At the time, people all over the city thought that the men of the hated State Security Authority were responsible, but according to some researchers, they were shooting from the rooftops on orders from General Serov.

People ran for cover under the arcades of the neoclassical Ministry of Agriculture, until at last only the wounded and the dead remained on the square in front of Parliament.

In the early afternoon of the following day, a Friday, Secretary of State Dulles, the U.S. president, and their advisors evaluated the Hungarian situation. At a meeting of the National Security Council, Harold E. Stassen, the president's advisor on disarmament, had advised that like Austria, the satellite states should also be made neutral. And let us add that at the time the Hungarians were hoping against hope that the great powers would treat them the way they had treated Austria. Approach them through President Tito, Stassen advised the secretary of state, or use some other diplomatic channel, but let the Russians know that if the Eastern European states achieved freedom and independence, it would not jeopardize the security of the Soviet Union. Dulles felt that they need not go quite that far. He parried Stassen's advice by saying that he wouldn't like the Hungarian revolutionaries to think that the State Department was negotiating with the Russians behind their back. However, the documents that were declassified fifty years later indicate that the secretary of state wished to do even less than the diplomatic minimum, and his comments should be understood as a maneuver in that direction. And when President Eisenhower called him an hour later, it must have been out of rhetorical consideration only that Dulles told him that it was extremely difficult to decide how the matter should be handled. Whereas he knew how to handle it. After all, the following day, on Saturday, in his speech in Dallas, he made no bones about his approach.

Regardless of the strength of collective emotions just then, regardless of the upsurge of revolutionary fervor throughout Europe and the major American cities, Secretary of State Dulles's sense of reality functioned as surely as a sleepwalker's. I know several men of my own age, specifically one Dane, one Dutch, one Swiss, and one French, who with their friends sprang into action during these same hours in various parts of Europe; they wanted guns or actually got their hands on guns so they could set off, like the Swiss Rudolf Stamm, who later became the Eastern European correspondent for the *Neue Züricher Zeitung*, and no wonder. But except for the Dutchman, whose name was Rob van Gennep, who later became a well-known publisher, and two others, the rest didn't make it to Vienna, a couple of well-aimed slaps from their parents kept them home. Dulles's diplomatic hesitation, backed by his clever rhetoric and steady pragmatism, is causing a lot of problems for Hungarians to this day, but in those critical October days it was more in line with the balance of power as well as international treaties than any action based on emotional considerations.

On Thursday of the following week, the old-school Communist Imre Nagy succumbed to the dynamics of the revolution when he solemnly if despairingly announced Hungary's withdrawal from the Warsaw Pact. He further declared the country's neutrality, which made his compatriots happy for a couple of hours, except neither the declaration nor the elation had any international reality, and thus, led nowhere. The previous Saturday, Dulles had made his views crystal clear. He could afford to do so, in Dallas he was speaking before an informed and discerning audience.

In his speech, Dulles emphasized that the Atlantic Charter and the United Nations Declaration bound all allies to ensure the right to self-determination in all those places where it had been taken away earlier by force. He made it very clear that in Eastern Europe one type of occupation had simply been replaced by another, and he called the Soviet oppression imperialist. He left no doubt about the fact that the United States sympathized with those patriots who valued freedom even above their own lives, but he also left no doubt about where, as far as the United States was concerned, the geographical limits of U.S. responsibility lay. Furthermore, the United States does not consider these nations, meaning the Hungarians and the Poles, potential military allies of the United States. The United States does not insist on any concrete social setup as a condition for economic ties. Needless to say, he made no mention of the possibility of neutrality. But he did announce that along with other nations, the United States had already taken the matter before the UN Security Council.

Though the democratic world could not decide, either then or later, what to think of the Hungarian revolution, or what to make of it, on Friday and Saturday, Dulles had hit the nail on the head; with respect to both practice and practicality, he decided in good time. It was certainly not the first time the reality of great-power politics had come up against the reality of sentiments and passions. And if the enlightened tradition of revolutionary thinking had been badly shaken by this rhetorical shillyshallying, which did not leave the words of Secretary of State Dulles unaffected, then in fact, it was shaken by the balance of power of the superpowers, coupled with the reality of free-trade interests; it wouldn't have been the first time, nor the last, that in the history of civil societies these values were clearly at odds. A satisfactory end to the repeatedly interrupted social revolution, something to be wished for in the eastern parts of Europe, was no longer on the table in its western and northern regions, where it had been achieved and was no longer of concern, even though its ethical and emotional traditions were not to be denied for cultural and religious reasons, among others. At the same time, satisfying the commitment to the tradition of freedom was impossible without going against free-trade interests and the balance of power, meaning the two pillars of social organization, or without conjuring the specter of a third world war. On the level of political practice, this meant the reaffirmation of the status quo with the attendant epoch-making separation of the western half of Europe from the eastern half of Europe, from which there was no point of return. In the short run, democratic Europe benefited from this loss, and in its pragmatic, shortsighted manner, by ignoring the intellectual and moral loss it incurred, it is benefiting from it to this day. In effect, it succeeded in separating the less economically developed region of Europe from the rest of the world, thereby stabilizing, both with regard to culture and geography, the part of the Yalta Agreement with respect to the spheres of influence in Europe, something that the Soviet power structure would not have been able to achieve on its own. With this separation, Yalta had increased and not decreased the financial mobility of the democratic European states.

On that early Sunday morning, when Budapest was enveloped in a wintry fog and the Soviet army reappeared on the streets with its hastily replaced armored divisions, in my Uncle István Nádas's Pozsonyi Street apartment, where I stayed the night, the earsplitting noise made me leap out of bed only to find my uncle sitting by the radio fully dressed, *Vnimaniye, Vnimaniye, Achtung, Achtung,* they were marching in with their unending stream of tanks, *Attention, Attention,* to show the world how to lay to ruin to a big city attempting to realize its tradition of freedom and which had not yet recovered fully from the devastation of the Second World War. With this act the Cold War tactic of the separation of Europe was now carved in stone, but the Hungarian government was still asking for help in several foreign languages.

No wonder the emotional and moral reticence of the democratic European societies left the debate about the definition of the Hungarian revolution in abeyance. Was it a revolution or a popular uprising, was it a freedom fight or an insurrection, or possibly an anti-Communist antirevolution, or a senseless hunger revolt. These are not unfounded questions. Although with the shape they took and the fates they determined, these two weeks determined my career and fate as well, I say in all honesty that I understand the incomprehension, the perplexity, and the reticence. It was not due to indifference, it was not due to the embarrassing lapse of historical memory, rather, it was due to a well-considered caution that makes us embrace things that are not quite appropriate emotionally, while they are questionable morally.

There is uncertainty in people's minds regarding the Hungarian revolution both at home and abroad, though perhaps more so at home.

Revolutions are not known for their intelligence. They are like natural phenomena. We don't ask an earthquake or a bolt of lightning if it knows what it is doing. Accordingly, we can't very well claim that the Hungarian revolution was an especially well considered or clear-cut mass movement. It brought all sorts of hysteria to the surface, it jump-started its share of pogroms and murders, but these never became dominant, as if some reticent common sense were protecting society from the forces of chaos, which was neither advantageous nor disadvantageous; rather, it was a genealogical given of that Tuesday's mass movement from which, considering what I had experienced up till then, I couldn't have kept myself away from, had I tried. We must accept it as it is, with its intellectual dullness, its bloody hysterics, and its silence. This revolution did not know what it was doing, nor did it gain insight into its actions later; it did not know why it did something or why it did something when it did it. And by the time it could have clarified all this, in line with the survival of the Communist world movement on the one hand, and the system of values of the anti-Communist world movement on the other, it distorted things in two directions at once, until the generations to follow couldn't see straight from all the different distortions. The years of reprisal did not offer sufficient explanation for its innate silence and dullness either. Okay, fine, freedom, but what sort of freedom, whose freedom, and at whose expense, what sort of tradition of freedom are we talking about. The ideal of freedom spearheaded by the revolution of 1956 was akin to the idea of freedom that sparked the freedom fight of 1848 against the Habsburgs, but it was not unlike the idea of freedom that spearheaded the revolution in Paris or the one in Vienna, and so it should be considered a Hungarian independence movement rather than a freedom movement, because its idea of freedom was tied not to the freedom of the individual but to the freedom of the nation. It was a freedom movement, but not a popular freedom movement, its concept of freedom tied it not to the freedom of the individual, nor to the free association of free individuals and their juridic contracts, but to the striving for national independence. Accordingly, the revolution did not provide an answer to the question of what it could do after more than one hundred years with an idea of freedom that is dependent neither on personal freedom nor on personal responsibility. The free world wasn't interested in the question either, and so those who followed the revolution from the outside did not engage in the missing analytical undertakings themselves. On the other hand, because of their own idea of freedom, which they considered universal, they did not realize the qualitative difference between these two concepts of freedom to begin with.

At the same time, the Hungarian revolution exhibited certain characteristics that theoreticians consider the givens of an intelligently functioning revolution. It had a relatively long incubation phase of about a year and a half with an appreciably rich theoretical and political content, and the way was paved by intellectuals, most of them young and almost exclusively Communist. For the most part, non-Communist intellectuals watched from the sidelines. Considering their experience in the previous years, they had plenty to be wary of. They considered the anti-Stalinist struggles the Communists' internal affair. After all, the debates of the young Communists were centered not on reinstating the civil world order, nor on launching a civil revolution, but on reorganizing the Communist movement. They talked about the need for cleansing within the Party and the mistakes that would need to be corrected. Géza Losonczy, meaning Pug Nose, who'd spent time in his comrades' prison, led the debates about renewal and the rectification of the mistakes hand in hand with here-lies-a-pile-of-shit Márton Horváth, when they should have been talking about irreparable crimes at home and the series of mass murders and genocides in Soviet Russia. And yet the public at large followed the internal strife of the Communists with lively interest; their evasive circumlocutions and maneuvers were not exactly fruitful, but they were entertaining. They're at each other's throats, and that's good for us, people thought. As for the non-Communist intellectuals or those intellectuals who were disillusioned with communism, they were hoping that the stupid Communists who were risking their lives in the struggle against the Stalinists would pull the chestnuts out of the fire for them.

The average age of the participants in the debates was thirty-six years. About 80 percent were members of the Communist Party, meaning the Hungarian Workers Party. About a third had participated in the antifascist resistance, and the same number had been in the prisons and internment camps of the dictatorship as Communists. The loosely allied intellectual groups, all of whom hailed from the same political circle and similar professional and intellectual backgrounds, spontaneously organized themselves around a group that they initially called the Bessenyei Circle, then the Petőfi Circle, in honor of the revolutionary poet of 1848–1849. Whether by intention or otherwise, they had close intellectual ties to the great reform generation of the Enlightenment that paved the way for the Hungarian freedom fights of 1848. They were fully aware of the intellectual parallels as well as the shared emotional and historical traditions. Freedom and equality were at the center of the values they cherished. Nonetheless, the methodology of their activities was centered not on preparation for a civil revolution but on the reformist transformation of Hungarian society. They analyzed, they judged, they made suggestions, they got lost in the details and the details of the details. They knew that they must come up with a program for the fundamental transformation of the prevailing order. They also knew that they must implement the radical reforms in the face of opposition from the political elite of the Stalinist dictatorship and its secret police. They retained their role as the Communist Party opposition in their reasoning, but did not shed their Stalinism and dogmatism, which in most cases was doomed to failure for the lack of culturally defined civilian modes of behavior they could have used as a model. They practiced self-criticism; they made their personal selves invisible behind the stage setup of their party, whereas they should have concerned themselves with themselves, and then, having reviewed their previous actions, they might have been able to separate the regime-specific and the personal within themselves. They blurred the lines. They passed the buck. They created scapegoats, and they pointed the finger at the guilty only within limits; after all, their mortal enemies were themselves inside the Communist movement. But even so, with all this blurring of the lines, their influence kept growing, and as it grew, they lost their ties to the Communist movement in proportion to the growth of their influence. They organized debates for economists, historians, teachers, and philosophers. They organized debates on literature, agrarian reform, and technological development. The interdisciplinary debates brought emotional and attitudinal changes in their wake. The participants couldn't agree on where their intention to bring about change and the attendant methodology had its place in Hungarian history, what world movements of whatever size they could join, or else, what they should reject and keep at bay, and yet more and more people from different walks of life came to agree that in the name of socialism and communism, the country was ruled not only by hordes of professional dilettantes, but by common criminals as well.

They also conceded that no change could be brought about without a free press, and that a free press must be free of Party interests and Party directives. On the other hand, it would have been difficult to imagine Márton Horváth leading a debate without his Communist fury thrown in. They would have had to empty the bitter cup of their ties to the Communist movement to the last drop, but they were not prepared to do so either emotionally or intellectually; after all, they were the driving force behind Communist revolutionary renewal. When the press debate was held back in June 1956 at the eclectic-style Budapest Officers Club, formerly the Royal Hungarian Officers Casino, in front of a packed audience, the police cordoned off the building for safety reasons, but the crowds that had gathered in nearby Váci and Veres Pálné streets crashed through the gates so they could be present in the stairwell and the main hall at least. The debate was meant for a small circle, but the outside world no longer tolerated being barred from anything whatsoever. The need for change gave them more and more prominence, but their program was never even properly worked out, probably not for lack of time, but rather because the debaters didn't have, nor could they have had, the appropriate language for it.

The mass movement that ran parallel to the various debates over a free press, and which began in earnest on the streets of Budapest that Tuesday in October, absorbed and practically nullified the movement of the Communist intellectuals incapable of renewal and equally incapable of realizing it. They had a vehicle fitted with loudspeakers, but this had no effect on the crowd because not only did they lack a ready program that they could have transmitted from the vehicle in faltering phrases, they lacked figures of consequence who might have understood the precedents as well as the repercussions from the perspective of a mass movement. The revolution had its very own spirit, but it did not have independent and free individuals who could have given this spirit an individual voice, whereas the revolutionary spirit requires compelling voices and compelling individuals. The movement of the Communist intellectuals and the revolutionary popular movement were not compatible and were never in a position to sustain a dialogue. The Hungarian revolution was both victorious and vanquished, but the intellect doesn't like to be confronted by such ambiguities. The brilliant triumph of the republican spirit against the dictatorship became the devastating debacle of the democracies pitted against the brutal power machinery of autocratic systems. Even today, Hungarians can't laud their brilliant short-lived triumph without having to confront themselves with the destructive and self-destructive results of its defeat, which is another dilemma the intellect would rather not have to consider. Let it be either defeat or victory, that's what the simplistic romantic mind likes. As for others, seeing the defeat of the Hungarian republicans and the world's democrats, they can't have a bad conscience without considering the reasons for the innate weaknesses of democracies forever at the mercy of absolutism, something that, taking into account the very real danger of atomic warfare and the concrete danger of the Cold War, perhaps no one could have attempted with a sane mind.

A mutual and joint reckoning of this nature is not in the cards, nor will it be, ever.

In the series of the revolts, rebellions, and mass movements of increasing discernment with which the subjugated peoples of Europe attempted to break out of the isolation caused by the Yalta Agreement and to rid themselves of Russian imperialism so they could return to constitutionalism and self-determination, the Hungarian revolution of 1956 takes center stage. And yet, half a century later, the significance and exemplary nature of the Hungarian revolution still stands in need of clarification, whereas the answer lies in its prehistory, the history of the mostly pointless Cold War politics of the great powers, and the history of unorganized isolation and organized separation, or it can be explained with recourse to its post-history as an event that though it did not bring about a new state of affairs, yet it acted as a break, or a pause. The Hungarian revolution forced a qualitative change in the relationship of the great powers to each other. For instance, President Truman had to send a message to First Secretary Khrushchev to the effect that he would honor the Yalta Agreement, and so he sent it. As for First Secretary Khrushchev, he had to rush off to see Tito, who in the name of the neutral nations assured him that he could go right ahead and put down the revolution, just as long as he chose the cowardly, pusillaminous, and underhanded János Kádár and not the heavy-handed and cheerful Ferenc Münnich as head of Hungary. They did the typecasting in Belgrade, and the great powers who until then had represented clashing interests now offered their help. The new state of affairs put an end to the first, hard phase of the Cold War, diminished the danger of atomic warfare, and brought about the era of peaceful coexistence that was seen by the opposing sides as the acceptable minimum. But it did not bring all this about through the triumph of republicanism or the triumph of democracy, it brought it about through the defeat of republicanism and of democracy. The Hungarian revolution of 1956 remained a memento, a negative experience that is part of European experience, but an experience that its sense of reality would rather not retain in the foreground of its consciousness, and so it has exiled it from that same consciousness. At the same time, its significance can also be explained, and indeed must be explained, as a contributing factor to the historical tradition of European and North American revolutions and social movements, except that would yield even more embarrassing results. The truth is that the Hungarian revolution was the last European revolution, the embarrassing and bloody denouement in the romantic and idealistic history of many centuries of revolution. Societies dependent on free trade and the continued growth of their efficiency have banished utopia from their originally utopian social contracts. And along with the banished utopia, there is no past and there is no future, and so we are left with the present as our sole reality. There is nowhere to go from here. This is why the memory of the Hungarian revolution is dead. As a symbol it has survived the era of retribution, but it survived only as the memento of the most primitive type of anti-Communist propaganda, a Jack Pudding, a buffoon, a clown, a memento mori, but it could not survive the false idyll of peaceful coexistence, and to this extent, as far as political thinking is concerned, it was not merely a significant interlude but a significant loss as well. Ever since, thinking about it has been restricted to thinking within a given framework. There is no God, or else God's existence is a matter of free choice. There is no utopia, after all, we've seen where social utopias lead. There is only the present, with the government at the helm. With the Hungarian revolution, the rival and debating partner of pragmatic thinking bled to death. Without the tradition of revolutionary change, we are left with the tradition of conformity and opportunism, and under the sign of this ab ovo shameful tradition, a person cannot reflect either on the vulnerability of republicanism nor the vulnerability of democracy. Those intent on a brighter future shoot their dick into an empty sky, to quote the well-known poet once again.

At the risk of exaggerating, we might say that in October 1956 the peoples and the legitimate governments of Europe and North America decided jointly that the era of revolutionary change had ended once and for all. And they were right. Something really did end. In order to avert another world war, the various systems had to integrate social and political dissatisfaction into their agenda. They integrated it into a bipolar world meant to last for all time to come; each system integrated its own dissatisfactions in its own way. This became the epoch-making Commandment. And so, amid profuse apologies and bleeding hearts, but with unerring foresight and fully cognizant of their moral responsibility, they failed to support, whether through diplomacy, volunteers, or weapons, Hungarian democracy's desperate and overdue noncivilian revolution. But even above and beyond the danger of another world war, the peoples and the legitimate governments of Europe and North America had good reason not to support it. Had they done so, in due course it would have turned out that even independent of the ideological hysteria of Russian imperialism, with the Hungarian revolution, the dichotomy of capitalism and socialism would have remained in force. At most, it would have bolstered the Titoist version, which was not in the interest of the Euro-Atlantic powers, to say the least. The fact is that despite all views to the contrary, the Hungarian revolution was not an antisocialist revolution, despite all its anti-Communist excesses it was not antisocialist, and at first, it wasn't even anti-Communist. Only the anti-Communists, who in the days of the revolution weren't in the saddle in Budapest, labeled the revolution anti-Communist after the fact, an endeavor in which János Kádár helped them when he returned to Budapest with the Russian troops. It was an anti-Stalinist revolution, it didn't want Russian imperialism, it wanted to divest itself of the foreign Byzantine element. It was a democratic revolution that put up neither with foreign rule, nor autocracy, nor the tyranny of the various collectives, but it was not a civil revolution. The Arrow Cross and the fascists had routed, persecuted, and murdered the Hungarian middle class, then the Communists ousted, persecuted, and murdered those who were left, deprived them of their fortunes, and effectively made their lives impossible. As a first step, the revolution would have continued to support public ownership and the self-determination of the working class. It would have liked to return small plants and workshops to their owners, but not the factories. It hastened to return small estates to their previous owners as well, and in many places it didn't even wait for new laws or decrees; rural Hungary wanted no cooperatives, everyone wanted their own farm; on the other hand, it didn't want large estates, nor estates that once belonged to the Church. The memory was still fresh, people knew where such things would lead. It would lead to feudalism. Servitude. The gendarmerie. Poverty. Humiliation. At any rate, at first anticapitalism and antifeudalism were at the top of the revolutionary agenda. This was and has remained its most independent and most striking intellectual yield, which it disgorged from itself in the delirium of just a couple of days, and without the participation of important theoreticians. Despite the reprisals, at the time of the great nationwide strikes in November and December, the agenda fought for workers' self-management and self-government. Surely, setting limits on ownership must have alienated European democracies, provided that the news reached their big cities to begin with, where, if for no other reason than because they didn't understand, they let things take their course, they let the revolution bleed to death.

I say this, and I say it without pathetic overtones or regrets, that my life was spent under the sign of this double bloodletting, and that I have come to hate tyranny ever since, nor can I look the other way when I see the weaknesses, cheap theatrics, and self-destructive prejudices of republicanism and democracy. So much the worse for us.

A NOTE ABOUT THE AUTHOR

Péter Nádas was born in Budapest in 1942. Among his works translated into English are the novels *Parallel Stories*, *A Book of Memories*, *The End of a Family Story*, and *Love*, as well as a collection of stories and essays, *Fire and Knowledge*; *A Lovely Tale of Photography*; and *Own Death*. He lives with his wife in Gombosszeg, in western Hungary.

A NOTE ABOUT THE TRANSLATOR

Judith Sollosy, an editor, an academic, and a literary translator, is best known for her translations of the contemporary Hungarian authors Péter Esterházy, Mihály Kornis, Péter Nádas, and István Örkény. Her own writing on translation has appeared in *PEN America*, *Asymptote*, and *Words Without Borders*, among other publications.